THE ROUGH GUIDE TO

Brittany & Normandy

This twelfth edition written and researched by

Greg Ward

ROUGH GUIDES

roughguides.com

Contents

Introduction to
Brittany & Normandy

Each quintessentially French yet cherishing its own unique identity, Brittany and Normandy rank among the most intriguing and distinctive regions of France. Exploring either or both offers visitors a wonderful opportunity to experience the best the country has to offer: sheltered white-sand beaches and wild rugged coastlines; mighty medieval fortresses and mysterious megaliths; graceful Gothic cathedrals and breathtaking contemporary architecture; heathland studded with wildflowers and deep ancient forests. Best of all, perhaps, there's the compelling and exuberant cuisine, from the seafood extravaganzas in countless little ports to the rich pungent cheeses of rural Normandy.

Both provinces are ideal for **cycle** touring, with superb scenery yet short distances between each town and the next, so you're never too far from the next hotel, restaurant or market. Otherwise, a **car** is the best alternative; public transport options tend to be very limited.

Where to go

Long a favourite with French and foreign tourists alike, **Brittany** is known above all for its glorious **beaches**. Here stretching languidly in front of elegant resorts, there nestled into isolated crescent coves, they invite endless days of relaxation. The Breton coastline winds its way around so many bays, peninsulas and river estuaries that it makes up over a third of the total seaboard of France, so it's always possible to find a strand to yourself, or to walk alone with the elements. The finest beaches of all tend to be along the more sheltered southern coast, all the way from **Bénodet** and **Le Fôret-Fouesnant** in the west, past the **Gulf of Morbihan**, and down to **La Baule** near the mouth of the Loire, but there are also plenty of wonderful spots tucked into the exposed Atlantic headlands of **Finistère**, or amid the extraordinary red rocks of the **Côte de Granît Rose** in the north.

ABOVE RIVER SEINE AND LES ANDELYS SEEN FROM CHÂTEAU GAILLARD

As well as exploring the mainland resorts and seaside villages – each of which, from ports the size of **St-Malo** or **Vannes** down to lesser-known communities such as **Erquy** or **Ploumanac'h**, can be relied upon to offer at least one welcoming hotel or restaurant – be sure to take a boat trip out to one or more of Brittany's **islands**. Magical **Bréhat** is just a ten-minute crossing from the north coast near Paimpol, while historic **Belle-Île**, to the south, is under an hour from Quiberon. Other islands are set aside as bird sanctuaries, while off Finistère, **Ouessant**, **Molène** and **Sein** are remote, strange and utterly compelling.

Brittany was the "Little Britain" of King Arthur's realm – Petite Bretagne, as opposed to Grande Bretagne – and an otherworldly element still seems entrenched in the land and people. That's especially apparent in **inland Brittany**, where the moors and woodlands are the very stuff of legend, with the **forests** of Huelgoat and Paimpont in particular being identified with the tales of Merlin, the Fisher King and the Holy Grail. Modern Brittany, though, also holds the vibrant modern cities of **Rennes**, noteworthy for its superb music festivals, and its former capital **Nantes**, where the amazing steampunk contraptions known as the **Machines de l'Île** should not be missed.

Normandy has a less harsh appearance and a more mainstream, prosperous history. It too is a seaboard province, first colonized by Norsemen and then colonizing in turn; during the eleventh and twelfth centuries, the likes of **William the Conqueror** exported the ruthless Norman formula to England, Sicily and parts of the Near East, while centuries later Norman seafarers established the French foothold in Canada. Normandy

FROM CATHEDRALS TO CHAPELS

Thanks to the wealth accrued by its warriors, Normandy can boast some of the most imposing and resplendent church architecture in France – the Gothic cathedrals of **Coutances**, **Bayeux** and **Rouen**, and the monasteries of **Mont-St-Michel** and **Jumièges**.

In Brittany, by contrast, it's often the tiny rural chapels and roadside crosses that are the most intriguing. Breton Catholicism has always had an idiosyncratic twist, incorporating Celtic, Druidic, and possibly prehistoric elements. Though hundreds of its saints have never been approved by the Vatican, their brightly painted wooden figures adorn every church, along with skeletal statues of death's workmate, **Ankou**, and their stories merge with tales of moving menhirs, ghosts and sorcery. Noteworthy village churches include those of **Kermaria-an-Isquit** and **Kernascléden**, both of which hold frescoes of the **Dance of Death**, and the *enclos paroissiaux* or "parish closes" of Finistère, where the proximity of the dead to the living seems to echo the beliefs of the megalith builders.

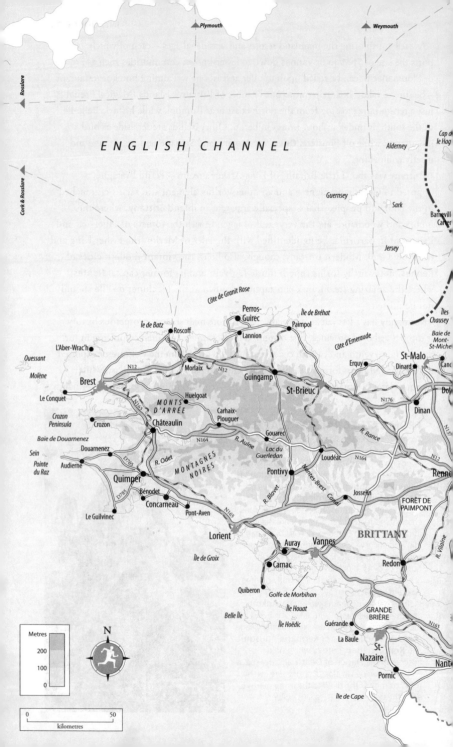

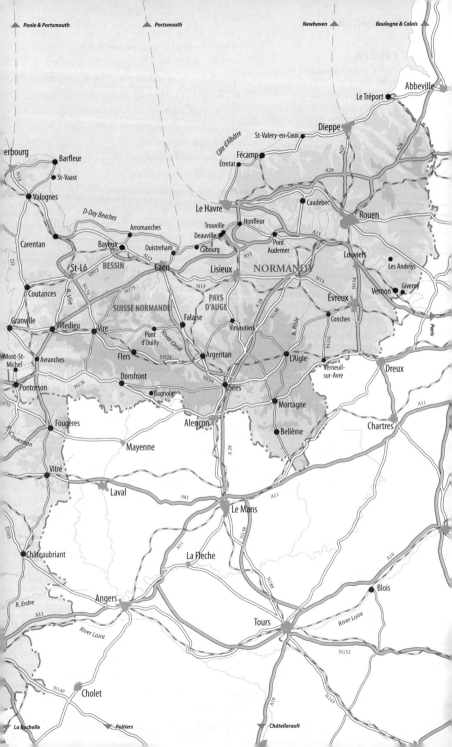

has always boasted large-scale **ports**: Rouen, on the Seine, is as near as ships can get to Paris, while Dieppe, Cherbourg and Le Havre have important transatlantic trade. **Inland**, it is a wonderfully fertile belt of tranquil pastureland, where most visitors head straight for the restaurants of the Pays d'Auge and the Suisse Normande.

The pleasures of Normandy are perhaps less intense than those of Brittany, but it too has its fair share of **beaches**, ranging from the shelving shingle of pretty **Étretat** to the vast sandy swathes that line the western **Cotentin peninsula**. Sedate nineteenth-century resorts like Trouville and Houlgate have their own considerable charms, but it's the delightful ancient ports like **Honfleur** and **Barfleur** that are most likely to capture your heart, and numerous coastal villages remain unspoiled by crowds or affectations. Lovely little towns lie tucked away within 20km of each of the major Channel ports – the headlands near **Cherbourg** are among the best, and least explored, areas – while the banks of the **Seine**, too, hold several idyllic resorts.

Normandy also boasts extraordinary **architectural** treasures, although only its much-restored traditional capital, **Rouen**, has preserved a complete medieval centre. The absolute jewel of the region is the abbey of **Mont-St-Michel**, which over the course of several centuries became so closely moulded to its tiny island home that the entire island now seems like a single stunningly integrated building. Jumièges and Caen hold further monasteries, while Richard the Lionheart's castle towers above the Seine at Les Andelys, and **Bayeux**, in addition to its vivid and astonishing **Tapestry**, holds a majestic cathedral. Many other great Norman buildings survived into the twentieth century, only to be destroyed during the **D-Day** landings of 1944 and the subsequent **Battle of Normandy**, which has its own legacy in a series of war museums, memorials and cemeteries. While hardly conventional tourist attractions, as part of the fabric of the province these are moving and enlightening.

OPPOSITE CLOCKWISE FROM TOP FAÏENCE LOBSTERS, QUIMPER; BOTTLES OF CALVADOS; CARNAC

AVERAGE DAILY TEMPERATURES AND MONTHLY RAINFALL

	Jan	Feb	Mar	Apr	May	Jun	Jul	Aug	Sep	Oct	Nov	Dec
BREST (BRITTANY)												
Av Temp (°C)	6	6	7	9	12	14	15	16	15	12	9	7
Rainfall mm	132	106	101	73	72	58	49	68	85	110	127	148
NANTES (BRITTANY)												
Av Temp (°C)	5	6	8	10	13	17	19	19	16	12	8	6
Rainfall mm	78	60	60	53	60	53	50	53	68	88	91	86
CHERBOURG (NORMANDY)												
Av Temp (°C)	5	5	6	7	11	13	15	16	14	12	8	6
Rainfall mm	90	79	78	56	65	48	44	47	80	99	110	103
ROUEN (NORMANDY)												
Av Temp (°C)	3	3	6	8	12	14	17	17	15	11	6	4
Rainfall mm	59	47	46	47	52	54	58	61	57	65	66	64

When to go

Every French town or district seems to promote its own *micro-climat*, maintaining that some meteorological freak makes it milder or balmier than its neighbours. On the whole, however, Normandy and Brittany follow a broadly set pattern. **Summer**, more reliable than in Britain, starts around mid-June and can last through to mid-October. **Spring** and **autumn** are mild but sporadically wet. If you come for a week in April or November, it could be spoiled by rain, though rainy spells seldom last more than a couple of days. **Winter** is not too severe, though in western Brittany especially the coast can be damp and very misty.

Sea temperatures, however, are far from Mediterranean – certainly in the Channel waters off the Norman coast, where any perceived greater warmth compared to the south of England is more likely to be psychological than real. The south coast of Brittany is a different matter – consistently warm through the summer, with no need for you to brace yourself before going into the sea.

On the coast, the **tourist season** gets going properly around July, reaches a peak during the first two weeks of August, and then fades quite swiftly; try to avoid the great *rentrée* at the end of the month, when cars returning to Paris jam the roads. Inland, the season is less defined; while highlights such as Monet's gardens at Giverny and parts of the Nantes–Brest canal can be crowded in midsummer, some smaller hotels close in August so their owners can take their own holidays by the sea. Conversely, those seaside resorts that have grown up without being attached to a genuine town take on a distinctly ghostlike appearance in winter, and can often be entirely devoid of facilities.

Author picks

For many years, our author has been exploring Brittany and Normandy from the cider farms of Calvados to the crêperies of Quimper, and the hedgerows of the Bocage to the heathlands of Cap Fréhel. Here are some of his favourite experiences:

Castles Both Brittany and Normandy abound in mighty castles and impregnable fortresses. The largest, at Fougères (p.206) and Falaise (p.164), are undeniably impressive, but don't forget the pocket-sized châteaux of Pirou (p.130) and Fort la Latte (p.209).

Treehouses If you're partial to the outdoor life but don't quite fancy sleeping under the stars, how about spending a night or two in a treehouse? Options include the *Village la Plage* in Penmarc'h (p.279); *Camping Lez Eaux* near Granville (p.134); and *Le Renardière* in the Perche countryside (p.154).

Festivals Brittany's annual festivals cater to every musical taste imaginable, from the massive Inter-Celtic jamboree at Lorient (p.320) to jazz at Châteaulin (p.288), world music on the Crozon peninsula (p.262), sea shanties at Paimpol (p.219), and even Art Rock at St-Brieuc (p.216).

Islets While big-name islands like Belle-Île attract the most attention, countless tiny offshore outcrops also make appealing day-trip destinations. Prime examples in Brittany include the Île de Batz (p.239), Houat (p.334) and Hoëdic, while Normandy chips in with the Îles Chausey (p.135), Tatihou (p.127) and the most famous of the lot, Mont-St-Michel (p.137).

Brontosauruses To tell the truth, there aren't all that many brontosauruses in Brittany and Normandy, but you won't want to miss the amazing topiary one in Villers-sur-Mer (p.98), and there's another gigantic thunder lizard at Malansac in Brittany (p.307).

> Our author recommendations don't end here. We've flagged up our favourite places – a perfectly sited hotel, an atmospheric café, a special restaurant – throughout the guide, highlighted with the ★ symbol.

FROM TOP LA POINTE D'EN TAL, ÎLE DE HOUAT; FESTIVAL DU BOUT DU MONDE, CROZON; TOPIARY BRONTOSAURUS IN VILLERS-SUR-MER

19

things not to miss

It may not be possible to sample everything that Brittany and Normandy have to offer in a single trip – but you can have a great time trying. What follows, in no particular order, is a selective taste of the regions' highlights: outstanding scenery, picturesque villages, remarkable history and fabulous fresh produce. Each entry has a page reference to take you straight into the guide. Coloured numbers refer to chapters in the Guide section.

1 THE INTER-CELTIC FESTIVAL
Page 320

For anyone who loves Breton music, or all things Celtic, Lorient's August extravaganza is the unmissable highlight of the year.

2 ROUEN
Page 69

Explore the vibrant medieval core of Rouen, which contains a superb cathedral as well as the spot where Joan of Arc met her death.

3 LE GRAND ÉLÉPHANT
Page 315

Trumpeting, squirting water, and carrying 49 passengers on its mighty back, Nantes' sensationally preposterous pachyderm is worth travelling a very, very long way to see.

4 THE SEINE
Page 65

Broadening as it approaches the Channel, the premier river of northern France becomes languidly rural, lined by lovely little-known villages such as Villequier.

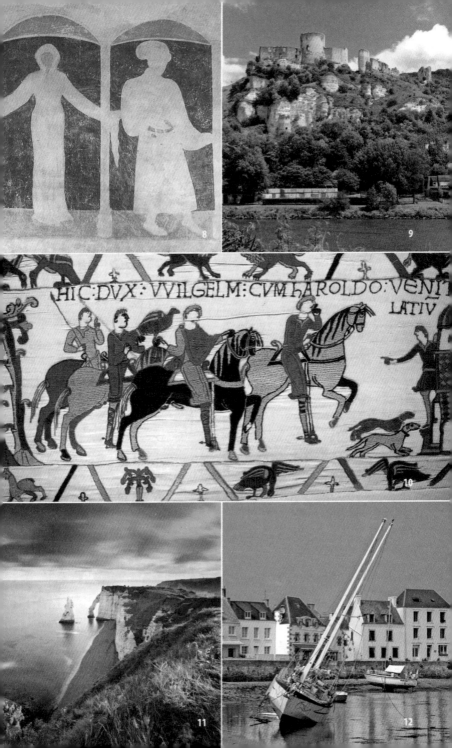

HIC · DVX · VVILGELM · CVM HAROLDO · VENIT
LATIV

13

14

15

16

CANOPUS

13 ST-MALO
Page 178

The finest town on the Breton coast, walled St-Malo proudly commands a lovely estuary.

14 THE PAYS D'AUGE
Page 155

With its crumbling half-timbered farmhouses, lush meadows and fertile orchards, the Pays d'Auge encapsulates Normandy's rural splendour.

15 CYCLING
Page 27

Slow your pace and cycle through quiet country lanes, undulating hills and enchanted forests.

16 NANTES–BREST CANAL
Page 288

Meander along Brittany's inland waterways and soak up the stunning scenery.

17 HIKING THE CÔTE DE GRANIT ROSE
Page 225

Lined by bizarre rock formations, this stretch of the northern Breton seashore offers dramatic coastal hikes.

18 MONT-ST-MICHEL
Page 137

The glorious medieval abbey that tops this tiny Norman island ranks among the most recognizable silhouettes in the world.

19 HONFLEUR
Page 92

Normandy's most charming little port has long attracted artists and photographers.

Itineraries

You could spend a lifetime exploring Brittany and Normandy and still not have seen every castle, cathedral and megalith, stayed beside every ancient harbour or unspoiled beach, or sampled every delicious variation on seafood, cider or cheese. In a single week, you'd do best to restrict yourself to the highlights of a single region. Two will give you time to see the best of both, but you'll need three or more to cover the entire area.

THE GRAND TOUR

Allow at least a fortnight to relax into the true pleasures of visiting Brittany and Normandy, while touring the major sights and the most stunning scenery.

❶ **Étretat** Squeezed between meadow-clad cliffs, this charming resort provides a great first taste of Normandy. **See p.58**

❷ **Honfleur** The harbour in this gorgeous old port is surrounded by ravishing medieval high-rises. **See p.92**

❸ **Bayeux** The world-famous Tapestry offers a unique record of how Normandy managed to conquer all of England. **See p.106**

❹ **D-Day beaches** Now lined by sedate resorts, these low-lying beaches abound in memories of the Allied invasion of 1944. **See p.110**

❺ **Mont-St-Michel** Newly restored to island status, this breathtaking monastery is an absolute jewel. **See p.137**

❻ **Dinan** A perfect medieval town, complete with castle, turreted walls, and a pretty river port. **See p.191**

❼ **Côte de Granit-Rose** A wonderland of rose-tinted rocks, coastal footpaths and inviting beaches. **See p.223**

❽ **Carnac** These impassive megaliths have guarded their secrets for more than seven thousand years. **See p.335**

❾ **Nantes** Brittany's historic capital has a dynamic energy – and where else can you ride a colossal mechanical elephant? **See p.310**

❿ **The Perche** It's hard to imagine a more peaceful patch of countryside – it even holds the original Trappist monastery. **See p.153**

⓫ **Giverny** Monet's gardens, complete with waterlily pond, remain preserved much as the artist knew them. **See p.83**

IN THE FOOTSTEPS OF CONQUERORS

Since time immemorial, raiders, invaders and mighty armies have swept through Normandy; a week's tour makes a great introduction to its hyperactive history.

❶ **Pegasus Bridge** The iconic site where the Allied invasion began, just south of the ferry port at Ouistreham. **See p.112**

❷ **Arromanches** Remains of Churchill's Mulberry Harbour stud a huge beach that's popular with holiday-makers. **See p.116**

❸ **Colleville-sur-Mer** The largest US military cemetery remains a sobering spectacle. **See p.117**

ABOVE FORÊT DE PAIMPONT

❹ Pointe du Hoc This shell-shattered clifftop is a vivid reminder of the sheer ferocity of the D-Day fighting. **See p.118**

❺ Bayeux Vibrant and colourful, this thousand-year-old comic strip brings the Norman Conquest to life. **See p.106**

❻ Caen A lively city that's home to William the Conqueror's tomb and a comprehensive World War II museum. **See p.101**

❼ Château de Falaise The redoubtable fortress where William the Conqueror was born is now a cutting-edge museum. **See p.163**

❽ Château Gaillard The stark ruins of Richard the Lionheart's castle command stunning views over the Seine. **See p.82**

BRITTANY'S SPECTACULAR COAST

It takes around ten days to do justice to Brittany's superb beaches, some sheltering in lush estuaries, others exposed to the crashing sea.

❶ St-Malo Cross-Channel ferries dock right alongside this dramatic walled town. **See p.178**

❷ Erquy A delightful family resort, cradling a sandy crescent beach. **See p.209**

❸ Île de Bréhat The easy day-trip to these twin balmy islets is rewarded with wonderful walking and scenery. **See p.221**

❹ Côte de Granit Rose You could while away a week here, amid the extraordinary profusion of glowing, pink-granite boulders. **See p.223**

❺ Crozon peninsula Vast sweeping beaches, rugged clifftop walks, charming resorts and ancient megaliths; this peninsula's convoluted shoreline has it all. **See p.258**

❻ Île de Sein Swirling out of the Atlantic mists, this haunting islet seems to lie beyond the everyday world. **See p.270**

❼ Forêt-Fouesnant A tracery of beaches and villages, linked by coastal footpaths, ideal for a classic seaside holiday. **See p.280**

❽ Belle-Île Brittany's largest island combines historic towns and sheltered beaches with windswept cliffs and wild walks. **See p.329**

❾ Carnac Europe's most famous megalithic site has an unlikely summer job – splendid beaches mean it's also a major holiday destination. **See p.335**

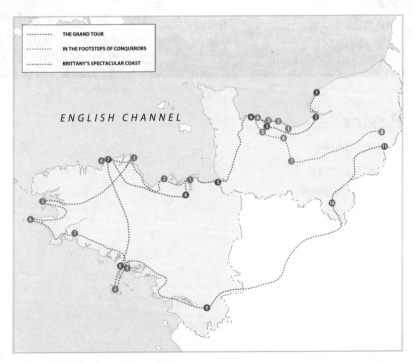

THE GRAND TOUR
IN THE FOOTSTEPS OF CONQUERORS
BRITTANY'S SPECTACULAR COAST

ENGLISH CHANNEL

LANGOUSTINES, LE GUILVINEC, FINISTÈRE

Basics

Getting there

It's easy to reach Brittany and Normandy from Britain. The main ferry operator, Brittany Ferries, crosses to Caen, Cherbourg, Le Havre, St-Malo and Roscoff, while other ferries connect Newhaven with Dieppe and Portsmouth with Le Havre, and the Channel Tunnel provides rapid access to Normandy. In addition, airlines offer well-priced flights to Brest, Caen, Deauville, Dinard, Nantes, Quimper and Rennes.

Irish visitors can choose between a handful of direct ferry services between Ireland and France, most active in summer; flying with Ryanair to Nantes; or travelling via England and/or Paris.

If you're coming to Brittany and Normandy from anywhere outside Europe, you'll almost certainly have to start by flying to Paris, and travel onwards from there.

From the UK

Six commercial ferry ports line up along the coastline of Brittany and Normandy, and seven regional airports are served by direct flights. While the cheapest ferry routes cross the Channel further east, between Dover and Calais, and the Channel Tunnel starts outside Folkestone, which route is most convenient for you will depend on where you're starting from.

Ferries

Motorists, cyclists and pedestrians heading to Normandy or Brittany can either catch a ferry directly to any of four Norman and two Breton ports, or take a shorter crossing further east, and travel via Calais or Dunkerque. All these services are detailed on p.22.

Ferry fares vary so enormously with the season – each sailing tends to be priced individually – that it's all but impossible to predict what you will actually pay. Most operators charge a flat fare for a vehicle with two adults, then additional per-person charges for further passengers, and for any "accommodation" required, from a seat for £5 to as much as £50 for a cabin berth.

Booking ahead is strongly recommended for motorists, certainly in high season; foot passengers and cyclists can normally just turn up and board, at any time of year. You can compare prices and find cut-price fares online at Ⓦferrysavers.com.

The Channel Tunnel

The Channel Tunnel, which burrows beneath the English Channel at its narrowest point – the Pas-de-Calais, well to the east of Normandy – plays host to two distinct services. Eurostar trains carry foot passengers only, with its principal routes being from London to Paris or Brussels, while Eurotunnel simply conveys cars and other vehicles between Folkestone and Calais, in direct competition with the ferries.

Eurostar

Eurostar **trains** from London St Pancras International take two hours five minutes to reach **Paris** Gare du Nord. Travellers heading for Brittany and Normandy can change at Lille, 1 hour 20 minutes out from London, for destinations in the two regions. Tickets can be bought directly from Eurostar (Ⓦeurostar.com), or from all main train stations in Britain.

Eurostar offers concessionary fares to young people (under 26), over-60s and holders of international rail passes. Bicycles can be carried free of charge in the carriage provided that they can fold; if not, they should be declared as "Registered Baggage" a day in advance (£25 per cycle per journey).

Eurotunnel

The Channel Tunnel also provides the fastest and most convenient way to take your car to France. For motorists, the tunnel entrance is less than two hours' drive from London, off the M20 at Junction 11A, just outside Folkestone. Once there, you drive your car onto a two-tier railway carriage; you're then

---

A BETTER KIND OF TRAVEL

At Rough Guides we are passionately committed to travel. We feel that travelling is the best way to understand the world we live in and the people we share it with – plus tourism has brought a great deal of benefit to developing economies around the world over the last few decades. But the growth in tourism has also damaged some places irreparably, and climate change is exacerbated by most forms of transport, especially flying. All Rough Guides' trips are carbon-offset, and every year we donate money to a variety of charities devoted to combating the effects of climate change.

free to get out and stretch your legs during the 35 minutes (45min for some night trains) before you emerge from the darkness at Coquelles, just outside Calais. The sole operator, **Eurotunnel** (☎08443 353535, ⒲eurotunnel.com), offers a continuous service with up to four departures per hour (1 per hr midnight–6am). While it's not compulsory to buy a ticket in advance, it's highly advisable in midsummer or during school holidays. You must arrive at least thirty minutes before departure.

Fares are calculated per car, regardless of the number of passengers. Rates depend on time of year, time of day and length of stay (the cheapest ticket is for a day-trip, followed by a five-day return). In low season, travelling at antisocial hours, you can make the round trip for around £100; a return fare in July or August, with weekend departures, can reach £300. You can travel with a bicycle for £18 each way; call ☎01303 282 201 for all bike reservations.

While the tunnel journey itself is fast and efficient, drivers heading for Brittany or Normandy should not underestimate how long it takes to drive across northern France from the tunnel exit. Just to reach Le Tréport, the eastern extremity of Normandy, takes a good two hours, while western Brittany would take more like eight hours.

Combined train/ferry routes

You can buy connecting tickets from any British station to any French station, via any of the ferry routes. Details and prices (again with various special

SEA CROSSINGS FROM THE UK

Route	Operator	Crossing Time	Frequency
BRITTANY			
Portsmouth–St-Malo	Brittany Ferries	10hr 45min	1 daily in summer, 3 weekly in winter
Poole–St-Malo (via Jersey or Guernsey)	Condor Ferries	6hr 40min	1–3 daily May–Sept
Plymouth– St-Malo	Brittany Ferries	10hr 30min	Thurs, Oct–March
Plymouth–Roscoff	Brittany Ferries	6–11hr	1–2 daily in summer, 2–3 weekly in winter
Weymouth–St-Malo (via Jersey or Guernsey)	Condor Ferries	6hr 20min	2–7 weekly, May–Dec
NORMANDY			
Newhaven–Dieppe	DFDS Seaways	4hr	2 daily
Portsmouth–Cherbourg	Brittany Ferries	5hr	daily, late April to mid-Sept
Poole–Cherbourg	Brittany Ferries	4hr 15min	daily
Portsmouth–Caen	Brittany Ferries	6–8hr	2–3 daily
Portsmouth–Le Havre	Brittany Ferries	3hr 45min–5hr 30min	0–2 daily in summer, no service Jan–March
Portsmouth–Le Havre	DFDS Seaways	5hr 30min–8hr	1 daily
PAS-DE-CALAIS			
Dover–Calais	P&O Ferries	1hr 30min	23 daily
Dover–Calais	DFDS Seaways	1hr 30min	10 daily
Dover–Dunkerque	DFDS Seaways	2hr	9–12 daily

FERRY OPERATORS

Brittany Ferries ☎0871 244 0744, ⒲brittanyferries.com
Condor Ferries ☎0845 609 1024, ⒲www.condorferries.co.uk
DFDS Seaways ☎0800 917 1201, ⒲dfdsseaways.co.uk
P&O Ferries ☎0871 664 6464, ⒲poferries.com

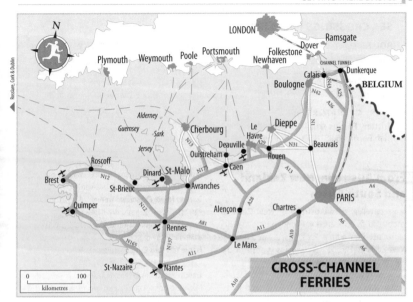

Rosslare, Cork & Dublin

CROSS-CHANNEL FERRIES

N

LONDON
Ramsgate
Plymouth Weymouth Poole Portsmouth Folkestone Dover
Newhaven
Calais Dunkerque
Boulogne BELGIUM
Alderney
Guernsey Sark
Jersey
Cherbourg Le Havre Dieppe
Deauville Beauvais
Roscoff Ouistreham Rouen
Brest Dinard St-Malo Caen
St-Brieuc Avranches PARIS
Quimper Alençon Chartres
Rennes
St-Nazaire Nantes Le Mans

0 100
kilometres

and seasonal offers) are obtainable from any British Rail travel centre. Students and anyone under 26 can buy heavily discounted tickets from Eurotrain outlets such as STA Travel and most student travel agents.

Rail travellers catching ferries from **Portsmouth** should be warned that "Portsmouth Harbour" station is nowhere near the cross-Channel ferry terminals, and the only connecting bus service is very intermittent.

By air

British European (W flybe.com) flies to Brest from Birmingham and Southampton, to Caen from Southend, to Nantes from Manchester and Southampton, and to Rennes from Exeter, Manchester, Southampton and Southend. **Easyjet** (W easyjet .com) connects Brest with London Gatwick, and Nantes with both Gatwick and Manchester, while **Ryanair** (W ryanair.com) links Dinard with London Stansted and East Midlands. From London City Airport, **Cityjet** (W cityjet.com) offers direct flights to Brest, Deauville and Nantes; **British Airways** (W ba.com) flies to Quimper; and **Air France** (W airfrance.com) to Nantes.

From Ireland

Three operators run ferries direct to Brittany and Normandy from Ireland. Services from both Rosslare and Dublin to **Cherbourg** operate year-round,

while in summer it's also possible to sail from Cork or Rosslare to **Roscoff**.

By air

Aer Lingus (W aerlingus.ie) flies direct from Dublin and Cork to Paris CDG, while Ryanair (W ryanair .com) flies from Dublin to Nantes, and from several Irish airports to London Stansted, where you can pick up onward flights to Dinard as well.

From the US and Canada

Getting to France from the US or Canada is straightforward; direct flights connect over thirty major North American cities with Paris. From there, it's simple to continue to Brittany or Normandy by rail – Rouen is just over an hour away, while super-fast TGV trains get to either Rennes or Nantes in around two hours – or by air. A connecting flight to Brest, the remotest Breton city, costs approximately US$150 extra.

Although flying to London is usually the cheapest way to reach Europe, price differences are so minimal that there's no point travelling to France via London unless you've specifically chosen to visit the UK as well.

An off-season midweek direct return flight to Paris can cost US$1000 from New York, and US$1200 from Los Angeles or Houston. From Canada, prices to Paris start at around CAN$1000 from Montréal or Toronto.

SEA CROSSINGS FROM IRELAND

ROUTE	OPERATOR	CROSSING TIME	FREQUENCY
Cork–Roscoff	Brittany Ferries	14hr	1 weekly, mid-March to Oct
Dublin–Cherbourg	Irish Ferries	19hr	1 weekly
Rosslare–Cherbourg	Irish Ferries	18hr 30min	3–4 weekly
Rosslare–Roscoff	Irish Ferries	16hr	2 weekly May–Sept

FERRY OPERATORS
Brittany Ferries ☎ 021 427 7801, ⓦ brittanyferries.ie
Irish Ferries ☎ 0818 300 400, ⓦ irishferries.com

From Australia, New Zealand and South Africa

Most travellers from **Australia** or **New Zealand** choose to fly to France via London; the majority of airlines can add a Paris leg to an Australia/New Zealand–Europe ticket. Flights via Asia or the Middle East, with a transfer or overnight stop in the airlines' home ports, are generally the cheapest option; those routed through the US tend to be slightly pricier. The cheapest return fares start at around Aus$2000 from Sydney, Perth and Darwin, and NZ$2700 from Auckland.

From **South Africa**, Johannesburg is the best place to start, with Air France flying direct to Paris from around R8000 return; from Cape Town, they fly via Amsterdam and cost from around R10,000. BA, flying via London, costs upwards of R9500 from Johannesburg and R10,000 from Cape Town.

AGENTS AND OPERATORS

Allez France ⓦ allezfrance.com. UK tour operator offering accommodation-only deals, as well as short breaks and other holiday packages.
Austin-Lehman Adventures ⓦ austinlehman.com. Bike and walking tours in Normandy for family groups or solo travellers.
Backroads ⓦ backroads.com. Cycling tours for families and singles, with the emphasis on going at your own pace. Accommodation ranges from campsites to luxury hotels.
Belle France ⓦ bellefrance.co.uk. Walking, cycling and boating holidays in Brittany and Normandy.
Bonnes Vacances Direct UK ⓦ bvdirect.co.uk. Agent for property owners in France for self-catering and B&B accommodation.
Brittany Travel ⓦ brittany.co.uk. Self-catering holidays throughout Brittany, and especially the Morbihan.
Canvas Holidays ⓦ canvasholidays.co.uk. Tailor-made caravan and camping holidays.
Chez Nous ⓦ cheznous.com. Thousands of self-catering and B&B properties.
Classic Journeys ⓦ classicjourneys.com. Seven-day coastal walking holidays in Normandy and Brittany, incorporating 3–4 hours of walking a day.

Cycling for Softies ⓦ cycling-for-softies.co.uk. Easy-going cycle holiday operator, offering rural jaunts in Normandy.
Discover France ⓦ discoverfrance.com. Self-guided cycling and walking holidays in both Normandy and Brittany.
Eurocamp UK ⓦ eurocamp.co.uk. Camping holidays with kids' activities and single-parent deals.
France Vacations ⓦ francevacations.net. Air/hotel and fly-drive packages to Normandy.
French Connections ⓦ frenchconnections.co.uk. Website offering holiday rentals throughout Brittany and Normandy, arranged direct with the owners at advantageous rates.
The French Experience ☎ 1 800 283 7262, ⓦ frenchexperience .com. US operator offering flexible escorted and self-drive tours, châteaux, apartment and cottage rentals, plus day-trips from Paris to destinations in Normandy.
French Travel Connection ⓦ frenchtravel.com.au. Australian operator offering a large range of holidays to France.
Gîtes de France ⓦ en.gites-de-france.com. Comprehensive listings of houses, cottages and chalets throughout both regions.
Headwater ⓦ headwater.com. Walking and cycling tours in Brittany.
Holiday France ⓦ holidayfrance.org.uk. Website that allows you to search for French tour operators by holiday type and location.
Holt's Battlefield Tours ⓦ holts.co.uk. Definitive guided battlefield tours; five-day tours to Normandy, covering the D-Day landings or other aspects of the invasion, depart from London.
Inntravel ⓦ inntravel.co.uk. Walking and cycling tours in Brittany.
Le Boat ⓦ leboat.com. Self-drive canal holidays in Brittany.
Locaboat ⓦ locaboat.com. French company that offers holidays on *pénichettes* (scaled-down replicas of commercial barges) on the Nantes–Brest canal.
Matthews Holidays ⓦ matthewsholidays.co.uk. Self-drive mobile-home holidays on good-quality campsites in southern Brittany.
North South Travel ⓦ northsouthtravel.co.uk. Friendly, competitive travel agency, offering discounted fares worldwide. Profits are used to support projects in the developing world, especially the promotion of sustainable tourism.
Saddle Skedaddle ⓦ skedaddle.co.uk. Inexpensive, week-long, self-guided cycle tours in Brittany, and epic guided trips all the way from St-Malo to Nice.
Travel.com ⓦ travel.com.au. Comprehensive Australian travel company.
Viking River Cruises ⓦ vikingrivercruises.com. Week-long river cruises along the Seine, from Paris to Rouen.

Getting around

The best way to travel around Brittany and Normandy is with a car or a bike. Public transport is far from impressive. SNCF trains are efficient, as ever in France, and the Atlantique TGV has reduced the Paris–Rennes journey to a mere two hours fifteen minutes, but the rail network circles the coast and, especially in Brittany, barely serves the inland areas.

Buses complement the trains to some extent – SNCF buses often pick up routes that trains no longer follow – but on the whole their timetables are geared more to market, school or working hours than the needs of tourists, and it can take a very long time to get where you want to go. If you come without your own transport, the ideal solution is to make longer journeys by train or bus, then to rent a bike (never a problem) to explore a particular locality.

By car

Car rental in France costs upwards of €250 per week (from around €70 a day); few British travellers see it as an economic alternative to bringing their own vehicle across the Channel. However, the major international rental chains are found throughout the region, including at the ferry ports.

North Americans and Australians should be forewarned that it is very difficult to rent a car with **automatic transmission**; if you can't drive a stick-shift, try to book an automatic well in advance, and expect to pay a much higher price for it. Most rental companies will only rent cars to customers aged under 25 on payment of a young-driver surcharge of around €20–25 per day; you still must be over 21 and have driven for at least one year.

Petrol/gas (*essence*) or diesel (*gazoil*) is least expensive at out-of-town superstores, and most expensive on the autoroutes. At night, many stations are unmanned, and often their automated 24-hour pumps will only accept French bank cards.

Autoroute driving, while fast, tends to be boring when it's not hair-raising, and the tolls in Normandy are expensive.

If you run into **mechanical difficulties**, all the major car manufacturers have garages and service stations in France. If you have an accident or break-in, make a report to the local police (and keep a copy) in order to make an insurance claim.

For motoring vocabulary, see p.384.

Legal requirements

British, Irish, Australian, Canadian, New Zealand and US **driving licences** are valid in France, though an International Driver's Licence makes life easier. If the vehicle is rented, its registration document (*carte grise*) and the insurance papers must be carried. The **minimum driving age** is 18, and provisional licences are not valid.

The vehicle registration document and the **insurance papers** must be carried; only the originals are acceptable. It's no longer essential for motorists from other EU countries to buy a green card to extend their usual insurance. If you have insurance at home then you have the minimal legal coverage in France; whether you have any more than that, and (if not) whether you want to buy more, is something to discuss with your own insurance company.

If your car is right-hand drive, you must have your **headlight dip** adjusted to the right before you go and, as a courtesy, change or paint them to yellow or stick on black glare deflectors. Similarly, you must also affix **GB plates** if you're driving a British car, and carry a red warning triangle, a single-use breathalyser and a spare set of headlight bulbs in your vehicle, as well as a reflective jacket that must be stored within reach of the driver's seat. Shops at the ferry terminals, and on the boats themselves, sell all the required equipment.

Seat belts are compulsory for the driver and all passengers; children under 10 can only sit in the front seat if they're in approved rear-facing child seats.

Rules of the road

The French **drive on the right**. Most drivers used to driving on the left find it easy to adjust. The biggest problem if you're driving a British car tends to be visibility when you want to overtake; you can buy special forward-view mirrors that may help.

Although the law of *priorité à droite* – which said you have to give way to traffic coming from your right, even when it is coming from a minor road – has largely been phased out, it still applies on some roads in built-up areas, so be vigilant at junctions. A sign showing a yellow diamond on a white background indicates that you have **right of way**, while the same sign with an oblique black slash warns you that vehicles emerging from the right have priority. **Stop signs** mean stop completely; *Cédez le passage* means "Give way". Other signs warning of potential dangers include *déviation* (diversion), *gravillons* (loose chippings), *boue* (mud) and *chaussée déformée* (uneven surface).

> ### ROAD INFORMATION
> Up-to-the-minute traffic information for all French roads can be obtained from the Bison Futé free-dial recorded information service (☎ 08 00 10 02 00; French only) or website ⓦ bison-fute.gouv.fr. Information on autoroutes is also available on the bilingual website ⓦ autoroutes.fr.

The main French national **speed limits**, which apply unless otherwise posted, are 130kph (80mph) on the tolled autoroutes; 110kph (68mph) on dual carriageways; and 90kph (56mph) on other roads. In wet weather, and for drivers with less than two years' experience, these limits are 110kph (68mph), 100kph (62mph) and 80kph (50mph) respectively. There's also a ceiling of 50kph (31mph) in towns, and on autoroutes when fog reduces visibility to less than 50m. Many towns and villages have introduced traffic calming and 30kph limits, and fixed and mobile radars are widely used. SatNav systems that identify the location of speed traps are illegal.

The **alcohol limit** is 0.05 percent (0.5 grams per litre of blood), and random breath tests and saliva tests for drugs are common. There are stiff **penalties** for driving violations, ranging from on-the-spot **fines** for minor infringements to the immediate confiscation of your licence and/or your car for more serious offences.

By scooter and motorbike

Scooters are relatively easy to find, and are ideal for pottering around local areas. Places that rent out bicycles often also rent scooters; expect to pay around €45 a day for a 50cc machine, less for longer periods. You only need a **motorbike licence** for bikes larger than 50cc. Rental prices for a motorbike are around €65 a day for a 125cc bike; expect to leave a hefty deposit – over €1000 is the norm – by cash or credit card too. **Crash helmets** are compulsory on all bikes, whatever the size, and the headlight must be switched on at all times. You are recommended to carry a first-aid kit and a set of spare bulbs.

By train

French **trains**, operated by the nationally owned SNCF (☎ 3635, ⓦ sncf.com), are by and large clean, fast and frequent, and their staff both courteous and helpful. All but the smallest stations (*gares SNCF*) have an information desk, while many also rent out bicycles.

Regional **timetables** and leaflets covering particular lines are available free at stations. "Autocar" (often abbreviated to "car") at the top of a column means it's an SNCF bus service, on which rail tickets and passes are valid. **Fares** are reasonable; children under 12 travel half-price and under-4s free. The ultra-fast TGVs (*Trains à Grande Vitesse*) require a supplement at peak times. The slowest trains, marked *Autotrain* in the timetable, stop at all stations.

Try to use the counter service for buying tickets, rather than the complicated computerized system; the latter changes the price of TGV tickets depending on demand, and you may find you've bought an expensive ticket without realizing that a later train is cheaper.

All tickets – but not passes – must be date-stamped in the orange machines at station platform entrances. It is an offence not to follow the instruction to *Compostez votre billet* ("Validate your ticket"). Train journeys may be broken for up to 24 hours at a time for as long as the ticket is valid (usually two months); if you plan longer stopovers, it's best to indicate this when buying your ticket.

Discounts and rail passes

French train **timetables** are divided into *période blanche* (normal or white period), and the cheaper *période bleue*, (off-peak or blue period), and a large number of additional **discounts** are also available. SNCF itself offers a range of travel cards, which can be purchased online or from main *gares SNCF*, and are valid for one year. Over-60s can get the Carte Senior (€60), which entitles the holder to up to fifty percent off tickets on TGVs, subject to availability, or other journeys starting during blue periods, and a 25 percent reduction on normal, white-period fares. The same percentage reductions are available for anyone under 28 (Carte 12–27; €50) and for up to four people travelling with a child under 12 (Carte Enfant Plus; €75). Those aged between 28 and 59 years can purchase a Carte Weekend (€75), which entitles the holder and a companion to limited reductions on weekend trips.

By bus

Buses cover far more Breton and Norman routes than the trains – and even when towns do have a rail link, buses are often quicker, cheaper and more direct. They are almost always short distance, however, requiring you to change if you're going further than from one town to the next. And timetables tend to be constructed to suit working, market and school hours – often dauntingly early when they do run, and prone to stop just when tourists need them most, becoming virtually non-existent on Sundays.

Larger towns usually have a central **gare routière** (bus station), most often found next to the *gare SNCF*. However, private bus companies don't always work together and may leave from an array of different points. The most convenient lines are those run by SNCF as an extension of rail links, which always run to/from the SNCF station (assuming there is one).

By bike

Bicycles have high status in France. Car ferries and SNCF trains carry them for a minimal charge, and the French respect cyclists – both as traffic, and, when you stop off at a restaurant or hotel, as customers. French drivers normally go out of their way to make room for you; it's the great British caravan you might have to watch out for.

Most importantly, distances in Brittany and Normandy are not great, the hills are sporadic and not too steep, cities like Rennes and Nantes have useful networks of **cycle lanes**, and the scenery is nearly always a delight. Even if you're quite unused to it, cycling sixty kilometres per day soon becomes very easy – and it's a good way to keep yourself fit enough to enjoy the rich regional food.

For a **short cycling break** straight off the ferry, the areas around **Cherbourg** and **Dieppe** are especially recommended. Dieppe is also the start of an increasingly popular cycle route to Paris; you can find full details at Ⓦdonaldhirsch.com /dieppeparis.pdf.

Most foreign visitors use **mountain bikes**, which the French call VTTs (*Vélos Touts Terrains*), for touring holidays, although if you've ever made a direct comparison you'll know it's much less effort, and much quicker, to cycle long distances and carry luggage on a traditional touring or racing bike. Whichever you prefer, do use cycle panniers; a backpack in the sun is unbearable.

Restaurants and hotels along the way are nearly always obliging about looking after your bike, even to the point of allowing it into your room. Most large towns have well-stocked retail and repair shops, where parts are normally cheaper than in Britain or the US. However, if you're using a foreign-made bike, it's a good idea to carry spare tyres, as French sizes are different. It can be harder to find parts for mountain bikes, the French enthusiasm

being directed towards racers instead. Bikes are often available to **rent** from campsites and hostels, as well as from cycle shops, some tourist offices and train stations and from seasonal stalls on islands, from perhaps €12 per day.

For cycling vocabulary, see p.384.

Taking bikes on French trains

Full details on taking your bike on the French **train network** can be found on Ⓦvelo.sncf.com. Broadly speaking, all trains will carry a folded or dismantled bike packed into a bag that measures no more than 120cm by 90cm; in addition, certain trains, including some TGVs, carry bikes free, either in dedicated bike racks or in the luggage van.

Boat trips and inland waterways

Boat trips on many of Brittany and Normandy's rivers, as well as out to the islands, are detailed throughout this book. More excitingly, you can **rent a canoe**, boat or even **houseboat** and make your own way along sections of the Nantes–Brest canal. Useful websites include Ⓦbretagne-info-nautisme.fr, Ⓦbretagne-fluviale.com and Ⓦlocaboat.com.

There is no charge for use of the waterways in Brittany or Normandy, and you can travel by boat without a permit for up to six months in a year. For information on maximum dimensions, documentation, regulations and so forth, see Ⓦvnf.fr.

Walking

Neither Brittany nor Normandy quite counts as serious hiking country, in that there are no mountains or extensive wilderness areas, and casual rambling along the clifftops and beside the waterways is the limit of most people's aims. However, 21 of the French GR long-distance walking trails – the *sentiers de grande randonnée* – run through the area. The GRs are fully signposted and equipped with campsites and rest huts along the way. The most interesting are the GR2 (*Sentier de la Seine*), which runs from Le Havre to Les Andelys; the GR341 (*Sentier de Bretagne*) along the Granit-Rose coast between Lannion and St-Brieuc; and the GR347 (*Val d'Oust au pays Gallo*) between Josselin and Redon.

Each GR path is described in a *Topo-guide*, produced by the principal French walkers' organization, the Fédération Française de la Randonnée Pédestre (Ⓦffrandonnee.fr), which gives a detailed account of the route (in French), including maps, campsites, sources of provisions and so on.

The **Brittany Walks** website, ⓦbrittanywalks.com, is an excellent resource for anyone planning local, coastal or long-distance hiking in Brittany. In addition, many tourist offices provide guides to local footpaths.

Accommodation

Accommodation is plentiful in both Brittany and Normandy, and for most of the year visitors can expect to be able simply to turn up in a town and find a room in a hotel or a place on a campsite. Many hoteliers and campsite managers, and almost all hostel managers, speak some English.

Problems arise mainly between July 15 and the end of August, when the French take their own vacations *en masse* – the first weekend of August is the busiest time of all. That said, the whole of July and August, extending in the more touristy areas to the period from mid-June to mid-September, is **high season** for the hotels. With campsites, which are generally open from around Easter to October or November, you can be more relaxed, unless you're touring with a caravan or camper van.

The tourist season in Brittany and Normandy runs roughly from Easter until the end of September; while hotels in the cities remain open all year, those in smaller towns and, especially, seaside resorts often close for several months in winter (Nov–March, for instance). It's quite possible to turn up somewhere in January or February to find that every hotel is closed; in addition, many family-run places close each year for two or three weeks sometime between May and September, and some hotels in smaller towns and villages close for one or two nights a week, usually Sunday or Monday.

Hotels

French **hotels** tend to be better value for money than they are in Britain and much of northern Europe, but not as good as in North America. In most towns, you'll be able to get a double room for around €50 (£42), or a single for around €40 (£33), though that may mean sharing a shower and/or toilet. A comfortable en-suite double room in a city is likely to cost from €70 (£58), while in a seafront hotel you'll probably pay around €80 (£66) in low season, and €100 (£84) in July or August.

The prices we give for each establishment listed in the Guide are, unless otherwise stated, for the **cheapest double room in high season**. Almost every hotel is likely to offer other rooms at higher prices, most obviously those that have extra facilities such as sea views, while off-season prices are likely to be significantly lower.

All French hotels are graded from zero to five stars. The price more or less corresponds to the number of stars, though the system is a little haphazard, having more to do with ratios of bathrooms per guest and so forth than genuine quality; ungraded and single-star hotels can be very good. North American visitors accustomed to staying in hotel rooms equipped with items like coffee-makers, safes and refrigerators should not automatically expect the same facilities in French hotels, even the more expensive ones. Lifts are also very much the exception rather than the rule in Normandy and Brittany. Genuine single rooms are rare; lone travellers normally end up in an ordinary double let at a slightly reduced rate. On the other hand, most hotels willingly equip rooms with extra beds, for three or more people, at a good discount.

Breakfast tends to be poor value at French hotels these days, though there is no obligation to take it. Many charge €8–10 per person for nothing more than fresh bread, jam and a jug of coffee or tea, while those that offer a more substantial buffet spread tend to charge more like €12–15.

The cost of eating dinner in a hotel's restaurant can be a more important factor to bear in mind when picking a place to stay. Officially, hotels are

---

TOP TEN PLACES TO STAY

These ten hotels, B&Bs and campsites are personal favourites, and span all budgets.

BESIDE THE SEA

Flaubert (hotel), Trouville, p.98
La Marine (hotel), Arromanches, p.117
Beau Séjour (hotel), Trégastel-Plage, p.228
Villa Tri Men (hotel), Ste-Marine, p.279
Bot Conan Lodge (campsite), Beg-Meil, p.281

IN THE COUNTRY

Manoir d'Archelles (hotel), Arques-La-Bataille, p.50
Château de la Ferté-Fresnel (B&B), La Ferté-Fresnel, p.152
Au Site Normand (hotel), Clécy, p.170
Jardins de l'Abbaye (hotel), St-Gelven, p.298
Relais de Brocéliande (hotel), Paimpont, p.306

not supposed to insist that you take meals, but they often do, and in busy resorts you may not find a room unless you agree to *demi-pension* (half-board). If you are unsure, ask to see the menu before checking in; cheap rooms aren't so cheap if you have to eat a €30 meal.

One of the great pleasures of travelling in the region is the sheer quality of **village hotels**. The fixtures and fittings may not always date from the twentieth century, let alone the twenty-first – at the bottom of the range, you'll find corduroy carpets creeping up the walls, blotchy linoleum curling from buckled wooden floors and clanking great brass keys that won't quite turn in the ill-fitting doors. However, the standards of service are consistently high, and it's rare indeed to stay in a hotel that doesn't take pride in maintaining a well-appointed and good-value restaurant serving traditional local food. **Wifi** is very widely available in hotels.

In recent years, outlets of several French **motel** chains have begun to proliferate, usually located alongside major through-routes on the outskirts of larger towns. Other than close to the ferry ports, there are fewer of these in Brittany and Normandy than elsewhere in the country, but those that do exist make a good alternative option for motorists, especially late at night.

The largest and most useful of the French **hotel federations** is Logis de France (ⓦ logishotels.com), an association of over 2800 independent hotels, promoted together for their consistently good food and reasonably priced rooms; they're recognizable on the spot by a green-and-yellow logo of a hearth. Two other, more upmarket federations worth mentioning are Châteaux & Hôtels de France (ⓦ chateauxhotels.com) and Relais du Silence (ⓦ relaisdusilence.com).

Bed and breakfast, rented accommodation and gîtes

In country areas, in addition to standard hotels, you will come across *chambres d'hôtes*, **bed-and-breakfast** accommodation in someone's house or farm. These vary in standard, but are rarely especially cheap; they usually cost the equivalent of a two-star hotel. However, they can be good sources of traditional home cooking. Average prices range between €60 and €120 for two people including breakfast; payment is almost always expected in cash. Some offer meals on request (*tables d'hôtes*), usually evenings only.

It's also worth considering renting **self-catering** accommodation. This will generally consist of self-contained country cottages known as *gîtes* or *gîtes ruraux*. Many *gîtes* are in converted barns or farm outbuildings, though some can be quite grand.

Both *gîtes* and *chambres d'hôtes* are listed on the Gîtes de France website (ⓦ gites-de-france.fr); you can search by type or theme as well as area, for example choosing a *gîte* near fishing or riding opportunities. Tourist offices maintain lists of places in their area that are not affiliated to Gîtes de France, and self-catering accommodation, often foreign-owned, is also easy to find online.

Hostels, foyers and gîtes d'étapes

At around €12–26 per night for a **dormitory bed**, usually with breakfast included, *Auberges de Jeunesse* – **hostels** – are invaluable for single travellers on a budget. For couples, however, and certainly for groups of three or more people, they'll not necessarily work out less than the cheaper hotels – particularly if you've had to pay a bus fare out to the edge of town to reach them. However, many hostels in Normandy and Brittany are beautifully sited, and they do allow you to cut costs by preparing your own food in their kitchens, or eating in cheap canteens.

As well as the two rival **French hostelling associations** – the Fédération Unie des Auberges de Jeunesse (FUAJ; ⓦ fuaj.org), and the smaller Ligue Française pour les Auberges de Jeunesse (LFAJ; ⓦ auberges-de-jeunesse.com) – there are also plenty of independent hostels, though these tend to be party places with an emphasis on good times rather than sleep.

Normally, to stay at FUAJ or LFAJ hostels you must show a current Hostelling International (HI) **membership card**. Visit ⓦ hihostels.com for details of your national youth hostel association and membership prices, as well as for worldwide booking facilities.

A further hostel-type alternative exists in the countryside, especially in hiking or cycling areas, in the form of the **gîtes d'étapes**. Less formal than hostels, these are often run by the local village or municipality, and provide basic beds and simple kitchen facilities from around €17. They are marked on the large-scale IGN walkers' maps and listed in individual GR *Topo-guides*. For more information, visit ⓦ gites-refuges.com.

Camping

Practically every village and town in the country has at least one **campsite**, to cater for the thousands of

French people who spend their holiday under canvas. Lists of sites in Brittany and Normandy are available from regional and local tourist boards, and on the Camping France website (@campingfrance.com).

The prices given for each site listed in the Guide are for two adults with a vehicle and a tent. The cheapest option – at around €12 per site per night – is usually the **Camping municipal**, run by the local municipality. In season or when they are officially open, they are always clean, with plenty of hot water, and often situated in the prime local position. Out of season, many of them don't even bother to have someone around to collect the overnight charge.

At superior categories of campsite, found especially on the coast, you'll pay prices similar to those of a budget hotel for the facilities – bars, restaurants, and often swimming pools. Many visitors spend their whole holiday at one site, in which case it's well worth booking ahead. Reckon on paying at least €15 per head with a tent, €20 with a vehicle.

Note, too, that almost all commercial campsites these days offer some form of cabin or bungalow for rent, typically at a similar cost to a hotel room.

Inland, *camping à la ferme* – on somebody's farm – is another (generally facility-less) possibility. The *Camping Qualité* designation (@campingqualite .com) indicates campsites with particularly high standards of hygiene, service and privacy, while the *Clef Verte* (@laclefverte.org) label is awarded to sites run along environmentally friendly lines.

Finally, a word of caution: never camp rough (*camping sauvage*, as the French call it) on anyone's land without first asking permission.

Food and drink

If you enjoy France's world-famous food, you're certain to love Brittany and Normandy. In ports like Dieppe and Honfleur in Normandy, and St-Malo, Roscoff and Quiberon in Brittany, fresh-caught fish and shellfish dominate almost every menu, while away from the sea, every village seems to hold a high-class restaurant. The emphasis in rural Normandy is on rich dairy produce, from meat prepared in thick creamy sauces, to signature cheeses like Camembert, Livarot and Pont l'Evêque.

With no wine production in Normandy, and only the Muscadet-style whites coming from the

southeast of Brittany, the most interesting local **alcohol** is derived from the region's orchards. Cider is made everywhere, along with its pear equivalent, *poiré*, while Normandy is renowned for its **Calvados** (apple brandy) and Fécamp's **Benedictine** liqueur.

Breton food

Brittany's proudest contribution to world cuisine has to be the (white-flour) **crêpe**, and its savoury (buckwheat) equivalent, the **galette**. Both are readily available in crêperies throughout the region, where a typical set menu, consisting of one of each, is likely to cost around €10. Despite the English translation, buckwheat, known in French as *blé noir* or *sarrasin*, is not a type of wheat, and is therefore OK to eat if you're gluten-intolerant.

Gourmets are more likely to be enticed to Brittany by its magnificent array of **seafood**, and above all its **shellfish** – mussels, oysters, clams, and scallops, to name but a few. Restaurants in resorts such as St-Malo and Quiberon jostle for the attention of fish fanatics, while some smaller towns – such as Cancale, which specializes in oysters (*huîtres*), and Erquy, with its scallops (*Coquilles St-Jacques*) – depend on a single specific mollusc for their livelihood.

Although they can't claim to be uniquely Breton, two appetizers feature on every self-respecting menu. These are **moules marinière**, giant bowls of succulent orange mussels steamed open in white wine, shallots and parsley (and perhaps enriched with cream or crème fraîche to become *moules à la crème*), and **soupe de poissons**, served with a pot of the garlicky mayonnaise known as *rouille* (coloured with pulverized sweet red pepper) and a bowl of croûtons. Jars of *soupe de poissons* – or crab, or lobster – are always on sale in seaside *poissonneries*, and make an ideal way to take a taste of France home with you. Seaside restaurants also offer the

For a comprehensive glossary of French food and drink terms, see p.385.

assiette de fruits de mer, a mountainous heap of langoustines, crabs, oysters, mussels, clams, whelks and cockles, most of them raw and all (with certain obvious exceptions) delicious. Main courses tend to be plainer than in Normandy, with fresh local fish being prepared with relatively simple sauces. Skate served with capers, or salmon baked with a mustard or cheese sauce, are typical dishes, while even the *cotriade*, a stew containing such fish as sole, turbot or bass, as well as shellfish, is distinctly less rich than the Mediterranean bouillabaisse.

Brittany is also better than much of France in maintaining its respect for fresh green vegetables, thanks to the extensive local production of peas, cauliflowers, artichokes and the like. Only with the desserts can things get rather too heavy; *far Breton*, considered a great delicacy, is a stodgy baked concoction of sponge, custard and chopped plums, while a *kouïgn-amann* is a rich cake containing multiple layers of folded butter.

Norman food

The food of Normandy owes its distinguishing feature – its gut-bursting, heart-pounding richness – to the lush orchards and dairy herds of the region's agricultural heartland, and especially the area known as the **Pays d'Auge**. Menus abound in meat such as veal (*veau*) cooked in *vallée d'Auge* style, which consists largely of the profligate addition of cream and butter. Many dishes also feature orchard fruit in its natural state or in more alcoholic forms – either as apple or pear **cider**, or further distilled to produce **brandies** (Calvados in the case of apples, *poiré* for pears).

Normans have a great propensity for blood and guts. In addition to game such as rabbit and duck, they enjoy such intestinal preparations as **andouilles**, the blood sausages known in English as chitterlings, and tripe, stewed for hours *à la mode de Caen*.

A full blowout at a country restaurant will also traditionally entail a pause or two between courses for the *trou normand* – a glass of Calvados while you catch your breath before struggling on with the feast.

Normandy's long coastline ensures that it, too, is a great destination for **seafood**. Many of the larger ports and resorts hold long waterfront lines of restaurants. Honfleur is the most enjoyable of these, but Dieppe, Cherbourg and Trouville also offer endless eating opportunities.

The most famous products of Normandy's meadow-munching cows are of course its gooey, pungent, irresistible **cheeses**. All the best-known varieties come from the Pays d'Auge, where monks were already making cheese a thousand years ago. Among them are the soft, square Pont-l'Évêque; the firmer and smellier Livarot; and, the queen of the crop, **Camembert**, a variation of Brie that dates from the 1790s. It's since been copied all over the world, but nothing can match the creamy taste and sharp smell of a fresh-made Camembert in its native land.

Restaurants and cafés

Both Brittany and Normandy hold countless **restaurants**, and in many towns **brasseries** add to the choice. There's no distinction between the two in terms of quality or price range, though brasseries, which resemble cafés, serve quicker meals at most hours of the day; restaurants tend to stick to the traditional meal times of noon until 2pm and 7 to 9.30pm. For the more upmarket places it's wise to make reservations – easily done on the same day. In small towns it may be impossible to get anything other than a bar sandwich after 10pm; in major cities, central brasseries will serve until 11pm or midnight and one or two may stay open all night. Restaurants usually close on one day each week (often Mon), in addition to the odd lunch time or evening. During low season (in other words, outside July & Aug) in seasonal resorts, closing times might extend to a couple of days per week. Don't forget that hotel restaurants are open to non-residents, and are likely not only to offer the best food in town but also to do so at good-value prices; the green-and-yellow **Logis de France** symbol is always worth looking out for.

Prices have to be posted outside. Almost all restaurants, and many brasseries, serve one or more **set menus**, for which you pay a fixed overall price for a certain number of courses, with a limited

> ### VEGETARIANS
>
> On the whole, **vegetarians** can expect a somewhat lean time in Brittany and Normandy. One or two towns have specifically vegetarian restaurants, but elsewhere you'll have to hope you find a sympathetic restaurant (crêperies can be good standbys). Sometimes they're willing to replace a meat dish on the *menu fixe* with an omelette; other times you'll have to pick your way through the *carte*.
>
> If you are **vegan**, however, you should probably forget about eating in French restaurants altogether and try to cook your own food.

WEEKLY MARKETS

The list below features the biggest and best markets of Brittany and Normandy, with an emphasis on those specializing in **fresh food** and **local produce**. Bear in mind that in addition to the specific days listed here, most large cities – **Rennes**, **Rouen** and **Caen**, for example – tend to have markets every day (with the occasional exception of Mon).

	NORMANDY	BRITTANY
Monday	Bricquebec, Carentan, Pont-Audemer, Pont-L'Éveque, St-Pierre-sur-Dives, Torigni-sur-Vire, Vierville-sur-Mer, Vimoutiers	Auray, Benodet, Combourg, Concarneau, Douarnenez, Moncontour, Pontivy, Questembert, Redon, St-Quay, Vitré
Tuesday	Alençon, Argentan, Bagnoles, Balleroy, Cherbourg, Deauville, Grandcamp-Maisy, Portbail, Thury-Harcourt, Villedieu-les-Poêles, Villers-sur-Mer, Vire	Dinard, Le Conquet, Locmariaquer, Paimpol, Pont-Aven, St-Malo, St-Pol, La Trinité
Wednesday	Bayeux, Bernay, Cabourg, Carrouges, Évreux, Granville, Honfleur, Isigny-sur-Mer, St-Hilaire, St-Lô, Trouville, Vernon, Yport	Audierne, Broons, Carnac, Douarnenez, Guérande, Quimper, Roscoff, St-Brieuc, Tréguier, Vannes
Thursday	Alençon, Bellême, Brionne, Cherbourg, Conches-en-Ouche, Coutances, Étretat, Forges-les-Eaux, Houlgate, Lisieux, Livarot, Ste-Mère-Église	Binic, Dinan, Dinard, Hennebont, Huelgoat, Lamballe, Lannion, Malestroit, Pont l'Abbé
Friday	Alençon, Argentan, Cabourg, Deauville, Caen, Domfront, Eu, Pont-Audemer, St-Hilaire, St-Lô, St-Valery, Valognes, Vimoutiers, Vire	Concarneau, Douarnenez, Fouesnant, Guingamp, Jugon-les-Lacs, Perros-Guirec, Ploërmel, Quimperlé, St-Malo, La Trinité, Le Val-André
Saturday	Avranches, Bagnoles, Bayeux, Beuvron-en-Auge, Caudebec, Cherbourg, Deauville, Dieppe, Dives, Falaise, Fécamp, Granville, Honfleur, Les Andelys, Ry, Sées, St-Lô, Verneuil-sur-Avre	Audierne, Carhaix, Dinard, Dol, Douarnenez, Erquy, Fougères, Guérande, Guingamp, Josselin, Locmariaquer, Morlaix, St-Brieuc, Quiberon, Quimper, Rennes, Vannes, Vitré
Sunday	Alençon, Argentan, Brionne, Cabourg, Caen, Conches-en-Ouche, La Ferrière-sur-Risle, Pirou Port-en-Bessin, St-Valery, Trouville	Auray, Baud, Cancale, Carnac, Plélan-le-Grand, Quimper, St-Brieuc

range of options for each, and service included. Perhaps confusingly for English speakers, the French term for this is *menu*. Reviews in the Guide that mention restaurants having "menus at €20 and €25" etc are referring to these set menus.

The French term for the full printed list of every dish – what the English would call the "menu" – is *la carte*. Hence the expression *à la carte*, to describe ordering individual dishes rather than a full meal.

Finally, at **lunch time**, many restaurants offer a daily special known as the *plat du jour*, typically costing around €10, and/or a set menu, which may be called either a *formule* or a *menu*, for €12–15.

Along the coast, in summer, you can also almost always find somewhere selling mussels and chips (*moules frites*) for €10 or so. Most bars and cafés – there's no real difference – advertise *les snacks*, or *un casse-croûte* (a bite), with pictures of omelettes, fried eggs, hot dogs or various sandwiches. Even when they don't, they'll usually fill a half or third of a baguette with such ingredients as *jambon* (ham), *fromage* (cheese), *thon* (tuna), *saucisson* (sausage) or *poulet* (chicken). Toasted sandwiches – most commonly *croques-monsieur* (cheese and ham) or *croques-madame* (the same thing with an egg on top) – are widely available.

In the evening, virtually any restaurant will serve you a good three-course **dinner** for €18–30, while four-course blowouts, including a starter as well as separate meat and fish courses, cost anything from €25 to €75.

North American visitors should bear in mind that in France an *entrée* is an appetizer or starter; the main course of the meal is the *plat principal*. In the French sequence of courses, salad usually comes separate from the main dish, and cheese precedes a dessert. You will be offered coffee, which almost always costs extra, to finish off the meal.

Service compris (s.c.) means the **service charge** is included, which is usually the case on all set menus; *service non compris (s.n.c.)*, or *service en sus*, means that it isn't, and you need to calculate an additional fifteen percent. **Wine** (*vin*) or a drink (*boisson*) is unlikely to be included, although a glass is occasionally thrown in with cheaper menus.

The French not only offer reduced-price menus for **children**, they also create an atmosphere, even in otherwise fairly snooty establishments, that positively welcomes kids. It's seen as self-evident that large family groups should be able to eat out together. That said, you may well be obliged to order the children's menu rather than a single, cheaper item à la carte, so things can work out expensive. A rather murkier area is that of **dogs** in the dining room; it can be quite a surprise in a provincial hotel to realize that the majority of your fellow diners are attempting to keep dogs concealed beneath their tables. One final note is that, no matter what you were taught in school, you should always call the waiter or waitress *Monsieur* or *Madame* (*Mademoiselle* if a young woman), never *garçon*.

Picnics and takeaways

For **picnic** and **takeaway food**, nothing beats buying fresh ingredients in a local **market**. Failing that, even the smallest village will hold a **charcuterie** selling cooked meats, prepared snacks such as *bouchées de la reine* (seafood vol-au-vents), ready-made dishes and assorted salads. You can buy by weight or ask for *une tranche* (a slice), *une barquette* (a carton) or *une part* (a portion). The cheapest, in towns, are the supermarkets' charcuterie counters.

Salons de thé, which open from mid-morning to late evening, serve brunches, salads, quiches, etc, as well as cake and ice cream and a wide selection of teas. They tend to be a good deal pricier than cafés or brasseries – you're paying for the ritzy surroundings.

Patisseries, of course, have impressive arrays of cakes and pastries, often using local cream to excess. In addition to standard French pastries, the Bretons specialize in heavy, pudding-like affairs, dripping with butter, such as *kouïgn-amann* and *gaufres* – cream-drenched waffles.

Drinking

Where you can eat you can invariably **drink**, and normally vice versa. Drinking is done at a leisurely pace, whether as a prelude to food (*apéritif*), a sequel (*digestif*), or the accompaniment.

Every bar or café is obliged to display a full price list, which will usually show progressively increasing prices for drinks at the bar (*au comptoir*), sitting down (*la salle*), and on the terrace (*la terrasse*).

Wine (*vin*) is the regular drink. Red is *rouge*, white is *blanc*, or there's *rosé*. *Vin de table* – house wine – is generally drinkable and always cheap. Restaurant mark-ups for quality wines can be outrageous, in a country where wine is so cheap in the shops; if you're worried about the cost, ask for *vin ordinaire*. You should in any case be given the house wine (or *cuvée*) unless you specify otherwise. Remember you can usually buy not only by the bottle and by the glass, but also by the carafe – ask for *un quart* or *un pichet* (quarter-litre), *un demi-litre* (half-litre) or *une carafe* (a litre). In bars, you normally buy by the glass.

Strictly speaking, no wine is produced in Brittany or Normandy. However, along the lower Loire Valley, the *département* of Loire-Atlantique, centred on Nantes, is still generally regarded as "belonging" to Brittany. Vineyards here are responsible for the dry white **Muscadet** – which is what normally goes into *moules marinière* – and the even drier **Gros-Plant**. You'll find a brief account of how to visit some of the vineyards where they are made on p.313.

Cider (*cidre*) is extremely popular. In Brittany it's a standard accompaniment to a meal of crêpes and may be offered on restaurant set menus. Normans more often consume it in bars. Most of the many varieties are very dry and very wonderful. *Poiré*, pear cider, is also produced, but on a small scale and is not commercially distributed.

The familiar Belgian and German brands account for most of the **beer** you'll find. Draught (*à la pression*, usually Kronenbourg) is the cheapest drink you can have next to coffee and wine – ask for *un demi* (defined as 25cl). Bottled beer is exceptionally cheap in supermarkets.

British-style ales and stouts are also popular. Every town seems to have some Celtic-affiliated bar that sells Guinness, and good pubs can be found in cities like Brest, Rennes and Quimper. There are even home-grown Breton beers, such as Coreff from Morlaix, and Britt, a white beer brewed in Concarneau.

Strong alcohols are drunk from 5am as pre-work fortifiers, right through the day; Bretons have a reputation for commitment to this. Brandies and dozens of *eaux de vie* (spirits) and liqueurs are always available. In Normandy, the most famous are **Calvados**, brandy distilled from apples and left to mature for anything upwards of ten years, and **Benedictine**, distilled at Fécamp from an obscure mix of ingredients (see p.56). Measures are generous, but they don't come cheap, especially in restaurants (where Calvados is traditionally drunk as the *trou Normand*, or "hole", between courses). The same applies to imported spirits like whisky (Scotch).

Bottles of mineral water (*eau minérale*) and spring water (*eau de source*) – either sparkling (*pétillante*) or still (*eau plate*) – abound, from the best-seller Perrier to the obscurest spa product. But there's not much wrong with the tap **water** (*eau du robinet*).

Coffee in Normandy is invariably espresso and very strong; in Brittany, particularly in villages, it is sometimes made in jugs, very weak. *Un café* or *un express* is black, *un crème* is white, *un café au lait* (served at breakfast) is espresso in a large cup or bowl filled up with hot milk. Most bars will also serve *un déca*, decaffeinated coffee. You can get ordinary **tea** (*thé*), usually Lipton's, everywhere, while herb teas (*tisanes*) are also widely available. The more common ones are *verveine* (verbena), *tilleul* (lime blossom) and *camomille* (camomile). *Chocolat chaud* (hot chocolate) lives up to the high standards of French food and drink, and can be ordered in any café.

The media

For anyone who can read French, or understand it when spoken, the print and electronic media in France match any in the world. English-language newspapers are widely available, many hotels offer English-language TV and BBC radio can easily be picked up.

Newspapers and magazines

British and North American **newspapers** – at the very least, the *International Herald Tribune* – are generally widely available, especially in summer and in larger towns. As for the **French press**, the widest circulations are enjoyed by the regional dailies. Throughout Normandy and Brittany, the most important and influential paper is *Ouest-France* (W ouest-france.fr). Based in Rennes, this publishes numerous local editions, worth picking up for their listings supplements, at the very least. Of the national dailies, *Le Monde* (W lemonde.fr) is the most intellectual and respected, with few concessions to entertainment, but a meticulously styled French that is probably the easiest to understand. *Libération* (W liberation.com; *Libé* for short), which has its own Rennes edition, is moderately left-wing, pro-European, independent and more colloquial, with good, if specific, coverage.

Weekly **magazines** include the wide-ranging left-leaning *Le Nouvel Observateur* (W nouvelobs.com), its right-wing counterpart *L'Express* (W lexpress.fr) and the centrist with bite, *Marianne* (W marianne.net). The best, and funniest, investigative journalism is in the satirical *Canard Enchaîné* (W lecanardenchaine.fr), unfortunately almost incomprehensible to non-native speakers.

Radio

The main **radio** provider, Radio France (W radio-france.fr), operates seven stations, including the regional France Bleu network, France Culture, France Info for news and France Musique. Other major private stations include Europe 1 (W europe1.fr) for news, debate and sport and NRJ (W nrj.fr) for relentless chart music.

English-language broadcasts are available from the BBC (W bbc.co.uk/worldservice), Radio Canada (W rcinet.ca) and Voice of America (W voa.gov). See their websites for local frequencies.

TV

French **terrestrial TV** has six channels: three public (France 2, France 3 and Arte/France 5); one subscription (Canal Plus – with some unencrypted programmes); and two commercial open broadcasts (TF1 and M6). Of these, TF1 (W tf1.fr) and France 2 (W france2.fr) are the most popular channels, showing a broad mix of programmes.

Cable and **satellite** channels you may find available in hotels include CNN, BBC World and BBC Prime, Eurosport, MTV, Planète, which specializes in documentaries, and Jimmy. The main French-run music channel is MCM.

Festivals and events

The most interesting Breton events are without doubt the region's cultural festivals. At the largest, the Lorient Festival Inter-Celtique (Aug), music, performance, food and drink of all seven Celtic nations are featured in a completely authentic gathering that pulls in cultural nationalists (and ethnic music fans) from Ireland to Spain.

Look out also for local club events put on by individual **Celtic folklore** groups – Cercles, Bagadou or, best of the lot, **Festou-Noz**. These are most prolific in Nantes, but wherever you are in the province, the listings pages of *Ouest-France* are worth scrutiny. The "Breton music" section at the end of this book recommends clubs and venues to check out.

Religious **pardons**, sometimes promoted as tourist attractions in Brittany, are rather different affairs. These are essentially church processions, organized by a particular community on the local saint's day. Though generally small-scale, some, like that at Ste-Anne-d'Auray, have over the centuries taken on region-wide status as pilgrimages. Rather than being carnivals or fêtes, they are primarily very serious, centred on lengthy and rather gloomy church services. If you're not interested in the religious aspects, only the food and drink stalls are likely to hold any great appeal.

By and large, **Normandy** lacks any specific cultural traditions to celebrate, but does its best to make up with celebrations of related historic events – births and deaths of William the Conqueror, Ste Thérèse, etc. The **D-Day** (June 6) landings along the Invasion Beaches are always marked in some way.

In both Normandy and Brittany, avoid the *Spectacles*, camp and overpriced outdoor shows on some mythical theme or other, held most regularly (and most tackily) at Bagnoles and Elven.

On the more mainstream cultural side, the larger cities – Rouen, Rennes and Nantes – have active theatre, opera and classical music seasons, though little happens during the summer. Cinema is most interesting in these cities, too, and the region is host to perhaps the most accessible French **film festival** – Deauville's American Film Festival (Sept).

Calendar of events

JANUARY TO APRIL

Carnival Granville, Feb/March; Ⓦ carnavaldegranville.fr. See p.133.
La Route du Rock St-Malo, mid-Feb; Ⓦ laroutedurock.com. See p.186.

La Route du Rock Rennes, mid-Feb; Ⓦ laroutedurock.com. See p.205.
Les Hivernautes music and film festival Quimper, March; Ⓦ hivernautes.com. See p.277.
Festival Panoramas music festival Morlaix, April; Ⓦ festivalpanoramas.com. See p.242.
Scallop Festival Erquy, late April; Ⓦ erquy-tourisme.com. See p.209.
Scallop Festival St-Quay-Portrieux, late April; Ⓦ saintquayportrieux.com. See p.217.

MAY AND JUNE

Jazz Sous Les Pommiers Coutances, late May; Ⓦ jazzsouslespommiers.com See p.131.
St-Yves Pardon Tréguier, third Sun in May; Ⓦ tregor-cotedajoncs -tourisme.com. See p.223.
Art Rock Festival St-Brieuc, end May/early June; Ⓦ artrock.org. See p.216.
Étonnants Voyageurs festival of travel books and films St-Malo, end May/early June; Ⓦ etonnants-voyageurs.com. See p.186.
D-Day Ceremonies Invasion Beaches, June 6, Ⓦ ddayfestival.com. See p.110.
Le Rock dans tous ses Etats Évreux, last weekend in June; Ⓦ lerock.org. See p.148.

JULY AND AUGUST

Astropolis electronic music festival Brest, first weekend of July; Ⓦ astropolis.org. See p.258.
Medieval Fair Bayeux, first weekend in July; Ⓦ bayeux-bessin-tourisme.com. See p.106.
Tombées de la Nuit theatre and music festival Rennes, first three weekends of July; Ⓦ lestombeesdelanuit.com. See p.205.
Troménie Pardon Locronan, second Sun in July; Ⓦ locronan -tourisme.com. See p.266.
Fête de St-Clair La Haye du Routot, July 16; Ⓦ lahayederoutot .com. See p.66.
Fête des Remparts Dinan, third weekend in July, even-numbered years only; Ⓦ fete-remparts-dinan.com. See p.191.
Les Vieilles Charrues Rock festival Carhaix, third weekend in July; Ⓦ vieillescharrues.asso.fr. See p.292.
Festival de Cornouaille Quimper, late July; Ⓦ www.festival -cornouaille.com. See p.277.
Pardon Ste-Anne-d'Auray, July 26; Ⓦ sainteanne-sanctuaire.com. See p.343.
Pont du Rock festival Malestroit, last weekend in July; Ⓦ aupontdurock.com. See p.306.
Temps Fête Maritime festival Douarnenez, last weekend in July; Ⓦ tempsfete.com. See p.267.
Fest Jazz Châteauneuf-du-Faou, last weekend in July; Ⓦ fest-jazz .com. See p.288.
Jazz Festival Vannes, late July/early Aug; Ⓦ jazzavannes.fr. See p.348.
Festival du Bout du Monde World Music Festival, Crozon peninsula, early Aug; Ⓦ festivalduboutdumonde.com. See p.262.
Cheese Fair Livarot, first weekend Aug; Ⓦ livarot-tourisme.com. See p.157.

Medieval Fair Moncontour, Aug; ⓦ tourisme-moncontour.com. See p.214.

Festival Inter-Celtique Lorient, first to second Sun, Aug; ⓦ festival-interceltique.com. See p.320.

Festival des Traversées Folk music, Île de Tatihou, first fortnight in Aug; ⓦ tatihou.manche.fr. See p.127.

Festival du Chant de Marin Paimpol, second weekend in Aug; ⓦ paimpol-festival.fr. See p.219.

Fête Brièronne Île de Fedrun, early Aug; ⓦ saint-joachim.com. See p.353.

Semaines Musicales Quimper, first three weeks in Aug; ⓦ semaines-musicales-quimper.org. See p.277.

La Route du Rock St-Malo, middle weekend in Aug; ⓦ laroutedurock.com. See p.186.

Les Filets Bleus Breton music festival Concarneau, middle weekend in Aug; ⓦ festivaldesfiletsbleus.fr. See p.281.

Normandy Horse Show Saint-Lô, mid-Aug; ⓦ normandie-horse-show.fr. See p.171.

Saint Loup Breton Dance Festival Guingamp, mid-Aug; ⓦ dansebretonne.com. See p.214.

Festival of the Sea St-Valery-en-Caux, mid-Aug; ⓦ ville-saint-valery-en-caux.fr. See p.55.

Onion Festival Roscoff, late Aug; ⓦ roscoff.fr. See p.237.

Festijazz Houlgate, late Aug; ⓦ ville-houlgate.fr. See p.99.

SEPTEMBER TO DECEMBER

Pardon Le Folgoët, first Sun in Sept; ⓦ notre-dame-folgoet.cef.fr. See p.246.

Kite-flying festival Dieppe, early Sept, even-numbered years only; ⓦ dieppe-cerf-volant.org. See p.47.

American Film Festival Deauville, first week in Sept; ⓦ festival-deauville.com. See p.97.

Pardon de Nôtre-Dame-de-Roncier Josselin, Sept 8; ⓦ josselin-communaute.fr. See p.300.

Holy Cross cattle and animal fair Lessay, second weekend in Sept; ⓦ canton-lessay.com. See p.130.

Archangel Michael Festival Mont-St-Michel, Sun nearest Sept 29; ⓦ ot-montsaintmichel.com. See p.137.

Cider Festival Caudebec, last Sun in Sept; ⓦ caudebec-en-caux.fr. See p.65.

Wild Mushroom Festival Bellême, first weekend in Oct; ⓦ mycologiades.com. See p.154.

Les Bordées de Cancale music festival Cancale, first weekend in Oct; ⓦ lesbordees.fr. See p.195.

British Film Festival Dinard, first week in Oct; ⓦ festivaldufilm-dinard.com. See p.190.

Fête du Ventre food festival Rouen, mid-Oct; ⓦ feteduventre.com. See p.77.

Cider Festival Beuvron-en-Auge, last Sun in Oct; ⓦ beuvron cambremer.com. See p.156.

Le Goût du Large food festival Port-en-Bessin, early Nov; ⓦ portenbessin-huppain.fr. See p.117.

Herring Festival St-Valery-en-Caux, third Sun in Nov; ⓦ ville-saint-valery-en-caux.fr. See p.55.

Yaouank festival geared towards young ("youank", in Breton) local musicians, Rennes, first three weeks in Nov; ⓦ yaouank.com. See p.205.

Les Transmusicales international rock festival Rennes, first week in Dec; ⓦ lestrans.com. See p.205.

Travel essentials

Beaches

Beaches are public property within 5m of the high-tide mark, so you can walk past private villas and set foot on islands. Another law, however, forbids you to camp.

Costs

While France as a whole ranks among the more expensive European countries for visitors, the price of food and accommodation in Brittany and Normandy is still lower than in Britain, and distances – and thus transport costs – remain relatively small.

On a shoestring level, camping and eating at least one picnic meal a day, taking buses or cycling, two people travelling together could get by on €60 (£50/$80) per person per day. Moving slightly more upmarket, staying in modest hotels, spending a bit on restaurants and driving, you should reckon on perhaps €110 (£90/$150) per person per day.

Accommodation is likely to represent the bulk of your expenditure. Hotels average around €55 (£45/$75) for the simplest double room in the cheapest places. If you're sharing, that works out at little more per person than the €18–26 per person charged by hostels. Camping, of course, can cut costs dramatically, so long as you avoid the plusher private sites; the local *Camping municipal* rarely asks for more than €10 a head.

As for eating out, you should always be able to find a good three-course meal for €20–25, or a takeaway for a lot less. Fresh food from shops and markets is surprisingly expensive in relation to low restaurant prices, but it's always possible to save money with a basic picnic of bread, cheese and fruit. More sophisticated meals – takeaway salads and ready-to-heat dishes – can be put together for reasonable prices if you shop at charcuteries (delis) and supermarkets. On the other hand, drinks in cafés and bars can make a severe hole in your pocket. Nowhere in the region matches Paris prices, but €5 cups of coffee are not unheard of, and a cognac costs double that. Note, however, that drink prices in most cafés are lower when ordering and drinking at the bar as opposed to occupying a table and being served by a waiter.

Transport costs obviously depend entirely on how (and how much) you travel, but note that car rental tends to be more expensive in France than elsewhere.

Admission charges for sites and museums can be high enough to make you picky as to what you visit – even with a student card (many museums have reduced admission for all under-26s, and not just students). But this is no special hardship: the region's attractions lie as much in its towns and landscapes as in anything fenced off or put in a showcase.

Discounts

Once obtained, various official and quasi-official youth/student ID cards soon pay for themselves in savings. Full-time students are eligible for the **International Student ID Card** (ISIC, Ⓦ isic.org) which entitles bearers to special air, rail and bus fares and discounts at museums and for certain services. You have to be 25 or younger to qualify for the **International Youth Travel Card (IYTC)**, while teachers are eligible for the **International Teacher Card (ITIC)**.

Crime and personal safety

Although compared to Paris or the south of France, crime is a low-key problem, you still need to take normal precautions against petty theft. To report a theft, go to the local *gendarmerie* (police station), and ask for the requisite piece of paper (the *constat de vol*) for a claim. The two main types of French police, the Police Nationale and the Gendarmerie Nationale, are for all practical purposes indistinguishable; you can go to either.

Drivers are obviously vulnerable, with the ever-present risk of a break-in. Vehicles are rarely stolen, but luggage left in cars makes a tempting target, and foreign number plates are easy to spot.

For non-criminal driving violations such as speeding, the police can impose on-the-spot fines. Should you be arrested on any charge, you have the right to contact your nearest consulate. Although the police are not always as cooperative as they might be, it is their duty to assist you – likewise in the case of losing your passport or all your money.

Officially, you're supposed to carry identification documents at all times, and the police are entitled to stop you and demand it.

From a safety point of view, hitching is definitely not advisable.

Electricity

Almost always 220V, using plugs with two round pins. If you need a transformer, it's best to buy one before leaving home, though you can find them in big department stores in France.

Entry requirements

Citizens of **EU countries** can enter France freely on a valid passport or national identity card, while those from many **non-EU countries**, including Australia, Canada, New Zealand and the United States, do not need a visa for a stay of **up to ninety days**. South African citizens require a short-stay visa for up to ninety days, which should be applied for in advance and costs €60.

All non-EU citizens who wish to remain **longer than ninety days** must apply for a long-stay visa, for which you'll have to show proof of – among other things – a regular income, or sufficient funds to support yourself, and medical insurance. Be aware, however, that the situation can change and it's advisable to check with your nearest French embassy or consulate before departure. For further information about visa regulations consult the Ministry of Foreign Affairs website: Ⓦ diplomatie.gouv.fr.

FRENCH EMBASSIES AND CONSULATES

Australia Canberra Ⓦ ambafrance-au.org.
Britain London and Edinburgh Ⓦ ambafrance-uk.org.
Canada Montréal Ⓦ consulfrance-montreal.org; Toronto Ⓦ consulfrance-toronto.org.
Ireland Dublin Ⓦ ambafrance-ie.org.
New Zealand Wellington Ⓦ ambafrance-nz.org.
South Africa Johannesburg Ⓦ consulfrance-jhb.org.
USA Washington Ⓦ ambafrance-us.org.

Fishing

You get fishing rights by becoming a member of an authorized fishing club – tourist offices have details. The main areas for river fishing are in Brittany, in the Aulne River around Châteaulin and in the Morbihan.

Gay and lesbian travellers

France tends to have liberal attitudes to homosexuality. The age of consent is 15, and same-sex couples can marry and adopt children. Brittany and Normandy, however, have little conspicuous gay life; the best source for clubs and meeting places is the *Gai Pied Guide* (Ⓦ gayvox.fr). *Têtu* (Ⓦ tetu .com) is a highly rated gay/lesbian magazine with events listings and contact addresses; you can buy it in bookshops or through their website, which is also an excellent source of information.

Health

Visitors to France have little to worry about as far as health is concerned. No vaccinations are required, there are no nasty diseases and tapwater is safe to drink. The worst that's likely to happen to you is a case of sunburn or an upset stomach from eating too much rich food. And if you do need treatment, you should be in good hands.

Under France's excellent **health system**, all services, including doctor's consultations, prescribed medicines, hospital stays and ambulance call-outs, incur a charge which you have to pay upfront. EU citizens are entitled to a refund (usually 70 percent) of medical and dental expenses, providing the doctor is government-registered (*un médecin conventionné*) and provided you have the correct documentation (the European Health Insurance Card – EHIC; application forms available from main post offices in the UK or on Ⓦ dh.gov.uk). Note that every member of the family, including children, must have their own card. Even with the EHIC card, it's a good idea to have additional insurance to cover the shortfall, which can be especially substantial after a stay in hospital. All non-EU visitors should ensure they have adequate medical insurance cover.

For **minor complaints**, go to a *pharmacie*, signalled by an illuminated green cross. There's at least one in every small town, and even some villages. In larger towns, at least one (known as the *pharmacie de garde*) is open 24 hours according to a rota; details are displayed in all pharmacy windows.

For anything more serious you can get the name of a **doctor** from a pharmacy, local police station, tourist office, or your hotel. Consultation fees are usually around €25. You'll be given a *Feuille de Soins* (Statement of Treatment) for later insurance claims. Any prescriptions will be fulfilled by the pharmacy and must be paid for.

In serious **emergencies** you will always be admitted to the nearest general hospital (*centre hospitalier*). For an ambulance, call ☎ 15.

Insurance

Even though EU citizens are entitled to health-care privileges in France, they would do well to take out an **insurance policy** before travelling in order to cover against theft, loss, illness or injury. Before paying for a new policy, however, it's worth checking whether you are already covered: some all-risks home insurance policies may cover your possessions when overseas, and many private medical schemes include cover when abroad.

After investigating these possibilities, you might want to contact a **specialist travel insurance** company. A typical travel insurance policy usually provides cover for the loss of baggage, tickets and – up to a certain limit – cash or cheques, as well as cancellation or curtailment of your journey. Most exclude so-called **dangerous sports** unless an extra premium is paid.

Rough Guides has teamed up with World Nomads to offer you **travel insurance** that can be tailored to suit the length of your stay. There are also annual **multi-trip** policies for those who travel regularly. You can get a quote on our website (Ⓦ roughguides.com/website/shop).

Internet access

Even the cheapest French hotels these days, along with many cafés and bars, offer **wifi**; if it's important to you, make sure that it's both available and working when you check in. Hotels also often hold a computer or two for guest use. Internet cafés are much less common than they used to be, but on the other hand almost every **tourist office** has free wifi access.

Living in Brittany and Normandy

Although EU citizens are in theory free to move to France and find jobs with exactly the same pay, conditions and union rights as French nationals, for anyone who isn't a specialist, casual work in Brittany or Normandy is hard to come by and poorly paid.

Visitors from North America or Australasia without a prearranged job offer would be foolish to imagine they have any chance of finding paid employment. For EU citizens who arrange things in advance, however, there are work possibilities in au-pairing, teaching English as a foreign language and in the holiday industry.

The **national employment agency** (Ⓦ anpe.fr), with offices all over France, advertises temporary jobs in all fields and, in theory, offers a whole range of services to job-seekers open to all EU citizens, but is not renowned for its helpfulness to foreigners. Non-EU citizens will have to show a work permit (*autorisation de travail*) to apply for any of their jobs.

Finding a job **teaching English** is best done in advance, in late summer. Courses and jobs are listed on Ⓦ tefl.com, while the best places to live and teach are probably St-Malo, Quimper, Rennes and Rouen.

Au pair work is usually arranged through an agency, who should sort out any necessary paperwork; you'll find agencies listed on ⓦiapa.org. **Terms and conditions** are never very generous, but should include board, lodging and pocket money. Prospective employers are required to provide a written job description, so there is protection on both sides.

It's relatively easy to be a **student** in France. Foreigners pay no more than French nationals to enrol for a course, and the only problem then is to support yourself, though you'll be eligible for subsidized accommodation, meals and all the student reductions. For details and prospectuses of French universities, contact the Cultural Service of any French embassy or consulate. The **British Council** (ⓦbritishcouncil.org) runs a programme for British university students hoping to study in France.

Language schools in both Brittany and Normandy provide intensive French courses for foreigners. Options include CIEL Bretagne in Brest (ⓦciel.fr); French in Normandy in Rouen (ⓦfrenchinnormandy.com); LFIF, just outside Bayeux (ⓦlfif.co.uk); the École des Roches in Verneuil-sur-Avre (ⓦecoledesroches.com); and the three-week summer school run by the University of Rennes (ⓦuhb.fr).

Mail

French **post offices**, known as La Poste or PTTs (ⓦlaposte.fr), and identified by bright yellow-and-blue signs, are generally open from around 9am to 6pm Monday to Friday, and 9am to noon on Saturday. However, these hours aren't set in stone: smaller branches and those in rural areas are likely to close for lunch (generally noon to 2pm) and finish at 5pm, while central city branches may be open longer.

Sending a standard letter (20g or less) or postcard in France and beyond costs €0.57; to other European Union countries a charge of €0.05 per 10g is added to the basic fee for heavier letters and of €0.11 per 10g to all other countries. You can also buy stamps from *tabacs* and newsagents.

Maps

Though their town maps are often very good, tourist office handouts rarely contain usable regional maps. To supplement them – and the maps in this guide – you will probably want a reasonable road map. The *Michelin* 1:200,000 area maps of Brittany (512) and Normandy (513) are very good for driving and other purposes; virtually every road they show is passable by any car, and those that are tinged in green are usually reliable as "scenic routes".

If you're planning to walk or cycle, check the *IGN* maps – either the green (1:100,000 and 1:50,000) or the more detailed purple (1:25,000) series. The *IGN* 1:100,000 is the smallest scale available with contours marked, though the bizarre colour scheme makes it hard to read. *Michelin* maps have little arrows to indicate steep slopes, which is all the information most cyclists will need.

Money

France's currency, the **euro**, is divided into 100 cents (often still referred to as *centimes*). There are seven notes – in denominations of 5, 10, 20, 50, 100, 200 and 500 euros – and eight different coins – 1, 2, 5, 10, 20 and 50 cents, and 1 and 2 euros.

By far the easiest way to access your money in France is to use your credit or debit card to withdraw cash from an **ATM** (known as a *distributeur* or *point argent*); machines are every bit as ubiquitous as in Britain or North America, and most give instructions in several languages. Check with your bank before you leave home if you're in any doubt, and note that there is often a transaction fee, so it's more efficient to take out a sizeable sum each time rather than making lots of small withdrawals.

Similarly, all major **credit cards** are almost universally accepted in hotels, restaurants and shops, although some smaller establishments don't accept cards, or only for sums above a certain threshold. Visa – called Carte Bleue in France – is almost universally recognized, followed by MasterCard (also known as EuroCard). American Express ranks a bit lower.

Opening hours and public holidays

Basic **hours of business** are Monday to Saturday 9am until noon, and 2 to 6pm. In big city centres, shops and other businesses stay open throughout the day, while in July and August most tourist offices and museums are open without interruption. Otherwise almost everything – shops, museums, tourist offices, most banks – closes for a couple of hours at midday.

If you're looking to buy a picnic lunch, you'll need to get into the habit of buying it before you're ready to eat. Small food shops often don't reopen until halfway through the afternoon, then close again around 7.30 or 8pm.

PUBLIC HOLIDAYS

January 1 New Year's Day
Easter Sunday
Easter Monday
Ascension Day (forty days after Easter)
Whit Monday (seventh Monday after Easter)
May 1 May Day/Labour Day
May 8 Victory in Europe Day
July 14 Bastille Day
August 15 Assumption of the Virgin Mary
November 1 All Saints' Day
November 11 Armistice Day 1918
December 25 Christmas Day

The standard closing days are Sunday and Monday. Food shops tend to close on Monday rather than Sunday, but in smaller towns you may well find everything except the odd boulangerie (bakery) shut on both days.

Museums are not very generous with their hours, tending to open around 10am, close for lunch, and then run through until only 5 or 6pm. The closing days are usually Monday or Tuesday, sometimes both.

Phones

To call **to France** from your home country, dial ☎00 33 from the UK or Ireland, ☎011 33 from the USA, Canada or Australia, or ☎00 44 33 from New Zealand, and then the last nine digits of the ten-digit French number (thus omitting the initial 0).

To make a phone call **within France** – local or long-distance – simply dial all ten digits of the number. Numbers beginning with ☎08 00 up to ☎08 05 are free; those beginning ☎08 10 and ☎08 11 are charged as a local call; anything else beginning ☎08 is premium-rated (typically €0.34 per minute). None of these ☎08 numbers can be accessed from abroad. Calls to mobile phones (numbers starting with ☎06) are also charged at premium rates.

To speak to the operator dial ☎13; directory enquiries, both national and international, are on ☎12; medical emergencies, ☎15; the police, ☎17; fire, ☎18.

Mobile or cell phones

Most foreign **mobile/cell phones** automatically connect to a local provider as soon as you reach France. If you have any concerns, contact your phone provider in advance, and make sure you know what the call charges are – they tend to be pretty exorbitant, and you're likely to be charged to receive calls as well as make them. Be wary, too, of roaming charges for internet use while you're on the road.

Smoking

Smoking is banned in all public places, including public transport, museums, cafés and restaurants.

Time

France is in the Central European Time Zone (GMT+1). Daylight Saving Time (GMT+2) in France lasts from the last Sunday in March to the last Sunday in October.

Tourist information

The **French Government Tourist Office** (Atout France) has offices throughout the world, each with its own website holding general country-wide information. For practical details on a specific location, such as hotels, campsites, activities and festivals, contact the relevant regional or departmental tourist offices; contact details can be found online at ⓦ fncrt.com and ⓦ rn2d.net respectively.

In France itself, practically every town and many villages have a tourist office – usually an **Office du Tourisme** (OT) but sometimes a **Syndicat d'Initiative** (SI). These provide local information, including hotel and restaurant listings, leisure activities, car and bike rental, bus times, laundries and countless other things; many can also book accommodation. Most can provide a town plan, and sell maps and local walking guides.

FRENCH GOVERNMENT TOURIST OFFICES

Australia and New Zealand ⓦ au.rendezvousenfrance.com
Britain ⓦ uk.rendezvousenfrance.com
Canada ⓦ ca.rendezvousenfrance.com
USA ⓦ us.rendezvousenfrance.com.

CALLING HOME FROM FRANCE

Note that the initial zero is omitted from the area code when dialling the UK, Ireland, Australia and New Zealand from abroad.
UK 44
Republic of Ireland 353
US and Canada 1
Australia 61
New Zealand 64
South Africa 27

REGIONAL TOURIST BOARDS

Brittany Tourist Board ⓦ brittanytourism.com
Normandy Tourist Board ⓦ normandie-tourisme.fr
Calvados (Normandy) ⓦ calvados-tourisme.com
Côtes d'Armor (Brittany) ⓦ cotesdarmor.com
Eure (Normandy) ⓦ tourisme28.com
Finistère (Brittany) ⓦ finisteretourisme.com
Ille-et-Vilaine (Brittany) ⓦ bretagne35.com
Manche (Normandy) ⓦ manchetourisme.com
Morbihan (Brittany) ⓦ morbihan.com
Orne (Normandy) ⓦ ornetourisme.com
Seine Maritime (Normandy) ⓦ seine-maritime-tourisme.com

Travellers with disabilities

While the French have improved facilities for travellers with disabilities, adding ramps or other forms of access to hotels, museums and other public buildings, haphazard parking habits and stepped village streets remain serious obstacles for anyone with mobility problems. All hotels are required to adapt at least one room to be wheelchair accessible. APF, the French paraplegic organization, is the most reliable source of information on accommodation with disabled access and other facilities.

Eurotunnel (see p.22) offers the simplest option for **travelling to France** from the UK, as you can remain in your car. Alternatively, Eurostar trains have a limited number of wheelchair spaces in first-class for the price of the regular second-class fare; reserve well in advance. While airlines are required to offer access to travellers with mobility problems, the level of service provided by discount airlines may be fairly basic. All cross-Channel ferries have lifts to and from the car deck, but moving between the different passenger decks may be more difficult.

Within France, most train stations now make provision for travellers with reduced mobility. SNCF produces a free booklet outlining its services, available at main stations and on its website for travellers with disabilities: ⓦaccessibilite.sncf.com. Note that you need to give 48 hours advance warning to receive assistance from the beginning to the end of your trip.

Drivers of **taxis** are legally obliged to help passengers in and out of the vehicle and to carry guide dogs. Specially adapted taxi services are available in some towns: contact local tourist offices, or the organizations listed below, for further information. All the big **car hire** agencies can provide automatic cars if you reserve sufficiently far in advance. while Hertz offers cars with hand controls in certain locations – reserve well in advance.

As for finding suitable **accommodation**, guides produced by Logis de France and Gîtes de France

(see p.24) indicate places with specially adapted rooms; check when booking that the facilities meet your needs.

Up-to-date **information** about accessibility, special programmes and discounts is best obtained before you leave home from the organizations listed below. French readers might want to get hold of the *Handitourisme* guide, published by Petit Futé (ⓦpetitfute.com).

USEFUL CONTACTS

Access Travel ⓦ access-travel.co.uk. UK tour operator that arranges flights, transfer and accommodation in both Normandy and Brittany.
Association des Paralysés de France (APF) ⓦ apf.asso.fr. National association that can answer general enquiries and put you in touch with their departmental offices.
Fédération Française Handisport ⓦ handisport.org. Among other things, this federation provides information on sports and leisure facilities for people with disabilities.
Society for the Advancement of Travellers with Handicaps (SATH) ⓦ sath.org. US non-profit educational organization with information and tips on travelling abroad.
Tourism For All ⓦ tourismforall.org.uk. Masses of information, including useful advice for prospective travellers to France.

Travelling with children

Children and babies are generally welcome everywhere, including most bars and restaurants. Hotels charge by the room, and many either hold a few large family rooms, or charge a small supplement for an additional bed or cot. Family-run places will often babysit or offer a listening service while you eat or go out. Especially in seaside towns, most restaurants have children's menus or cook simpler food on request. SNCF charge nothing on trains and buses for under-4s, and half-fare for 4–11s. Most tourist offices have details of specific activities for children – in particular, many resorts supervise "clubs" for children on the beach. Something to be aware of – not that you can do much about it – is the difficulty of negotiating a child's buggy over the large cobbles that cover many of the older streets in town centres.

Travelling with pets from the UK

If you wish to take your dog or cat to France, the **Pet Travel Scheme (PETS)** enables you to avoid putting it in quarantine when re-entering the UK, so long as certain conditions are met. For details, visit ⓦgov.uk/take-pet-abroad or call the PETS Helpline (☎0370 241 1710).

Seine-Maritime

THE FALAISE D'AVAL, ÉTRETAT

1

Seine-Maritime

Stretching north from the fertile Seine Valley to the undulating cliffs that line the Channel coast, the *département* of Seine-Maritime is largely distinct from the rest of Normandy. Though scattered with the usual Norman half-timbered houses and small farms, the landscape is stark along the seashore, while relentlessly flat on the chalky Caux plateau behind. Only along the sheltered ribbon to either side of the Seine do you find the greenery, and profusion of flowers and fruit, that you would normally expect of Normandy.

It's well worth taking time to explore, however. Near the pleasant ferry port of **Dieppe** several low-key but popular resorts on the **Côte d'Albâtre** make appealing overnight stops, with occasional surprises behind their windswept and tide-chased walks. **Étretat**, for example, boasts spectacular stacks and arches of rock, flanking one of the nicest little coastal towns in Normandy; **Fécamp** holds the absurd Gothic monstrosity of the Benedictine distillery; and **Varengeville** offers the wonderful house designed by architect Edwin Lutyens at **Bois des Moutiers**.

While motorists tend to hurry through the hinterland just south of the coastal cliffs, for **cyclists** the gentle valleys and expansive grain fields are ideal for a few days' undemanding pedalling through pastoral French countryside. Even **Le Havre**, on the Seine estuary, while hardly conventionally attractive, is home to some noteworthy modern architecture and art.

The extravagant meanders of the **River Seine**, however, shape most itineraries. **Rouen**, by far the largest of the river towns, was the scene of the trial and execution of Joan of Arc, and remains one of the major provincial capitals of France; a combination of contemporary verve and its restored medieval centre makes it by far the most interesting city in Normandy. Elsewhere along the valley and riverbanks there is plenty to delay your progress: tranquil villages such as **Villequier** and **La Bouille**; the evocative Romanesque abbey ruins of **St-Wandrille** and **Jumièges**; the English frontier-stronghold of **Château Gaillard** looming above **Les Andelys**; and, an unmissable last stop before Paris, **Monet's garden** and waterlilies at **Giverny**.

Dieppe

Squeezed between high cliff headlands, **DIEPPE** makes an enjoyably small-scale port at which to arrive in France. Quintessentially French yet long associated with England, it's certainly not a place where you'd regret spending an afternoon or evening. With kids in tow, the aquariums of the **Cité de la Mer** are the obvious attraction; otherwise, you could settle for admiring the cliffs and the castle as you stroll the seafront lawns.

Dieppe took on its current shape early in the nineteenth century, when its ancient circuit of walls was knocked down, and the modern town was laid out along three still-evident axes. The **boulevard de Verdun** runs for over a kilometre

---

Operation Jubilee: the raid on Dieppe p.48

Harfleur p.63

The loss of the *Latham 47* p.65

Joan of Arc p.72

Bringing the beach to the city: Rouen sur Mer p.73

Claude Monet at Giverny p.84

RUE MARTAINVILLE, ROUEN

Highlights

❶ Hôtel de la Terrasse Lovely clifftop hotel in Varengeville that makes a perfect first- or last-night stopover for ferry passengers. **See p.54**

❷ Étretat Normandy's most attractive little resort, offering great walks to spectacular cliff formations. **See p.58**

❸ Pont de Normandie Vertiginous bridge across the Seine that's both an architectural marvel and an exhilarating thrill to walk over. **See p.64**

❹ Rouen Despite war damage, this fine old medieval city would still seem familiar to Joan of Arc, who perished in its main square. **See p.69**

❺ Aître St-Maclou Ghoulish Dance of Death carvings adorn this centuries-old courtyard in central Rouen. **See p.71**

❻ Château Gaillard The atmospheric ruins of Richard the Lionheart's mighty fortress dominate a sweeping curve of the River Seine. **See p.82**

❼ Giverny Claude Monet's house and garden remain just as he left them, though these days his lovingly tended waterlilies are more photographed than painted. **See p.83**

HIGHLIGHTS ARE MARKED ON THE MAP ON P.46

1

along the seafront, with the twin turrets of the only one of seven city gates to survive, **Les Tourelles**, still guarding its western end, alongside the casino and below the fifteenth-century **château**. A short way inland, the **rue de la Barre** and its pedestrianized continuation, the **Grande Rue**, run parallel to the seafront. That line is extended along the harbour's edge by **quai Henri IV**, with its colourful backdrop of cafés, brasseries and restaurants.

Brief history

As the closest harbour and beach to Paris, 170km southeast, Dieppe has had an eventful history. The abbey of Mont Ste-Catherine-de-Rouen acquired the area in 1030, for an annual rent of five thousand smoked herrings. William the Conqueror, as king of England, used the port regularly, and it returned to French control in 1195 when Philippe Auguste burned Richard the Lionheart's fleet in the harbour.

Adventurers from Dieppe were at the forefront of French **naval explorations**. Dieppois navigators supposedly reached the coast of Guinea in 1384, and Brazil in 1488; less questionably, the Italian Giovanni da Verrazzano sailed from here in 1524

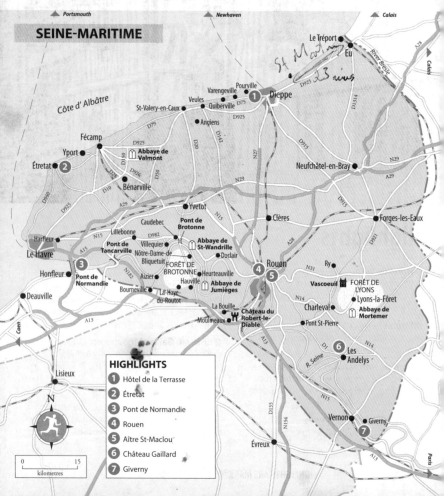

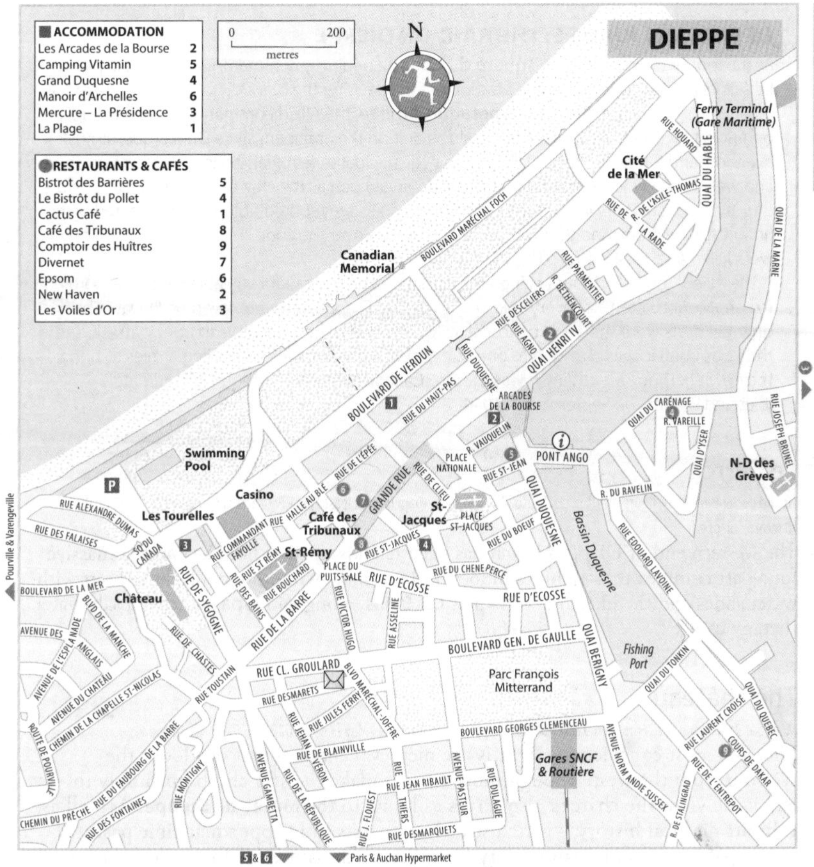

DIEPPE
ACCOMMODATION
Les Arcades de la Bourse 2
Camping Vitamin 5
Grand Duquesne 4
Manoir d'Archelles 6
Mercure – La Présidence 3
La Plage 1
RESTAURANTS & CAFÉS
Bistrot des Barrières 5
Le Bistrôt du Pollet 4
Cactus Café 1
Café des Tribunaux 8
Comptoir des Huîtres 9
Divernet 7
Epsom 6
New Haven 2
Les Voiles d'Or 3
0 200
metres
N
Ferry Terminal (Gare Maritime)
Cité de la Mer
Canadian Memorial
Swimming Pool
Casino
Les Tourelles
Château
Café des Tribunaux
St-Rémy
St-Jacques
Arcades de la Bourse
Pont Ango
Bassin Duquesne
N-D des Grèves
Fishing Port
Parc François Mitterrand
Gares SNCF & Routière
Boulevard Maréchal Foch
Boulevard de Verdun
Quai Henri IV
Quai Duquesne
Quai du Hable
Quai de la Marne
Grande Rue
Rue d'Ecosse
Boulevard Gen. de Gaulle
Boulevard Georges Clemenceau
Pourville & Varengeville
5 & 6
Paris & Auchan Hypermarket

to found what later became New York. Early emigrants to Canada used the port, too, establishing links with the French colony there that endured long after the French lost Canada to the British in 1759.

Soon after the railway from Paris reached Dieppe in 1848 the Newhaven Packet started a daily cross-Channel service from England. The town became a fashionable **seaside resort**, attracting French aristocracy and British royalty; French visitors would promenade along the seafront, while the English colony indulged in the peculiar pastime of bathing in the sea.

The beach

Dieppe's wide, steeply shelving **shingle beach** was deposited by a freak tide long after the rest of the town took shape. Hence the extravagant clear space between the seafront and the first buildings, taken up partly by windswept grassy lawns and partly by car parks where departing ferry passengers munch last-minute picnics.

Every two years, this large open space serves as the venue for a **kite festival**, the Festival International de Cerf-Volant, which spreads across two weekends during the early September of even-numbered years (Ⓦdieppe-cerf-volant.org). Dieppe's sister town, the Dieppe in New Brunswick, Canada, hosts a similar festival.

1

> ### OPERATION JUBILEE: THE RAID ON DIEPPE
>
> At the foot of the château, the **square du Canada** originally commemorated the role played by sailors from Dieppe in the colonization of Canada. After the last war, however, it acquired an additional significance, thanks to **Operation Jubilee**, the Allied commando raid on Dieppe, on August 19, 1942. In the first large-scale assault on the continent since Dunkerque, almost five thousand Canadian troops launched a near-suicidal series of landings and attacks up sheer and well-fortified cliff faces. Many were cut down as soon as they left their landing craft, before they even touched dry land; some German defenders are reputed not to have bothered with firing their weapons, and simply dropped projectiles over the edge. In total, 907 Canadians were killed and 1874 captured.
>
> The Allied Command later justified the carnage as having taught valuable lessons; according to Lord Mountbatten, "for every soldier who died at Dieppe, ten were saved on D-Day". The Channel ports were shown to be too heavily defended to be vulnerable to frontal attack, and the invasion plan was changed to one that required the amphibious landing armies to bring their own harbour with them. It was the 2nd Canadian Infantry Division who ultimately liberated Dieppe, on September 1, 1944.

Le Carré

101 bd de Verdun • Daily, hours vary, but pools usually open from 10am until at least 7pm • Pool access €6.20 • ☎ 02 35 82 80 90, Ⓦ lecarre-dieppe.fr

The western end of Dieppe's beach has been relandscaped to hold **Le Carré**, a massive four-part complex that includes indoor and outdoor swimming pools, kitted out with water slides and the like, and known as **Les Bains**, along with **Spa Manche**, a salt-water therapy centre.

The château

Mon–Sat 9am–noon & 2–6pm, Sun 9am–noon & 2–5pm; closed Tues Oct–May • €4 • ☎ 02 35 06 61 99, Ⓦ dieppe.fr

Dieppe's most conspicuous sight is the medieval **château** that overlooks the seafront from the west. Though most visitors make the stiff climb up simply to enjoy the view, the château also serves as home to the **Musée de Dieppe**. As well as exhibits on local history – which stretches, thanks to Dieppe's maritime past, to encompass pre-Columbian pottery from Peru – the museum houses two showpiece collections. The first is a group of **carved ivories**. Dieppois "explorers" shipped ivory home from Africa in such quantities that during the seventeenth century over three hundred craftsmen-carvers lived here. Earlier pieces tend to be exquisite miniature portraits and classical scenes; later on, the sculptors were concentrating instead on souvenirs.

The other permanent exhibition is made up of a hundred or so prints by the co-originator of Cubism, **Georges Braque**, who went to school in Le Havre, spent his summers in Dieppe, and is buried nearby at Varengeville-sur-Mer (see p.54). Around a quarter tend to be displayed at any one time. Other galleries upstairs hold assorted paintings of local scenes, while a newer wing stages temporary exhibitions.

The port

Dieppe remains a busy port; its sheer bustle and verve is striking to any visitor. Vast quantities of fruit from all over the world – and forty percent of all shellfish eaten in France – are unloaded at its commercial docks, but the quayside fish stalls near the tourist office are what really grab the eye. Each morning the previous night's catch is displayed with mouthwatering French flair, an appetizing profusion of sole, turbot and the local speciality, scallops.

Cité de la Mer

1

37 rue de l'Asile-Thomas • Mon–Fri 9.30am–6pm, Sat & Sun 9.30am–12.30pm & 1.30–6pm • €7 • ☎ 02 35 06 93 20, Ⓦ www
.estrancitedelamer.fr

The grandly named **Cité de la Mer**, or "City of the Sea", is in fact simply a museum.
Housed in a white concrete block, in the tangle of streets just west of the harbour
mouth, it's designed both to entertain children and serve as a centre for scientific
research. Kids are bound to enjoy learning the principles of navigation by operating
radio-controlled boats (€2 for 3min). The museum then traces the history of seagoing
vessels, leading from the great Norman voyages of exploration and conquest up to a
sketchy account of the insides of a nuclear-powered submarine. Next comes a very
detailed geological exhibition covering the formation of the local cliffs, from which we
learn how to convert shingle into sandpaper.

Visits culminate with large **aquariums**, filled with the marine life of the Channel:
flatfish with bulbous eyes and twisted faces, retiring octopuses, battling lobsters and
hermaphrodite scallops (a caption helpfully explains that the white part is male, and
the orange, female).

The old town

The **place du Puits-Salé**, at the heart of Dieppe's old town, is dominated by the spruce
half-timbered *Café des Tribunaux* (see p.50). From here, rue St-Jacques leads to
St-Jacques church. The original church, built in the twelfth century to greet English
pilgrims heading for the shrine of St James at Santiago de Compostela, burned down
a hundred years later, so its oldest part today is the fourteenth-century lantern tower.
Inside, the chapel to the "Canadian Martyrs", dedicated in 1951, has nothing to do
with World War II; instead it's devoted to two Dieppe priests, shown in modern
stained glass being hacked to death by "Mohawks" in 1648. Nearby, the **Mur de Trésor**
bears intricate seventeenth-century carvings of Brazilian Indians, which sadly are too
high and weathered to see clearly.

ARRIVAL AND DEPARTURE

DIEPPE

By train The *gare SNCF* is 500m south of the tourist office,
on boulevard Clemenceau.
Destinations Paris-St-Lazare (19 daily; 2hr 10min) via
Rouen (16 daily; 50min).
By bus The *gare routière* is on boulevard Clemenceau, by
the train station.
Destinations Fécamp (4 daily; 2hr 20min); Le Tréport

(4 daily; 30min); St-Valery (5 daily; 1hr).
By ferry LD Lines (Ⓦ ldlines.co.uk) sails between Dieppe's
gare maritime, 500m east of the centre, and Newhaven in
England (2 daily; 4hr). Motorists coming off the boats are
directed away from the town, and have to double back
west to reach it; foot passengers can walk to the centre.

INFORMATION AND GETTING AROUND

Tourist office On Pont Ango, which crosses the pleasure
port to connect the town centre with the ferry harbour
(April–June & Sept Mon–Sat 9am–1pm & 2–6pm, Sun
9.30am–1pm & 2–5.30pm; July & Aug Mon–Sat
9am–7pm, Sun 9.30am–1pm & 2–5.30pm; Oct–March
Mon–Sat 9am–12.30pm & 1.30–5pm; ☎ 02 32 14 40 60,

Ⓦ dieppetourisme.com).
By bike Vélo Service rents out inexpensive bikes from 27
rue de Stalingrad, near the *gare SNCF*, and, in summer, from
a bus just across the bridge from the tourist office (€1 per
hr, €5.50 per day; electric bike €11 per day; ☎ 02 35 04 92
40, Ⓦ acrept.fr/veloservice.

ACCOMMODATION

Dieppe holds plenty of **hotels**. The more expensive options are concentrated along the seafront – which is surprisingly
quiet at night – especially at its western end, closest to the château. Hotels with their own restaurants tend to insist on half
board, or even full board, in season.

Les Arcades de la Bourse 1–3 arcades de la Bourse
☎ 02 35 84 14 12, Ⓦ lesarcades.fr. Long-established

central hotel under the arcades facing the port; you
couldn't ask for a more convenient location. Cheaper rooms

1

face the street, but it's worth paying €10 more for a harbour view. The downstairs restaurant serves full, good-value menus from €22. **€72**

Camping Vitamin 865 Rue des Vertus, St-Aubin-sur-Scie ☎ 02 35 82 11 11, ⊛ camping-vitamin.com. Three-star site, well south of town in an unremarkable setting, with indoor and outdoor pools. It's really only convenient for motorists, though it is served by bus #2. Closed mid-Oct to March. **€22.40**

Grand Duquesne 15 place St-Jacques ☎ 02 32 14 61 10, ⊛ augrandduquesne.free.fr. This small, central hotel is unusually plain for the *Logis de France*, offering eight slightly old-fashioned en-suite rooms at bargain rates, plus two larger family suites. All are only accessible via steep stairs. Vegetarian and meat-rich menus in its highly rated restaurant start at under €20. **€54**

★ **Manoir d'Archelles** Route de Neufchâtel, Arques-La-Bataille ☎ 02 35 83 40 51, ⊛ manoir-darchelles.fr. This irresistibly eccentric old château is set in gorgeous gardens, 6km southeast of central Dieppe. The rooms are simple, but they have a certain faded charm – some are circular, for a start – and include some larger family suites. The owners also run a good restaurant beside the front gate, with menus from €21.50. **€75**

Mercure – La Présidence 1 bd de Verdun ☎ 02 35 84 31 31, ⊛ hotel-la-presidence.com. Dieppe's most upscale hotel, immediately below the château at the west end of the promenade, offers very comfortable sea-view rooms with attractive seaside decor, and has its own restaurant. **€108**

La Plage 20 bd de Verdun ☎ 02 35 84 18 28, ⊛ plage-hotel-dieppe.com. Seafront hotel with helpful management and rooms to suit all budgets, from the upmarket sea-view options with balconies to smaller but perfectly pleasant courtyard-facing doubles. No restaurant. **€65**

EATING AND DRINKING

If you like to stroll and compare menus of a summer's evening, the most promising area to look for **restaurants** in Dieppe is not the beach, which holds nothing beyond a couple of open-air bistro-type cafés and a handful of crêpe stands, but the quai Henri IV, overlooking the port. For the very best food in town, though, it's worth heading a little further afield, to one of the places listed below. Things tend to shut early in Dieppe, though a handful of **bars** do manage to keep busy.

Dieppe's principal **shopping streets** are rue de la Barre and the Grande Rue. Saturday sees an all-day open-air **market** in the place Nationale and along Grande Rue, while the largest of several local **hypermarkets** is Auchan (Mon–Sat 8.30am–9.30pm), south of town at the Centre Commercial du Belvédère on the route de Rouen (RN 27), or reached by bus #2 from the tourist office.

Bistrot des Barrières 5–7 Arcades de la Poissonerie ☎ 02 35 40 46 83. Welcoming little restaurant near the tourist office, where, apart from the great-value €16 lunch menu, everything is à la carte, with daily fish specials for around €17 and a highly recommended *marmite Dieppoise* (seafood pot, with shellfish and white fish) for €24. Tues–Sat noon–2pm & 7.30–9.30pm.

Bistrot du Pollet 23 rue de la Tête du Boeuf ☎ 02 35 84 68 57, ⊛ bistrotdupollet.fr. Little local restaurant not far east of Pont Ango, renowned for its seafood and especially cosy on a winter's evening. Weekday lunch menus from €19, dinner from €30. Tues–Sat noon–2pm & 7.30–9.30pm; closed second fortnight in April and second fortnight in Aug.

Cactus Café 71 quai Henri IV ☎ 02 35 82 59 38. Lively café, squeezed between the quayside restaurants with plenty of outdoor seating, offering a regular diet of reggae and Latin music. Mon–Thurs & Sun 10am–midnight, Fri & Sat 10am–2am. Closed Jan & Feb.

Café des Tribunaux Place du Puits-Salé ☎ 02 32 14 44 65. Cavernous café, built as an inn towards the end of the seventeenth century. Two hundred years later, it was favoured by painters and writers such as Renoir, Monet, Sickert, Whistler and Pissarro, but for English visitors, its most evocative association is with the exiled and unhappy Oscar Wilde, who drank here regularly. These days it's a popular hangout for students. Daily 8am–8pm.

Comptoir des Huîtres 12 cours de Dakar ☎ 02 35 84 19 37. It's worth seeking out this local bistro, tucked away in a slightly rundown dockside district just south of the fishing port, to enjoy its fresh-caught seafood. Dinner menus from €20, but it's worth paying à la carte prices to sample specialities like oysters and scallops. Mon–Sat noon–2pm & 7–9.30pm.

Divernet 138 Grande Rue ☎ 02 35 84 13 87, ⊛ divernet.fr. Chic *patisserie*, brasserie and tea room, with pavement seating on Dieppe's main shopping street. Delicious cakes and desserts, and simple lunch *formules* from €8.50. Daily 9am–7pm; closed Mon Sept to mid-July.

Epsom 11 bd de Verdun ☎ 02 35 84 12 27. Seafront brasserie, putting on live jazz on some Thurs. Mon–Thurs & Sun noon–1am, Fri & Sat noon–2am.

New Haven 53 quai Henri IV ☎ 02 35 84 89 72, ⊛ restaurantdieppe.fr. Reliable seafood specialist, towards the quieter end of the quayside, with good menus from €19.50, and a plentiful array of mixed shellfish platters. Mon & Wed–Sun noon–9.30pm, Tues noon–3pm; closed Mon & Wed in winter.

Les Voiles d'Or 2 chemin de la Falaise, Neuville-lès-Dieppe ☎ 02 35 84 16 84, ⊛ lesvoilesdor.fr. Menus at this modern, pricey but exquisite Michelin-starred restaurant, atop the cliffs immediately above the ferry port,

15min walk west of the centre, focus on whatever's freshest each day – though there's always plenty of seafood. Lunch costs €38 including two glasses of wine; a five-course dinner for the entire table is €55 per person, or à la carte mains cost €30–35. Wed–Sat noon–2pm & 7.30–9pm, Sun noon–2pm.

The Côte d'Albâtre

Thanks to its high white cliffs, the Norman coast between Picardy in the east and Le Havre in the west is known as the **Côte d'Albâtre** – the Alabaster coast. This whole shoreline is eroding at such a ferocious rate that the small resorts here, tucked in at the mouths of successive valleys, may not last another century. For the moment, however, they are quietly prospering, with casinos, sports centres and marinas ensuring a modest but steady summer trade.

If you're setting out to tour Normandy, it might seem counter-intuitive to head **east** from Dieppe towards Calais and Boulogne, but doing so gives the opportunity to see a couple of surprising old towns: venerable **Le Tréport** and, just inland, the village of **Eu**, with its thick forest surround. Head **west**, on the other hand, and the coast road dips into a series of pretty little ports, with **Étretat** the pick of the bunch.

Le Tréport

Thirty kilometres east of Dieppe, at the mouth of the River Bresle – the border with Picardy – **LE TRÉPORT** is an atmospheric old seaside resort that springs creakily to life each summer. Already something of a bathing spot when the railways arrived in 1873, it was duly promoted as "the prettiest beach in Europe, just three hours from Paris", and remained the capital's favoured resort until the 1950s.

Le Tréport divides into three distinct sections: the flat wedge-shaped seafront area, bounded on one side by the Channel, on another by the harbour at the canalized river mouth, and on the third by imposing hundred-metre chalk cliffs; the old town, higher up the slopes on safer ground; and the modern town further inland. The actual **seafront** is entirely taken up by a concrete 1960s apartment block, with one or two snack bars, but no other sign of life, facing the casino and a drab grey shingle beach. It's the more sheltered harbourside **quai François 1er** around the corner that holds most of the action, lined with restaurants, souvenir shops and cafés, plus a venerable little brick fish market. The assorted stone jetties and wooden piers around the harbour are enjoyable to stroll around, as you watch the comings and goings of the fishing boats that still keep Le Tréport bustling.

It's even more fun to take a ride up (indeed through) the cliffs on the téléphérique (see below), though if you walk to the top of the cliffs instead, climbing 365 steps, not far up from the *quai* you'll pass the heavily nautical **Église St-Jacques**, built in the fifteenth century to replace an eleventh-century original that crumbled into the sea, along with the cliff on which it stood.

The téléphérique

July & Aug daily 7.45am–12.45am; Sept–June Sun–Fri 7.45am–8.45pm, Sat 7.45am–12.45am • Free

The restored **téléphérique**, or funicular railway, tunnels into the rock to re-emerge in the open air up top. As well as views to either side of the decaying mansions of Le Tréport, you can see across to the longer beach of **Mers-les-Bains**, which, being in Picardy, falls outside the scope of this book.

ARRIVAL AND INFORMATION   **LE TRÉPORT**

By train Le Tréport's *gare SNCF*, on the far side of the harbour, a short walk from the main *quai*, is served by around 10 trains per day from Abancourt (1hr), which has connections to Rouen and Amiens.

Tourist office Quai Sadi-Carnot (April & May Mon–Sat 10am–noon & 2–6pm, Sun 10am–12.30pm & 2.30–5pm;

1

June & Sept Mon–Sat 9.30am–12.30pm & 2–6pm, Sun 10am–12.30pm & 2.30–5pm; July & Aug daily 9.30am–7pm; Oct–March Mon–Sat 10am–noon & 2–6pm, Sun 9.30am–12.30pm; ☎02 35 86 05 69, ⓦville-le-treport.fr).

ACCOMMODATION AND EATING

Numerous consistently tempting seafood **restaurants** line the *quai*, each boasting of its fresh *assiette de fruits de mer* and serving similar meals from around €20.

De Calais 1 rue de Paris ☎02 27 28 09 09, ⓦhotel decalais.fr. This friendly, slightly eccentric family-run place, overlooking the port, offers Le Tréport's best-value accommodation. The cheapest rooms are en-suite and overlook the harbour, while the fanciest have whirlpool baths and great sea views. €61

Les Délices d'Alice 6 rue Duc de Penthièvre ☎02 35 83 46 75. Bistro, very slightly back from the harbour, that's the best option for a straightforward, good-value meal, with large mixed salads and *moules frites* alike costing around €10. Tues–Sun noon–2pm & 7–9pm.

Le Homard Bleu 45 quai François 1er ☎02 35 86 15 89, ⓦle-homard-bleu.fr. The pick of the many harbourfront seafood restaurants, serving top-notch fish and shellfish on menus from €20. July & Aug daily noon–2pm & 7.30–9.15pm, Sept–June Tues–Sat noon–2pm & 7.30–9.15pm, Sun noon–2pm.

Villa Marine 1 place Pierre-Sémard ☎02 35 86 02 22, ⓦhotel-lavillamarine.com. Renovated hotel, across the harbour from the centre, near the station, where the simple contemporary rooms are decorated in appealing seaside-style pastels and exposed wood. Several have sea views, but there's wifi in public areas only. Dinner menus in the attractive restaurant – closed Sun – start at €22. €59

Eu

Queen Victoria twice visited Le Tréport with Albert; she didn't come to play on the beach, though, but to stay at the château at **EU**, a couple of kilometres inland. When she did so the first time, in the original "Entente Cordiale" in 1843, she became the first English monarch to make an official visit to France since Henry VIII arrived for the Field of the Cloth of Gold.

Today, Eu is something of a backwater, consisting of a few pedestrian streets at the top of a hill, and a straggle of newer districts reaching down the slopes. The sixteenth-century château (mid-March to early Nov Mon, Wed, Thurs, Sat & Sun 10am–noon & 2–6pm, Fri 2–6pm; €5; ☎02 35 86 44 00, ⓦchateau-eu.fr) at its heart holds a museum devoted to its glory years as the summer residence of French monarch Louis Philippe, between 1830 and 1848. Of Eu's previous château, burned in 1475, only the tiny chapel remains, which was the site of William the Conqueror's marriage to Mathilda.

Unlikely as it may sound, Eu's Gothic church, **Notre-Dame et St-Laurent**, is dedicated to St Lawrence O'Toole, an archbishop of Dublin who died here in 1181 while en route to visit Henry II of England in Rouen. His effigy still lies in the brightly lit and eerie crypt.

For an enjoyable afternoon, venture into the **forest of Eu**, a mysterious and ancient tangled woodland dominated by tall beeches, where a lost Roman city supposedly lies hidden.

ARRIVAL AND INFORMATION   EU

By train Eu is on the Le Tréport rail line, with its *gare SNCF* 500m downhill from the centre.

Tourist office On the central place Guillaume le Conquérant (May to mid-June Mon–Sat 9.30am–12.30pm & 2–6pm, Sun 10am–12.30pm; mid-June to mid-Sept Mon–Sat 9.30am–6pm, Sun 10am–12.30pm; mid-Sept to April Mon 2–5pm, Tues–Sat 10am–noon & 2–5pm; ☎02 35 86 04 68, ⓦville-eu.fr).

ACCOMMODATION AND EATING

Camping Municipal Parc du Château ☎02 35 86 20 04, ⓦville-eu.fr. The town campsite spreads across the lawns of a wonderfully well-shaded enclave in the grounds of the castle, with a new shower block plus vending machines and bakery. Closed Nov–March. €9.20

Centre des Fontaines Rue des Fontaines ☏ 02 35 86 05 03, ⓦ centredesfontaines.fr. FUAJ hostel in the former royal kitchens, which serves breakfast for €4.50 plus lunch and dinner for groups only, and acts as a general resource for local youngsters. **€14.50**

De la Poste 5 rue de la Poste ☏ 02 35 86 10 78. Bright-yellow, central bistro, facing the post office, which serves a great-value lunch menu, including a buffet of hors d'oeuvres, for €11.50. Tues–Sat noon–2pm & 7–9pm, Sun noon–2pm. Closed early July to early Aug.

Pourville-sur-mer

Immediately **west** of Dieppe, the coastal D75 drops in a majestic sweep after 3km down a steep green hill, to reach the resort of **POURVILLE-SUR-MER**. An extremely tranquil last- or first-night stop for ferry passengers, it's no more than a long straight beach at the mouth of a broad valley that briefly interrupts the line of cliffs. It lacks any form of port, but the wave conditions are enough to attract hordes of **surfers**. The beach itself was painted by Monet, a reproduction of whose *La Plage à Pourville* is displayed at the centre of the promenade. Most of the few buildings lining the seafront road through Pourville are **hotels**.

ACCOMMODATION AND EATING   POURVILLE-SUR-MER

l'Huîtrière ☏ 02 35 84 36 20. Beyond its ugly white concrete exterior, this seafront restaurant is a delight. As the name suggests, it serves delicious fresh oysters (€1 or so each), from the owners' own oyster beds, on its raised sea-view terrace. Full menus are also available. Daily 10am–8pm.
Le Marqueval ☏ 02 35 82 66 46, ⓦ camping lemarqueval.com. Set in the fields a little way back from the sea, this three-star campsite has cabin rentals as well as tent places, along with a sauna and three heated

outdoor pools (mid-May to mid-Sept). Closed mid-Oct to mid-March. **€22.40**
Produits de la Mer ☏ 02 35 84 38 34, ⓦ auxproduits delamer.com. All eight of the simple, somewhat faded, rooms in this *Logis de France*, next to its own crazy-golf course, have showers or baths. The name, which simply means "seafood", might seem strange for a hotel, but all becomes clear in the restaurant (closed Tues & Wed), where the simplest menu costs €25. Closed Dec & Jan. **€50**

Varengeville-sur-mer

The charming village of **VARENGEVILLE-SUR-MER**, which stretches parallel to the clifftops, 8km west of Dieppe, has long been popular with **artists**, including at different times Monet, Dufy, Miró and the painter parents of British Prime Minister Anthony Eden, who was born here. For art-lovers, the principal attraction now is the tomb of **Georges Braque**, beside the St-Valéry church holding a stained-glass window that he designed, but Varengeville also holds a couple of fascinating summer houses from widely separated eras, the sixteenth-century **Manoir d'Ango** and the twentieth-century **Bois des Moutiers**, while on a down-to-earth note it's also simply a lovely place to spend the night.

Manoir d'Ango

First half of April & Oct Sat & Sun 10am–12.30pm & 2–6pm; mid-April to Sept daily 10am–12.30pm & 2–6pm • €5 • ☏ 02 35 83 61 56, ⓦ manoirdango.fr

The **Manoir d'Ango**, signposted 300m south from the main road through Varengeville, was the "summer palace" of the leading shipbuilder in sixteenth-century Dieppe. Jean Ango outfitted such major expeditions as Verrazzano's, which "discovered" the site of New York in 1524, and made his riches from pillaging treasure ships out on the Spanish Main. His former home consists of a rectangular ensemble of fine brick buildings arranged around a central courtyard.

The intricate patterning of red bricks, shaped flint slabs, stone blocks and supporting timbers is at its finest in the remarkable central **dovecote**, topped by a dome that rises to an elegant point, which is aflutter with pigeons. Parts of the various houses are given over to temporary art exhibitions each summer.

1

Bois des Moutiers

Route de l'Église • Mid-March to mid-Nov daily: house 10am–noon & 2–6pm, gardens 10am–8pm • €10 • ☎ 02 35 85 10 02, ⊕ boisdesmoutiers.com

Head coastwards from the main road at the east end of Varengeville, and you'll soon come to the **Bois des Moutiers**. The house here, built for local landowner Guillaume Mallet from 1898 onwards and un-French in almost every respect, was one of architect **Edwin Lutyens**' first commissions. Then just 29, and heavily influenced by the "Arts and Crafts" ideas of William Morris, Lutyens was at the start of a career that culminated during the 1920s when he laid out most of New Delhi.

The chief reason to visit, however, is to enjoy the magnificent **gardens**, designed by Mallet in conjunction with Gertrude Jekyll, and at their most spectacular in the second half of May. Enthusiastic guides lead you through the highly innovative engineering of the house and grounds, full of quirks and games. The colours of the Burne-Jones tapestry hanging in the stairwell were copied from Renaissance cloth in William Morris's studio; the rhododendrons were chosen from similar samples. Paths lead through vistas based on paintings by Poussin, Lorrain and other eighteenth-century artists; no modern roses, with their anachronistic colours, are allowed to spoil the effect.

Thanks in part to its hugely complicated legal status, being co-owned by an ever-increasing number of Mallet's descendants, the Bois des Moutiers was up for sale as this book went to press, and there's a significant possibility it will not remain open to visitors.

Église St-Valéry

The pioneer Cubist painter **Georges Braque** (1882–1963), a great devotee of Varengeville, lies buried alongside the Église St-Valéry, a twelfth-century church that's perched spectacularly above the cliffs 650m north of the Bois des Moutiers. Braque's smooth marble tomb is topped by a sadly decaying mosaic of a white dove in flight. More impressive is his vivid-blue *Tree of Jesse* stained-glass window inside the church, through which you can see the sun rise in summer.

ACCOMMODATION AND EATING	VARENGEVILLE-SUR-MER

★ De la Terrasse Route de Vastérival ☎ 02 35 85 12 54, ⊕ hotel-restaurant-la-terrasse.com. Irresistible Logis de France, perched high above the cliffs at the end of a dead-end right turning just west of town. Fish menus in its panoramic dining room start at €25, and you can follow footpaths down through narrow cracks in the cliffs to reach the rocky beach below. Rates are for two people, including breakfast and dinner, and It has some large family rooms. Closed mid-Oct to mid-March. **€125**

Veules-les-Roses

As you follow the coastal road west of Varengeville, **Quiberville**, the main name on the map, is popular with windsurfers, but in itself is little more than an overgrown caravan park. **VEULES-LES-ROSES** is rather more promising, a delightful little seaside town that boasts of being located on the shortest river in France, the kilometre-long Veules itself. Apart from walks along the riverbank and the wide shingle beach, the chief pleasure here is dining at the superb local seafood **restaurants**. **Angiens**, not far beyond, is another attractive village with a flower-bedecked square.

ACCOMMODATION AND EATING	VEULES-LES-ROSES

Camping Les Mouettes Avenue Jean-Moulin ☎ 02 35 97 61 98, ⊕ camping-lesmouettes-normandie.com. Verdant campsite, 300m back from the sea, with bar, grocery, sauna and covered heated swimming pool, and bungalows and cabins sleeping up to 6, as well as its hedge-separated tent sites. Closed Nov to early April. **€28.30**

Les Galets 3 rue Victor-Hugo ☎ 02 35 97 61 33, ⊕ restaurant-lesgalets-veuleslesroses.com. Rather chic, highly recommended gourmet restaurant, just footsteps from the sea, and serving exquisite menus from €39. In addition to the expected seafood, they're known for their foie gras. Mon & Wed–Sun noon–1.45pm, 7.30–9.15pm; closed Wed in winter.

St-Valery-en-Caux

1

The first sizeable community west of Dieppe, **ST-VALERY-EN-CAUX** is a rebuilt but still attractive port where open-air stalls along the quayside of the narrow harbour sell fresh-caught fish daily. The bulk of the town lies on the east side; its central square holds a modern church that's made almost entirely of stained glass, with a giant sailing boat motif above its entrance. The square itself is the site of lively **markets** on Fridays and, in summer only, Sundays as well, while the town plays host to both a **festival of the sea** in mid-August, complete with Viking boats, and a **herring festival** on the third Sunday in November.

St-Valery is fronted by a large **beach**, much used by local families, on which grey shingle slopes down to a broad expanse of sand that's only exposed as the tide goes out. The seafront promenade that lines it has been appealingly zested up with wooden decking, benches and picnic tables, while a prominent casino occupies prime position in the middle. Crumbling, brown-stained cliffs stretch away along the coast in either direction.

St-Valery also provides a clear reminder of the fighting – and massive destruction – during the Allied retreat of 1940. A monument on the western heights pays tribute to the French division who faced Rommel's tanks on horseback, brandishing their sabres with hopeless heroism, and beside the ruins of a German artillery emplacement on the opposite cliffs a second monument commemorates a Scottish division, the 51st Highlanders, rounded up while fighting their way back to the boats home.

ARRIVAL AND INFORMATION
ST-VALERY-EN-CAUX

By bus No trains serve St-Valery, but SNCF buses connect with trains to and from Rouen at Yvetot, 27km south. Destinations Dieppe (3–5 daily, 1hr); Fécamp (3–5 daily, 1hr 20min).

Tourist office 1 quai d'Amont (April–Sept daily 9.30am–12.30pm & 2–6.30pm; Oct–March Mon–Sat 9.30am–12.30pm & 2–6pm; ☎02 35 97 00 63, ⓦville-saint-valery-en-caux.fr).

ACCOMMODATION

Du Casino 14 av Clemenceau ☎02 35 57 88 00, ⓦhotel-casino-saintvalery.com. Huge modern hotel, 500m back along the pleasure port. Its 149 rooms are faultlessly comfortable, if a little characterless, and can be a godsend in high season, when the few resources along this stretch of coast are strained to the limit. **€95**

Eden 21 place du Marché ☎02 35 97 11 44. One of several small hotels around the market square, above a lively brasserie serving full meals from €11; the cheapest rooms have WCs but not shower. **€35**

D'Étennemare 21 Hammeau d'Étennemare ☎02 35 97 15 79, ⓦvacances-seasonova.com. Large three-star municipal campsite, set back from the sea, southwest of the harbour, with a covered, heated swimming pool plus a bakery, bike rental and a handful of cabins. Closed mid-Nov to March. **€15**

★**Maison des Galets** 22 rue le Perrey ☎02 35 97 11 22, ⓦlamaisondesgalets.com. Though housed in the unremarkable concrete block that lines St-Valery's beach, this charming hotel has a distinct prewar, Art Deco flavour. All the simple, tasteful rooms, of which half enjoy sea views, have good bathrooms; they also have some cheap single rooms, facing inland. A panoramic ground-floor space operates as a tearoom year-round, and a decent bistro in summer only. **€70**

EATING AND DRINKING

La Boussole 1 rue Max-Leclerc ☎02 35 57 16 28. Pretty, blue, half-timbered house near the tourist office, with tables in a narrow conservatory or outdoors on the seaview terrace, and serving a great-value €19 lunch menu, with choices ranging through snails, curry and chicken with camembert, as well as the expected seafood. Daily noon–2pm & 7.30–9.30pm; closed Mon–Wed in winter.

La Passerelle 1 promenade Jacques-Couture ⓦ02 35 57 84 11, ⓦcasino-saintvalery.com. Classy casino restaurant, enjoying splendid views over the beach, and serving seafood-rich menus from €18 for lunch (weekdays only) and €23 for dinner. The bouillabaisse is especially recommended. Daily noon–2pm & 7.30–10pm.

Restaurant du Port 18 quai d'Amont ☎02 35 97 08 93. Harbourfront restaurant, with a few quayside tables amid the traffic and plenty more room indoors. There's a simple but delicious €25.80 menu, and a more extravagant five-course €46 one, featuring a seafood platter and the day's fresh catch – you're in luck if it's grilled turbot or scallops. Tues, Wed, Fri & Sat noon–1.45pm & 7.30–9.30pm, Thurs & Sun noon–1.45pm.

1

Fécamp

FÉCAMP, roughly halfway between Dieppe and Le Havre, is, like Dieppe, a serious fishing port, albeit one with a modern sideline as a holiday resort. First chartered in 875 AD as Fiscannum, from the Germanic for "fish", it has been a centre for shipbuilding ever since. These days, it's a striking rather than pretty town, with high, overhanging cliffs to either side.

Approaching from inland, you'll come into Fécamp beside the Valmont River, which disappears when it reaches the port into successive canalized channels and artificial harbours, filled with yachts and fishing boats jostling for position. The town proper, focused on the venerable church known as the **Abbatiale de la Sainte-Trinité**, sprawls up the slopes near the port, while the sea lies a few hundred yards further on, reached via a long harbourside street that holds most of Fécamp's best restaurants.

A sturdy sea wall shields the seafront road from the Channel itself. In summer, visitors stroll along the broad promenade that runs atop its full length, and spend time on the steeply shelving shingle beach on the far side. As so often along this coast, windsurfing is more appealing than bathing.

Immediately inland, everyday life continues year-round; only a block or two back from the sea, you'll find rundown residential terraces. Tucked in among them, however, is the town's chief tourist attraction, the incongruous and rather amazing **Benedictine Distillery**.

Note that the long-standing **Musée des Terre-Neuvas et de la Pêche**, near the seafront in Fécamp, closed forever in 2012. Its displays on the local fishing fleet, which for many centuries sailed en masse to Newfoundland every summer, are due to form part of a new **Musée des Pêcheries**, under construction in the docks. The museum will also cover more general history and culture, and may well have opened by the time you read this.

The Benedictine Distillery

110 rue Alexandre-le-Grand • Daily: mid-Feb to mid-April & mid-Oct to mid-Nov 10.30am–12.30pm & 2.30–5.30pm; mid-April to early July & early Sept to mid-Oct 10am–1pm & 2–6.30pm; early July to early Sept 10am–7pm; mid-Nov to early Jan 10.30am–12.30pm & 2.30–5pm; last admission always 1hr before closing; closed early Jan to mid-Feb • €8; fully guided tour at 3.30pm, €12 • ☎ 02 35 10 26 10, ⓦ benedictine.fr

A bizarre mock-Gothic monstrosity, Fécamp's **Benedictine Distillery** somehow squeezes into a backstreet parallel to the port. It was built at the end of the nineteenth century by entrepreneur Alexandre le Grand – no relation to Alexander the Great – who had made a fortune from reviving the manufacture of the sweet liqueur known as Benedictine, originally invented three centuries earlier in the local abbey.

The appeal of visiting this sprawling palace is as much to enjoy the sheer eccentricity of the building as to learn about Benedictine itself. The entire world production of the liqueur does still take place right here, though, even if these days the process is so automated as to require just four full-time employees.

Tours consist of three separate stages. First of all, you wander at your own pace through the ornate upstairs galleries, bursting with treasures and oddities that range from altarpieces, statues and Renaissance paintings to serpentine musical instruments, a wall of framed fourteenth-century keys, and a kitsch stained-glass window depicting monsieur le Grand being treated to a bottle of his favourite tipple by a passing angel. There's also a huge model of the distillery, sadly with its windows closed so you can't see whether it contains another smaller model in turn.

Next you meet up with a guide to be escorted through the production area, where you get to sniff the various herbs, spices and flavourings that feature in Benedictine's complex secret recipe, and see the resultant brew maturing in huge kegs down in the cellars. Finally comes a free tasting, of either Benedictine or its sister drink B&B, a brandy blend, in a newer area that also holds a gleaming white-walled gallery of contemporary art.

1

Abbatiale de la Sainte-Trinité

Place des Ducs Richard • Daily: April–Sept 9am–7pm; Oct–March 9am–noon & 2–5pm • Free; guided visits July & Aug only, Thurs & Sun 3pm, €3 • ☎ 02 35 28 84 39

The medieval abbey church of the **Abbatiale de la Sainte-Trinité** is light and almost frail with age, its bare nave echoing to the sound of birds flying free beneath the high roof. The wooden carvings are tremendous, in particular the dusty wooden bas-relief *Dormition of the Virgin*. The abbey also has a fine selection of saintly fingers and sacred hips, authenticated with wax seals, and even a drop of the Precious Blood itself, said to have floated all the way here in a fig tree dispatched by Joseph of Arimathea. Until Mont-St-Michel was built, this was the religious centre of Normandy; Edward the Confessor may have lived here at some point before his coronation as king of England.

ARRIVAL AND DEPARTURE   FÉCAMP

By train Fécamp's *gare SNCF* is on boulevard de la République, on the left bank of the river at the inland end of the port, just north of the town centre.

Destinations Bréauté-Beuzeville (10 daily; 20min) with connections to Le Havre (total journey 1hr) or Rouen (total journey 1hr 30min).

By bus The *gare routière* is on boulevard de la République, near the *gare SNCF*. Buses from Le Havre arrive on avenue Gambetta, opposite St-Étienne church.

Destinations Étretat (10 daily; 40min), with connections to Le Havre (11 daily; 1hr 20min); Yport (8 daily; 15min).

INFORMATION AND TOURS

Tourist office Quai Sadi-Carnot (Sept–March Mon–Fri 9am–12.30pm & 2–5.30pm, Sat 10am–1pm & 3–5pm, Sun 9.30am–12.30pm in school hols only; April–June Mon–Fri 9am–6pm, Sat & Sun 10am–6.30pm; July &

Aug daily 9am–6.30pm; ☎ 02 35 28 51 01, ⓦ fecamp tourisme.com).

Boat trips Ask at the tourist office about each week's programme of sea cruises, typically priced at €25.

ACCOMMODATION

Fécamp's hotels tend to be set back away from the sea, on random side streets. It's a popular place, so you'll need to reserve a room in summer.

Angleterre 91–93 rue de la Plage ☎ 02 35 28 01 60, ⓦ hotelangleterre.com. Long-established hotel, just back from the sea above a crêperie, which looks unattractive from the outside but holds nicely refurbished sea-view rooms, all en suite, as well as a lively "English pub" with a large outdoor terrace. The ambience is more suited to young budget travellers than those seeking seaside tranquillity, and there's no lift. Parking costs extra, but you should be able to find a space nearby. **€98**

Camping de Reneville Chemin de Nesmond ☎ 02 35 28 20 97, ⓦ campingdereneville.com. Lovely campsite, with beautiful views along the coast, located just a short walk out of town on the western cliffs. One-week minimum stay in summer. Closed early Nov to March. **€18.50**

Grand Pavois 15 quai de la Vicomté ☎ 02 35 10 01 01, ⓦ hotel-grand-pavois.com. Large, grey, modern hotel,

on the quayside facing the port, with bright comfortable well-equipped rooms, many with harbour-view balconies. No restaurant but plenty nearby; €16 buffet breakfasts. **€101**

De la Mer 89 bd Albert 1er ☎ 02 35 28 24 64, ⓦ hotel -dela-mer.com. Eight plain but bright and good-value rooms on the seafront – some with balconies, though the cheapest have toilet but no bath – above *La Frégate* bar, just short of the casino. Closed first three weeks of Feb. **€60**

De la Plage 87 rue de la Plage ☎ 02 35 29 76 51, ⓦ hoteldelaplage-fecamp.com. Behind its somewhat drab exterior, this hotel holds some surprisingly genteel rooms, including larger family options. Each is decorated to a single dominant colour; watch out for the pink one. Only the higher ones have sea views, and the cheapest have shower but not WC, but all are comfortable, the breakfast is good, and the location is quiet. **€48**

EATING AND DRINKING

In summer, Fécamp welcomes enough visitors to keep several restaurants in business; not surprisingly, the fish tends to be good. The most promising area is along the *quais* fronting the harbour; the seafront boulevard has a relatively meagre selection.

Chez Nounoute 3 place Nicolas-Selle ☎ 02 35 29 38 08. The blue chairs of this friendly, good-value bistro, housed in a former fishmonger's, spread across a nice little square by

the port; fill yourself up with *moules frites* for €10, or get the €13 lunch menu. Mon, Tues & Thurs–Sat noon–9pm, Sun noon–2.30pm.

La Marée 77 quai Bérigny ☎02 35 29 39 15, ⓦrestaurant-maree-fecamp.fr. Well-priced quayside fish restaurant, attached to a fish shop and offering a recommended €29 menu, as well as assorted seafood platters. Tues, Wed, Fri & Sat noon–2pm & 7–9.30pm, Thurs & Sun noon–2pm.

La Marine 23 quai de la Vicomté ☎02 35 28 15 94. Friendly little quayside restaurant, not far from the beach, but with indoor seating only, in a smart dining room.

Predominantly seafood €15 lunches and dinners costing up to €35; the excellent *choucroute de la mer* is €14. Daily except Wed noon–2pm & 7–9.30pm.

Les Terre-Neuvas 63 bd Albert 1er ☎02 35 29 22 92, ⓦlesterreneuvas.com. The one high-class seafood option on Fécamp's seafront, occupying a panoramic dining room above the *Filibuster* snack bar; menus from €28 to €56, plus lovely sunset views. Tues–Sat noon–1.30pm & 7–9.30pm, Sun noon–1.30pm.

Yport

The tiny fishing community of **YPORT**, tucked into a narrow gap in the chalky cliffs 6km west of Fécamp, makes an appealing and very peaceful overnight stop. To look at, it's something of a cross between Fécamp and Étretat – much smaller and more attractive than Fécamp, from which it's actually visible along the shoreline, without being as photogenic (or crowded) as Étretat.

Yport is not a natural port. With no river reaching the sea at this point, the seafront consists of an unbroken shelf of shingle, and when the tide goes out it reveals an expanse of seaweed-covered rocks. Traditionally, fishing boats would simply be hauled up onto the beach, and while there's no active fleet these days, small boats scattered along the beach provide a welcome splash of colour. In summer, they're joined by an array of snack, drink and equipment-rental shacks, while a row of beach huts unveil their striped awnings, and the whole place turns into a low-key but very pleasant little resort.

In theory, you could walk at the foot of the cliffs all the way to Fécamp. Owing to the ever-present danger of rock falls, however – as evidenced by the big piles of fresh rubble visible at frequent intervals – visitors are forbidden to venture along the beach east of Yport.

Local legend has it that Yport was colonized over two thousand years ago by Greek fishermen from Asia Minor, who for some reason were not deterred by its complete lack of a harbour. Their descendants have remained ever since, meaning that Yport has a reputation for being insular.

INFORMATION

YPORT

Tourist office Rue Alfred-Nunes (April–June daily 9.30am–12.30pm & 2–6pm; July & Aug daily 9.30am–12.30pm & 2.30–6.30pm; Sept–March Mon–Fri 9am–12.30pm & 2–5.30pm, Sat 10am–1pm & 3–5pm; ☎02 35 29 77 31, ⓦville-yport.fr).

ACCOMMODATION

Normand 2 place J-P Laurens ☎02 35 27 30 76, ⓦhotel-normand.fr. Logis de France, painted to appear half-timbered, on a corner 200m back from the sea. Menus in the restaurant, some tables of which are in a narrow courtyard, start at €18; the €23 option includes some excellent fish fishes. The very cheapest rooms have shower but not WC. Closed mid-Jan to mid-Feb. **€48**

★ **La Sirène** 7 bd Alexandre-Dumont ☎02 35 27 31 87, ⓦhotel-sirene.com. Jaunty seafront hotel, where several of the simple but comfortable and spacious en-suite rooms enjoy sweeping beachfront views. Guests eat in a peaceful, nautical-themed upstairs dining room with panoramic windows, while there's also a restaurant and terrace downstairs; high-quality seafood menus at both cost €19.50 or €29. Closed Dec & Jan. **€75**

Étretat

It's at the delightful little town of **ÉTRETAT**, 18km west of Fécamp and 12km west of Yport, that the alabaster cliffs reach their most spectacular. Hollowed out by the waves to form arches and tunnels, or carved into solitary pinnacles like the "needle" immediately offshore, they adorn countless tourist brochures, and Étretat itself has grown up simply as a pleasure resort.

Much like Yport, Étretat doesn't have a port of any kind; nothing interrupts the curving concrete promenade that stretches along the seafront, above another shingle beach. At one time, wooden boats were dragged up here each summer and thatched over to serve as seasonal bars. Now the boats are permanent fixtures, cemented into place and roofed over, but they still add a charming touch.

However, it's not just the waterfront, and the breathtaking clifftop walks to either side, that make Étretat truly special, but its central core of attractive old timber buildings, grouped a few metres inland around the market square, **place Foch**. The old wooden market *halles* still dominate the square, the ground floor now converted into souvenir shops, while the beams of the balcony and roof remain bare and ancient. **Market** day locally is Thursday, with most of the stalls spreading across the larger car park to the west.

Falaise d'Aval

As soon as you step onto the beach at Étretat you're confronted by the stunning **cliffs**. The coastline here runs roughly northeast to southwest; the largest of the natural waterfront arches, and the lone needle, thrust out on the town's southwestern side, at the foot of the cliff known as the **Falaise d'Aval**.

A straightforward, if precarious, walk leads up the crumbling side of the cliff. On the inland side lie the lush lawns and pastures of a golf course, while on the shoreward edge, old German fortifications extend to the point where the turf abruptly stops. From the windswept top you can see further rock formations and possibly even glimpse Le Havre, but the views back to the town sheltered in the valley, and the matching cliff on its northeastern side, are what stick in the memory.

Falaise d'Amont

Maupassant compared the profile of the smaller arch at the base of Étretat's northeastern cliffs – known as the **Falaise d'Amont**, and painted by Monet among others – to an elephant dipping its trunk into the ocean. Except at high tide, it's possible to stroll along the shingle beyond the town proper to within a few metres of the arch.

Alternatively, an extraordinarily picturesque footpath winds to the top of the cliff, a demanding climb up the green hillside that leads to the little chapel of **Notre Dame**. Just beyond that, a futuristic white arch commemorates French aviators **Nungesser and Coli**, who set out from Paris in the *Oiseau Blanc* in May 1927, hoping to make the first east–west transatlantic flight, and were last seen over Étretat. What happened to them is not known – there are suggestions that they crashed somewhere in deepest Maine, New England – but a mere eighteen days later Charles Lindbergh arrived coming from the opposite direction (see p.130) and went into the history books. In the turf alongside the arch, a life-size aeroplane is set in concrete relief, and a tiny museum nearby tells the story (mid-June to mid-Sept daily 10am–noon & 2–6pm; free).

ARRIVAL AND INFORMATION

ÉTRETAT

By bus Coastal buses stop just outside the tourist office. Destinations Fécamp (10 daily; 40min) via Yport (25min); Le Havre (11 daily; 35min).

By car The biggest drawback to visiting Étretat is that it gets so crowded; in theory there's plenty of central parking, especially at the northern end of the seafront, but in summer you may have to use overflow car parks that stretch back a *long* way from the sea.

Tourist office Back from the sea, on the main road through town, on place Maurice Guillard (mid-March to mid-June & mid-Sept to mid-Nov Mon–Sat 10am–noon & 2–6pm; mid-June to mid-Sept daily 9.30am–6.30pm; mid-Nov to mid-March Fri & Sat 10am–noon & 2–6pm; ☎ 02 35 27 05 21, ⓦ etretat.net).

ACCOMMODATION

Étretat is hardly short of hotels, but they struggle to cope with demand during high season, so it's well worth booking in advance.

Camping Municipal 69 rue Maupassant ☎ 02 35 27 07 67. Spacious individual pitches in Étretat's campsite spread amid the trees to the east of the D39, 1km inland from the town centre. Closed mid-Oct to March. **€19.80**

1

Détective 6 av George V ☎ 02 35 27 01 34, ⓦ detective hotel.com. It's hard to resist being arrested by this quirky hotel, where each room is themed to celebrate a different fictional detective, ranging from Étretat's own Arsène Lupin via Sherlock Holmes and Tintin to Charlie's Angels and Inspector Clouseau. Set 200m back from the sea, it's among the cheapest options in town, but with its strong eco-friendly emphasis and all-round charm, it's great value. **€69**

Dormy House Route du Havre ☎ 02 35 27 07 88, ⓦ dormy-house.com. Grand, modern establishment perched above town on the coastal road to the west, situated as much for the golf course as the beach. Comfortable rooms, some with superb views, and a good restaurant with lovely outdoor seating. **€107**

Rayon Vert 1 rue Général-Leclerc ☎ 02 35 10 38 90, ⓦ hotelrayonvertetretat.com. Nicely restored Victorian-era hotel in the middle of the seafront. Not all rooms face the sea, but those that do, especially on the top floor (no lift), have truly exceptional views, and charge premium prices. There's a brasserie downstairs, under separate management. **€89**

La Résidence 4 bd René-Coty ☎ 02 35 27 02 87, ⓦ hotels -etretat.com. Dramatic half-timbered old mansion just off place Foch, moved in its entirety from Lisieux a century ago, with beautiful wooden carvings decorating its every nook and cranny. Though refurbished, the guest rooms vary enormously; the cheapest option has a toilet but no other en-suite facilities, while others are positively luxurious, costing three times the price and holding four-poster beds and whirlpool baths. **€45**

EATING AND DRINKING

Fierce competition keeps **restaurant** prices in Étretat appealingly low. Even the succession of seafront terraces offer good value for money, while away from the sea, bargains can be had at both ends of the spectrum.

Crêperie Lann-Bihoué 45 rue Notre-Dame ☎ 02 35 27 04 65, ⓦ etretat-lannbihoue.fr. Cheerful, traditional crêperie, at the south end of town, that's Étretat's best bet for a good-value family meal. A *formule* of one galette and one sweet crêpe costs €10.50. Mon, Tues & Thurs–Sun noon–2pm & 7–9pm; closed Tues in low season, plus 3 weeks in Dec.

L'Effet Mer 11 rue Traz-Périer ☎ 02 35 27 02 82, ⓦ etretatrestaurant.com. Panoramic first-floor dining room, at the foot of the steps up the Falaise d'Aval, which makes the perfect setting for an absolute blowout on seafood (though they do also offer meat dishes). Three-course menus start at €34 (with options including nine oysters followed by a seafood *cassolette*), and mixed seafood platters at €39.50 per person. Daily noon–2pm & 7–9pm.

Le Galion Boulevard René-Coty ☎ 02 35 29 48 74, ⓦ etretat-legalion.fr. Étretat's finest restaurant, adjoining the *Résidence* hotel just off the square, serves classic Norman dishes such as oysters poached in Camembert cream or champagne in a gloriously weathered medieval hall, on menus from €25 to €47. Daily noon–1.30pm & 7.30–9pm; closed Tues & Wed in winter.

La Salamandre 4 bd René-Coty ☎ 02 35 27 17 07. This organic restaurant, downstairs from the *Résidence* hotel, but run by separate management, serves stylish modern cuisine amid ravishing medieval trappings, with a good-value €16.80 lunch special, à la carte choices including €13 *moules frites*, and a full dinner menu at €37. Daily noon–2pm & 7–9pm.

Le Havre

While **LE HAVRE**, at the mouth of the Seine, may not be the most picturesque or tranquil place in Normandy, neither is it the soulless urban sprawl some travellers suggest. Yes, its port, the second largest in France after Marseille, takes up half the Seine estuary, but the town itself at the core, home to a population of around 175,000, has become a place of pilgrimage for devotees of **contemporary architecture**. As such, it was added in its entirety to UNESCO's World Heritage List in 2005.

The city was originally built by François I in 1517, to replace the ancient ports of Harfleur and Honfleur, then already silting up. Its name soon changed from Franciscopolis to Le Havre – "the Harbour" – and it became the principal trading post of northern France, importing cotton, sugar and tobacco. In the years before the outbreak of war in 1939, it was the European home of the great trans-Atlantic liners such as the *Normandie*, *Île de France* and *France*.

During World War II, Le Havre suffered heavier damage than any other port in Europe. Following its all but total destruction by Allied bombing, it was rebuilt by a single architect, **Auguste Perret**, between 1946 and 1964. That makes it a rare entity, and one that with its utter dependence on **reinforced concrete** is visibly circumscribed by constraints of time and money. Nonetheless, its sheer sense of space can be

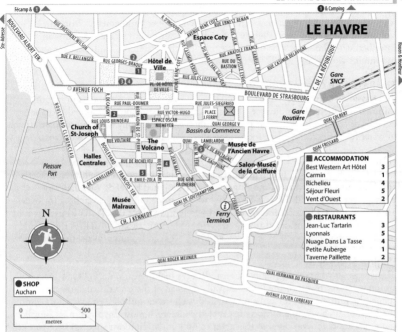

exhilarating, the showpiece monuments have a dramatic and winning self-confidence, and the few churches and other relics that survive of the old city have been sensitively integrated into the whole. While the skyline has been kept deliberately low, the endless mundane residential blocks, which simply had to be erected as economically and swiftly as possible, can get dispiriting. However, with the sea visible at the end of almost every street, and open public space and expanses of water at every turn, even those visitors who ultimately fail to agree with Perret's famous dictum that "concrete is beautiful" may enjoy a stroll around his city.

Downtown Le Havre

It's easy to travel to and from Le Havre without ever seeing its **downtown** area, and thus be left with an impression of an interminable industrial sprawl. Take the time to explore a little, however, and the city's underlying appeal should rise to the surface. Many people's impression changes for the better as soon as they reach the 2km stretch of shingle **beach**, 1.5km west of the *gare SNCF*, fronted on one side by a lively promenade and on the other by some surprisingly clean water. In summer especially, this is by far the most pleasant part of town.

The Volcano

Le Havre's boldest example of modern architecture, the cultural centre known as the **Volcano** – or, less reverentially, the "yoghurt pot" – dominates the **Espace Oscar Niemeyer** at the end of the Bassin du Commerce. The Brazilian architect after whom the *espace* is named – who was best known for overseeing the construction of Brasilia, and remained hard at work right up until he died just short of his 105th birthday in 2012 – designed this slightly asymmetrical, smooth, gleaming-white cone during the 1970s. Cut off abruptly just above the level of the surrounding buildings, its curving planes are undisturbed by doors or windows; the entrance is concealed beneath a white walkway in the open plaza below. A large, green, copper hand emerges from the Volcano just above its base, slightly cupped and pouring out water as a fountain, inscribed with the sentiment that "One day, like this water, the land, beaches and mountains will belong to all".

The Bassin du Commerce

The **Bassin du Commerce**, which stretches away east from the Volcano, is in fact of minimal commercial significance, though a couple of permanently moored boats serve as clubs or restaurants. It's all surprisingly quiet, existing mainly as an appropriate stretch of water for the graceful white footbridge of the Passarelle du Commerce to cross.

Hôtel de Ville

Le Havre's characteristic **urban greenery** is typified by the pergola walkways, flowerbeds and fountains that surround the Auguste Perret-designed **Hôtel de Ville**, halfway between the beach and the *gare SNCF*: a low, flat-roofed building stretching for over 100m and topped by a seventeen-storey concrete tower. Not that Perret himself would have approved; he considered trees and plants to be unnecessary obstacles that would impair the appreciation of his edifices, and they were added after his death in 1954.

L'Église St-Joseph

The steeple of what was arguably Auguste Perret's major creation, **L'Église St-Joseph**, rises not far southwest of the Hôtel de Ville. Instead of the traditional elongated cross shape, the four arms of the cross on which this church is built are equally short. From the outside, it's a very plain mass of speckled concrete, almost Egyptian in its simplicity, the main doors thrown open to the street to hint at dark interior spaces. Once you get inside, it all makes sense. The altar is in the centre, with the hundred-metre bell tower rising directly above it. Simple patterns of stained glass, all around the church and right the way up the tower, produce a bright interplay of coloured light, all focusing on the altar to create the effect of a church in the round.

Musée d'Art Moderne André Malraux – MuMa

2 bd Clemenceau • Mon & Wed–Fri 11am–6pm, Sat & Sun 11am–7pm • €5 • T 02 35 19 62 62, W muma-lehavre.fr

The **Musée d'Art Moderne André Malraux**, overlooking the harbour entrance and widely known as **MuMa**, ranks among the best designed art galleries in France. It uses natural light to full advantage to display an enjoyable assortment of nineteenth- and twentieth-century French paintings.

The principal highlight upstairs is a collection of over two hundred canvases by **Eugène Boudin**. Two years after the painter's death, his brother Louis gave the museum the entire contents of Eugène's studio. Although many of the works were neither signed nor dated, and some are no bigger than postcards, they range from throughout the artist's career. Most are arranged by theme, so one wall consists almost entirely of miniature cows, but there are also greyish landscapes from all along the Norman and Breton coastlines, including views of Trouville, Honfleur and Étretat.

Downstairs, the focus shifts to a lovely set of works by **Raoul Dufy** (1877–1953). In his case, the artist's widow left two hundred of his paintings to be divided between three museums – the national modern art museum in Paris, the one in Nice, and this gallery in Dufy's home town. Each curator was allowed to pick a single piece in turn, with the result that Le Havre ended up with a collection of images of itself that make it seem positively radiant. Dufy depicts his native city at play, with drawings and paintings of festivals and parades, and even a panorama of the whole city framed beneath an arching rainbow.

Other treasures include several Monets – including scenes of Westminster and Varengeville, plus a few waterlilies and a snowscape sunrise – as well as works by Corot, Courbet, Pissarro (one of which was painted within a few metres of this spot), Sisley, Léger, Braque and Lurçat.

HARFLEUR

The once-great port of **Harfleur** is now no more than a suburb of Le Havre, 6km upstream from the centre. While visibly older than the modern city that engulfs it, it's no longer sufficiently distinctive to be worth visiting. It earned an undying place in history, however, as the landing place of Henry V's English army in 1415, en route to victory at Agincourt. During a month-long siege of the town, two thousand English soldiers died from eating contaminated seafood from the surrounding marshes. Harfleur surrendered in late September, following a final English onslaught spurred on – according to Shakespeare – by Henry's cry of "Once more unto the breach, dear friends…".

ARRIVAL AND INFORMATION

By train The *gare SNCF* is a 10min walk from the centre down boulevard de Strasbourg, not far from the ferry port. If you're travelling west, you have to change at Rouen – a very circuitous route. Commuter services run regularly to Harfleur in around five minutes.

Destinations Paris (11 daily; 2hr 30min); Rouen (15 daily; 50min).

By bus The *gare routière*, alongside the *gare SNCF*, is the base for local and express buses.

Destinations Caen (2 daily express services; 1hr 25min); Étretat (12 daily; 45min); Fécamp (11 daily; 1hr 20min); Honfleur (7 daily; 30min).

LE HAVRE

By ferry Frequent sailings from Portsmouth are operated by DFDS Seaways (⍵ dfdsseaways.co.uk) and Brittany Ferries (⍵ brittanyferries.com). Shuttle buses connect the ferry terminal with the *gare SNCF*.

Tourist office 186 bd Clemenceau, in an inconspicuous and not very central location on the main seafront drag (July & Aug daily 9am–7pm; April–June & Sept Mon–Sat 9.30am–12.30pm & 2–6.30pm, Sun 10am–12.30pm & 2.30–6.30pm; Oct–March Mon–Sat 9.30am–12.30pm & 2–6pm, Sun 10am–12.30pm & 2.30–5pm; ☏ 02 32 74 04 04, ⍵ lehavretourisme.com).

ACCOMMODATION

One consequence of Le Havre's lack of idiosyncratic old buildings is that its hotels tend to be hidden away behind indistinguishable concrete facades. There are two main concentrations of hotels: one group faces the *gare SNCF*, while most of the rest lie within walking distance of the ferry terminal.

Best Western Art Hôtel 147 rue Louis Brindeau ☏ 02 35 22 69 44, ⍵ www.art-hotel.fr. Very smart, comfortable hotel in a Perret-designed building on the north side of the Espace Oscar Niemeyer, facing the Volcano cultural centre. Rooms do indeed have arty touches, and the largest have outdoor terraces. **€98**

Carmin 15 rue Georges Braque ☏ 02 32 74 08 20, ⍵ hotelcarmin.com. Good-value hotel in a relatively quiet neighbourhood, not too far back from the sea; the large rooms may not be fancy, but they're comfortable. Buffet breakfasts €9. **€75**

Richelieu 132 rue de Paris ☏ 02 35 42 38 71, ⍵ hotel lerichelieu.fr. For a mid-priced hotel in a very central location, where the comfortable rooms have bright, colourful quilts and tapestries, and in some instances balconies,

this friendly, family-run place is hard to beat. **€56**

Séjour Fleuri 71 rue Émile-Zola ☏ 02 35 41 33 81, ⍵ hotelsejourfleuri.fr. On a side road off rue de Paris, close to the ferry terminal; not as "flowery" as the name might suggest but cheered up by bright-red shutters and window boxes, and holding small, minimally furnished but perfectly clean rooms, the very cheapest of which lack en-suite facilities. **€45**

★**Vent d'Ouest** 4 rue de Caligny ☏ 02 35 42 50 69, ⍵ ventdouest.fr. Le Havre's smartest hotel is a stylishly designed boutique affair, housed in a cream-coloured cement building beside the main entrance to the St-Joseph church. All the comfortable, well-equipped rooms are decorated with a nautical or mountain theme. Apartments sleeping four are also available. **€100**

EATING AND DRINKING

The area around the *gare SNCF* is the best place to head for bars, cafés and brasseries, while all sorts of restaurants, from traditional French to Japanese, fill the back streets of the waterside St-François district.

Jean-Luc Tartarin 73 place Foch ☏ 02 35 45 46 20, ⍵ jeanluc-tartarin.com. Stylish, but not too formal restaurant, with two Michelin stars and prices to match. The inventive cuisine ranges across meat and game, as well as

seafood, and is renowned for its creative use of fruit, as with adding passion fruit to lentils. The limited-choice lunch menu costs €35, while dinner is €58, €99 or €155. Tues–Sat noon–2pm & 7.30–9pm; closed first 2 weeks in Aug.

1

Lyonnais 7–9 rue de Bretagne ☎ 02 35 22 07 31. Small, cosy restaurant with chequered tablecloths and a welcoming atmosphere. The speciality is baked fish, though dishes from Lyon, such as *andouillettes*, are also available on menus that start at €13.40 at lunch, €17.50 at dinner. Tues–Fri noon–2pm & 7–10pm, Sat noon–2pm.

Nuage Dans La Tasse 93 av Foch ☎ 02 35 21 64 94. Close to the town hall, the "storm in a teacup" serves huge salads, baked quiches and flans and simple, good-value bistro meals. Mon–Wed noon–2pm, Thurs–Sat noon–2pm & 7–10pm.

Petite Auberge 32 rue de Ste-Adresse ☎ 02 35 46 27 32, ⊕ lapetiteauberge-lehavre.fr. High-class traditional

French cooking, aimed more at local businesspeople than at tourists, and offering few surprises but no disappointments. Lunch costs €22, while dinner menus start at €28. Tues & Thurs–Sat noon–1.30pm & 7.30–9pm, Wed 7.30–9pm, Sun noon–1.30pm.

Taverne Paillette 22 rue Georges Braque ☎ 02 35 41 31 50, ⊕ taverne-paillette.com. This venerable Bavarian brasserie can trace its roots – and its beer – back to the sixteenth century, even if its present incarnation is a post-war reconstruction. The twin specialities are *choucroute* and elaborate seafood platters; there's also a changing daily lunch menu for €14.20. Daily noon–midnight.

SHOPPING

The best place to buy fresh fruit and vegetables, fish and meat in downtown Le Havre is the city's covered marketplace, the **Halles Centrales**, on rue Bernardin de St-Pierre just east of the Espace Oscar Niemeyer.

Auchan Mont Gaillard Centre Commercial ☎ 02 35 54 71 71, ⊕ magasins.auchan.fr. The largest local hypermarket is the obvious place for ferry passengers to stock up on food and drink to take home, and also holds an outlet

of the chain self-service cafeteria, *Flunch*. Get here by following cours de la République beyond the *gare SNCF*, through the tunnel. There's another smaller Auchan, at Montivilliers, east of the centre. Mon–Sat 8.30am–10pm.

The Lower Seine Valley

As far back as the Bronze Age, the **River Seine** was a crucial part of the "Tin Road" that linked Cornwall to Paris. Fortresses and monasteries lined its banks from the Roman era onwards. These days, with the threat of its tidal bore and treacherous sandbanks long gone, heavy ships make their serene way up its sinuous course from the Channel to the provincial capital of **Rouen**, and although both Le Havre and Rouen have become vast industrial conurbations, long stretches of the river bank between the two remain remarkably unspoiled and tranquil.

Whether you follow the Seine by car, bus or bicycle, this is a journey to take equally slowly. With only a few scattered bridges and the occasional ferry en route, you have to choose which bank appeals to you. The **south (left) bank** holds the vast majority of the **Parc Naturel Régional de Brotonne**, where peaceful rolling hillsides are evenly divided between bucolic agricultural fields and dense woodlands, while the **north (right) bank**, lined by dramatic chalky bluffs, makes a much more direct route to Rouen, and the riverside road leads past such sights as the venerable towns of **Villequier** and **Caudebec**, and the magnificent ruined abbey of **Jumièges**.

The Pont de Normandie

When you first leave Le Havre, the refineries and cement works seem to go on forever; to reach the river, drivers have first to negotiate a long approach road that twists its way over the Canal du Havre. Beyond that, the huge, humpback **Pont de Normandie** spans the mouth of the Seine to connect Le Havre with Honfleur, offering direct access between the coasts of Upper and Lower Normandy for a one-way toll of €5.40. An amazing spectacle, it stretches a total of 2143m across, with a central span over the Seine itself of 856m, and the roadway climbing 50m above sea level. When completed in 1995, it was the longest cable-stayed bridge in the world, but it has since been surpassed by rivals in Japan and Greece.

Beyond the similarly immense **Pont de Tancarville** suspension bridge (toll €2.50), 20km upriver, only one more bridge crosses the extravagant loops of the Seine before Rouen – the **Pont de Brotonne** (free), near Caudebec. Further upstream, however,

1

intermittent *bacs* (car **ferries**) cross the river. They charge minimal tolls, and tend to leave on the hour (and have long lunch breaks).

Villequier

The first riverbank town you come to on the D982 along the north bank is quite undeservedly one of the least known – **VILLEQUIER**. While there's nothing very much to do in Villequier, watching the extraordinary array of boats great and small that pass by, towering above the riverbank, is deliciously hypnotic.

An enjoyable riverside pedestrian promenade runs the length of the village, which has a bohemian vibe with its higgledy-piggledy old houses. Several hundred metres upstream from the centre, near the southern end of the waterfront, a mournful statue of Victor Hugo, so weathered as to make the author appear naked, peers out into the Seine, to the spot where his daughter and her husband drowned in 1843, just six months after their marriage. A small pavilion nearby is inscribed with the words of Hugo's poem about visiting his daughter's grave in Villequier, Demain dès l'aube.

The couple's former home, back in town, now serves as the **Musée Victor Hugo** (April–Sept Mon & Wed–Sat 10am–12.30pm & 2–6pm, Sun 2–6pm; Oct–March Mon & Wed–Sat 10am–12.30pm & 2–5.30pm, Sun 2–5.30pm; €3.50, under-18s free; ☏02 35 56 78 31, ⓦmuseevictorhugo.fr) probably of interest only to fluent French speakers with a passion for Hugo's writings.

Caudebec-en-Caux

Just over 4km upstream from Villequier, **CAUDEBEC-EN-CAUX** is significantly larger and busier. The magnificent flamboyant **Notre Dame church**, with its octagonal spire circled by three separate *fleurs-de-lis* crowns, still dominates the main square, which has been the site of a **market** every Saturday since 1390. On the last Sunday in September of each year, Caudebec comes alive with a large **Cider Festival**.

Maison des Templiers

rue Thomas Bassin • April–Sept Wed–Fri & Sun 2.30–6.30pm, Sat 10am–noon & 2.30–6.30pm • €5 • ☏02 35 96 95 91, ⓦmaisondestempliers.over-blog.com

Caudebec's thirteenth-century **Maison des Templiers**, 100m back from the river, was one of the few buildings in this old town to survive the firestorm devastation of World War II. It now serves as a museum of local history, with plenty of old photos and "one of the most important collections of chimney plaques in France".

The Pont de Brotonne

Slightly upstream from Caudebec, the magnificent span of the **Pont de Brotonne**, completed in 1977 as the world's highest and steepest humpback bridge, climbs out above the Seine. It has an unexpectedly appealing colour scheme – the suspension

---

THE LOSS OF THE *LATHAM 47*

A short way south of Caudebec, close to the Pont de Brotonne, a **stone aeroplane** propels itself out of the cliff face across the water. This is the **Latham 47 Monument**, erected in 1931 to commemorate a tragedy from the heyday of the great aviators.

In 1928, a twin-engined flying boat, the *Latham 47*, was being prepared here for an attempt at what would have been the first east–west transatlantic flight. But shortly before it was due to set off, the Norwegian polar explorer **Roald Amundsen**, famous for being the first man to reach the South Pole, issued a worldwide appeal for help to rescue some Italian sailors who had been shipwrecked off Spitsbergen in the Arctic. The French government offered the plane, and its four crewmen left with Amundsen. Two days later they were lost.

1

cables are custard yellow, the rails pastel green, the walkway maroon, and the vast concrete columns left bare. If you don't lose both heart and hat to the sickening drop and the seaborne winds, walking across it is one of the big treats of Normandy. From a distance, its stays refract into strange optical effects, while far below small tugs flounder in the wash of mighty cargo carriers.

Parc Naturel Régional des Boucles de la Seine Normande

Maison du Parc April–June & Sept Mon–Fri 9am–6pm, Sat & Sun 1–6pm; July & Aug Mon–Fri 9am–6.30pm, Sat & Sun 10am–6.30pm; Oct–March Mon–Fri 9am–12.30pm & 1.30–6pm • ☎ 02 35 37 23 16, ⓦ pnr-seine-normande.com

The **Parc Naturel Régional des Boucles de la Seine Normande**, most but not quite all of which lies south of the Seine, ranks among the most beautiful tracts of the Norman countryside. While not entirely rural, it shelters a wide range of conservation projects and traditional industry initiatives, run by local people, alongside its more obvious abbey and château sites. Full details on all its aspects can be obtained from the very helpful Maison du Parc in the small village of **NÔTRE-DAME-DE-BLIQUETUIT**, immediately east of the southern end of the Pont de Brotonne.

The most compelling section of the park is concentrated into a mighty meander on the southern bank of the Seine, across from Caudebec. Here the slopes are covered by the deep thick woods of the **Forêt de Brotonne**, perfect for cyclists and hikers. The pretty little village of **AIZIER** nestles beside the river at the western limit of the forest, with the edges of the Vernier marshes, grazed by Camargue horses and Scottish Highland cattle, just beyond.

Moulin de Pierre

2 rte du Moulin, Hauville • Late April to June & first three weeks in Sept Sun 2.30–6.30pm; July & Aug daily 2–6.30pm • €2.50 • ☎ 02 32 56 57 32, ⓦ moulinavent27.wix.com

The southern border of the Forêt de Brotonne marks the dividing line between the *départements* of Seine-Maritime and Eure. Still under the auspices of the park, outside the small community of **HAUVILLE** (and signposted towards the even tinier village of La Mare-Guérard), you can look round what's said to be the oldest still-functioning **windmill** in France, known as the **Moulin de Pierre**. One of six owned by the monks of Jumièges, who farmed and forested this area in the Middle Ages, its existence was first recorded in 1258. Its outline – based on contemporary castle towers – looks like a kid's drawing.

La Haye de Routot

The churchyard in the village of **LA HAYE DE ROUTOT**, 4km west of Hauville, is a real oddity, featuring a pair of thousand-year-old yew trees that are still alive but have been sufficiently hollowed out to shelter a chapel and grotto. Every year, on July 16, the feast of St Clair, the village stages the dramatic **Fête de St-Clair** (ⓦ lahayederoutot.com). Its centrepiece is a towering, conical bonfire, topped by a cross which must survive to ensure a good year. The smouldering logs are taken home to serve as protection against lightning. Should you miss the big day, you can see footage in the local **crafts museum** (March–June & Sept–Nov Sun 2–6pm; July & Aug daily 2–6.30pm; €2.50; ☎ 02 32 57 59 67, ⓦ lahayederoutot.com), at 15 Grande Rue, which numbers among its separate sections a traditional functioning bread oven, adjacent to the church, and a clog-specialist shoemaker opposite.

Abbaye de St-Wandrille

Daily 5.15am–1pm & 2–9.15pm; guided tours Easter–June & Sept–early Nov Mon–Sat 3.30pm, Sun 11.30am & 3.30pm; July & Aug daily 11.30am, 3pm & 4pm; services Mon–Sat 5.25am, 7.30am, 9.45am, 12.45pm, 2.15pm, 5.30pm & 8.35pm; Sun 5.25am, 7.30am, 10am, 12.45pm, 2.30pm, 5pm & 8.35pm • €6 • ☎ 02 35 96 23 11, ⓦ st-wandrille.com

According to legend, the **Abbaye de St-Wandrille** was founded by a seventh-century count who, with his wife, renounced all earthly pleasures on the day of their wedding.

MONET'S GARDEN, GIVERNY (P.84) >

1

Still an active monastery, it can be reached by following a side road – marked "St-Wandrille-Rançon" – that climbs 2km up from the north bank of the Seine, just beyond the Pont de Brotonne.

While not such an obvious tourist destination as nearby Jumièges, the abbey complex nonetheless makes an attractive if curious architectural ensemble: part ruin, part restoration and, in the case of the main buildings, part transplant – a fifteenth-century barn brought in a few years ago from another Norman village. It's now home to fifty or so Benedictine monks who, in addition to their spiritual duties, turn their hands to money-making tasks that range from candle-making to running a reprographic studio.

Ideally, time your visit to coincide with one of the **guided tours** in which monks show visitors around the abbey; otherwise the admission fee simply entitles you to wander through the grounds on your own, while you can hear **Gregorian chanting** at services in their new church.

Abbaye de Jumièges

24 rue Guillaume-le-Conquérant, Jumièges • Daily: mid-April to mid-Sept 9.30am–6.30pm; mid-Sept to mid-April 9.30am–1pm & 2.30–5.30pm • €6, ages 18–25 €4, under-18s free • ☎ 02 35 37 24 02, ⓦ www.abbayedejumieges.fr

Deliberately destroyed during the Revolution, and now a haunting skeleton hailed as "the most beautiful ruins in France", the **Abbaye de Jumièges** stands 12km upstream from St-Wandrille, in the next loop of the Seine. Founded by St Philibert in 654 AD, just five years after St-Wandrille, it was burned by Vikings in 841, then rebuilt a century later. Its main surviving shell, however, as far as it can still be discerned, dates from the eleventh century; William the Conqueror attended its reconsecration in 1067. The twin towers, over 52m high, are still standing. So too is one arch of the roofless nave, while a one-sided yew tree stands in the centre of what were once the cloisters.

These bleached bones can be explored on hourly guided tours, in French only, or you can take an unescorted ramble across the lawns; in either case, you're obliged for the most part to keep well clear of the precarious walls themselves. Though it survived the Revolution intact, the grand **abbot's residence** that commands a nearby eminence – built in the seventeenth century, by which time the abbot was appointed directly by the king rather than being elected by his fellow monks – is not open to visitors. The grounds, however, are sometimes used for temporary art exhibitions.

The river itself now flows roughly a kilometre west of the ruins. A tiny, free *bac* (ferry) crosses the Seine at this point to Heurteauville on the left bank, half-hourly in summer and hourly in winter.

INFORMATION   **LOWER SEINE VALLEY**

CAUDEBEC-EN-CAUX

Tourist office Slightly south of the centre, in place Charles de Gaulle by the river (June–Sept daily 10am–12.30pm & 1.30–6.30pm; Oct–May Tues–Sat 10am–12.30pm & 1.30–5pm; ☎ 02 32 70 46 32, ⓦ caudebec-en-caux.com).

JUMIÈGES

Tourist office Rue Guillaume-le-Conquérant (April–Sept Tues–Sun 10am–12.30pm & 2–6pm; Oct–March Tues–Sat 10am–noon & 2–5pm; ☎ 02 35 37 28 97, ⓦ jumieges.fr).

ACCOMMODATION AND EATING

VILLEQUIER

Barre Y Va Route de Villequier ☎ 02 35 96 26 38, ⓦ camping-barre-y-va.com. Two-star riverside campsite, halfway between Villequier and Caudebec, with a bakery and grocery store onsite, and a pool nearby. Closed late Oct to early April. **€21.30**

★ **Grand Sapin** 12 rue Louis le Gaffric ☎ 02 35 56 78 73, ⓦ legrandsapin.fr. Until a few years ago, this gorgeous rambling old riverside building held a hotel. Sadly, that now seems to be permanently closed, but its restaurant remains a magical setting for traditional Norman meals. Dishes such as rabbit *millefeuille* figure on the main €25 dinner menu, while the set weekday lunch costs €15. Tables in the riverside garden are laid out under the shade of the eponymous *grand sapin* itself – not the original, but a rather frail pine that has had its thunder stolen by a giant magnolia nearby. Mon & Thurs–Sun 12.15–2.15pm & 7.15-9.15pm, Tues 12.15–2.15pm.

Maison Blanche 11 rue Louis le Gaffric ☎ 02 35 56 76 82, ✉ gabrielcraquelin@orange.fr. Imposing sixteenth-century white-stone mansion, facing the river, which now holds two grand B&B rooms, one equipped with a four-poster bed, and serves splendid breakfasts. **€100**

CAUDEBEC-EN-CAUX

Cheval Blanc 4 place René-Coty ☎ 02 35 96 21 66, ⓦ le-cheval-blanc.fr. Logis de France, set a little way back from the river on the western edge of town, 200m north of the Hôtel de Ville. Rooms are slightly old-fashioned, and some are rather small too, but they're perfectly comfortable, while good-value menus start with a €19.50 option that features fish poached in *poiré*. Closed late Dec. **€62**

Normandie 19 quai Guilbaud ☎ 02 35 96 25 11, ⓦ le-normandie.fr. Central, family-run hotel with a commanding view of the river and some family-sized rooms. Much like its neighbours, it offers decent but uremarkable rooms, and a good restaurant, with a simple €24 dinner and a €34.50 regional menu that includes kidneys flambéed in Calvados. **€65**

Normotel La Marine 18 quai Guilbaud ☎ 02 35 96 20 11, ⓦ normotel-lamarine.fr. Somewhat severe concrete riverfront hotel, with great views out over the Seine. The rooms are a little faded but acceptable, and the restaurant serves classic food, at its best on the €32.50 dinner menu; at lunch time it's a brasserie, with set meals for €16. Look for good deals online. **€59**

JUMIÈGES

Auberge du Bac 2 rue Alphonse Callais ☎ 02 35 37 24 16. Riverbank restaurant, next to the *bac*, that makes a lovely lunch time halt, serving excellent menus from €13.50 (lunch only) up to €36. Wed–Sat noon–2pm & 7–9pm, Sun noon–2pm.

★ **Auberge des Ruines** 17 place de la Mairie ☎ 02 35 37 24 05, ⓦ auberge-des-ruines.fr. A relaxing and truly superb restaurant, with outdoor seating on a shaded terrace across from the abbey. Menus range from the "Discovery" at €28 up to the €97 "Symphony". Mon, Tues & Thurs–Sat noon–2pm & 7–9pm, Sun noon–2pm.

Rouen

Capital of both the Seine-Maritime *département* and all Upper Normandy, **ROUEN** is one of France's most ancient and historic cities. Standing on the site of Rotomagus, built by the Romans at the lowest bridge-able point on the Seine, it was laid out by the Viking Rollo, the first duke of Normandy, in 911. Captured by the English in 1419, after a long siege, it became the stage in 1431 for the trial and execution of Joan of Arc, before returning to French control in 1449.

Bombing during the fierce onslaught that preceded the D-Day landings in 1944 destroyed all Rouen's bridges, the area between the cathedral and the *quais*, and much of the left bank's industrial quarter. The city has since been almost entirely rebuilt, turning its inner core of streets, a few hundred metres north of the river, into the closest approximation to a medieval city that modern imaginations could conceive. Rouen today can be very seductive, its lively and bustling centre well equipped with impressive churches and museums. The effect is enhanced by the fact that in the last few years they've at long last got round to restoring the riverfront.

While Rouen proper is home to a population of 110,000, its metropolitan area holds five times that number. The city spreads deep into the loop of the Seine, with its docks and industrial infrastructure stretching endlessly away to the south, and has expanded up into the hills to the north as well. As the nearest point that large container ships can get to Paris, this remains the fourth-largest port in the country; it's also the biggest exporter of foodstuffs in the European Union, and the biggest in the world for wheat.

Cathédrale de Notre Dame

April–Oct Mon 2–6pm, Tues–Sat 9am–7pm, Sun 8am–6pm; Nov–March Mon 2–6pm, Tues–Sat 9am–noon & 2–6pm, Sun 8am–6pm

Rouen's focal point, the **Cathédrale de Notre Dame**, stands on the site of a Roman place of worship, erected in the third century AD at a major crossroads. Despite the addition of all sorts of towers and spires, it remains at heart the Gothic masterpiece that was built in the twelfth and thirteenth centuries. Later accretions include the flamboyant **Tour du Beurre**, named for the erroneous belief that it was paid for by the granting of

1

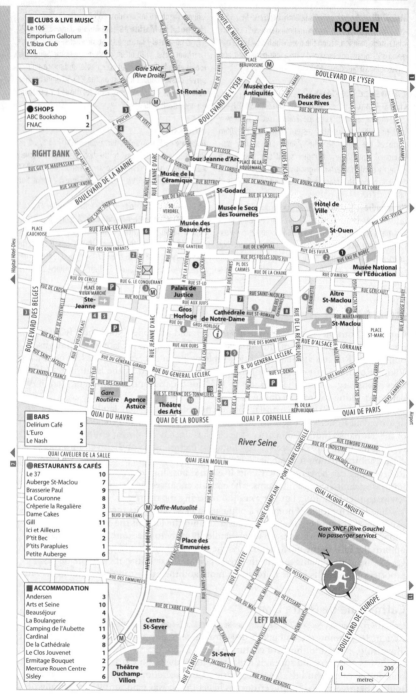

ROUEN

CLUBS & LIVE MUSIC
Le 106	7
Emporium Gallorum	1
L'Ibiza Club	3
XXL	6

SHOPS
ABC Bookshop	1
FNAC	2

BARS
Delirium Café	5
L'Euro	4
Le Nash	2

RESTAURANTS & CAFÉS
Le 37	10
Auberge St-Maclou	7
Brasserie Paul	9
La Couronne	8
Crêperie la Regaliere	3
Dame Cakes	5
Gill	11
Ici et Ailleurs	4
P'tit Bec	2
P'tits Parapluies	1
Petite Auberge	6

ACCOMMODATION
Andersen	3
Arts et Seine	10
Beauséjour	4
La Boulangerie	5
Camping de l'Aubette	11
Cardinal	9
De la Cathédrale	8
Le Clos Jouvenet	1
Ermitage Bouquet	2
Mercure Rouen Centre	7
Sisley	6

Hôpital Hôtel-Dieu

RIGHT BANK

LEFT BANK

Gare SNCF (Rive Droite)

St-Romain

Musée des Antiquités

Théâtre des Deux Rives

BOULEVARD DE L'YSER

Tour Jeanne d'Arc

Musée de la Céramique

St-Godard

Musée le Secq des Tournelles

Hôtel de Ville

St-Ouen

Musée des Beaux-Arts

Musée National de l'Education

Palais de Justice

Gros Horloge

Cathédrale de Notre-Dame

Aître St-Maclou

St-Maclou

Gare Routière

Agence Astuce

Théâtre des Arts

River Seine

Gare SNCF (Rive Gauche) No passenger services

Joffre-Mutualité

Place des Emmurées

Centre St-Sever

St-Sever

Théâtre Duchamp-Villon

0	200
	metres

dispensations that allowed wealthy churchgoers to eat butter during Lent, and the nineteenth-century iron **spire** of the central lantern tower. Cast in the foundries of Conches, it was built to replace a tower that burned down in 1822, and was at the time, at 151m, the highest in France.

The ongoing **restoration** of the cathedral has been an immense task, rendered more complex when one of the spire's four greenish supports was detached by a hurricane in 1999, and fell, piercing the roof of the cathedral itself and destroying a section of the medieval choir stalls below. Intricately sculpted like the rest of the exterior, the west facade of the cathedral was **Monet's subject** for over thirty studies of changing light, one of which hangs in the Musée des Beaux Arts (see p.74). Monet might not recognize it now, however – it's been scrubbed a gleaming white, free from the centuries of accreted dirt he so carefully recorded.

The interior

Inside the cathedral, the carvings of the misericords in the choir depict fifteenth-century life, in secular scenes, as well as the usual mythical beasts. The chapel dedicated to Joan of Arc, and paid for by an English committee in 1956, contains a statue of Joan at the stake. The **ambulatory** and **crypt** – closed on Sunday mornings and during services – hold the assorted tombs of various recumbent royal figures, stretching back as far as **Duke Rollo**, who died "enfeebled by toil" in 933 AD. Rollo's effigy was destroyed by the bombs of 1944, and has now been replaced by a nineteenth-century copy of someone else's. Both he and **Richard the Lionheart** – whose heart is actually in a lead box in the treasury – have detachable feet, which are occasionally removed for cleaning.

Cathédrale de Lumière

Daily: mid-June to end July 11pm; first half of Aug 10.30pm, second half of Aug 10pm; first 3 weeks of Sept 9.30pm • Free • ☎ 02 35 71 51 23, Ⓦ cathedrale-rouen.net

On summer nights, under the name of **Cathédrale de Lumière**, spectacular thirty-minute light shows are projected onto the cathedral façade; one show draws on Monet's paintings to creat giant Impressionist canvases, while another depicts the story of Joan of Arc.

Église St-Maclou

April–Oct Mon & Fri–Sun 10am–noon & 2–6pm; Nov–March Mon, Sat & Sun 10am–noon & 2–5.30pm

The intricate wooden panelling in the porch of the fifteenth-century church of **St-Maclou**, a short way east of the cathedral, is the highlight of what is often cited as the most spectacular example of Gothic flamboyant architecture in France. The whole building was so badly damaged by bombs on June 4, 1944 that it only reopened in 1980; thankfully, the ornate stone stairway up to the organ inside remains as ethereal as ever. The interior is so light partly because most of its stained glass was destroyed, and the windows are now clear. St Maclou himself – more familiar as St Malo – was a seventh-century missionary from Wales.

Aître St-Maclou

188 rue Martainville • April–Oct Sat & Sun 9am–7pm; Nov–March Sat & Sun 9am–6pm; plus Mon–Fri 9am–6pm all year, during school hols only • Free

Near the Église St-Maclou, though its entrance is a little hard to find between nos. 184 and 186 rue Martainville, the **Aître St-Maclou** was built between 1526 and 1533, in an era of mass plague deaths, as a cemetery and charnel house. The ground floor was used as an open cloister while the bare bones of victims were exposed to view in the rooms above.

1

JOAN OF ARC

Joan of Arc stands alone, and must continue to stand alone... There is no one to compare her with, none to measure her by... There have been other young generals, but they were not girls; young generals, but they have been soldiers before they were generals; she began as a general; she commanded the first army she ever saw; she led it from victory to victory, and never lost a battle with it; there have been young commanders-in-chief, but none so young as she: she is the only soldier in history who has held the supreme command of a nation's armies at the age of 17.   Mark Twain, Joan of Arc

When the 17-year-old peasant girl known to history as **Joan of Arc** arrived at the French court in Chinon early in 1429, the Hundred Years War had already dragged on for over ninety years. Most of northern France was in the grip of an Anglo-Burgundian alliance, whose major strongholds were the châteaux of the Loire. Since 1425, Joan had been hearing voices in her native village of Domrémy, in Lorraine, near France's eastern frontiers. Convinced that she alone could save France, she came to Chinon to present her case to the as-yet-uncrowned Dauphin. Partly through recognizing him despite a simple disguise he wore to fool her at their first meeting, she convinced him of her divine guidance; and after a remarkable three-week examination by a tribunal of the French *parlement*, she went on to secure command of the armies of France. In a whirlwind campaign, which culminated in the raising of the siege of Orléans on May 8, 1429, she broke the English hold on the Loire Valley. She then escorted the Dauphin deep into enemy territory, with town after town rallying to her standard as they advanced, so that in accordance with ancient tradition he could be crowned King Charles VII of France in the cathedral at Reims, on July 17.

Within a year of her greatest triumph, Joan was captured by the Burgundian army at Compiègne in May 1430, and held to ransom. Chivalry dictated that any offer of payment from the vacillating Charles must be accepted, but in the absence of such an offer Joan was handed over to the English for 10,000 ducats. On Christmas Day 1430, she was imprisoned in the château of Philippe-Auguste at Rouen.

Charged with heresy, on account of her "false and diabolical" visions and refusal not to wear men's clothing, Joan was put on trial for her life on February 21, 1431. For three months, a changing panel of 131 assessors – only eight of whom were English-born – heard the evidence against her. Condemned, inevitably, to death, Joan recanted on the scaffold in St-Ouen cemetery on May 24, and her sentence was commuted to life imprisonment. The presiding judge, Bishop Pierre Cauchon of Beauvais, reassured disappointed English representatives that "we will get her yet". The next Sunday, Joan was tricked into breaking her vow and putting on male clothing, and taken to the archbishop's chapel in rue St-Romain to be condemned to death for the second time. On May 30, 1431, she was burned at the stake in the place du Vieux-Marché; her ashes, together with her unburned heart, were thrown into the Seine.

Charles VII finally recaptured Rouen in 1449. Seeing the verdict against Joan as reflecting on the legitimacy of his own claim to the French throne, he instigated a Procès en Nullité, which took evidence from all the surviving witnesses, and resulted in a papal declaration of Joan's innocence in 1456. Joan herself passed into legend, until the discovery and publication of the full transcript of her trial in the 1840s. The forbearance and devout humility she displayed throughout her ordeal added to her status as France's greatest religious heroine. She was canonized as recently as 1920, and soon afterwards became the country's patron saint.

As this book went to press, Rouen was planning to open a new museum dedicated to Joan of Arc on the place du Vieux-Marché.

At first sight it looks very picturesque – a tranquil garden courtyard of half-timbered houses – but look closely at the carvings on the beams of the lower storey and you'll see they bear traces of a macabre **Dance of Death**, everywhere adorned with fading skulls and crossbones. A case to the right of the entrance contains a mummified cat. The buildings are still in use, and still stimulating morbid imaginations, not as a morgue but as Rouen's Fine Arts school. It's therefore closed to visitors during teaching times. The square outside holds several good antique bookshops and a few art shops.

Place du Vieux-Marché

1

A small plaque and a huge cross, 20m high, adorn the **place du Vieux-Marché**, the public square in which **Joan of Arc** was burned to death on May 30, 1431. Louis Arretche designed the adjacent memorial **church** (daily: April–Oct 10am–noon & 2–6pm; Nov–March 10am–noon & 2–5.30pm) to the saint. A wacky, spiky-looking thing, said to represent either an upturned boat or the flames that consumed Joan, it was dedicated in 1979. An indisputable triumph, it's part of an ensemble that also incorporates a covered **food market**, open daily except Monday, and intended less for practical shopping than for show – everything in it does indeed look mouthwateringly appetizing.

The theme of the church's fish-shaped windows continues in the scaly tiles of its hugely elongated roof, which forms a covered walkway across the square. On the lawns, where a flowerbed marks the precise spot of Joan's martyrdom, the foundations of the church of St-Vincent, destroyed in the war, remain visible. Some sixteenth-century stained glass removed from the vanished church was incorporated into one facade of its replacement. It's now displayed beautifully, even though the windows that hold it are an entirely different shape. The square itself is surrounded by fine old brown-and-white half-timbered houses; many of those on the south side now serve as restaurants.

Gros Horloge

Rue du Gros-Horloge • Daily except Mon: April–Oct 10am–1pm & 2–7pm; Nov–March 2–6pm; last admission 1hr before closing • €6 •
⊕ 02 32 08 01 90, Ⓦ rouen.fr/gros-horloge

Until it was lowered to straddle the rue du Gros Horloge in 1529, to allow the citizens of Rouen to see it better, the colourful one-handed clock known as the **Gros Horloge** used to adorn the Gothic belfry alongside. Visitors now climb, via several rooms that explain the history of both clock and city, up a stone spiral staircase, to emerge on a narrow but safely railed boardwalk around the very top. Here you can admire the clock's intricate workings, and enjoy marvellous views of the old city, with its startling array of towers and spires. The bell at the top, cast in 1260, still rings what's known as the "Conqueror's Curfew" at 9pm daily.

Abbatiale St-Ouen

Place du Général-de-Gaulle • Tues–Thurs, Sat & Sun: April–Oct 10am–noon & 2–6pm; Nov–March 10am–noon & 2–5pm • Free

Rouen's last great church, **St-Ouen**, stands next to the Hôtel de Ville in a large open square north of the cathedral. Despite being larger, it has far less decoration; as a result, its Gothic proportions and the purity of its lines have that instant impact with which nothing built since the Middle Ages can compete.

BRINGING THE BEACH TO THE CITY: ROUEN SUR MER

Rouen is finally falling in love with the Seine again. Ever since World War II, when its riverfront buildings, and especially its bridges, were devastated by Allied bombing, the banks of the Seine have held little more than congested highways that offered nothing to lure visitors away from the old city core. Now, however, through traffic is being steered clear of central Rouen, and much of the riverside area is taken up instead by attractive pedestrian promenades.

Every summer, a large stretch of the Seine's left bank becomes **Rouen sur Mer** ("Rouen on Sea"; mid-July to mid-Aug Mon 2–8pm, Tues–Thurs, Sat & Sun 2–8pm, Fri 2–10.30pm; free; Ⓦ rouensurmer.fr). Modelled on a successful similar scheme in Paris, the city authorities strew sand along the quai Saint-Sever, between the Boieldieu and Jeanne d'Arc bridges, to create an artificial **beach**. Every afternoon, local kids flock to play at being on the seaside; there's no access to the river itself, but the bank holds giant waterslides plus games and rides of all kinds, along with ice-cream and snack stalls and lots of room for sunbathing. On Friday evenings, it stays open late for a live concert.

1

Originally it was a seventh-century Benedictine abbey church, founded before the Viking invasion. The present building was begun in 1318 and completed in the sixteenth century; its main entrance is known as the "Porch of the Marmosets" because its ornate carvings are thought to represent monkeys. Inside, it holds some stunning fourteenth-century stained glass, though much was destroyed during the Revolution – hence the 1960 *Crucifixion* in the choir, by Max Ingrand.

Immediately north of St-Ouen is the city's **Hôtel de Ville**, outside which parades an equestrian statue of Napoleon, weathered to an eerie green and looking like death incarnate.

Rue Eau-de-Robec

Running east from rue Damiette just south of St-Ouen, **rue Eau-de-Robec** was described by one of Flaubert's characters as a "degraded little Venice". It's now a textbook example of how Rouen has been restored. Where once a shallow stream flowed beneath the raised doorsteps of venerable half-timbered houses, a thin trickle now makes its way along a stylized cement bed crossed by concrete walkways. It remains an attractive ensemble, if a rather ersatz one, and the houses themselves are now predominantly inhabited by antique dealers, interspersed with the odd café.

Musée National de l'Éducation

185 rue Eau de Robec • Mon & Wed–Fri 10am–12.30pm & 1.30–6pm, Sat & Sun 2–6pm • €3 • ⓦ cndp.fr/musee

Centering on a fine old mansion, the **Musée National de l'Éducation** tells the story of the last five centuries of schooling in France, with photos, paintings, ancient textbooks and a mocked-up schoolroom. As this book went to press, it was undergoing extensive restoration and expansion, which should be complete by the time you read this.

Tour Jeanne d'Arc

Rue Bouvreuil • April–Sept Mon & Wed–Sat 10am–12.30pm & 2–6pm, Sun 2–6.30pm; Oct–March Mon & Wed–Sat 10am–12.30pm & 2–5pm, Sun 2–5.30pm • €1.75 • ⓣ 02 35 98 16 21, ⓦ www.tourjeannedarc.fr

The pencil-thin **Tour Jeanne d'Arc**, a short way southeast of the *gare SNCF*, is all that remains of the castle of Philippe-Auguste, built in 1205 and scene of the imprisonment and trial of Joan of Arc. It served as the castle's keep and entranceway, and was itself fully surrounded by a moat. It was not, however, Joan's actual prison – that was the Tour de la Pucelle, demolished in 1809. The trial took place first of all in the castle's St-Romain chapel, and then later in its great central hall, both of which were destroyed in 1590.

Joan came to this building only once, on May 9, 1431, to be confronted with the fearsome torture chamber in its lowest level. Threatened by Bishop Cauchon with the words "There is the rack, and there are its ministers. You will reveal all, now, or be put to the torture", she responded: "I will tell you nothing more than I have told you; no, not even if you tear the limbs from my body. And even if in my pain I did say something otherwise, I would always say afterwards that it was the torture that spoke and not I".

The tall, sharp-pointed tower was bought by public subscription in 1860, and restored to its present state. After seeing a small collection of Joan-related memorabilia, you can climb the steep spiral staircase to the very top, but you can't see out over the city, let alone step outside into the open air.

Musée des Beaux Arts

Esplanade Marcel-Duchamp • Daily except Tues 10am–6pm • €5; temporary exhibitions may cost extra • ⓣ 02 35 71 28 40, ⓦ mbarouen.fr

Rouen's imposing **Musée des Beaux Arts** commands the square Verdrel from just east of the central rue Jeanne d'Arc. Even this grand edifice is not quite large enough to display some of its medieval tapestries, which dangle inelegantly from the ceilings to trail along the floor, but the collection as a whole is consistently absorbing. Unexpected highlights include dazzling Russian icons from the sixteenth century onwards, and an entertaining three-dimensional eighteenth-century Nativity from Naples.

Many of the biggest names among the painters – Caravaggio (the centrepiece *Flagellation of Christ*), Velázquez, Rubens – tend to be represented by a single minor work, but there are several Modiglianis and a number of Monets, including *Rouen Cathedral* (1894), the *Vue Générale de Rouen* and *Brume sur la Seine* (1894), as well as canvases by Blanche Hoschedé-Monet, who was both the daughter of Claude Monet's mistress Alice and the wife of his son Jean. The central sculpture court, roofed over but very light, is dominated by a wonderful three-part mural of the course of the Seine from Paris to Le Havre, prepared by Raoul Dufy in 1937 for the Palais de Chaillot in Paris.

Musée de la Céramique

I rue Faucon • Daily except Tues 2–6pm • €3 • ☎ 02 35 07 31 74, ⓦ museedelaceramique.fr

Rouen's history as a centre for *faïencerie*, or earthenware pottery, is recorded in the **Musée de la Céramique**, facing the Beaux Arts. A series of beautiful rooms, some incorporating sixteenth-century wood panelling rescued from the nunnery of St-Amand, display specimens from the seventeenth century onwards. Until polychrome appeared in 1698, everything was blue; at that time, Rouen's main rivals and influences were the cities of Delft and Nevers, well represented here. Assorted tiles and plates reflect the eighteenth-century craze for chinoiserie, although the genuine Chinese and Japanese pieces nearby possess a sophistication contemporary French craftsmen could only dream of emulating. The mood changes abruptly in the Revolutionary era, as witnessed by fascinating plates bearing slogans from both sides of the political fence.

Musée Le Secq des Tournelles

2 rue Jacques-Villon • Daily except Tues 2–6pm • €3 • ☎ 02 35 88 42 92, ⓦ museelesecqdestournelles.fr

Behind the Beaux Arts, the old and barely altered church of St-Laurent holds an interesting and unusual museum of ironmongery, the **Musée Le Secq des Tournelles**. Its gloriously eccentric and uncategorizable collection includes wrought-iron objects of all dates and descriptions, among them nutcrackers and door knockers, locks and gates, nineteenth-century toys and jewellery, spiral staircases that lead nowhere, and hideous implements of torture.

Musée des Antiquités

Rue Beauvoisine • Tues–Sat 1.30–5.30pm, Sun 2–6pm; also open Tues–Sat 10am–12.15pm during school hols • €3.50 • ☎ 02 35 98 55 10, ⓦ www.museedesantiquites.fr

The **Musée des Antiquités**, a short walk north of the centre, provides a comprehensive run-through of ancient artefacts found in or near Rouen. Starting with an impressive pointed helmet from the Bronze Age and an assortment of early iron tools, it continues with some remarkably complete Roman mosaics from villas unearthed in Lillebonne and the Forêt de Brotonne. Then comes a long gallery filled with woodcarvings rescued from long-lost Rouen houses – including a lovely bas-relief of sheep that served as the sign for a medieval draper's shop – and some fine fifteenth-century tapestries.

Musée Flaubert et de l'Histoire de la Médicine

Hôtel-Dieu Hospital, 51 rue de Lecat • Tues 10am–6pm, Wed–Sat 10am–noon & 2–6pm • €3 • ☎ 02 35 15 59 55, ⓦ chu-rouen.fr

The **Musée Flaubert et de l'Histoire de la Médicine**, five minutes' walk west of the place du Vieux-Marché, provides a wonderful insight into the writings of Gustave Flaubert.

1

Flaubert's father was chief surgeon and director of the medical school, living with his family in this house within the hospital; Gustave himself was born here in 1821. Even during the cholera epidemic when he was 11, the young Gustave and his sister were not stopped from running around the wards or climbing along the garden wall to look into the autopsy lab. Some of the medical exhibits would certainly have been familiar objects to him – a phrenology model, a childbirth demonstrator resembling a giant ragdoll, and the sets of encyclopedias. There's also one of his stuffed parrots, as featured in Julian Barnes' novel *Flaubert's Parrot*.

ARRIVAL AND INFORMATION

By train Rouen's main *gare SNCF*, Gare Rive Droite, stands at the north end of rue Jeanne-d'Arc. Gare Rive Gauche on the south bank only handles goods traffic.

Destinations Caen (7 daily; 1hr 30min); Clères (16 daily; 20min); Dieppe (12 daily, 50min); Le Havre (13 daily, 1hr 10min); Lisieux (7 daily, 1hr 5min); Paris-St-Lazare (25 daily; 1hr 20min); Vernon (12 daily; 30min); Yvetot (15 daily; 30min) with connecting bus to St-Valery (total 1hr 30min).

By bus The *gare routière* is tucked away behind the riverfront on rue des Charrettes, one block west of rue Jeanne-d'Arc and immediately behind Agence Astuce, the headquarters of the local bus network.

Destinations Clères (6 daily; 45min); Évreux (hourly; 1hr); Le Havre (hourly; 2hr 45min), via Jumièges (30min); Lisieux (2 daily; 2hr 30min).

ROUEN

By car Rouen is a difficult and frequently congested city to drive into. With many of the central streets pedestrianized, it's best to park as soon as you can – there are plenty of central underground car parks, especially near the cathedral and the place du Vieux-Marché – and explore the city on foot.

By air Rouen's airport, at Boos 9km southeast (⊛ rouen .aeroport.fr), does not currently receive any flights from the UK.

Tourist office 25 place de la Cathédrale, in the early sixteenth-century "House of the Exchequer" (May–Sept Mon–Sat 9am–7pm, Sun 9.30am–12.30pm & 2–6pm; Oct–April Mon–Sat 9.30am–12.30pm & 1.30–6pm; ☎ 02 32 08 32 40, ⊛ rouentourisme.com). They also offer free wifi and a bureau de change.

GETTING AROUND

On foot The city centre of Rouen, north of the Seine, is small enough to stroll around with little effort.

By métro Rouen's métro system (⊛ reseau-astuce.fr) is more useful to commuters than tourists. It follows the line of the rue Jeanne-d'Arc south from the *gare SNCF*, making two stops before resurfacing to cross the river by bridge; thereafter, the tracks dip below and above ground like a rollercoaster. Tickets for individual journeys, valid for both métro and bus, cost €1.60; a book of ten tickets is €13.30, or you can buy a 24hr pass for €4.70.

By bus All local buses from the *gare SNCF* except #2A run

down rue Jeanne-d'Arc to the centre, which takes 5min. Agence Astuce, the headquarters of the bus network, is just north of the river.

By bike The city-sponsored Cy'clic network (⊛ cyclic .rouen.fr) enables credit-card holders to unlock a simple bike from "stations" scattered along the streets, and leave it at any other station; journeys of less than 30min are free.

Tours A motorized "*petit train*" makes a forty-minute tour from the tourist office in summer (April–Oct daily 10am, 11am, noon, 2pm, 3pm, 4pm & 5pm; €6.50, ages 3–11 €4.50).

ACCOMMODATION

With more than three thousand **hotel** rooms in town, there should be no difficulty in finding accommodation in Rouen, even at the busiest times. Few of the city's hotels have restaurants, chiefly because there's such a wide choice of places to eat.

Andersen 4 rue Pouchet ☎ 02 35 71 88 51, ⊛ hotel andersen.com. Friendly, somewhat faded old budget hotel with plenty of character, set back beyond a small gravel yard a short walk west of the main railway station. The exterior is run-down, and the bathrooms a little basic, but the bedrooms are large, light and colourful. **€58**

Arts et Seine 6 rue St-Étienne-des-Tonneliers ☎ 02 35 88 11 44, ⊛ artsetseine.com. Inexpensive hotel, a block north of the river not far from the cathedral, redecorated in vaguely Asian style by friendly owners. Clean, well-equipped rooms of varying levels of comfort, accessible

via stairs only, plus good buffet breakfasts. **€65**

Beauséjour 9 rue Pouchet ☎ 02 35 71 93 47, ⊛ hotel -beausejour-rouen.fr. Good-value hotel near the station (turn right as you come out). Beyond the orange facade and nice garden courtyard, the rooms are nothing fancy, but they're crisply decorated with large-screen TVs. The cheapest double room lacks its own shower, and they have even cheaper singles. Closed second half of July. **€48**

La Boulangerie 59 rue St-Nicaise ☎ 06 12 94 53 15, ⊛ laboulangerie.fr. Very welcoming three-room B&B, just north of St-Ouen and set above a half-timbered,

red-painted boulangerie where the owners bake bread and serve breakfast. Bedrooms feature exposed beams, comfy beds, and in two instances bathtubs open to the room; one suite sleeps up to five. **€82**

Camping de l'Aubette 23 rue du Vert Buisson in St-Léger du Bourg-Denis ☎ 02 35 08 47 69. Basic site, dominated by tent campers, in a somewhat inaccessible rural setting 4km east of town on bus route #8. Credit cards not accepted. **€10**

Cardinal 1 place de la Cathédrale ☎ 02 35 70 24 42, ⓦ cardinal-hotel.fr. Very good-value hotel in a stunning location – albeit potentially noisy – facing the cathedral. Rooms are spacious and clean, with good en-suite facilities and flatscreen TVs. Two family rooms are available. All have views of the cathedral (the higher ones from balconies). Ample buffet breakfasts for €9. **€88**

De la Cathédrale 12 rue St-Romain ☎ 02 35 71 57 95, ⓦ hotel-de-la-cathedrale.fr. Attractive hotel, in a pedestrian lane beside the cathedral, with a pleasant olde-worlde theme, nice breakfast room and flower-filled courtyard. The rooms are plainer than the public spaces might suggest, but it's still a peaceful haven. Discounts at public car park nearby. Buffet breakfasts €11. **€90**

★ **Le Clos Jouvenet** 42 rue Hyacinthe Langlois ☎ 02 35 89 80 66, ⓦ leclosjouvenet.com. Four beautifully decorated, comfortable rooms in an immaculate nineteenth-century house a 10min walk east of the train station. Breakfast is served in the conservatory, overlooking the enclosed garden. Rates drop for 2nd night onwards. **€113**

Ermitage Bouquet 58 rue Bouquet ☎ 02 35 12 30 40, ⓦ hotel-ermitagebouquet.com. Very comfortable wood-panelled rooms and suites, with air-conditioning and power showers or whirlpool baths, in a spacious red-brick town-house a short walk up from the station. Courtyard parking and lavish buffet breakfasts. **€119**

Mercure Rouen Centre 7 rue Croix de Fer ☎ 02 35 52 69 52, ⓦ mercure.com. Large chain hotel in the heart of the old city. It's a lot more comfortable and stylish than might appear from the outside, though the rates mean it's largely the preserve of business travellers. Extras such as breakfast, and parking in the *very* cramped underground garage, can mount up considerably. **€115**

Sisley 51 rue Jean Lecanuet ☎ 02 35 71 10 07, ⓦ hotel sisley.fr. Very central little budget hotel, an easy walk from the station, where each of the thirteen bright, comfortable double rooms is decorated in keeping with a different Impressionist painter, and has a shower rather than a bath. **€62**

EATING AND DRINKING

Rouen has a good reputation for food, with its most famous dish being *canard rouennais* – prepared by strangling a particular crossbreed of duck from the Seine Valley and cooking it with all its blood, which results in a much meatier taste than usual. Unlike the hotels, which sometimes have cheaper weekend rates, the city's upmarket restaurants tend to charge more over weekends, when families eat out. In mid-October each year, the **Fête du Ventre** festival (ⓦ feteduventre .com) celebrates the city's culinary traditions.

You can buy fresh fish, fruit and cheese at the daily **food market** in place du Vieux-Marché, while the area just north is full of Tunisian takeaways, crêperies, and so forth. There are also sumptuous patisserie shops everywhere, while if you've had enough of all things continental, the rue du Gros-Horloge holds a half-timbered *McDonald's*.

Auberge St-Maclou 224–226 rue Martainville ☎ 02 35 71 06 67. Half-timbered building in the shadow of St-Maclou church, with outdoor tables on a busy pedestrian street, and an old-style ambience. Well-priced traditional French menus – lunch is €13.50/€16.50, dinner €23/€29. Tues–Fri noon–2pm & 7–10pm, Sat noon–2.30pm & 7–10.30pm, Sun noon–2.30pm.

Brasserie Paul 1 place de la Cathédrale ☎ 02 35 71 86 07, ⓦ brasserie-paul.com. Rouen's definitive bistro, an attractive belle époque place with lots of outdoor seating, facing the cathedral. You pay slightly over the usual odds, but the setting makes it worth it. Daily lunch specials, with a €17 *formule* or Simone de Beauvoir's favourite goat's cheese and smoked duck salad for €14. Mon–Thurs & Sun 10am–11pm, Fri & Sat 10am–midnight.

La Couronne 31 place du Vieux-Marché ☎ 02 35 71 40 90, ⓦ lacouronne.com.fr. The pick of the restaurants on the square, this claims to be the oldest auberge in France, serving food since 1345, a century before Joan of Arc's time.

If you find the interior a little too stuffy and formal, opt for one of the few tables on the square itself. Menus at €25 for lunch and €35 or €49 ("Harmonie Gourmande") for dinner. Daily noon–2.30pm & 7–10.30pm.

Crêperie la Régalière 12 rue Massacre ☎ 02 35 15 33 33. This quaint, inexpensive but good-quality crêperie, in a quiet but very picturesque backstreet just north of the Gros-Horloge, is one of central Rouen's best bargains, with a lunch menu at €8.50 and good-value deals later on. They also serve a surprising array of fine teas. Tues–Sat 11.45am–11pm.

Dame Cakes 70 rue St-Romain ☎ 02 35 07 49 31, ⓦ damecakes.fr. Rather exquisite tearoom, with a little garden, on a quiet street next to the cathedral, tempting the tastebuds with delicious desserts, savoury tarts and salads, as well as tea in all varieties, plus espresso coffee and nine kinds of hot chocolate. Mon–Fri 10.30am–7pm, Sat 10am–7.30pm.

Gill 8–9 quai de la Bourse ☎ 02 35 71 16 14, ⓦ gill.fr. A showcase for celebrated local chef Gilles Tournadre, this

1

ultra-smart quayside restaurant boasts two Michelin stars. The Asian-influenced food is presented with all the fancy trimmings and extras that it might suggest; it can be hard to tell what you're eating, but it tastes sublime. There's a €38.50 weekday lunch menu, while set dinners cost €70 or €98. Tournadre's other Rouen restaurants include the cheaper and less formal *37*, in the street behind at 37 rue St-Etienne-des-Tonneliers. Tues–Sat noon–1.45pm & 7.30–9.45pm; closed 2 weeks in April and 3 weeks in Aug.

Ici et Ailleurs 31 rue Damiette ☎02 35 62 18 46, ⓦici-ailleurs.com. Very welcoming café/library, with tables out on the pedestrianized street and a cosy reading room inside, where the shelves are lined with (French-only) travel guides. As well as tea, coffee and chocolate, they serve breakfast and lunch, including soup, quiche and other baked goods, with a €10 *plat du jour*. Tues–Sat 10.30am–7pm, Sun 10am–6pm.

★La Marmite 3 rue de Florence ☎02 35 71 75 55, ⓦlamarmiterouen.com. Smart little place just north of the place du Vieux-Marché, offering beautiful, elegantly presented gourmet dishes on well-priced menus at €31, €41 (featuring hot foie gras), and €58 (the seven-course Dégustation Surprise). Tues 7–9.30pm, Wed–Sat noon–2pm & 7–9.30pm, Sun noon–2pm.

P'tit Bec 182 rue Eau-de-Robec ☎02 35 07 63 33, ⓦleptitbec.com. Friendly brasserie that's especially popular at lunch time. Simple menus at €13 and €16.50 include a fish or meat main course, plus vegetarian options, or you can get a salad for €11. There's seating indoors as well as out on the pedestrianized street, in view of several fine half-timbered mansions. June–Aug Mon noon–2.30pm, Tues–Sat noon–2.30pm & 7–10.30pm; Sept–May Mon–Wed noon–2.30pm, Thurs–Sat noon–2.30pm & 7–10.30pm.

P'tits Parapluies 46 rue Bourg-l'Abbé, place de la Rougemare ☎02 35 88 55 26, ⓦlesptits-parapluies .com. Elegant, secluded, half-timbered restaurant not far north of the Hôtel de Ville, on the edge of an attractive little square. Counting your calories (or your pennies) is not really an option; set menus start at €29 for lunch, €36 for dinner, and include oysters or duck carpaccio as a starter. Just €6 extra buys two glasses of wine per person. Tues–Fri noon–1.45pm & 7.45–10pm, Sat 7.45–10pm, Sun noon–1.45pm.

Petite Auberge 164 rue Martainville ☎02 35 70 80 18, ⓦrestaurant-petite-auberge.fr. Attractive, old-fashioned, indoor restaurant, serving delicious traditional Norman cuisine at very reasonable prices; they're very proud of their snails, but there are plenty of alternatives. Weekday lunch *formule* €12.80, dinner menus from €17 on weekdays, €21 at weekends. Tues–Sun noon–1.30pm & 7.15–10pm.

NIGHTLIFE AND ENTERTAINMENT

As a city with a strong student population, and one renowned for its (largely rock-oriented) **music scene**, Rouen enjoys a far-from-provincial nightlife. Some of the city's most appealing **bars** lie in the maze of streets between rue Jean Lecanuet and place du Vieux-Marché. Incoming sailors used to head straight for this area of the city – the small bars are still there, even if the sailors aren't. New **clubs** are springing up all the time, though most are some distance from the centre.

BARS

Delirium Café 30 rue des Vergetiers ☎02 32 12 05 95, ⓦdeliriumcafe.be. In a splendid half-timbered house right under the big clock, this student-oriented pub, part of a Belgian chain, focuses entirely on beer, with a couple of dozen on draught – largely Belgian – and plenty more besides. Mon–Sat 1pm–2am.

L'Euro 41 place du Vieux-Marché ☎02 35 07 55 66, ⓦl-euro.fr. Upscale cocktail bar/lounge, occupying a multistorey half-timbered building on the western corner of the place du Vieux-Marché, with outdoor chill-out sofas on the square itself, and EDM DJs up on the second floor in winter. Daily 10pm–2am.

Le Nash 97 rue Écuyère ☎02 35 98 25 24. Relaxed bar that's popular with trendy young locals. The interior has a lounge-like feel with its mood lighting and zebra stripes, while the outdoor terrace is much more akin to a classic French café, and serves light snacks. Music from ambient to Latin, with jazz on Tuesday evenings in summer. Tues–Sat 6pm–2am.

CLUBS

Emporium Galorium 151 rue Beauvoisine ☎02 35 71 76 95, ⓦemporium-galorium.com. Busy, half-timbered student-dominated bar, a short walk north of the centre, hosting small-scale gigs and theatrical productions. Wed–Sat 8pm–4am.

XXL 25–27 rue de la Savonnerie ☎02 35 88 84 00, ⓦxxl-rouen.com. Gay (very largely male) club near the river, just south of the cathedral, with theme nights and a small basement dancefloor. Tues–Sun 10.30pm–4am.

LIVE MUSIC

Le 106 106 quai Jean-de-Béthancourt ☎02 32 10 88 60, ⓦle106.com. City-owned hangar-like venue with two halls, used for large gigs, as well as meetings and exhibitions, on the southern side of the river 15 mins' walk from the centre, and served by night buses N2 and N3.

L'Ibiza Club 29 bd des Belges ☎02 35 07 76 20, ⓦibiza-club76.com. Despite the name, not an Ibiza-style club, but a three-storey complex, set in a mansion that once belonged to the king of Belgium, and incorporating a restaurant, lots of karaoke rooms, and a basement club where the emphasis is on the Seventies and Eighties. Thurs 8pm–2am, Fri & Sat 8pm–5am.

THEATRE

As you would expect in a conurbation of half a million, there's always plenty going on in Rouen, from classical concerts in churches to alternative events in community and commercial centres. The city has several theatres, which mainly work to winter seasons.

Hangar 23 pied du Pont Flaubert ✆ 02 32 76 23 23, ⓦ hangar23.fr. Major south-bank venue used by local and touring theatre companies, and also hosting dance, world music and jazz.

Théâtre des Arts 7 rue du Dr-Rambert ✆ 02 35 98 74 78,

ⓦ operaderouen.com. This highbrow venue puts on a varied programme of opera, ballet and concerts.

Théâtre Charles Dullin Allée des Arcades, Grand Quévilly ✆ 02 35 68 48 91, ⓦ dullin-voltaire.com. Well south of the river, staging touring theatre productions as well as concerts, this theatre can be accessed via the metro, direction "Georges Braque".

Théâtre des Deux Rives ✆ 02 35 70 22 82, ⓦ cdr2rives .com. Home to an adventurous repertory company, this small theatre, opposite the Antiquités museum at the top end of rue Louis Ricard, also hosts touring productions.

SHOPPING

Most of the classier **shops** in Rouen are in the pedestrian streets near, and slightly north of, the cathedral. Rue Jeanne d'Arc and rue du Gros-Horloge is the area to look for fancy foodstuffs, patisserie, chocolates and the like. For **hypermarkets** and cheap clothes, head south of the river to the multistorey St-Sever complex. There's an open-air antiques and bric-a-brac **market** nearby in the place des Émmurées.

ABC Bookshop 11 rue des Faulx ✆ 02 35 71 08 67, ⓦ abc-bookshop.info. Bookshop close to St-Ouen church, specializing in English titles. Tues–Sat 10am–6pm.
FNAC Espace du Palais mall, 8 allée Eugène Delacroix ✆ 08 92 35 04 05, ⓦ fnac.com. Rouen's largest bookshop,

entirely underground and immediately north of the Palais de Justice, stocks a fine selection of local maps and guides, largely in French, plus English-language titles and a wide range of CDs, DVDs and computer paraphernalia. Mon–Sat 10am–7pm.

Around Rouen

While pleasant small towns well worth an overnight stop lie within a few minutes of Rouen in either direction along the river, such as Villequier (see p.65) or Les Andelys (see p.82), a number of places only just outside the city proper make **good day-trips** if you are based in Rouen itself.

La Bouille

Ten kilometres southwest from central Rouen along the southern riverbank, the small village of **LA BOUILLE** stands near a magnificent sweeping bend in the Seine. Little more than a couple of narrow twisting lanes lined with gnarled half-timbered houses, pressed hard against the steep hillside, it's a complete contrast to the noise and bustle of the city, and makes a perfect place to spend a couple of nights for anyone not dependent on public transport. Not far north, a little *bac* (ferry) crosses the river (14 daily, Mon–Sat) to the small Forêt de Roumare, which makes for a pleasant stroll.

Clères château and zoo

Daily: March & Oct 10am–noon & 1.30–6.30pm; April–Sept 10am–7pm; Nov 10am–noon & 1.30–5.30pm • €7 • ✆ 02 32 82 99 20, ⓦ parcdecleres.net

The pretty village of **CLÈRES**, 16km northeast of Rouen and accessible by train or bus, has centred since the eleventh century on an imposing **château**, though the stout walls that now remain date back a mere five hundred years. The spacious and beautifully landscaped grounds are home to a popular **zoo**; while not holding a very wide range of species, it displays them in idyllic surroundings. The whole place is something of a Garden of Eden, in that peacocks, antelope and wallabies can wander at will in the absence of predators; families with pushchairs, however, may well struggle with some of

1

the steeper gravel footpaths. Exotic birds kept in ageing aviaries include emus, rheas and kookaburras, while the château itself plays host to temporary art exhibitions.

The infamous French writer Colette made the impenetrable but presumably positive remark that "at Clères, in the zoo park, it is easy to lose the melancholy feeling of inevitability".

The Forêt de Lyons

The **Forêt de Lyons**, around 25km east of Rouen, was a thousand years ago a favoured hunting ground of William the Conqueror and other dukes of Normandy. Parts of the forest feel as though they have changed little in the intervening millennium – remarkable considering its proximity not only to Rouen but also to Paris.

Henry I of England died in the forest's central village, **Lyons-la-Forêt**, in 1135, of a surfeit of lampreys consumed after a late-November hunting expedition. The village itself is a picturesque place, while a few kilometres to the north and south respectively, a château and abbey are worth visiting. Almost any of the little roads through these dense woods rewards exploration by cyclists or walkers.

Lyons-la-Forêt

At the heart of the forest, the little hill village of **LYONS-LA-FORÊT**, actually situated not in Seine-Maritime but the neighbouring *département* of Eure, was once the site of a castle belonging to William the Conqueror, which is now completely indiscernible. It still retains, however, a superb ensemble of half-timbered Norman houses dating from around 1610. In the centre of the village stand the plain old wooden *halles*, while the roads around abound in splendid rural mansions. One, the house named *Le Fresne* on rue d'Enfer, was much used by the composer Ravel in the 1920s.

Abbaye de Mortemer

Daily: May to mid-Sept 11am–6.30pm, mid-Sept to April hours vary; guided tours half-hourly, May to mid-Sept daily 2–6pm, mid-Sept to April Sat & Sun 2–5.30pm • €6 admission, €9 with tour • ☎ 02 32 49 54 37, Ⓦ mortemer.fr

The ruins of the twelfth-century Cistercian **Abbaye de Mortemer**, clearly signed off a main road half a dozen kilometres south of Lyons, amount to little more than heaps of rubble scattered across gentle lawns, amid a landscape of rolling parklands. Plenty of outbuildings survive, however, including a round stone *pigeonnier*, with a spider's-web tangle of wood inside, and little niches for hundreds of pigeons (bred by the monks for food); a cast-iron pigeon stands permanently on top.

A **museum** in the eighteenth-century château that dominates the grounds displays models of the abbey as it is now, and an audiovisual show of life as it used to be, complete with plenty of tales of hauntings and bumps in the night. Beyond the abbey, which was quarried after the Revolution to build the nearby village of Lisors, a couple of marshy lakes are populated by geese and swans and surrounded by woods and lawns that accommodate free-roaming deer.

The abbey grounds also host all sorts of spectacles and events in summer, including a medieval fair in the middle of August and "ghost nights" on Saturdays in August and September.

Château de Vascoeuil

On the northwest edge of the Forêt de Lyons • April–June & Sept–Nov Wed–Sun 2.30–6pm; July & Aug daily 10.30am–1pm & 2–6.30pm • €9.50 • ☎ 02 35 23 62 35, Ⓦ chateauvascoeuil.com

The small but graceful **Château de Vascoeuil**, 12km from Lyons, is known to have existed as early as 1050, and was home during the nineteenth century to the historian Michelet. These days, it's renowned for top-quality temporary **art exhibitions**. Each summer usually sees two large shows, as well as special events such as concerts and performances, and there's often a crafts fair during the weeks leading up to Christmas.

Ry

1

The village of **RY**, 4km northwest of the Château de Vascoeuil, is immortalized in literary history as the real-life home of Flaubert's fictionalized Madame Bovary. A monument in its churchyard commemorates Delphine Couturier, who committed suicide in Ry in 1849, having married a local doctor ten years previously, at the age of 17.

Ry consists of one main street, with green hills rising at either end, and a church to one side with an unusual carved wooden porch. Delphine's husband is buried in the churchyard, and Madame Bovary is evident throughout the village, which seems to have had little else to celebrate for a century or so. The local florist is Emma's, the video shop is Bovary, while the pharmacy was Delphine's real house.

Musée des Automates

Place Gustave Flaubert • May–June & Sept–Oct Sat & Sun 2.30–6pm; July & Aug daily except Mon 2.30–6pm • €5 • ☎ 02 35 23 61 44, ⓦ musee-bovary.net

The **Musée des Automates**, next to a pretty bridge over the River Crevon, is most likely to appeal to young children, though some of its mannequins do, rather jerkily, act out the less explicit moments of Madame Bovary's career.

INFORMATION

LYONS-LA-FORÊT
Tourist office 20 rue de l'Hôtel de Ville, with information on the whole forest area (Easter to mid-Oct Mon–Sat

9.30am–noon & 2–6pm, Sun 10am–12.30pm & 2–5pm; mid-Oct to Easter Tues–Sat 10am–noon & 2–5pm; ☎ 02 32 49 31 65, ⓦ paysdelyons.com).

ACCOMMODATION AND EATING

LA BOUILLE
★ **Bellevue** 13 quai Hector-Malot ☎ 02 35 18 05 05, ⓦ hotel-le-bellevue.com. Exquisite and smartly renovated hotel, overlooking the river across the main road through the village. The cheapest rooms face away from the river, so it's worth paying €10 extra to enjoy a fabulous view. A superb dining room serves classic French cuisine, with weekday lunches from €17, dinner from €27. **€76**

Maison Blanche 1 quai Hector-Malot ☎ 02 35 18 01 90, ⓦ restaurant-lamaisonblanche.com. Good restaurant, with a panoramic first-floor dining room, and a dash of north African spices and flavourings providing a flourish to its traditional Norman food, on menus from €17 at midday, €26 in the evening. Wed–Sat noon–1.45pm & 7.15– 9pm, Sun noon–1.45pm.

St-Pierre 4 place du Bateau ☎ 02 35 68 02 01, ⓦ restaurantlesaintpierre.com. Elegant and expensive

riverfront restaurant, offering refined French cuisine on dinner menus that start at €37; the *Palette Gourmande*, available for the entire table only, costs €67. Wed–Sat 12.15–1.30pm & 7.15–9pm, Sun 12.15–1.30pm.

LYONS-LA-FORÊT
La Licorne 27 place Bensérade ☎ 02 32 48 24 24, ⓦ hotel -licorne.com. Elegant hotel in the main village square, near the *halles*, aimed at weekenders from Paris and featuring a garden spa with outdoor pool. The rooms aren't quite as fancy as they look on the website, while gourmet dinners in the grand dining room start at €43. **€180**

Lions de Beauclerc 7 rue de l'Hôtel de Ville ☎ 02 32 49 18 90, ⓦ hotel-restaurant-lyons.fr. Small red-brick village hotel near the tourist office, offering six opulent, antique-furnished en-suite bedrooms, plus a pleasant little garden and good-value meals. **€85**

Upstream from Rouen

Upstream from Rouen towards Paris, high cliffs on the north bank of the Seine imitate the coast, looking down on waves of green and scattered river islands. By the time you reach **Les Andelys**, the site of Richard the Lionheart's ruined castle fortress, accommodation and eating options tend to be geared towards affluent weekend- and day-trippers. Claude Monet's celebrated gardens at **Giverny** attract even more visitors from the capital, but deservedly so – no visitor to Normandy should miss them.

1

Pont St-Pierre

The first point south of Rouen at which the Seine begins to be enticing again is
PONT ST-PIERRE, where it's joined by the River Andelle. The spectacularly sharp **Côte
des Deux Amants** soars above the confluence of the two rivers. This sheer escarpment,
topped by a high plateau, takes its name from a twelfth-century legend in which a cruel
king stipulated that the man who would marry his daughter must first run with her in
his arms to the top of this hill. Noble Raoul sprinted up carrying the fair Caliste, then
dropped dead; out of sympathy, so did she. That story provides precious little incentive
for anyone else to make the climb – but rumour has it that the view from the top does.

Les Andelys

As the name implies, **LES ANDELYS**, 25km along the Seine from Rouen, consists in fact
of two separate towns. **Petit Andely**, the birthplace in 1594 of Nicolas Poussin, is a
gorgeous little village, overshadowed by the magnificent Château Gaillard. Its main
street, parallel to the Seine, is lined with ancient half-timbered houses, while from the
grassy riverbank itself views stretch north to some imposing white bluffs as well as
south to the castle. **Grand Andely**, 1.5km inland, at the far end of a long boulevard,
holds little of interest for tourists, apart from its shops and bars, and Saturday **market**.

Château Gaillard

Les Andelys • Mid-March to mid-Nov daily except Tues 10am–1pm & 2–6pm • €3, grounds free all year • ⓦ lesandelys.com/chateau-gaillard

The single most dramatic sight anywhere along the Seine short of Paris – especially awesome
and magical by night – has to be **Château Gaillard**, perched high above Les Andelys.

The château was constructed in the space of a single year, 1196–97, under the
auspices of Richard the Lionheart. A previous truce had expressly forbidden the
construction of a castle here, but Richard went ahead anyway, seizing the rock on
which it stands from Archbishop Walter of Rouen, then bribing the pope for
permission to build. His objective was to deny the king of France access to Rouen by
controlling all traffic along the Seine, by both road and river. In a design feature unique
for the time, the ramparts were rounded into nineteen separate curving segments,
which enabled defenders to shoot arrows at any angle while depriving besiegers of
vulnerable targets for their projectiles.

After Richard's death, Philippe-Auguste managed to capture the château in 1204, when
his soldiers gained access via the latrines. The structure might well have survived intact,
however, had Henry IV not ordered its destruction in 1603. Even then, it would have
taken more recent devices to reduce Château Gaillard to rubble. The stout flint walls of its
keep, roughly 4m thick, remain reasonably sound, and the outline of most of the rest is
still clear, arranged over assorted green and chalky knolls. The castle was originally divided
into two separate segments, linked by a bridge across a moat that was never intended to be
filled with water – you can still explore the storage caves hidden in its depths.

On foot, you can make the steep climb up via a path that leads off rue Richard
Coeur-de-Lion in Petit Andely. The only route for motorists is extraordinarily convoluted,
following a long-winded one-way system that starts opposite the church in Grand Andely.

INFORMATION   LES ANDELYS

Tourist office 24 rue Reymond Phélip, between Petit and
Grand Andely (March Mon–Fri 2–6pm, Sat 10am–1pm &
2–5pm; April & May Mon–Sat 10am–noon & 2–6pm, Sun
10am–1pm; June–Sept Mon–Sat 10am–noon & 2–6pm,
Sun 10am–noon & 2–5pm; Oct Mon–Fri 2–6pm, Sat
10am–noon & 2–5pm; Nov–Feb Mon–Fri 2–6pm, Sat
10am–1pm; ⓣ 02 32 54 41 93, ⓦ lesandelys-tourisme.fr).

ACCOMMODATION AND EATING

La Canotière 5 rte des Falaises, Petit Andely
ⓣ 06 26 56 73 66, ⓦ lacanotiere.net. Gorgeous,
thatched, half-timbered Norman house, facing the river at
the foot of the cliffs, and offering four light and very

charming B&B rooms, plus sumptuous breakfasts. **€110**
★**Chaîne d'Or** 25 rue Grande, Petit Andely ☎ 02 32 54
00 31, ⓦ hotel-lachainedor.com. Les Andelys' most
upscale hotel, this luxurious old coaching inn is arrayed
around a courtyard beside the river, opposite the thirteenth-
century St-Sauveur church; the much nicer Seine-view
rooms cost from €35 extra. Its restaurant (closed Wed all
year, plus Sun eve & Tues mid-Oct to mid-April) serves
wonderful food on menus priced €52 and up. **€95**
Fort de Thé 3 rue Richard Coeur-de-Lion, Petit Andely
☎ 02 32 54 03 61. Welcoming little tea-room where the
riverside terrace makes a delightful spot for organic tea,
coffee, juices and cake on a summer afternoon. Wed–Sun
2–7pm.

L'Île des Trois Rois 1 rue Gilles-Nicole, Petit Andely
☎ 02 32 54 23 79, ⓦ camping-troisrois.com. Lovely
three-star campsite, stretching out beside the river far
below the château, with a pool and snack bar. The riverfront
pitches are a delight, but the site as a whole is a little short
on showers & toilets. Closed mid-Nov to mid-March. **€26**
Paris/Le Castelet 10 av de la République, Grand
Andely ☎ 02 32 54 00 33, ⓦ hotel-andelys.fr. This
unassuming hotel, in a rather Gothic red-brick townhouse
well back from the river, offers comfortable, nicely
refurbished rooms and a friendly family atmosphere. The
big attraction, though, is its top-notch dining room,
Le Castelet, in which dinner menus start at €26 (restaurant
closed Sun eve, Mon lunch & Wed). **€67**

Giverny

Had it not caught the eye of Claude Monet from a passing train carriage, the little
village of **GIVERNY** might by now have decayed into insignificance; instead, it ranks
among the most-visited tourist attractions in Normandy. Standing a few hundred
metres from the right bank of the Seine, 20km south of the ancient fortifications of
Les Andelys and a mere 40km from Paris, it welcomes a constant stream of traffic in
summer. Between November and March, however, when Monet's house and gardens
are closed to visitors, everything else seems to close down too.

The road south to Giverny from Les Andelys crosses a flat plain dotted with lovely
little hamlets. **Port Mort** in particular, where the road is lined by an almost unbroken
stone wall, is well worth a stop.

Fondation Claude Monet

84 rue Claude Monet, Giverny • April–Oct daily 9.30am–6pm; last entry 5.30pm • €9.50, ages 7–12 €5; to avoid queues, book ahead online •
☎ 02 32 51 28 21, ⓦ fondation-monet.fr

The former home of Claude Monet is open to visitors as the **Fondation Claude Monet**.
If anything, art lovers who make the pilgrimage here are outnumbered by **garden**
enthusiasts. No original Monet paintings are on display – the largest collections are in
the Orangerie and Musée d'Orsay in Paris – whereas the gardens that many of his
friends considered to be his masterpiece are still lovingly tended in all their glory.

Visits start in the huge **studio**, built in 1915, where Monet painted the last and
largest of his many canvases depicting waterlilies (in French, *nymphéas*). It now serves
as a well-stocked book and gift shop.

The house

A gravel footpath leads from Monet's studio to his actual **house**, a long two-storey
structure that faces down towards the river, and is painted pastel pink with green
shutters. Monet's bedroom is bedecked with family photos and paintings by friends
and family, while the washed-out reproductions in his *salon* include a depiction by
Renoir of Monet at work in his earlier, less perfect garden at Argenteuil in 1875,
and one by Monet himself of his dream closer to realization in the garden at Vétheuil
in 1881.

All the other main rooms are crammed almost floor-to-ceiling with his collection of
Japanese prints, especially works by Hokusai and Hiroshige. While most of the original
furnishings are gone, you get a real sense of how the dining room used to look, with all
its walls and fittings painted a glorious bright yellow; Monet designed his own yellow
crockery to harmonize with the surroundings. By contrast, the stairs and upstairs
rooms are a pale blue.

1

CLAUDE MONET AT GIVERNY

Claude Monet first rented the Giverny home that now houses the Fondation Claude Monet in 1883. At the age of 43, he was exactly halfway through his life. Born in Paris in 1840, he had grown up in Le Havre, and had spent the previous decade living in Argenteuil, Vétheuil and Poissy. Although his reputation as a painter was already established – the movement known as **Impressionism** had taken its name from a critic's somewhat contemptuous response to his work *Impression, Sunrise*, shown in Paris in April 1874 as part of the First Impressionist Exhibition – his personal and financial circumstances were far from settled.

The Monet ménage, who arrived by houseboat in Giverny on April 29, 1883, consisted of ten people. As well as Claude's two sons by his wife Camille, who had died in 1879, he was now also responsible for the six children of his long-term mistress **Alice Hoschedé**. Her husband Ernest was a former patron of the Impressionists who had fallen on hard times; she finally married Monet after Ernest's death in 1891.

Monet was to find both artistic and commercial success in Giverny. In his early years, he continued to travel to paint landscapes not only throughout Normandy but also in Brittany, on the Riviera and in England. As time went by, however, his advancing physical frailty and failing eyesight made extended trips increasingly daunting, while his growing prosperity enabled him to tailor his immediate environment to meet his needs as a painter.

In 1890, Monet began to produce sequences of reworkings and renditions of the same scene, shown at different times of the day or seasons of the year. The first such series consisted of 25 views of the **haystacks** on a neighbouring farm; all were arranged side by side in his studio, to be worked on simultaneously. Designed to be seen en masse, they went on show in Paris early in 1891, and proved hugely popular. The individual paintings sold out quickly, and from then on visiting American collectors – and would-be students – were a constant feature of life at Giverny.

In 1891, Monet painted a sequence showing the poplar trees that stood along the banks of the River Epte, roughly 1.5km south of his home. By now he was rich enough to buy the trees, for as long as his work was in progress, from a local timber merchant who was due to fell them. Having purchased his house outright, for 22,000F, he went on to buy a further plot of land, across the main road. With permission from the local authorities, he dammed the stream known as the Ru to feed an artificial pond, which he planted with **waterlilies** and spanned with a Japanese footbridge.

A team of gardeners worked to keep different sections of his **flower gardens** in bloom for as much of the year as possible, so he would always have a suitable subject on which to work. One man had the full-time responsibility of tending the waterlilies to Monet's specifications, depending, for example, on whether he planned to use square or rectangular canvases. Monet would work outdoors for around six hours each day, avoiding the midday sun, and went on to paint over 250 versions of his waterlilies (*nymphéas*), not to mention the canvases he destroyed in disgust. One set of 48 waterlily pictures is said to have hung in his studio for six years, being constantly reworked, before it was exhibited in 1909.

Photographs of Monet in his later years show him as very much the white-bearded patrician, not only presiding over his studio and household but also playing host to leading painters and politicians. Despite a series of operations on his eyes, he continued to work almost until his death in December 1926. The house at Giverny passed to his son, Jean Monet, who married his half-sister Blanche Hoschedé. He left it in turn to the Académie des Beaux Arts in 1966, and it reopened as a museum in 1980.

The gardens

Lined with trellised walkways, scattered with shady bowers, Monet's colourful **flower gardens** stretch down from the house. Originally, the main footpath led straight to the **waterlily pond**; now, however, visitors have to reach the *jardin d'eau* by burrowing beneath the main road by way of a dank underpass. Once there, paths around the perimeter of the pond, as well as arching Japanese footbridges of course, offer differing views of the waterlilies themselves, cherished by gardeners in rowing boats.

May and June, when the rhododendrons flower, and the wisteria that winds over the Japanese bridge is in bloom, are the best times to visit. Whenever you come, however, you'll have to contend with camera-happy crowds jostling to capture their own impressions of the waterlilies. These same crowds are the cause of long waits to enter the house during the busy summer period.

Musée des Impressionismes

99 rue Claude Monet, Giverny • April–Oct daily 10am–6pm • €7, free first Sun of each month • ☎ 02 32 51 94 65, ⓦ mdig.fr

Giverny's **Musée des Impressionismes**, reached by heading left as you leave Monet's house, and walking for a few minutes up the main village street, sets out to put Monet's work in its contemporary context. The exterior is far from attractive, but inside you'll find a spacious and well-lit gallery where the primary focus is on changing temporary exhibitions.

When it first opened, the museum was known as the "Musée d'Art Américain", and was largely devoted to American artists who made their homes in France, and Giverny in particular, during the late nineteenth century. While its remit is now broader, its permanent collection is much smaller; how rewarding you find it to visit will depend on the scope of whatever exhibition is current.

Vernon

The small town of **VERNON** straddles the Seine 5km north of Giverny. Riverside footpaths are laid out along both banks, but the town centre is on the opposite side to Giverny. But for the fact that it holds the closest *gare SNCF* to Monet's house, served by trains between Rouen and Paris, there'd be no real reason to visit Vernon, let alone stay; as it is, the town is busy throughout the summer with day-trippers. Elvis Presley's dad was called Vernon.

ARRIVAL AND DEPARTURE   GIVERNY

By train The closest station to Giverny, 5km north at Vernon, is on the line that runs northwest to Rouen (14 daily; 40min) and southeast to Paris-St-Lazare (17 daily; 50min). Shuttle buses (☎ 02 32 54 57 78; €4 each way), timed to connect with Paris trains, leave the *gare SNCF* daily at 9.25am, 11.25am, 1.25pm and 3.50pm for the 20min trip to Monet's house, and

leave Giverny for the return trip at 9.55am, 11.55am, 2.15pm, 3.20pm, 4.15pm, 5.15pm and 6pm. You can also rent rather poor-quality bikes at *Café du Chemin de Fer* (☎ 02 32 21 16 01; €15 per day), directly opposite Vernon's *gare SNCF.*

By car There's free parking close to Monet's house; don't be fooled by signs for private car parks elsewhere in Giverny.

ACCOMMODATION AND EATING

GIVERNY

Eating in the grounds of Monet's house or the Musée des Impressionismes is forbidden, and the surrounding countryside is not particularly appealing for picnicking. Otherwise, the charcuterie at 60 rue Claude-Monet, a few doors down from *Au Bon Maréchal*, makes delicious sandwiches, while the restaurant inside the Musée des Impressionismes has a peaceful garden terrace.

Au Bon Maréchal 1 rue du Colombier ☎ 02 32 51 39 70, ⓦ giverny.fr. Former café, 100m to the right as you leave the Musée des Impressionismes, that's now a very friendly B&B, holding three colourful rooms surrounded by an attractive garden. **€80**

Jardin des Plumes 1 rue du Milieu ☎ 02 32 54 26 35, ⓦ lejardinsdesplumes.fr. Luxurious half-timbered country hotel, set in extensive gardens, 500m from Monet's house, which allow guests plenty of private space, and offers smart contemporary rooms with lots of polished wood and exposed brickwork. Dinner menus start at €39. Hotel closed Nov–March; restaurant closed Mon & Tues. **€160**

Musardière 123 rue Claude-Monet ☎ 02 32 21 03 18, ⓦ lamusardiere.fr. Ten comfortable en-suite rooms in a fine old rosy-hued townhouse a couple of hundred metres

from Monet's house. Dinner menus in its restaurant start at €26. Its terrace, abundantly shaded by the surrounding trees, makes a nice spot for lunch, and it also offers crêpes and snacks during the day. Closed Christmas–Jan. **€84**

Les Nymphéas 109 rue Claude-Monet ☎ 02 32 21 20 31, ⓦ giverny-restaurant-nympheas.fr. Pleasant little tearoom and restaurant opposite the Fondation Claude Monet, which, as well as afternoon tea and pastries, serves a reasonable range of quiches, baked goods and salads. Daily 9am–6pm; closed Nov–March.

VERNON

D'Évreux 11 place d'Évreux ☎ 02 32 21 16 12. Classic old-fashioned hotel in the central square. The rooms are a bit past their prime, and come at widely varying prices – the cheapest share bathrooms – but there's a good restaurant. **€50**

Restaurant les Fleurs 71 rue Sadi Carnot ☎ 02 32 21 29 19, ⓦ bistrodesfleurs-vernon.jimdo.com. Friendly little local restaurant close to the river, offering a simple dinner for €20, and a fancier five-course tasting menu, including five glasses of wine, for €36. You can also order à la carte in the adjoining bistro. Tues–Sat noon–1.45pm & 7.15–9pm.

The Lower Normandy Coast

HONFLEUR

The Lower Normandy Coast

The coast of Lower Normandy changes progressively in character as you move from east to west. Along the Côte Fleurie, from Honfleur to Cabourg, it is moneyed and elegant, with the so-called Norman Riviera, concentrated on Deauville and Trouville, styling itself as a northern counterpart to the Côte d'Azur. Then, through the much flatter Côte de Nacre and into the Bessin, around Caen and Bayeux, the shoreline is lower key: though the coastal strip remains built up, few towns amount to more than slender ribbons sandwiched between the broad sandy Invasion Beaches and the featureless scrub inland. West again, beyond a series of marshes, is the Cotentin Peninsula, with charming harbour villages along its east front, cliffs across the north, and vast dunes and wild beaches to the west. Finally comes the southern bay of Mont-St-Michel, where the island abbey is swept by treacherous tides.

The most enjoyable destination along the Côte Fleurie is **Honfleur**, a real gem of a medieval port, familiar from the paintings of Eugène Boudin, Monet and other Impressionists. Each of its neighbours, such as **Trouville**, **Deauville** and **Cabourg**, has its own nineteenth-century charm, but all are also rather dominated by affluent Parisian visitors in summer.

Further west, the pivotal role of the Côte de Nacre and the Bessin in the **D-Day Landings** is commemorated in numerous museums, memorials and cemeteries. Successive small-scale seaside towns here, all the way from **Ouistreham** to **Grandcamp-Maisy**, make charmingly atmospheric places to spend a few days. Just inland, the venerable cathedral city of **Bayeux** would be a destination to savour even without the bonus of its world-famous **tapestry**, while its much larger neighbour **Caen** also boasts an abundance of impressive medieval architecture.

The main city of the Cotentin Peninsula, **Cherbourg**, is home to the fascinating Cité de la Mer, while arriving ferry passengers can choose between the lovely little villages to the east, especially **Barfleur**, and the magnificent beaches and dunes of the peninsula's western coastline (popular with windsurfers). Such distractions serve to delay progress towards the glorious island abbey of **Mont-St-Michel**, visible across the bay from the hilltop fortress of **Granville** onwards.

The Côte Fleurie and the Norman Riviera

The stretch of the coast that lies immediately west of the Seine, known as the **Côte Fleurie** nearer the river and then the **Norman Riviera** further west, holds two very distinct sorts of community. Old ports such as **Honfleur** and **Dives** have, over the centuries, been pushed further and further back from the sea by heavy deposits of silt from the Seine, though still retaining their historic medieval buildings, while newer resorts like **Trouville** and **Deauville** have been unimaginatively laid out alongside the resultant sandy beaches. The happiest balance is found at places

Proust at the Grand Hôtel, Cabourg p.100
War museums p.111
D-Day Tours p.112
The war cemeteries p.113

The Kearsarge and the Alabama p.124
Death of an English prince p.126
Island museums p.140

BAYEUX TAPESTRY

Highlights

❶ Les Maisons Satie Surreal museum devoted to the avant-garde composer in the beautiful harbour town of Honfleur. **See p.94**

❷ The Bayeux Tapestry An extraordinary historical document, embroidering the saga of William the Conqueror in colourful detail. **See p.107**

❸ Arromanches The remains of Winston Churchill's Mulberry Harbour – the key to the invasion of 1944 – still litter the beach at Arromanches. **See p.116**

❹ The war cemeteries Memories of D-Day abound in Normandy, but nowhere more poignantly than in the monumental American cemetery at Colleville-sur-Mer. **See p.118**

❺ Cité de la Mer Holding a genuine nuclear submarine, fascinating displays on the *Titanic*, and assorted aquariums and thrill rides, Cherbourg's Art Deco passenger terminal should not be missed. **See p.123**

❻ Barfleur A delightful little grey-granite fishing port that makes a great stop for ferry passengers. **See p.126**

❼ Mont-St-Michel Second only to the Eiffel Tower as France's best-loved landmark, the island abbey of Mont-St-Michel is a magnificent spectacle. **See p.137**

HIGHLIGHTS ARE MARKED ON THE MAP ON PP.90–91

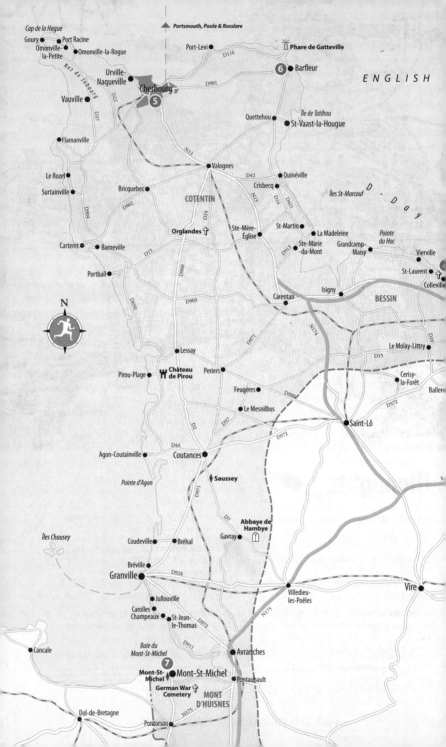

Portsmouth, Poole & Rosslare

E N G L I S H

Cap de la Hague
Goury
Port Racine
Omonville-la-Petite
Omonville-la-Rogue
Port-Levi
Phare de Gatteville
Urville-Naqueville
6 Barfleur
Vauville
Cherbourg
5
Nez de Jobourg
D22
D37
Flamanville
Quettehou
Île de Tatihou
St-Vaast-la-Hougue
N13
Valognes
D42
Quinéville
Le Rozel
Bricquebec
COTENTIN
Crisbecq
Surtainville
D902
N13
D14
D421
Carteret
Barneville
D15
Orglandes
Ste-Mère-Église
St-Martin
La Madeleine
Ste-Marie-du-Mont
Îles St-Marcouf
D - Day
Grandcamp-Maisy
Pointe du Hoc
Vierville
Portbail
D900
St-Laurent
Colleville
D650
D903
Carentan
Isigny
BESSIN
Le Molay-Littry
N174
D15
N
D971
Lessay
Cerisy-la-Forêt
D572
Ballero
Pirou-Plage
Château de Pirou
Periers
Feugères
D900
Le Mesnilbus
Saint-Lô
D2
D57
D972
Agon-Coutainville
D44
Coutances
Pointe d'Agon
Saussey
Îles Chausey
D7
Abbaye de Hambye
Coudeville
Bréhal
Gavray
D971
Bréville
Granville
D924
Villedieu-les-Poêles
Vire
Jullouville
Carolles
Champeaux
St-Jean-le-Thomas
D973
N175
D911
Baie du Mont-St-Michel
Avranches
Cancale
7
Mont-St-Michel
Pontaubault
Mont-St-Michel
German War Cemetery
MONT D'HUISNES
Dol-de-Bretagne
N175
Pontorson

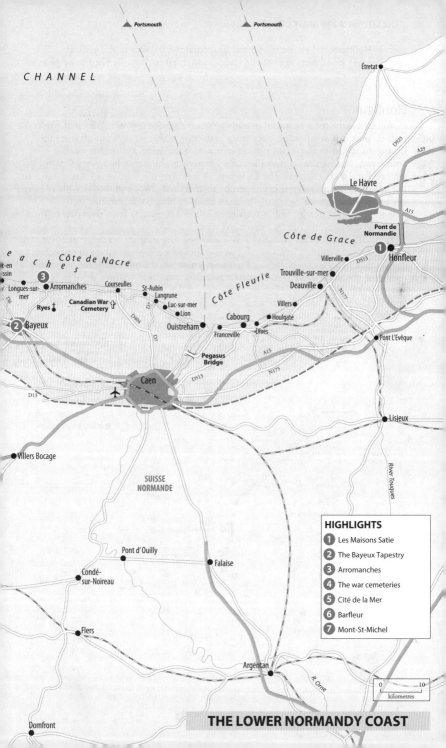

THE LOWER NORMANDY COAST

2

such as **Houlgate**, where development has remained low-key and the rocky coastline has stood firm against the river – which gives the added bonus of pleasant corniche drives.

Honfleur

HONFLEUR is the most beautiful of all Normandy's seaside towns, and its best-preserved historic port. All that holds it back from perfection is that it's now cut off from the Channel itself; with the accumulation of silt from the Seine, the sea has steadily withdrawn, leaving the eighteenth-century waterfront houses of boulevard Charles V stranded and a little surreal. The ancient port, however, still functions – the channel to the beautiful Vieux Bassin is kept open by regular dredging – and though only pleasure craft now use the moorings in the harbour basin, fishing boats continue to tie up alongside the pier nearby. Fish is usually on sale either directly from the boats or from stands on the pier, still run by fishermen's wives.

Honfleur is picturesque enough to have adorned magazine covers the world over, and attracts summer tourists in droves. It has also moved steadily upmarket since becoming connected to Le Havre via the vast **Pont de Normandie**, the toll-bridge that spans the mouth of the Seine (see p.64). Despite now being just a few minutes' drive from the city, however, the old port still feels not so very different to the fishing village that appealed so greatly to artists in the second half of the nineteenth century, notably Eugène Boudin, who taught Monet and Cézanne.

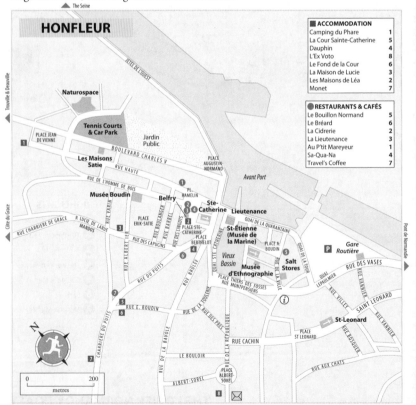

HONFLEUR

■ ACCOMMODATION	
Camping du Phare	1
La Cour Sainte-Catherine	5
Dauphin	4
L'Ex Voto	8
Le Fond de la Cour	6
La Maison de Lucie	3
Les Maisons de Léa	2
Monet	7

● RESTAURANTS & CAFÉS	
Le Bouillon Normand	5
Le Bréard	6
La Cidrerie	2
La Lieutenance	3
Au P'tit Mareyeur	1
Sa-Qua-Na	4
Travel's Coffee	7

The Vieux Bassin

Visitors to Honfleur inevitably gravitate towards the old centre, around the **Vieux Bassin**, where slate-fronted houses, each one or two storeys higher than seems possible, harmonize despite their tottering and ill-matched forms.

All serve as a splendid backdrop for the **Lieutenance** at the harbour entrance, the former dwelling of the King's Lieutenant, which has been the gateway to the inner town since at least 1608, when Samuel Champlain sailed from Honfleur to found Québec. Further architectural and historic treasures lie tucked away in the tangled medieval streets and squares to either side of the *bassin*. Two seventeenth-century **salt stores** on rue de la Ville, which held the precious commodity during the days of the much-hated *gabelle*, or salt tax, are now used for art exhibitions.

Musée de la Marine

Quai St-Etienne • Mid-Feb to March, Oct & Nov Tues–Fri 2.30–5.30pm, Sat & Sun 10am–noon & 2.30–5.30pm; April–Sept Tues–Sun 10am–noon & 2–6.30pm • €3.90, €5.10 with Musée d'Ethnographie, €10.10 with Musée d'Ethnographie, Musée Eugène Boudin and Les Maisons Satie • Ⓣ 02 31 89 14 12, Ⓦ musees-honfleur.fr

Honfleur's **Musée de la Marine** somehow manages to squeeze into the fourteenth-century church of **St-Étienne**, on the eastern side of the *bassin*. This one-room museum, which still retains some of its stained glass, traces the story of the town's intimate association with the sea, including its role in the slave trade as well as its history of fishing and commerce, and explains how the port itself took shape. The most prominent exhibits are the large-scale replicas of sailing ships and a cumbersome early diving suit.

Musée d'Ethnographie

Rue de la Prison • Mid-Feb to March, Oct & Nov Tues–Fri 2.30–5.30pm, Sat & Sun 10am–noon & 2.30–5.30pm; April–Sept Tues–Sun 10am–noon & 2–6.30pm • €3.90, €5.10 with Musée de la Marine, €10.10 with Musée de la Marine, Musée Eugène Boudin and Les Maisons Satie • Ⓣ 02 31 89 14 12, Ⓦ musees-honfleur.fr

Alongside the Musée de la Marine, on tiny rue de la Prison, a nice little ensemble, consisting of a half-timbered house that once held Honfleur's prison along with several tumbledown structures alongside, serves as the **Musée d'Ethnographie**. Its ten rooms, themed as the Weaver's Room, the Costume Room, and so on, hold an engaging assortment of everyday artefacts from old Honfleur. Among the highlights are the Sailor's Room, which for some reason holds a spinning wheel as well as an anchor; the Printer's Room, with an eighteenth-century press; and the final Haberdasher's Room, where a waxwork effigy toils at his desk in front of an array of buttons, feathers and swatches. There's also a copper bath on wheels, shaped like a clog, that's identical to the one in which Jacobin leader Jean-Paul Marat was assassinated by Charlotte Corday in 1793.

Église Ste-Catherine

Church Daily: summer 8.30am–7pm; winter 8.30am–6pm **Belfry** Mid-March to May & Sept Mon & Wed–Sun 10am–noon & 2–6pm; June–Aug Mon & Wed–Sun 10am–12.30pm & 2–6pm; Oct to mid-March Mon & Wed–Fri 2.30–5.30pm, Sat & Sun 10am–noon & 2.30–5.30pm • €2, or free with Musée Eugène Boudin

Honfleur's most remarkable building has to be the church of **Ste-Catherine**, with its distinctive detached **belfry**, which ranked among Monet's favourite subjects in his younger days. The church was built almost entirely of wood during the Hundred Years War, when stone was reserved for military use; the town's shipbuilders, experienced in working with wood, took responsibility for its construction. All the timbers inside are now exposed to view, having been sheathed in white plaster during the nineteenth century, when an incongruous four-columned porch (long since removed) was added to the front. The changing patterns on its tiles, both along the main body and the belfry, delineate Christian symbols. It all makes a change from the great stone Norman churches, and has the added peculiarity of being divided into twin naves, with one balcony running around both.

The belfry now holds a fairly random assortment of ethnographic oddities, and visitors are not permitted above ground level.

2

Musée Eugène Boudin

Place Érik-Satie • Mid-March to Sept Mon & Wed–Sun 10am–noon & 2–6pm; Oct to mid-March Mon & Wed–Fri 2.30–5.30pm, Sat & Sun 10am–noon & 2.30–5.30pm • €6.50, €10.10 with Les Maisons Satie, Musée de la Marine and Musée d'Ethnographie • ☎ 02 31 89 54 00, ⓦ musees-honfleur.fr

Honfleur's artistic past, and its present concentration of galleries and painters, owes most to **Eugène Boudin**, forerunner of Impressionism. Born in Honfleur in 1824 – his father worked on the ferries between Honfleur and Le Havre – Boudin continued to paint here throughout his life. He taught the 18-year-old Monet and was joined for various periods by Pissarro, Renoir and Cézanne.

Boudin was among the founders of what's now the **Musée Eugène Boudin**, west of the port, and left 53 works to it after his death in 1898. His pastel seascapes and sunsets, some of which are juxtaposed with nineteenth-century photographs of the same scenes, hold an especial resonance in this setting, where panoramic windows on the top floor offer superb views of the Seine estuary and the Pont de Normandie. Several other artists with local connections are also represented, including Dufy, while Fernand Herbo's hellish 1956 vision of workers streaming out of Le Havre's Shell refinery adds a contemporary edge.

Les Maisons Satie

67 bd Charles-V • Mon & Wed–Sun: mid-Feb to April & Oct–Dec 10am–6pm; May–Sept 10am–7pm; last entry 1hr before closing • €6.50, €10.10 with Musée Eugène Boudin, Musée de la Marine and Musée d'Ethnographie • ☎ 02 31 89 11 11, ⓦ musees-honfleur.fr

The red-timbered former home of composer **Érik Satie**, just down the hill from the Musée Boudin, forms part of a row of stately shipbuilders' residences that once lined the Honfleur waterfront; now they look across reclaimed flatlands to the industrial desert of Le Havre's docks in the distance. From the outside, it looks unchanged since Satie was born here in 1866. Step inside, however, and you'll find yourself in Normandy's most unusual and enjoyable museum.

As befits a close associate of the Surrealists, Satie is commemorated by means of all sorts of weird interactive surprises, and under many of his self-adopted aliases, including for example "Esoterik Satie". It would be a shame to give too many of them away here; suffice it to say that you're immediately confronted by a giant pear, bouncing into the air on huge wings to the strains of his best-known piano piece, *Gymnopédies*, and said to represent Satie's soul leaving his body after his death in Paris on July 1, 1925. To make the most of the whole thing, it's well worth listening to the complementary soundtrack on the headphone sets lent to all visitors.

The Côte de Grace

Honfleur's seafront can be reached by an easy three-minute walk from the Maisons Satie – more like ten minutes from the town centre. Follow boulevard Charles-V northwest, then walk through the car park of the Naturospace butterfly exhibit, and you swiftly come to the **Jardin des Personnalités**, a free public garden devoted to the memory of the town's painters, artists and historical figures. Immediately to the left here, steps lead down from the sea wall to a broad and very pleasant **beach** that's a great spot for picnics but not a very enticing place to swim, facing the mouth of the Seine.

The beach marks the eastern end of the **Côte de Grace**, which stretches west from Honfleur as far as the Côte Fleurie. At low tide, it's possible to walk the 6km from here all the way to Villerville. Beautiful wooded hills rise tantalizingly above you inland, where the grand old houses of ancient aesthetes, and the **Chapelle Notre Dame de Grâce** in Équemauville, beloved of the Impressionists, nestle dry-footed in the forests.

ARRIVAL AND INFORMATION   **HONFLEUR**

By train The nearest train station, 20km south at Pont-l'Évêque, is connected to Honfleur by the Lisieux bus #50 (20min).

By bus The *gare routière* is 10min walk east of the Vieux Bassin (☎ 08 10 21 42 14, ⓦ busverts.fr).

Destinations Caen (12 daily; 1–2hr); Le Havre (10 daily; 30min); Lisieux (5 daily; 30min) via Pont-l'Évêque (20min).

INFORMATION AND TOURS

Tourist office Quai Le Paulmier (Easter–June & Sept Mon–Sat 9.30am–12.30pm & 2–6.30pm, Sun 10am–12.30pm & 2–5pm; July & Aug Mon–Sat 9.30am–7pm, Sun 10am–5pm; Oct–Easter Mon–Sat 9.30am–12.30pm & 2–6pm, Sun 10am–1pm in school hols only; ☏ 02 31 89 23 30, ⓦ ot-honfleur.fr).

Guided tours The tourist office offers a wide programme of guided walks around the town, costing €5–8; see ⓦ ot-honfleur.fr for current schedules.

River cruises In summer, several cruises sail upriver each day from well-signposted departure points either side of the Avant-Port, for a closer look at the Pont de Normandie (45min trip €6, 1hr 30min €8.50). Visit ⓦ ot-honfleur.fr for full listings.

ACCOMMODATION

Honfleur is an expensive destination, especially in summer; many budget travellers choose simply to visit for the day. No hotels overlook the harbour itself, while motorists will find it hard to park anywhere near most central hotels.

Camping du Phare Place Jean-de-Vienne, boulevard Charles V ☏ 02 31 89 10 26, ⓦ campings-plage.fr. Honfleur's relatively low-key two-star campsite is set just off the main road to the west, an easy walk from the heart of town. Closed Oct–March. **€20.70**

★ **La Cour Sainte-Catherine** 74 rue du Puits ☏ 02 31 89 42 40, ⓦ coursaintecatherine.com. Beautiful B&B tucked down a quiet street beyond Ste-Catherine church. Comfortable, well-decorated rooms around a plant-filled courtyard, and some larger apartments; substantial buffet breakfasts served in the old cider press. **€90**

Dauphin 10 place Berthelot ☏ 02 31 89 15 53, ⓦ hotel dudauphin.com. Grey-slate townhouse around the corner from Ste-Catherine church, offering assorted rooms above a tearoom. All have recently been spruced up with contemporary decor; the cheapest are in the rather impersonal annexe, while the fanciest come with jacuzzis, and there are also some larger family options. The creaky floorboards and thin walls are universal, however. **€73**

L'Ex Voto 8 place Albert-Sorel ☏ 02 31 89 19 69. Four clean, well-priced rooms, reached via a precarious spiral staircase above a friendly family-run café/bar, a short walk inland along the main road from the Vieux Bassin. Two are en suite, the others share a shower and toilet. Rates include breakfast. Closed Nov & Dec. **€60**

Le Fond de la Cour 29 rue Eugène-Boudin ☏ 06 72 20 72 98, ⓦ lefonddelacour.com. Secluded little complex, run by a friendly Scottish couple and set around a courtyard a short walk from the centre, consisting of tastefully furnished rooms and suites in a former stables, plus a garden cottage sleeping up to four. Rates shown are for B&B guests, who enjoy excellent breakfasts served in the conservatory, but you can stay on a self-catering basis if you prefer. **€90**

La Maison de Lucie 44 rue des Capucins ☏ 02 31 14 40 40, ⓦ lamaisondelucie.com. Delightful boutique hotel, tucked away just seconds from the centre, in a beautiful restored eighteenth-century townhouse furnished with hints of 1930s-style decadence. The nine regular rooms are spacious and comfortable – some have private terraces – and there's a larger suite and a duplex apartment, as well as a spa. **€170**

★ **Les Maisons de Léa** Place Ste-Catherine ☏ 02 31 14 49 49, ⓦ lesmaisonsdelea.com. This magnificent hotel spreads through four seventeenth-century houses on Honfleur's central square. Rooms range from spacious doubles to family suites and a self-catering cottage; each has its own quirks and treasures, and all are luxurious. They also have a spa, while menus in the high-class on-site restaurant, which has some tables on the square itself, start at €29. **€170**

★ **Monet** Rue Charrière du Puits ☏ 02 31 89 00 90, ⓦ hotel-monet-honfleur.com. Spruce, modern en-suite rooms in a very quiet spot 10min walk uphill from the centre, with courtyard parking available. Some are in the original old townhouse, the remainder in various new extensions, and the management is exceptionally helpful. **€98**

EATING AND DRINKING

Honfleur supports an astonishing number of restaurants, most specializing in seafood and many very good at it. Surprisingly few face onto the harbour itself; the narrow buildings around the edge are largely devoted to snack bars, crêperies, cafés and ice-cream parlours, where you can get reasonable food and drink at substantial prices, but rarely a good-value or high-quality restaurant meal.

Le Bouillon Normand 7 rue de la Ville ☏ 02 31 89 02 41, ⓦ aubouillonnormand.fr. Old-fashioned bistro, with indoor and outdoor seating, in a spacious and relatively quiet cobbled square just back from the basin behind St-Étienne church. Fish, cider and cheese are prominent on simple, good-value menus at €22 and €30. Mon, Tues & Fri–Sun noon–2pm & 7–9.30pm, closed 3 weeks in Jan.

Le Bréard 7 rue du Puits ☏ 02 31 89 53 40, ⓦ restaurant -lebreard.com. Highly creative, contemporary take on classic French cuisine, in a fine old mansion that's been hollowed out and remodelled from the inside, located just off the church square. Don't expect to be bludgeoned with

2

heavy sauces and huge portions; here things are very much lighter and more delicate, on dinner menus at €31–55. Tues 7–9.30pm, Wed–Sun noon–2pm & 7–9.30pm; closed 3 weeks in Dec.

La Cidrerie 26 place Hamelin ☎ 02 31 89 59 85, ⓦ creperie-lacidrerie-honfleur.com. This lively and convivial old cider bar, set back just off the square, also serves a wide range of crêpes and galettes costing around €6, and has an €11 lunch menu. It might look like a tourist trap, but once you get deep inside it's a pleasantly cosy spot. Daily noon–10pm; closed Tues & Wed in low season.

La Lieutenance 12 place Ste-Catherine ☎ 02 31 89 07 52, ⓦ restaurant-honfleur.com. Not in fact by the Lieutenance, despite the name, but facing both church and belfry on the cobbled pedestrian square, with plenty of outdoor seating. Gourmet dining with a heavy emphasis on oysters; lunch menus start at €23 and dinner at €31, and there's always at least one good vegetarian starter and main course. Tues–Sun noon–2pm & 7.30–9.30pm; also closed Tues in winter, plus all Jan.

Au P'tit Mareyeur 4 rue Haute ☎ 02 31 98 84 23, ⓦ auptitmareyeur.fr. No distance from the centre, but all the seating is indoors and there are no views. Very good fish dishes, plus plenty of creamy *pays d'Auge* sauces and superb desserts. Menus from €28 for lunch, €35 for dinner, or you can get a sumptuous bouillabaisse for €38. Mon & Thurs–Sun noon–2pm & 7.30–9.30pm; closed Jan.

Sa-Qua-Na 22 place Hamelin ☎ 02 31 89 40 80, ⓦ alexandre-bourdas.com. While the exotic-sounding name is simply an abbreviation for chef Alexandre Bourdas' guiding principles – *saveur, qualité, nature* – there's definitely something different about the Asian-influenced cuisine that has rapidly earned Honfleur's premier gourmet restaurant two Michelin stars. Expect Japanese-style flavours and techniques, plus Thai and Indian herbs and seasoning, on the two changing daily menus, priced at €75 and €115. Reservations essential. Thurs–Sun noon–2pm & 7.30–9.30pm.

Travel's Coffee 6 place des Puits ☎ 06 37 51 86 55. Friendly, peaceful little café, with some outdoor tables on a sleepy square. The good-value €8 breakfast deal includes a delicious little apple tart; add a slice of quiche as well and it becomes a €14 brunch. A plate of cheese, pâté or charcuterie also costs €8. Cash only. Mon, Tues & Thurs–Sun 8am–5pm.

Villerville

For the 15km **west along the corniche** from Honfleur to Trouville-sur-Mer, green fields and fruit trees line the land's edge, and cliffs rise from sandy beaches. The **resorts** aren't cheap, but they're relatively undeveloped, and if you want to stop by the seaside this is the place to do it.

The most conspicuous community is **VILLERVILLE**, 10km west of Honfleur, a coastal village whose narrow twisting streets, filled with old mansions, front onto a huge sandy beach that unfortunately faces straight across the mouth of the Seine to the refineries of Le Havre.

ACCOMMODATION AND EATING

VILLERVILLE

Bellevue 12 rue du Général-Leclerc ☎ 02 31 87 20 22, ⓦ bellevue-hotel.fr. Grand old hotel, dropping down the hillside from the main D513 just east of town, with some very comfortable but rather anonymous rooms in its seafront annexe, and cheaper ones in its main building. Good fish menus in the sea-view restaurant start at €29. Dinner nightly, lunch Mon & Fri–Sun only. **€105**

Le Cabaret Normand 2 rue Daubigny ☎ 02 31 87 20 57. Bar/restaurant that's a place of pilgrimage for fans of French cinema, being barely changed since its appearance in the 1962 movie *Un Singe en Hiver*, starring Jean Gabin and Jean-Paul Belmondo. Even if that reference is lost on you, it's worth dropping in for a good solid meal in these deeply authentic, old-fashioned surroundings; expect to pay around €15 for a menu featuring the likes of mussels and fish soup. In the afternoon, between meal times, only drinks are available. Summer Tues–Sun noon–9.30pm; winter Sat & Sun noon–9.30pm.

Trouville-sur-Mer and Deauville

The towns of **Trouville-sur-Mer** and **Deauville** lie within a stone's throw of each other to either side of the mouth of the River Touques, sharing many of their amenities, and also their rather exclusive reputations.

Trouville-sur-Mer

Though **TROUVILLE-SUR-MER** retains some semblance of a real town, with a constant population and industries other than tourism, it has primarily been a resort ever since

Napoléon III first brought his court here for the summer during the 1860s. (His empress, Eugénie, fled France from here in 1870 in the yacht of an English admirer.) These days, the whole place retains a charming Belle Époque feel.

The beach and promenade

As the main road through town crosses the River Touques 800m inland from the sea, your first impression is likely to be of the long row of shops and restaurants that lines the east bank of the river. Trouville's crowning glory, though, is its magnificent, broad **beach** of fine sand, popular these days with surfers as well as bucket-and-spade-toting families, and scattered with striped bathing huts, children's activity centres, snack bars and fully fledged restaurants.

A long **promenade** marks the boundary between the sands and the spectacular villas that run parallel to the shoreline. Prime among these is the chic former **Hôtel des Roches Noires** (now a private residence), patterned with complex brickwork and topped by ornate turrets. Several buildings here were painted by Monet during a visit in 1870.

Rue des Bains and the fish market

The tangle of busy pedestrian streets that lie a short way back from the promenade are alive with shops, restaurants and hotels. **Rue des Bains**, at the epicentre, is the scene of open-air concerts on Saturday nights in summer, while many of the stalls in the picturesque **fish market**, next to the river, double as bars, thereby providing an unusually congenial opportunity to sample a few fresh oysters. A €1 *bac* (ferry) crosses the river nearby, sparing pedestrians heading to and from Deauville the long walk via the road bridge.

Deauville

One of Emperor Napoleon's dukes, looking across the river from Trouville-sur-Mer, saw not marshlands but money, and lots of it, in the form of a **racecourse**. His vision materialized, and villas appeared between the racecourse and the sea to become **DEAUVILLE**, Trouville-sur-Mer's grander and more exclusive neighbour, which likes to style itself as the *21e arrondissement* of Paris.

Now you can lose money on the horses, cross five streets to lose more in the **casino** (formal attire compulsory; temporary membership around €15), where Winston Churchill spent the summer of 1906 gambling every night until 5am, and finally lose yourself in the broad band of private bathing huts that intervene before the *planches*. Beyond this stretch of boardwalk, rows of primary-coloured parasols obscure the sea.

The **American Film Festival**, held in Deauville over ten days in early September (ⓦfestival-deauville.com), is the antithesis of Cannes, with public admission to a wide selection of previews, while still attracting big-name stars.

ARRIVAL AND INFORMATION   TROUVILLE-SUR-MER AND DEAUVILLE

By train and bus Trouville and Deauville share their *gare SNCF* and *gare routière*, located between the two just south of the marina.

Destinations (train) Lisieux (5 daily in winter, much more frequently in summer; 20min); Paris (5 daily in winter, much more frequently in summer; 2hr).

Destinations (bus) Caen (hourly; 1hr 15min); Honfleur (10 daily; 30min).

By plane In summer only, CityJet (ⓦcityjet.com) flies from

London's City Airport direct to Deauville (4 weekly; 1hr).

Tourist office 32 quai Fernand Moureaux, Trouville (July & Aug Mon–Sat 9.30am–7pm, Sun 10am–6pm; Sept–June Mon 2.30–6pm, Tues–Sat 10am–6pm, Sun 10am–1.30pm; ☏02 31 14 60 70, ⓦtrouvillesurmer.org); 112 rue Victor Hugo, Deauville (mid-July to mid-Sept Mon–Sat 9am–7pm, Sun 10am–6pm; mid-Sept to mid-July Mon–Sat 10am–6pm, Sun 10am–1pm & 2–5pm; ☏02 31 14 40 00, ⓦdeauville.org).

ACCOMMODATION

As you might imagine, hotels in Trouville and Deauville tend to be luxurious, or overpriced, or indeed both. For lesser mortals, however, there are a few cheaper options.

2

★**Flaubert** Rue Gustave-Flaubert, Trouville ☎ 02 31 88 37 23, ⓦ flaubert.fr. If you fancy staying right on the seafront, it's hard to beat this great-value faux-timbered mansion at the start of Trouville's boardwalk, where the spacious, comfortable rooms have large bathrooms and in many cases balconies. The bistro downstairs is separately owned, but the hotel has its own tearoom, which becomes a bar in the evening. Sea-view rooms cost €10 extra, and they have some large family suites. **€100**

Normandy Barrière 38 rue Jean-Mermoz, Deauville ☎ 02 31 98 66 22, ⓦ www.lucienbarriere.com. Not surprisingly, this enormous, rambling timbered hotel, the fanciest in either town, is where the stars stay during the film festival. Even the indoor swimming pool is half-timbered, and there's a splendid dining room, *La Belle Époque*, where dinner menus start at €55. **€255**

Des Sports 27 rue Gambetta, Deauville ☎ 02 31 88 22 67. Nine well-priced and comfortable en-suite rooms, two of which have balconies, above a popular local bar/ restaurant behind Deauville's fish market. Closed March & Nov, plus Sun in winter. **€70**

Trouville 1 rue Thiers, Trouville ☎ 02 31 98 45 48, ⓦ hotelletrouville.fr. Trouville's best budget option, a friendly place 50m back from the beach, offers en-suite rooms graded to four different categories, including small singles; the cheapest are pretty basic, it has to be said, so the "comfort" ones, which have balconies, are preferable. They also rent out bicycles. Closed Jan. **€65**

Vallée de Deauville Route de Beaumont-en-Auge, St-Arnoult ☎ 02 31 88 58 17, ⓦ camping-deauville.com. The nearest campsite to the twin resorts, 3km from the centre of Deauville, is a large and very luxurious five-star affair, with a restaurant and grocery, as well as a large spa and waterpark, plus self-catering rentals. Closed Nov–March. **€31.50**

EATING AND DRINKING

Chez Miocque 81 rue Eugène-Colas, Deauville ☎ 02 31 88 09 52, ⓦ chez-miocque.fr. Everyone who's anyone in Deauville drops in at some point to this bustling, top-quality Parisian-style bistro, to snack on anything from hard-boiled eggs to steak and chips, or to enjoy a full three-course meal for €40. Feb–Dec daily noon–11pm; closed Tues & Wed in winter.

L'Inattendu 89 rue des Bains, Trouville ☎ 02 31 88 74 04, ⓦ inattendu-trouville.fr. Friendly little neighbourhood restaurant on a lively pedestrianized street, with some outdoor tables. Each day they chalk up a wide-ranging €25 menu of classic local dishes, including salads and all kinds of seafood; you can also simply drop in for a coffee or drink, and there's live jazz on the last Friday of the month. Daily 9am until late; closed Tues & Wed Sept–June.

La Petite Auberge 7 rue Carnot, Trouville ☎ 02 31 88 11 07, ⓦ lapetiteaubergesurmer.fr. Small, intimate restaurant a short walk inland from the beach, where seafood is the speciality but the menus, from €40 in the evenings, always include some hearty meat dishes, too. Mon & Thurs–Sun 12.15–1.45pm & 7.15–9.30pm; also open Wed in Aug.

Les Vapeurs/Les Voiles 160 bd F. Moureaux, Trouville ☎ 02 31 88 15 24, ⓦ lesvapeurs.fr. Hard-to-resist pair of indistinguishable, co-owned and co-run old-fashioned brasseries, whose red-and-yellow chairs line a long pavement terrace facing the attractive half-timbered fish market. Non-stop service of everything from salads at around €10 or mussels and oysters for €13–15 up to meat and fish dishes for €18–36 and seafood platters costing up to €94. Daily noon–1am.

Villers-sur-Mer

West of Deauville, the shoreline at first stays flat, and the main coast road passes through a succession of what are almost suburban resorts – less snobbish than Trouville and Deauville, but equally crowded and equally short of inexpensive hotels.

The largest of these, **VILLERS-SUR-MER**, is noteworthy both for straddling the Greenwich meridian, and for the giant topiary brontosaurus, complete with calf, which stalks the little roundabout at the western end of the beach.

Paléospace

Avenue Jean-Moulin • May & June daily 10am–6pm; July & Aug daily 10am–7pm; Sept Mon & Wed–Sun 10am–6pm; mid-Feb to April and Oct to late Nov Wed–Sun 10am–6pm; Dec to early Jan Sat & Sun 10am–6pm; closed early Jan to mid-Feb • €7.70, ages 5–14 €4.80 • ☎ 02 31 81 77 60, ⓦ paleospace-villers.fr

An attractively landscaped park, 100m from the sea at the eastern end of Villers, is home to **Paléospace**, a new museum devoted to the fossils discovered in the Falaise des Vaches Noires, along the coast to the west. Nineteenth-century palaeontologists struggled to account for the so-called "crocodiles of Honfleur"; some specimens were later identified as ichthyosaurs, as now illustrated by an all-but-complete fossil brought here from Wyoming. The permanent displays are translated into English, and also explain the freshwater marshlands visible through the windows.

ACCOMMODATION VILLERS-SUR-MER

Camping de Bellevue Route de Dives ☎02 31 87 05 21, ⓦcamping-bellevue.com. Four-star campsite, through the middle of which, incidentally, the Greenwich meridian runs right through, and which has a covered heated pool plus a bar and restaurant. Closed Nov–March. **€26**

★**Outre-Mer** 1 rue du Maréchal-Leclerc ☎02 31 87 04 64, ⓦhoteloutremer.com. Venerable hotel, where each bedroom is decorated in a distinctive, contemporary colour scheme; some have sea-view balconies. Downstairs they have a tearoom rather than a restaurant, which stays open until 10.30pm in summer and occasionally features jazz bands. **€120**

Houlgate

A century ago, **HOULGATE**, 7km west of Villers-sur-Mer, was every bit as glamorous and sophisticated as its neighbours. What makes it different today is that it has barely changed since then. Its long straight beach remains lined by a stately procession of ornate Victorian villas, with what few commercial enterprises the town supports confined to the narrow parallel street, the **rue des Bains**, 50m inland.

As a result, Houlgate is the most relaxed of the local resorts, ideal if you're looking for a peaceful family break where the only stress is deciding whether to paddle or play mini-golf. Come in late August if you want to see it at its most active; that's when they celebrate the annual **Festijazz**.

So long as you keep an eye on the tides, it's possible to walk between Villers and Houlgate along the foot of the **Vaches Noires** (Black Cows) cliffs, which force the main road at this point up and away from the sea. However, industrial Le Havre is a bit too visible across the water for it to be an especially picturesque stroll.

INFORMATION HOULGATE

Tourist office 10 bd des Belges, back from the sea at the east end of town (Easter–June & Sept Mon–Sat 10am–1pm & 2–6pm, Sun 10.30am–1pm & 2–4pm; July & Aug daily 10am–1pm & 2–6.30pm; Oct–Easter Mon–Sat 9.30am–1pm & 2–5.30pm; ☎02 31 24 34 79, ⓦville-houlgate.fr).

ACCOMMODATION AND EATING

Le 1900 17 rue des Bains ☎02 31 28 77 77, ⓦhotel1900 -houlgate.com. Formal but nonetheless friendly red-brick hotel where rooms offer varying levels of comfort, and dinner menus in the glassed-in *Belle Époque* bistro start at €24. **€100**

Ferme Auberge des Aulnettes ☎02 31 28 00 28, ⓦaubergedesaulnettes.fr. Lovely half-timbered country house, set in pleasant gardens, well back from the corniche road above the cliffs east of town. The cheapest rooms have a shower but share a WC, and there's a good restaurant with outdoor seating, serving lunch from €15, and dinner menus from €18.50 to €35. Closed Dec & Jan. **€69**

Hostellerie Normande 11 rue E-Deschanel ☎02 31 24 85 50, ⓦhotel-houlgate.com. Pretty but rather impersonal little hotel, just off the rue des Bains and covered with ivy and creeping flowers, with a €16.50 lunch menu on which you can follow fish soup with *moules frites* or tripe. **€80**

Dives

Immediately west of Houlgate, the main D513 is forced to detour away from the open sea when it reaches the mouth of the River Divette. Just 1km along, the venerable little port of **DIVES** was the spot from which William the Conqueror sailed for Hastings, by way of St-Valery; contemporary chronicles tell of vast stockpiles of supplies accumulating on the beach in the days preceding the invasion. Now, like Honfleur, pushed well back from the sea, Dives is older and less commercialized than Cabourg, its haughty aristocratic neighbour across the river.

A lively **Saturday market** focuses on the ancient wooden *halles*, tucked away south of the main through road. The steep tiled roof of the *halles* must be five times the height of its walls, and its venerable weather-beaten timbers are held together by tight metal bands; it's crammed with mouthwatering delicacies and Norman specialities, while more mundane produce and imported jeans are sold in the square alongside and on the narrow streets.

ACCOMMODATION | DIVES

Camping du Golf Route de Lisieux ⊙ 02 31 24 73 09, ⊚ campingdugolf.com. Peaceful, attractive campsite, tucked into the woods 2km inland, off the route de Lisieux. Closed late Sept to mid-April. **€13**

Ibis Budget Promenade de la Dives ⊙ 08 92 68 08 54,

⊚ etaphotel.com. Large, fully refurbished chain hotel, very close to the bridge that connects Dives with Cabourg, with basic but good-value rooms, plus buffet breakfasts and a Japanese garden. **€65**

Cabourg

CABOURG is not so much a seaside resort as an exercise in formal geometry, laid out at much the same time as Deauville and catering for much the same elderly clientele. There's an awful lot of town planning, but not really any town.

At the centre of the straightest promenade in France, the **Grand Hôtel**, which once regularly accommodated Marcel Proust, looks out towards the sea, while behind it the crescent that defines the formal **Jardin du Casino** is the first of several concentric crescents, spreading out like ripples and lined with large, placid, undistinguished houses.

Other than on its splendid sandy **beach**, the one area where Cabourg really comes to life is along the **Avenue de la Mer**, the single, long commercial street that connects the Casino gardens with the main traffic route along the coast. In summer, the shops, bars and restaurants are filled dawn to dusk with browsing day-trippers. Should you feel the urge to escape the crowds and daydream over your own Proustian *madeleine*, stop off at the *Dupont Patissier*, at no. 6.

Cabourg makes an unlikely twin town for the notoriously raucous gambling resort of Atlantic City, New Jersey; for example, notices request that you "avoid noise on the beach", where picnicking is forbidden.

ARRIVAL AND INFORMATION | CABOURG

By train Trains run all the way from Paris-Gare-St-Lazare, via Trouville-Deauville, to the *gare SNCF* that Cabourg shares with Dives, every day in July and August, and otherwise at weekends only.
Destinations Trouville-Deauville (July & Aug 6 daily, rest of year 2 daily Sat, Sun & national hols only; 30min) via Houlgate (6min) and Villers (20min).

By bus Cabourg is also on the Caen–Honfleur bus route, #20.

Tourist office In the Casino gardens (May, June, Sept & Oct Mon–Sat 10am–12.30pm & 2–5.30pm, Sun 10am–noon & 2–4pm; July & Aug daily 9.30am–7pm; Nov–April Mon & Wed–Sat 10am–12.30pm & 2–5.30pm, Sun 10am–noon & 2–4pm; ⊙ 02 31 06 20 00, ⊚ cabourg.net).

ACCOMMODATION AND EATING

★**Le Baligan** 8 av Alfred Piat ⊙ 02 31 24 10 92, ⊚ lebaligan.fr. Modernized to add abundant space and light, this hugely popular gourmet restaurant is off the

beaten track, 500m east of Cabourg's main drag, but it's filled with eager in-the-know diners, here for well-priced menus – from €17.50 at lunch, €29 for dinner – of succulent

---

PROUST AT THE GRAND HÔTEL, CABOURG

As both child and adult, between 1881 and 1914, **Marcel Proust** stayed repeatedly at the *Grand Hôtel* in Cabourg. The town is the "Balbec" of *Du Côté de Chez Swann*, and the hotel itself – now officially located on the promenade Marcel-Proust – thrives on its Proustian connection. All guests are served with a *madeleine* for breakfast, and you can even sleep in Proust's own room, meticulously refurbished in line with the author's descriptions. The main dining room, which has a superb sea view, is now called *Le Balbec*. The ambivalent Proust referred to it as "the aquarium"; each night locals would press their faces to its window in wonder at the luxurious life within, "as extraordinary to the poor as the life of strange fishes or molluscs".

contemporary dishes like cucumber gazpacho served with tomato sorbet, or the substantial seafood *cassoulet*. Daily noon–2pm & 7.30–9pm.

★**Banc des Oiseaux** 105 route de Cabourg, Merville Franceville ☎ 02 50 01 32 37, ⓦ bancdesoiseaux.com. Secluded beachfront mansion, just off the coast road 4km west of Cabourg, which holds five very comfortable B&B rooms, each decorated to match a specific world destination, from Nairobi to New York (Kuala Lumpur is a lovely four-person suite). The beachfront setting is superb, but it's 3km to the nearest restaurant. Rates include breakfast, and drop for stays of more than one night. **€110**

Grand Hôtel Mercure Promenade Marcel-Proust ☎ 02 31 91 01 79, ⓦ mgallery.com. If money is no object, the famous seafront *Grand Hotel* is very much *the* place to stay in Cabourg. Both the views and the prices are tremendous, and you can even stay in Proust's own room. **€205**

Paris 39 av de la Mer ☎ 02 31 91 31 34, ⓦ hotel-paris-cabourg.com. Large and very central half-timbered hotel, above the *Café de Paris* brasserie on Cabourg's only commercial (semi-pedestrianized) street, and holding plain en-suite rooms, some with balconies. Closed Jan. **€73**

Caen

Few visitors spend much time in **CAEN**, capital and largest city of Basse Normandie (although it's the closest city to the Landing Beaches, there's plenty of accommodation along the coast), but it remains in parts highly impressive. Its central feature is a ring of ramparts that no longer has a castle to protect, and, though there are the scattered spires and buttresses of two abbeys and eight old churches, roads and roundabouts fill the wide spaces where prewar houses stood. Approaches are along thunderous highways through industrial suburbs, prospering thanks to an influx of high-tech newcomers.

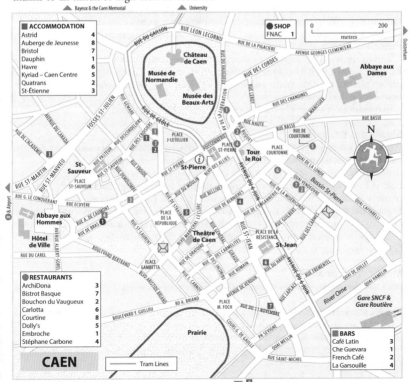

The nineteenth-century **Bassin St-Pierre**, a short walk south of the Abbaye aux Dames, now serves as Caen's **pleasure port**, and marks the end of the canal that links the city to the sea. In summer, this is one of the liveliest areas in town.

Brief history

Appropriately enough for a city that has been fought over throughout its long history, the name Caen originally came from a Celtic word meaning "battlefield". The town's site was first fortified in 1060 by **William the Conqueror**, because the navigable River Orne afforded safe access to the Channel. Over the ensuing centuries Caen repeatedly changed hands, and was twice sacked by the English. It was Henry VI of England who founded the university here in 1432, but Caen has been French since Charles VII took it back in 1450.

The modern city began to take shape when a canal to the sea was completed in 1850, running parallel to the heavily silted Orne. At the same time, the Bassin St-Pierre was built, creating a central marina, and the smaller River Odon was covered over. **World War II**, however, devastated the city. Historians still argue as to quite why the prime target of the 1944 landings took so long to capture. The "Battle of Caen" lasted two full months – even once the Canadians had entered the city, four weeks after D-Day, the southern bank of the river remained in enemy hands. Three-quarters of the town had to be destroyed before they were finally dislodged.

Château de Caen

Although almost nothing remains of the eleventh-century **Château de Caen**, its ancient **ramparts** are still in place. Walking the complete circuit gives a good overview of the city, with a particularly fine prospect of the reconstructed fourteenth-century facade of the nearby church of **St-Pierre**.

Within the walls, it's possible to visit the former **Exchequer**, which once hosted a banquet thrown by Richard the Lionheart en route to the Crusades, and inspect a garden planted with the herbs and medicinal plants that would have been cultivated here during the Middle Ages.

Two modern structures inside the castle precinct hold **museums**.

Musée des Beaux-Arts

Daily except Tues 9.30am–6pm • €3.20, special exhibitions extra; under-26s free • ☎ 02 31 30 47 70, ⓦ mba.caen.fr

The **Musée des Beaux-Arts** is housed in a light 1960s stone building, kept deliberately low to avoid topping the castle walls. Its upstairs galleries trace a potted history of European art from Renaissance Italy through such Dutch masters as Bruegel the Younger up to grand portraits from eighteenth-century France. Downstairs brings things up to date with a diverse range of twentieth-century and contemporary art – though there are few big-name works – as well as paintings by Monet, Bonnard and Gustave Doré (represented by a spectacular Scottish landscape).

Musée de Normandie

Daily 9.30am–6pm; closed Tues Nov–May • €3.20, special exhibitions extra; under-26s free • ☎ 02 31 30 47 60, ⓦ musee-de -normandie.eu

The **Musée de Normandie** provides a surprisingly cursory overview of Norman history, ranging from archeological finds like stone tools from the megalithic period and glass jewellery from Gallo-Roman Rouen to artefacts from the Industrial Revolution. It also hosts two or three temporary exhibitions per year, covering particular themes in much greater detail.

Abbaye aux Hommes

Rue St-Pierre • Mon–Sat 9.30am–12.30pm & 2–6.30pm, Sun 2–6.30pm; 1hr 15min guided tours leave adjacent Hôtel de Ville; tours in English July & Aug Mon–Fri 11am, 1.30pm & 4pm; tours in French all year, times vary • Free; tours €7 • ☎ 02 31 30 42 81, ⓦ caen-tourisme.fr

When William the Conqueror married Mathilda in Eu (see p.52), in 1051, both incurred excommunication. The precise nature of their offence remains obscure – they may have been distant cousins – but Pope Nicholas II only agreed to sanction their marriage in 1059 on the solemn vow that each would build an abbey in Caen.

William's, the **Abbaye aux Hommes** west of the city centre, is focused on the Romanesque church known as the Abbatiale St-Étienne. The abbey was originally designed to hold William's tomb, but his burial here, in 1087, was hopelessly undignified. The funeral procession first caught fire and was then held to ransom, as various factions squabbled over his rotting corpse for any spoils they could grab. A further interruption came when a man halted the service to object that the grave had been constructed without compensation on the site of his family house, and the assembled nobles had to pay him off before William could finally be laid to rest. His tomb still occupies pride of place in front of the main altar, though as the church was ransacked both by Protestants in 1562 and during the Revolution, it now holds at most a solitary thighbone rescued from the river. Still, the building itself serves as a wonderful monument and is also home to a fine collection of seventeenth- to nineteenth-century paintings. As you explore, look out for the huge wooden clock to the left of the altar.

To see the entire complex, you have to join one of the **guided tours** that leave from the **Hôtel de Ville** alongside, housed in what used to be its convent buildings.

Abbaye aux Dames

Rue des Chanoines • Daily 2–5.30pm; guided tours, in French, 2.30pm & 4pm • Free • ☎ 02 31 06 98 45, ⓦ caen-tourisme.fr

The **Abbaye aux Dames**, on the east side of central Caen, holds the tomb of Mathilda, William the Conqueror's queen. She had commissioned the building of the abbey church, La Trinité, well before the Conquest. It's starkly impressive, with a gloomy pillared crypt, superb stained glass behind the altar, and odd sculptural details like the fish curled up in the holy-water stoup.

The Caen Memorial

Avenue Marshal-Montgomery • Late Jan to early Feb, Nov & Dec daily except Mon 9.30am–6pm; early Feb to Oct daily 9am–7pm; closed 3 weeks in Jan; last entry 1hr 15min before closing • €19, family pass €49 • ☎ 02 31 06 06 44, ⓦ memorial-caen.fr • Bus #2 from stop "Tour le Roi" in central Caen

Just north of Caen, the **Caen Memorial** stands on a plateau named after General Eisenhower, on a clifftop beneath which the Germans had their HQ in June and July 1944. Originally a "museum for peace", its brief has expanded to cover history since the Great War; allow two hours at the very least for a visit. It also organizes very detailed tours of the Landing Beaches (see p.112). In summer, especially when the weather is not so good, queues can be very long, but at least there's a good-value self-service restaurant.

All visitors to the museum itself have to follow a prescribed route, which, with a slightly heavy-handed literalism, leads on a downwards spiral from World War I and the Treaty of Versailles towards the maelstrom of World War II. Hitler's image recurs with increasing size and frequency on screens beside you as the events of the 1920s and 1930s are recounted.

The war is superbly documented, with a greater emphasis on the minutiae of everyday life in occupied France than on military technology. Nothing is glossed over in the attempt to provide a rounded picture of the nation under occupation and at war; the collaborationist Vichy government, for example, is set in context without being excused. Secret Nazi reports show how Resistance activity in Normandy grew as the

2

war continued, and what reprisals were taken. Most of the captions throughout the museum, though not always the written exhibits, are well translated into English.

Visits to the memorial's **upper section** culminate with **films** in separate auditoriums. One, a harrowing account of D-Day and the ensuing battle to liberate Normandy, starts with the screen split in two to show, on one side, the preparations of the Allied forces on the eve of the invasion and, on the other, those of the Germans, then traces the course of the Battle of Normandy.

Finally, a short lift ride from the Memorial proper takes you down to the former **German bunkers.**

ARRIVAL AND DEPARTURE   CAEN

By air Caen's small airport (ⓦ caen.aeroport.fr), served by British European flights from Southend (ⓦ flybe.com), is 7km west on the D9, just outside Carpiquet.

By boat The Brittany Ferries (ⓟ 02 31 36 36 36, ⓦ brittany -ferries.com) service from Portsmouth (2–3 daily; 6–8hr), which is promoted as sailing to Caen, in fact docks at Ouistreham, 15km north (see p.111). Buses from Caen's *gare routière* connect with each sailing, and Bus Verts' express bus #1 runs the same route.

By train Caen's *gare SNCF* is 1km south of the centre, across the River Orne.

Destinations Cherbourg (10 daily; 1hr 15min), via Bayeux (20min) and Valognes (1hr); Lisieux (21 daily; 30min); Le Mans (5 daily; 2hr), via Argentan (45min) and Alençon (1hr 15min); Paris-St-Lazare (11 daily; 2hr 10min); Rennes (4 daily; 3hr), via Bayeux (20min), St-Lô (50min), Coutances (1hr 15min) and Pontorson (2hr); Rouen (6 daily; 2hr);

Tours (1 daily; 3hr).

By bus The *gare routière* is alongside the *gare SNCF*, 1km south of the centre. The main inland bus networks are operated by Bus Verts (ⓦ busverts.fr), who cover Calvados in particular; timetables for all regional routes can be found on ⓦ commentjyvais.fr.

Destinations Arromanches (1 daily; 1hr 10min); Bayeux (3 daily; 50min); Clécy (4 daily; 50min); Falaise (10 daily; 1hr); Flers (4 daily; 1hr 20min) via Thury-Harcourt (40min) and Clécy (50min); Honfleur (9 daily; 2hr), via Cabourg (50min), Houlgate (1hr) and Deauville (1hr 15min), of which 5 continue to Le Havre (2hr 30min); Le Havre (3 daily express services; 1hr 20min), via Honfleur (1hr); Luc-sur-Mer (12 daily; 40min); Ouistreham (20 daily; 30min); Pont-L'Évêque (3 daily; 1hr 10min); Thury-Harcourt (5 daily; 40min); Vire (connections for Brittany; 3 daily; 1hr 30min) via Aunay-sur-Odon (1hr).

GETTING AROUND

By bus and tram Caen's buses and trams are run by TWISTO (ⓟ 02 31 15 55 55, ⓦ twisto.fr). Single journeys cost €1.40, and a 24-hour pass €3.90 per adult, €5.95 per family or group of 2–5 passengers. The main tram route

connects the southern and northern suburbs, running through the centre from the *gare SNCF* up avenue du 6-Juin to the university and beyond.

INFORMATION AND TOURS

Tourist office Place St-Pierre (March Mon–Sat 9.30am– 1pm & 2–6.30pm; April–June & Sept Mon–Sat 9.30am– 6.30pm, Sun 10am–1pm; July & Aug Mon–Sat 9am–7pm, Sun 10am–1pm & 2–5pm; Oct–Feb Mon–Sat 9.30am–1pm & 2–6pm; ⓟ 02 31 27 14 14, ⓦ caen-tourisme.fr).

Guided tours In July and August, the tourist office offers

excellent €6 tours, in French only, that focus mainly on William the Conqueror's connections with Caen. Between mid-July and early Sept, they also put on "dramatized visits", in which actors perform short historical sketches, again in French only (Thurs & Sat 9pm; €14), and even all-singing musical tours (Wed & Fri 9pm; €11).

ACCOMMODATION

Astrid 39 rue de Bernières ⓟ 02 31 85 48 67, ⓦ hotel _astrid.club.fr. Smart, central little two-star budget hotel with spacious rooms, though rather compact bathrooms; the cheapest have private showers but share toilets. The friendly owner provides tourist information. **€48**

Auberge de Jeunesse Foyer Robert-Remé, 68bis rue Eustache Restout, Grâce-de-Dieu, ⓟ 02 31 52 19 96, ⓦ fuaj.org/Caen. Lively and welcoming hostel in a sleepy area 2km southwest of the *gare SNCF*, on tramline B. Beds in four-bed dorms or two-bed private rooms. Reception

5–9pm. Closed Oct–May. Dorms **€12**; doubles **€24**

Bristol 31 rue du 11-Novembre ⓟ 02 31 84 59 76, ⓦ hotelbristolcaen.com. Efficient, spruce and friendly hotel, in a quiet location an easy walk across the river from the train station. Rooms are small, but not bad for the price, and a substantial buffet breakfast is served in a pleasant dining room. **€89**

Dauphin 29 rue Gémare ⓟ 02 31 86 22 26, ⓦ le-dauphin -normandie.com. Upmarket *Best Western* hotel, part of which was a priory during the eighteenth century, not that you'd ever guess. The public areas are impressive, while the rooms are comfortable but relatively compact, at least at the lower end of the price scale. Sauna and fitness facilities are available – for a price – and a grand restaurant serves dinner menus from €25 to €55. **€140**

★**Havre** 11 rue du Havre ☎ 02 31 86 19 80, ⊛ hotel duhavre.com. Modern, cosy, and very good-value budget hotel, a block south of St-Jean church, close to the trams and with free parking. Rooms range from small singles to larger triples. **€72**

Kyriad – Caen Centre 1 place de la République ☎ 02 31 86 55 33, ⊛ hotel-caen-centre.com. Large, comfortable, spacious and very central chain hotel, with no restaurant but

copious buffet breakfasts. There's an underground car park, but on-street parking is free at weekends. **€70**

Quatrans 17 rue Gémare ☎ 02 31 86 25 57, ⊛ hotel -des-quatrans.com. Renovated hotel in an anonymous modern setting, a very short walk from the tourist office and the château. The pastel theme of the facade continues inside; some might find it a bit cloying, but the service is friendly, and everything works well. **€95**

St-Étienne 2 rue de l'Académie ☎ 02 31 86 35 82, ⊛ hotel-saint-etienne.com. Friendly budget hotel in a venerable stone house in the characterful St-Martin district, not far from the Abbaye aux Hommes. The rooms are far from fancy, but all are en-suite. **€49**

EATING AND DRINKING

The centre of Caen offers two major dining areas. The attractive pedestrianized **quartier Vaugueux** covers world cuisines from couscous to curry, pizzas to crêpes, while streets such as rue des Croisiers and rue Gémare off **rue de Geôle**, near the western ramparts, house more traditional French restaurants. The pleasure port, and **quai Vendeuvre** in particular, is packed with lively bars, pubs and clubs, and there's another concentration in the town centre a few hundred metres west.

ArchiDona 17 rue Gémare ☎ 02 31 85 30 30, ⊛ archidona.fr. This classy and atmospheric restaurant, adjoining the *Quatrans* hotel, serves delightfully fresh Mediterranean-influenced cuisine, ranging from simple entrée-plus-dessert meals at €18 up to the €39 "seduction" and €49 "emotion" menus. Tues–Thurs noon–1.30pm & 7–9.30pm, Fri & Sat noon–1.30pm & 7–10pm.

Bistrot Basque 24 quai Vendeuvre ☎ 02 31 38 21 26, ⊛ le-bistrot-basque.com. Opposite the pleasure port, an atmospheric restaurant with a bright interior, serving tasty Basque-influenced cooking, such as grilled cod with chorizo, with lunch menus from €16, dinner from €25, and a range of tasty tapas for €6–8. Mon–Thurs noon–2pm & 7.30–10.30pm, Fri & Sat noon–2pm & 7.30–11pm.

★**Bouchon du Vaugueux** 12 rue Graindorge ☎ 02 31 44 26 26, ⊛ bouchonduvaugueux.com. You'll need to reserve in advance for this intimate but hugely popular little brasserie in the Vaugueux quarter, which offers well-prepared French classics, such as duck with peaches, on just two menus (€21 and €33). Tues–Thurs noon–2pm & 7–10pm, Fri & Sat noon–2pm & 7–10.30pm.

Café Latin 135 rue St-Pierre ☎ 02 31 85 26 36. Convivial, invariably packed tapas bar in the town centre. Upstairs the theme of the decor is Mexican; downstairs, both inside and on the street terrace, it is much more French. The huge plates of tapas are very good and the music is not so loud as to drown out conversation. Mon–Sat 9am–1am.

Carlotta 16 quai Vendeuvre ☎ 02 31 86 68 99, ⊛ lecarlotta.fr. Smart, busy, fashionable Parisian-style brasserie beside the pleasure port, which serves good Norman cooking both à la carte and on dinner menus at €24.50 (not Fri & Sat), €30.50 and €40. Mon–Thurs 12.15–2.30pm & 7.15–10.30pm, Fri & Sat 12.15–2.30pm & 7.15–11pm.

Che Guevara 6–8 rue du Tour-de-Terre ☎ 02 31 85 10 75. Lively Cuban-themed cocktail bar, kitted out to evoke a Caribbean beach. Naturally, rum-based drinks are the house speciality. Tues–Thurs 6pm–1am, Fri & Sat 6pm–3am.

Courtine 16 rue Caponière ☎ 02 31 79 19 16. Behind a simple side-street shopfront, a short walk west of the Abbaye aux Hommes, this friendly local restaurant serves up a different short menu daily; €22 buys a full meal of excellent local cuisine, with an emphasis on fresh salads as well as the expected meat and fish. Tues, Wed, Fri & Sat noon–2pm & 7.30–9.30pm, Thurs noon–2pm.

Dolly's 18 av de la Libération ☎ 02 31 94 03 29. Very popular, very central, English-style café and tearoom, serving not only tea and coffee but good salads, with lots of vegetarian options, and Anglophile snacks like fish'n'chips for €12.50. Mon 11am–6pm, Tues 10am–7pm, Wed–Sun 10am–10.30pm.

Embroche 17 rue de la Porte au Berger ☎ 02 31 93 71 31. Cosy little place, where the open kitchen whips up simple regional specialities in full view of appreciative diners, with lunch from €18.50 and dinner from €25; there are also a few outdoor tables. Tues–Fri noon–2pm & 7–9.30pm, Sat 7–10pm.

French Café 32 quai Vendeuvre ☎ 02 31 50 10 02. Trendy, antique-filled bar facing the pleasure port along-side the *Carré* nightclub (run by the same management), serving cocktails and reasonable tapas, all you can eat on some evenings. A lot of 1980s music and rock, with the occasional French golden oldie thrown in for good measure. Tues–Sat 7pm–2am.

La Garsouille 11–13 rue Arcisse-de-Caumont ☎ 02 31 86 80 27. Hip, happening bar that also hosts live music and movie nights. Mon–Sat 4pm–1am.

Stéphane Carbone 14 rue de Courtonne ☎02 31 28 36 60, ⓦstephanecarbone.fr. Stylish, up-to-the-minute, Michelin-starred restaurant, specializing in Asian-influenced cuisine with a flair for both presentation and flavour. The most expensive menu, at €98, is devoted entirely to lobster, but you can sample Stéphane Carbone's cooking on menus from €26 at lunch time, €39 in the evening. Tues–Fri noon–2pm & 7.30–10pm, Sat 7.30–10pm.

ENTERTAINMENT

Caen's **cinemas** include the Café des Images, 4 square du Théâtre, Hérouville (ⓦcafedesimages.fr); Pathé Lumière, 15 bd Maréchal-Leclerc, and Pathé Malherbe, 55 rue des Jacobins (both ⓦcinemasgaumontpathe.com); and Cinéma Lux, 6 av Ste-Thérèse (ⓦcinemalux.org).

Théâtre de Caen 8 place St-Pierre ☎02 31 30 48 00, ⓦtheatre.caen.fr. A complete programme of music, opera, dance and drama. Closed July & Aug.

SHOPPING

Most of central Caen is taken up with busy modern shopping developments and pedestrian precincts, where the cafés are distinguished by such names as *Fast Food Glamour Vault*. The shops are good, possibly the best in Normandy or Brittany, if Parisian style is what you're after. Rue Écuyère has a fine assortment of shops full of unusual and cheap oddments, **antiques**, stuff for collectors and jokes. The main city **market** takes place on Sunday, filling place Courtonne by the Bassin St-Pierre, while another large one spreads along both sides of Fossés St-Julien every Friday.

FNAC Centre Paul-Doumer, rue de Bras ☎02 31 02 00 20, ⓦfnac.com. If you're looking for books, maps, music, movies or tech stuff, or tickets for local events, this central outlet is your best one-stop shop. Mon–Fri 10am–7pm, Sat 10am–7.30pm.

DIRECTORY

Hospital C.H.U. Avenue Côte de Nacre (☎02 31 06 31 06, ⓦchu-caen.fr).
Launderette Lavomatique, 16 rue Écuyère (daily 7am–8pm).
Pharmacy Grande Pharmacie du Progrès, 2 bd des Alliés (Mon–Sat 8am–8pm; ☎02 31 27 70 17; ⓦgrandepharmacieduprogres.pharminfo.fr).
Post office Place Gambetta (Mon–Fri 8am–7pm, Sat 8.30am–12.30pm; ☎02 31 39 35 76).
Swimming pools Chemin Vert, 42 rue Champagne (☎02 31 73 08 79; ⓦcaenlamer.fr); Stade Nautique, boulevard Yves-Guilleau (☎02 31 30 47 47; ⓦcaenlamer.fr).

Bayeux

Home to a perfectly preserved medieval ensemble, magnificent **cathedral** and world-famous **tapestry**, the city of **BAYEUX** is 23km west of Caen – a mere twenty-minute train ride. It's a smaller and much more intimate place, and, despite the large crowds of summer tourists, a far more enjoyable place to visit.

Bayeux's surprisingly diminutive core is basically oriented to either side of one long street, which starts from the place St-Patrice in the west (scene of a Saturday market). As the **rue St-Malo** and **rue St-Martin**, this is lined with the busy little shops of a typical Norman town; it then crosses the attractive canalized River Aure, passing the tourist office and the old watermill, Moulin Crocquevieille, to become **rue St-Jean**, which is pedestrianized in summer on the east side. Filled with cafés, brasseries, restaurants and souvenir shops, it, too, is the site of a market, on Wednesdays.

Both Bayeux's principal attractions lie south of this main thoroughfare. The **Cathédrale Notre Dame** is in an attractive tangle of old streets, best reached along rue des Cuisiniers – look out for the magnificent fourteenth-century half-timbered house that overhangs the street at no. 1, on the corner with rue St-Martin – while the **tapestry** is on the other side of the river.

Standing just 10km in from the coast, Bayeux was the first French city to be liberated in 1944, the day after the D-Day landings. It was occupied so quickly – before the

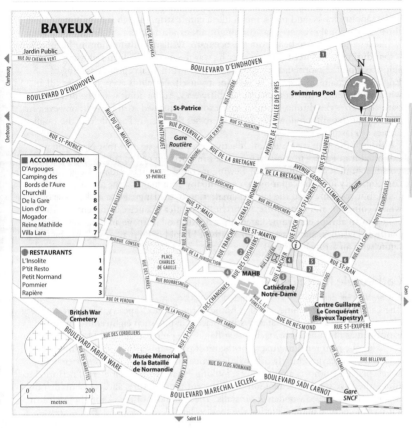

BAYEUX

Jardin Public
RUE DU CHEMIN VERT
Cherbourg
BOULEVARD D'EINDHOVEN
BOULEVARD D'EINDHOVEN
RUE DE BEAUVAIS
RUE DU DR. MICHEL
RUE ST-PATRICE
Cherbourg
St-Patrice
RUE D'ETERVILLE
Gare
Routière
PLACE
ST-PATRICE
RUE DES BILLETTES
RUE ROYALE
RUE MONTFIQUET
RUE CARBONG
RUE D'ARPRAY
RUE ST-QUENTIN
RUE DE LA BRETAGNE
RUE DES BOUCHERS
AVENUE DE LA VALLÉE DES PRÉS
RUE LOUVIÈRE
Swimming Pool
RUE DU PONT TRUBERT
N
RUE ST-LAURENT
Aure
R. DE LA BRETAGNE
AVENUE GEORGES CLEMENCEAU
ROUTE DE COURSEULLES
RUE ST-MALO
RUE DU GEN. DE GAS
RUE DES URSULINES
R. GEMAS DU HOMME
RUE DES BOUCHERS
RUE ST-LAURENT
RUE FOCH
AVENUE CONSEIL
RUE DE LA JURIDICTION
RUE FRANCHE
RUE ST-MARTIN
RUE DES CUISINIERS
RUE LARCHER
RUE DE LA CAVE
PLACE
CHARLES
DE GAULLE
RUE DES TERRES
RUE BOURBESNEUR
MAHB
RUE AUX COQS
RUE ST-JEAN
RUE DE VERDUN
RUE DE LA POTERIE
R. DES CHANOINES
RUE L. LE
FORESTIER
Cathédrale
Notre-Dame
RUE DU PETIT ROMAN
Caen
British War
Cemetery
BOULEVARD FABIEN WARE
RUE DES MARETTES
RUE DES CORDELIERS
RUE ST-LOUP
RUE TARDIF
Centre Guillaume
Le Conquérant
(Bayeux Tapestry)
RUE DE NESMOND
RUE ST-EXUPÉRÉ
RUE DE CRENEL
RUE BELLEVUE
Musée Mémorial
de la Bataille
de Normandie
RUE SEC DE NORMAND
RUE DU CLOS NORMAND
BOULEVARD MARECHAL LECLERC
BOULEVARD SADI CARNOT
Gare
SNCF
0   200
metres
Saint Lô

ACCOMMODATION

D'Argouges	3
Camping des Bords de l'Aure	1
Churchill	5
De la Gare	8
Lion d'Or	6
Mogador	2
Reine Mathilde	4
Villa Lara	7

RESTAURANTS

L'Insolite	1
P'tit Resto	4
Petit Normand	5
Pommier	2
Rapière	3

Germans had got over their surprise – that it escaped serious damage, and briefly became capital of Free France.

Bayeux Tapestry

13bis rue de Nesmond • Daily: first week of Jan, Feb to mid-March & mid-Nov to Christmas 9.30am–12.30pm & 2–6pm; mid-March to April & Sept to mid-Nov 9am–6.30pm; May–Aug 9am–7pm; closed last 3 weeks of Jan; last admission 45min before closing • €9; €12 with either MAHB or Musée Mémorial de la Bataille de Normandie; €15 with both • ☎ 02 31 51 25 50, ⊕ bayeuxmuseum.com

A grand eighteenth-century seminary, remodelled as the **Centre Guillaume le Conquérant**, houses the extraordinary **Bayeux Tapestry**. Unexpectedly, and unceremoniously, the first thing you see on entry is the tapestry itself, with an interesting audio-guided commentary to explain the events it so vividly depicts. Only afterwards comes an exhibition and film show that tell you more about it.

Known to the French as the *Tapisserie de la Reine Mathilde*, the tapestry is a seventy-metre strip of linen that was created over nine centuries ago to recount the story of the Norman Conquest of England. The brilliance of its coloured wools has barely faded, and the tale is enlivened throughout with scenes of medieval life, popular fables and mythical beasts. Technically, it's not really a tapestry at all, but an embroidery; the skill of its draughtsmanship, and the sheer vigour and detail, are stunning. The work is thought to have been carried out by nuns in England, commissioned by Bishop Oddo, William's half-brother, in time for the inauguration of Bayeux Cathedral in 1077.

2

The tapestry looks, and reads, much like a comic strip, though it has a strong three-dimensional presence that you might not expect from all the flat reproductions. While it's considered to be historically accurate, William's justification for his invasion – that during an enforced sojourn after he was rescued by William following a shipwreck on the Normandy coast, Harold had sworn to accept him as King of England – remains in dispute. In the tapestry itself, Harold is every inch the villain, with his dastardly little moustache and shifty eyes. At the point when he breaks his oath and seizes the throne, Harold looks extremely pleased with himself; however, his comeuppance swiftly follows, as William crosses the Channel and defeats the English armies at Hastings.

Although the tapestry is such an effective piece of propaganda that Napoleon exhibited it in Paris – to show that a successful invasion of England was indeed possible – much of the pleasure of viewing it comes from its incidental vignettes of contemporary life. The captions that accompany each major scene are of course in Latin, but you only need the faintest smattering of the language to make sense of what's going on, and in any case, audio headsets offer a concise commentary. The saga comes to an abrupt end immediately after the turmoil, carnage and looting of the Battle of Hastings, and of course the death of Harold (who may or may not be the figure with an arrow in his eye).

Cathédrale Notre Dame

Daily: Jan–March 9am–5pm; April–June & Oct–Dec 9am–6pm; July–Sept 9am–7pm · Free

The **Cathédrale Notre Dame**, the first home of the Bayeux Tapestry, is a short and very obvious walk away from its latest resting place. Despite such eighteenth-century vandalism as the fungoid baldachin that flanks the pulpit, Bishop Oddo's original Romanesque plan remains intact, for the most part sensitively merged with Gothic additions. The crypt, entirely original, is particularly wonderful, with its frescoes of angels playing trumpets and bagpipes, looking exhausted by their eternal performance. Along the nave is some tremendous twelfth-century sculpture, and you shouldn't miss the beautifully carved wooden choir stalls. The tiled floor of the chapterhouse features a fifteenth-century maze depicting the road to Jerusalem.

The courtyard that adjoins the northern facade of the cathedral is dominated by the **Liberty Tree**, a 200-year-old plane tree planted with much Revolutionary rejoicing in 1797.

MAHB – Musée d'Art et d'Histoire Baron Gérard

137 rue du Bienvenu · Daily: first week of Jan, mid-Feb to April & Oct–Dec 9.30am–12.30pm & 2–6pm; May–Sept 9.30am–6.30pm; closed early Jan to mid-Feb; last admission 45min before closing · €7; €12 with either Tapestry or Musée Mémorial de la Bataille de Normandie; €15 with both · ☎ 02 31 92 14 21, ⊚ bayeuxmuseum.com

Alongside the cathedral, and incorporating the former palace of the archbishops of Bayeux as well as modern extensions, the **Musée d'Art et d'Histoire Baron Gérard**, or **MAHB** for short, is a large museum complex that covers local history from prehistoric axe-heads up to the present, and also includes the city's fine-art collection.

It's a slightly odd assortment, made all the more peculiar because it makes no mention of the one thing everyone knows about Bayeux – the Tapestry. All in all, though, there's plenty here to like, from the easily missed private chapel of the bishops in the old building, with its wood panelling and ceiling frescoes, to the very fancy displays of "bobbin" lace and drawers filled with butterflies in the new part.

Paintings on display include works by Eugène Boudin, while in one room visitors can lift large leather flaps to reveal lithographs by Matisse, Bonnard and Utrillo. You'll even find a Sioux peace pipe and some Inuit boots, brought home by a nineteenth-century explorer.

Musée Mémorial de la Bataille de Normandie

Boulevard Fabian Ware • Daily: mid-Feb to April & Oct–Dec 10am–12.30pm & 2–6pm; May–Sept 9.30am–6.30pm; closed Jan to mid-Feb • €6; €12 with either Tapestry or MAHB; €15 with both • ☎ 02 31 51 46 90, ⓦ bayeuxmuseum.com

Set behind massive guns, next to the ring road on the southwest side of town, Bayeux's **Musée Mémorial de la Bataille de Normandie** provides a readily accessible, visceral and highly visual, overview of the Battle of Normandy. Rather than endless military hardware, it's filled with colour photos, maps and display panels that trace the development of the campaign, with especially good sections on German counter-attacks and the role of the press.

It also includes an account of the career of **Général de Gaulle**, who for many years had his own museum in Bayeux to commemorate the fact that this was the first place he landed in Free France, on June 14, 1944. That visit was a day-trip undertaken in the face of opposition from the Allied commanders; his arrival was so unexpected that the first two civilians he encountered, two policemen wheeling their bicycles, failed to recognize him.

The understated and touching **British War Cemetery** stands immediately across the road (see p.113).

ARRIVAL AND INFORMATION

BAYEUX

By train The *gare SNCF* is a 15min walk southeast of the town centre, just outside the ring road.

Destinations Caen (very frequent; 20min); Cherbourg (6 daily; 55min); Dol (6 daily; 2hr).

By bus Buses stop both at the *gare SNCF* and across town, on the north side of place St-Patrice.

Destinations Arromanches (6 daily; 20min); Courseulles (4 daily; 40min); Grandcamp-Maisy (6 daily; 45min);

Port-en-Bessin (5 daily; 20min).

Tourist office In the former fish market on the arched pont St-Jean, in the town centre (Jan–March, Nov & Dec Mon–Sat 9.30am–12.30pm & 2–5.30pm, Sun 10am–1pm & 2–5.30pm; April–June, Sept & Oct Mon–Sat 9.30am–12.30pm & 2–6pm, Sun 10am–1pm & 2–6pm; July & Aug Mon–Sat 9am–7pm, Sun 9am–1pm & 2–6pm; ☎ 02 31 51 28 28, ⓦ bayeux-bessin-tourisme.com).

ACCOMMODATION

D'Argouges 21 rue St-Patrice ☎ 02 31 92 88 86, ⓦ hotel-dargouges.com. Quiet, central and very stylish eighteenth-century building, with an imposing courtyard entered via an archway on the west side of place St-Patrice, and a well-kept garden around the back. Several rooms are very grand, with magnificent exposed wooden beams; all have bath plus shower. No restaurant. **€140**

Camping des Bords de l'Aure Boulevard d'Eindhoven ☎ 02 31 92 08 43, ⓦ camping-bayeux.fr. Large three-star municipal campsite, near the river on the northern ring road (RN13). Well-shaded tent sites, rental cabins, and free access to the local swimming pool alongside. Closed early Nov to early April. **€14.10**

★**Churchill** 14–16 rue St-Jean ☎ 02 31 21 31 80, ⓦ hotel-churchill.fr. Perfectly situated in the heart of town, with its own free parking, this beautifully furnished 32-room hotel has no restaurant, but offers personal and friendly service plus a daily return shuttle to Mont-St-Michel, costing €60, in conjunction with its sister hotel, *Villa Lara*. Closed Dec to mid-Feb. **€125**

De la Gare 26 place de la Gare ☎ 02 31 92 10 70, ⓦ hotel-delagare-bayeux.fr. Set beside the station, a 15min walk from the cathedral, this is a basic but perfectly adequate hotel, with fourteen en-suite rooms (showers not baths) and a simple brasserie. Tours of D-Day beaches arranged through Normandy Tours (see p.112), who are based here. **€44**

Lion d'Or 71 rue St-Jean ☎ 02 31 92 06 90, ⓦ liondor-bayeux.fr. Grand old coaching inn, dating from 1734 and affiliated to the "Relais du Silence" organization, that's set back behind a courtyard just beyond the pedestrianized section of rue St-Jean. The rooms themselves are brighter and newer than the exterior suggests; the one snag is that there's no parking. Dinner menus from €28, lunch from €15. Hotel closed mid-Dec to late Jan. Restaurant closed for lunch on Mon, Tues & Sat. **€109**

Mogador 20 rue Chartier ☎ 02 31 92 24 58, ⓦ hotel-mogador-bayeux.fr. Friendly little hotel facing Bayeux's main square, with free parking alongside; the fourteen varied rooms are simple but very presentable, with the quieter ones overlooking the inner courtyard. Some sleep three or four. **€62**

Reine Mathilde 23 rue Larcher ☎ 02 31 92 08 13, ⓦ hotel-reinemathilde.com. Simple but well-equipped en-suite rooms backing onto the canal, between the Tapestry and the cathedral. There's a nice open-air brasserie/crêperie downstairs. **€85**

Villa Lara 6 place du Québec ☎ 02 31 92 00 55, ⓦ hotel-villalara.com. A new luxury hotel, tucked into a peaceful square close to the Tapestry. All its 28 large, exceptionally comfortable rooms enjoy cathedral views; there's no restaurant, but staff prepare and serve excellent breakfasts. A mini-van makes the day-trip to Mont-St-Michel daily for €60. **€270**

EATING AND DRINKING

L'Insolite 16 rue des Cuisiniers ☎ 02 31 51 71 16. Cheap but chic crêperie serving an imaginative range of savoury galettes, with flavours such as salmon with *crème fraiche* (€8), followed by sweet crêpes. Set menus at €16 and €21. Tues–Sun noon–2pm & 7–9.30pm.

P'tit Resto 2 rue du Bienvenu ☎ 02 31 51 85 40, ⓦ restaurantbayeux.com. Stylish contemporary restaurant all but across from the cathedral, where the "creative cuisine" extends to veal chop fried in wasabi, and rolled monkfish with tandoori stuffing. Menus from €16 at lunch, €22 at dinner. Mon–Sat noon–2pm & 7–9.30pm, closed Mon in low season.

Le Petit Normand 35 rue Larcher ☎ 02 31 22 88 66. Below the cathedral, offering good traditional cooking, with seafood specialities and local cider. Lunch menus

from €16, dinner from €21.50. Mon–Sat noon–1.30pm & 7–9.30pm; closed mid-Dec to Jan.

Pommier 38–40 rue des Cuisiniers ☎ 02 31 21 52 10, ⓦ restaurantlepommier.com. Traditional restaurant that spreads through two buildings close to the cathedral, with terrace seating all the way along. Meat- and dairy-rich Norman cuisine on menus from €15 (lunch only) up to €39.50, including an all-vegetarian option from €25. Daily noon–2.30pm & 7–9.30pm; closed Nov to mid-March.

★ **Rapière** 53 rue St-Jean ☎ 02 31 21 05 45, ⓦ larapiere .net. Hidden away just off the main pedestrianized street, this cosy little restaurant feels as though it's been here forever – certainly its old-fashioned Norman cooking remains as dependable as ever, on copious €29, €40 and €50 dinner menus. Tues–Sat noon–1.30pm & 7–9.30pm.

The D-Day Beaches

At dawn on **D-Day**, June 6, 1944, Allied troops landed at points along the Norman coast from the mouth of the Orne to the eastern Cotentin Peninsula. For the most part, the shoreline here consists of innocuous beaches backed by gentle dunes, and yet this foothold in Europe was won at the cost of 100,000 lives. The various beaches are still often referred to by their wartime code names. The British and Commonwealth forces landed on **Sword**, **Juno** and **Gold** beaches between Ouistreham and Arromanches; the Americans, further west on **Omaha** and **Utah** beaches.

That the invasion happened here, and not nearer to Germany, was partly due to the failure of the Canadian raid on Dieppe in 1942 (see p.48), which demonstrated the even more appalling casualties that would have resulted from an assault on a cliff-dominated coastline. The ensuing **Battle of Normandy** killed thousands of civilians and reduced nearly six hundred towns and villages to rubble, but within a week of its eventual conclusion, Paris was liberated.

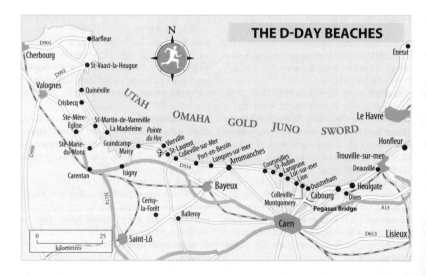

WAR MUSEUMS

The events of 1944 still draw countless visitors to lower Normandy. Few substantial traces of the actual fighting on D-Day now remain, apart from at the **Pointe du Hoc** (see p.118), where the cliff heights are still deeply pitted with German bunkers and shell-holes, and **Arromanches** (see p.116), where the ruins of the vast prefabricated Mulberry harbour will take centuries to disappear.

However, **museums** and **monuments** are opening at a faster rate than ever. No single museum or site can tell the whole story of the invasion, but the largest and most significant ones are listed below.

2

Caen Caen Memorial (see p.103)
Bayeux Musée Mémorial de la Bataille de Normandie (see p.109)
Ouistreham Musée du Mur de l'Atlantique (see p.112)
Ouistreham Musée No 4 Commando (see p.112)
Ranville-Bénouville Mémorial Pegasus (see p.112)
Courseulles Centre Juno Beach (see p.114)
Arromanches Musée du Débarquement (see p.116)
Arromanches Arromanches 360 (see p.117)
Longues-sur-Mer La Batterie de Longues-sur-Mer (see p.117)
Port-en-Bessin Musée des Épaves Sous-Marines du Débarquement (see p.118)

St-Laurent Omaha Beach Museum (see p.118)
Grandcamp-Maisy Batterie de Maisy (see p.119)
Grandcamp-Maisy Musée des Rangers (see p.119)
Catz Normandy Tank Museum (see p.119)
St-Côme-du-Mont Centre Historique des Parachutistes (see p.120)
Ste-Marie-du-Mont Musée du Débarquement d'Utah-Beach (see p.120)
Quinéville Mémorial de la Liberté Retrouvée (see p.120)
Crisbecq Musée de la Batterie de Crisbecq (see p.120)
Ste-Mère-Église Musée Airborne (see p.121)
Cherbourg Musée de la Libération (see p.124)

Even if the events of D-Day are not your primary reason for visiting, the towns and villages offer their own rewards. They are traditional seaside resorts – old-fashioned villages, with rows of boarding houses and little wooden bathing huts. And of course the **beaches** themselves are great for young families, though **windsurfing** is better suited to these north-facing resorts than chilly bathing. Attractive seaside **hotels** are scattered all along the coast, typically with simple rooms upstairs above a large glass-fronted sea-view dining room.

GETTING AROUND
THE D-DAY BEACHES

By bus Bus Verts (☎08 10 21 42 14, ⊛busverts.fr) run all along this coast; for timetables, visit ⊛commentjyvais.fr. From Bayeux, bus #74 goes to Arromanches, Courseulles and Ouistreham, and bus #70 to the Pointe du Hoc, the US cemetery at Colleville-sur-Mer and Port-en-Bessin. From Caen, bus #30 runs inland to Bayeux, and bus #3 to Courseulles.

Ouistreham-Riva Bella

Although **OUISTREHAM-RIVA BELLA**, on the coast 15km north of Caen, has been connected by ferry with Portsmouth, England since 1986, it remains at heart a small seaside village. From the port itself at its eastern end, it's easy to drive straight out of town, on the fast dual carriageway towards Caen.

Head west instead from the place de Gaulle, immediately outside the terminal, and you'll soon come to the handful of charming old streets at the heart of the old town. The sea itself lies a couple of hundred metres north of here, along the semi-pedestrianized **Avenue de la Mer**, home to several inexpensive snack bars and restaurants. Strictly speaking, the waterfront, backing a long straight beach, is a separate community known as **Riva Bella**. Its large central **casino**, on place Alfred-Thomas, has been remodelled as a 1930s passenger liner, housing an

2

D-DAY TOURS

The Caen Memorial (see p.103) organizes bilingual **guided tours** of the beaches in summer (June–Aug Tues, Wed, Fri & Sat; departs 1pm; €39, ages 2–9 €30; ☎ 02 31 06 06 45, ⓦ memorial -caen.fr); the price includes admission to the Memorial, which doesn't have to be on the same day, and to the 360° cinema in Arromanches.

Other operators offering D-Day tours, at typical prices of around €50/half-day and €90/day, include Normandy Sightseeing Tours (☎ 02 31 51 70 52, ⓦ normandy-sightseeing-tours.com), Victory Tours (☎ 02 31 51 98 14, ⓦ victorytours.com), and Normandy Tours (☎ 02 31 92 10 70, ⓦ normandy-landing-tour.com). All three are based in Bayeux, while D-Day Battle Tours (☎ 02 33 01 26 12, ⓦ ddaybattletours.com) start from Ste-Mère-Église.

---

expensive restaurant and cocktail bar, while gloriously old-fashioned bathing huts face onto the sands.

If you're **cycling** from Ouistreham, the obvious direction to take for a gentle start to your holiday is west along the coast, but if you head south towards Caen, you'll find the designated cycle path that follows the canal all the way to Caen city centre is far more pleasant than the main road.

Musée du Mur de l'Atlantique

Avenue du 6-Juin • Daily: Feb, March & Oct–Dec 10am–6pm; April–Sept 9am–7pm • €7.50 • ☎ 02 31 97 28 69, ⓦ normandiememoire.com

Housed in a lofty bunker – hence its alternative name, the Grand Bunker – the **Musée du Mur de l'Atlantique** was the headquarters of the several German batteries that defended the mouth of the River Orne; after brief resistance, it fell to Allied forces on June 9, 1944. Displays inside the heavily restored bunker recreate living conditions, with newspapers, cutlery and packets of cigarettes adding a welcome human touch to the moderately interesting explanations of the workings of the generators, gas filters and radio room.

Musée No 4 Commando

Place Alfred-Thomas • Daily mid-March to late Oct 10.30am–6pm • €5 • ☎ 02 31 96 63 10, ⓦ musee-4commando.org

Close to the casino, the **Musée No 4 Commando** details the story of the 117 Free-French commandos who landed at what's now Colleville-Montgomery on June 6, 1944; a documentary film covers their training as well as the actual invasion.

Pegasus Bridge

Five kilometres south of Ouistreham, the main road towards Caen passes close by the site now known as **Pegasus Bridge**. Just after midnight on the night before D-Day, the twin bridges here that cross the Caen canal and the River Orne were the target of a daring **glider assault**. Seizing them intact was a crucial Allied objective, because it both enabled the invaders to advance east along the coast and blocked potential German reinforcements. Three of the six Horsa gliders that were towed from Dorset, England, landed close enough for what was then Bénouville Bridge to be captured within half an hour, although Lieutenant Brotheridge, leading the charge, became the first British casualty of D-Day in the process.

Mémorial Pegasus

Avenue du Major Howard • Daily: Feb, March, & Oct to mid-Dec 10am–5pm; April–Sept 9.30am–6.30pm • €7 • ☎ 02 31 78 19 44, ⓦ memorial-pegasus.org

The original Pegasus Bridge, which was replaced in 1994, now spans a hole in the lawns outside the **Mémorial Pegasus** immediately east of its former site. This vaguely glider-shaped museum holds the expected array of helmets, goggles, medals and other memorabilia, most captioned in English, as well as various model bridges used in planning the attack, and a replica Horsa glider.

ARRIVAL AND INFORMATION

By boat Brittany Ferries connect Ouistreham with Portsmouth (2–3 daily; 6–8hr; ☎02 31 36 36 36, ⓦbrittany -ferries.com). Buses, timed to connect with each sailing, run to Caen.

OUISTREHAM-RIVA BELLA

Tourist office Esplanade Lofi, alongside the casino (April–June & Sept daily 10am–1pm & 2–6.30pm; July & Aug daily 10am–7pm; Oct–March Mon–Sat 10am–1pm & 2.30–5.30pm; ☎02 31 97 18 63, ⓦouistreham.fr).

ACCOMMODATION AND EATING

Ouistreham makes a perfectly pleasant place to spend a night before or after a ferry crossing. The little square right by the ferry terminal – which is neither by the sea nor particularly pretty, with nothing but car parking in the centre – holds a copious assortment of hotels, restaurants and *mouleries*, and there are more hotels near the beach in Riva Bella.

2

Normandie 71 av Michel-Cabieu ☎02 31 97 19 57, ⓦlenormandie.com. Faded but convenient hotel, just off the square that's closest to the ferry port, where the rooms are comfortable but a little thin-walled for light sleepers, and the restaurant (closed Sun eve, plus Mon Nov–March) serves good three-course menus from €27. Closed Jan. **€73**

De la Plage 39–41 av Pasteur ☎02 31 96 85 16, ⓦhotel-ouistreham.com. Bright, good-value rooms in an imposing red-brick villa, in a peaceful location barely 100m from the casino near the Commando museum. No restaurant. Closed Dec to mid-Feb. **€59**

St-Georges 51 av Andry ☎02 31 97 18 79, ⓦlesaint georges.fr. Spacious, well-equipped rooms near the casino, many with great sea views, plus a garden – complete with chickens – and good food on menus from €27. Closed three weeks in Jan. **€69**

THE WAR CEMETERIES

The World War II **cemeteries** that dot the Norman countryside are filled with foreigners; most of the French dead are buried in the churchyards of their home towns. After the war, some felt the soldiers should remain in the makeshift graves dug where they fell. Instead, their remains were gathered into cemeteries devoted to the separate warring nations. In total, over 140,000 young men were disinterred; more than half of the 31,744 US casualties were repatriated.

The 27 **British** and **Commonwealth** cemeteries are magnificently maintained, and open in every sense. They tend not to be screened off with hedges or walls, or to consist of endless expanses of manicured lawn, but are instead intimate, punctuated with bright flowers. The family of each soldier was invited to suggest an inscription for his tomb, making each grave very personal, and yet part of a common attempt to bring meaning to the carnage. Some epitaphs are questioning – "One day we will understand"; some are accepting – "Our lad at rest"; some matter-of-fact, simply giving the home address. Interspersed among them all is the chilling refrain of the anonymous: "A soldier… known unto God". Thus the cemetery outside **Ryes**, northeast of Bayeux, where so many graves bear the date of D-Day, and so many victims are under 20, remains immediate and accessible – each grave clearly contains a unique individual. Even the monumental sculpture is subdued, a very British sort of fumbling for the decent thing to say (to reach it, head 2km southeast of the village on the D87 towards Bazenville). The understatement of the memorial at **Bayeux**, with its contrived Latin epigram commemorating the return as liberators of "those whom William conquered", conveys deep humility and sadness.

What the **German** cemeteries might have been like had the Nazis won doesn't bear contemplation. As it is, they are sombre places, inconspicuous in order to minimize the bitterness they still arouse. At **Orglandes**, 10km south of Valognes on the Cotentin Peninsula, ten thousand lie buried, three to each of the plain headstones set in the long flat lawn, almost hidden behind an anonymous wall. There are no noble slogans and the plain entrance lacks a dedicatory monument. Another 21,000 Germans lie buried at **La Cambe**, just off the N13/E46 9km south of Grandcamp-Maisy, around a six-metre hill topped by an imposing granite cross. At the superb site of **Mont d'Huisnes**, 6km east of Mont-St-Michel, ten thousand more are filed away in the cold concrete tiers of a circular mausoleum. There is no attempt to defend the indefensible, and yet one feels an overpowering sense of sorrow – that there is nothing to be said in such a place bitterly underlines the sheer waste.

The largest **American** cemetery, at **Colleville-sur-Mer** near the Pointe du Hoc, and likely to be familiar from the opening sequences of *Saving Private Ryan*, is described on p.118.

Sword and Juno beaches

The coastline west of Ouistreham, along Sword and Juno beaches, is also known to the French as the **Côte de Nacre**. Although the landscape is predominantly flat and featureless, the towns themselves are welcoming. A long promenade curves by the sea all the way from Ouistreham to Lion – it's built up, though always in a low-key way, and makes a pleasant walk straight from the ferry.

Colleville-Montgomery, the first village after the port, is one of the few "Montgomeries" in the area to be named after the British general rather than his Norman ancestors. It's not otherwise distinguished.

Luc-sur-Mer

If you're looking for atmosphere – albeit sedate – **LUC-SUR-MER**, 11km from Ouistreham, has much to recommend it. It's a gentle resort with a small wooden pier, neon-lit crêpe-stands, and tearooms along the pedestrian promenade that runs parallel to its long straight beach.

Maison de la Baleine

45 rue de la Mer • April–June & Sept daily 3–6pm; July & Aug Mon–Sat 10am–12.30pm & 2.30–6.30pm, Sun 2.30–6.30pm • Free • ☎ 02 31 97 55 93, ⓦ maisondelabaleine.com

In the early hours of January 15, 1885, an enormous **whale** washed up on the beach at Luc-sur-Mer. A rorqual, measuring over nineteen metres from tip to tail, and twelve metres around what you might call its waist, it weighed forty tons, and not surprisingly caused an absolute sensation. Its skeleton is now displayed in the park in the heart of town; alongside, the **Maison de la Baleine** ("house of the whale") tells the whole story and provides copious information on whales in general.

Courseulles

COURSEULLES is a sizeable and lively yachting port, with an enjoyable Friday **market** in an old square set back from the sea, and, allegedly, the best oysters in Normandy.

Rather too many holiday apartments have been constructed in recent years, but the seafront remains recognizable as **Juno Beach**. This section of Norman coast was allocated to the fourteen thousand Canadian soldiers who took part in the D-Day landings; within ten days of its capture, Winston Churchill and King George VI visited the beach on morale-boosting excursions.

Centre Juno Beach

Daily: Feb, Nov & Dec 10am–1pm & 2–5pm; March & Oct 10am–6pm; April–Sept 9.30am–7pm; closed Jan; tours April, May, Sept & Oct daily 10.30am & 2.30pm; June–Aug daily 10.30am, 11.30am, 2.30pm & 4.30pm • €7, tours €5.50, or €11 with museum admission • ☎ 02 31 37 32 17, ⓦ junobeach.org

The **Centre Juno Beach**, next to Juno Beach, commemorates the Canadian contribution to World War II, focusing not so much on what happened at Juno itself as on every aspect of the Canadian war effort. In summer, the Centre also conducts **tours** of the ruins of the Atlantic Wall, down on the actual beach.

The beautiful **Canadian Cemetery**, which holds many of the 359 Canadians who died on D-Day itself, is 3km inland at **Bény-sur-Mer**, on flat ground from which you can see the sea.

INFORMATION SWORD AND JUNO BEACHES

LUC-SUR-MER
Tourist office Rue Docteur Charcot (mid-June to mid-Sept Mon & Thurs–Sat 9.30am–12.30pm & 2–7pm, Tues & Wed 9.30am–12.30pm & 2–6.30pm, Sun 10am–12.30pm & 2.30–6.30pm; ☎ 02 31 97 33 25, ⓦ luc-sur-mer.fr).

ACCOMMODATION AND EATING

LUC-SUR-MER

★**Beau Rivage** 1 rue Docteur Charcot ☎02 31 96 49 51, ⓦhotel-beaurivage-lucsurmer.fr. Rooms in Luc's most reasonably priced hotel, rose-coloured and splendidly sited right on the seafront, are comfortable enough, even if they aren't decorated in the most modern of styles. Sea views cost €20 extra. Dinner menus cost €19 or €27. Closed mid-Dec to mid-Jan. **€69**

La Capricieuse ☎02 31 97 34 43, ⓦcamping lacapricieuse.com. This large four-star campsite doesn't have a pool, what with being just 50m from the beach, but there is a tennis court, and it also has rental cabins. Closed Oct–March. **€17.55**

Des Thermes et du Casino 3 rue Guynemer ☎02 31 97 32 37, ⓦhotelresto-lesthermes.com. This grand-looking hotel, towards the western end of the seafront, has seen better days, and the decor is fading, but those rooms that have large sea-view balconies only cost a little more than the standard ones, and there's a heated pool in the garden around the back. Closed mid-Nov to mid-March. **€110**

LANGRUNE

De la Mer 2 rue de la Mer ☎02 31 96 03 37, ⓦhotel restaurantdelamer.com. Virtually on the beach, this tastefully renovated hotel has nine small but pleasant, good-value rooms and a nice sea-view restaurant serving seafood-rich menus from €22 to €44. **€65**

ST-AUBIN-SUR-MER

Clos Normand 89 rue Louis Pasteur ☎02 31 97 30 47, ⓦclosnormandhotel.com. Large, peaceful ivy-covered hotel, stretching from the main road all the way to the pedestrian beachside promenade, with small but attractive rooms and rather thin walls. Its restaurant spreads onto a separate terrace on the beach itself and serves three- to eight-course menus at €27.50–70. Closed Jan to mid-Feb. **€85**

COURSEULLES

Crémaillère-Le-Gytan 23–25 av de la Combattante ☎02 31 37 46 73, ⓦla-cremaillere.com. The pick of Courseulles' small array of hotels, with the best sea views, and pleasant rooms, a number of them in a nearby beachfront annexe (where some face the garden). The restaurant serves menus at €25–56, and specializes in scallops. **€98**

La Pêcherie 7 place du 6 Juin ☎02 31 37 46 73, ⓦla-pecherie.fr. This half-timbered hotel, just back from the sea, has quite a history, having been a station and a cinema. It now offers six jazzy modern rooms – some with startling purple decor, others with exposed stonework, and some squeezed in under the rafters – as well as a good restaurant, with a €19.50 menu and some unusual fish specialities at around €29.50. **€110**

Arromanches

While basically a little seaside village, **ARROMANCHES**, 13km west of Courseulles and 10km northeast of Bayeux, has the strongest identity of all the resorts along this stretch of shoreline. That's partly because it's given a clear geographical definition by the cliffs that rise to either side, finally breaking the monotonous flatness of the Côte de Nacre.

However, the real reason that it's become the centre of the D-Day tourism industry is that this was the location of the artificial **Mulberry harbour**, "Port Winston", that facilitated the landings of two and a half million men and half a million vehicles. Two of these prefab concrete constructions were built in segments in Britain, while "doodlebugs" blitzed overhead, then submerged in rivers away from the prying eyes of German aircraft, and finally towed across the Channel at 6kph as the invasion began. Meanwhile, the British 47 Royal Marine Commando were storming Arromanches itself to clear the way.

Arromanches is quite a cheerful place to stay, with a lively pedestrian street of bars and brasseries, and a long expanse of sand where you can rent windsurf boards.

Musée du Débarquement

Place du 6 Juin • Daily: Feb, Nov & Dec 10am–12.30pm & 1.30–5pm; March & Oct 9.30am–12.30pm & 1.30–5.30pm; April 9am–12.30pm & 1.30–6pm; May–Aug 9am–7pm; Sept 9am–6pm • €7.90 • ☎02 31 22 34 31, ⓦmusee-arromanches.fr

The seafront **Musée du Débarquement** recounts the story of Arromanches's role in the invasion by means of models, machinery and movies – and the evidence of your own eyes. A huge picture window stares straight out to where the bulky remains of the harbour stretch away along the coast, making a strange intrusion on the beach and shallow seabed. Its sheer scale is impossible to appreciate at this distance; for three months after D-Day, this was the largest port in the world. (The other such harbour, slightly further west on Omaha Beach, was broken up within two weeks by a huge storm, but this one was repairable.)

Arromanches 360

Chemin du Calvaire • Daily: Feb, March, & mid-Nov to Dec 10am–5.30pm; April & Oct to mid-Nov 10am–6pm; May–Sept 9.30am–7pm; closed Jan; shows at 10 and 40 minutes past each hour • €5 • ⓦ www.arromanches360.com

Perhaps the most striking of Arromanches's many war memorials is the statue of the Virgin Mary that's sited high on the cliffs above the invasion site (parking €4). Alongside, a steel dome contains **Arromanches 360**, a wraparound cinema which at half-hourly intervals, under the slogan of "eighteen minutes of total emotion", plunges viewers into the heart of the fighting. Despite the lack of contemporary footage, the effect, with the action running simultaneously on separate screens, is undeniably impressive.

2

INFORMATION   ARROMANCHES

Tourist office Just back from the sea at 2 rue Maréchal-Joffre (Feb, March, Nov & Dec daily 10am–noon & 2–5pm; April, Sept & Oct Mon–Sat 9.30am–12.30pm & 2–6pm, Sun 10am–12.30pm & 2–6pm; May–Aug daily 9.30am–12.30pm & 2–7pm; closed Jan ☎ 02 31 22 36 45, ⓦ ot-arromanches.fr).

ACCOMMODATION AND EATING

Arromanches 2 rue du Colonel René Michel ☎ 02 31 22 36 26, ⓦ hoteldarromanches.fr. Comfortable hotel, just back from the sea across the main square, with a variety of rooms in both traditional and contemporary styles; the *Pappagall* restaurant has menus from €16. **€97**

Camping Municipal av de Verdun ☎ 02 31 22 36 78, ⓦ arromanches.com. Spacious, well shaded two-star local campsite, 200m back from the seafront, with cabin rentals and playground but no swimming pool. Closed Nov–March. **€14.50**

★**La Marine** 1 quai du Canada ☎ 02 31 22 34 19, ⓦ hotel-de-la-marine.fr. At the centre of Arromanches's seafront, ideally placed for the D-Day sights and the beach, this comfortable hotel offers bright, sizeable, pastel-painted sea-view rooms and a high-class restaurant, sprawling through the entire ground floor, which serves fishy menus from €24.50. **€106**

Omaha Beach

West of Arromanches, and especially beyond Port-en-Bessin, the coastline becomes steadily hillier. As **Omaha Beach** it presented a stiff challenge to the American forces on D-Day. Stark reminders of the task they faced remain visible at the **Pointe du Hoc**, while the US cemetery at **Colleville-sur-Mer** holds over nine thousand American dead.

Longues-sur-Mer

Tours April, May, Sept & Oct Sat & Sun 10.15am, 11.45am, 2.15pm & 3.45pm; July & Aug daily 10.15am, 11.45am, 2.15pm & 3.45pm • €4 • ☎ 02 31 21 46 87, ⓦ bayeux-bessin-tourisme.com

Six kilometres west of Arromanches, a minor road leads 1.5km north of the village of **LONGUES-SUR-MER** to the best-preserved German defensive post to survive the war. **La Batterie de Longues-sur-Mer** consists of four concrete Nazi pillboxes, from which mighty gun barrels still point out across the Channel. Visitors are free to wander in and over the bunkers, and there are guided tours in English, French and German in summer.

Port-en-Bessin

PORT-EN-BESSIN, 11km west of Arromanches, and the nearest point on the coast to Bayeux (on bus route #70), has a thriving fishing industry and – rare on this coast – a sheltered, enclosed site. The fish, caught off Devon and Cornwall, are auctioned three times a week. Despite lacking a beach, it's a nice enough place, with an intriguing round watchtower at its eastern end.

Port-en-Bessin doesn't make an obvious base for visitors, though it does play host to a large food festival in early November, **Le Goût du Large**.

Musée des Épaves Sous-Marines du Débarquement

Route de Bayeux, Port-en-Bessin • May Thurs–Sun 10am–1pm & 2–7pm; June–Sept daily 10am–1pm & 2–7pm; Oct Sat & Sun 10am–1pm & 2–7pm • €6 • ☎ 02 31 21 17 06, ⓦ normandiememoire.com

A kilometre back from the sea in Port-en-Bessin, en route to Bayeux, the **Musée des Épaves Sous-Marines du Débarquement** displays miscellaneous artefacts salvaged from D-Day shipwrecks. Film and photos explain how they were brought back to the surface.

Normandy American Cemetery and Memorial

Outside Colleville-sur-Mer, above Omaha Beach, 21km west of Arromanches • Daily: mid-April to mid-Sept 9am–6pm; mid-Sept to mid-April 9am–5pm • Free • ☎ 02 31 51 62 00, ⓦ abmc.gov

The clifftop village of **COLLEVILLE-SUR-MER**, 7km west of Port-en-Bessin and not far from the Pointe du Hoc, marks the start of the long approach road to the larger of Normandy's two American war cemeteries. In the vast **Normandy American Cemetery and Memorial**, neat rows of crosses cover the clifftop lawns. There are no individual epitaphs, just gold lettering for a few exceptional warriors. At one end, a muscular giant dominates a huge array of battlefield plans and diagrams covered with surging arrows and pincer movements. Barack Obama is the latest of many US presidents to have paid his respects here; another president's son, General Theodore Roosevelt Jr, is among those buried.

A high-tech visitor centre explains the events of 1944 and the American role in them. Poignant multimedia displays focus on the personal angle, highlighting the stories of both casualties and survivors.

St-Laurent

At the first point west of the American cemetery where road access to the sea becomes possible – **ST-LAURENT**, 2.5km further on – a colossal flat beach stretches away beneath the cliffs. An abstract but evocative stainless-steel sculpture by French artist Anilore Banon, erected in 2004 and named *Les Braves*, emerges from the sands at its centre.

Omaha Beach Museum

St-Laurent • Daily: mid-Feb to mid-March 10am–12.30pm & 2.30–6pm; mid-March to mid-May & mid-Sept to mid-Nov 9.30am–6.30pm; mid-May to June & first fortnight of Sept 9.30am–7pm; July & Aug 9.30am–7.30pm; last admission 1hr before closing • €6.20 • ☎ 02 31 21 97 44, ⓦ musee-memorial-omaha.com

The small **Omaha Beach Museum**, 100m uphill from the seafront at St-Laurent, displays a fine assortment of photos taken on D-Day itself, but few artefacts of any interest.

Vierville

Immediately west of St-Laurent, **VIERVILLE**, like Arromanches, was chosen as a site for the building of an artificial harbour. Codenamed "Gooseberry" to Arromanches's "Mulberry", this one, however, only lasted thirteen days before breaking up in an unprecedented storm. A memorial to the US National Guard stands atop a ruined German pillbox where the road from the village proper drops down to the sea.

Pointe du Hoc

Site access Daily 24hr • Free • **Visitor centre** Daily: mid-April to mid-Sept 9am–6pm; mid-Sept to mid-April 9am–5pm • Free • ☎ 02 31 51 62 00, ⓦ abmc.gov

The most dramatic American landings took place along the cliff heights of the **POINTE DU HOC**, 6km west of Vierville, which are still today deeply pitted with German bunkers and shell-holes. Standing amid the scarred earth and rusty barbed wire, looking down to the rocks at the base of the cliff, it seems inconceivable that the first US sergeant was at the top five minutes after landing, and the whole complex taken within another quarter of an hour.

There's a small **visitor centre** next to the large car park, set well back from the cliffs, but access to the site, which legally belongs to the US, is free and unrestricted.

Grandcamp-Maisy

GRANDCAMP-MAISY, 3km west of Pointe du Hoc, was extensively damaged in the war. Centring on a compact fishing harbour, rebuilt in severe grey stone, it makes fewer concessions to tourism than its neighbours, but that somehow lends it a perverse, austere appeal. It's home to two **war museums**: the **Musée des Rangers** (mid-Feb to April daily except Mon 1–6pm; May–Oct Tues 1.30–6.30pm, Wed–Sun 10am–1pm & 2.30–6.30pm; €4.40; ⓦgrandcamp-maisy.fr) tells the story of the American landings at the Pointe du Hoc, while the **Batterie de Maisy** (April–Sept daily 10am–4pm; €6; ⓦmaisybattery.com), just off the D514 towards Isigny, is a secret German gun emplacement that was only rediscovered sixty years after the war.

2

ACCOMMODATION AND EATING

OMAHA BEACH

PORT-EN-BESSIN

De la Marine 5 quai Letourneur ⓣ02 31 21 70 08; ⓦhoteldelamarine.fr. Classic seaside hotel, with plain rooms but exceptionally comfortable beds – those with a view over the fishing port cost €15 extra – and a restaurant serving menus from €17. Closed second fortnight in Nov, plus three weeks in Feb. **€57**

ST-LAURENT-SUR-MER

D-Day House 1 rue Désiré Lemier ⓣ02 31 92 66 49, ⓦd-dayhouse.com. Overlooking the beach, with fourteen comfortable rooms, many with sea-view balconies, a pool and a terrace restaurant with menus from €12. **€70**

La Sapinière 100 rue de la 2ième-Infanterie ⓣ02 31 92 71 72, ⓦla-sapiniere.fr. Modern hotel facing Omaha Beach, where rooms are grouped in twos and threes in wooden cabins, and each has its own terrace area, plus a good brasserie/restaurant. Closed Nov to mid-March. **€90**

VIERVILLE

Du Casino bd de Cauvigny ⓣ02 31 22 41 02. Logis de France right on Omaha Beach, surveying the scene from the foot of the cliff. The rooms are a little faded but have been refurbished with modern bathrooms, and there's a restaurant and snack bar. Closed mid-Nov to March. **€126**

GRANDCAMP-MAISY

Belle Marinière 9 rue Petit Maisy ⓣ02 31 22 61 23. Simple, friendly, old-fashioned restaurant, a minute's walk back from the seafront, serving classic cuisine like your grandmother would have made, had she only been Norman, on menus from €19. Roasted oysters in a cream and cheese sauce, ham in cider, and a *salade paysanne* that's a meal in itself. Daily 11.45am–1.30pm & 7.45–10pm; closed Dec & Jan.

Camping du Joncal quai du Petit Nice ⓣ02 31 22 61 44, ⓦcampingdujoncal.com. Large, well-shaded three-star seafront campsite, immediately west of the harbour, with no pool. Very unusually, it's first-come, first-served; reservations are not accepted. Closed Oct–March. **€17.70**

Duguesclin 4 quai Crampon ⓣ02 31 22 64 22, ⓦleduguesclin.eu. Small hotel just east of the port, where a panoramic sea-view dining room serves menus from €15, though most of the accommodation is in the annexe behind. Closed Mon in winter, plus all Jan. **€70**

La Marée 5 quai Henri-Charon ⓣ02 31 21 41 00, ⓦrestolamaree.com. Nice restaurant, facing the port, with some outside tables, and a recommended €27 menu that features roasted scallops as starter and/or main course. Daily noon–2pm & 7–10pm; closed Jan to mid-Feb.

Isigny-sur-Mer and Carentan

A marshy inlet, at the mouths of several small rivers, separates Omaha Beach from Utah Beach. Two unremarkable market towns stand a dozen kilometres apart here, each set well back from the sea. **ISIGNY-SUR-MER**, 11km southwest of Grandcamp-Maisy at the western edge of the *département* of Calvados, is renowned for producing Normandy's butter, while **CARENTAN** is also best known as a centre of dairy farming.

Normandy Tank Museum

Avenue du Cotentin, Catz • Daily: Feb, March, Nov & Dec 10am–5pm; April–Oct 9am–6pm; closed Jan • €9 • ⓣ02 33 44 39 45, ⓦnormandy-tank-museum.fr

Halfway between Isigny-sur-Mer and Carentan, the **Normandy Tank Museum** fills a former World War II airfield at Catz with a huge array of tanks and armoured vehicles. For groups of five or more, it's even possible to take a ride in a small tank.

2

Centre Historique des Parachutistes du Jour-J

2 village de l'Amont, St-Côme-du-Mont • May–Sept daily 9am–6pm; Oct–April Mon–Sat 9am–6pm • €5.95 • ☎ 02 33 42 00 42,
Ⓦ paratrooper-museum.org

Four kilometres north of Carentan on the D974, just south of Saint-Côme-du-Mont, the **Centre Historique des Parachutistes du Jour-J** centres on a house that acted on June 6, 1944 as the HQ for German paratroopers, and passed that day into the hands of US paratroopers of the 101st Airborne Division. Marking a crucial road junction between the battlefields, this spot became known as **Dead Man's Corner**, and the museum itself also uses that name.

Utah Beach

The westernmost of the Invasion Beaches, **Utah Beach** stretches up the eastern shore of the Cotentin Peninsula, running 30km north towards St-Vaast (see p.127). Operations here on D-Day started at 4.30am, with the capture of the uninhabited **Îles St-Marcouf**, clearly visible 6km offshore; from 6.30am onwards, 23,000 men and 1700 vehicles landed on the beach itself. A minor coast road, the D421, traces the edge of the dunes and enables visitors to follow the course of the fighting, though in truth there's precious little to see these days. Ships that were deliberately sunk to create artificial breakwaters are still visible at low tide, while markers along the seafront commemorate individual fallen heroes.

Musée du Débarquement d'Utah-Beach

Ste-Marie-du-Mont • Daily: June–Sept 9.30am–7pm; Oct–May 10am–6pm; last admission 45min before closing • €8 • ☎ 02 33 71 53 35,
Ⓦ utah-beach.com

The single best opportunity to learn about the Utah Beach landings comes at the southern end of the D421, in **STE-MARIE-DU-MONT**. Built over a former German bunker, the **Musée du Débarquement d'Utah-Beach** explains operations in exhaustive detail, with huge sea-view windows to lend immediacy to its copious models, maps, films and diagrams. Visitors can sit in a genuine landing vehicle, while the foaming surf is at high tide just a few metres away.

Mémorial de la Liberté Retrouvée

18 av de la Plage • Quinéville • Daily: April, May, Sept, and two weeks around start of Nov 10am–1pm & 1.30–7pm; June–Aug
10am–7pm; closed first 3–4 weeks of Oct plus mid-Nov to March • €7 • ☎ 02 33 95 95 95, Ⓦ memorial-quineville.com

At the northern end of the D421, in **QUINÉVILLE**, the **Mémorial de la Liberté Retrouvée** is a museum that focuses on the everyday life of Normandy under Nazi occupation. Its central reconstruction of a village street is adorned with German posters announcing the strict nightly curfew, or offering a 30,000-franc reward for anyone turning in a saboteur. Displays covering their American liberators include some fine shots of aircrews sporting Mohican haircuts. All the captions and explanations are in French only, but there's so much to look at and absorb – including, it has to be said, the fact that many of the mannequins clearly started life as fashion dummies – that non-Francophones are unlikely to mind.

Musée de la Batterie de Crisbecq

Route des Manoirs • Daily: April, Oct & Nov 11am–6pm; May, June & Sept 10am–6pm; July & Aug 10am–7pm; closed Dec–March • €7 •
☎ 06 68 41 09 04, Ⓦ batterie-marcouf.com

Four kilometres south of Quinéville, heading inland from the coast road towards **Crisbecq** soon brings you to the **Musée de la Batterie de Crisbecq**, where you can visit a complex of German bunkhouses, connected by trenches and now inhabited by mannequins.

Ste-Mère-Église

These days, the market town of **STE-MÈRE-ÉGLISE**, a short way inland from Utah Beach on the main road between Valognes and Carentan, seems to attract more D-Day tourists than any other town. Its church was immortalized in the film *The Longest Day*, thanks to scenes of an unfortunate US paratrooper dangling from its steeple during the heavy fighting. That incident was based on fact, and the man in question, John Steele, used to return occasionally to re-enact and commemorate his ordeal. He's now dead, but a uniformed mannequin is permanently entangled on the roof in his stead. The new stained glass above the main door of the church also depicts American parachutists, surrounding the Virgin and Child.

Musée Airborne

2

14 rue Eisenhower • Daily: Feb, March & Oct–Dec 10am–5pm; April–Sept 9am–6.45pm; closed Jan • €7 • ☎ 02 33 41 41 35, ⓦ airborne-museum.org

Just behind Ste-Mère's central church, the approximately parachute-shaped **Musée Airborne** (Airborne Troops Museum) tells the story of the landings, complete with tanks, jeeps, and even a troop-carrying plane.

INFORMATION
UTAH BEACH

STE-MÈRE-ÉGLISE
Tourist office Facing the church at 6 rue Eisenhower (April–June Mon–Sat 9am–1pm & 2–6pm, Sun 10am–1pm; July &

Aug Mon–Sat 9am–6.30pm, Sun 10am–4pm; Sept Mon–Sat 9am–1pm & 2–6pm; Oct–March Mon–Sat 9.30am–12.30pm & 1.30–5pm; ☎ 02 33 21 00 33, ⓦ ot-baieducotentin.fr).

ACCOMMODATION AND EATING

QUINÉVILLE
De la Plage 7 av de la Plage ☎ 02 33 21 43 54, ⓦ hotel delaplagequineville.com. A short way back from the beach, this hotel offers six plain but pleasant guest rooms and serves well-priced menus from €15. Closed Mon in winter. **€60**

STE-MARIE-DU-MONT
Camping La Baie des Veys Le Grand Vey ☎ 02 33 71 56 90, ⓦ campinglabaiedesveys.com. Small campsite, separated by a large hedge from the seafront, with verdant tent pitches plus assorted rental cabins and a lovely little brightly painted gypsy caravan, which just has room for a bed. There's no swimming in the sea at this point – the nearest beach is 6km away – but they do have a heated pool. Closed Oct–March. Camping **€24**, gypsy caravan **€55**

STE-MÈRE-ÉGLISE
Auberge John Steele 4 rue Cap de Laine ☎ 02 33 41 41 16, ⓦ aubergejohnsteele.com. This ivy-covered inn, just north of the church, offers seven simple rooms plus high-quality meals at €18.50–32. Closed Sun eve & all Mon, except July & Aug. **€59**

Du Six Juin 11 rue des Clarons ☎ 02 33 21 07 18, ⓦ hotel-du-6-juin.com. Simple, modern hotel behind the church, with friendly staff and clean rooms, but no restaurant. Closed Nov–Jan. **€61**

Sainte-Mère 8 rue Richedoux ☎ 02 33 21 00 30, ⓦ hotel-sainte-mere.com. Large and rather ugly modern *logis*, south of the centre at the intersection of the main street with N13, with sizeable, well-equipped rooms. The restaurant, *La Cotentine*, puts on buffet spreads of hors d'oeuvres and desserts; have both for €18, or either one with a main course for €21.50. **€72**

The Cotentin Peninsula

Hard against the frontier with Brittany, and cut off from the rest of Normandy by difficult marshy terrain, the **Cotentin Peninsula** has traditionally been seen as something of a backwater, far removed from the French mainstream. The local *patois* has a special pejorative word for "stranger", applied indiscriminately to foreigners, Parisians and southern Cotentins alike, while official disdain for the region might explain why the Cap de la Hague, the peninsula's westernmost tip, was chosen as the site for a controversial nuclear reprocessing plant. The Cotentin nonetheless makes a rewarding goal for travellers, and one that by sea at least is very easily accessible. Ferries from England and Ireland still dock at the peninsula's major port, **Cherbourg**, with a plethora of attractive little villages nestled amid the hills to both east and west.

The long western flank of the peninsula, with its flat beaches, serves as a prelude to **Mont-St-Michel**, with hill towns such as **Coutances** and **Avranches** cherishing historical

2

relics associated with the abbey. Halfway down, the approaches to the Baie du Mont-St-Michel are guarded by the walled port of **Granville**, a sort of small-scale mirror-image of Brittany's St-Malo.

Cherbourg

Though its heyday as a transatlantic passenger port is now long in the past, the sizeable town of **CHERBOURG** still makes an appealing place to arrive in France. Although many visitors head straight out and on, lured in part by the truly delightful little villages that lie within a few kilometres to either side, there's a lot to like about Cherbourg, both in its historic core, and also in the impressive **maritime museum** that's housed in its former Art Deco ferry terminal.

The **old town**, immediately west of the quayside, is an intriguing maze of pedestrian alleys that abounds in shops and restaurants. The tempting array of small shops and boutiques clustered round the place Centrale includes a place to buy the city's most

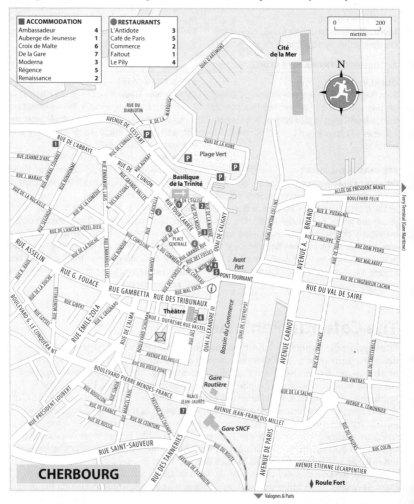

■ ACCOMMODATION		● RESTAURANTS	
Ambassadeur	4	L'Antidote	3
Auberge de Jeunesse	1	Café de Paris	5
Croix de Malte	6	Commerce	2
De la Gare	7	Faitout	1
Moderna	3	Le Pily	4
Régence	5		
Renaissance	2		

CHERBOURG

famous product, the genuine **Cherbourg umbrella**, at 30 rue des Portes, while the excellent Thursday **market** is held on and off rue des Halles, near the majestic theatre with its Belle Époque facade. A pleasant stroll north of the commercial zone leads to the Basilique de la Trinité and the former town beach, now grassed over to form the "Plage Vert".

It was Napoleon who inaugurated the transformation of what had previously been a rather poor, but perfectly situated, natural harbour into a major port, by means of massive artificial breakwaters. An equestrian statue commemorates his boast that in Cherbourg he would "recreate the wonders of Egypt".

2

La Cité de la Mer

Gare Maritime Transatlantique • Daily: May, June & Sept 9.30am–6pm; July & Aug 9.30am–7pm; Oct–Dec & Feb–April 10am–6pm, with variations including longer hours in school hols, and Mon closures in March, Nov & Dec; last entry 1hr before closing • €18 • ☎ 02 33 20 26 69, ⓦ citedelamer.com

Just across the pleasure port from the town centre, the **Cité de la Mer** maritime museum centres on Cherbourg's former trans-Atlantic ferry terminal. This massive Art Deco extravaganza opened in 1933 to serve what was then one of the world's greatest ports, and closed down in the 1970s. It's now divided into several sections, each large enough to rank as a major attraction in its own right. Allow at least half a day for a thorough visit.

The Titanic exhibition

The permanent **Titanic, Return to Cherbourg** exhibition opened in 2012, a hundred years after the *Titanic* called here for two hours on her maiden voyage. Almost three hundred passengers joined the ill-fated ship at Cherbourg, including John Jacob Astor IV, Benjamin Guggenheim, and "the unsinkable" Molly Brown. Rather than reconstruct the entire *Titanic*, superb mock-ups of her wireless room, mailroom, and a first-class cabin offer an "immersive experience" that fortunately stops short of a dunking in icy waters. A film simulation of the view from the upper decks shows the departure from Cherbourg and the collision itself.

Underwater exploration

A separate building tells the story of **underwater exploration** in history and fiction, ranging from Alexander the Great descending into the Bay of Bengal in a diving bell in 352 BC, via Jules Verne and H.P. Lovecraft, to Jacques Cousteau, pictured with his diving saucer "shaped like a giant lentil" in 1959. Various fish tanks hold species such as jellyfish, seahorses and large (though sadly not giant) squid, while walkways enable you to peer into a vast cylindrical aquarium at ever greater depths.

The Redoutable submarine

In a dry dock alongside the museum, the **Redoutable** was France's first ballistic-missile submarine. With an audio commentary from its former captain, visitors can scramble through its labyrinth of tube-like walkways and control rooms, though as the nuclear generator that once powered it has been removed, there's a cavernous empty space at its heart. The cramped crew quarters will feel very familiar if you've just shared a cabin on an overnight ferry crossing, while the plush carpeting and moulded chairs in the living room are remarkably reminiscent of Elvis's Graceland.

Walking into the Depths

Entry to the **Walking into the Depths** section, aimed primarily at children, is by timed admission. An over-long film explaining your "mission", to help an underwater explorer in his latest expedition, is followed by a ride in a submarine simulator. The whole experience lasts around 45 minutes, and culminates with a final "surprise".

Musée de la Libération

Fort du Roule • Feb–Nov Tues–Sat 10am–noon & 2–6pm, Sun 2–6pm; closed Jan & Dec • €4 • ☎ 02 33 20 14 12, ⊕ ville-cherbourg.fr

Southeast of the centre of the Cherbourg, you can climb up to the **Fort du Roule** for a view of the whole port. The fort itself contains the **Musée de la Libération**, which, with the usual dry maps and diagrams but also plenty of contemporary newsreel footage – much of it, for once, in English – commemorates the period in 1944 when, despite the massive destruction wrought by the Nazis before they surrendered, Cherbourg briefly became the busiest port in the world.

ARRIVAL AND INFORMATION
CHERBOURG

By ferry Brittany Ferries and Irish Ferries sail into Cherbourg's *gare maritime*, not far east of the town centre and served by regular shuttle buses.

Destinations Portsmouth (daily, late April to mid-Sept; 5hr) and Poole (daily; 4hr 15min), with Brittany Ferries (⊕ brittanyferries.com); Rosslare, with Irish Ferries (⊕ irish ferries.com; 3–4 weekly; 18hr 30min).

By train The *gare SNCF* is on av J-F Millet, a short walk south of the town centre.

Destinations Lison (12 daily; 45min), with connections to St-Lô (total 1hr 5min), and Coutances (1hr 40min);

Paris (7 daily; 3hr), via Valognes (15min) and Caen (1hr 15min).

By bus The *gare routière* is opposite the *gare SNCF*.

Destinations Barneville-Carteret (3–4 daily; 1hr 10min); Coutances (2 daily; 1hr 20min); St-Lô (3 daily; 1hr 30min), via Valognes (30min) and Carentan (1hr); St-Vaast (3 daily; 1hr 10min), via Barfleur (1hr).

Tourist office 2 quai Alexandre III (mid-June to mid-Sept Mon–Sat 9.30am–7pm, Sun 10am–5pm; mid-Sept to mid-June Mon–Sat 10am–12.30pm & 2–6pm, Sun 10am–1pm; ☎ 02 33 93 52 02, ⊕ cherbourgtourisme.com).

THE KEARSARGE AND THE ALABAMA

In June 1864, Cherbourg played host to one of the most extraordinary incidents of the **US Civil War** – a pitched **naval battle** between two rival warships, the Union *Kearsarge* and the Confederate *Alabama*.

The **Alabama** had been cruising the Atlantic for a year, harassing ships carrying supplies to the northern United States. By the time it docked at Cherbourg, it had captured, destroyed or held to ransom over eighty Yankee merchant vessels. The **Kearsarge**, meanwhile, had been prowling the coasts of Europe in pursuit; **Captain John A. Winslow** heard of the *Alabama*'s arrival while in Amsterdam, and was anchored off Cherbourg within two days.

Both vessels spent several days preparing for the inevitable duel. **Captain Raphael Semmes** of the *Alabama* – known as "Old Beeswax" – noted that "the combat will no doubt be contested and obstinate, but the two ships are so evenly matched that I do not feel at liberty to decline it". Cherbourg buzzed with excitement: its hotels filled with eager spectators brought by special trains from Paris, and hundreds more camped along the quaysides.

Sunday being Semmes' lucky day, he ordered the *Alabama* out of the harbour on the morning of Sunday June 12. At first, the *Kearsarge* seemed to retreat; then it turned, and charged the *Alabama* at full steam. The *Alabama* was the first to fire its guns. One shell lodged in the sternpost of the *Kearsarge*, but it failed to explode. Instead, a slow, steady barrage from the *Kearsarge* began to pound the *Alabama* to pieces.

To Captain Semmes' bewilderment, the *Alabama*'s shells kept bouncing off the *Kearsarge*. When it later transpired that the *Kearsarge* was lined below the water level with iron chains, he furiously expostulated that "It was the same thing as if two men were to go out and fight a duel, and one of them, unknown to the other, were to put on a suit of mail under his own garment".

Eventually, the doomed *Alabama* attempted to flee. Its escape was cut off, but Semmes himself managed to get away. As his ship went down, he whirled his sword above his head and flung it into the Channel, then leaped into the sea. Together with several members of his crew, he was picked up by a British holiday-maker who had watched the battle from his yacht, and taken to Southampton. Hailed by *The Times* as a "set of first-rate fellows", the defeated Confederates in due course managed to return home.

Captain Winslow – whose ship had suffered just three casualties, as opposed to the *Alabama*'s 43 – brought the *Kearsarge* into Cherbourg harbour after the battle. Their previous Confederate sympathies conveniently forgotten, the local citizens hailed him as a hero, before he made his way to a celebration banquet in Paris.

ACCOMMODATION

By Norman standards, room rates in Cherbourg are very reasonable. It makes a lively place to pass an evening – though the crowds and traffic can get a bit much, and the lack of daytime parking space is a problem for motorists. Few hotels maintain their own restaurants.

Ambassadeur 22 quai de Caligny ☎ 02 33 43 10 00, ⓦambassadeurhotel.com. Inexpensive, good-value central hotel on the quayside, with four storeys of en-suite rooms, many with harbour views (there's a lift). There are some good-value family rooms, and double-glazing keeps the noise down. Decent buffet breakfasts cost €9. **€60**

Auberge de Jeunesse 55 rue de l'Abbaye ☎ 02 33 78 15 15, ⓦfuaj.org/Cherbourg-Octeville. Well-equipped red-brick hostel, a 15min walk west of the centre and on bus routes #3 and #5. Two rooms are designed for visitors with limited mobility. Breakfast included. Check-in 9am–1pm & 6–11pm. Closed 3 weeks over Christmas and early Jan. **€21.50**

Croix de Malte 5 rue des Halles ☎ 02 33 43 19 16, ⓦhotelcroixmalte.com. Simple hotel on three upstairs floors, one block back from the harbour and around the corner from the theatre. Clean renovated rooms – all have TV and at least a shower – with the cheapest rates being for the windowless but perfectly acceptable ones in the attic. **€49**

De la Gare 10 place Jean Jaurès ☎ 02 33 43 06 81. This conspicuous blue-trimmed budget hotel is surprisingly quiet for such a convenient location, close to the *gares* SNCF and *routière*. The rooms may not be exactly stunning, but have en-suite facilities, and family-sized rooms are available. **€57**

Moderna 28 rue de la Marine ☎ 02 33 43 05 30, ⓦhotel-moderna.com. Friendly, small hotel, set slightly back from the harbour, with reasonably well-priced en-suite rooms of all sizes. **€66**

Régence 42 quai de Caligny ☎ 02 33 43 05 16, ⓦlaregence.com. Slightly more upmarket than Cherbourg's other offerings, with antique-style British furnishings, this family-run Logis de France has neat, well-equipped rooms overlooking the harbour. The dining room downstairs starts with a reasonable €19.50 menu, and ranges up to €36; it's not the best restaurant along the *quai*, but there's something to be said for eating where you sleep. **€82**

Renaissance 4 rue de l'Église ☎ 02 33 43 23 90, ⓦhotel-renaissance-cherbourg.com. Nicely refurbished rooms, all with either shower or bath and some with sea views, in a friendly hotel facing the port in the most appealing quarter of town. Garage parking available. The "Église" of the address is the attractive Trinité. **€77**

EATING AND DRINKING

Cherbourg's restaurants divide readily into the glass-fronted seafood places along the quai de Caligny, each with its "copious" *assiette de fruits de mer*, and the more varied, less expensive little places tucked away in the pedestrianized streets and alleyways of the Old Town. This is also where you'll find some animated bars, especially on rue de l'Union.

If you want to stock up on food or wine, your best bets for large-scale shopping are the Auchan hypermarket at the junction of RN13 and N13, south of town, or the Carrefour, on the southeast corner of the Bassin du Commerce.

L'Antidote 41 rue au Blé ☎ 02 33 78 01 28, ⓦrestaurant-cherbourg.com. Friendly little restaurant whose multi-coloured tables squeeze into a small courtyard just off the market square. As well as offering full dinner menus from €21.50, it's a good place to drop in for a quick daytime snack, with a dish of the day, such as *choucroute de la mer*, for €9.50, and some excellent desserts. The bar section stays open longer hours, serving cocktails. Tues–Sat 11.30am–3pm & 7–11pm.

Café de Paris 40 quai de Caligny ☎ 02 33 43 12 36, ⓦrestaurantcafedeparis.com. Diners at this grand Belle Époque café, with quayside tables, can savour fish-heavy menus (€22.50–39), or work their way up through the ranks of *assiettes de fruits de mer*, from the €21.50 *Matelot* to the *Corsaire* at €63.50 for two and the *Amiral* at €118. Mon 7–9pm, Tues–Sat noon–1.45pm & 7–9.45pm.

Commerce 42 rue François-la-Vieille ☎ 02 33 53 18 20, ⓦbrasserie-du-commerce.fr. If you're tired of white tablecloths and over-attentive service, this in-town brasserie, much larger than it looks from the outside, serves huge portions of good food from 11am until late, with cheap menus from €14 and plenty of à la carte options. The home-made pâté is recommended. Mon–Sat 11am–midnight.

★**Faitout** 25 rue Tour-Carrée ☎ 02 33 04 25 04, ⓦrestaurant-le-faitout.com. Stylish, faux-rustic, fishing-themed restaurant that offers traditional French cuisine, centring on local specialities such as scallops, with lunch for €19 and good dinner menus at €25 and €39, plus a seasonal all-lobster menu for €89. Reservations advised in summer. Mon 7.15–10pm, Tues–Sat noon–2pm & 7.15–10pm.

Le Pily 39 rue Grande Rue ☎ 02 33 10 19 29, ⓦrestaurant-le-pily.com. This tiny but smart little Michelin-starred restaurant, in the tangled heart of the old town, is a showcase for imaginative contemporary Norman cuisine, with a focus on fish and meat. Weekday lunch menu €29, dinner from €40.50. June–Sept Mon 7–9pm, Tues–Fri noon–1.45pm & 7–9pm, Sat 7–9pm; Oct–May Tues–Fri noon–1.45pm & 7–9pm, Sat 7–9pm, Sun noon–1.45pm.

East from Cherbourg: the Val de Saire

East from Cherbourg, the D901, which switchbacks through a series of pretty valleys, is the most direct route to the old ports of **Barfleur** and **St-Vaast**. Following the D116 along the coast, however – signposted throughout as the **Route du Val de Saire** – takes you past a succession of stunning viewpoints and some really lovely quasi-fortified villages, shielded from the sea winds by stout stone walls.

Abundant footpaths make this a great area for walking; one particularly appealing stroll leads five kilometres from the magnificent crescent bay of **L'Anse du Brick** to the stark but pretty little harbour of **Port-Levi**, near Fermanville.

Barfleur

Seven centuries ago, the pleasant little harbour village of **BARFLEUR**, 25km east of Cherbourg, was the biggest port in Normandy. The population has since dwindled from nine thousand to around six hundred, and fortunes have diminished alongside. It's now a low-key place, whose grey granite quayside and formal main street retain an appealing elegance that if anything is boosted by their relative austerity. Although the broad, sweeping crescent of the main harbour sees little tourist activity, clusters of tiny fishing vessels tie up alongside, and fresh fish is often for sale.

At the far left-hand end of the harbour, the stocky church of **St-Nicolas** stands in a tiny walled enclosure; it's worth looking inside to admire its chief treasure, a sixteenth-century *pietà*. A lichen-covered rock on the shoreline nearby commemorates the fact that, when William the Conqueror embarked for southern England in 1066, it was in a ship constructed at Barfleur – the *Mora* – and piloted by a Barfleurais, Étienne.

Gatteville lighthouse

Daily: Feb, first two weeks in Nov & last two weeks in Dec 10am–noon & 2–4pm; March & Oct 10am–noon & 2–5pm; April & Sept 10am–noon & 2–6pm; May–Aug 10am–noon & 2–7pm; closed mid-Nov to mid-Dec & all Jan • €3 • ☎ 02 33 23 17 97, ⓦ phare-de-gatteville.fr

Since 1834, the rock upon which prince William of England came to grief, north of Barfleur – see below – has been guarded by the **Gatteville lighthouse**. A pleasant footpath leads there in thirty minutes from town, starting beside what was in 1865 the first lifeboat station to be built in France. At 75m, the lighthouse is the second tallest in both France and Europe – the tallest is near L'Aber-Wrac'h in Brittany – with a beam that in reaching 50km overlaps with that of its opposite number on the Isle of Wight. Energetic visitors can climb the 365 steps to the top.

INFORMATION   **BARFLEUR**

Tourist office Next to the church (April–June & Sept Mon–Sat 10am–noon & 2–6pm; July & Aug daily 10am–noon & 2–6pm; Oct–March Tues–Sat 10am–noon & 2–5pm; ☎ 02 33 54 02 48, ⓦ ville-barfleur.fr).

DEATH OF AN ENGLISH PRINCE

On November 25, 1120, both King Henry I of England, and his 17-year-old son **William Aetheling**, the grandson of William the Conqueror and heir to the English throne, set sail from Barfleur to return home after a visit to France.

Each sailed in a different vessel, but young William spent the day drinking and carousing in Barfleur, and delayed his departure until after dark, confident that he would swiftly catch up with the rest of the English fleet. According to a contemporary account, his ship, the *Blanche Nef* "flew swifter than the winged arrow…but the carelessness of the intoxicated crew drove her onto a rock, which rose above the waves not far from the shore".

William reached the safety of a small lifeboat, but turned back to sea upon hearing the cries of his sister, and was **drowned** together with three hundred of his companions. The desolate Henry I was thus left without a male heir, which precipitated a period of strife over the succession known to historians as **The Anarchy**.

ACCOMMODATION AND EATING

Café de France 12 quai Henri Chardon ☎ 02 33 54 00 38. Good old-fashioned bistro on the northern side of the harbour, across from the sea near the church, and attracting devoted crowds of locals with a €13.50 *plat du jour*, and classic set menus at €18.50 and €23, featuring oysters followed by mussels, tripe or steak tartare. April–June & Sept daily except Wed 8am–7.30pm, July & Aug daily 8am–midnight.

★**Comptoir de la Presqu'Île** 30 quai Henri Chardon ☎ 02 33 20 37 51, ⓦ comptoirdelapresquile.overblog .com. Relaxed, friendly waterfront brasserie, with lots of seating both indoors and out. Seafood enthusiasts can opt for seafood platters at €34 and €48, or a substantial bowl of *moules Barfleuraise* for €10; mussels also feature on the one set menu, at €28, and there's occasional live jazz. Daily noon–2.30pm & 7.30–10pm.

★**Le Conquérant** 16–18 rue St-Thomas-à-Becket ☎ 02 33 54 00 82, ⓦ hotel-leconquerant.com. Welcoming family-owned hotel, set in an elegant old stone-built townhouse on the main street, a few steps inland from the harbour. Ten relatively simple rooms, of which the six that overlook the garden are larger and nicer, and have appealing Norman touches. No restaurant. Closed mid-Nov to mid-March. **€90.50**

La Ferme du Bord du Mer 23 rte du Val de Saire, Gatteville-le-Phare ☎ 02 33 54 01 77, ⓦ camping -gatteville.fr. This basic but appealing campsite, a couple of kilometres north of Barfleur, is exactly what its name suggests: a farm beside the sea, alongside a scruffy flat beach. As well as tent sites, it also has a few mobile homes for rent. **€13**

St-Vaast-la-Hougue

ST-VAAST-LA-HOUGUE, 11km south of Barfleur, is more of a resort, with lots of tiny Channel-crossing yachts moored in the bay where Edward III landed on his way to Crécy. It's still a fishing port as well, though, its quayside busy with men in oilskins washing down gleaming boatloads of squid and mussels.

The narrow spit of sand called **La Hougue**, south of the centre, holds various sporting facilities, such as tennis courts and a diving club, although the tip itself is a sealed-off military installation; the fortifications are graceful, courtesy (as ever) of the celebrated seventeenth-century military architect Vauban. The whole area is at its best at high tide; low tide reveals, especially on the sheltered inland side, bleak muddy flats dotted with some of the country's best-loved **oyster beds**.

Île Tatihou

Ferry tickets only available from Accueil Tatihou office on quai Vauban, St-Vaast • April–June, Sept & early Oct daily 10am–4pm; July & Aug daily 10am–7pm; late March Sat & Sun 1–4.30pm; Nov & Feb only during school hols • €6 return • ☎ 02 33 23 19 92, ⓦ tatihou.manche.fr

In 1692, a French and Irish army gathered at St-Vaast and set sail for Britain in an attempt to restore the deposed Stuart King James II to the English throne. However, the fleet was destroyed by a combined Anglo-Dutch force, before it could get any further than La Hougue. The battle took place just off the sandy flat island of **TATIHOU**, very close to the mainland, which now doubles as a bird sanctuary and the location of an ecologically minded **Musée Maritime** (daily 10am–12.45pm & 1.30–5.30pm; €9 with ferry).

A limited number of visitors each day are carried across to Tatihou by amphibious mud-wallowing "**ferries**" from St-Vaast; the exact schedule is determined by the state of the tides. It's also possible to **walk** to Tatihou when the tide is low enough; check at the same office for current advice.

Tatihou hosts a **folk-music festival**, the Festival des Traversées, during the first fortnight of each August.

INFORMATION   ST-VAAST

Tourist office | place Général-de-Gaulle, at the southern end of the seafront quai Vauban (July & Aug daily 10am–12.30pm & 2–6.30pm, Sept–June Tues–Sat 10am–noon & 2–6pm; ☎ 02 33 23 19 32, ⓦ ot-pointedesaire.com).

ACCOMMODATION AND EATING

ST-VAAST

De France et des Fuchsias 18 rue du Maréchal-Foch ☎ 02 33 54 40 41, ⓦ france-fuchsias.com. Sprawling back from the main road a few blocks short of the sea, this popular hotel has splendid gardens, and with rooms of all sizes and degrees of comfort it makes an ideal stopover for ferry passengers. The cheapest menu in the excellent restaurant, at €24, is reserved for guests only. Closed Jan, plus Mon in winter. €69

La Granitière 74 rue du Maréchal Foch ☎02 33 54 58 99, ⊚hotel-la-granitiere.com. A very nice hotel in a fine old townhouse, set in an attractive garden, offering nine spacious, brightly decorated rooms and buffet breakfasts. €89

TATIHOU

Hébergement du Tatihou Île de Tatihou ☎02 33 54 33 33, ⊚tatihou.manche.fr. The only accommodation on Tatihou is offered in this large hall-like building, not so very different from a university hall of residence, which holds 34 simple en-suite rooms that can sleep 1–3 people. Rates are per person, and include ferry and museum admission, plus breakfast and an evening meal. €89

Valognes

VALOGNES, around 18km through the woods from St-Vaast on the main road south from Cherbourg, is described in tourist handouts, with a dose perhaps of wishful thinking, as "the Versailles of Normandy". The tag might have had some meaning before the war, when the region was full of aristocratic mansions, but thanks to the bombing that preceded D-Day, only a scattering of fine old houses remain, along with the very scant ruins of a Gallo-Roman settlement called Alauna. Nonetheless, spending a few hours here is a quiet, convenient alternative to waiting around in Cherbourg, and the surrounding country lanes make for a pleasant stroll.

All Valognes has to show for itself is a big empty square, enlivened only for the Friday **market**, a little public garden, and a **cider museum** housed in an old watermill (April–June & Sept Mon & Wed–Sat 10am–noon & 2–6pm, Sun 2–6pm; July & Aug Mon–Sat 10am–noon & 2–6pm, Sun 2–6pm; Oct–March groups by appointment; €4.50; ☎02 33 40 22 73). The museum is crammed with bizarre old wooden implements and ancient warped barrels, including a particularly obscene example upstairs.

ACCOMMODATION AND EATING   **VALOGNES**

De l'Agriculture 18 rue L-Delisle ☎02 33 95 02 02, ⊚hotel-agriculture.com. This rambling, ivy-coated hotel is the best of several inexpensive options in Valognes. All the rooms are en suite, and its restaurant (closed Sun eve) serves top-quality food on menus that start at €18.50. €63

West from Cherbourg: the Cap de la Hague

The stretch of coast immediately west of Cherbourg is similar to that to the east, although it holds no harbour town to compare with Barfleur or St-Vaast. The main goal for most visitors is the windswept **Cap de la Hague** at its westernmost tip. However, the old villages of **Omonville-la-Petite** and **Omonville-la-Rogue**, 20km out of Cherbourg, are lovely places to stroll around, and all the way along you'll find wild and isolated countryside where you can lean against the wind, watch waves smashing against rocks or sunbathe in a spring profusion of wild flowers, while a whole range of activities are on offer.

The real drawback of the area around **Cap de la Hague** is that the discharges of "low-level" radioactive waste from the **nuclear reprocessing plant** may discourage you from swimming. In 1980, the Greenpeace vessel *Rainbow Warrior* chased a ship bringing spent Japanese fuel into Cherbourg harbour. The *Rainbow Warrior*'s crew were arrested, but all charges were dropped when three thousand Cherbourg dockers threatened to strike in their support. In the spring of 1985, the French secret service finally took their revenge on the *Rainbow Warrior* by sinking it in Auckland harbour, killing a member of the crew in the process.

The main road, the D901, continues a couple of kilometres beyond the plant to **GOURY**, where the fields finally roll down to a craggy pebble coastline, a splendidly windswept spot.

From the cape of **La Hague** itself, the northern tip of the peninsula, bracken-covered hills and narrow valleys run south to the cliffs of the **Nez de Jobourg**, claimed in wild local optimism to be the highest in Europe. South of that, a great curve of sand – some of it military training ground – takes the land's edge to **Flamanville** and another nuclear installation.

Château de Vauville

Vauville · April–June & Sept daily 2–6pm; July & Aug daily 2–7pm; Oct Sat & Sun 2–6pm · €7 · ☎ 02 33 10 00 00, ⓦ jardin-vauville.fr

Just north of Flamanville, in the picturesque village of **VAUVILLE**, the tropical-looking garden at the **Château de Vauville** is famed for its huge palm-grove, a sure sign of the area's mild microclimate.

INFORMATION
CAP DE LA HAGUE

Tourist office 45 rue Jallot, Beaumont-Hague (July & Aug Mon–Fri 9.30am–12.30pm & 2–5.30pm, Sat & Sun 10am–12.30pm; Sept–June Mon–Fri 9.30am–12.30pm & 2–5pm, Sat 10am–12.30pm; ☎ 02 33 52 74 94, ⓦ lahague-tourisme.com).

ACCOMMODATION AND EATING

URVILLE-NACQUEVILLE

★ **Le Landemer** 2 rue des Douanes ☎ 02 33 04 05 10, ⓦ le-landemer.com. This long-defunct seaside hotel, alongside the coastal footpath 12km west of Cherbourg, reopened in 2014 after a complete top-to-bottom restoration. Bright and very comfortable rooms, many with superb sea views, plus decked outdoor space and fine dining, with dinner at €39. **€139**

PORT RACINE

★ **L'Erguillère** Port Racine, St-Germain des Vaux ☎ 02 33 52 75 31, ⓦ hotel-lerguillere.com. Delightful, peaceful and very rural hotel, poised on a seafront hillside overlooking what's said to be the smallest port in France, as well as a gorgeous little beach. Ten

well-equipped, individually styled modern rooms, most with sea views, plus a bar/tearoom that spreads out onto the expansive terrace; no on-site restaurant, but there's one 200m away. **€98**

POINT DE GOURY

Auberge de Goury Point de Goury ☎ 02 33 52 77 01, ⓦ aubergedegoury.com. Facing an octagonal lifeboat station and looking out towards a slate-grey lighthouse, this ancient stone cottage, close to the northwest tip of the peninsula, has a real edge-of-the-world feel. It serves fresh seafood on menus ranging from a €25 option, featuring local crab and grilled bream, to a €67 blow-out with a shellfish platter and an entire lobster. Between mealtimes, it serves a brasserie menu all afternoon. Daily noon–9pm.

Barneville and Carteret

The next two sweeps of beach down to Carteret, backed by sand dunes like miniature mountain ranges, are among the best **beaches** in Normandy – all you need is transport and a desire for solitude. **CARTERET** itself, sheltered by a rocky headland, is the nearest harbour to the English-speaking island of **Jersey**, just 25km away across seas made treacherous by the fast Alderney current.

Carteret's old port area is not especially attractive, but does have several seafront **hotels**. Visitors who prefer to be beside a beach, however, should head for Carteret's twin community of **BARNEVILLE**, directly across the mouth of the bay but a few kilometres away by road. Here an endless (and quite exposed) stretch of clean, firm sand is backed by a long row of weather-beaten villas and the odd hotel.

ARRIVAL AND INFORMATION
BARNEVILLE AND CARTERET

By ferry Manche Îles Express offers boat trips from the harbour to both Jersey and Guernsey, to very erratic schedules (day return €53.50 in high season; ☎ 08 25 13 10 50, ⓦ manche-iles-express.com).

Tourist office 15bis rue Guillaume-le-Conquérant, Barneville (Jan to mid-April & Oct–Dec Mon & Wed–Fri 9.30am–12.30pm & 2–5.30pm, Sat 9.30am–12.30pm;

mid-April to June & Sept Mon–Sat 9.30am–12.30pm & 2–6pm, Sat & Sun 9.30am–12.30pm; July & Aug Mon–Sat 9.30am–1pm & 2–7pm, Sun 9.30am–1pm; ☎ 02 33 04 90 58, ⓦ otcdi.com); 2 place Flandres-Dunkerque, Carteret (July & Aug Mon, Tues, Thurs &Sat 10am–1pm & 3–7pm, Wed, Fri & Sun 3–7pm; ☎ 02 33 04 94 54, ⓦ otcdi.com).

2

ACCOMMODATION AND EATING

Le Cap 6 rue du Port, Carteret ☎02 33 53 85 89, ⓦhotel-le-cap.fr. Cosy, good-value hotel close to the seaward tip of the promenade in Carteret, offering simple but attractive rooms, several of which, costing €25 extra, have great views, plus a restaurant serving decent food – including a definitive chocolate mousse – on dinner menus at €19 and €29. €54

★**Des Isles** 9 bd Maritime, Barneville ☎02 33 04 90 76, ⓦhoteldesisles.com. Light, airy, New England-style seaside hotel, all white paint, wooden decking and huge terraces, near the northern end of the beach, with a heated outdoor swimming pool and a superb restaurant that offers views clear to the Channel Islands on fine evenings.

Menus range from €18 to €35 and include oysters stewed in *pommeau*. Closed Feb. €139

Les Mielles 80 route des Laguettes, Surtainville ☎02 33 04 31 04, ⓦcamping-municipal-normandie.com. Three-star municipal campsite, with rental mobile homes as well as tent and caravan space, very close to the beach in the dunes, a dozen kilometres north of Carteret. €10.05

Des Ormes Promenade Barbey d'Aurévilly, Carteret ☎02 33 52 23 50, ⓦhoteldesormes.fr. Elegant, very tastefully restored hotel in a nineteenth-century townhouse facing the port, with small but attractive rooms and a good restaurant, *Le Rivage*, which doubles as a garden tearoom (closed Mon). €159

Portbail

Five kilometres further down the coast from Barneville, the dunes are interrupted once again by the broad estuary of the Ollonde River. Set slightly back from the sea, **PORTBAIL** is a delightful village where the tiny Romanesque church is now deconsecrated and hosts temporary art exhibitions in summer. Its streets are thronged on summer Tuesdays with a bustling **market**, where, as well as buying spit-roasted chickens and fresh oysters, you can pick up a dining table or have your chairs re-upholstered. Access to two fine beaches is by way of an old stone bridge, beneath which fishermen wade thigh-deep in the river.

The first French beach that **Charles Lindbergh** crossed as he completed the first solo transatlantic flight in 1927, just south of Portbail, is now called plage Lindbergh.

ACCOMMODATION AND EATING   PORTBAIL

Aux XIII Arches 9 place Castel ☎02 33 04 87 90, ⓦ13arches.com. Good-value rooms, of varying sizes and degrees of luxury, but all with sea views, above an attractive café-restaurant that serves mussels from €11.

They also have some appealing self-catering apartments nearby, on the ground floor with outdoor space. Room €95, apartment €125

Lessay

South of Carteret, the road around the headland joins the main D900 at **LESSAY**, where an important Romanesque **monastery** stands right in the heart of town. Until the war it was one of the few early Norman churches still intact. When it had to be rebuilt from scratch afterwards, guided by photographs, the job was done using not only the original stone but also authentic tools and methods. The square central tower of Lessay is similar to that which collapsed centuries ago on Mont-St-Michel. The abbey hosts a series of evening concerts, under the umbrella title **Heures Musicales**, in July and August (☎02 33 45 14 34, ⓦlesheuresmuses.blogspot.co.uk), while its monks sing Gregorian chant each Sunday. They're also very much in evidence at the **Holy Cross Fair** in the first half of September, which celebrates cattle and other animals (ⓦcanton-lessay.com).

Château de Pirou

South of Lessay · Daily except Tues: 2nd half of March, 2nd half of Oct, and a few days in mid-Nov 10am–noon & 2–5pm; April–Sept 10am–noon & 2–6.30pm; closed mid-Nov to mid-March · €5.50 · ☎02 33 46 34 71, ⓦchateau-pirou.org

Off the main coastal road, the D650, roughly 2km south of the junction for Lessay, turns inland for a few hundred metres to reach the **Château de Pirou**. Although you see nothing from the road, once you've passed through its three successive fortified gateways you are confronted by a ravishing little castle. Some historians have suggested that this is the oldest castle in Normandy, dating back to the earliest Viking raids; it's thought to have taken its current form around the twelfth century.

Considering that it was converted into a farm, and then for centuries forgotten and all but submerged in ivy, it remains remarkably complete. Originally built of wood, on the coast, it was later remodelled in stone and now stands encircled by a broad moat, its towers rising sheer from the water. At your own risk, you can pick your way up to the top of the keep and look out over the surrounding fields.

Between mid-June and September, a modern **tapestry** depicting the 1091 Norman invasion of Sicily, embroidered in the style of the Bayeux Tapestry, is displayed in a barn opposite the drawbridge.

Pirou-Plage

Heading towards the sea instead of inland, at the turn-off for the Château de Pirou, brings you to a dead end in a couple of hundred metres at the tiny community of **PIROU-PLAGE**. When the tide is low, you can see the *buchôts*, poles used in the cultivation of shellfish, poking up from the six-kilometre strip of endless flat sand that stretches away to either side.

ACCOMMODATION AND EATING   PIROU-PLAGE

De la Mer 2 rue Ferdinand Desplanques ☎ 02 33 46 43 36, ⓦ restaurantdelamer.com. This seafront restaurant is the ideal place to sample the local produce, with weekday lunches from €24, and substantial menus at €33.50 and €43.50, all featuring Pirou oysters. Mon, Tues, Thurs & Sun noon–2pm, Fri & Sat noon–2pm & 7.30–9.30pm; closed Jan.

Coutances

The old hill town of **COUTANCES**, 65km south of Cherbourg and confined by its site to just one main street, has on its summit a landmark for all the surrounding countryside – the **Cathédrale de Notre Dame**, whose twin towers stand in magnificent silhouette against the sky. Essentially Gothic, it is very Norman in its unconventional blending of architectural traditions; Louis XIV's master architect Vauban said the lantern tower must be "the work of a madman". In summer, guided tours explore the cathedral's otherwise inaccessible upper levels (mid-July to Aug Mon–Fri 11am & 3pm, Sun 3pm; €7; ☎ 02 33 19 08 10).

In late May each year, assorted indoor and outdoor venues all over Coutances play host to a large-scale jazz festival, **Jazz Sous Les Pommiers** (ⓦ jazzsouslespommiers.com).

Jardin Public

Museum • July & Aug Mon & Wed–Sat 10am–noon & 2–6pm, Sun 2–6pm; Sept–June Mon & Wed–Sat 10am–noon & 2–5pm, Sun 2–5pm • €2.50 • ☎ 02 33 07 07 88, ⓦ ville-coutances.fr

Walk the length of the main square that faces Coutances's cathedral, then head either to the right and slightly downhill, or a short way left, to reach the fountained **Jardin Public**, highly formal gardens with smooth rolling lawns, a well of flowers, a fountain of obelisks and an odd pyramid of hedges. Pleasantly illuminated (and left open) on summer nights, they enclose the small **Musée Quesnel-Marinière**, which has a rather dull collection of permanent paintings but also puts on lively temporary art exhibitions.

ARRIVAL AND INFORMATION   COUTANCES

By train Coutances's *gare SNCF*, an important junction, is 1.5km southeast of the centre, at the bottom of the steep hill.
Destinations: Caen (7 daily; 1hr 15min); Granville (6 daily; 35min); Rennes (7 daily; 1hr 45min).
By bus All buses stop outside Coutances's *gare SNCF*.
Destinations: Agon-Coutainville (1–2 daily; 20min).

Tourist office Place Georges-Leclerc, behind the Hôtel de Ville (July & Aug Mon–Fri 9.30am–6.30pm, Sat 10am–12.30pm & 2–6pm, Sun 10am–2pm; Sept–June Mon, Wed & Fri 9.30am–12.30pm & 2–6pm, Tues & Thurs 9.30am–12.30pm & 2–5pm, Sat 10am–12.30pm & 2–5pm; ☎ 02 33 19 08 10, ⓦ tourisme-coutances.fr).

ACCOMMODATION AND EATING

Cositel 29 rue de St-Malo ☎02 33 19 15 00, ⊕hotel cositel.fr. Large and exceptionally comfortable modern hotel, architecturally uninspiring but equipped with stylish rooms and spacious gardens, halfway up the hill towards Agon on the western outskirts of town. **€91**

Tanquerey de la Rochaisière 13 rue St-Martin ☎06 50 57 22 55, ⊕bandb-hotel-coutances.fr. Very charming B&B, in a seventeenth-century townhouse in a quiet street close to the cathedral, offering two huge antique-furnished rooms, one with shower and one with bath, plus a court-yard garden and sumptuous breakfasts. **€125**

Taverne du Parvis 18 place du Parvis ☎02 33 45 13 55, ⊕hotel-restaurant-taverne-du-parvis.com. Unexciting but adequate rooms, several of them family-sized, in an unbeatable location facing the cathedral on the main square, above a reasonable brasserie that serves a Norman menu for €17. Hotel & restaurant closed Sun. **€50**

Les Vignettes 27 rue de St-Malo ☎02 33 45 43 13, ⊕ville-coutances.fr. Excellent little year-round municipal campsite, offering lush pitches on a wooded hill just west of town. **€10.50**

Agon-Coutainville

AGON-COUTAINVILLE, 10km west of Coutances and its nearest resort, is crammed in summer with visitors. This is an utterly nondescript stretch of coast, where the open sea batters against an endless, featureless beach. Huge tides expose massive sandflats, while behind the line of dunes dull holiday homes are punctuated by the occasional snack bar, campsite or motel.

A long walk south from town, fighting against the wind, brings you after three or four kilometres to the **Pointe d'Agon**, where a lighthouse commands a view of the dune environment at its most ecologically unspoiled.

ACCOMMODATION AND EATING   AGON-COUTAINVILLE

Les Fresques 9 rue de l'Amiral-Tourville ☎02 33 47 05 77, ⊕hotellesfresques.fr. Simple hotel, 100m back from the sea in the heart of town, which can get noisy in high summer. Rooms have plain modern furnishings, and several English TV channels. There's no on-site restaurant,

but plenty nearby. **€71**

Marais Boulevard Lebel Jehenne ☎02 33 47 05 20, ⊕agoncoutainville.fr. Three-star municipal campsite, 600m back from the beach and 300m out of town. Closed Sept–June. **€13.70**

Abbaye de Hambye

Route de l'Abbaye • April–June & Sept daily except Tues 10am–noon & 2–6pm; July & Aug daily 10am–6pm; Oct daily except Tues 10am–noon & 2–5pm • €5 • ☎02 33 61 76 92, ⊕patrimoine.manche.fr

What's left of the **Abbaye de Hambye** stands in a very sylvan setting 20km southeast of Coutances and 10km northwest of Villedieu, with little lawns laid out in front, an orchard alongside, and cows grazing in the adjacent meadows.

Very reminiscent of Yorkshire abbeys such as Rievaulx, the abbey was constructed as a Cistercian monastery in the second half of the twelfth century, just as builders were about to abandon the Romanesque tradition in favour of the new Gothic style. Much of the structure was quarried for stone and left in ruins after the Revolution; nineteenth-century prints show the walls drowning in rampant ivy. However, the central tower still stands foursquare above the high narrow walls of the nave, and a few delicate buttresses remain in place, the whole ensemble crammed in tight against a wooded hillside and inhabited mostly by crows. To explore the ruins themselves, beyond the little exhibition in the entrance room above the ancient gateway, you have to join a guided tour (no extra charge).

ACCOMMODATION AND EATING   ABBAYE DE HAMBYE

Auberge de l'Abbaye Le Pont de l'Abbaye ☎02 33 61 42 19, ⊕aubergedelabbayehambye.com. Luxurious but very well priced rural hotel, 100m from the abbey, just off the D51. There being few alternative ways to pass an

evening here, its restaurant serves up extravagant and expensive gourmet dinners (€28–€69). Closed Mon, plus mid-Feb to mid-March; restaurant also closed Sun eve. **€71**

Granville

The striking fortified coastal town of **GRANVILLE** is in many ways the Norman equivalent to Brittany's St-Malo, with a similar history of piracy and an imposing, severely elegant citadel – known as the **haute ville** – guarding the approaches to the bay of Mont-St-Michel across from Cancale. Here, however, the fortress was originally built by the English, early in the fifteenth century, as the springboard for an attack on Mont-St-Michel that never came to fruition.

Granville these days has become a deservedly popular destination for tourists. Thanks in part to the long **beach** that stretches away north of town, which disappears almost completely at high tide, it's the most popular resort in the area. Traffic in the maze-like new town, down below the headland, can be nightmarish, but the beaches are excellent, with facilities for watersports of all kind, while the *haute ville* makes a fascinating and much more peaceful refuge. Riotous four-day **carnival** celebrations take over the town at Mardi Gras each year (ⓦcarnavaldegranville.fr).

Granville had an unexpected brush with destiny on March 9, 1945, when it was overrun for an hour and a half by German commandos from Jersey, long after the invading Allied forces had swept on to Germany.

The Haute Ville

The great difference between Granville and St-Malo is that Granville's walled, fortified citadel, the **haute ville**, stands separate from the modern town, and remains resolutely uncommercialized. Although – or rather, because – it holds only a handful of shops and restaurants, and no hotels, it's an intriguing enclave, well worth a couple of hours of your time.

Sheltered behind a rocky outcrop that juts out into the Channel, the *haute ville* is reached by flights of roughly 150 steep steps from alongside the beach and casino, or circuitous climbing roads from the port. Once up here, you'll find three or four long narrow parallel streets of grey-granite eighteenth-century houses – some forbidding and aloof, some adorned with brightly painted shutters – that lead to the church of Notre Dame. The views up and down the coast, across to Mont-St-Michel and out to the Îles Chausey, are dramatic. Ornamental gardens close to the headland boast a statue of the city's best-known pirate, **Georges Pléville le Pellay**, splendidly complete with peg leg and cutlass.

Musée d'Art et d'Histoire

2 rue le Carpentier · Feb, March & Oct–Dec Wed, Sat & Sun 2–6pm; April–June & Sept daily except Tues 10am–noon & 2–6pm; July & Aug daily except Tues 10am–noon & 2–6.30pm · €1.80 · ☏ 02 33 50 44 10, ⓦ ville-granville.fr

Set into the citadel walls directly above the port, the **Musée d'Art et d'Histoire** holds three floors of rather dry displays on local history. The main feature downstairs, amid old postcards and paintings, is a model of Granville as it appeared in 1912; higher up, antique coiffes and costumes jostle for space with hefty wooden Norman furniture, while the top level is devoted to the history of the Newfoundland cod fisheries.

Musée d'Art Moderne Richard Anacréon

Pl de l'Isthme · April–Sept daily except Mon 11am–6pm; Oct–March Wed–Sun 2–6pm · €3 · ☏ 02 33 51 02 94, ⓦ ville-granville.fr

In pride of place at the inland end of the *haute ville*, the **Musée d'Art Moderne Richard Anacréon** houses art accumulated by the eponymous M. Anacréon, who was born in Granville in 1907 and opened his L'Originale bookshop in Paris in 1940. Filled with sketches and autographs from the likes of Jean Cocteau and André Derain – and one or two Picasso *eau-fortes* – it's not all that compelling, but the gallery itself is impressive and hosts interesting temporary exhibitions.

Musée Dior

Rue d'Estouteville • May to late Sept daily 10am–6.30pm • €7 • ⓦ musee-dior-granville.com

The family home of perhaps the most famous Granvillais – the couturier **Christian Dior**, who was responsible for the "New Look" – overlooks the beach a few hundred metres northeast of the citadel. A striking orange-and-pink-painted Belle Époque mansion, it can be reached along a coastal footpath that continues another 6.5km to St-Martin de Bréhal. Its tranquil, flower-filled gardens enjoy sweeping views, while the interior of the actual house has been stripped bare and is refitted each summer for changing annual exhibitions on aspects of twentieth-century fashion, focusing on Dior in particular.

ARRIVAL AND DEPARTURE GRANVILLE

By train and bus Granville's *gare SNCF*, well east of the centre on avenue du Maréchal-Leclerc, stands at the end of a spur line from Coutances (6 daily; 35min); change there for all other directions. Buses stop here, too.

By ferry Services from the harbour to Jersey, Guernsey and Sark are operated by Manche Îles Express (day return €59.50 in high season; ⓣ 08 25 13 10 50, ⓦ manche-iles -express.com), and to the Îles Chausey (see opposite) by Jolie France (ⓣ 02 33 50 31 81, ⓦ vedettejoliefrance.com).

GETTING AROUND AND INFORMATION

By bike Bikes can be rented from O Cycle Hop, 41 bd des Amiraux (ⓣ 02 33 79 15 69, ⓦ ocyclehop.com).

Tourist office 4 cours Jonville, below the citadel (April–June & Sept Mon–Sat 9am–12.30pm & 2–6pm; July & Aug Mon–Sat 9am–6.30pm, Sun 10am–1pm & 2–5pm; Oct–March Mon & Wed–Sat 9am–12.30pm & 2–5.30pm, Tues 10am–12.30pm & 2–5.30pm; ⓣ 02 33 91 30 03, ⓦ granville-tourisme.fr).

ACCOMMODATION

Les Bains 19 rue Clemenceau ⓣ 02 33 50 17 31, ⓦ hoteldesbains-granville.com. Smart hotel, facing the casino beside the beach, at the foot of the stairs up to the old town. Several of its 54 contemporary rooms have sea-view balconies, and there's a Tex-Mex restaurant and cocktail lounge. **€73**

Camping Lez Eaux 340 av de Lez-Eaux, St-Aubin-des-Préaux ⓣ 02 33 51 66 09, ⓦ lez-eaux.com. Five-star campsite in the grounds of a nineteenth-century château, 8km southeast and inland of Granville, with indoor and outdoor swimming pools and a waterpark, plus rental cabins and, best of all, some thrilling and very comfortably appointed wooden treehouses, reached by spiralling staircases. Closed late Sept to March. Camping **€43**, treehouse **€130**

Centre Régional de Nautisme bd des Amiraux ⓣ 02 33 91 22 60, ⓦ crng.fr. This modern, oceanfront building, 1km south of the station in the town centre, serves as Granville's hostel, with dorms and private rooms. Closed Sat & Sun Nov–Feb. Dorms **€17.40**, doubles **€53**

Logis du Roc 13 rue St-Michel ⓣ 06 18 35 87 42, ⓦ lelogisduroc.com. This nicely furnished townhouse B&B, run by a fluent English-speaker, is the only accommodation option in Granville's peaceful old citadel, though its three attractive and spacious en-suite rooms are complemented by a separate flat and small house for rent. **€60**

EATING AND DRINKING

La Citadelle 34 rue du Port ⓣ 02 33 50 34 10, ⓦ restaurant-la-citadelle.com. Good seafood restaurant facing the port, with dinner menus from €28 for three courses, €20 for two. The sumptuous €34 option features veal with chorizo or monkfish with aioli. Daily except Wed 12.15–2pm & 7.15–9.30pm.

L'Échauguette 24 rue St-Jean ⓣ 02 33 50 51 87, ⓦ echauguette-granville.fr. Cosy, stone-walled old-town crêperie, which serves good simple meals, grilled over an open fire. Unusually, it's open for lunch only. Galettes cost under €10, and meat main courses more like €14. Daily 11.30am–3pm.

★**Mer et Saveurs** 49 rue du Port ⓣ 02 33 50 05 80, ⓦ meretsaveurs.fr. The pick of the fine crop of waterfront restaurants that line Granville's commercial port; its mouthwatering assortment of fishy menus, from €14.50 for lunch, €25.50 dinner, changes daily. Tues–Sun noon–2pm & 7–9.30pm; closed Sun eve in low season.

Restaurant du Port 19 rue du Port ⓣ 02 33 50 00 55, ⓦ restaurant-du-port.com. Seafood place in the small-boat harbour, with a mouthwatering assortment of very fishy menus, and an unbelievably garlicky fish soup as its speciality. Menus range from €16.50 up to €31.50; the good-value €27.50 menu features nine stuffed oysters and roasted duck in caramel sauce. Tues–Sat noon–2pm & 7–10pm, Sun noon–2pm.

Îles Chausey

Nowadays visited for their long beaches of fine sand, the myriad low-lying **Îles Chausey** were the site of the quarries that provided the granite that built Mont-St-Michel. They originally formed part of the ancient Forest of Scissy, until exceptional tides at the spring equinox of 709 AD, combined with strong north winds, flooded the entire region.

The only inhabited island, the **Grande Île**, which, as the name suggests is by far the largest of the archipelago, holds the one (summer-only) **hotel**. Other accommodation is available in either private or municipal *gîtes*, the latter run by the tourist office in Granville (see opposite).

2

ARRIVAL AND DEPARTURE
ÎLES CHAUSEY

By ferry Ferries are operated by Jolie France (April–Sept up to 5 daily, Oct–March 1–5 weekly; ☎ 02 33 50 31 81, ⓦ vedettejoliefrance.com). Timings and frequencies depend on the tides, and the trip takes just under an hour. Day returns cost €25.60.

ACCOMMODATION AND EATING

Du Fort et des Îles ☎ 02 33 50 25 02, ⓦ hotel-chausey .com. This lonely hotel has eight simple rooms, four of which have sea views and two of which share a bathroom, plus a restaurant serving menus from €26, and only accepts guests on at least a *demi-pension* basis. Closed late Sept to mid-April, restaurant closed Mon. Two people, *demi-pension* **€154**

Around Granville

If you prefer to base yourself out of town rather than in Granville itself, the coastal countryside is best to the **north**, although the villages tend to be non-events. As well as windsurfers, the huge flat sands of villages like **Coudeville** attract hordes of sand-yachters.

Jullouville and Carolles

Eight kilometres south of Granville, **Jullouville** is geared more towards young families. Its main through road, a block inland from the sea, is lined with generally downmarket snack bars, but the seafront promenade makes for a very pleasant stroll.

Carolles has a good beach, but little more; its one hotel is uninviting, but there are alternatives in the hilltop community of Champeaux just beyond.

St-Jean-le-Thomas

The village of **St-Jean-le-Thomas**, downhill from Champeaux and a total of 17km from Granville, promotes itself as "le Petit Nice de la Manche". In fact it's remarkably unlike Nice, in that it consists of a single street leading up to a beach. Thanks to the fact that the village proper lies just off the through coastal roads, it's a delightfully sleepy little place, and walking to the seafront from its tiny commercial hub is a pleasant 500m stroll.

The sea here retreats so far at low tide that it's possible to walk across to Mont-St-Michel. However, this is not a walk to take on impulse; only do it with a licensed guide (see p.140).

ACCOMMODATION AND EATING
AROUND GRANVILLE

COUDEVILLE

Dunes Coudeville ☎ 02 33 51 76 07, ⓦ coudevillesurmer .fr. Good two-star campsite, with mobile-home rentals, beside a long beach that has lifeguards in July & Aug. Closed Nov–March. **€10.57**

JULLOUVILLE

Promenade place du Casino ☎ 02 33 90 80 20. Delightful old-style restaurant, where the large dining room is replete with 1930s' atmosphere, in the former casino building. Seafood-rich menus start at €26.50. Daily except Mon noon–2pm & 7.15–9.30pm.

2

CHAMPEAUX

Les Hermelles 18 rte des Falaises ☎ 02 33 61 85 94, ⓦ hotel-leshermelles.com. Roadside hotel in clifftop village, a short, steep climb up from Carolles, which enjoys truly spectacular views out across the bay; guests check in at its run-of-the-mill restaurant, the *Marquis de Tombelaine*, on the other side of the road. Closed Tues eve & Wed, plus mid-Dec to March. **€62**

ST-JEAN-LE-THOMAS

★**Des Bains** 8 allée Clemenceau ☎ 02 33 48 84 20, ⓦ hotelrestaurantdesbains.com. This great-value hotel, 500m from the sea in the village centre, has been much extended over the years. The rooms are simple but have decent facilities; there's a large heated pool, and good traditional food is served either indoors or on an oddly unadorned garden terrace, with a good-value no-choice €16.50 menu. **€69**

Avranches

Perched high above the bay on an abrupt granite outcrop, **AVRANCHES** is the nearest large town to Mont-St-Michel. It has always had close connections with the abbey. The Mont's original church was founded by an eighth-century bishop of Avranches, spurred on by the Archangel Michael, who supposedly became so impatient with the lack of progress that he prodded a hole in the bishop's skull. Subsequently gold-plated, that skull now forms part of the *trésor* of Avranches's St-Gervais basilica. Robert of Torigny, a later abbot of St-Michel, played host in the town on several occasions to Henry II of England, the most memorable being when Henry – bare-footed and bare-headed – did public penance for the murder of Thomas à Becket, on May 22, 1172. Henry's act of contrition took place in **Avranches Cathedral**. Designed by Robert himself, though without expertise, it eventually "crumbled and fell for want of proper support"; all that now marks the site of Henry's humbling is a fenced-off platform.

The ruins of Avranches's old **castle** dominate the entire central area of the town; the highest point of all is the former keep, which, together with the vestiges of a small section of ramparts, has been landscaped into a small garden. From the very top, you get long views over Avranches itself, and the Mont away to the west. The terrace of Avranches's large formal public gardens, the **Jardin des Plantes** across town, is another good vantage point for the Mont.

A monument to **General George Patton**, southeast of the town centre, commemorates the spot where he stayed the night before his crucial Avranches breakthrough, at the end of July 1944. This small plot of land was ceded to the USA, so technically the statue stands on US soil – and it does literally as well, earth having been brought across the Atlantic to create a memorial garden.

Scriptorial d'Avranches

Place d'Estouteville • Feb–April & Oct–Dec Tues–Fri 10am–12.30pm & 2–5pm, Sat & Sun 10am–12.30pm & 2–6pm; May–June & Sept daily except Mon 10am–12.30pm & 2–6pm; July & Aug daily 10am–12.30pm & 2–7pm; closed Jan; last admission 1hr before closing • €7 • ☎ 02 33 79 57 00, ⓦ scriptorial.fr

For a vivid evocation of Normandy's medieval splendours, be sure to examine the illuminated manuscripts, mostly created on the Mont, displayed in the state-of-the-art museum known as the **Scriptorial d'Avranches**. Additional exhibits trace the history of Avranches, and bring the story up to date by covering modern book-production techniques.

ARRIVAL AND INFORMATION   AVRANCHES

By train Avranches's *gare SNCF* is a long way below the town centre; the walk up discourages most rail travellers from stopping here at all.

Destinations Caen (2 daily; 1hr 40min); Dol (1 daily; 30min) via Pontorson (for Mont St-Michel; 15min).

By bus Buses to Mont St-Michel (1 daily; 45min) and

Granville (1 daily; 30min) stop on the main town square, and also outside the *gare SNCF*.

Tourist office 2 place Général-de-Gaulle (July & Aug Mon–Sat 9.30am–6.30pm, Sun 10am–5pm; Sept–June Mon–Sat 9.30am–12.30pm & 2–6pm; ☎ 02 33 58 00 22, ⓦ avranches.fr).

ACCOMMODATION AND EATING

★**Croix d'Or** 83 rue de la Constitution ☎02 33 58 04 88, ⓦhoteldelacroixdor.fr. Gloriously old-fashioned hotel, consisting of a rambling former coaching inn plus a newer annexe hidden away in the beautiful hydrangea-filled gardens at the back. Good-value rooms, and the best restaurant in town, where dinner menus start at €27.50. Closed Jan, plus Sun eve in winter. €87

Littré 8 rue du Dr-Gilbert ☎02 33 58 01 66, ⓦlelittre.fr. The best option for a quick meal in Avranches, this unassuming but always busy place, right beside the main square, incorporates a brasserie and a coffee shop as well as a fully-fledged restaurant

that serves a great-value €16 *menu du jour* at lunch time. Tues–Sat 9am–11pm.

Patton 93 rue de la Constitution ☎02 33 48 52 52, ⓦhotel-patton-avranches.fr. Family-run hotel where the rooms have been nicely renovated to create a very acceptable budget alternative. Off-street parking is limited, and costs €3 extra, and there's no restaurant. €55

Vallée de la Sélune 7 rue Maréchal Leclerc, Pontaubault ☎02 33 60 39 00. Very welcoming, two-star, English-owned campsite, 7km south of Avranches, that makes a good base for campers visiting the Mont. Closed mid-Oct to March. €14

Pontorson

There's very little to attract anyone's attention to the likeable but ordinary inland town of **PONTORSON**, other than its status as the closest town – and closest railway station – to Mont-St-Michel. That, of course, is enough to keep it busy with visitors year-round.

The most direct route from Pontorson to the Mont, 6km north, runs alongside the **River Couesnon**, which marks the Normandy–Brittany border. The sands at the river mouth are those from which Harold can be seen rescuing two floundering soldiers in the Bayeux Tapestry, in the days when he and William were still getting on. The sheep that graze on the scrubby pastures of the marshes at the sea's edge provide meat for the local delicacy, *mouton pré-salé*.

A more roundabout road to the abbey can take you to the **German war cemetery** at **MONT D'HUISNES**, a grim and unforgettable concrete mausoleum on a tiny hill (see p.113).

ARRIVAL AND DEPARTURE   PONTORSON

By train Pontorson's *gare SNCF* is on the line that connects Caen with Rennes. Shuttle buses timed to coincide with

trains take 15min to make the trip to Mont-St-Michel itself (€3.10).

ACCOMMODATION AND EATING

Centre Duguesclin 21 rue du Général-Patton ☎02 33 60 18 65, ⓦhifrance.org. Huge and rather forbidding hostel near the cathedral, 1km west of the station. Closed Oct to early April. Non-members pay €3 extra. Dorms €12

Montgomery 13 rue du Couesnon ☎02 33 60 00 09, ⓦhotel-montgomery.com. Fine sixteenth-century ivy-covered mansion in the heart of Pontorson, now offering comfortable, tastefully furnished rooms. Courtyard garden

but no restaurant. Closed last two weeks in Nov. €96

Tour Brette 8 rue de Couesnon ☎02 33 60 10 69, ⓦlatourbrette.fr. Friendly and exceptionally inexpensive Logis de France at the western end of the central drag, with 9 simple en-suite rooms (with multiple English TV channels) and a restaurant that serves good lunch menus from €13, and dinner at €18–35. Restaurant closed Wed Oct–June. €50

Mont-St-Michel

The stupendous abbey of **MONT-ST-MICHEL** was first erected on an island at the very frontier of Normandy and Brittany more than a millennium ago. Until recently, however, that island was attached to the mainland by a long causeway, topped by a road. Now it has become an island once more, thanks to a vast hydraulic and reconstruction project aimed at "Restoring the Maritime Character" of the Mont.

A futuristic curved bridge, surfaced with wooden decking, now connects the island to the shore; crucially it has enabled tidal waters to sweep all around, and thus flush away centuries of accumulated sand.

Apart from restoring the natural integrity of the Mont, the real point of all this work was to control access for the millions of tourists who come here each year, and get rid of the acres of unsightly car parks that had come to surround the island. It's therefore no longer possible to drive all the way to Mont-St-Michel in your own vehicle; instead you have to park on the mainland, roughly 2km away, and access the island either on foot, by bike, or riding in a shuttle bus or horse-drawn carriage.

Bear in mind, incidentally, that there's a difference between visiting the island – which is effectively a small and very commercialized town, filled with shops, hotels and restaurants, and circled by various parapets and walls that enclose a number of peaceful parks and gardens – and the abbey itself, surmounting it all. Amazingly enough, fewer than a third of all visitors make the climb up to reach the abbey itself.

Brief history

The abbey of Mont-St-Michel dates back to the eighth century, when the archangel appeared to a bishop of Avranches, Aubert, who duly founded a monastery on the island poking out of the Baie du Mont-St-Michel. This eighty-metre-high rocky outcrop was known as "the Mount in Peril from the Sea", and many a medieval pilgrim was drowned or sucked under by quicksand while trying to cross the bay to reach it. The Archangel Michael was its vigorous protector, the most militant spirit of the Church Militant, ever ready to leap from rock to rock in his titanic struggles against Paganism and Evil.

Since the eleventh century – when work on the sturdy church at the peak commenced – new buildings have been grafted onto the island to produce a fortified hotchpotch of Romanesque and Gothic buildings, piled one on top of the other and clambering to the pinnacle of the graceful church, to form the most recognizable silhouette in France after the Eiffel Tower.

Over the course of its long history, the island has been besieged many times. However, unlike all the rest of northern France, it was never captured, not even during the 27 years, from 1423 to 1450, when the English had a permanent fort on nearby Tombelaine. Although the abbey was a fortress town, home to a large community, even at its twelfth-century peak it never housed more than sixty monks, who said Mass for pilgrims and ran their own school of art. The Revolution ultimately closed the monastery down, and converted it into a prison, renaming the island "Free Mount".

In 1966, exactly a thousand years after Duke Richard the First originally brought the order to the Mont, the Benedictines were invited to return, but they departed again in 2001, having found that the present-day island does not exactly lend itself to a life of quiet contemplation. In their place, a dozen nuns and monks from the Monastic Fraternity of Jerusalem now maintain a presence.

The Island

The base of Mont-St-Michel rests on a primeval slime of sand and mud. Just above that, you pass through the heavily fortified **Porte du Roi** onto the narrow **Grande Rue**, climbing steadily around the base of the rock, and lined with medieval gabled houses that now hold a bewildering succession of hotels and restaurants, along with a jumble of postcard and souvenir shops, and a cluster of heavily commercialized museums. A plaque near the main staircase records that Jacques Cartier was presented to King François I here on May 8, 1532, and charged with exploring the shores of Canada.

It's much more fun, and less crowded, to leave the main street and walk instead atop the castellated **walls** that still protect much of the island's perimeter. Large crowds gather each day at the **North Tower** to watch the tide sweep in across the bay. During the high tides of the equinoxes (March & Sept), the waters are said to rush in like a foaming galloping horse. Seagulls wheel away in alarm, and those foolish enough to be wandering too late on the sands toward Tombelaine have to sprint to safety.

If you're impatient to escape all the jostling, you can also duck through St-Pierre church to reach the **gardens**. From the various footpaths here, popular with picnickers, you can see the giant ramp up the side of the hill, up which prisoners used to haul supplies for the abbey by walking around a treadmill at the top.

The Abbey

Daily: May–Aug 9am–7pm; Sept–April 9.30am–6pm; last admission 1hr before closing; night visits July & Aug Mon–Sat 7pm–midnight; closed Jan 1, May 1 and Dec 25 • €9, EU citizens aged under 26 free, non-EU citizens aged 18–25 €5.50; fee includes optional 1hr 15min guided tour, available in English all year; night visits €9, or €13.50 with daytime admission, ages 18–25 €5.50/€8 • ☎ 02 33 89 80 00, ⓦ mont-saint-michel.monuments-nationaux.fr

The **abbey**, an architectural ensemble incorporating the high-spired archangel-topped church and the magnificent Gothic buildings known since 1228 as the **Merveille** ("The Marvel") – which in turn includes the entire north face, with the cloister, Knights' Hall, Refectory, Guest Hall and cellars – is visible from all around the bay, but it becomes, if anything, more awe-inspiring the closer you approach.

All visitors to the abbey itself pay for admission at its lowest level, and then keep on climbing to reach the large open-air terrace that spreads in front of the **church**, and offers fabulous views to all sides. To get a clearer sense of the abbey's historical development, it's worth pausing in the reception area immediately below, where intriguing scale models depict it during four different epochs.

Most people who opt to see the complex at their own pace scoot through in well under an hour; if you join a tour it'll take more like ninety minutes.

The Mont's rock comes to a sharp point just below what is now the transept of the church, a building in which the transition from Romanesque to Gothic is only too evident in the vaulting of the nave. In order to lay it out in the traditional shape of the cross, supporting crypts had to be built up from the surrounding hillside, and in all

2

ISLAND MUSEUMS

Four museums punctuate Mont-St-Michel's single winding street; all are over-priced, and pall in comparison to the abbey itself. The rather dry **Musée de la Mer et de l'Écologie** offers an insight into the island's ties with the sea, while the multimedia trickery of the **Archéoscope** allows the Archangel Michael to lead visitors on a fifteen-minute voyage through space and time.

Further along the Grande Rue and up the steps towards the abbey church, close to the eleventh-century **church of St-Pierre**, the **Musée Historique** displays the island's original prison, along with sundry torture implements, and the **Maison Duguesclin** recreates the home of a fifteenth-century knight. All are open daily 9am–6pm, apart from the Archéoscope (daily Feb–June & Sept to mid-Nov 9am–5.30pm; July & Aug 9am–6.30pm). Entry to each museum is €9; a four-museum pass costs €18. See ⓦlemontsaintmichel.info for more information.

---

construction work the Chausey granite has had to be sculpted to match the exact contours of the hill. Space was always limited, and yet the building has grown through the centuries, with an architectural ingenuity that constantly surprises in its geometry – witness the shock of emerging into the light of the **cloisters** from the sombre Great Hall.

Not surprisingly, the building of the monastery was no smooth progression; the original church, choir, nave and tower all had to be replaced after collapsing. The style of decoration has varied, too, along with the architecture. That you now walk through halls of plain grey stones is a reflection of modern taste. In the Middle Ages, the walls of public areas such as the refectory would have been festooned with tapestries and frescoes, while the original coloured tiles of the cloisters have long since been stripped away to reveal bare walls.

All visitors exit the abbey on its north, seaward side; as you follow the circling footpath back to the mayhem below, you pass beneath what Victor Hugo described as "the most beautiful wall in Europe".

ARRIVAL AND DEPARTURE   MONT-ST-MICHEL

By car All visitors have to park on the mainland (cars €12.30, motorbikes €4.10). Rates include the shuttle ride to the island; the buses leave from alongside the information centre, as do horse-drawn carriages known as Maringotes, which operate to varying schedules year-round and charge €5.20 per person. You can also walk the 2km to Mont-St-Michel; it's a lovely walk, but bear in mind there's quite a lot of walking – and climbing stairs – on the island itself.

By train The nearest *gare SNCF* is at Pontorson, 6km south (see p.137).

By bus Shuttle buses connect the *gare SNCF* in Pontorson with Mont-St-Michel itself (€3.10). In addition, Keolis Emeraude (☎02 99 26 16 00, ⓦdestination-montsaint michel.com) runs scheduled services to Mont-St-Michel from the *gares SNCF* in Dol (2 daily; 30min) and Rennes (4 daily; 1hr 15min).

INFORMATION AND TOURS

Information centre Adjoining the parking areas and shuttle-bus stop on the mainland, with (free) left-luggage lockers and displays on the restoration project (daily 9am–7pm; ☎02 14 13 20 15, ⓦbienvenueaumontsaint michel.com).

Tourist office The island's own tourist office is in the lowest gateway (April–June & Sept Mon–Sat 9am–12.30pm & 2–6.30pm, Sun 9am–noon & 2–6pm; July & Aug daily 9am–7pm; Oct–March Mon–Sat 9am–noon & 2–6pm, Sun 10am–noon & 2–5pm; ☎02 33 60 14 30, ⓦot-montsaintmichel.com).

Walking tours Schedules for guided walks across the bay from Genêts to Mont-St-Michel vary according to the tides.

With Chemins de la Baie (☎02 33 89 80 88, ⓦchemins delabaie.com), the standard guided trip, to the Mont and back (a total of 13km), takes 4hr 30min and costs €6.90 without a commentary; for a shorter walk, though much the same total time, you can make the return trip by bus (€11.90). The same walk with a commentary costs €10.90, while other options include themed tours, and night or dawn walks. Similar tours are available with Dans Les Pas Du Guide (☎02 33 58 44 82, ⓦlespasduguide.com; no under-13s), Didier Lavadoux (☎02 33 70 84 19, ⓦtraversee-baie.com) and La Maison du Guide (☎02 33 70 83 49, ⓦdecouvertebaie.com).

ACCOMMODATION AND EATING

Mont St-Michel holds a surprising number of **hotels**, albeit not enough to cope with the sheer number of visitors. Most are predictably expensive, and all charge extra for a view of the sea. Drivers have to leave their vehicles in the mainland parking lots; spare yourself a long walk with heavy luggage by only bringing an overnight bag to the island. You'll also find plenty of accommodation on the mainland: the area known as **La Caserne**, along the D976 at the end of the bridge to the Mont, is lined with large and virtually indistinguishable hotels and motels. Many share booking engines, so if you try to reserve online you may well be directed to another hotel.

Sadly, the **restaurants** on Mont-St-Michel, both independent and in the hotels, are consistently worse than almost anywhere in France. It's impossible to make any confident recommendations, other than that ideally you should aim to eat elsewhere – for example, Cancale (see p.194), which has a fabulous selection of restaurants.

2

MONT ST-MICHEL

Croix Blanche Grande Rue ☎ 02 33 60 14 04, ⓦ hotel-la-croix-blanche.com. This little hotel is the nicest on Mont St-Michel itself, with nine small but sprucely decorated rooms, reached via steep stairs. Expect to pay €20 extra for a sea view, and €17 for breakfast. €192

Du Guesclin Grande Rue ☎ 02 33 60 14 10, ⓦ hotel duguesclin.com. The cheapest option on the island, a Logis de France with ten old-fashioned and mostly small en-suite rooms, of which five have sea views. Closed mid-Nov to March. €80

Mouton Blanc Grande Rue ☎ 02 33 60 14 08, ⓦ lemoutonblanc.fr. Wood-panelled fourteenth-century house, now a hotel with fifteen small and somewhat plain rooms, and a large old-fashioned restaurant. €145

ON THE MAINLAND

Camping du Mont-St-Michel Route du Mont-St-Michel ☎ 02 33 60 22 10, ⓦ camping-montsaintmichel.com.

Three-star, 350-pitch campsite, on the mainland just short of the bridge, with well-shaded pitches separated by hedges. Closed mid-Nov to Feb. €15

De la Digue Route du Mont-St-Michel ☎ 02 33 60 14 02, ⓦ ladigue.eu. Century-old, ivy-covered Logis de France hotel, with 35 spacious but unremarkable rooms and a terrace restaurant that has views towards the Mont. €115

Gabriel Route du Mont-St-Michel ☎ 02 33 60 14 13, ⓦ hotelgabriel-montsaintmichel.com. Modern hotel resembling an American motel, with a huge gleaming glass facade facing the Mont, and rooms sprucely decorated in a knowing Pop-art style. €85

Vert La Caserne 8, rte du Mont-St-Michel ☎ 02 33 60 09 33, ⓦ hotelvert-montsaintmichel.com. Low-slung, anonymous but perfectly adequate motel, set a little back from the road behind the *Rôtisserie* restaurant and bar, and offering 54 pastel-toned rooms of varying sizes. €82

Inland Normandy

CLÉCY, SUISSE NORMANDE

Inland Normandy

For anyone exploring inland Normandy, seeking out specific highlights is not really the point. The pleasure of a visit lies not so much in show-stopping sights, or individual towns, as in the feel of the landscape – the lush meadows, orchards and forests of the Norman countryside. On top of that, of course, there's the food, a major attraction in these rich dairy regions. To the French, the Pays d'Auge, Calvados and the Suisse Normande are synonymous with cheeses, cream, apple and pear brandies, and ciders.

3

Other sensory pursuits can also be indulged. There are spas, forests, rivers and lakes for lazing or stretching the muscles in, and, everywhere, classic half-timbered houses and farm buildings. If you are staying on the Norman coast, trips inland – even just ten to twenty kilometres – will pay dividends, while if you arrive at a Norman port intending to head straight for Brittany or southern France you may well find yourself tempted to linger.

Travelling from **east to west**, you pass through a succession of distinct regions. **South of the Seine**, and natural targets from Le Havre, Dieppe or Rouen, lie the **river valleys** of the **Eure**, **Risle** and **Charentonne**. While certain areas – especially along the Charentonne – have been disfigured by industrial development, the valleys remain for the most part rural and verdant. The occasional château, castle ruin or abbey provides a focus, most memorably at **Bec-Hellouin**, near Brionne, and at the country town of **Conches**. Further south lie the wooded hills and valleys of **the Perche**, home of the mighty Percheron horse and also of the original Trappists.

Following the rivers northwest, on the other hand, as they flow towards the sea near Honfleur or Cabourg, brings you into the classic cheese and cider country of the **Pays d'Auge**, all rolling pastoral hills, grazing meadows and orchards. **Livarot**, **Pont-l'Évêque** and **Camembert** here are renowned throughout the world for their cheeses, while **Lisieux**, the home little more than a century ago of Sainte Thérèse, has become one of the major pilgrimage towns of France.

To the **south** of the Pays d'Auge extend the forests of the **Parc Naturel Régional de Normandie-Maine**, with the sedate and famous spa at **Bagnoles** and the national stud at **Le Pin**, as well as the historic towns of **Argentan** and **Alençon**.

Further west, on the routes inland from either Caen or Cherbourg and the Cotentin, comes something of a shift. Around Thury-Harcourt and stretching south to Pont d'Ouilly and Putanges lies the area dubbed the **Suisse Normande**, for its "alpine" valleys and thick woods; fine walking country, if not genuinely mountainous. To its west, the **Bocage** begins with grim memories of war around **St-Lô** – this was the main 1944 invasion route – but subsides into a pastoral scene once more as you hit the gastronomic centres of the **Vire**.

CHÂTEAU DE FALAISE

Highlights

❶ Abbaye de Bec-Hellouin One of the most venerable monasteries in Christendom sets the tone for an idyllic rural valley. **See p.151**

❷ Crèvecoeur-en-Auge Evoking the Middle Ages as they never were, this recreated village juxtaposes beautiful half-timbered farm buildings with a twelfth-century château. **See p.156**

❸ Camembert See the cows that eat the grass that make the milk that makes the cheese that made the name of Normandy. **See p.158**

❹ Le Pin-au-Haras If you love horses, you won't be able to resist the French National Stud, laid out in the eighteenth century. **See p.160**

❺ Château de Falaise The imposing castle where William the Conqueror was born is now a top-class exhibition centre. **See p.163**

❻ Domfront Charming hilltop village, complete with ruined castle and a rather extraordinary modern church. **See p.166**

❼ Suisse Normande This oh-so-scenic quasi-Alpine valley, and the river that runs through it, form inland Normandy's most enticing destination for active travellers. **See p.167**

HIGHLIGHTS ARE MARKED ON THE MAP ON PP.146–147

South from the Seine

South across the Seine from Rouen, the long and featureless **Neubourg plain** consists of intensively farmed agricultural land where the crumbling barns, Tudor-style houses and occasional grazing horses look oddly out of place. The first sizeable town you come to, war-ravaged **Évreux**, provides little incentive to stop, so most visitors choose instead to press on as far as the attractive medieval communities of **Conches**, tucked snugly into the forest, and **Verneuil**.

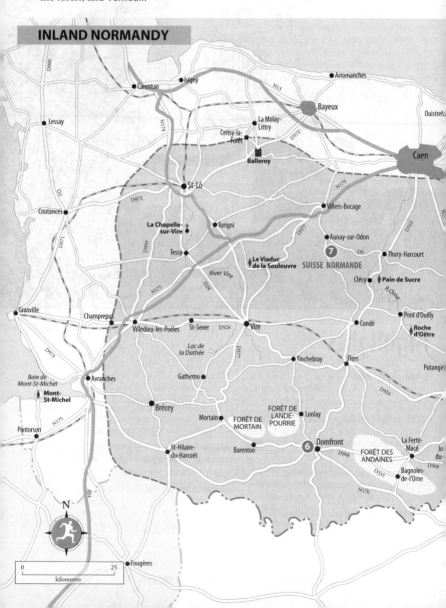

INLAND NORMANDY

Arromanches
Isigny
Carentan
Bayeux
Ouistreh
Lessay
La Molay-Littry
Cerisy-la-Forêt
Caen
Balleroy
St-Lô
Villers-Bocage
Coutances
La Chapelle-sur-Vire
Torigni
Aunay-sur-Odon
Thury-Harcourt
Tessy
Le Viaduc de la Souleuvre
7 SUISSE NORMANDE
Clécy **Pain de Sucre**
River Vire
Granville
Champrepus
Villedieu-les-Poêles
St-Sever
Vire
Condé
Pont d'Ouilly
Roche d'Oëtre
Lac de la Dathée
Tinchebray
Flers
Putange
Baie de Mont-St-Michel
Avranches
Gathemo
Mont-St-Michel
Brécey
Mortain
FORÊT DE MORTAIN
FORÊT DE LANDE-POURRIE
Lonlay
Pontorson
6 Domfront
La Ferté-Macé
Jo du-
St-Hilaire-du-Harcoët
Barenton
FORÊT DES ANDAINES
Bagnoles-de-l'Orne

N

0   25
kilometres

Fougères

Château du Champ-de-Bataille

5km northwest of Le Neubourg • **Château** Easter–June, Sept & Oct Sat & Sun 3.30–5.30pm; July & Aug daily 3.30–5.30pm **Gardens**
Easter–April & Oct Sat & Sun 2–6pm; May, June & Sept daily 2–6pm; July & Aug daily 10am–6pm • Gardens €12, château & gardens €24 •
☎ 02 32 34 84 34, ⓦ chateauduchampdebataille.com

Just off the D39, near the only significant town on the Neubourg plain, **LE NEUBOURG**
itself, stands the enormous seventeenth-century **Château du Champ-de-Bataille**. Since
the early 1990s, as a colossal labour of love, interior designer Jacques Garcia has
revamped both the château itself, which has been meticulously kitted out with period

furnishings, and, more playfully and imaginatively, its extensive gardens, which now feature contemporary flourishes like a topiary chess board. In late June each year, the estate plays host to a weekend of **open-air opera** (ⓦoperaenpleinair.com).

Évreux

The venerable town of **ÉVREUX**, 20km southeast of Le Neubourg, is the capital of the Eure *département*, despite not being on the Eure river itself. Throughout history, it has suffered violent reversals of fortune – as early as the fifth century, its affluent Gaulish community made an inviting target for rampaging Vandals.

Bombing raids by both sides during World War II reduced much of the city to rubble, however, and Évreux today is disconcertingly lifeless. Even so, an afternoon's wander in the vicinity of the **cathedral** – a minor classic with its flamboyant exterior decoration and original fourteenth-century windows – and along the ramparts by the Iton riverbank is pleasant enough.

Conches-en-Ouche

The classic old Norman town of **CONCHES-EN-OUCHE**, which can have changed little since the nineteenth century, stands above the River Rouloir on a spur so narrow and abrupt that the railway line is forced to tunnel right beneath its centre. Arriving by train, you're barely aware that the place exists at all; all you see is the cutting, deep into the hill.

On the highest point of the spur, in the middle of a row of medieval houses on the main rue Ste-Foy, the **church of Ste-Foy** is topped by a cast-iron spire. Conches was formerly renowned for its metal foundries, which were responsible for the iron spire added to Rouen Cathedral in 1876. The windows of the church hold a sequence of Renaissance stained glass. Venture into the gift shop opposite, and you'll find an unlikely secret; the stone spiral staircase in the back room leads to a labyrinth of eleventh-century cellars that extends under most of its neighbours.

Behind the church, in the gardens of the **Hôtel de Ville**, a robust, if anatomically odd, stone boar gazes proudly out over a spectacular view, raising its eyes to the horizon far beyond the sewage works. Next to the Hôtel de Ville, you can scramble up the slippery steps of the ruined twelfth-century **castle**, though it's too dangerous to go inside. Twice captured by the English during the Hundred Years War, this was one of the many haunts of the ubiquitous Bertrand du Guesclin (see p.365). Such sights ensure that Conches remains firmly rooted in the past, but the town is given an added contemporary flavour, too, by the pieces of modern sculpture that you come upon around seemingly every corner.

On the other side of the main road from the castle, you'll find a long **park**, with parallel avenues of trees, a large ornamental lake and fountain. On Thursdays, both this and the main street are taken up by a **market**.

Verneuil-sur-Avre

Southwest of Conches, the towns of Rugles and L'Aigle are both industrial and uninteresting. However, 25km due south on the D840 you come to the pretty little hilltop town of **VERNEUIL-SUR-AVRE**. While now marking nothing more significant than the transition from the Ouche to the Perche, this was, during the Hundred Years War, a crucial fortified outpost between (English-held) Normandy and France proper. Traces of its former ramparts and deep moat can still be seen along boulevard Casati on the west side of town, while the three main streets and numerous alleyways are lined with venerable half-timbered houses.

As you approach along the arrow-straight D840 from the north, the solid bell tower of **La Madeleine** is perfectly framed for several kilometres' distance by the avenue of trees. The actual church of La Madeleine, to which it is somewhat inelegantly attached, stands in the main square, completely dwarfed by the belfry, which opens for occasional visits (call ☎02 32 32 06 56 to arrange a visit).

Following the pedestrian lanes that lead away from the square will bring you out at the **Notre Dame** church in the southeast, built of crude red agglomerate stone in the twelfth century, or to the sixteenth-century **Tour St-Jean** to the southwest, a former church spire separated by wartime bombing from its Gothic porch.

ARRIVAL AND INFORMATION   SOUTH FROM THE SEINE

ÉVREUX
By bus and train Évreux's *gares SNCF* and *routière* are side by side, 400m south of the cathedral.
Tourist office 1 place de Gaulle, 300m north of the cathedral (mid-June to mid-Sept Mon–Sat 9.30am–6.30pm, Sun 10am–12.30pm; mid-Sept to mid-June Mon–Sat 9.30am–6pm; ☎02 32 24 04 43, ⓦ grandevreuxtourisme.fr).

CONCHES-EN-OUCHE
Tourist office Place Aristide-Briand, near the castle 200m south of the church (March–Oct Tues–Fri 2–5.30pm, Sat

9.30am–12.30pm & 2–5.30pm; Nov–Feb Mon–Fri 2–5.30pm; ☎02 32 30 76 42, ⓦ conches-en-ouche.fr).

VERNEUIL-SUR-AVRE
By train Verneuil's *gare SNCF*, five minutes' walk north of the centre, is served by four daily trains from Paris (1hr).
Tourist office 129 place de la Madeleine (April–Sept Mon–Sat 9.30am–1pm & 2–6pm, plus Sun 9.30am–1pm & 2–6pm in July & Aug; Oct–March Mon–Sat 9.30am–1pm & 2–5pm; ☎02 32 32 17 17, ⓦ verneuil-sur-avre.fr).

ACCOMMODATION AND EATING

LE NEUBOURG
Au Grand St-Martin 68 rue de la République ☎02 32 35 04 80, ⓦ au-grand-saint-martin.com. Central Logis de France hotel that's home to a traditional restaurant and a brasserie. The whole establishment is closed on Sun Sept–March; restaurant/brasserie closed Mon pm & Fri pm all year. **€55**
Le Soleil d'Or 1 rue de Brionne ☎02 32 35 00 52. Good, half-timbered hotel-restaurant, with appealing old-fashioned decor. Sumptuous menus in the dining room start at around €22. Closed Mon, and Sun lunch time. **€55**

ÉVREUX
De l'Étape 1 rue Isambard, Pacy-sur-Eure ☎02 32 36 12 77, ⓦ etapedelavallee.pagesperso-orange.fr. Traditional hotel in a lovely riverside village, 13km east of Évreux towards Giverny, with comfortable rooms and tasty menus from €18.50 lunch, €28.50 dinner. Restaurant closed Sun eve & Mon). **€76**
La Gazette 7 rue St-Sauveur ☎02 32 33 43 40, ⓦ restaurant-lagazette.fr. Menus in Évreux's finest restaurant range from the "green", vegetable-rich €24 option to an all-lobster €49 blow-out. Tues–Fri noon–2pm & 7–9pm, Sat 7–9pm.
De l'Orme 13 rue des Lombards ☎02 32 39 34 12, ⓦ hotel-de-lorme.fr. This modernized hotel offers the best-value accommodation in the centre of town, with simple but bright and cheerful rooms, and a bar but no restaurant. **€74**

CONCHES-EN-OUCHE
Le Cygne 2 rue Paul Guilbaud ☎02 32 30 20 60, ⓦ lecygne.fr. Logis de France arranged around a courtyard at the north end of the main street, with spruced-up rooms

and menus starting at €19.50. Restaurant closed Fri lunch time, Sun eve & all Mon. **€50**
Grand'Mare 13 av Croix de Fer ☎02 32 30 23 30, ⓦ lagrandmare.com. Recently revamped hotel in a green and quiet location beside the park, with comfortable rooms and large family suites, plus a classy restaurant that serves a €22 menu rich in local flavours. Restaurant closed Sun eve, Tues eve & all Mon. **€61**
Normandie 1 place Paul Doumer ☎02 32 30 04 58, ⓦ conches-hotel.com. Very welcoming hotel near the tourist office, where the well-equipped modern rooms are in a motel-like annexe at the back, and the spacious dining room serves excellent traditional food from €21.50, with house-prepared foie gras on the €30.50 option. Restaurant closed Mon lunch time, Sun eve & all Fri. **€62**

VERNEUIL-SUR-AVRE
Hostellerie Le Clos 98 rue de la Ferté-Vidame ☎02 32 32 21 81, ⓦ leclos-normandie.com. Bizarre little patterned château set in attractive gardens near the Notre Dame church, which has a fabulous restaurant (menus from €36) and phenomenally expensive rooms – the fanciest suite costs €675. Closed mid-Jan to mid-Feb; restaurant closed Tues lunch and all Mon. **€196**
Le Saumon 89 place de la Madeleine ☎02 32 32 02 36, ⓦ hoteldusaumon.fr. Cream-coloured hotel that glows an inviting pink at sunset, and offers well-equipped and comfortable rooms, all en suite, at very reasonable rates. A tankful of live lobsters nervously await patrons of the more expensive menus; in midweek especially, the lower-priced menus are very good value, though you need to spend at least €37 to be sure of avoiding a surfeit of innards. Hotel & restaurant closed Sun eve, plus mid-Dec to early Jan. **€48**

3

The Charentonne and the Risle

The **River Risle** drains down from the Ouche region, north of the Perche, and passes initially through traditional and now very faded ironworking towns such as L'Aigle. Roughly 30km northwest of Conches, it's joined by a fast-flowing tributary, the **Charentonne**. In the area to either side of the confluence, and from then on northwards as the newly strengthened Risle heads towards the sea near Honfleur, several small riverside towns are worth visiting.

Broglie

The southernmost town of any size along the Charentonne is **BROGLIE**, pronounced "Broy", 12km east of Orbec (see p.157). Its charming little central square, the place des Trois Maréchaux, holds the half-Roman, half-Gothic church of **St-Martin**.

The impressive private **château** that stands on the brow of the hill above Broglie is the ancestral home of the de Broglie family. Its last-but-one owner, Prince Louis, won the Nobel Physics Prize for demonstrating that matter, like light, has wavelike properties. His work – to "seek the last hiding places of reality", as he put it – subsequently formed the foundation of the whole discipline of quantum mechanics. Originally a medieval historian, Louis was attracted to his great theory "purely on the grounds of intellectual beauty".

Immediately **downstream from Broglie**, the Charentonne sprawls between its banks on a wide flood plain. It is classic inland Normandy, uneventful and totally scenic; the one flaw in the whole thing is the unseemly preponderance of porcelain donkeys in people's front gardens.

Bernay

As you approach **BERNAY**, 11km northeast of Broglie, factories and warehouses line both sides of the river. The town itself, however, has a few humpback footbridges and picturesque half-timbered old streets, and one of those churches typical of the region with a spire that looks like a stack of inverted octagonal ice-cream cones. An impressive Romanesque twelfth-century **abbey church** forms part of the town museum (Tues–Sun: June–Sept 11am–6pm; Oct–May 2–5.30pm; €4).

Bernay has few claims to renown, though Edith Piaf lived here as a child, and a local baker found fame for **running** each stage of the Tour de France during the night before the cyclists raced over it.

Beaumont-le-Roger

BEAUMONT-LE-ROGER is set beside the Risle, 25km northwest of Conches and 17km east of Bernay, shortly before the Risle meets the Charentonne. Its ruined thirteenth-century priory **church** is gradually crumbling to the ground, the slow restoration of one or two arches unable to keep pace. Little happens in the village beyond the hourly hammering of the church bell – next door to the abbey – by a nodding musketeer; and with each passing hour, the ruins crumble a little more.

Brionne

The small town of **BRIONNE**, 15km north of Beaumont-le-Roger and the first stop on the rail line to Rouen, plays host to large regional **markets** on Thursday and Sunday. The fish hall is on the left bank; the rest by the church on the right bank. Above them both, with panoramic views, is a **donjon**, or old castle keep, spotlit by the setting sun. Should you decide to climb up the hill to reach it, you'll find a *table d'orientation* with arrows pointing out local landmarks.

Abbaye du Bec-Hellouin

Le Bec-Hellouin • Daily 7am–7pm; guided tours Mon–Sat 10.30am, 3pm & 4pm, plus 5pm June–Sept only; Sun & hols noon, 3pm & 4pm • Free; tours €5.30 • ☎ 02 32 43 72 62, ⓦ abbayedubec.com

Following the Risle north towards Honfleur and the sea, the **D39** is lined with perfect timbered farmhouses. Five kilometres from Brionne, the size and tranquil setting of the **ABBAYE DU BEC-HELLOUIN** lend a monastic feel to the whole valley. Bells echo between the hills and white-robed monks go soberly about their business. From the eleventh century onwards, the abbey was one of the most important centres of intellectual learning in the Christian world. An intimate association with the court of William the Conqueror meant that three of its early abbots – Lanfranc, the philosopher Anselm, and Theobald – became archbishops of Canterbury. Recent archbishops of Canterbury have maintained tradition by coming here on retreat.

Owing to the Revolution, most of the monastery buildings are relatively new – the monks only returned in 1948 – but some have survived amid the appealing clusters of stone ruins, while fragments of medieval lettering are still visible on the solitary tower, topped by a beehive spire. Visitors are welcome to wander through the grounds for no charge; to get a better sense of what you're seeing, join a **guided tour**.

Pont-Audemer

At the northernmost major crossing point over the Risle, **PONT-AUDEMER**, medieval houses lean out at alarming angles over the crisscrossing roads, rivers and canals. It's an attractive little place, the scene of busy markets on Mondays and Fridays.

From Pont-Audemer you have the choice of making for the sea at **Honfleur** (see p.92), passing some tottering Giacometti-style barns on the way to St-Georges-du-Vièvre 15km or so to the south along the thickly wooded valleys of the D38, or going on towards the **Seine**. If you plan to cycle north across the Forêt de Brotonne towards Caudebec, follow a map, not the road signs; to discourage motorists from spoiling the nicest part of the forest, the signs direct you the long way round, via La Mailleraye.

Pont-l'Évêque

There was little left after the war of the old **PONT-L'ÉVÊQUE**, 35km west of Pont-Audemer and technically the northernmost town of the Pays d'Auge (see p.155). One or two ancient houses remain, most notably along rue St-Michel where some have been repainted in the bright colours of the Middle Ages, and the whole place comes alive on **market** day, Monday, when plenty of stalls sell the town's namesake **cheese**. However, in the main, it's too much of a turmoil of major roads to linger in for too long.

Cormeilles

The village of **CORMEILLES**, 17km southeast of Pont-l'Évêque, makes a more appealing destination for a pleasant stroll, having been left relatively unscathed by fighting. Each Friday sees a **market** in its tiny centre, and there are several half-timbered restaurants scattered around.

ARRIVAL AND INFORMATION   THE CHARENTONNE AND THE RISLE

By train Brionne is served by trains between Rouen (3 daily; 40min) and Caen (3 daily; 1hr).

Tourist office 27 place des Trois Maréchaux, Broglie (April–June, Sept & Oct Tues–Fri 2.30–5.30pm, Sat 10am–noon & 2.30–5.30pm, Sun 10am–noon; July & Aug Wed–Fri 2.30–5.30pm, Sat 10am–noon & 2.30–5.30pm, Sun 10am–noon & 3–6pm; Nov–March Tues–Sat 2.30–5.30pm; ☎ 02 32 46 27 52, ⓦ cc-broglie.fr); 29 rue Thiers, Bernay (mid-June to mid-Sept Mon–Sat 9.30am–6pm, Sun 10am–1pm; mid-Sept to mid-June Mon–Sat 9.30am–12.30pm & 2–5.30pm; ☎ 02 32 43 32 08, ⓦ bernaytourisme.fr).

3

ACCOMMODATION AND EATING

LA FERTÉ-FRESNEL

★**Château de la Ferté-Fresnel** La Ferté-Fresnel ☎ 02 33 24 23 23, ⓦ chateau.fertefresnel.free.fr. Neat and very charming little nineteenth-century château, in a small town in the southern reaches of the Charentonne valley 12km northwest of L'Aigle, which holds one of Normandy's most unusual, and magnificent B&Bs. The château itself stands at the end of a majestic avenue of trees, and is set in superb formal grounds, while the huge, high-ceilinged guest rooms are reached via a graceful curving double staircase. €90

BERNAY

Camping Municipal Rue des Canadiens ☎ 02 32 43 30 47, ⓦ ville-bernay27.fr. Municipal campsite, on the southwest edge of town beside a former railway track that's been converted into a lush footpath, offering fifty well-shaded sites, plus indoor and outdoor pools. Closed Oct–April. €14.50

Lion d'Or 48 rue Général-de-Gaulle ☎ 02 32 43 12 06, ⓦ hotel-liondor-bernay.com. Conventional, good-quality hotel in a former coaching inn, with decent rooms and lots of restaurants within easy walking distance. €66

Moulin Fouret 2 rte de Moulin-Fouret, St-Aubin-le-Vertueux ☎ 02 32 43 19 95, ⓦ moulin-fouret.com. This sixteenth-century riverside windmill, 3km south of Bernay, is primarily a restaurant, serving menus at €26 (lunch only) and €45, with some lovely outdoor seating in summer, but it also has a few simple en-suite rooms, making it the nicest place to stay in the vicinity. Closed Sun eve & Mon. €50

BEAUMONT-LE-ROGER

La Calèche 54 rue St-Nicolas ☎ 02 32 45 25 99, ⓦ lacalechetraiteur.com. Top-quality and very friendly restaurant at a prominent crossroads, which offers menus at €25 and €35. Mon & Thurs–Sat noon–1.45pm, Sun noon–1.45pm; closed three weeks in July.

Lion d'Or 91 rue St-Nicolas ☎ 02 32 46 54 24, ⓦ hostel lerieduliondor.com. Sixteenth-century coaching inn with some quiet and comfortable courtyard rooms, and a restaurant charging just €14 for lunch, and €24 for dinner. Restaurant closed Sun eve & Mon. €52

BRIONNE

Auberge du Vieux Donjon 19 rue de la Soie ☎ 02 32 44 80 62, ⓦ auberge-vieux-donjon.fr. Lovely old half-timbered hotel, facing the marketplace, where the food, on menus from €15 at lunch, €20 for dinner, is significantly better than the accommodation – watch out for sagging mattresses. Restaurant closed Mon, Sat & Thurs eve. €55

Logis de Brionne 1 place St-Denis ☎ 02 32 44 81 73, ⓦ lelogisdebrionne.com. Modern hotel, close to the *gare SNCF* but a long way west of the centre, with an excellent restaurant where dinner menus start at €35. Restaurant closed Mon, plus Wed lunch, Sat lunch and Sun dinner. €96

LE BEC-HELLOUIN

Auberge de l'Abbaye 12 place Guillaume le Conquérant, Bec-Hellouin ☎ 02 32 44 86 02, ⓦ hotel bechellouin.com. Pretty, half-timbered hotel-restaurant in the tiny and rather twee village adjacent to the Abbaye du Bec-Hellouin, bedecked in flowers and offering ten rooms of varying degrees of luxury, plus a spa. Closed Tues, plus all Dec & Jan, & Wed Oct–March. €89

PONT-AUDEMER

De l'Agriculture 84 rue de la République ☎ 02 32 41 01 23, ⓦ lagriculture.free.fr. Basic but welcoming riverside hotel, offering cheap en-suite rooms plus a lunch-only café. Closed Sun eve in winter. €45

Belle-Isle-sur-Risle 112 rue de Rouen ☎ 02 32 56 96 22, ⓦ bellile.com. Set in a grand nineteenth-century mansion on an island in the river, amid gorgeous grounds, this luxurious hotel has an opulent glassed-in dining room, serving menus from €33 at lunch time and €44 in the evening. Closed mid-Nov to mid-March. €149

Erawan 4 rue de la Seule ☎ 02 32 41 12 03, ⓦ resto -erawan.jimdo.com. What's surely Normandy's only traditional half-timbered Thai restaurant, just across the river from the centre, serves a simple €12 lunch *formule*. Mon–Sat noon–1.30pm & 7–9.30pm.

PONT-L'ÉVÊQUE

Eden Park Avenue de la Libération ☎ 02 31 64 64 00, ⓦ edenparkhotel.com. This large Logis de France, housed in a sprawling complex of buildings beside its own lake 2km southwest of the centre, makes an ideal overnight stop for families. The standard dinner menu in its restaurant costs €26.50; its outdoor terrace is at its best on a summer evening. €98

CORMEILLES

Auberge du Président 70 rue de l'Abbaye ☎ 02 32 57 80 37, ⓦ hotel-cormeilles.com. An efficient hybrid on the southern edge of town, featuring motel-style rooms around the back and a very traditional, formal and good plush-velvet restaurant in the old building facing the street, with menus from €22. Closed Mon lunch. €88

Gourmandises 29 rue de l'Abbaye ☎ 02 32 20 63 42. The very best restaurant in town, in what used to be a cheese shop, where you can watch the enterprising chef hard at work whipping up ultra-fresh Normandy specialities in the open kitchen, served on lunch menus from €29 and dinner menus from €47. Wed 7.30–9.30pm, Thurs–Sun 12.30–2pm & 7.30–9.30pm.

The Perche

All roads south of Verneuil start to undulate alarmingly as you enter the region known as the **Perche**, which lies within the *département* of Orne. This offers some of Normandy's most bucolically appealing countryside, with green valleys nestled between heavily forested hills. Despite its apparent fertility, however, it has never been a particularly prosperous area.

It's well known for the mighty **Percheron horses**, the strongest workhorses in the world, while its remoteness and seclusion made it an ideal home for the first **Trappist** monks, who took their name from the Forêt de la Trappe. The most famous local dish hereabouts is the black *boudin noir*, a crumbly black pudding or blood sausage with a healthy dose of fat and tripe thrown in.

Mortagne-au-Perche

MORTAGNE-AU-PERCHE, the largest town of the Perche region, stands on a hill set in the heart of the forests. Although it has lost virtually all of its fortifications, it remains an appealing country town, with a pleasant ensemble of stone townhouses. The one part of the ramparts to survive is a fifteenth-century arch known as the **Porte St-Denis**.

In Mortagne's liveliest square, the **place de Gaulle**, the nineteenth-century market hall has been imaginatively converted into a cinema, with some postmodern spiral staircases attached to either side. Nearby stands an unusual modern fountain, looking like an open mummy case made of copper. If you cross from here through the main gates of the Hôtel de Ville to reach the flower-filled gardens around the back, which are filled with sculpture old and new, you can enjoy fine views over the Perche hills.

THE TRAPPISTS

The **Abbaye de la Trappe** is set in open rolling fields on the fringes of the Forêt de la Trappe – a minor appendage of the Forêt du Perche – just beyond a fishing lake and 10km north of Mortagne, outside Soligny-la-Trappe. This was the original home of one of the world's most famous – yet deliberately self-effacing, and consistently misunderstood – Christian monastic orders.

Although the abbey was founded in the thirteenth century, its monks only began to follow the principles for which the Trappists are known today in 1664, following reforms instigated by the **Abbé Rancé**. Reacting against the excesses of the time, he set out to recreate the lives of the **"Desert Fathers"** of the first few centuries after Christ, who lived in contemplative isolation in the Sinai, and to follow St Benedict's precept that true monks should live by the labour of their own hands.

The monks were driven out by the Revolution, successively to Switzerland, Poland, Russia and as far as the United States. That they succeeded in returning to their devastated abbey in 1815, still led by Dom Augustin l'Estrange, made them the only order of monks in France not to be wiped out.

The abbey as it exists today is a nineteenth-century creation. The monks live communally – they don't have individual cells – and not in the absolute silence of popular myth, but speaking only for the necessities of work and community life and spending the rest of their time in quiet reflection. Tourists are not encouraged to disturb them, but you can watch a video in a reception room beside the entrance.

There's also an unusual **shop** (July & Aug Mon–Sat 10.30am–noon & 3–6.30pm, Sun 11.45am–1pm & 3–6.30pm; Sept–June Mon–Sat 10.30am–noon & 2.45–5.45pm, Sun 11.45am–1pm & 2.45–6.30pm; ☎02 33 84 17 00, Ⓦlatrappe.fr) which sells all things monk-made: herbal teas, muesli, shampoo, furniture wax – even local *boudin* (pork blood sausage) and coffee grown in Cameroon (by different monks).

Musée de l'Émigration Française au Canada
15 rue Mondrai, Tourouvre • April–Oct Tues–Sun 10am–12.30pm & 2–6pm • €3 • ☎ 02 33 25 55 55, ⓦ hautperche.fr/muséales

During the seventeenth century, times in the Perche were hard enough for much of the population to emigrate to **Canada**, or New France. The **Musée de l'Émigration Française au Canada** in the small town of **TOUROUVRE**, 10km northeast of Mortagne, traces the entire story, following the individual tales of 246 local inhabitants who left the region in just 22 years.

Bellême

Tiny **BELLÊME**, 17km due south of Mortagne on the switchback D938, is actually the capital of the Perche despite being very much smaller. In many ways it's more attractive, too, crammed so tightly onto the top of a sharp hill that the views are consistently superb.

As in Mortagne, hardly anything survives of the fortifications that once ringed the very crest of the hill. The one exception is the forbiddingly thick **Porche** – now the home of the local library, but still equipped to take a portcullis if things turn bad – reached by an alleyway leading off from a corner of the place de la République near the St-Sauveur church.

At the start of each October, Bellême's annual four-day **Mycology Festival** (ⓦmycologiades.com) celebrates the more obscure mushrooms of the surrounding forests.

ARRIVAL AND INFORMATION   THE PERCHE

By bus Regular buses connect Mortagne with Bellême (1–4 daily; 20min).

Tourist office In the former market hall, at 36 place Général de Gaulle, Mortagne-au-Perche (mid-May to mid-June & 2nd half of Sept Tues–Sat 9.30am–12.30pm & 2.30–6pm; mid-June to mid-Sept Mon 10am–12.30pm & 2.30–6pm, Tues–Sat 9.30am–12.30pm & 2.30–6pm, Sun 10am–12.30pm; Oct to mid-May Tues–Sat 10am–12.30pm & 3–6pm; ☎ 02 33 83 34 37, ⓦ ot-mortagneauperche.fr); boulevard Bansard des Bois, Bellême (April–June & Sept Tues 2.30–6.30pm, Wed–Sun 10am–12.30pm & 2.30–6.30pm; July & Aug daily 10am–12.30pm & 2–7pm; ☎ 02 33 73 09 69, ⓦ cdcpaysbellemois.fr). Appealingly, Bellême's tourist office doubles as the headquarters of the adjoining miniature golf course.

ACCOMMODATION AND EATING

MORTAGNE-AU-PERCHE

★ **Ferme du Gros Chêne** Le Gros Chêne ☎ 02 33 25 02 72, ⓦ fermedugroschene.com. This working farm, just outside Mortagne on the D8 towards Logny-au-Perche, has five comfortable, colourful and imaginatively deco-rated guest rooms in a converted barn, plus the option of a three-course dinner for €23. **€68**

★ **Du Tribunal** 4 place du Palais ☎ 02 33 25 04 77, ⓦ hotel-tribunal.fr. The nicest hotel in Mortagne, on a sleepy little tree-lined square, consists of two or three old stone buildings with a few exposed timbers, crammed together on the corner of an alleyway leading to Porte St-Denis. As well as tasteful, if slightly old-fashioned, rooms with good updated bathrooms, it has a fine restaurant, with outdoor seating, and menus starting at €30. **€75**

Camping Monaco Parc Route de Monceaux, Longny-au-Perche ☎ 02 33 23 37 35, ⓦ campingmonacoparc .com. By far the nicest campsite in the vicinity, open year-round and set in a gorgeous wooded valley roughly 15km east of Mortagne, with a huge, opulent swimming pool. **€26.80**

BELLÊME

Relais St-Louis 1 bd Bansard des Bois ☎ 02 33 73 12 21, ⓦ www.relais-st-louis.com. Behind its grand façade, Bellême's best hotel is an elegant place, and its seven guest rooms are even spacious enough to boast proper armchairs. The light dining room downstairs, serving menus from €14 to €46, looks out on one side to a flowery garden, and across the town's diminutive ring road on the other to a small vestige of moat. Restaurant closed Sun eve. **€82**

La Renardière Bellou-le-Trichard ☎ 02 33 25 57 96, ⓦ perchedansleperche.com. Perhaps the most unusual accommodation in Normandy, and the most ideally suited to its location, this split-level treehouse, which sleeps up to five guests, is wrapped around an ancient chestnut tree overlooking rich pasture and woodland, with superb views from its open decks. At weekends, it's available for two-night stays only. **€150**

The Pays d'Auge

The pastures of the **Pays d'Auge**, the region that extends south from the ancient cathedral city of **Lisieux** – itself now almost entirely preoccupied with the cult of Ste Thérèse – are the lushest in all of Normandy, renowned for producing the world-famous **cheeses** of Camembert, Livarot and Pont-l'Évêque. Its rolling hills and green twisting valleys are scattered with magnificent **half-timbered manor houses**. Each sprawling farm is liable to consist of a succession of such treasures, each family house, as it becomes too dilapidated to live in, being converted for use as a barn, and replaced by a new one built alongside. In addition to grazing land, the area has acres of orchards, which yield the best of Norman ciders, both apple and pear (*poiré*), as well as Calvados apple brandy.

Much of the appeal lies in the scope just to wander, and it's easy to fill the days following signs down the back roads to farms where you can sample home-made ciders and cheeses. In addition, the manor houses of **Beuvron-en-Auge**, **Crèvecoeur-en-Auge** and **Montpinçon** are well worth finding, while at **Cambremer**, 20km west of Lisieux, there is a special crafts market on Sunday mornings in July and August.

3

Lisieux

LISIEUX, the main town of the Pays d'Auge, was a regional capital successively under the Gauls, the Romans and the Franks. However, it was obliterated by barbarians in 275 AD, and again by the Allies in 1944, with the result that what had once been a beautiful market town is now for the most part nondescript. Although it still boasts a Norman Gothic cathedral built in 1170, which holds a chapel erected by Pierre Cauchon, the judge who sentenced Joan of Arc to death, these days Lisieux's identity is thoroughly wrapped up in the life and death of **Sainte Thérèse**.

Pilgrims come to Lisieux in considerable numbers, and even a casual visitor will find the Thérèse cult inescapable. The garish and gigantic **Basilique de Ste-Thérèse**, crowning a slope southwest of the centre, was modelled on the Sacré-Coeur in Paris. Completed in 1954, it was the last major religious building in France to be erected solely by public subscription. Thérèse is in fact buried in the chapel of the Carmelite convent roughly opposite the tourist office on rue du Carmel, though her presence in the Basilica is ensured by selected bones from her right arm and by countless photographs, Thérèse being one of the few saints to have lived since the invention of the camera. The huge

---

SAINTE THÉRÈSE

Born at Alençon in 1873, **Thérèse Martin** lived for the last nine years of her short life in the Carmelite convent in Lisieux, until she died of TB at the age of 24. She had felt the call to take holy orders when only 9, but it took a pilgrimage to Rome and a special dispensation from the pope before she was allowed into the convent at the age of 15. The prioress said then that "a soul of such quality should not be treated as a child".

Thérèse owes her fame to her book *Story of a Soul*, in which she describes the approach to life she called her "Little Way" – a belief that all personal suffering, thankless work and quiet faith is made holy and worthwhile as an offering to God. Her reflections proved astonishingly popular after her death, in light of the worldwide attempt to make sense of the vast suffering of World War I, and she was rapidly beatified.

In 1945, Thérèse was declared France's second patron saint, after her heroine Joan of Arc. In fact, she wrote several poems to Joan, and there are even photographs of her dressed as the imprisoned saint chained to a wall. Her continuing relevance to Catholics was celebrated by the late Pope John Paul II, who made his own pilgrimage to Lisieux and declared Thérèse to be the 33rd "Doctor of the Church". This highest of theological honours had only previously been conferred on two women, Catherine of Siena and Theresa of Avila. Her relics regularly tour the world, and attracted crowds of devotees in Britain in 2009.

modern mosaics that decorate the nave are undeniably impressive, but the overall impression is of a quasi-medieval hagiography.

If Thérèse isn't your prime motivation, Saturday is the best day to visit, for the large **street market**, stacked with Pays d'Auge cheeses. Otherwise, the most appealing place to spend a little time in the town is the delightful flower-filled park, raised above street level behind the restrained and sober Cathédrale St-Pierre. To get a glimpse of Lisieux's former glories, take a look at the fading photos in the **Musée d'Art et d'Histoire**, 38 boulevard Pasteur (daily except Tues 2–6pm; €4).

Château de Crèvecoeur-en-Auge

April–June & Sept daily 11am–6pm; July & Aug daily 11am–7pm; Oct Sun 2–6pm · €7 · ☎ 02 31 63 02 45, ⊕ www.chateau-de-crevecoeur.com

While it's always fun simply to stumble across dilapidated old half-timbered farms in the Pays d'Auge, here and there it's possible to visit prime specimens that have been beautifully restored and preserved. An especially fine ensemble has been gathered just west of **CRÈVECOEUR-EN-AUGE**, 17km west of Lisieux on the N14, in the grounds of the small twelfth-century **Château de Crèvecoeur-en-Auge**. Around the pristine lawns of a recreated village green, circled by a shallow moat, this photogenic group of golden adobe structures includes a manor house, a barn, an attractive little twelfth-century chapel, and a tall thin dovecote that date from the fifteenth century. They were brought here by the Schlumbergers, a local family of German origin, who made their fortune from the 1920s onwards by pioneering the use of electricity in prospecting for petroleum. That process is described in exhaustive detail in the barn.

The most interesting displays are in the manor house, including a fascinating exhibition on the music and instruments of the Middle Ages, and several rooms that have been meticulously recreated to their medieval appearance. Unfortunately, almost all the explanatory captions are in French.

For eight days starting on the first Sunday of each August, volunteers recreate the life of a medieval village in the château grounds, complete with a daily mystery for children to solve.

Beuvron-en-Auge

Few villages anywhere can be as pretty as **BEUVRON-EN-AUGE**, 7km north of the N13 halfway between Lisieux and Caen, which consists of an oval central *place*, ringed by a glorious ensemble of multicoloured half-timbered houses. The largest of these, the yellow-and-brown sixteenth-century **Vieux Manoir** at the south end of the village, backs onto a stream and open fields. The beams around its first storey bear weatherbeaten carvings, including one of a Norman soldier.

A map in the main square details suggested **walking routes** through the countryside nearby, while if you step off the square into the alleyway known as **rue de la Catouillette**, opposite the Vieux Manoir, you'll find another set of lovely half-timbered structures clustered around a tiny courtyard.

Beuvron-en-Auge stages its own **Cider Festival**, with a huge local market in the square, on the last Sunday in October each year.

Château de St-Germain-de-Livet

7km south of Lisieux, off the D579 · **Château tours** April–June & Sept to early Nov daily except Mon 11am, noon, 2pm, 3pm, 4pm & 5pm; July & Aug daily 10am–7pm, every half hour; early Nov to March Sat & Sun 2pm, 3pm, 4pm & 5pm · €7.10 **Gardens** April–June & Sept to early Nov daily except Mon 11am–1pm & 2–6pm; July & Aug daily 10am–7pm; early Nov to March Sat & Sun 2–6pm · €2· ☎ 02 31 31 00 03

The **château de St-Germain-de-Livet** is an appealing blend of fifteenth- and sixteenth-century architectural elements. From the main gate, its half-timbered older wing – home to some stirring military frescoes – is largely concealed by the more imposing later addition, with its cheerful checked facade of coloured stones and brick. The whole edifice is topped by classic pointed grey-slate turrets, circled by a moat, and surrounded by immaculate lawns.

Orbec

The most attractive of the larger Pays d'Auge towns, **ORBEC** lies just a few kilometres along a valley from the source of its river, the Orbiquet, 19km southeast of Lisieux. Consisting of little more than its main road, the rue Grande, with the huge tower of Notre Dame church at its southern end, it epitomizes the simple pleasures of the region.

On rue Grande, you'll see several houses in which the gaps between the timbers are filled with intricate patterns of coloured tiles and bricks. Debussy composed *Jardin sous la Pluie* in one of these, and the oldest and prettiest of the lot – a tanner's house dating back to 1568, and called the **Vieux Manoir** – holds a museum of local history (April–Sept Wed–Sun 10am–12.30pm & 3–6pm; €2). On the whole, though, it's more fun just to walk down behind the church to the river, and its watermill and paddocks.

Fromagerie Graindorge

42 rue Général-Leclerc, Livarot • April–June, Sept & Oct Mon–Sat 9.30am–1pm & 2–5.30pm; July & Aug Mon–Sat 9.30am–1pm & 2–5.30pm, Sun 9.30am–1pm & 3–5.30pm; Nov–March Mon–Fri 10am–noon & 2–5pm, Sat 9.30am–noon • Free • ☎ 02 31 48 20 10, Ⓦ graindorge.fr

The centre of the cheese country is the old crossroads village of **LIVAROT**, 18km south of Lisieux, where the **Fromagerie Graindorge** gives you a closer look at how Livarot's eponymous cheese is made, with free samples doled out at the end of each visit. For the best views of the valley, climb up to the thirteenth-century church of **St-Michel de Livet**, just above the town. The local **cheese fair** falls on the first weekend of August.

St-Pierre-sur-Dives

ST-PIERRE-SUR-DIVES, 16km west of Livarot, is noteworthy for two fine old architectural treasures, both of which date back to the twelfth century. The wooden *halles* in its vast open marketplace – which still plays host to a large traditional **market**

THE CHEESE OF THE PAYS D'AUGE

The tradition of cheesemaking in the Pays d'Auge started in monasteries during the Dark Ages, and by the eleventh century the characteristics of the local product had become fairly standard. At first, it was variously known as either *Augelot* or *Angelot*; the *Roman de la Rose* in 1236 referred to *Angelot* cheese, which was identified with a small coin depicting a young angel killing a dragon. This cheese was the forerunner of the principal modern varieties, which began to emerge in the seventeenth century – **Pont-l'Évêque**, which is square, with a washed crust, and is soft but not runny, and **Livarot**, which is round, thick and firm, with a stronger flavour.

Although Marie Herel is generally credited with having invented **Camembert** in the 1790s, a smaller and stodgier version of that cheese had already existed for some time. Apparently, one Abbé Gobert, a priest fleeing the Revolutionary Terror at Meaux, stayed in Mme Herel's farmhouse at Camembert and watched the methods she used for making cheese. He suggested modifications in line with the techniques he'd seen employed to produce Brie de Meaux – a slower process, gentler on the curd and with more thorough drainage. The rich full cheese thus created was an instant success in the market at Vimoutiers, and the development of the railways (and the invention of the chipboard cheesebox in 1880) helped to give it worldwide popularity.

every Monday, and an antiques market on the first Sunday of each month – were burned to the ground in 1944, but had been rebuilt by 1949. Only traditional techniques were used, so there's not a single nail or screw in the place – the timber frame rests on low stone walls and is held together by chestnut pegs alone.

Just across the central street stands a Gothic-Romanesque church, whose windows depict the history of the town. The Benedictine abbey of which it forms part is progressively being restored, and its former convent buildings now house the **Musée des Techniques Fromagères** (mid-April to mid-Oct Mon–Fri 9.30am–12.30pm & 1.30–6pm, Sat 10am–noon & 2.30–5pm; mid-Oct to mid-April Mon–Fri 9.30am–12.30pm & 1.30–5.30pm; free; ☎02 31 20 57 50), a slightly academic complement to the practical-minded *fromagerie* at Livarot.

Vimoutiers

3

The pretty little town of **VIMOUTIERS** lies 10km south of Livarot. A statue in the main square honours **Marie Harel**, who, at the nearby village of **Camembert**, developed the original cheese early in the nineteenth century, promoting it with a skilful campaign that included sending free samples to Napoleon. There's a photo in the town's Musée du Camembert of the statue with its head blown off after a US air raid in June 1944; its replacement was donated by the cheesemakers of Ohio. Marie is confronted across the main street by what might be called the statue of the Unknown Cow.

Vimoutiers hosts a **market** on Monday afternoons.

Musée du Camembert

10 av Général-de-Gaulle • April–Oct Thurs–Mon 2–5.30pm • €3 • ☎02 33 39 30 29, ⓦ vimoutiers.fr

No tyrosemiophile – cheese-label collector (they do exist) – should miss the quirky **Musée du Camembert**'s glorious collection, which boasts Camembert stickers ranging from remote Chilean dairies to Marks & Spencer. Nibblers beware, though – most of the cheese on display turns out to be polystyrene.

Camembert

CAMEMBERT itself, 3km southeast of Vimoutiers, is tiny, hilly and very rural. Consisting of little more than a sloping square, surrounded by an awful lot of fields, it's home to far more cows than humans.

La Maison du Camembert

Mid-Feb to March Fri–Sun 10am–noon & 2–5pm; April & Oct Wed–Sun 10am–noon & 2–5pm; May–Sept daily 10am–noon & 2–5.30pm • €3.50 • ☎02 33 12 10 37, ⓦ fermepresident.com

On one side of Camembert's little central square, the largest local cheese producers, **La Ferme Président**, run their own, surprisingly amateurish, museum. Aptly called **La Maison du Camembert**, it whirls through the history of the cheese and the methods, both traditional and modern, used to make it. Afterwards comes a cheese tasting, in their café.

Fromagerie Durand

Ferme de la Hérronière • Mon–Sat 10am–12.30pm & 3–5pm • €6 • ☎02 33 39 08 08

The **Fromagerie Durand**, 7km south of Camembert on the road towards Trun, offers a visit to the last farm in the region that makes Camembert in the traditional way, using unpasteurised milk. An interesting film explains – you've guessed it – the cheese production process, while four windows allow visitors to view the cheese at various stages in its life, and you're also likely to catch a glimpse of the artisan at work. The end product and other local produce are on sale in the shop. Call ahead if you're travelling in a small party in low season.

Gacé

The **D26** runs along the **valley of the Vie** south of Vimoutiers – a route that is something of a microcosm of Norman vernacular architecture, lined with ramshackle old barns, outhouses and farm buildings. Faded orange clay crumbles from between the weathered wooden beams of these flower-covered beauties.

Although **GACÉ** itself, just off the A28 motorway 18km from Vimoutiers, is not wildly exciting, this area has a certain renown as being the original home of **Alphonsine Plessis**, a celebrated courtesan whose lovers included Alexandre Dumas and Franz Liszt. Born in **Nonant-le-Pin**, 12km south of Gacé, in 1824, she was only 23 when she died, but served as the inspiration for Dumas' *La Dame aux Camélias* and Verdi's *La Traviata*. A museum is devoted to her in Gacé's château.

ARRIVAL AND INFORMATION

LISIEUX

By train Lisieux's *gare SNCF* is on the south side of town, below the Basilica.

Destinations Caen (20 daily; 30min); Paris (11 daily; 1hr 40min); Rouen (8 daily; 1hr 5min) via Bernay (20min) and Brionne (35min).

By bus Buses from the place Mitterand, adjoining the cathedral, connect Lisieux with towns throughout the region.

Destinations Le Havre (2 daily; 1hr 30min); Orbec (6 daily; 35min); Pont-l'Évêque (4 daily; 25min) and on to Honfleur (50min); Vimoutiers (4 daily; 40min) via Livarot (30min).

Tourist office 11 rue d'Alençon (mid-June to Sept Mon–Sat 8.30am–6.30pm, Sun 10am–12.30pm & 2–5pm; Oct to mid-June Mon–Sat 8.30am–noon & 1.30–6pm; ☎02 31 48 18 10, ⊛lisieux-tourisme.com).

ORBEC

Tourist office 6 rue Grande (July & Aug Mon–Sat 9.30am–12.30pm & 2–6.30pm, Sun 10am–12.30pm; Sept–June Mon–Fri 9.30am–12.30pm & 2–5.30pm, Sat 10am–12.30pm & 2.30–5.30pm; ☎02 31 32 56 68, ⊛tourisme-normandie.fr).

LIVAROT

Tourist office 1 place Georges-Bisson (Mon 2–6pm, Tues–Sat 9.30am–12.30pm & 2–6pm; ☎02 31 63 47 39, ⊛livarot-tourisme.com).

ST-PIERRE-SUR-DIVES

Tourist office Sharing space with the cheese museum, in the convent on rue St-Benoist (mid-April to mid-Oct Mon–Fri 9.30am–12.30pm & 1.30–6pm, Sat 10am–12.30pm & 2.30–5pm; mid-Oct to mid-April Mon–Fri 9.30am–12.30pm & 1.30–5.30pm; ☎02 31 20 97 90, ⊛www.mairie-saint-pierre-sur-dives.fr.

VIMOUTIERS

Tourist office 21 place de Mackau (June–Sept Mon 2–6pm, Tues–Sat 9.30am–12.30pm & 2–6pm, Sun 10am–12.30pm & 2–6pm; Oct–May Mon 2–5.30pm, Tues–Sat 10am–12.30pm & 2–5.30pm; ☎02 33 67 49 42, ⊛vimoutiers.fr).

ACCOMMODATION AND EATING

LISIEUX

Aux Acacias 13 rue de la Résistance ☎02 31 62 10 95. Lisieux's best stand-alone place to eat, assuming you can put up with its twee pastel decor; menus range from €18 to €36. Tues–Sat noon–2pm & 7–9.30pm, Sun noon–2pm.

Coupe d'Or 49 rue Port-Mortain ☎02 31 31 16 84, ⊛la-coupe-dor.com. Welcoming, good-value hotel just off the southeast corner of the central place de la République, with decent rooms and a good restaurant that serves a lighter take on Norman cuisine. Restaurant closed Fri eve, Sat lunch & Sun eve. **€66**

St-Louis 4 rue St-Jacques ☎02 31 62 06 50, ⊛hotel saintlouis-lisieux.com. Friendly and ultra-enthusiastic new owners have transformed this budget hotel, which has fourteen individually decorated rooms – of which the cheapest lack en-suite facilities – and serves excellent organic breakfasts for €9. **€75**

De la Vallée Rue de la Vallée ☎02 31 62 00 40. Large, three-star municipal campsite, 1.5km north of town. In truth, though, campers would probably be better off somewhere more rural, such as Livarot or Orbec. Closed early Oct to Easter. **€13**

CRÈVECOEUR-EN-AUGE

Auberge du Cheval Blanc 44 rue de St-Pierre-sur-Dives ☎02 31 63 03 28. Very hospitable five-room village hotel, housed in a former coaching inn, which serves fine regional food. Hotel closed mid-Jan to mid-Feb, restaurant closed Mon & Tues lunch. **€62**

BEUVRON-EN-AUGE

Clos Fleuri 23 place Vermugnen ☎02 31 39 00 62, ⊛leclosfleuri-14.fr. Lovely and very comfortable little two-room B&B, in a venerable half-timbered farmhouse

3

opposite the Vieux Manoir. **€67**

★ **Pavé d'Auge** ☎ 02 31 79 26 71, ⓦ pavedauge.com. Top-notch restaurant in Beuvron's timber-framed medieval market hall, in the central square, serving rich and opulent Norman cuisine on changing menus from €39.50; it also offers five comfortable B&B rooms, from €115 per night, in the separate *Pavé d'Hôtes*. July & Aug daily except Mon noon–1.45pm & 7.30–9.30pm; Sept–June Wed–Sun noon–1.45pm & 7.30–9.30pm.

ORBEC

Le Caneton 32 rue Grande ☎ 02 31 32 73 32, ⓦ aucaneton.fr. The best restaurant in town, in the half-timbered house at the narrowest point of rue Grande, serves top-quality menus from €26. Wed–Sat noon–2pm & 7–9pm, Sun noon–2pm.

Les Capucins Avenue du Bois ☎ 02 31 32 76 22. Small and deliciously peaceful two-star municipal campsite. Closed early Sept to late May. **€9**

Côté Jardin 62 rue Grande ☎ 02 31 32 77 79, ⓦ cote-jardin-lorette.com. B&B that focuses on a central mansion, set in lovely gardens, and holding two very cosy split-level suites, each capable of sleeping three. **€80**

Manoir de l'Engagiste 15 rue de St-Rémy ☎ 02 31 32 57 22, ⓦ manoir-engagiste.fr. Gorgeous half-timbered B&B, dating back to the sixteenth century, offering four very comfortable rooms, decorated in styles ranging from "Kimonos" to "Hemingway", arrayed around a peaceful courtyard. **€120**

LIVAROT

Camping Municipal Rue du Général Leclerc ☎ 06 77 43 09 83. Tiny, old-fashioned one-star municipal campsite, close to the village centre and only staffed 7.30–8pm daily. Closed Sept–April. **€7**

De La France 9 place de la Gare ☎ 02 31 31 59 35. This half-timbered hotel at Livarot's northern end, the one accommodation option in the village, holds six simple rooms, one of which sleeps three. **€50**

ST-PIERRE-SUR-DIVES

Les Agriculteurs 118 rue de Falaise ☎ 02 31 20 72 78, ⓦ lesagriculteurs.com. Ten-room Logis de France that's St Pierre's best bet for both accommodation and food, with plain en-suite rooms and menus from €12.50 at lunch time, €16.90 in the evening. Restaurant closed Sun eve. **€49**

VIMOUTIERS

La Campière Boulevard Docteur-Dentu ☎ 02 33 39 18 86, ⓦ vimoutiers.fr. Clean and very cheap two-star campsite, a short walk north of the town centre. Closed Nov–March. **€9.55**

L'Escale du Vitou Route d'Argentan ☎ 02 33 39 12 04, ⓦ domaineduvitou.com. Attractive half-timbered hotel, in a delightful rural setting not far south of Vimoutiers towards Camembert, where the lake known as the Escale du Vitou offers everything you need for windsurfing, swimming and horseriding. Seventeen rooms, a couple of rental cottages, and a decent restaurant, closed Mon. **€70**

Argentan and around

Although the small town of **ARGENTAN** has a long and venerable history, it was so comprehensively obliterated in August 1944, during General Patton's bid to close the "Falaise pocket", that there's virtually nothing for modern visitors to see. Its sole landmark is the **church of St-Germain**, which dominates all approaches, and took well over fifty years to restore.

You won't find it unless you look hard, but the crest of a hill that overlooks the central place du Marché holds the vestiges of a **ruined castle**. This was where Henry II of England received the news on New Year's Day 1171 that four of his knights had taken him at his word and murdered Thomas à Becket.

Although Argentan makes an enjoyable enough halt when its Tuesday **market** is in full swing, or for boat trips on the River Orne, the main reason anyone comes here is not monuments but **horses**. Outside the town are numerous equestrian centres, with riding schools, stables, racetracks and studs.

Le Pin-au-Haras

March & Oct Sat & Sun 2–5pm; April–Sept daily 10am–6pm; additional openings in off-season school hols • €7; €11.50 with self-guided Discovery Trail • last tour 1hr before closing • ☎ 02 33 36 68 68, ⓦ www.haras-national-du-pin.com

LE PIN-AU-HARAS, 15km east of Argentan on the N26, is an essential stop for horse lovers: it's the home of the **National Stud** (*Haras National*). The plan for the stud was

originally conceived by Louis XIV's minister, Colbert, and the grounds subsequently laid out by André Le Nôtre from 1715 to 1730. It can be approached via a number of woodland avenues, the most impressive being the D304, which climbs slowly from the hippodrome and is lined with jumps and hedges.

While the buildings are magnificent, they're nowhere near as sumptuous as the residents, around thirty of them – incalculable investments that include champions of Epsom and Longchamp, as well as prize specimens of the indigenous Norman Percheron.

Hour-long **tours** of the stud leave every thirty minutes from the main entrance. Visitors are escorted by a groom through stables full of stomping, snorting, glistening stallions, rooms of polished harnesses and fine carriages, and great doorways labelled in stone, until eventually you come out to a pastoral vision of the horses grazing in an endless succession of gardens and paddocks. If you find it hard to follow the rapid French-only commentary, you can amuse yourself by watching the way everybody scrupulously affects not to notice the rampant sexuality – which, of course, is the *raison d'être* of the whole place.

For an additional fee, you stay on after the tour to explore the so-called **Discovery Trail**, a high-tech exhibition on the science of modern horse breeding that's housed in a disused stable.

Every Thursday in summer, the horses parade to music in the main courtyard (late May to Sept, Thurs 3pm; €6.50), and there are also special events on three or so Sundays during September and October, as well as a few other summer weekends.

As for the **château** itself, it's only open during school holidays, not including the summer holidays (Feb–May & Oct–Dec Thurs 2–5pm; €10.50 with the stud).

Château d'O

Mid-July to mid-Sept daily 10am–4pm; hours vary considerably year to year • Free • ☎ 02 33 35 30 81

Just outside Mortrée, 15km southeast of Argentan on the N158, and 6.5km northwest of Sées, the postcard-perfect **Château d'O** is a turreted château, whose grey-slate roof rises to a cluster of sharp pencil-points, with a full moat that widens out into a lake. The house dates from the end of the fifteenth century and, unusually, was designed purely as a domestic residence, with no military pretensions.

Visits take in selected portions of the interior, including the Great Gallery and Marble Salon, as well the ornate central courtyard, but really nothing beats the overall views you get from the outside, as you stroll through its spacious gardens.

Sées

SÉES, midway between Argentan and Alençon near the intersection of the A88 and A28 motorways, has long had an air of being lost in its own history. A succession of dusty and derelict squares, all with medieval buildings intact, surround its great Gothic, white-ceilinged **cathedral**, which is the fifth to stand on the site and is magnificently illuminated every summer evening. One of its predecessors was burned down by its own bishop, attempting to smoke out a gang of thieves – much to the scorn of the pope.

Musilumières

July Fri & Sat 10.30pm; Aug Wed, Fri & Sat 10pm; Sept Fri & Sat 9.30pm, but check website for latest times • €14 • ⓦ musilumieres.org

Between July and September, the cathedral reopens late in the evening for **Musilumières**, a spectacular sound-and-light show that explains and illuminates its history and architecture.

ARRIVAL AND INFORMATION

ARGENTAN

By train Argentan's *gare SNCF* is across the Orne, a short way southwest of the centre.

Destinations Granville (6 daily; 1hr 15min) via Vire

(45min) and Villedieu (1hr).

By bus Alençon (1–2 daily; 1hr 15min) via Sées (40min); Carrouges (1–3 daily; 45min); Domfront (1–3 daily;

1hr 50min) via Bagnoles (1hr).

Tourist office 6 place du Marché, in the old chapel St-Nicolas, Argentan (July & Aug Mon 9am–12.30pm & 1.30–6pm, Tues–Sat 9am–6.30pm; Sept–June Mon–Fri 9.30am–12.30pm & 2–6pm, Sat 9.30am–12.30pm &

1.30–5.30pm; ☎02 33 67 12 48, ⓦwww.argentan.fr); Place du Général de Gaulle, Sées (Mon–Sat 9.30am– 12.30pm & 2–6pm, plus Sun 2–6pm in July & Aug; ☎02 33 28 74 79, ⓦsees.fr).

ACCOMMODATION AND EATING

Donjon 1 rue de l'Hôtel-de-Ville ☎02 33 67 03 76. Thoroughly renovated budget hotel, right by the castle keep, offering simple but tasteful rooms above a brasserie, where full dinner menus start at just €14. *Restaurant closed Sun eve.* **€52**

Renaissance 20 av 2e Division-Blindée ☎02 33 36 14 20, ⓦhotel-larenaissance.com. Stylish and very comfortable hotel with sauna, hammam and pool, plus a good restaurant that serves menus from €21 for lunch, €30 for dinner. **€89**

Falaise

Poised between two of Normandy's most scenic regions, the Pays d'Auge and the Suisse Normande, **FALAISE**, 40km southwest of Lisieux, is a small town with a big history. The entire town was devastated in August 1944, during the struggle to close the "Falaise Gap". This was the climax of the Battle of Normandy, as the Allied armies sought to encircle the Germans and cut off their retreat. By the time the Canadians entered Falaise on August 17, they could no longer tell where the roads had been and had to bulldoze a new four-metre strip straight through the middle.

Falaise is best known, however, for an event that took place almost a thousand years earlier – the birth of **William the Conqueror**, or William the Bastard, as he is more familiarly known to Normans. Some time around 1028, William's mother, Arlette, a laundress and daughter of a tanner, was spotted by his father, Duke Robert of Normandy, at the washing place below the mighty **château** that remains the town's major feature. A shrewd woman, Arlette scorned secrecy in her eventual assignation by riding publicly through the main entrance to meet him. During her pregnancy, she dreamed of bearing a mighty tree that cast its shade over Normandy and England.

Château Guillaume-le-Conquérant

Daily: July & Aug 10am–7pm; Sept–June 10am–6pm; last admission 1hr before closing • €7.50 • ☎02 31 41 61 44, ⓦchateau-guillaume
-leconquerant.fr

From a distance, the sheer-walled keep of the **Château Guillaume-le-Conquérant**, firmly planted on the massive rocks of the cliff (*falaise*) that gave Falaise its name, and towering over the **Fontaine d'Arlette** down by the river, looks all but impregnable. Nonetheless, it was so heavily damaged during the war that it took over fifty years to reopen the castle for regular visits.

Huge resources were eventually lavished on restoring the central *donjon* – reminiscent of the Tower of London, with its cream-coloured Caen stone – in accordance with cutting-edge contemporary concepts. A guiding principle was to avoid any possible confusion between what was original and what was new.

Steel slabs, concrete blocks, glass floors and tent-like canvas awnings have been slapped down atop the bare ruins, and metal staircases even squeezed into the wall cavities. The raw structure of the keep, down to its very foundations, lies exposed to view, while the new rooms are used for changing exhibitions that focus on the castle's fascinating past. Visitors are given – well, loaned – individual tablet computers that display virtual images of each room with its original furnishings, decor and colour scheme.

Add the superb views of the town and surroundings from the battlements, and you have one of Normandy's most rewarding historical sites.

Musée des Automates

Boulevard de la Libération • Early Feb to March, Oct & Nov Sat, Sun & hols 10am–12.30pm & 1.30–6pm; April–June, Sept & Dec daily 10am–12.30pm & 1.30–6pm; July & Aug daily 10am–6pm; • €7 • ☎ 02 31 90 02 43, ⓦ automates-avenue.fr

Also known as "Automates Avenue", the **Musée des Automates** preserves mechanical window displays that graced the department stores of Paris between the 1920s and 1950s. The highlight is a mock-up of a real-life collision that took place in a tiny village between the cyclists of the Tour de France and a herd of pigs.

INFORMATION   FALAISE

Tourist office Boulevard de la Libération (May–Sept Mon–Sat 9.30am–12.30pm & 1.30–6.30pm; late June to mid-Sept also open Sun 10am–12.30pm & 2–4pm; mid-Sept to April Mon–Sat 9.30am–12.30pm & 1.30–5.30pm; ☎ 02 31 90 17 26, ⓦ falaise-tourisme.com).

ACCOMMODATION AND EATING

Camping Municipal Rue du Val d'Ante ☎ 02 31 90 16 55, ⓦ falaise-tourisme.com. This well-equipped three-star municipal campsite is in a superb location, immediately below the castle, next to Arlette's fountain and the local swimming pool complex, to which guests get cut-price access. Closed Oct–April. __€14.30__

Poste 38 rue Georges-Clemenceau ☎ 02 31 90 13 14, ⓔ hotel.delaposte@orange.fr. Falaise's best-value rooms, in an imposing white-painted hotel near the tourist office, are traditional rather than fancy, but the dining room downstairs serves great food on menus from €17. Hotel closed Jan, restaurant closed Fri eve, Sun eve & Mon. __€70__

Alençon and around

ALENÇON, a fair-sized and busy town, is best known for its traditional – and now largely defunct – **lacemaking** industry. Good **restaurants**, cafés and shops are scattered through the handful of pedestrianized streets in the town centre. Thanks to wartime bombardment, however, little is left of the buildings that once stood on the banks of the River Sarthe.

Although the **Château des Ducs**, the old town castle, looks impressive, it doesn't encourage visitors. Only its forbidding gateway now survives, and it remains in use as a prison – indeed the Gestapo incarcerated captives here during World War II.

Stained glass in the **Notre Dame** church on the place de La Magdeleine shows the medieval guilds of craftsmen who paid for each specific window, and the baptism of **Ste Thérèse** is commemorated in the chapel in which it took place. If you haven't already had a surfeit of the saint at Lisieux, you can also wander over to her **birthplace**, at 50 rue St-Blaise, just in front of the *gare routière* (daily except Mon: April–Oct 9am–noon & 2–6pm, Nov–March 10am–noon & 2–5pm; free, donation requested; ☎ 02 33 26 09 87, ⓦ louiszeliemartin-alencon.com).

Alençon was the first town in France to be liberated by French forces alone, and a monument right next to the Pont-Neuf honours their leader, the aristocratic **Général Leclerc** (whose headmaster at school was Général de Gaulle's father). Directly behind the general's statue the movements of his army are chronicled through the deserts of North Africa, via Utah Beach, to reach Alençon on August 12, 1944. Within two weeks he was in Paris; within a year, in Berlin; and by 1946 he was in Hanoi. He died in a plane crash in North Africa in 1947.

Musée des Beaux-Arts et de la Dentelle

Cour Carrée de la Dentelle • July & Aug daily 10am–noon & 2–6pm; Sept–June closed Mon • €4.10 • ☎ 02 33 32 40 07, ⓦ museedentelle -alencon.fr

Housed in a former Jesuit school, Alençon's **Musée des Beaux-Arts et de la Dentelle** has all the best trappings of a modern museum. It holds a highly informative history of lace-making, with examples of numerous different techniques, juxtaposed with an incongruous collection of gruesome Cambodian artefacts, spears and lances, tiger skulls and elephants' feet, gathered by a "militant socialist" French governor at the turn of the twentieth century.

The paintings in its Beaux Arts section are fairly nondescript, except for a touching Nativity by the Norman artist, Latouche, and a few works by Courbet and Géricault.

Forêt d'Écouves

Easily reached (under your own steam) from Alençon or Sées, the **Forêt d'Écouves** is the centrepiece of the Parc Régional Normandie-Maine, an amorphous area that stretches from Mortain in the west to within a few kilometres of Mortagne-au-Perche in the east. A dense mixture of old spruce, pine, oak and beech, set on high hills a few kilometres north of Alençon, the Écouves forest is one of the most attractive in Normandy. These commanding heights were bitterly fought over during the war, and a Free French tank still guards the **Croix-de-Médavy** at their very apex.

Unfortunately, the forest is now a favoured spot of the military – and, in autumn, of deerhunters too. To avoid risking life and limb, check with the park's offices to find the safe routes. You can usually ramble freely along the cool paths, happening on wild mushrooms and even the odd wild boar.

3

Carrouges

The appealing little town of **CARROUGES** stretches along the top of a hill at the western end of the Forêt d'Écouves, 28km northwest of Alençon. Its one significant attraction, however, a fine medieval castle, is down below, in the lush rolling countryside at the foot of the hill.

Château de Carrouges

Daily: April to mid-June & Sept 10am–noon & 2–6pm; mid-June to Aug 9.30am–noon & 2–6.30pm; Oct–March 10am–noon & 2–5pm • €7.50 • ☎ 02 33 27 20 32, ⓦ carrouges.monuments-nationaux.fr

The twin highlights of visiting the fourteenth-century **château de Carrouges** are a superb restored brick staircase, and a room in which hang portraits of fourteen successive generations of the Le Veneur family, an extraordinary illustration of the processes of heredity. The spacious landscaped grounds are also worth a look, while local craftsmen sell their work in the **Maison de Métiers**, once the castle chapel.

Bagnoles de l'Orne

The spa town of **BAGNOLES DE L'ORNE**, 17km west of Carrouges, lies at the heart of a long, narrow wood, the Forêt des Andaines. Broad avenues radiate into the forest from the town centre, where a forbidding nineteenth-century building holds the town's famed **thermal baths**. Bagnoles attracts the sick from all over France; its springs are such big business that they maintain a booking office next to the Pompidou Centre in Paris. Treatments in what's known officially known as **B'O Resort** (ⓦbo-resort.com) start at around €50, but can easily run into hundreds of euros; the tourist office can arrange all-inclusive packages.

Although life in the town is conducted at a phenomenally slow pace, it is all surprisingly jolly, redolent with aged flirtations and gallantry. The lakeside gardens are the big scene, with pedalos, horse-drawn *calèches* and an enormous casino, and there are also Tuesday and Saturday **markets**. Innumerable cultural events, concerts and stage shows take place throughout the summer; the ostensible high spot, the annual *Spectacle* in July – a tedious mock-historical pageant – is one of the less enthralling.

Away from its main roads, the **Forêt des Andaines** is pleasant, with scattered and unspoiled villages, such as Juvigny and St-Michel, and the secluded, private **Château de Couterne**, a visual delight even from the gates, with its lake and long grass-floored avenue approach.

Note that the town as a whole operates to a season that lasts roughly from early April to the end of October; arrive in winter, and you may find everything shut.

Domfront

The road west through the forest from Bagnoles, the D335 and then the D908 climbs above the lush woodlands and progressively narrows to a hog's back before entering the rather delightful village of **DOMFRONT**, 22km on. Less happens here than at Bagnoles, but the countryside is prettier.

A public park, near the long-abandoned former train station, leads up to some redoubtable **castle ruins** perched on an isolated rock. Henry II and his queen, Eleanor of Aquitaine, often visited this castle; their daughter, also called Eleanor, was born here in October 1162. Thomas à Becket came to stay for Christmas 1166, saying Mass in the Notre-Dame-sur-l'Eau church down by the river, which has sadly been ruined by vandals. The views from the flower-filled gardens that surround the mangled keep are spectacular, including a very graphic panorama of the ascent you've made to get up.

A slender footbridge connects the castle with the narrow little **village** itself, which boasts an abundance of attractive half-timbered houses. Near its sweet little central square stands the modern **St-Julien** church, a quite extraordinary building, somewhat resembling a stack of inverted ice-cream cones, which was constructed out of concrete segments during the 1920s. Its interior is bursting with exciting "neo-Byzantine" mosaics, which culminate in the vast *Christ in Majesty* above the altar.

ARRIVAL AND INFORMATION

ALENÇON

By train The *gare SNCF* is northeast of the centre, on rue Denis Papin.
Destinations Caen (8 daily; 1hr 10min) via Sées (12min) and Argentan (30min); Le Mans (11 daily; 40min); Tours (4 daily; 1hr 50min).
By bus The *gare routière* is a little short of the *gare SNCF*, northeast of the centre; for bus schedules, visit ⓦ vtni61.fr.
Destinations Bagnoles (3 daily; 1hr); Bellême (1–2 daily; 1hr); Carrouges (3 daily; 40min); Évreux (1 daily; 2hr), via L'Aigle (1hr 40min); Mortagne (2–3 daily; 1hr); Vimoutiers (1–3 daily; 1hr 55min) via Sées (35min).
Tourist office In the dramatic fifteenth-century Maison d'Ozé on the central Place de La Magdelaine (April–June Mon–Fri 9.30am–12.30pm & 1.30–6.30pm, Sat 9.30am–12.30pm & 2–6.30pm; July & Aug Mon–Sat 9.30am–7pm, Sun 10am–12.30pm & 2–4.30pm; Sept–March Mon–Sat 9.30am–12.30pm & 2–6pm; ☏ 02 33 80 66 33, ⓦ paysdalencontourisme.com).

ALENÇON AND AROUND

BAGNOLES-DE-L'ORNE

By train Briouze (3 daily; 40min) for Argentan (1hr 15min) and Paris (3hr).
Tourist office Place du Marché (April–June, Sept & Oct Mon–Sat 9.30am–12.30pm & 2–6pm, Sun 10am–12.30pm & 2.30–6.30pm; July & Aug Mon–Sat 9.30am–6.30pm, Sun 10am–12.30pm & 2.30–6.30pm; Nov–March Mon–Sat 9.30am–12.30pm & 2–6pm; ☏ 02 33 37 85 66, ⓦ bagnolesdelorne.com).

DOMFRONT

Tourist office Beside the castle at 12 place de la Roirie (April–Oct Mon–Sat 10am–12.30pm & 2–6pm; also open Sun 10.30am–12.30pm & 1.30–4.30pm in midsummer; Nov–March Tues–Sat 10am–noon & 2–5pm; ☏ 02 33 38 53 97, ⓦ ot-domfront.com). In summer, they offer weekly guided tours of old Domfront (mid-June to mid-Sept Wed 3pm).

ACCOMMODATION AND EATING

ALENÇON

Chapeau Rouge 3 bd Duchamp ☏ 02 33 26 00 51, ⓦ lechapeaurouge.net. Just across the river west of the centre, this hotel offers rather plain but large and comfortably furnished rooms, with parking but no restaurant. **€67**
Château de Sarceaux Valframbert ☏ 02 33 28 85 11, ⓦ chateau-de-sarceaux.com. Grand, yet comfortable and very welcoming eighteenth-century château, 3km north of central Alençon. Family-owned and run as an intimate B&B, it holds four luxurious antique-furnished rooms and copious breakfasts. Opulent dinners, served communally, are available for an additional €49 per person. **€130**

Le Hangar 12 place à l'Avoine ☏ 02 33 82 04 27. This popular local rendezvous, near the lace museum, serves high-quality but affordable Normandy cuisine, à la carte or on menus from €25. Mon–Fri noon–2pm & 7.30–10pm.
De Paris 26 rue Denis-Papin ☏ 02 33 29 01 64, ⓦ hotel deparis-alencon.com. Perfectly presentable rooms in a simple hotel above a bar facing the *gare SNCF*. All rooms have showers, but some don't have toilets. **€38.50**

CARROUGES

Du Nord Rue Ste-Marguerite ☏ 02 33 27 20 14, ⓦ hotel -restaurant-du-nord.fr. On the narrow street that runs through the heart of Carrouges – a noisier location than it might look – this unprepossessing hotel, above the village bar, offers reasonably large en-suite rooms at low rates, and delicious local cuisine on menus from €12 at lunch, €16 in the evening. Dining room closed Fri eve, plus Sun eve Sept–June; hotel closed mid-Dec to mid-Jan. **€55**

Ô Gayot 2 av de la Ferté-Macé ☎ 02 33 38 44 01, ⓦ ogayot.com. Bagnoles' nicest hotel, alongside the tourist office, offers a contemporary take on the spa experience with its minimalist rooms, and has a pleasant bistro/restaurant (closed Thurs) with outdoor garden seating. **€55**

BAGNOLES-DE-L'ORNE

Beryl 1 rue des Casinos ☎ 02 33 38 44 44, ⓦ hotel -bagnoles.com. Strange-looking, but well equipped and very comfortable hotel in an unbeatable location, with spacious rooms rising in balconied tiers across from the lake, a lake-view restaurant serving menus from €24, and spa facilities. **€109**

Camping de la Vée Avenue du Président Coty ☎ 02 33 37 87 45, ⓦ campingbagnolesdelorne.com. Rather forlorn three-star campsite, south of town. Closed mid-Nov to early March. **€12.80**

DOMFRONT

Camping du Champs Passais ☎ 02 33 37 37 66, ⓦ camping-municipal-domfront.jimdo.com. Domfront's two-star municipal campsite is exceptionally small. Closed Oct to late March. **€6.30**

France 7 rue du Mont-St-Michel ☎ 02 33 38 51 44, ⓦ hoteldefrance-fr.com. Old-fashioned but perfectly comfortable *logis* on the main road below the old town, where it's somewhat exposed to traffic noise. Affordable rooms above a nice bar and good-value restaurant, with a garden at the back. **€53.50**

The Suisse Normande

The area known as the **Suisse Normande** starts roughly 25km south of Caen, stretching along the gorge of the River **Orne** between **Thury-Harcourt** and **Putanges**. While the name, with its allusion to the Alps, may be a little far-fetched – there are certainly no mountains – it's a distinctive and highly attractive region, with cliffs and crags and wooded hills at every turn. The energetic race along the Orne in canoes and kayaks, their lazier counterparts contenting themselves with pedalos or a bizarre species of inflatable rubber tractor, while high above them climbers dangle from thin ropes and claw desperately at the sheer rock face. For mere walkers, the Orne can be frustrating: footpaths along the river are few and far between, whatever maps may say, and often entirely overgrown with brambles. At least one road sign in the area warns of unexploded mines from World War II, so tread carefully.

The Suisse Normande is most usually approached from Caen or Falaise, and contrasts dramatically with the prairie-like expanse of wheatfields en route. **Bus** Verts #34 can take you to Thury-Harcourt or Clécy on its way from Caen to Flers, and **SNCF** run occasional special summer train excursions from Caen. If you're **cycling** head out of Caen via the village of Ifs, following signs for Falaise. The least stressful approach is to follow the D212, cruising across the flatlands to Thury-Harcourt, though swooping down the D23 from Bretteville, with thick woods to either side, is exhilarating. **Touring** the Suisse Normande on a bike, however, is an exhausting business: the minor roads do not follow the gorge floor, but undulate endlessly over the surrounding slopes.

Thury-Harcourt

THURY-HARCOURT is really two separate towns: a little village around a bridge across the Orne, and a larger market town on the hill that overlooks it. In summer, the grounds of the local manor house are open to visitors, providing access to the immediate riverside (March, April & Oct Sun 2.30–6.30pm; May–Sept daily 2.30–6.30pm; €5).

Aunay-sur-Odon

AUNAY-SUR-ODON, 14km west of Thury-Harcourt and the river, is no one's idea of a holiday destination; all but obliterated during the war, it was rebuilt from scratch in functional concrete. In summer, however, when all the **accommodation** possibilities in

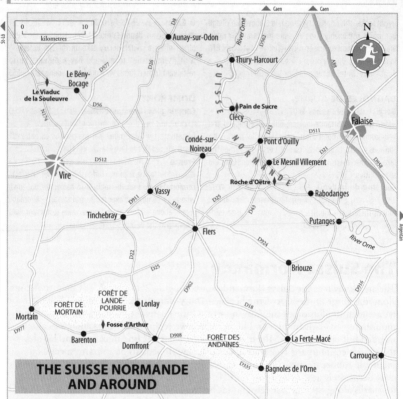

THE SUISSE NORMANDE AND AROUND

the Suisse Normande proper tend to be wildly over-subscribed, you may well be glad of finding a room.

Clécy

The small village of **CLÉCY**, 10km south of Thury-Harcourt, is perched on a hill about 1km up from the point where the D133A crosses the River Orne by means of the Pont du Vey. On the way up, the Parc des Loisirs holds a **Musée du Chemin de Fer Miniature** (mid-April to mid-May Mon & Fri 2–6pm, Tues–Thurs, Sat & Sun 10am–noon & 2–6pm; mid-May to early July Tues–Thurs, Sat & Sun 10am–noon & 2–6pm, Fri 2–6pm; early July to end Aug daily 10am–6.15pm; Sept daily except Mon 2–5pm; €8, ages 3–12 €6; ☎02 31 69 07 13, ⓦchemin-fer-miniature-clecy.com), featuring a gigantic model railway certain to appeal to children.

Clécy is a better bet than Thury-Harcourt for finding a **room**, although its visitors outnumber residents in high season and the whole area can get much too crowded for comfort.

The Pain de Sucre

Across from Clécy, the **east bank** of the Orne is dominated by the exposed rock face of the giant **Pain de Sucre**, or Sugarloaf, looming above the river. Small footpaths, and the tortuous Route des Crêtes, wind up to its flat top, making for some fabulously enjoyable walks. Picnic sites and parking places along the crest hold orientation maps so weather-beaten as to be almost abstract, but the views down to the flat fields of the Orne Valley are stupendous. This is a prime site for **hang-gliders**; disconcertingly, at two points paved concrete ramps, built to facilitate launches, lead right to the edge of the precipice.

Pont d'Ouilly

For anyone who's planning to walk, or cycle, **PONT D'OUILLY**, a dozen or so kilometres upriver from Clécy, where the main road from Vire to Falaise crosses the river, makes a good starting point. It's just a village, with a few basic shops, an old covered market hall and a promenade (with bar) slightly upstream alongside the weir.

Alternatively, a pleasant walk leads 3.5km south along the riverside to the pretty little village of **Le Mesnil Villement**. A Grand Pardon de St-Roch takes place along the river on the third Sunday in August.

The Roche d'Oëtre

A short way south of Pont d'Ouilly, the high rock known as the **Roche d'Oëtre** affords a tremendous view, not over the Orne but into the deep and totally wooded gorge of the Rouvre. The rock itself is private property, though you're under no obligation to visit the café there.

The river widens soon afterwards into the **Lac du Rabodanges**, formed by the many-arched Rabodanges Dam. It's a popular spot, where grassy picnic slopes lead down to the water's edge, and the occasional bather risks a swim among the waterskiers, speedboats, windsurfers, canoes and kayaks. The imposing Rabodanges château, higher up the hillside, is now a stud farm.

Putanges

While the town of **PUTANGES** lies somewhat south of the main attractions of the Suisse Normande, it makes a pleasant stop, with a few bars and pavement cafés. Just upstream from its central bridge lie the weirs over which the Orne appears from its source a short way south.

ARRIVAL AND INFORMATION   THE SUISSE NORMANDE

THURY-HARCOURT

By bus Bus Verts #34 stops in Thury-Harcourt and Clécy en route between Caen and Flers.

Bike and canoe rental Kayak Club Thury-Harcourt, at the waterfront Base de Canoe (❶02 31 79 40 59, ⓦkcth.fr), rents out bikes and canoes.

Tourist office 2 place St-Sauveur (May, June & Sept Tues–Sat 10am–12.30pm & 2.30–6.30pm, Sun 10am–12.30pm; July & Aug also open Mon; Oct–April Tues–Fri 10am–12.30pm & 2.30–5pm, Sat 10am–12.30pm; ❶02 31 79 70 45, ⓦot-suisse-normande.com).

CLÉCY

Tourist office Place du Tripot, behind the church (second half of April Tues–Sat 10am–12.30pm & 2.30–5pm; May, June & first half of Sept Tues–Sat 10am–12.30pm & 2.30–6.30pm, Sun 10am–12.30pm; July & Aug also open Mon;

second half of Sept Tues–Fri 10am–12.30pm, Sat 10am–12.30pm & 2.30–5pm; ❶02 31 69 79 95, ⓦot-suisse-normande.com).

PONT D'OUILLY

Bike and canoe rental Canoes, kayaks and mountain bikes can be rented at the riverside Base de Plein Air (❶02 31 69 86 02, ⓦpontdouilly-loisirs.com).

Tourist office in the market square (May & June Sat 10am–1pm & 2–6pm; July & Aug Tues–Sat 10am–1pm & 2–6pm, Sun 10am–1pm; ❶02 31 90 17 26, ⓦfalaise-tourisme.com).

PUTANGES

Tourist office 1 Grande Rue (Mon–Sat 9.30am–12.30pm & 2–6pm, Sun 10.30am–12.30pm; closed Sun Oct–March; ❶02 33 35 86 57, ⓦoffice-tourisme-putanges.com).

ACCOMMODATION AND EATING

THURY-HARCOURT

Relais de la Poste 7 rue de Caen ☎ 02 31 79 72 12, ⓦ hotel-relaisdelaposte.com. Elegant old country-house hotel, holding a dozen rooms of all shapes and sizes, plus an opulent restaurant (closed Thurs & Fri lunch times in summer, Fri and Sun eves in winter) that's perfect at the end of a long day. Dinner menus start at €29. €65

Vallée du Traspy Rue du Pont-Benoit ☎ 02 31 79 61 80, ⓦ campingdutraspy.fr. Attractive four-star campsite beside the river, with restaurant and mobile home rental. Closed Oct–March. €16.25

AUNAY-SUR-ODON

De la Place 10 rue du 12-Juin-1944 ☎ 02 31 77 60 73, ⓦ hotelrestaurantdelaplace.com. Comfortable hotel in the town centre, with unremarkable rooms and a good restaurant, where the excellent €30 menu includes scallops in cider. Restaurant closed Sun eve mid-Nov to March. €54

CLÉCY

★ **Au Site Normand** 2 rue des Châtelets ☎ 02 31 69 71 05, ⓦ hotel-clecy.com. Village hotel, facing the church, with pleasant, comfortable rooms in a modern annexe, and a stylish modern dining room in the main timber-framed building, serving good menus from €26.50 (restaurant closed Sun pm & all Mon). The river is 1km away, down the hill. €62

Les Rochers des Parcs La Cours, le Vey ☎ 02 31 69 70 36, ⓦ camping-normandie-clecy.fr. Two-star municipal campsite in a lovely waterfront location, at the end of the brief splurge of restaurants, takeaways and snack bars that lines the western riverbank. The tent sites are great, but the mobile homes are too expensive for what you get. Closed Oct–March. €18.60

PUTANGES

Camping du Val d'Orne Putanges-Pont-Ecrepin ☎ 02 33 35 00 25, ⓦ office-tourisme-putanges.com. Small, attractive riverfront campsite. Closed Oct–March. €9.15

Lion Verd Place de l'Hôtel de Ville ☎ 02 33 35 01 86, ⓦ lionverd.fr. Inexpensive hotel, very near the river, with an array of simple old-fashioned rooms, and a good restaurant with splendid views and outdoor seating. Closed Sun eve & Mon, plus all Jan. €39

The Bocage

The region that centres on **St-Lô**, west of Caen and just south of the Cotentin, is known as the **Bocage Normand**. The word *bocage* refers to a type of cultivated countryside common in the west of France, in which fields are delineated by tight hedgerows rooted into walls of earth well over a metre high.

An effective form of smallhold farming, at least in pre-industrial days, the *bocage* also proved to be a perfect system of anti-tank barricades. When the Allied troops tried to advance through the region in 1944, it was almost impenetrable – certainly bearing no resemblance to the East Anglian plains where they had trained. The war here was hand-to-hand, inch-by-inch slaughter; the destruction of villages often wholesale.

St-Lô

The city of **ST-LÔ**, a transport junction 60km south of Cherbourg and 36km southwest of Bayeux, played a crucial wartime role in the Allied breakout from the Cotentin, and has been known ever since as the "Capital of the Ruins". Black-and-white postcards of the wartime devastation are on sale everywhere, and you come across memorial sites at every turn.

In the main square, the gate of the old prison commemorates Resistance members executed by the Nazis, citizens deported east to the concentration camps, and soldiers killed in action. When the bombardment of St-Lô was at its fiercest, the Germans refused to take any measures to protect the prisoners; the gate was all that survived. In similar vein, behind the cathedral, a monument to the dead of World War I is pitted with shrapnel from World War II. Less depressingly, at the foot of the rock under the castle you can see the entrance to caves where locals sheltered from the onslaught, while somewhere far below lie great vaults used by the German command. In Studs Terkel's book, *The Good War*, a GI reminisces about the huge party thrown there after the

Americans found vast stockpiles of champagne; Thomas Pynchon's *Gravity's Rainbow* has a crazed drinking scene based on the tale. **Samuel Beckett** was here during the battle and after, working for the Irish Red Cross as interpreter, driver and provision-seeker – for such items as rat poison for the maternity hospitals. He said he took away with him a "time-honoured conception of humanity in ruins".

The newness of so much in St-Lô reveals the scale of fighting. It took sixty years for the canalized channel of the Vire, running in between the *gare SNCF* and the castle rock, to be extensively relandscaped, Now known as **Port-St-Lô**, it's become an attractive area to walk around, and pedalos are even available for rent. But the most visible – and brilliant – reconstruction is the **Cathédrale de Notre Dame**. The main body of this, with its strange southward-veering nave, has been conventionally repaired and rebuilt. Between the shattered west front and base of the collapsed north tower, however, a startling sheer wall of icy green stone makes no attempt to mask the destruction.

By way of contrast, a lighthouse-like 1950s folly spirals to nowhere on the main square, place Général-de-Gaulle. Should you feel the urge to climb its 157 steps, make your way into the labyrinth of glass at its feet, which houses St-Lô's tourist office, and pay the €2 admission fee.

In mid-August each year, St-Lô plays host to the **Normandy Horse Show** (⊚ normandie-horse-show.fr).

Musée des Beaux Arts

Place du Champ du Mars • Wed–Sun 2–6pm • €2.75 • ☎ 02 33 72 52 55, ⊚ saint-lo.fr

St-Lô's **Musée des Beaux Arts**, around the back of the Mairie, is full of treasures. Standouts include a Boudin sunset; a Lurçat tapestry depicting his dog, entitled *Nadir et les Pirates*; works by Corot, van Loo, Moreau; a Léger watercolour, *Anniversaire*; and a fine series of sixteenth-century Flemish tapestries.

Northeast from St-Lô

Travellers heading **northeast from St-Lô**, towards Bayeux, pass close to two remarkable buildings: the **Abbaye de Cerisy-la-Forêt** and the **Château de Balleroy**. Neither is easy to get to without transport, but if you have a bike or car they shouldn't be missed.

Abbaye de Cerisy-la-Forêt

Rue Sangles, Cerisy-la-Fôret • April daily except Mon 11am–6pm; May– Aug daily 10am–6pm; Sept Wed–Sun noon–6pm; Oct to mid-Nov Sat & Sun noon–6pm; guided tours May–Sept Wed 3pm • €4; guided tours €6 • ☎ 02 33 57 34 63, ⊚ abbaye-cerisy.fr

The village of **CERISY-LA-FORÊT** stands at the edge of its forest 6km west of the D572 and a total of 20km northeast of St-Lô. Its eleventh-century Romanesque **abbaye St-Vigor** was founded by William the Conqueror's father on the site of an already venerable monastery. Set on a hill, overlooking an attractive pond just east of Cerisy itself, its triple tiers of windows and arches, lapping light onto its cream stone, can make you sigh in wonder at the skills of medieval Norman masons. The abbey these days functions as the local parish church, and following extensive recent renovations it's looking more splendid than ever.

Château de Balleroy

Château Daily: April–June & Sept 10.30am–12.30pm & 2–6.30pm; July & Aug 10.30am–6.30pm **Museum and gardens** April–Sept daily 10.30am–6.30pm • Château €7, museum €4.50, both €9 • ☎ 02 31 21 06 76, ⊚ chateau-balleroy.fr

The village of **BALLEROY**, 8.5km east of Cerisy across the D572, and 21km northeast of St-Lô, harks back to an era when architects ruled over craftsmen. Its main street leads straight to the **château**, masterpiece of the celebrated seventeenth-century architect François Mansard. The formal gardens were laid out by André le Nôtre, also responsible for those at Versailles.

3

In keeping with its ostentatious past, the château was bought in 1970 by the late American press magnate Malcolm S. Forbes (1919–90), pal of presidents Nixon, Ford and Reagan. You can tour the house to see its eclectic furnishings, pieces of modern sculpture and an original *salon*, which holds superb royal portraits by Mignard.

Forbes devoted a museum at Balleroy to his principal passion, **ballooning**. The historical exhibits are truly fascinating, even if there is rather too much emphasis on Forbes himself.

The Vire Valley

Once St-Lô was taken in the Battle of Normandy, the armies moved speedily on to their next confrontation. Consequently, the **Vire Valley**, trailing south from St-Lô, saw little action – and indeed its towns and villages have rarely been touched by any historic or cultural mainstream. The motivation in coming to this landscape of rolling hills, occasional gorges, and orchards of apples and pears, is essentially to consume the region's cider, Calvados and butter-rich fruit pastries.

Between St-Lô and Vire

The finest section of the Vire is the valley that stretches south from St-Lô through the Roches de Ham to Tessy-sur-Vire. A pair of sheer rocky promontories high above the river, known as the **Roches de Ham**, are promoted as a "viewing table", though the pleasure lies as much in the walk up, through lanes lined with blackberries, hazelnuts and rich orchards.

Just downstream from the Roches, in the tiny village of **LA CHAPELLE-SUR-VIRE**, the church that towers majestically above the river has been an object of pilgrimage since the twelfth century, though in its current incarnation it dates from 1886. There's a weir nearby and a scattering of grassy islands.

The spacious country town of **TORIGNI-SUR-VIRE**, 5km northeast of La Chapelle, was home to the Grimaldi family before they achieved quasi-royal status upon moving on to the principality of Monaco. Other than a few grand buildings, however, there's little to the town itself.

Vire

The pride and joy of the people of the hill town of **VIRE** are their *andouilles*, the highly spiced sausages known in English as chitterlings. If you can avoid these hideous parcels of pigs' intestines, and the assortment of abattoirs that produce them, it's possible to have a good time; in fact, Vire is worth visiting specifically for its food, and for its Friday **market** in particular.

The only problem is what to do when you're not eating. As testified by a memorial in the **belfry** that stands alone in the town centre, the town was all but destroyed on D-Day, at a cost of five hundred lives. That stunted tower houses temporary exhibitions each summer (July & Aug Mon–Thurs 2–6pm, Fri & Sat 10am–noon & 2–6pm; free), while down the hill towards the river, the **Museum of Vire** (May–Oct Wed–Sun 10am–12.30pm & 2–6pm; €3; ☎02 31 66 66 50, ⓦmuseedevire.blogspot.co.uk) in the place Ste-Anne holds furniture, costumes and paintings by regional artists. Nearby, you can wander by the little scrap of **canal**, equipped with twee floating houses for the ducks, which lies just below the one stark finger that survives of the castle.

THE UNLIKELY BIRTHPLACE OF VAUDEVILLE

The small industrial area immediately north of Vire, where the Vire and Varenne valleys meet, holds a remarkable place in the history of popular music. As the **Vaux de Vire**, this became a centre during the fifteenth century for the manufacture of cloth. The drinking songs composed by one of the textile workers, Olivier Basselin, acquired such popularity throughout medieval Europe that the district gave its name to a new kind of entertainment – **vaudeville**.

BUNGY-JUMPING FROM THE VIADUC DE LA SOULEUVRE

The former railway viaduct of **Le Viaduc de la Souleuvre**, 10km north of Vire, at the eastern end of the sinuous Vire gorge, was designed by Gustave Eiffel. Only the six supporting granite pillars of Eiffel's original structure remain – the railway closed down in 1970 – but a wooden boardwalk has been relaid across half the span of the bridge, on which visitors can cross to the deepest part of the gorge. Once there, 61m up, they are expected to jump off – this is A.J. Hackett's **bungy-jumping** centre (hours vary, but open April–June & Sept–Nov Sat, Sun & hols; July & Aug daily; first jump €129, additional jumps on same day €49; reservations essential ☎ 02 31 66 31 66, ⓦ www.ajhackett.fr). Less intrepid souls can walk down to the meadows immediately beneath the viaduct and watch the plummeting from there.

Lac de la Dathée

Set in open country, 6km south of Vire along the D76, the **Lac de la Dathée** is circled by footpaths. In summer it sometimes dries up completely, but when it's wet it can also be crossed by rented sailing boat, kayak or windsurf board (daily June–Sept; ☎ 02 31 66 01 58, ⓦ mjc-vire.org).

St-Sever

The village of **ST-SEVER**, 14km west of Vire along the D524, is backed by a dark and magical **forest** that holds a dolmen, an abbey, and a scattering of good picnic spots marked by signs showing a champagne bottle in a hamper.

Villedieu-les-Poêles

VILLEDIEU-LES-POÊLES – literally "City of God the Frying Pans" – is a lively place, usually busy with tourists, 28km west of Vire. Much of this ancient town still retains significant elements of its medieval appearance, especially in its backstreets, where perfectly preserved old courtyards are tucked away behind unprepossessing wooden gateways.

Ever since the twelfth century, Villedieu has been a centre for **metalworking**, despite the fact that with no mines in Normandy the only source of copper came from melting down unwanted artefacts. To this day, copper souvenirs and kitchen utensils gleam from its rows of shops, and the tourist office can provide lists of dozens of local ateliers for more direct purchases.

Musée de la Poeslerie

Cour du Foyer, 25 rue Général-Huard April–Oct Mon–Sat 10am–12.30pm & 2–6pm, plus Sun 2–6pm in July & Aug • €5 • ☎ 02 33 69 33 44, ⓦ museesvilledieu.sitew.com

Displays at the **Musée de la Poeslerie**, set in a pretty little courtyard, illustrate the historical development of copperware hereabouts; the same ticket also gets you into the **Musée de la Dentellière** (lace-making) in the same building. Paying an extra €2 entitles you to admission to the **Musée du Meuble Normand** (mid-May to late Sept same hours) a museum of Norman furniture, down the street in place du Pussoir Fidèle.

Atelier du Cuivre

54 rue Général-Huard Mon–Fri 9am–noon & 1.30–6pm, Sat 9am–noon & 2–5.30pm • €5.50 • ☎ 02 33 51 31 85, ⓦ atelierducuivre.fr

The **Atelier du Cuivre**, or copper workshop, gives visitors a rare opportunity to see copper craftsmen at work, and to buy the results. First, however, you have to watch a twenty-minute film about the process. If possible, don't come on a Saturday, when fewer of the actual artisans are likely to be here.

Fonderie de Cloches

13 rue du Pont-Chignon • Mid-Feb to mid-July & late Aug to mid-Nov Tues–Sat 10am–12.30pm & 2–5.30pm; mid-July to late Aug daily 9.30am–6.30pm • €6.50 • ☎ 02 33 61 00 56, ⓦ cornille-havard.com

Even if all Villedieu's emphasis on copper pots and pans is starting to seem obsessive, it's well worth making time to visit the **Fonderie de Cloches**, one of the twelve remaining **bell foundries** in Europe. Work here is only part-time due to limited demand, but you may find the forge lit nonetheless. Expert craftsmen will show you the moulds, composed of an unpleasant-looking combination of clay, goats' hair and horse manure.

Zoo Champrepus

D924, 8km west of Villedieu • Mid-Feb to mid-March, second half of Sept, & second half of Oct daily 11am–6pm; second half of March & first half of Oct Sat & Sun 11am–6pm; mid-April to mid-Sept daily 10am–7pm • €15.50, ages 3–12 €9.50 • ☎ 02 33 61 30 74, ⓦ zoo-champrepus.com

An arch across the main road at **CHAMPREPUS**, west of Villedieu, serves as both a sign announcing, and a bridge between the two sections of, Normandy's finest **zoo**. This displays a vast array of species in remarkably natural surroundings, starting a little disappointingly with domestic and farm animals such as bunnies and donkeys, but swiftly moving on to tigers and chimps, ostriches and otters, and even giraffes.

In this typically pastoral Norman landscape, it's oddly shocking to encounter zebras grazing in the meadows, wallabies hopping around the orchards, and lions making their homes amid dolmens.

In the most unusual section, visitors are free to stroll among large groups of sleepy-eyed **lemurs**, with nothing to stop you touching them apart from their prominently bared canine teeth. Children are invited to milk an artificial cow or bounce on an inflatable elephant, and there's a little grill-restaurant on site.

Forêt de Lande-Pourrie

South from Vire, anyone heading for Fougères (see p.206) or Domfront (see p.166) passes through the **Forêt de Mortain** and its continuation, the **Forêt de Lande-Pourrie**. The **Fosse d'Arthur**, a remote spot in the forest east of Mortain, is one of many unlikely claimants to King Arthur's death scene. A couple of waterfalls disappear into deep limestone caverns, but there's little to see.

Mortain

The war-ravaged town of **MORTAIN** perches high above the very deep gorge of the Cance, 24km south of Vire. It's not a place to linger very long, but the views, especially from the south end of the main street, are spectacular. A short walk west out of town leads into some lovely countryside, with two **waterfalls** – known as the Grande Cascade and the Petite Cascade – interrupting the river itself. Head up the high rocky bluff to the east, on the other hand, and from the tiny chapel at the top the neighbouring province of Maine spreads before you. On a clear day, you can even see Mont-St-Michel.

St-Hilaire-du-Harcoët

The thriving (Wed) market town of **ST-HILAIRE-DU-HARCOËT**, 28km north of Fougères in Brittany (see p.206), amounts to little more than a crossroads near the big market square. It does, however, hold a few restaurants and hotels.

ARRIVAL AND INFORMATION   **THE BOCAGE**

ST-LÔ

By train The *gare SNCF* is on avenue Briovère, across the Vire river from the town centre.

Destinations Caen (12 daily; 50min), via Bayeux (25min);

Rennes (4 daily; 2hr 10min), via Coutances (20min) and Pontorson (1hr 15min).

By bus The *gare routière* is on rue des 80e et 136e, a short way south of the train station.

Destinations Bayeux (8 daily; 30min); Cherbourg (3 daily; 1hr 40min); Coutances (5 daily; 50min); Villedieu-les-Poêles (4 daily; 1hr 10min).

Tourist office 60 rue de la Poterne (Mon 2–6pm, Tues–Fri 9.30am–12.30pm & 2–6pm, Sat 10am–1pm; ☎ 02 14 29 00 17, ⓦ saint-lo-agglo.fr).

VIRE

By train Granville (6 daily; 35min) via Villedieu (15min); Paris (5 daily; 2hr 45min) via Argentan (50min) and L'Aigle (1hr 30min).

By bus Avranches (5 daily; 45min); Condé-sur-Noireau (2 daily; 30min); Fougères (4 daily; 1hr 30min); St-Hilaire-

du-Harcoët (4 daily; 1hr).

Tourist office Square de la Résistance (Easter–Nov Mon–Fri 9.30am–12.30pm & 1.30–6pm, Sat 9.30am–12.30pm & 1.30–5pm; Nov–Easter Mon & Wed–Fri 9.30am–12.30pm & 1.30–6pm, Tues 9.30am–12.30pm; ☎ 02 31 66 28 50, ⓦ bocage-normand.com).

VILLEDIEU-LES-POÊLES

Tourist office 8 place des Costils (July & Aug daily 9.30am–6pm; April–June & Sept daily 9.30am–12.30pm & 2–6pm; Oct–March Mon–Sat 9.30am–noon & 2–5.30pm; ☎ 02 33 61 05 69, ⓦ tourisme-villedieu.com).

ACCOMMODATION AND EATING

ST-LÔ

La Crémaillère 8 rue de la Chancellerie ☎ 02 33 57 14 68, ⓦ la-cremaillere-50.com. Economical hotel up in town, holding fifteen plain en-suite rooms, plus a good-value restaurant, where all the menus, which start at €9.50 for lunch and €12.50 for dinner, include a buffet of hors d'oeuvres. **€46**

Mercure Saint-Lô 1 av Briovère ☎ 02 33 05 10 84, ⓦ mercure.com. St-Lô's largest hotel, ranged atop a ridge beside the *gare SNCF*, just across the river. As well as 67 modern motel-style rooms, it's home to the *Tocqueville* restaurant, open for all meals on weekdays only, and serving menus from €19. **€90**

TORIGNI-SUR-VIRE

Le Lac des Charmilles Route de Vire ☎ 02 33 56 91 74, ⓦ camping-lacdescharmilles.com. Very appealing little campsite, within easy walking distance of town beside a lake that's circled by a cycle path, and offering a bar/restaurant and heated swimming pool. Closed Nov–Feb. **€22.50**

VIRE

De France 4 rue d'Aignaux ☎ 02 31 68 00 35, ⓦ hotel defrancevire.com. Central hotel, within sight of the tourist office, with a good dining room that serves several separate menus; the €33 menu focuses exclusively on *andouilles*, but no one's going to make you eat it if you don't want to. Closed mid-Dec to mid-Jan, plus Mon lunch. **€60**

La Manchevrette La Béchellerie, Gathemo ☎ 02 33 69 31 36, ⓦ la.manchevrette.free.fr. Your chance to sleep in a genuine Mongolian bed in a genuine Mongolian yurt, holding up to four people, on a working goat farm 12km southwest of Vire. **€75**

Au Vrai Normand 14 rue Armand-Gasté ☎ 02 31 67 90 99, ⓦ auvrainormand.com. Vire's best stand-alone restaurant, with lunch from €18 and a €30 dinner menu that includes a *Montgolfière de pêcheur*, a sort of fish stew covered with pastry. Mon & Thurs–Sat noon–2pm & 7.15–9pm, Tues & Sun noon–2pm.

VILLEDIEU-LES-POÊLES

Camping des Chevaliers 2 impasse Pré de la Rose ☎ 02 33 61 02 44, ⓦ camping-deschevaliers.com. Three-star campsite in the lush meadows beside the river, with its own bar/restaurant. Closed Oct–March. **€22.50**

Fruitier Place Costils ☎ 02 33 90 51 00, ⓦ le-fruitier .com. Modern hotel facing the tourist office, and serving good food on an open-air but not very exciting terrace. Closed Christmas to mid-Jan. **€81**

Le Pussoir 2 place du Pussoir Fidèle ☎ 02 33 51 94 58. Brasserie/grill with tables out on a delightful, pedestrianized floral square, just below the main street, with a great-value €13 lunch menu. Tues noon–2.30pm, Wed–Sat noon–2.30pm & 7–9.30pm.

Le Samovar 93 rue du Dr-Havard ☎ 02 33 51 46 73. This cosy, informal and very friendly little café/bistro places a strong emphasis on local and/or organic produce, served on a changing daily set menu priced at €13.50 for two courses, €17.50 for three, and also offers healthy mixed salads. Tues–Sat 10am–11.30pm.

St-Pierre et St-Michel 12 place de la République ☎ 02 33 61 00 11, ⓦ st-pierre-hotel.com. Very welcoming Logis, in the heart of the main street, housing a stylish restaurant that serves seriously gastronomic menus at €19.50 and €29.50. Closed mid-Jan to mid-Feb. **€56**

MORTAIN

De la Poste 1 place des Arcades ☎ 02 33 59 00 05, ⓦ hoteldelaposte-mortain.fr. The best place to stay in Mortain, facing the church with a restaurant serving good menus from €19 at lunch, €34 for dinner. Restaurant closed Fri, plus Sat pm & Sun pm. **€63**

ST-HILAIRE-DU-HARCOËT

Le Cygne et Résidence 99 rue Waldeck-Rousseau ☎ 02 33 49 11 84, ⓦ hotel-le-cygne.fr. Comfortable, modern *logis* on the main road into town from Fougères, with a swimming pool in the garden and an appealing set of menus from €19.50 to €80. Closed Sun eve & Fri eve Oct–March. **€80**

3

The North Coast and Rennes

HALF-TIMBERED HOUSES, DINAN

The North Coast and Rennes

The northern coast of Brittany is varied in the extreme. Long sections, open to the full force of the Atlantic, are spectacular but much too dangerous for swimming; others shelter superb natural harbours and peaceful resorts. The old *citadelle* port of St-Malo makes an attractive point of arrival, with plenty of nearby sights and diversions. It faces the sedate beach town of Dinard across the mouth of the spectacular estuary of the River Rance, while 20km upstream, the splendid medieval walls of Dinan guard the head of the river itself.

Towards Normandy, to the east, the **Baie du Mont-St-Michel** is dominated by the pinnacle of the Mont itself (see p.137), and swept by extraordinary tides that render swimming out of the question. **Cancale**, the most sheltered point along the Breton side of the bay, is a good spot from which to appreciate it all, ideally as you sample the town's famous oysters. Inland, further southeast, the redoubtable fortresses of **Fougères** and **Vitré** still glower at the Norman frontier.

At the heart of the *département* of Ille-et-Vilaine, the city of **Rennes** has after centuries of rivalry with Nantes finally established itself as the indisputable capital of Brittany. Rennes may not be the prettiest town in the province, but it is without doubt the liveliest. It hosts an important university and most of the major Breton political and cultural organizations; it's also renowned for **festivals**, devoting itself to ten days of theatre and music each July during the **Tombées de la Nuit**, and celebrating the **Transmusicales** rock festival in December.

The best of Brittany's northern **resorts** are concentrated along two separate stretches of coastline, the Côte d'Émeraude and the Côte de Granit Rose. As green as its name suggests, the **Côte d'Émeraude** remains largely unspoiled, at its wildest on the heather-covered headlands of Cap Fréhel. Thanks to gorgeous beaches, seaside towns such as **Erquy** and **Le Val-André** hold plenty of hotels and restaurants, while it's always possible to find a secluded campsite for a night or two's stopover.

Further west, beyond the placid **Baie de St-Brieuc**, the coastline erupts into a garish labyrinth of pink granite boulders, the famed **Côte de Granit Rose**. This harsher territory was once, at **Paimpol** and elsewhere, the home of cod and whaling fleets that ranged right across the Atlantic. Today it's reliant on tourism, especially around lovely coastal villages like **Ploumanac'h** and **Trégastel**. There are also plenty of places where you can avoid the crowds, such as **Loguivy** on the mainland, and, just offshore, the **Île de Bréhat**, which is among the most beautiful of all northern French islands.

St-Malo

The elegant, ancient, and beautifully positioned city of **ST-MALO** makes an essential stop on any tour of Brittany. Walled and built with the same grey granite stone as Mont-St-Michel, St-Malo was originally a fortified island at the mouth of the Rance,

CREUSES de CANCALE

4,20€ La dz

OYSTERS FOR SALE, CANCALE

Highlights

❶ St-Malo St-Malo's walled *citadelle* still feels like the romantic haunt of pirates and explorers. **See p.178**

❷ Dinan With its imposing walls and delightful lanes, Dinan is one of France's finest medieval towns. **See p.191**

❸ Cancale Cancale is thronged with seafood lovers; picnic on oysters from a harbourfront stall, or dine at a fine restaurant without breaking the bank. **See p.194**

❹ Binic Cute little seafront resort, with huge beaches, that's ideal for families and romantic couples alike. **See p.216**

❺ Île de Bréhat Even in high summer, a boat trip to this beautiful island enables you to escape the traffic and crowds. **See p.221**

❻ Sentier des Douaniers The spectacular coastal footpath between Perros-Guirec and Ploumanac'h passes extraordinary pink-granite scenery. **See p.225**

❼ Hôtel Beau Séjour What a combination – a quirky and friendly hotel beside a lovely beach, run by owners who are also fabulous bakers. **See p.228**

❽ Cairn de Barnenez A pair of step pyramids, predating those in Egypt, in a magnificent seafront setting. **See p.230**

HIGHLIGHTS ARE MARKED ON THE MAP ON PP.180–181

controlling not only the estuary but also the open sea beyond. Now inseparably attached to the mainland, it's the most popular destination in the region, thanks more to its superb **old citadelle** and sprawling **beaches** than to the **ferry terminal** that's tucked into the harbour nearby.

From outside the walls, the dignified ensemble of the old city might seem stern and forbidding, but passing through into the **intra-muros** ("within the walls") streets brings you into a busy, lively and very dynamic town, packed with hotels, restaurants, bars and shops. Yes, the summer crowds can be oppressive, but even then a stroll atop the

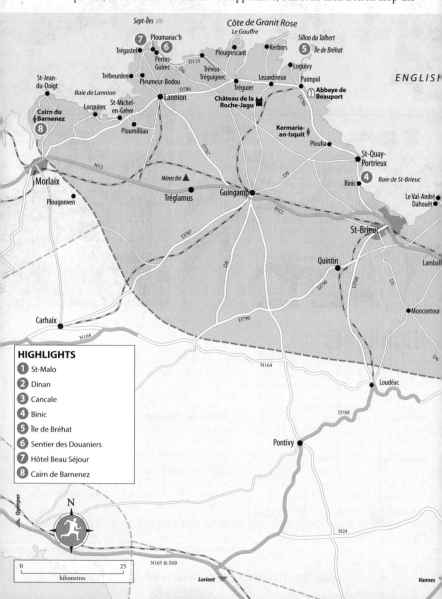

HIGHLIGHTS

1. St-Malo
2. Dinan
3. Cancale
4. Binic
5. Île de Bréhat
6. Sentier des Douaniers
7. Hôtel Beau Séjour
8. Cairn de Barnenez

N

0 ————— 25
kilometres

ramparts should restore your equilibrium, while the presence of vast, clean strands of sand right on the city's doorstep is a very big bonus if you're travelling with children. Having to spend a night here before or after a ferry crossing is a positive pleasure – so long as you reserve accommodation in advance.

Brief history

While the promontory fort of Alet, south of the modern centre in what's now **St-Servan**, commanded approaches to the Rance even before the arrival of the

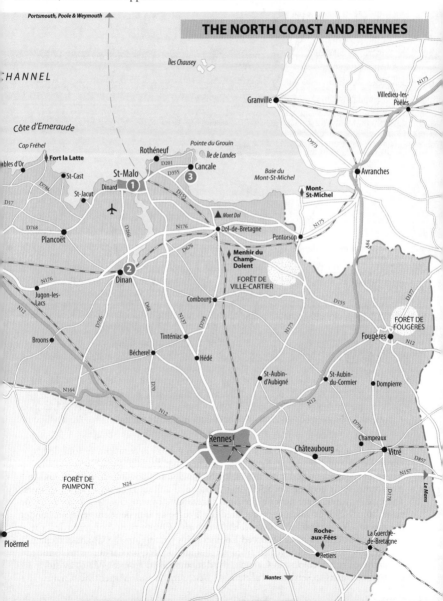

THE NORTH COAST AND RENNES

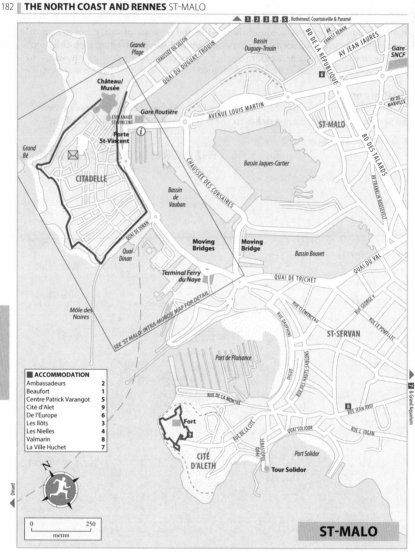

4

ST-MALO

ACCOMMODATION

Ambassadeurs	2
Beaufort	1
Centre Patrick Varangot	5
Cité d'Alet	9
De l'Europe	6
Les Ilôts	3
Les Nielles	4
Valmarin	8
La Ville Huchet	7

Romans, modern St-Malo traces its origins to a monastic community founded by saints Aaron and Brendan early in the sixth century. From 550 AD onwards the settlement was identified with the Celtic St Maclou (or possibly MacLow), and in later centuries it became notorious as the home of a fierce breed of **pirate-mariners**. These adventurers were never quite under anybody's control but their own; for four years from 1590, St-Malo even declared itself to be an independent republic, under the motto "*Ni Français, Ni Breton, Malouin Suis*". Over a period of centuries, the *corsaires* of St-Malo not only forced English ships passing up the Channel to pay tribute, but also brought wealth from further afield. **Jacques Cartier**, who founded the earliest French colony in Canada, lived in and sailed from St-Malo, as did the first colonists to settle the Falklands – hence the islands' Argentinian name,

Las Malvinas. Even when the Duke of Marlborough landed fifteen thousand men just up the coast near Cancale in 1758, and attempted to take the city by land, St-Malo's defences proved too formidable.

St-Malo intra-muros – the citadelle

Very much the prime destination for visitors, the **citadelle** of St-Malo was for many years joined to the mainland only by a long causeway, before the original line of the coast was hidden forever by the construction of the harbour basin. Although its cobbled streets of restored seventeenth- and eighteenth-century houses can be packed to the point of absurdity in summer – and the cobbles present quite a challenge to parents pushing buggies – away from the more popular thoroughfares random exploration is fun.

Owing to space limitations on this tiny peninsula, the buildings tend to be a little more high-rise than you might expect. Venerable as they may look, they are almost entirely reconstructed – photographs of the damage suffered in 1944, when General Patton bombarded the city for two weeks before the Germans surrendered, show barely a stone left in place. Eighty percent of the city had to be lovingly and precisely rebuilt, stone by stone.

Beneath grey skies, the narrow lanes can appear sombre, even grim, but in high summer or at sunset they take on a different, softer hue, much more in keeping with the *citadelle's* romantic atmosphere. In any case, you can always surface to the sunlight on the **ramparts** – first erected in the fourteenth century, and redesigned by the master builder Vauban four hundred years later – to enjoy wonderful views all round, especially to the west as the sun sets over the sea.

Musée d'Histoire de la Ville

St-Malo Château • April–Sept daily 10am–12.30pm & 2–6pm; Oct–March Tues–Sun 10am–noon & 2–6pm • €6, or €11 with Tour Solidor; free on first Fri of month • ☏ 02 99 40 71 57, ⓦ ville-saint-malo.fr

The main gate of the *citadelle* as you approach by road, the **Porte St-Vincent**, was constructed in 1709. Until 1770, the whole town was sealed off by a 10pm curfew; as you walk through the gateway, you pass the small room where latecomers were obliged to spend the night. Once inside, you'll see the forbidding stone walls of the **castle**, which houses the **Musée d'Histoire de la Ville**, something of a paean to the "prodigious prosperity" enjoyed by St-Malo during its days of piracy, colonialism and slave-trading.

Climbing the 169 steps of the castle keep – whose walls are up to 7m thick – you pass a fascinating mixture of maps, diagrams and exhibits. Among them are chilling handbills from the Nazi occupation, accounts of the "infernal machine" used by the English to blow up the port in 1693, and savage four-pronged *chaussetrappes*, thrown by pirates onto the decks of ships being boarded to immobilize their crews. A gull's-eye prospect at the top takes in the entire *citadelle*.

The beaches

It is possible to pass **through the ramparts** at a couple of points on the western side of the peninsula, where there are some small, sheltered **beaches**. On the open shore to the east of the *citadelle*, a huge beach stretches away beyond the resort-suburbs of **Courtoisville** and **Paramé**. Out to sea stands a procession of rocky islets, many of which still hold traces of medieval fortifications.

Grand Bé

When the tide is low, an easy short walk across the sands of the Plage de Bon Secours, past a seawater swimming pool refreshed by each high tide, leads to the small island of **Grand Bé**. It's such a popular stroll that you may even need to queue to get onto the short causeway. Solemn warnings are posted of the dangers of attempting to return from the island when the tide has risen too far – timetables are displayed by the Porte St-Pierre and elsewhere. If you're caught on the island, there you have to stay. Its one "sight" is the tomb of the nineteenth-century writer-politician **François-René du Chateaubriand**, who was born in St-Malo on Sept 4, 1768, and died in 1848.

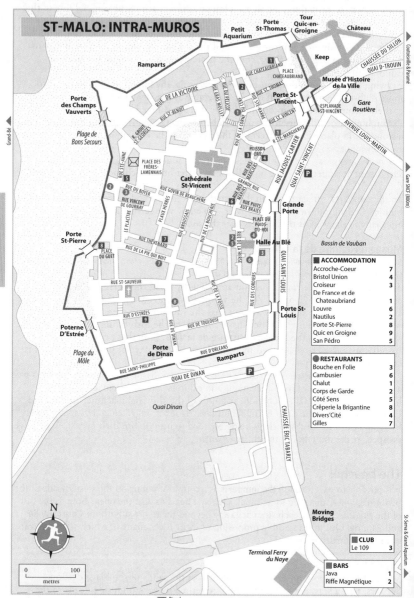

ST-MALO: INTRA-MUROS

Grand-Bé

Coutouville & Paramé

Gare SNCF (800m)

St-Servia & Grand Aquarium

Dinard

ACCOMMODATION

Accroche-Coeur	7
Bristol Union	4
Croiseur	3
De France et de Chateaubriand	1
Louvre	6
Nautilus	2
Porte St-Pierre	8
Quic en Groigne	9
San Pédro	5

RESTAURANTS

Bouche en Folie	3
Cambusier	6
Chalut	1
Corps de Garde	2
Côté Sens	5
Crêperie la Brigantine	8
Divers'Cité	4
Gilles	7

CLUB

Le 109	3

BARS

Java	1
Riffe Magnétique	2

Fort National

Opening hours vary, dependent on tides: Easter hols, plus June to mid-July & late Aug to Sept daily except Tues; mid-July to late Aug daily • €5 •
📞 06 72 46 66 26, 🌐 fortnational.com

The **Fort National**, a sturdy little fortress designed by Vauban in 1689, occupies a small island, just offshore from the château. Like Grand Bé, it's only accessible at low tide. It's open for guided tours in summer only.

St-Servan

The district of **St-Servan**, within walking distance along the corniche south from the *citadelle*, is actually older than St-Malo itself. It was on the site of the Gallo-Roman city of Alet that St Maclou established his church, and the seat of the bishopric only moved onto the impregnable island fortress when danger threatened in 1142. St-Servan is a very pretty little town in its own right, curving around successive small inlets and beaches to face the tidal power dam across the river.

Tour Solidor

April–Sept daily 10am–12.30pm & 2–6pm; Oct–March Tues–Sun 10am–noon & 2–6pm • €6, or €11 with Musée d'Histoire de la Ville; free on first Fri of month • 📞 02 99 40 71 58, 🌐 ville-saint-malo.fr

The main landmark in St-Servan, right by the waterfront with views over the town harbour and main beach, is the distinctive **Tour Solidor**. Built in 1382 and consisting of three linked towers, it looks in cross-section just like the ace of clubs.

Originally known in Breton as the *Steir Dor*, or "gate of the river", the Tour Solidor now holds a rather ramshackle **museum** of Cape Horn clipper ships. A haphazard assortment of paintings, models and artefacts tell the story of the European (well, mainly French) exploration of the Pacific, and of the four-masters that dominated the route during the early twentieth century. Curiosities on show include the decorative ceramic rolling pins that English sailors would traditionally leave with their sweethearts, wives or mothers, and various ships in bottles. Visits culminate with a superb view from the topmost ramparts.

Grand Aquarium

Avenue du Général-Patton • Daily: April–June & Sept 10am–7pm; first two weeks in July & second two weeks in Aug 9.30am–8pm; mid-July to mid-Aug 9.30am–9pm; Oct–March 10am–6pm as a rule, but closed most of Jan; last admission 1hr before closing • €16, ages 4–12 €12 • 📞 02 99 21 19 07, 🌐 aquarium-st-malo.com • Bus #5 from *gare SNCF*

Follow the main road due south from St-Servan, and at a roundabout high above town you'll come to the **Grand Aquarium**. This postmodern structure can be a bit bewildering at first, but once you get the hang of it it's an entertaining place, where you can either learn interesting facts about slimy monsters of the deep or simply pull faces back at them. Its eight distinct fish tanks, which hold fish from all over the world, include one shaped like a Polo mint, where dizzy visitors stand in the hole in the middle as myriad fish whirl around them.

The Barrage de la Rance

The road from St-Malo to Dinard crosses the Rance along the top of the world's first **tidal power dam**. Built in 1966, the Barrage de la Rance failed to set a non-nuclear example to the rest of the province, where at the end of the nineteenth century there were still five thousand working windmills. If you choose to cover the 4km between the centre of St-Malo and the *barrage* on foot or bicycle, try to make your way on the small roads through St-Servan, following the line of the estuary southwards, rather than the signposted (circuitous) inland route used by motorists.

4

Roches Sculptées

Chemin des Roches Sculptées, Rothéneuf • Daily except Wed: June–Sept 9am–7pm; Oct–May 10am–noon & 2–6pm • €3 • ☎ 02 99 56 23 95

Just inside the eastern end of St-Malo's city limits, as the D201 winds towards Cancale, signs direct visitors away from the central streets of suburban **Rothéneuf** to the **Roches Sculptées**, or "sculpted rocks". The hermit priest Abbé Fouré spent 25 years, from the 1870s onwards, carving these jumbled boulders into the forms of dragons, giants and assorted sea monsters.

Perched on a rocky promontory high above the water line, they're quite weathered now, and not all that compelling in themselves, but with the town well out of sight this makes an appealing spot to stop and admire the coastline. The gardens of the site also hold a small, sheltered café, and a shop that sells Breton pottery.

ARRIVAL AND DEPARTURE ST-MALO

By cross-channel ferry From the Terminal Ferry du Naye, Brittany Ferries (☎ 02 99 40 64 41, ⓦ brittany -ferries.com) sails to Portsmouth, while Condor Ferries (☎ 02 99 40 78 10, ⓦ condorferries.co.uk) connects with Weymouth and Poole (via Jersey or Guernsey).

By river ferry Between April and Oct, regular passenger ferries (10min) to Dinard operate from the quai Dinan, just outside the southernmost point of the ramparts (€4.90 single, €7.50 return; bikes cost double; ☎ 08 25 13 81 00, ⓦ compagniecorsaire.com). Compagnie Corsaire also conducts excursions up the river to Dinan (see p.191), and cruises along the Brittany coast to Cap Fréhel, St-Cast and the Île Cézembre, and out to Jersey and the Îles Chausey (see p.135).

By train St-Malo's *gare SNCF* is 2km inland from the *citadelle*, convenient neither for the old town nor the ferry. All trains to and from St-Malo pass through Dol. Most continue through to Rennes, so if you're heading west towards Dinan and St-Brieuc, or northeast into Normandy, you'll probably have to change at Dol.

Destinations Rennes (14 daily; 50min; connections for Paris on TGV). All trains pass through Dol (15min).

By bus Almost all local and long-distance buses stop on the esplanade St-Vincent, just outside the *citadelle*. Illenoo (☎ 08 10 35 10 35, ⓦ illenoo.fr) runs services to Dinard, Rennes and Mont-St-Michel; Tibus (☎ 08 10 22 22 22, ⓦ tibus.fr) serves Dinan and Dinard.

Destinations Cancale (6 daily; 45min); Combourg (2 daily; 1hr); Dinan (6 daily; 1hr); Dinard (10 daily; 30min); Fougères (3 daily; 2hr 15min); Mont St-Michel (4 daily; 1hr 30min); Pontorson (4 daily; 1hr 15min); Rennes (3 daily; 1hr 30min); St-Cast (2 daily; 1hr) via St-Jacut (35min).

By car The walled town is encircled by open-air car parks, and there's also a massive underground car park beneath the esplanade St-Vincent, but space can still be very hard to find in summer. If you're driving in to catch a ferry, keep well clear of the old town; the Chaussée de Corsaires, which links the *citadelle* with the ferry terminal, can be closed for long periods while its moveable bridge is opened to let boats out of the Bassin Jacques-Cartier.

INFORMATION AND ACTIVITIES

Tourist office Esplanade St-Vincent, just outside the *citadelle* (April–June & Sept Mon–Sat 9am–1pm & 2–6.30pm, Sun 10am–12.30pm & 2.30–6pm; July & Aug Mon–Sat 9am–7.30pm, Sun 10am–6pm; Oct–March Mon–Sat 9am–1pm & 2–6pm; ☎ 08 25 13 52 00, ⓦ saint-malo -tourisme.com). As well as good detailed city maps, it can provide information on annual festivals such as the Étonnants Voyageurs (Amazing Travellers; ⓦ etonnants -voyageurs.com), dedicated to the film and literature of travel and adventure, which takes place for three days in late May and/or early June, and the two annual Route du Rock music festivals, in mid-Feb and mid-Aug (ⓦ laroutedurock.com).

Bike rental Bicycles can be rented from Les Vélos Bleus, 19 rue Alphonse-Thébault (☎ 02 99 40 31 63, ⓦ velos-bleus.fr; closed Nov–March), who also offer a delivery service for taking luggage to neighbouring towns; or Espace Nicole, 11 rue R-Schuman, Paramé (☎ 02 99 56 11 06, ⓦ cyclesnicole.com).

Sailing St-Malo's Station Nautique can provide full information on all aspects of sailing in the vicinity, from lessons to rentals and cruises; the tourist office has advisers in summer (☎ 02 99 56 18 88, ⓦ nautisme-saint-malo.fr).

Scuba diving St-Malo Plongée Émeraude, Centre Bleu Émeraude, Terre Plein du Naye, St-Servan (☎ 02 99 19 90 36, ⓦ saintmaloplongee.com).

RIVER CRUISES

Le Chateaubriand (☎ 02 99 46 44 40, ⓦ www.chateaubriand.com) offers **sightseeing cruises** through the year in the Baie du Mont-St-Michel and up the Rance, starting from the Gare Maritime du Barrage de la Rance, at the Dinard end of the barrage (90min trip €17, 3hr €30). Gastronomic cruises, which include a full meal, cost €59–82.

Surfing and windsurfing Boards are available for rental from Surf School, 2 av de la Hoguette (☎02 99 40 07 47, ⓦsurfschool.org), or the Société Nautique de la Baie de St-Malo, quai du Bajoyer (☎02 23 18 20 30, ⓦsnbsm

.com). Most surfers make for the beaches further along the coast towards Cancale, the plage du Verger and the larger Anse du Guesclin.

ACCOMMODATION

St-Malo boasts more than a hundred hotels, including the seaside boarding houses just off the beach, along with several campsites and a hostel. In high season it needs every one of them, so make reservations well in advance. Some *intra-muros* hotels take advantage of summer demand by insisting you eat in their own restaurants. Cheaper rates can be found by the *gare SNCF*, or in suburban Paramé. There are two significant advantages to staying in a hotel outside St-Malo's city walls: prices are generally cheaper, and access is easier, whether you're travelling by train or car – especially an issue if you have heavy luggage. On the other hand, most of the after-dark activity takes place in the *citadelle*, and getting there from any of the surrounding suburbs requires a fair walk in through the docks. There are also a handful of nice beach hotels in St-Servan, and in suburban Courtoisville and Paramé to the east. If you don't have a reservation, don't demoralize yourself hunting around, and settle for spending the night somewhere else along the coast or nearby. Apart from the obvious alternatives of Dinard and Dinan, it's worth considering peaceful smaller towns such as Combourg, Cancale, Jugon-les-Lacs, St-Jacut or Erquy.

IN THE CITADELLE

Accroche-Coeur 9 rue Thévenard ☎02 99 40 43 63, ⓦaccrochecoeursaintmalo.fr; map p.184. Welcoming B&B in a quiet side street, in one of the city's few surviving authentic seventeenth-century townhouses. Five beautifully restored and updated rooms, with exceptionally helpful hosts and great breakfasts. **€125**

Bristol Union 4 place de la Poissonnerie ☎02 99 40 83 36, ⓦhotel-bristol-union.com; map p.184. Tall, somewhat upscale hotel, equipped with a lift, in a relatively quiet little square facing the former fish market, just off the Grande Rue. It offers appealing modernized rooms, some very small. Buffet breakfast €9. **€68**

Croiseur 2 place de la Poissonnerie ☎02 99 40 80 40, ⓦhotel-le-croiseur.com; map p.184. Contemporary-style hotel overlooking the old fish market, with sleek and spotless rooms, and a great bar and terrace on the ground floor. Friendly and very good value. **€69**

De France et de Chateaubriand 12 place Chateaubriand ☎02 99 56 66 52, ⓦhotel-fr-chateaubriand.com; map p.184. This imposing old hotel, in prime position behind a courtyard just off the main square, has been partially renovated. While the standard *confort* rooms are pretty ordinary, the *supérieure* – especially those with sea views – are well worth the extra €20 or so, and the old-fashioned public spaces are ideal for lazy days. Choose between a large, well-priced bistro downstairs and the fancier modern top-floor restaurant, *Le 5*. Breakfast costs €12 and parking €15. **€116**

Louvre 2 rue des Marins ☎02 99 40 86 62, ⓦhotel dulouvre-saintmalo.com; map p.184. Pleasant, upmarket place just off Grande Rue, between the Grande Porte and Cathédrale St-Vincent, with fifty nicely revamped rooms – some suitable for disabled visitors – and good €12.50 buffet breakfasts. **€78**

★**Nautilus** 9 rue de la Corne de Cerf ☎02 99 40 42 27, ⓦlenautilus.com; map p.184. Colourfully refitted hotel (with a lift), not far in from the Porte St-Vincent, with

small, bright, good-value rooms, all with shower and WC. Friendly staff ensure it's hugely popular with younger travellers in particular, but it's welcoming to all. Bar but no restaurant. Closed Nov to late Dec. **€72**

Porte St-Pierre 2 place du Guet ☎02 99 40 91 27, ⓦhotel-portestpierre.com; map p.184. Comfortable Logis de France, peeping over the walls of the *citadelle*, near the small Porte St-Pierre and very handy for the beach; the modernized rooms have new floors and in many cases sea views (€10 extra). One family room sleeps five. The owners also run a restaurant across the alley, recommended for seafood lovers. Closed mid-Nov to Feb. **€85**

★**Quic en Groigne** 8 rue d'Estrées ☎02 99 20 22 20, ⓦquic-en-groigne.com; map p.184. Friendly little hotel run by helpful owners, located at the far end of the *citadelle*, with attractive en-suite rooms, recently refreshed with good bathroom fittings. Closed mid-Dec to late Jan. **€85**

San Pédro 1 rue Ste-Anne ☎02 99 40 88 57, ⓦsanpedro-hotel.com; map p.184. Twelve compact but tastefully and stylishly furnished rooms in a nice quiet setting, just inside the walls in the north of the *citadelle*. Great breakfasts and friendly advice. Higher rooms (reached via a minuscule lift) enjoy sea views, and cost around €10 extra. Closed Dec to mid-March. **€75**

OUTSIDE THE WALLS

Ambassadeurs 11 chaussée du Sillon, Courtoisville ☎02 99 40 26 26, ⓦhotel-ambassadeurs-saintmalo .com; map p.182. Twenty-room, four-floor hotel, right on the seafront, with free parking nearby. The rooms may be small, but they've been very tastefully refreshed, and those facing the sea (around €20 extra) come with balconies directly over the waves, and there's also a rooftop bar with a fabulous terrace. **€80**

Beaufort 25 chaussée du Sillon, Courtoisville ☎02 99 40 99 99, ⓦwww.hotel-beaufort.com; map p.182.

Grand seaside hotel, half-an-hour's walk along the beach from the *citadelle*. Beautifully restored rooms – some with lovely sea-view balconies – and a fine restaurant. **€176**

Centre Patrick Varangot 37 av du Père-Umbricht, Paramé ☎ 02 99 40 29 80, ⓦ centrevarangot.com; map p.182. One of France's busiest hostels, near the beach 2km northeast of the *gare SNCF*, and usually dominated by lively young travellers. Dorm beds are in shared en-suite rooms that can also be rented privately; hostelling association membership required. Rates include breakfast, and there's also a cut-price cafeteria where you can get a three-course meal for €8.20, plus kitchen facilities and tennis courts. No curfew, open all year. Dorms **€24**

★ **Cité d'Alet** Allée Gaston Buy, St-Servan ☎ 02 99 81 60 91, ⓦ ville-saint-malo.fr/tourisme/les-campings; map p.182. The nicest local campsite is also by far the nearest to the *citadelle*, a municipally run gem in a dramatic location on the headland southwest of St-Malo, overlooking the city from within the wartime German fortified stronghold. Bus #1 from *gare SNCF* or Porte St-Vincent. Open July to late Sept, plus mid-April to mid-May; and mid-term holidays in June & Oct. **€15.70**

De l'Europe 44 bd de la République ☎ 02 99 56 13 42, ⓦ hoteldeleurope-saintmalo.com; map p.182. Year-round cheap but clean rooms (the cheaper ones don't have en-suite toilets) in a genuinely friendly, if noisy, hotel near the *gare SNCF*, with a cosy café. The rooms that hold four people work out cheaper than the hostel. **€57**

Les Îlots Avenue de la Guimorais, Rothéneuf ☎ 02 99 56 98 72, ⓦ ville-saint-malo.fr/tourisme/les-campings; map p.182. Green little municipal site, reserved for caravans and mobile homes only, 5min walk inland from either of two crescent beaches, and roughly 5km east of the *citadelle*. Closed mid-Nov to late March. **€10.60**

Les Nielles Avenue John Kennedy, Paramé ☎ 02 99 40 26 35, ⓦ ville-saint-malo.fr/campings; map p.182. Fifty-pitch municipal campsite on the beach at the smaller of Paramé's strands, the plage du Minhic, just a short walk from the town's facilities. Closed late Aug to early July. **€15.70**

Valmarin 7 rue Jean XXIII, St-Servan ☎ 02 99 81 94 76, ⓦ www.levalmarin.com; map p.182. Impressive eighteenth-century *malouinière* – sea captain's house – set in spacious flowery gardens 50m from the sea in St-Servan, that's now a hotel with a dozen very comfortable antique-furnished rooms. **€100**

La Ville Huchet Route de la Passagère ☎ 02 99 81 11 83, ⓦ lavillehuchet.com; map p.182. Four-star campsite in the grounds of a château, south of St-Malo on the road to Rennes, with an aquatic park, pool and bike rental. Closed mid-Sept to mid-April. **€17.15**

EATING AND DRINKING

Even more restaurants than hotels are crammed into *intra-muros* St-Malo, with a long crescent lining the inside of the ramparts between the Porte St-Vincent and the Grande Porte. In recent years, there's been a trend for gourmet seafood restaurants to be replaced by crêperies and snack bars, but prices are still probably higher than anywhere else in Brittany, especially on the open café terraces.

Bouche en Folie 14 rue du Boyer ☎ 06 72 49 08 89; map p.184. This little place offers classic, seasonal French dishes, with a good lunch menu for €15, and an excellent €30 dinner menu. Some outdoor seating. Mon & Thurs–Sun noon–2pm & 7–10pm.

Cambusier 6 rue des Cordiers ☎ 02 99 20 18 42, ⓦ cambusier.fr; map p.184. Creative contemporary cuisine from one of St-Malo's top chefs, with plenty of seafood – oysters and lobsters are particular favourites – but also rich duck and other meat dishes. A two-course lunch costs €16, dinner is €35 or à la carte. Mon, Tues & Thurs–Sat noon–2pm & 7–9pm, Sun noon–2pm.

Chalut 8 rue de la Corne de Cerf ☎ 02 99 56 71 58; map p.184. Blue-painted, fish-themed bistro a short way in from the Porte St-Vincent, where all the menus offer a limited choice, with perhaps one or two exclusively fishy main courses, and the odd meaty appetizer. The €29 weekday lunch menu centres on the catch of the day; otherwise you can pay €43 or €59 for a gourmet fish dinner, not quite as rich as the traditional norm, or €78 for a five-course menu of which three consist entirely of lobster. Reservations preferred. Wed–Sun noon–1.30pm & 7–9.30pm.

Corps de Garde 3 montée Notre Dame ☎ 02 99 40 91 46, ⓦ le-corps-de-garde.com; map p.184. The only restaurant that's right up on St-Malo's ramparts is a simple crêperie, serving delicious but far from unusual crêpes (€3–10). However, the views from its large open-air terrace (covered when necessary) are sensational, looking out over the beach to dozens of little islets. July & Aug noon–9.30pm; mid-Dec to June & Sept to mid-Nov noon–2pm & 7–9pm; closed mid-Nov to mid-Dec.

Côté Sens 16 rue de la Herse ☎ 02 99 20 08 12, ⓦ cote-sens.com; map p.184. Romantic, intimate little restaurant near the old market, run by a welcoming husband-and-wife team, and offering a delicious take on southern French as well as Breton cuisine, with a good €28 menu and a wider-ranging €45 one. Mon, Tues, Thurs, Fri & Sun noon–2pm & 7–9.30pm, Sat 7–11pm.

Crêperie la Brigantine 13 rue de Dinan ☎ 02 99 56 82 82, ⓦ la-brigantine.fr; map p.184. Sweet and savoury pancakes at very reasonable prices, with a strong emphasis on organic ingredients – the seafood fillings are exceptional. An individual crêpe can cost just €2.20, and there's a full menu for €10, including a glass of cider. Daily noon–10pm; closed Tues & Wed in low season.

Divers'Cité 18 rue des Cordiers ☎ 02 99 56 74 08; map p.184. Friendly, simply decorated little restaurant, with outdoor seating on a pavement terrace, where a hospitable French couple cook and serve delicious local cuisine – including excellent sole and cod dishes, and unforgettable profiteroles – on menus starting at €18. Tues–Sat noon–2pm & 7.15–9pm

Gilles 2 rue de la Pie-qui-Boit ☎ 02 99 40 97 25, ⓦ restaurant-gilles-saint-malo.com; map p.184. Bright, modern, good-value restaurant, just off the central pedestrian axis and lacking views or outdoor space. The €21 lunch

menu is fine; for dinner, €29 brings you *moules cassolette* or salmon tartare plus duck in cider. Mon, Tues & Fri–Sun noon–1.30pm & 7–9pm, Thurs noon–1.30pm.

Java 3 rue Ste-Barbe ☎ 02 99 56 41 90, ⓦ lajavacafe .com; map p.184. Among its many eccentric features, this entertaining and unique cider bar – to give it its full official name, *Le Café du Coin d'en bas de la Rue du Bout de la Ville d'en face du Port … La Java* – boasts a row of swings at the bar, old dolls on the wall, and an elevator door into the toilet. All is designed to keep the conversation flowing as smoothly as the drinks. Mon–Fri 8.31am–9.44pm, 11.42pm, or 12.52am "depending on the flexibility of the tail of the dog"; Sat & Sun opens 8.33am.

NIGHTLIFE AND LIVE MUSIC

Le 109 3 rue des Cordiers ☎ 02 99 56 81 09, ⓦ le-109 .com; map p.184. Flashy nightclub, decked out in fiery reds and yellows. Daily 6.30pm–3am; closed Sun & Mon Sept–June.

Riff Magnétique 20 rue de la Herse ☎ 02 99 40 85 70, ⓦ leriffmagnetique.com; map p.184. Lively, friendly bar, with a fine choice of wines plus regular café-concerts, and DJs at the weekend. Tues–Sun 6.30pm–3am.

SHOPPING

Butter St-Malo is famed for its butter; to buy the very best, drop in at the Maison du Beurre, 9 rue Orme (☎ 02 99 40 88 79; ⓦ lebeurrebordier.com).

Hypermarkets Carrefour, Centre Commercial La Madeleine ☎ 02 99 21 10 10 (closed Sun); Centre Leclerc, 55 bd des

Déportés, Paramé ☎ 02 99 19 97 97 (closed Sun).

Markets St-Malo, in the Halle au Blé within the walls (Tues & Fri); St-Servan (Mon & Fri); Paramé (Wed & Sat). St-Malo's fish market is on Saturday in the place de la Poissonnerie, within the walls.

Dinard

Formerly a fishing village, now a smart little resort blessed with several lovely beaches, **DINARD** sprawls around the western approaches to the Rance estuary, just across the water from St-Malo but a good twenty minutes' drive away. With its casino, spacious shaded villas and social calendar of regattas and ballet, it might not feel out of place on the Côte d'Azur. The nineteenth-century metamorphosis of Dinard was largely thanks to the tastes of affluent English and Americans. Although Dinard is a hilly town, undulating over a succession of pretty little coastal inlets, it attracts great numbers of older visitors; as a result, prices tend to be high, and pleasures sedate.

The beaches

Central Dinard faces north to the open sea, across the curving bay that holds the attractive **plage de l'Écluse**. As so often in Breton resorts, the buildings that line the waterfront are, with the exception of the casino in the middle, venerable Victorian-style villas rather than hotels or shops, and so the beach itself has a relatively low-key atmosphere, despite the summer crowds. Rows of delightful, blue-and-white-striped, tent-like sunshelters, which cost €15 to rent for the afternoon, add colour to the sands below.

Few casual visitors realize that some of **Pablo Picasso**'s most famous images, such as *Deux Femmes Courant sur la Plage* and *Baigneuses sur la Plage* – both of which look quintessentially Mediterranean with their blue skies and golden sands – were painted on this beach during the artist's annual summer visits in the 1920s.

Enjoyable **coastal footpaths** lead off in either direction. The path heading east – which is floodlit each evening between July and early October – leads up to the Pointe du Moulinet for views over to St-Malo, and then (as the **promenade du Clair de Lune**)

HITCHCOCK IN DINARD

You may find yourself wondering why the main access point to the plage de l'Écluse, in the centre of Dinard's seafront, is dominated by a statue of film director **Alfred Hitchcock**. Depicting Hitchcock standing on a giant egg, with a ferocious-looking bird perched on each shoulder, it's there to commemorate the town's annual **festival of English-language films**, held in early October (wfestivaldufilm-dinard.com). According to local legend, Hitchcock based Norman Bates's house in *Psycho* on a solitary villa high above the beach.

continues past the tiny and now exclusive port, and down to the estuary beach, the plage du Prieuré. Setting off west, on the other hand, takes you around more rocky outcrops to the secluded strand at neighbouring **St-Énogat**.

ARRIVAL AND DEPARTURE — DINARD

By plane Dinard's small airport, off the D168 near Pleurtuit, 4km southeast of the centre, is served by Ryanair flights from London Stansted and East Midlands, and by Aurigny Air services from Guernsey (waurigny.com). Illenoo buses stop nearby en route between Dinard and Rennes.

By boat Regular river ferries connect Dinard's pleasure port, below the promenade du Clair de Lune, 10 mins' walk east of the tourist office, with St-Malo (April–Oct; €4.90

one-way, €7.50 return; bikes cost double; ☎ 08 25 13 81 00, wcompagniecorsaire.com).

By bus Local buses run regularly between Dinard and St-Malo, across the dam, while long-distance buses, run by Illenoo (☎ 08 10 35 10 35, willenoo.fr) and Tibus (☎ 08 10 22 22 22, wtibus.fr), go from the former *gare SNCF* and "Le Gallic" stop (near the tourist office).

Destinations Cancale (2 daily; 1hr 30min); Dinan (6 daily; 40min); Rennes (4 daily; 1hr 30min); St-Brieuc (8 daily; 25min).

INFORMATION AND ACTIVITIES — DINARD

Tourist office 2 bd Féart (Mon–Sat 10am–12.30pm & 2.30–6pm, Sun 10am–12.30pm & 3–6.30pm; ☎ 02 99 46 94 12, wot-dinard.com).

Watersports Windsurfing equipment, paddleboards and kayaks are available for rent in summer at St-Énogat beach (☎ 06 35 96 18 55, wwindschool.fr).

ACCOMMODATION AND EATING

Camping Port Blanc Rue du Sergent-Boulanger ☎ 02 99 46 10 74, wcamping-port-blanc.com. Dinard's finest campsite, run by the municipality, has the plage du Port-Blanc, west of the centre almost to itself, with shady pitches right by the beach. Closed Oct–March. **€20.35**

Le Cancaven 3 place de la République ☎ 02 99 46 15 45. The tables of this busy all-day brasserie fill a glassed-in enclosure on the central square, and there's also cosy indoor seating. As well as à la carte dishes like *moules frites* (€10.50), or a dozen oysters (€12.50), they serve good set menus at €21 and €28. Daily 10am–11pm.

★ **Didier Méril** 1 place du Général-de-Gaulle ☎ 02 99 46 95 74, wrestaurant-didier-meril.com. High-quality gourmet restaurant, beside the main road on the edge of Dinard, just above a great beach. Open for lunch and dinner daily, it offers fancy menus from €31, and holds half-a-dozen stylish designer bedrooms, of which the two sumptuous sea-view suites are much the largest and nicest. Room **€85**, suite **€160**

La Gonelle Promenade du Clair de Lune ☎ 02 99 16 40 47, wlagonelle.com. Expensive, open-fronted seafood restaurant, where diners can bask in unobstructed views across to St-Malo as they savour à la carte specialities like fresh wild oysters from Cancale, mixed shellfish platters

costing up to €96, or well-cooked fish main courses for €18–25. Carnivores beware; there's not an ounce of meat on the menu. Mid-April to June & Sept, Mon & Thurs–Sun; July & Aug daily; closed Oct to mid-April.

La Plage 3 bd Féart ☎ 02 99 46 14 87, whoteldelaplage -dinard.com. Modern, good-value and very central hotel, just up from the main beach, and offering smart contemporary bedrooms with crisp white linens and spacious, well equipped bathrooms. Expect to pay up to €40 extra for a full-on sea view, though guests can enjoy the buffet breakfast on an open-air, beach-facing terrace in summer. **€75**

Printania 5 av George V ☎ 02 99 46 13 07, wprintania hotel.com. Good and very traditional mid-range hotel, a short walk from the centre on a quiet street that drops down to the port. Some rooms, and the excellent restaurant, which serves a particularly good €40 menu, face across the estuary to St-Malo. Closed mid-Nov to mid-March. Street view **€90**, sea view **€167**

la Vallée 6 av George V ☎ 02 99 46 94 00, whotel delavallee.com. Attractive Logis de France, down at sea level in the pleasure port, but unfortunately facing the wrong way for views of St-Malo. The most basic rooms look straight onto a bare cliff face, but in principle this is a nice spot, and the restaurant is good too. Street view **€125**, sea view **€140**

4

Dinan

The wonderful citadel of **DINAN** has preserved almost intact its three-kilometre encirclement of protective masonry, along with street upon colourful street of late medieval houses. However, despite its slightly unreal perfection – this would be the ideal film set for *The Three Musketeers*, say – it's seldom overrun with tourists. There are no essential museums, the most memorable architecture is vernacular rather than monumental, and time is most easily spent wandering from crêperie to café and down to the pretty port, admiring the overhanging half-timbered houses along the way.

During the third weekend of July, every even-numbered year, Dinan celebrates the **Fête des Remparts** with medieval-style jousting, banquets, fairs and processions, culminating in an immense fireworks display (ⓦfete-remparts-dinan.com).

Place du Guesclin and around

Dinan's large, central **place du Guesclin** is named in honour of the Breton warrior **Bertrand du Guesclin**, who fought and defeated the English knight Thomas of Canterbury in single combat here in 1364, and thereby settled the outcome of the siege of Dinan. An equestrian statue of du Guesclin now stands in the square, looking remarkably like an armour-clad Winston Churchill.

The square, if not the statue, comes alive on Thursdays, when together with the adjoining place du Champ Clos it's the scene of a large **market**; for the rest of the week,

DINAN

ACCOMMODATION

Arvor	5
Auberge de Jeunesse	2
Le d'Avaugour	6
Camping Municipal Chateaubriand	8
Challonge	7
Logis de Jerzual	3
De la Porte St-Malo	1
Théâtre	4

BARS

Bistrot d'en Bas	1
Saut de la Puce	2

RESTAURANTS

Crêperie Ahna	2
Cantorbery	5
Chez La Mère Pourcel	4
Fleur de Sel	6
L'Atelier Gourmand	1
Marmite de l'Abbaye	8
Mr Robert	3
St-Louis	7

it serves as the main central car park. The true heart of town consists of two much smaller squares, the **place des Merciers** and the **place des Cordeliers**, which hold Dinan's finest assortment of medieval wood-framed houses, painted in lively hues and with their upper storeys perching precariously on splintering wooden pillars that appear to buckle beneath the weight.

You can get a good general overview of Dinan's ramparts from the wooden balcony of the central **Tour de l'Horloge**, which dates from the end of the fifteenth century (daily: April & May 2–6pm; June–Sept 10am–6.30pm; €4). A small and uninteresting shopping mall has been created around the foot of the belfry's stout stone walls.

Château de Duchesse Anne

Daily: June–Sept 10am–6.30pm; Oct to early Nov & Easter–May 1.30–5.30pm; guided tours July & Aug daily 11am • €5 • ☎ 02 96 39 45 20, Ⓦ dinan.net/chateau-dinan

What's now known as the **Château de Duchesse Anne** is not so much a castle as the fourteenth-century keep that once protected Dinan's southern approach, along with two separate towers to which it offers access. The keep itself, or *donjon*, consists of four storeys, each of which holds an unexpected hotchpotch of items, including two big old looms and assorted Greek and Etruscan perfume jars; at ground level, well below the walls, there's a slender, closed drawbridge.

The more intriguing of the two neighbouring towers, the ancient **Tour de Coëtquen**, is all but empty. If you descend the spiral staircase to its waterlogged bottom floor, however, you'll find a group of stone fifteenth-century notables resembling some medieval time capsule, about to depetrify at any moment.

St-Sauveur church

On a little square not far above the imposing gateway of the **Porte du Jerzual**, **St-Sauveur church** sends the skyline of Dinan even higher. It's a real hotchpotch, with a Romanesque porch and an eighteenth-century steeple. Even its nine Gothic chapels feature five different patterns of vaulting in no symmetrical order; the most complex pair, in the centre, would make any spider proud.

By contrast, a very plain cenotaph on the left contains the heart of **Bertrand du Guesclin**, the fourteenth-century Breton warrior who later became Constable of France. Relics of his life and battles are scattered all over Brittany and Normandy; in death, he spread himself between four separate burial places for four different parts of his body (the French kings restricted themselves to three burial sites).

The one stretch of Dinan's medieval **ramparts** that's open to visitors leads from behind St-Sauveur church to the Tour du Sillon, overlooking the river.

Port de Dinan

Like St-Malo, the best way to approach Dinan is by boat, up the Rance. By the time the ferries get to the lovely **port de Dinan**, down below the thirteenth-century ramparts, the river has narrowed sufficiently to be spanned by a small but majestic old stone bridge. High above it towers the former railway viaduct now used by the D795.

The steep, cobbled **rue du Petit Fort** twists up from the artisans' shops and restaurants along the quay. Dotted with many stone benches where you can catch your breath, it makes a wonderful climb, passing ancient flower-festooned edifices of wood and stone, as well as several crêperies and even a half-timbered poodle parlour, before it enters the city through the Porte du Jerzual.

The **riverside path** that runs south from the port along the east bank of the Rance extends all the way to Rennes. For cyclists, that's a delightful ride; for walkers, the lovely village of **Léhon** – one of those places the French label a *petite cité de caractère* – makes a more realistic target, being reachable in around half an hour.

ARRIVAL AND INFORMATION

DINAN

By train or bus Both the Art Deco *gare SNCF* and the *gare routière* (☏ 08 10 22 22 22, ⌨ tibus.fr) are a 10min walk west of the walls, on place du 11-Novembre in the rather gloomy modern quarter.

Train destinations Dol (8 daily; 23min); St-Brieuc (5 daily; 50min).

Bus destinations St-Cast (3 daily; 1hr 5min); St-Jacut (3 daily; 45min); St-Malo (6 daily; 45min).

By boat Between May and Oct, boats sail along the Rance between Dinan's port and Dinard and St-Malo (☏ 08 25

13 81 00, ⌨ compagniecorsaire.com). The trip takes 2hr 45min, with the exact schedule varying according to the tides (adults €26, under-16s €15.70). It's only possible to do a day-return by boat (adults €32.50, under-16s €19.50) if you start from St-Malo or Dinard; starting from Dinan, you have to come back by bus or train.

Tourist office 9 rue du Château, just off the place du Guesclin (July & Aug Mon–Sat 9.30am–7pm, Sun 10am–12.30pm & 2.30–6pm; Sept–June Mon–Sat 9am–12.30pm & 2–6pm; ☏ 02 96 87 69 76, ⌨ dinan-tourisme.com).

ACCOMMODATION

Many of Dinan's hotels lie within the walled town or down by the port. Both locations are convenient if you're on foot, but motorists should note that parking can be difficult in summer. Most hotels are mid-range, with only a couple of genuine budget options.

Arvor 5 rue Pavie ☏ 02 96 39 21 22, ⌨ hotelarvordinan.com. Renovated eighteenth-century townhouse in the heart of town, with some surviving traces of the convent that previously occupied the site. The traditionally furnished guest rooms are smart, well-equipped and very comfortable, and include some plush family-sized suites. **€135**

Auberge de Jeunesse Moulin de Méen, 2 rue des Quatres Moulins, Vallée de la Fontaine-des-Eaux ☏ 02 96 39 10 83, ⌨ fuaj.org/dinan. Attractive, rural former watermill, beside the river in green fields below the town centre. No bus access: to walk there, follow the quay downstream from the port on the town side. Breakfast €4. Camping is permitted in the grounds. Closed Oct–March. Dorms **€14.90**, doubles **€29.80**

Le d'Avaugour 1 place du Champ Clos ☏ 02 96 39 07 49, ⌨ avaugourhotel.com. Smart, elegant hotel, entered from the main square but backing onto the ramparts, with very tasteful renovated rooms, lovely gardens, and exceptionally helpful staff. Closed Nov–Feb, plus Sun in low season. **€165**

Camping Municipal Chateaubriand 103 rue Chateaubriand ☏ 02 96 39 11 96. Verdant, minimally equipped little campsite, in a quiet spot just outside

the western ramparts, offering just fifty pitches. Closed Oct–May. **€11.70**

Challonge 29 place du Guesclin ☏ 02 96 87 16 30, ⌨ hotel-dinan.fr. The clean modern rooms feature slightly busy decor, but many have balconies, and they're above a good brasserie overlooking Dinan's main square. **€78**

Logis du Jerzual 25–27 rue du Petit Fort ☏ 02 96 85 46 54, ⌨ logis-du-jerzual.com. Friendly B&B, with a lovely garden terrace, halfway up the exquisite little lane that climbs from the port. The five rooms have wonderful character, with four-poster beds, modern bathrooms and romantic views over the rooftops. **€85**

★ **De la Porte St-Malo** 35 rue St-Malo ☏ 02 96 39 19 76, ⌨ hotelportemalo.com. Simple but spotless and very comfortable rooms in a hugely welcoming and tasteful small hotel just outside the walls, beyond the Porte St-Malo, away from the bustle of the centre. The €8.50 breakfasts are recommended. **€79**

Théâtre 2 rue Ste-Claire ☏ 02 96 39 06 91. Nine very basic rooms above a friendly (and generally early-closing) bar, right by the Théâtre des Jacobins; the very cheapest comes with only a sink and its own bathroom on the landing, but the rest have en-suite bathrooms. Closed Mon Oct–May. **€43**

EATING AND DRINKING

All sorts of specialist restaurants, including several ethnic alternatives, are tucked away in the old streets of Dinan. Take an evening stroll through the town and down to the port, and you'll pass at least twenty places. For bars, explore the series of tiny parallel alleyways between place des Merciers and rue du Marchix.

L'Atelier Gourmand 4 rue du Quai ☏ 02 96 85 14 18. This delightful riverside spot, beside the bridge, with indoor and outdoor seating, serves a well-priced menu of *tartines* (€11), *moules* (€11–14) and assorted main courses (€15–17). July–Sept Mon 6.30–9.30pm, Tues–Sat noon–1.30pm &

6.30–9.30pm, Sun noon–1.30pm; Oct–June closed Mon.

★ **Bistrot d'en Bas** 20 rue Haute Voie ☏ 02 96 87 34 71. This lively little pub and wine bar hosts popular jazz and folk performances, and serves salads and *tartines* too. Tues–Sat 10.30am–1am, Sun 11.30am–3pm.

Cantorbery 6 rue Ste-Claire ☎02 96 39 02 52. High-class food served in an old stone house with rafters, a spiral staircase and a real wood fire. Lunch from €16, while traditional dinner menus start with a good €31 option that includes fish soup and veal kidneys. June–Sept Mon–Sat noon–1.45pm & 7–9.30pm, Sun noon–1.45pm; Oct–May closed Wed.

Chez La Mère Pourcel 3 place des Merciers ☎02 96 39 03 80, ⊛chezlamerepourcel.com. Upstairs dining room in a beautiful half-timbered fifteenth-century house in the central square. Good à la carte options are served all day, while the dinner menus (€24–36), are gourmet class. May–Sept daily noon–2.30pm & 7–10pm; Oct–April Mon & Thurs–Sat noon–2.30pm & 7–10pm, Tues & Sun noon–2.30pm.

Crêperie Ahna 7 rue de la Poissonnerie ☎02 96 39 09 13, ⊛creperie-ahna.blogspirit.com. Smart central crêperie, with limited outdoor seating, that's hugely popular with lunching locals. Savoury pancakes cost €4–11, and they also serve potato blinis at similar prices, as well as grilled meats, including nice big sausages. Mon–Sat noon–2pm & 7–9.30pm.

Fleur de Sel 7 rue Ste-Claire ☎02 96 85 15 14. Central restaurant, just off the main square, that's a must for its quirky and inventive take on Breton cuisine, as evidenced by the onion tart starter that comes with goats'-milk ice cream. Highlights on its two set menus, at €22 and €34,

range from raw oysters to stewed beef cheeks, plus rich, creamy desserts. Tues–Sat noon–1.30pm & 7–9.30pm, Sun noon–2pm.

Marmite de l'Abbaye 15 le Bourg, Léhon ☎02 96 87 39 39. Work up an appetite by walking half an hour south from the port to attractive little Léhon, then enjoy good traditional French cooking at the village restaurant, with plenty of fish options, on menus from €15 for lunch, €24 in the evening. Wed–Sun noon–1.30pm & 7.30–9pm.

Mr Robert 11 place des Cordeliers ☎02 96 85 20 37, ⊛www.mrrobertrestaurant.fr. Named for its Irish chef-owner, this excellent central option offers a handful of tables on the square itself but plenty of room indoors. Classic French cuisine with subtle Asian-influenced flavourings, with a 3-course lunch at €16 and full dinner menus from €26.50. Tues–Sat noon–1.30pm & 7–9.30pm.

St-Louis 9–11 rue de Léhon ☎02 96 39 89 50. Good-value restaurant, just inside the Porte St-Louis, which specializes in buffets; both the €21 and €22 menus include extensive buffets of hors d'oeuvres and desserts, with a conventional main course in between. Mon, Tues & Fri–Sun noon–2pm & 7–10pm, Thurs 7–10pm

Saut de la Puce 15 rue de la Cordonnerie ☎02 96 39 36 11. A long-standing stalwart of Dinan nightlife, one of several similar hangouts along the ever-lively rue de la Cordonnerie, this contemporary Breton dive continues to attract nightly crowds of drinkers. Tues–Sun 5pm–1am.

Around the Baie du Mont-St-Michel

The **coastal road** D201 runs east from St-Malo to **Cancale**, past a succession of coves and beaches, where lines of dunes attempt to hang on against the battering from the sea. At the **Pointe du Grouin** – a perilous and windy height that also overlooks the bird sanctuary of the **Île de Landes** to the east – the line of cliffs turns sharply back on itself at one extremity of the **Baie du Mont-St-Michel**. This is a huge flat expanse of mud and sand, over which – in local legend at any rate – the tide can race faster than a galloping horse. It's dangerous to wander out too far, quite apart from the risk of quicksands, and, in the Breton part of the bay at least, the beaches have little appeal for bathers.

The course of the **River Couesnon**, which marks the border between Brittany and Normandy, has shifted repeatedly over the centuries. So too has the shoreline of the bay, in which traces of long-drowned villages can be seen when the tide is out. Bretons like to say that it is just an accident that the river now runs west of Mont-St-Michel; be that as it may, the Mont and Pontorson, the nearest town to it, are both in Normandy (see p.137). The pinnacle of La Merveille, however, remains clearly visible from every vantage point along the coast.

Cancale

The delightful harbour village of **CANCALE**, just south of the Pointe du Grouin less than 15km east of St-Malo, is not so much a one-horse as a one-mollusc town – the whole place is obsessed with the **oyster**, and with "*ostréiculture*". Its current population is, at around five thousand, less than it was a century ago, but thanks to all the visitors attracted by its edible hinged bivalves, it looks bigger than that might suggest.

Cancale is divided into two distinct halves. In the **old town** up on the hill, the streets behind the main church host the Sunday **market**. The port area of **La Houle**, down below, is smart and very pretty. Glass-fronted hotels and restaurants stretch the length of the waterfront, always busy with visitors, while fishing boats bob in the harbour itself. At its northern end, demarcated by a stone jetty, stalls with bright striped canvas awnings sell **fresh oysters**. Prices start at just €3 per dozen; you can have a plateful opened for another €0.50, and eat them right away as a seaside picnic. The town also has a fabulous range of restaurants for seafood-lovers.

When the sea recedes at low tide, it exposes the **parcs** where the oysters are grown. Behind, the rocks of the cliff are streaked and shiny like mother-of-pearl; underfoot, the beach is littered with countless generations of empty shells.

On the first weekend of October each year, Cancale puts on the **Bordées de Cancale** festival (w lesbordees.fr), featuring acoustic musicians and vocal groups from around the world.

Musée des Arts et Traditions Populaires

Daily: July & Aug 10am–12.30pm & 2.30–6.30pm: first 3 weeks of Sept 10am–noon & 2.30–6.30pm • €2.50 • ☎ 02 99 89 79 32, w museedecancale.fr

The church of **St-Méen**, at the top of the hill in Cancale's old town, holds a small, summer-only **Musée des Arts et Traditions Populaires**, documenting Cancale's oyster obsession with meticulous precision. Cancale oysters have been found in the camps of Julius Caesar, were taken daily to Versailles for Louis XIV, and even accompanied Napoleon on the march to Moscow. The most famous symbol of the town – and its oyster cultivation – is the stark rocky pinnacle known as the **Rocher du Cancale** just offshore; the museum lists all the *Rocher du Cancale* restaurants that have ever existed, including ones in Shanghai and Phnom Penh, and one in Moscow that closed in the 1830s.

Ferme Marine

L'Aurore, route de la Corniche • Mid-Feb to June & mid-Sept to Oct Mon–Fri at 3pm; July to mid-Sept daily at 11am, 3pm & 5pm, with an English-language tour at 2pm • €7 • ☎ 02 99 89 69 99, w ferme-marine.com

Follow the corniche road out of Cancale to the southwest, and you'll soon come to the **Ferme Marine**, a working *parc* where enjoyable guided tours explain the entire oyster-raising process. At one time, Cancale staged an annual event, La Caravanne, during which a huge flotilla of sailing vessels dragged nets along the bottom of the sea for wild oysters. These days, though, they're farmed like any other crop. The seabed is divided into countless segments of different sizes, each having an individual owner who has the right to sell what it produces, while the oysters are cultivated from year-old "spat" bought in from elsewhere.

ARRIVAL AND INFORMATION CANCALE

By bus There's no train service to Cancale, but buses connect it with St-Malo (6 daily; 45min; w illenoo.fr).

Tourist office Near the church square, at the top of the hill well above the port, at 44 rue du Port (July & Aug Mon–Sat 9am–7pm, Sun 9.30am–1pm; Sept–June daily 9am–1pm & 2.30–6pm; ☎ 02 99 89 63 72, w cancale-tourisme.fr). There's also a summer-only kiosk on the waterfront (July & Aug Mon–Sat 10am–noon & 4–7pm, Sun 4–7pm).

ACCOMMODATION

Auberge de Jeunesse Port Picain ☎ 02 99 89 62 62, w fuaj.org. Striking modern hostel, very close to the beach, 2km north of town, where rates include breakfast; camping space and kitchen facilities are also available. Closed Nov–March. Dorms **€28.13**

Camping Municipal de la Pointe du Grouin Port Picain ☎ 02 99 89 63 79, w cancale-tourisme.fr.

By far the best campsite in the vicinity, perched beside the sea just beyond the hostel north of town, and enjoying sensational views. Closed late Oct to early March. **€16.30**

La Pointe du Grouin ☎ 02 99 89 60 55, w hotelpointe dugrouin.com. Splendidly isolated Logis de France, very close to the spectacular Pointe du Grouin, 5km north of town. All the rooms have great views, and the restaurant serves menus from €24.50 to €84. Hotel closed mid-Nov to March; restaurant closed all Tues, plus Thurs eve in low season. **€90**

Le Querrien 7 quai Duguay-Trouin ⓣ 02 99 89 64 56, ⓦ le-querrien.com. Bright, large and colourful rooms,

above a restaurant at the middle of the quayside. **€89**

La Voilerie 8 rue Ernest-Lamort ⓣ 02 99 89 88 00, ⓦ hotel-lavoilerie.com. Twelve simple but good-value, wood-panelled rooms, in a hotel that stands very slightly uphill from the point where the road reaches the southern end of Cancale's waterfront. **€60**

EATING AND DRINKING

Chez Victor 8 quai Thomas ⓣ 02 99 89 55 84. Occupying a huge corner site, with indoor and outdoor tables beside the jetty and oyster stalls at the north end of the quayside, this all-day brasserie is a sure-fire option for good local seafood. There's a great-value €15.20 menu, featuring oysters and mussels, and an excellent €26 one, along with a wide range of mixed platters and *moules frites* for €12. Daily noon–9pm.

★ **Au Pied de Cheval** 10 quai Gambetta ⓣ 02 99 89 76 95. A ramshackle, gloriously atmospheric little place to sample a few oysters – it's named after the largest local variety – with great baskets of bivalves spread across its wooden quayside tables. There's no set menu, but while prices have crept up, and seafood sharing platters for two start at €52, you can still get a dozen raw oysters on

a bed of seaweed for around €8, and cooked mussels for little more. July & Aug Mon–Fri 9am–10pm, Sat & Sun 9am–6pm; Sept, Oct & mid-April to June Mon, Tues, Thurs & Fri 9am–10pm, Sat & Sun 9am–6pm.

La Table Breizh 7 quai Thomas ⓣ 02 99 89 56 46, ⓦ breizhcafe.com. Breton cuisine has not generally caused an international sensation, so this double café, which also has several branches in Japan, is a real oddity. Downstairs there's a crêperie, where galettes using organic ingredients cost €7–12, while the much pricier upstairs dining room is, if not quite a Japanese restaurant, then one that prepares Breton food in distinctly Japanese ways. Lunch menus cost €38 and €48, dinner €75 and €135, and feature all sorts of sliced raw seafood and seared meats. Mon & Thurs–Sun noon–1.30pm & 7–9pm.

4

Dol-de-Bretagne

The foundation of **DOL-DE-BRETAGNE**, 30km west of Mont-St-Michel, is attributed to St Samson, one of the many Celtic evangelists who flooded into Brittany around the sixth century. The Breton hero King Nominoë appointed its first official bishop during the ninth century, and the city remained an important bishopric throughout the Middle Ages.

Dol is no longer large enough to merit its own bishop, but Samson's name lives on in the fortified thirteenth-century **Cathédrale St-Samson**, with its strange, squat, tiled towers and ornate porches. An appealing handful of the older streets nearby are still packed with venerable buildings, most notably the pretty **Grande Rue des Stuarts**, just south of the cathedral, where one Romanesque edifice dates back as far as the eleventh century, assorted five hundred-year-old half-timbered houses look down on the bustle of shoppers below, and a laundry claims to have been visited by Victor Hugo in 1836.

Médiévalys

4 place de la Cathédrale • First half of March daily 2–6pm; mid-March to June & Sept daily 10am–1pm & 2–6pm; July & Aug daily 10am–7pm; Oct & Nov Sat & Sun 2–6pm • €6.80 • ⓣ 02 99 48 35 30, ⓦ medievalys.fr

Housed in a former school in the cathedral square, the ambitious **Médiévalys** is a high-tech modern museum that sets out to explore why and how the great cathedrals of Europe were built. That gives it scope to range through all aspects of medieval life, and reach into the homes of the architects, guildsmen and crafts workers responsible. The upper floors allow close-up views of Dol's own cathedral, and also hold displays explaining the imagery and symbolism with which it's permeated.

Mont Dol

All approaches to Dol from the bay are watched over by the former island of **Mont Dol**. This abrupt granite outcrop, now eight rather marshy kilometres in from the sea and looking mountainous beyond its size on such a flat plain, was the

legendary site of a battle between the Archangel Michael and the Devil. The site has been occupied since prehistoric times – flint implements have been unearthed alongside the bones of mammoths, sabre-toothed tigers and even rhinoceroses. Later on, it appears to have been used for worship by the druids, before becoming, like Mont-St-Michel, an island monastery. Traces of the abbey have long vanished, though the mythic battle may recall its foundation, with Christianity driving out the old religion.

It's possible to drive up a steep narrow road to the top of Mont Dol, from the attractive little village at the foot of the hill. Alternatively, it makes a pleasant climb on foot, via a footpath that winds up among the chestnuts and beeches. Just below the summit, the lawns of a crêperie-cum-bar hold crowds of summer day-trippers. A little further up, there's a tiny chapel, while the peak itself is crowned by a granite tower topped by a white statue of the Madonna and Child. Ascending the 55 tight little spiral steps within brings you to a viewing platform that commands immense views across the surrounding pancake-flat plains.

If you fancy an extended hike, you could pick up the long-distance **GR34** trail, on which both Dol and Mont Dol are located. You can head east to Mont-St-Michel (reckoned as an eight-hour stroll), or west along the coast way beyond St-Malo.

The Menhir du Champ-Dolent

A short way out of Dol to the south, a small picnic area fenced off among the fields contains the **Menhir du Champ-Dolent**. According to one legend, this 9.6-metre standing stone dropped from the sky to separate two brothers on the point of mutual fratricide. Another has it that the menhir is inching its way into the soil, and the world will end when it disappears altogether. It has to be said, this would not be a particularly interesting spot on which to experience the end of the world – the unadorned stone, big though it is in its banal setting, has little of the romance or mystery of the megalithic sites of the Morbihan and elsewhere.

The Forêt de Ville-Cartier

The *Circuit Touristique* signposted from Dol continues beyond the menhir and the village of Trans to the **Forêt de Ville-Cartier**. The pines and beech of the dense forest sweep down to a lake in which it is possible – in fact almost irresistible – to swim. Keeping to the *circuit*, along the D155, would lead eventually to Fougères.

INFORMATION   **DOL-DE-BRETAGNE**

Tourist office 5 place de la Cathédrale (June & Sept Mon–Sat 10am–12.30pm & 2–6pm, Sun 2–6pm; July & Aug daily 10am–1pm & 2–6pm; Oct–May Mon 2–6pm, Tues–Sat 10am–12.30pm & 2–6pm; ☎02 99 48 15 37, ⓦpays-de-dol.com).

ACCOMMODATION AND EATING

Bretagne 17 place Chateaubriand ☎02 99 48 02 03, ⓦhotel-de-bretagne35.fr. Refurbished hotel, next to the market east of Grande Rue des Stuarts, with rooms to suit all budgets, and sleeping up to five guests – those at the back look out across a vestige of ramparts towards Mont Dol – as well as decent food on menus from €12.50 to €32. Breakfast is poor value, though. €72

Castel Camping des Ormes ☎02 99 73 53 00, ⓦlesormes.com. Phenomenally luxurious campsite, set around a lake in the grounds of a château, 6km south towards Combourg on the N795, which arranges horse riding for its guests, and boasts its own golf course and even a cricket pitch. Camping closed late Sept to mid-April, facilities open year-round. €43.60

La Grabotais 4 rue Ceinte ☎02 99 48 19 89, ⓦrestaurant-dol-de-bretagne.com. Nice fish restaurant in an ancient house between Grande Rue des Stuarts and the cathedral, serving menus from €19 that feature fish as kebabs or *choucroute* and conventional meat dishes. Tues, Wed, Fri & Sat noon–2pm & 7–9pm, Sun noon–2pm.

Katédral 4 place de la Trésorerie ☎02 99 48 05 40, ⓦle-katedral.e-monsite.com. Lively and welcoming bar, between the church and museum, that puts on local music and also serves inexpensive crêpes. Daily 11am–11pm.

Inland to Rennes

Much the most direct route inland from the north coast to Rennes is the **D137**, which takes barely half an hour to drive from St-Malo. The D795 south from Dol however makes an appealing alternative, passing through the castle town of **Combourg**. The twin canalside towns of **Hédé** and **Tinténiac** also merit a brief detour.

Combourg

The pleasant little town of **COMBOURG**, 17km south of Dol, is very much dominated by its château. The tranquil, cypress-lined **lake** that stretches below both château and town, is, however, if anything, more appealing than the château itself. Misty and quiet early in the morning, busy only with anglers, it provides a welcome opportunity for leisurely countryside walks.

Château de Combourg

Guided tour only: April–June & Sept daily except Sat 2–5.30pm; July & Aug daily 10.45–11.30am & 2–5pm; Oct daily except Sat 2–5pm; gardens April–June & Sept daily except Sat 9.30am–12.30pm & 2–6pm; July & Aug daily 9.30am–12.30pm & 2–6pm; Oct daily except Sat 10am–noon & 2–5pm • Gardens €3.50, gardens & château €8 • ☎ 02 99 73 22 95, ⓦ www.chateau-combourg.com

Perched on a hill, overlooking magnificent landscaped gardens, the Château de Combourg was the childhood home of the writer Chateaubriand (now buried at St-Malo), and remains in the hands of his descendants. The castle's Tour du Chat is supposedly haunted by a ghost taking the form of a cat; Chateaubriand himself claimed it was haunted by the ghost of the wooden leg of a former lord – and that the cat was merely an acquaintance of this phantasmal limb. The entrance to the château is not where you expect it to be: turn right at the end of Combourg's main square instead of continuing straight towards the keep, and it's a short way up on the left.

Beside the canal: Hédé and Tinténiac

The D795 south from Combourg meets the D137 roughly 20km north of Rennes, close to the particularly pleasant stretch of the **Canal d'Ille-et-Vilaine** that connects the two old towns of **HÉDÉ** and **TINTÉNIAC**, both set on hills to the west of the canal.

There are tempting places to collapse in the sun between the many locks and lock-keepers' cottages, although the towpath isn't consistent enough to follow for any distance on foot, let alone bike.

INFORMATION   **INLAND TO RENNES**

Tourist office 23 place Albert-Parent, Combourg (April–Sept Mon–Sat 10am–1pm & 2.30–6.30pm, Sun 10am–12.30pm; Oct–March Tues–Sat 10am–1pm & 2.30–6pm; ☎ 02 99 73 13 93, ⓦ combourg.org).

ACCOMMODATION AND EATING

COMBOURG

Du Château 1 place Chateaubriand ☎ 02 99 73 00 38, ⓦ hotelduchateau.com. Faultlessly correct Logis de France, holding smart, updated – albeit somewhat chintzy – rooms of all sizes plus a good traditional restaurant where menus start at €28. Buffet breakfasts cost €11. Restaurant closed Mon lunch, Tues lunch & Sat lunch, plus all Sun in low season; hotel closed early Dec to early Jan. **€95**

Du Lac 2 place Chateaubriand ☎ 02 99 73 05 65, ⓦ hotel-combourg.com. Of the two top-notch (and not very imaginatively named) hotels that square off against each other in the square between château and lake, this one just has the edge, thanks to the lake views from most rooms, as well as from the restaurant, where dinner menus start at €26. Closed Fri lunch in summer, Sun eve & all Fri in low season, plus all Feb. **€67**

HÉDÉ

Hostellerie du Vieux Moulin ☎ 02 99 45 45 70, ⓦ levieuxmoulin-hede.com. Logis de France, in a lovely rural setting below the ruined ramparts of the town castle on the main road just north of Hédé; the guest rooms are pretty minimal for the price, but the restaurant is magnificent, with dinner menus starting at €26 and a two-course lunch for €12. Restaurant closed Thurs lunch, Sun eve & all Mon; hotel closed Sun & Mon Sept–June, plus first three weeks in Jan & last two weeks in Oct. **€67**

Restaurant le Genty-Home La Vallée de Hédé

📞02 99 45 46 07, 🌐restaurant-legentyhome.fr. Inexpensive but high-quality restaurant, in a flower-festooned stone cottage just off the highway between Tinténiac and Hédé, a couple of hundred metres north of the *Vieux Moulin*, where the enthusiastic chef prepares traditional meats and fish on menus from €16 at lunch time, €27 for dinner. Mon & Thurs–Sat noon–1.45pm & 7.15–9pm, Tues & Sun noon–1.45pm.

Rennes

For a city that has been the capital and power centre of Brittany ever since it was united with France in 1532, **RENNES** is – outwardly at least – uncharacteristic of the province, with its Neoclassical layout and grandiose major buildings. Much of its potential to be a picturesque tourist destination was destroyed in 1720, when a drunken carpenter managed to set light to virtually the whole city. The fire lasted a

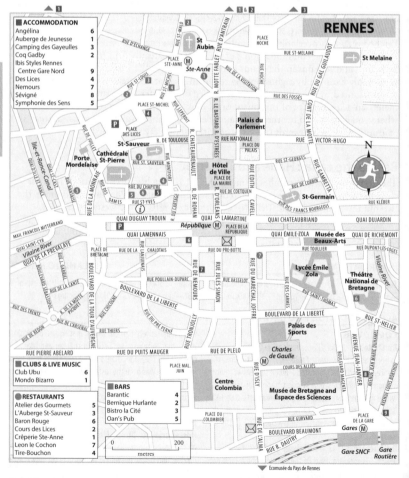

week, razing 33 streets and nine hundred houses. Only sections of the area known as **Les Lices**, at the junction of the canalized Ille-et-Rance and the River Vilaine, were left undamaged; fortunately, it was even then the oldest part of Rennes, so considerable traces of the medieval town survive.

The subsequent remodelling of the rest of the city left it, on the north side of the river at any rate, as something of a patchwork quilt, consisting of grand eighteenth-century public squares interspersed with intimate little alleys of half-timbered houses. It's a lively enough place though, with over forty thousand **students** at the two-part local university, based east of the centre, to help stimulate its political and cultural activity, and a couple of major annual **festivals**, the Tombées de la Nuit and the Transmusicales, to lure in outsiders.

Rennes was first laid out by the **Romans**, at a convenient ford in the Vilaine that was already home to the Celtic community of Condate; over thirty thousand Roman coins have been found in the riverbed, it being traditional for travellers to toss in an offering whenever they crossed water. Although it was ravaged by barbarian invaders in 276 AD, the city subsequently enjoyed over a thousand years of independence before it was captured by Charles VIII of France in 1491. That defeat obliged Duchess Anne to marry Charles, and led to the union of Brittany and France.

City Centre

Rennes' original **medieval core**, bordered by the canal to the west and the river to the south, was enclosed long before 1422. As much as a thousand years earlier, it was already known as the "ville rouge" on account of the red bricks used in its walls. Those walls were enlarged in 1440, when the **Porte Mordelaise** was constructed to serve as the ceremonial entrance to the city. While the gateway itself is now hidden away in a sleepy back alleyway, the old quarter remains the liveliest part of town, and it stays up late, particularly in the area around St-Aubin church and along rue St-Michel and rue de Penhöet.

The place des Lices

Just northeast of the *porte*, the **place des Lices**, now dominated by two usually empty market halls, comes alive every Saturday for one of France's largest **street markets**. The place was originally the venue for jousting tournaments, and on this spot in 1337 the hitherto unknown **Bertrand du Guesclin**, then aged 17, fought and defeated several older opponents. This set him on his career as a soldier, during which he was later to save Rennes during an English siege. However, after the Bretons were defeated at Auray in 1364, he fought for the French and twice invaded Brittany.

The magnificent medieval-style townhouses that overlook the place des Lices are not as old as they look: most were built in the late seventeenth century to house Brittany's parliamentarians. The streets immediately northeast offer a more genuine glimpse of ancient Rennes. Wander around the back of the excellent crêperie at 5 place Ste-Anne (see p.205), through an archway beside no. 7 rue Motte-Fablet, and you'll find an extraordinary specimen of medieval high-rise housing.

The south bank

The **Vilaine River** flows through the centre of Rennes, narrowly confined to a steep-sided channel, and even forced underground at one point. The city districts on its **south bank** are every bit as busy as those on the north. Just west of the *gare SNCF*, the vast **Centre Colombia** is packed with shops of all kinds, plus cafés and snack bars, while slightly nearer the river, **rue Vasselot** has its own array of half-timbered old houses.

DREYFUS IN RENNES

For a few weeks at the very end of the nineteenth century, the eyes of the Western world were focussed on a grey, school building, just south of the Vilaine in central Rennes, that's now the Lycée Émile Zola. This was the location of the second court martial of **Captain Alfred Dreyfus**, who had been found guilty in 1894 of supplying secret military information to the Germans.

Politicians, writers and intellectuals in France and beyond were by now convinced of what some insiders had known all along – that Dreyfus's conviction was a quite extraordinary miscarriage of justice, based on fabricated evidence and a wilful refusal to acknowledge the real culprit, and rooted in anti-Semitism in both Army and government. Thanks in part to the efforts of **Émile Zola**, who had risked his own freedom in writing the famous open letter "J'accuse", Dreyfus was released after four years of solitary confinement on Devil's Island, off the coast of French Guiana, and brought back to France.

The military and civil authorities who had reluctantly agreed to a second court martial remained adamantly convinced of Dreyfus's guilt. They chose Rennes as the site because Brittany was seen as the most Catholic and conservative part of France, and had witnessed violent anti-Dreyfus demonstrations the year before. Dreyfus himself arrived in Quiberon on June 30, 1899, and the court martial opened in August. Journalists from all over the world regaled their readers with every detail of the proceedings, from the military prosecutor who was accompanied by his own pet crow to the defence counsel who was shot by an unknown gunman as he walked beside the river, but was back in court within a few days. The various protagonists lodged in different parts of central Rennes, and their supporters soon began to gather daily in specific local cafés.

On September 9, to utter international outrage, the seven low-ranking military judges who heard the case – and entirely lacked legal qualifications or experience – found Dreyfus **guilty** once more, this time with unspecified "extenuating circumstances". At that point, French President Émile Loubet stepped in and granted Dreyfus a pardon; seven years later, he was finally exonerated after another military tribunal.

Palais du Parlement
Rue Hoche

The one central building to escape Rennes' 1720 fire was the **Palais du Parlement** on rue Hoche downtown. In 1994, however, the Palais was all but ruined by a mysterious conflagration, sparked by a flare during a demonstration by Breton fishermen. Now rebuilt and restored, the entire structure is once more topped by an impressive array of gleaming, gilded statues. Inside, its lobby stages temporary exhibitions.

Musée des Beaux-Arts
20 quai Émile-Zola • Tues 10am–6pm, Wed–Sun 10am–noon & 2–6pm • €5 • ☎ 02 23 62 17 45, ⓦ mbar.org

An imposing former university building on the south bank of the Vilaine houses Rennes' **Musée des Beaux Arts**. As its finest artworks – including drawings by Leonardo da Vinci, Botticelli, Fra Lippo Lippi and Dürer – are seldom on public display, it can't honestly be rated as a must-see art museum. The ground floor, however, holds some unexpected and intriguing other collections, including archeological treasures ranging from mummified Egyptian cats to Etruscan urns; a "Cabinet of Curiosities" assembled by Christophe-Paul de Robien (1698–1756); and some very definitely not-suitable-for-work nineteenth-century erotica.

The art itself, rather drearily exhibited in the upstairs galleries, largely consists of lesser-known Impressionist views of Normandy, by the likes of Boudin and Sisley, interspersed with anachronistic modern pieces. Among the occasional highlights are Pieter Boel's contemporary-looking seventeenth-century animal studies; Veronese's depiction of a flying *Perseus Rescuing Andromeda*; Pierre-Paul Ruben's *Tiger Hunt*; and a haunting 1850s landscape by Breton painter Théodore Caruelle d'Aligny, *La Solitude*, that's suffused with a delicate Maxfield-Parrish-style glow. Picasso also makes a cameo appearance, with a nude from 1923, a simple *Baigneuse à Dinard* from 1928, and a very late canvas from 1970.

Musée de Bretagne

10 cours des Alliés • July & Aug Tues–Fri 1–7pm, Sat & Sun 2–7pm; Sept–June Tues noon–9pm, Wed–Fri noon–7pm, Sat & Sun 2–7pm • €4 •
☎ 02 23 40 66 00, ⓦ www.musee-bretagne.fr

A state-of-the-art edifice known as **Les Champs Libres**, 500m south of the river, houses the high-tech – and highly recommended – **Musée de Bretagne**. Located up on the second floor, this provides a comprehensive overview of Breton history and culture. Displays start at the very beginning, with a hearth used by humans in a Finistère sea cave half a million years ago that ranks among the oldest signs of fire in the world. Then follows an entertaining skate through regional history, covering pottery from 4000BC, the dolmens and menhirs of the megalith builders, some magnificent jadeite axes and Bronze Age swords, and the arrival of first the Celts, next the Romans, and later still the spread of Christianity from the fifth century onwards. A separate section is devoted to the Dreyfus Affair (see opposite), and there's also extensive coverage of World War II, with harrowing photos of Resistance supporters hung in the streets by the Nazis, and a no-holds-barred account of how certain Breton nationalists sided with the German occupiers in the hope of gaining regional autonomy.

Espace des Sciences

Same address and hours as above • €5

Under the same roof as the Musée de Bretagne, the **Espace des Sciences** is a peculiar sort of scaly volcano that contains two floors of interactive scientific displays. These tend to change each year, and to be aimed very largely at children.

Ecomusée du Pays de Rennes

Route Chatillon sur Seiche • April–Sept Tues–Fri 9am–6pm, Sat 2–6pm, Sun 2–7pm; Oct–March Tues–Fri 9am–noon & 2–6pm,
Sat 2–6pm, Sun 2–7pm • €5, free 1st Sun of each month • ☎ 02 99 51 38 15, ⓦ ecomusee-rennes-metropole.fr • Métro line 1,
stop "Triangle"

For a distinctly Breton take on the past, head out to the **Ecomusée du Pays de Rennes**, just outside the ring road 5km south of the centre. This former farmhouse, the Ferme de la Bintinais, has been preserved as a monument to local rural history. Recounting the minutiae of five centuries of daily life, it shows the vital role Rennes has played in the evolution of Breton agriculture; living exhibits range from dairy cattle to honey bees.

ARRIVAL AND DEPARTURE
RENNES

By train Rennes' *gare SNCF*, on the Paris–Brest TGV line, is a 15min walk south of the Vilaine, and a little more from the medieval quarter.

Destinations Brest (11 daily; 2–2hr 30min); Caen (4 daily; 3hr) and Pontorson (1hr); Lille (2 daily; 3hr 45min); Morlaix (10 daily; 1hr 45min) via Lamballe (40min), St-Brieuc (50min), Guingamp (1hr 10min) and Plouaret (1hr 25min); Nantes (10 daily; 1hr 25min); Paris-Montparnasse (12 daily; 2hr 10min); Quimper (9 daily; 2hr 15min); St-Malo (14 daily; 50min); Vannes (6 daily; 1hr); Vitré (12 daily; 18–35min).

By bus The long-distance *gare routière* stands alongside the *gare SNCF* on boulevard Solférino; main operators include Illenoo (☎02 99 82 26 26, ⓦ illenoo.fr) and Keolis Emeraude (☎02 99 26 16 00, ⓦ destination-montsaintmichel.com).

Destinations Dinan (6 daily; 1hr 20min); Dinard (4 daily; 1hr 30min); Fougères (10 daily; 1hr); Mont St-Michel (4 daily; 1hr 15min); St-Malo (3 daily; 1hr 30min).

By car For drivers, it's best to park as soon as you reach the city centre; the most convenient car parks are beneath the place des Lices, and between the quais Duguay-Trouin and Lamennais.

INFORMATION AND GETTING AROUND

Tourist office In a disused medieval church, the Chapelle St-Yves, just north of the river at 11 rue St-Yves (July & Aug Mon–Sat 9am–7pm, Sun 11am–1pm & 2–6pm; Sept–June Mon 1–6pm, Tues–Sat 10am–6pm, Sun 11am–1pm

& 2–6pm; ☎02 99 67 11 11, ⓦ tourisme-rennes.com).

By metro and bus An efficient métro system connects the *gare SNCF*, the place de la République beside the canal in the heart of town, and the place Ste-Anne. Like the extensive local bus network, which radiates out from place de la République, it's run by STAR (single journey, with transfers €1.50, all-day pass €3.80; ⓦstar.fr).

By bike A free bike rental system is based at the *gare SNCF*.

This is a separate scheme to the one open only to city residents, under which locals are given special identity cards to unlock the free white bicycles you'll see parked all over town.

ACCOMMODATION

Angélina 1 quai Lammenais ☎02 99 79 29 66, ⓦangelina-hotel.com. On the third floor of what initially seems a run-down commercial building, this budget hotel offers large, great-value rooms, and a bright breakfast room; the one snag with its central location is the potential for late-night noise outside. **€60**

Auberge de Jeunesse 10–12 Canal St-Martin ☎02 99 33 22 33, ⓦfuaj.org/rennes. Welcoming, attractively positioned HI hostel, 3km north of the centre by the Canal d'Ille et Rance (bus #8 from place Ste-Anne métro station). It has a cafeteria and a laundry; hostelling association membership is compulsory. Closed Xmas to mid-Jan. **€21.50**

Camping des Gayeulles Rue du Prof-Maurice-Audin ☎02 99 36 91 22, ⓦcamping-rennes.com. An appealingly verdant municipal site, 1km east of central Rennes (bus #3, direction "St-Laurent"), in a park that offers good shade and a pool, with sporting facilities nearby. Open all year. **€15.70**

Coq Gadby 156 rue d'Antrain ☎02 99 38 05 55, ⓦlecoq-gadby.com. Family-run for four generations, this self-styled "urban resort" is in a somewhat inconvenient location, in a humdrum neighbourhood around 1.5km north of the centre. Spread between the original seventeenth-century building and a modern annexe, it holds 24 comfortable rooms, an open-fire lounge, a pool and spa, and a Michelin-starred restaurant that's closed Sun & Mon. **€136**

Ibis Styles Rennes Centre Gare Nord 15 place de la

Gare ☎02 99 67 31 12, ⓦibisstyles.com. Modern chain hotel, opposite the train station, used largely by business travellers. The hundred stylish, good-value rooms feature excellent showers, while rates include a buffet breakfast plus free hot and cold drinks. **€70**

Des Lices 7 place des Lices ☎02 99 79 14 81, ⓦwww .hotel-des-lices.com. Forty-eight small-ish modern rooms, all with balcony, in a very comfortable and friendly hotel in the prettiest part of old Rennes, handy for the place des Lices car park. **€88**

★**Nemours** 5 rue de Nemours ☎02 99 78 26 26, ⓦhotelnemours.com. Recast as a boutique hotel, this central option has spotless, stylish and well-lit rooms in white, green and earth tones, with comfortable beds. Friendly and professional service, and you can take good breakfasts (€10) in bed. **€72**

Sévigné 47 av Jean-Janvier ☎02 99 67 27 55, ⓦwww .hotellesevigne.fr. Smart, upmarket establishment 100m north of the *gare SNCF* en route to the centre, with buffet breakfasts, and a large brasserie next door. All rooms have good en-suite bathrooms, plus satellite TV; discounts at weekends. **€82**

★**Symphonie des Sens** 3 rue du Chapitre ☎02 99 79 30 30, ⓦsymphoniedessens.com. Irresistible B&B, set in Rennes' oldest surviving half-timbered building, dating from 1481. The various beautifully furnished en-suite rooms are accessed via an extraordinary ancient wooden staircase; the hosts are friendly, and the breakfasts superb. **€128**

EATING AND DRINKING

Most of Rennes' more interesting bars and restaurants are in the streets just south of place Ste-Anne, with the bar-lined rue St-Michel and rue Penhoët, each with a fine assemblage of ancient wooden buildings, forming the epicentre. Ethnic alternatives are concentrated along rue St-Malo just to the north, and also on rue St-Georges near the place du Palais. Rue Vasselot, south of the river, is similar.

Atelier des Gourmets 12 rue Nantaise ☎02 99 67 53 84. Simple, old-fashioned bistro on the western edge of the centre, serving beautifully prepared French standards in a homely atmosphere; the friendly chef-owner is more than happy to talk you through each day's changing menu, costing €26 for lunch and €29 for dinner. Tues, Thurs & Fri noon–2pm & 7.30–9.30pm, Wed noon–2pm, Sat 7.30–9.45pm.

Auberge St-Sauveur 6 rue St-Sauveur ☎02 99 79 32 56, ⓦrestaurant-lesaintsauveur.fr. Classy, romantic restaurant, in an attractive medieval house near the cathedral, with exposed beams in the dining room, and

pavement tables as well. Light lunches for €13 and richer, meaty dinners for €23, with Asian-flavoured dishes like weeping tiger beef. Mon noon–2pm, Tues–Sat noon–2pm & 7.30–11pm.

Barantic 4 rue St-Michel ☎02 99 79 29 24. One of the city's favourite bars, putting on occasional live music for a mixed crowd of Breton nationalists and boisterous students; if it's too full, you can head to half-a-dozen similar alternatives within spitting distance. Mon–Fri 9am–1am, Sat 7am–1am, Sun 2pm–1am.

Baron Rouge 15 rue du Chapitre ☎02 99 79 08 99, ⓦwww.lebaronrouge.fr. Traditional restaurant run by an

RENNES FESTIVALS

Rennes is at its best during the first three weekends of July, when the **Festival des Tombées de la Nuit** takes over the whole city to celebrate Breton culture with music, theatre, film, mime and poetry (ⓦlestombeesdelanuit.com). A pocket version of the same festival is also held in the week between Christmas and New Year.

Rock festivals take place in Rennes throughout the year, including **La Route du Rock** in mid-February (ⓦlaroutedurock.com); **Youank**, in the first three weeks of November (ⓦyaouank.com), which is geared towards young up-and-coming bands; and the **Transmusicales** in the first week of December (ⓦlestrans.com), which attracts big-name acts from all over the world, while retaining a Breton emphasis.

enthusiastic young chef, where you can dine outdoors in the heart of historic Rennes, enjoying lunch with a glass of wine for €15, or classic dinner menus at €25 and €30, featuring, say, oysters followed by veal or lamb. Tues–Sat noon–2pm & 7.30–10.30pm.

Bernique Hurlante 40 rue St-Malo ☎02 99 38 70 09, ⓦlaberniquehurlante.free.fr. This popular, yellow-painted haunt ranks among Rennes' most gay-friendly bars, and also serves as a rendezvous for local artists and activists. Daily 6pm–1am.

★**Bistro la Cité** 7 rue St-Louis ☎02 99 79 24 34. This great little bar/bistro, with art on the walls and friendly staff and clientele, is the ideal place for a cider, a stronger house brew, or a quick meal. They host live music to suit a range of tastes on Saturday nights. Tues–Sun 5pm–1am.

★**Cours des Lices** 18 place des Lices ☎02 99 30 25 25, ⓦlecoursdeslices.fr. Top-notch French restaurant, perfectly positioned to take advantage of the fresh produce in the adjoining market. Dinner menus at €18.50 (weekdays only), €30 and €44; the latter includes such dishes as poached foie gras and de-boned pigeon. Tues–Fri noon–2pm & 7.30–10pm, Sat 11.30am–2pm & 7.30–10pm.

Crêperie Ste-Anne 5 place Ste-Anne ☎02 99 79 22 72. Appealing crêperie nicely situated on place Ste-Anne opposite the church, with plenty of outdoor seating and a good selection of galettes for €4–10. Mon–Sat 11.45am–10.30pm.

Léon le Cochon 6 rue du Pré Botté ☎02 99 79 37 54, ⓦleonlecochon.com. Tasteful, contemporary but classically French restaurant; as the name suggests, there's a heavy emphasis on pigs, and their trotters in particular. The simple €12.50 lunch menu includes wine, while the dinner menu costs €23 on weekdays, €25 at weekends. Mon–Thurs & Sun noon–2.30pm & 7.30–10.30pm, Fri & Sat noon–2.30pm & 7.30–11pm. Closed Sun in July & Aug.

Oan's Pub 1 rue George-Dottin ☎02 99 31 07 51. Lively pub facing the tourist office, with a large open-air terrace and a huge array of beers. Mon–Sat 3pm–1am.

Tire-Bouchon 2 rue du Chapitre ☎02 99 79 43 43. Part bistro, part wine bar, this friendly local rendezvous chalks up a simple array of fresh-cooked dishes on its blackboard each day, from *tartines* to meat with pasta, and also offers ample plates of cheese or charcuterie. A full meal should cost around €20. Mon–Fri noon–2pm & 7–10.45pm.

LIVE MUSIC AND ENTERTAINMENT

Cinemas Schedules for all Rennes' cinemas are on ⓦcine35.com. Cinemas include the Gaumont, 8 quai Duguay-Trouin; L'Arvor, 29 rue d'Antrain, which shows films in English; and Ciné TNB, 1 rue St-Hélier.

Club Ubu 1 rue St-Hélier ☎02 99 31 12 10, ⓦubu-rennes .com. The city's principal venue for big rock concerts, open year round, is on the same site as the theatre, but in a separate auditorium.

Mondo Bizarro 264 av Général-Patton ☎02 99 87 22 00, ⓦmondobizarro.free.fr. Rock, metal and especially punk club, 1km northeast of the centre (bus line #5), and kept busy most nights with local bands and international punk stalwarts, plus a leavening of tribute bands, ska, reggae and jazz. Tues–Sat 5pm–3am.

Théâtre National de Bretagne 1 rue St-Hélier ☎02 99 31 12 31, ⓦt-n-b.fr. A stimulating programme of varied events – with dance and music as well as theatre – throughout the year, except in July and Aug.

LISTINGS

Bookshops Co-op Breizh, 17 rue Penhoët (☎02 99 79 01 87), stocks Breton and Celtic CDs along with books and posters; FNAC, Centre Commercial Colombier (ⓦfnac.fr).

Hospital Hôtel Dieu, 2 rue de l'Hôtel Dieu (☎02 99 28 43 21, ⓦchu-rennes.fr).

Pharmacy Pharmacie Colombia, Centre Commercial Colombia (Mon–Sat 9.30am–8pm; ☎02 99 65 08 08).

Post office Palais du Commerce in the heart of town on the place de la République (Mon–Fri 8am–7pm, Sat 8.30am–12.30pm); 27 bd du Colombier, just west of the *gare SNCF* (Mon–Fri 8am–7pm, Sat 8am–noon).

4

Fougères

FOUGÈRES, 50km east of Rennes on the main road into Brittany from Caen, promotes itself as the *"ville au joli nom"*, *fougères* being the French for "ferns". Its pride and joy, a magnificent medieval **castle** that claims to be the largest in all Europe, is worth going a long way out of your way to see.

Thanks to its split-level site, the topography of the town is almost impossible to grasp from a map. Streets that look a few metres long turn out to be precipitous plunges down escarpments, and lanes collapse into flights of steps; the only efficient way to get around is on foot.

The best approach to the castle is from **place des Arbres** beside St-Léonard's church off rue Nationale, the main street of the old fortified town. Footpaths, ramps and stairways drop down through successive tiers of formal public gardens, offering magnificent views of the ramparts and towers along the way, to reach the water meadows of the River Nançon. You cross the river itself beside a little cluster of medieval houses – the sculpted doorway at 6 rue de Lusignan is particularly attractive.

Château de Fougères

Feb–April & Oct–Dec Tues–Sun 10am–12.30pm & 2–5.30pm; May Tues–Sun 10am–7pm; June–Sept daily 10am–7pm; closed Jan • €8 • ☎ 02 99 99 79 59, ⓦ chateau-fougeres.com

Perhaps the oddest feature of Fougères' lay-out is the positioning of the **château**, sited in pre-artillery days well below the main part of the town, on a low spit of land that separates two mighty rock faces towering above. The massive structure was laid out in 1166 to replace a wooden fort destroyed by English invaders. Shielded by great curtain-walls, and circled by a hacked-out moat full of weirs and waterfalls, it was also protected in its heyday by the River Nançon. None of this, however, prevented it being captured several times by medieval adventurers such as du Guesclin. Today it remains a spectacular sight; the moat is still filled with water, while every crevice of the surrounding buildings seems to erupt with bright geraniums.

The large area that lies immediately within the castle walls, along with the château itself, has recently been overhauled and redesigned to turn visits into journeys through time as well as space. Several grand towers, and especially the main keep, hold multimedia displays on the history of both castle and town, while the majestic lawns, once occupied by a heavily populated settlement, remain tranquil havens for picnickers and sunbathers. Many nooks and crannies still lie in ruins, often overgrown with colourful wild flowers. Visitors can explore by themselves, pick up an audioguide, or join a guided tour for no extra charge.

The Forêt de Fougères

Northeast of Fougères, the **Forêt de Fougères**, stretching for roughly 8km on either side of the D177, which heads towards Vire (see opposite), is one of the most enjoyable in the province. The beech woods are spacious and light, with various megaliths and trails of old stones scattered among the chestnut and spruce. It's quite a contrast to their normal bleak and windswept haunts to see dolmens in such verdant surroundings. A good walk is to start at **Landéan**, about 8km northeast of Fougères on the D177, and head west through the forest for another 8km or so as far as **Le Chatellier**, a village set high in thick woods.

ARRIVAL AND DEPARTURE   **FOUGÈRES**

By bus The only public transport to serve Fougères are buses to and from Rennes (10 daily; 1hr) and Vitré (2 daily; 35min).

By car Several car parks lie around the perimeter of the castle; parking spaces in the town centre higher up are much harder to find.

INFORMATION AND ACTIVITIES

Tourist office 2 rue Nationale in the upper town (Easter–June, Sept & Oct Mon–Sat 9.30am–12.30pm & 2–6pm; July & Aug Mon–Sat 9am–7pm, Sun 10am–noon & 2–6pm; Nov–Easter Mon 2–6pm, Tues–Sat 10am–12.30pm &

2–6pm; ☎02 99 94 12 20, ⓦ ot-fougeres.fr).
Horseriding For a horseback tour of the Forêt de Fougères, contact the Base de Plein-Air in Chénedet, 2.5km south of Landéan (☎02 99 97 35 46).

ACCOMMODATION AND EATING

Balzac 15 rue Nationale ☎02 99 99 42 46, ⓦ en-balzachotel.fr. Friendly little hotel in a central grey granite townhouse, offering pleasant rooms at a very decent price. €58
Buffet 53bis rue Nationale ☎02 99 94 35 76. Great-value food from €12, including all-you-can-eat buffets of

hors d'oeuvres, cheeses and desserts. Mon, Tues & Thurs–Sat noon–2pm & 7–9pm, Wed noon–2pm.
Des Voyageurs 10 place Gambetta ☎02 99 99 08 20, ⓦ hotel-fougeres.fr. Particularly nice hotel, on the main road near the tourist office, with attractively renovated rooms – the quieter ones are at the back. €71

Vitré

A lesser rival to Dinan as the best-preserved **medieval town** in Brittany, **VITRÉ** stands just north of the Le Mans–Rennes motorway, 30km east of Rennes. Occupation of this site dates right back to the Romans, when a certain Vitrius owned a villa here. While its thirteenth-century **walls** are no longer quite complete, their effect is enhanced by the fact that what lies outside them has changed so little. To the north are stark wooded slopes, while into the western hillside beneath the castle burrow thickets of stone cottages that must once have been Vitré's medieval slums.

Vitré is a market town, with its principal **market** held on Mondays in the square in front of Notre Dame church. The old city is full of twisting streets of half-timbered houses, a good proportion of which are bars. The **rue de la Baudrairie**, between the church and the castle, and formerly the town's leather-working quarter, is the most picturesque of the streets, but the **rue d'En Bas**, which climbs up from the Rachapt quarter to the castle, has the best selection of bars.

Château de Vitré

April–June & Sept daily 10am–12.30pm & 2–6pm; July & Aug daily 10am–6pm; Oct–March Mon & Wed–Fri 10.30am–12.30pm & 2–5pm, Sat & Sun 2–5pm • €4 • ☎02 99 75 04 54, ⓦ ot-vitre.fr

In best fairy-tale fashion, the towers of the **château de Vitré**, which dominates the western end of the ramparts, have pointed slate-grey roofs that look like freshly sharpened pencils. First erected in 1060, the castle was remodelled to its present appearance two hundred years later. The **museum** inside shows off some fine Renaissance architecture and furnishings, but throws little light on the town's eventful past; instead, it's a ragbag of pretty much anything some nineteenth-century curator could get his hands on. The highlight is a collection of tatty **stuffed frogs** doing amusing things, such as fighting duels and playing billiards.

The admission fee for the castle also includes entry to a couple of other museums in the general vicinity (same fee and hours). The **Musée St-Nicholas**, on the western outskirts of town, occupies the huge former chapel of a fifteenth-century hospital, with a sober collection of medieval reliquaries and religious paraphernalia, while the **Château des Rochers-Sévigné**, 10km southeast, is a place of pilgrimage for French devotees of the seventeenth-century society letter-writer Madame de Sévigné, and holds little interest for anyone not familiar with her work.

Champeaux

The little town of **CHAMPEAUX**, 8km west of Vitré, consists of a central paved square, surrounded by stone houses, with an ornate well in the centre. Its fifteenth-century collegiate **church** contains a superb stained-glass *Crucifixion* by Gilles de la Croix-Vallée, the ornate tombs of its founding family, and some fine carved choir stalls.

The Roche-aux-Fées

About 15km south of Châteaubourg, not far from the road just off the D341 near Retiers, the **ROCHE-AUX-FÉES** is the least visited of the major megalithic monuments of Brittany. This "fairy rock" is a twenty-metre-long covered alleyway of purplish stones, with no apparent funerary purpose or, indeed, any evidence that it was ever buried. It's set on a high and exposed spot, guarded by just a few venerable trees, and it's thought the slabs had to be dragged a good 45km to get here. There's no admission charge.

Tradition has it that engaged couples should come to the Roche-aux-Fées on the night of a full moon and separately count the stones; if they agree on the total, things are looking good.

ARRIVAL AND INFORMATION   VITRÉ

By train Vitré's candy-striped *gare SNCF* is on the southern edge of the centre, where the ramparts disappear and the town blends into its newer sectors.
Destinations Rennes (12 daily; 18–35min)
Tourist office Place Général-de-Gaulle, left from the station (July & Aug Mon–Sat 9.30am–12.30pm & 2–6.30pm, Sun 10am–12.30pm & 3–6pm; Sept–June Mon 2.30–6pm, Tues–Fri 9.30am–12.30pm & 2.30–6pm, Sat 10am–12.30pm & 3–5pm; ☎02 99 75 04 46, ⊚ot-vitre.fr).

ACCOMMODATION AND EATING

Ar Milin 30 rue de Paris, Châteaubourg ☎02 99 00 30 91, ⊚armilin.com. Wonderful and rather exclusive hotel, straddling the River Vilaine in huge gardens halfway between Vitré and Rennes, and offering large contemporary-styled rooms. Breakfast, at €13, includes an enormous buffet of fresh pastries. The complex also includes a slightly cheaper sister hotel, *du Parc*, and two restaurants, one of which is always open. €119
Du Château 5 rue Rallon ☎02 99 74 58 59, ⊚hotel duchateauvitre.com. Inexpensive hotel, down below the castle, just outside the walls, and above a tearoom. All rooms are acceptable, but it's worth paying a little extra for those on the upper floors, which have views of the ramparts. €56
Petit Billot 5bis place du Général-Leclerc ☎02 99 75 02 10, ⊚hotel-vitre.com. Very friendly, good-value hotel, facing the station and offering clean, simple rooms of all shapes and sizes. €60
La Soupe aux Choux 32 rue Notre-Dame ☎02 99 75 10 86, ⊚restaurant-vitre.fr. Fine old house, with exposed stone walls, converted into a smart restaurant that offers simple but classic French food, with the occasional eccentricity like kangaroo cooked in cider (€15) thrown in. Dinner menu €26. Mon–Fri noon–2pm & 7.15–10pm, Sat 7.15–10pm.

The Côte d'Émeraude

Lush green for much of its length, interrupted by expanses of heather and indented by beach after magnificent beach, the splendidly attractive coast to the west of Dinard is known as the **Côte d'Émeraude**. This is one of Brittany's most traditional family resort areas, with old-fashioned holiday towns, safe sandy beaches and a plethora of well-organized campsites. None of the towns is of any significant size, and paying attractions or entertainments suitable for whiling away rainy afternoons are almost nonexistent. If you're lucky enough to be here on a fine summer's day, however, **St-Jacut**, **St-Cast**, **Erquy** and **Le Val-André** all make idyllically lazy seaside destinations, while **Cap Fréhel** offers a fine, if bracing, coastal walk.

St-Jacut-de-la-Mer

ST-JACUT, which takes up most of the tip of a narrow peninsula roughly 16km west of St-Malo, was founded over a thousand years ago by an itinerant Irish monk. The general shape, and many of the buildings, of the old fishing village are still here, though that's now mingled with the fine villas and promenades added when St-Jacut became a classic nineteenth-century bathing resort. A peaceful little spot, it holds everything young children could want – good sand, rocky pools to clamber about, and woods nearby to scramble in.

St-Cast-le-Guildo

The pleasant seaside community of **ST-CAST**, on the next promontory west of St-Jacut, is a thirty-kilometre drive from St-Malo, and connected by SNCF buses with the nearest train station, at Lamballe (see p.212). Most of its commercial activity takes place in the rather uninspiring **Bourg**, set back from the water, but the seaside area down below is very nice, with an enormous die-straight **beach** popular with families; the beach runs parallel to the pedestrianized, restaurant-lined rue du Duc d'Aiguillon. There's also a quiet, picturesque **port** north of the beach, with splendid walking along the coast towards the headland beyond.

Cap Fréhel

While the entire Côte d'Émeraude is ravishingly beautiful, the **Cap Fréhel**, a high, warm expanse of heath, cliffs and heather 9km north of the main D786, and a total drive of 24km west of St-Cast, is exceptional. Its western shoreline boasts a succession of spectacular sandy beaches; pull-offs along the road above offer drivers repeated opportunities to park and walk down to the enticing strands.

The unspoiled headland itself lies 400m walk from the road (parking €2), with no more than a few ruins of old buildings and a small "tearoom" nearby. The rocks, 60m down at the foot of the cliffs, busy with puffins and guillemots, officially constitute the Fauconnière **seabird sanctuary**. Offshore, the heather-covered islands are grand to look at, although too tiny to visit; the view from the cape's **lighthouse** (July & Aug daily 2–6pm; free) can extend as far as Jersey and the Île de Bréhat.

Fort la Latte

2km southeast of Cap Fréhel • Early July to late Aug daily 10.30am–7pm; April to early July & late Aug to Sept daily 10.30am–12.30pm & 2–6pm; Oct–March Sat, Sun & hols 1.30–5.30pm • €5.20 • ☏ 02 96 41 57 11, ⓦ castlelalatte.com

The fourteenth-century **Fort la Latte**, at the tip of a lesser headland 2km southeast of Cap Fréhel, is reached along a few hundred metres of hedge-lined footpath from its free car park. At the far end, as you re-emerge onto open heathland, is the fortified castle, a gorgeous little gem, restored by private owners in the 1930s. Visitors enter the enclosure across two drawbridges; outbuildings scattered within include a cannonball foundry, and there's also a medieval herb garden, but the highlight is the keep, which contains historical exhibits. Precarious walkways climb the outside of its roof to the very summit, for superb coastal views.

A lovely little open-air bar alongside the car park sells coffee and ice cream in summer.

Erquy

The delightful little family resort of **ERQUY** nestles into a vast natural bay around 20km west of Cap Fréhel, with a perfect crescent beach that curves through more than 180 degrees. At low tide, the sea disappears way beyond the harbour entrance, leaving gentle ripples of paddling sand. Adventurers equipped with suitable boots could walk right across its mouth, from the grassy wooded headland on the left side over to the picturesque little lighthouse at the end of the jetty on the right.

Erquy is best known in Brittany for its scallops, celebrated in late April each year with a **Scallop Festival**.

Le Val-André

The beach in the broader bay of **LE VAL-ANDRÉ**, 11km southwest along the coast from Erquy, is slightly larger than its neighbour's, much straighter, and composed of finer sand. Apart from the casino at its centre, fringed by modern apartment blocks, the pedestrian promenade that stretches along the seafront consists of huge old holiday villas undisturbed by shops or bars. However, Le Val-André is definitely more of a commercial town than Erquy, and rue Amiral-Charner, running parallel to the sea one street back, is lively with holiday-makers in summer.

For an enjoyable scenic **walk**, follow the 2km-long footpath around the headland to the small, secluded lagoon of **Dahouët** (see p.222 for details of summer sailings to the Île de Bréhat). The construction of a large yachting marina here has obliterated all significant traces of its past, but this lagoon is known to have been used by Viking raiders over a thousand years ago.

ARRIVAL AND INFORMATION
CÔTE EMERAUDE

ST-CAST-LE-GUILDO
Tourist office Place Charles-de-Gaulle, a couple of blocks back from the sea (July & Aug Mon–Sat 9.30am–7pm, Sun 10am–12.30pm & 3–6.30pm; Sept–June Mon–Sat 9.30am–12.30pm & 2–6pm; ☎02 96 41 81 52, Ⓦsaintcastleguildo.fr).

ERQUY
By bus Bus #2 (Ⓦtibus.fr) calls at Erquy 5 times daily en route between St-Brieuc and Lamballe (1hr & 35min west respectively) and the village of Fréhel (7min east).

Tourist office 3 rue du 19 Mars (April–June Mon–Sat 9.30am–12.30pm & 2–6pm, Sun 10am–12.30pm; July & Aug Mon–Sat 9.30am–1pm & 2–7pm, Sun 10am–1pm & 4–6pm; first fortnight of Sept Mon–Sat 9.30am–12.30pm & 2–6pm; mid-Sept to March Mon–Sat 9.30am–12.30pm & 2–5pm; ☎02 96 72 30 12, Ⓦerquy-tourisme.com).

LE VAL-ANDRÉ
Tourist office in the seafront casino (Mon–Sat 9.15am–12.30pm & 2.30–6pm; ☎02 96 72 20 55, Ⓦval-andre.org).

ACTIVITIES

ST-CAST-LE-GUILDO
Boat trips Compagnie Corsaire operates summer-only cruises along the coast, to St-Malo, Dinard and Cap Fréhel (Thurs only in recent years; €20.50; Ⓦcompagniecorsaire.com).

ERQUY
Boat trips Every Wed between April and September, and

also on Mon & Fri in July & Aug, Les Vedettes de Bréhat operates trips from Erquy to the Île de Bréhat (see p.221; departures 8.30am; €32; ☎02 96 55 79 50, Ⓦvedettesdebrehat.com).
Watersports Erquy holds schools of sailing, kayaking and windsurfing (all ☎02 96 72 32 62, Ⓦeverquy.org), and also diving (☎02 96 72 49 67, Ⓦhistoiredeauplongee.com).

ACCOMMODATION AND EATING

ST-JACUT-DE-LA-MER
Camping Municipal de la Manchette 24 rue de la Manchette ☎02 96 27 70 33, Ⓦmairie-saintjacutdelamer.com. Very simple local campsite, right beside both a pleasant beach and the village football pitch, with its own all-day snack bar. Closed Oct–March. **€13.25**
Vieux Moulin 22 rue du Moulin ☎02 96 27 71 02, Ⓦhotel-le-vieux-moulin.com. Distinctive hotel, atop the central spine of the peninsula. As it centres on a fifteenth-century windmill, two of its guest rooms are

completely round and offer sea views in two directions. The very cheapest have washbasin & WC but not shower or bath, and sadly there's no longer a restaurant. Closed Nov–Feb. **€52**

ST-CAST-LE-GUILDO
Le Bonheur est dans le Blé 17 rue du Duc d'Aiguillon ☎02 96 81 03 99, Ⓦlebonheurestdansleble.com. Popular crêperie that's known for its generous portions and imaginative fillings; reserve in advance during summer.

Daily noon 2.30pm & 7–9.30pm; closed Tues & Wed Sept–June.

Châtelet Rue des Nouettes ☎02 96 41 96 33, ⓦlechatelet.com. Four-star campsite facing the bay, 150m up from the beach, with a heated swimming pool. Closed mid-Sept to April. €36

Port Jacquet 32 rue du Port ☎02 96 41 97 18, ⓦport-jacquet.com. Attractive old hotel, perched on a hilltop between the port and the main beach, and linked to both by a coastal footpath. Small, good-value rooms with great views, a guests-only dining room, and large €8.50 buffet breakfasts. They also offer bike rental, and a baggage-carrying service for cyclists. €55

CAP FRÉHEL

Camping Municipal du Cap Fréhel Les Grèves d'en Bas, Pléherel ☎02 96 41 43 34, ⓦcamping-municipal-du-cap-frehel.webnode.fr. This ideal, isolated campsite is the nearest to the Cap, and is especially popular with walkers and surfers. Closed Sept to late June. €11.25

FORT LA LATTE

Maison Bellevue Fort la Latte ☎02 96 41 41 61, ⓦhotel-bellevue-ushuaia.fr. Family-run B&B that offers five tastefully furnished bedrooms, some with sea views, and has its own crêperie/tearoom. Closed Jan. €65

ERQUY

★**Beauséjour** 21 rue de la Corniche ☎02 96 72 30 39, ⓦbeausejour-erquy.com. Set in a seaside villa above the southern end of the beach, and festooned with dungaree-wearing teddy bears, the *Beauséjour* represents Erquy at its quirkiest. It no longer has its own restaurant, but the breakfasts are good, and the rooms very nice indeed. Closed mid-Nov to mid-April. €69

Camping de la Plage de St-Pabu Plage de St-Pabu ☎02 96 72 24 65, ⓦsaintpabu.com. The pick of the local campsites, right by the sea just beyond the second promontory southwest of town. The garden-like location incorporates a kids' playground but not a pool. Closed early Nov to March. €21.20

De la Plage 21 bd de la Mer ☎02 96 72 30 09, ⓦhotelplage-erquy.com. Modern hotel with bright, large rooms and an excellent restaurant serving lunch

from €13 and dinner menus from €27, and great buffet breakfasts. Sea-view rooms typically cost around €20 extra. €72

Reflet de la Mer 18 rue du Port ☎02 96 72 00 95. Jaunty little crêperie, at the north end of the beachfront as it starts to curve towards the port, with an outdoor terrace, blue shutters and even a picket fence. Daily noon–2pm & 7–9pm; closed Oct–March.

★**La Villa Nazado** 2 rue des Patriotes ☎02 96 63 67 14, ⓦvillanazado.com. Four very tasteful B&B rooms, in a grand, pastel-yellow, nineteenth-century villa, a couple of blocks back from the seafront in the heart of Erquy. €70

★**Le Vivier** 64 rue du Port ☎02 96 72 34 24, ⓦle-vivier-erquy.com. The best of a row of similar restaurants at the far northern, right-hand, end of the bay, beside the fishing port, with weekday lunches for €16.50, and seafood-rich dinner menus from €23; the €30 option includes sumptuous grilled oysters and a scallop stew. Daily noon–2pm & 7–9pm; closed Jan.

LE VAL-ANDRÉ

Biniou 121 rue Clemenceau ☎02 96 72 24 35, ⓦrestaurant-au-biniou.com. The best of several adjacent seafood restaurants just back from the casino, close to the beach; lunch costs €17, while the €27.50 dinner menu features salmon poached with saffron and coriander. Daily noon–2pm & 7–9pm; closed Tues & Wed Sept–June, plus 2 weeks in Feb.

De France 4 rue Pasteur, Pléneuf ☎02 96 72 22 52, ⓦpleneuf-hoteldefrance.com. Logis de France in the main church square of Pléneuf, the *bourg* associated with Le Val-André, 1.5km up the hill from the sea. The eccentric block of cheap rooms out the back, all accessed from open balconies, are marine-themed with knots, canvas and navy-blue trimmings. There's also a good restaurant hidden away, with menus from €18; the €30 menu includes three scallop courses. €60

De la Mer 63 rue Amiral-Charner ☎02 96 72 20 44, ⓦhotel-de-la-mer.com. Refurbished hotel, one block back from the beach, with plain but acceptable en-suite rooms, some of which have sea views. The same management operate the characterless *Nuit et Jour* motel nearby for guests without reservations. Motel €64, hotel €80

The inland route: west to Morlaix

Following the coast from Dinard and Dinan is by far the most scenic route westwards across Brittany, but it can also be pretty slow. Travellers in a hurry to reach Morlaix and Finistère can choose instead to head **inland**, either by branching onto the D768 just south of St-Jacut if coming from Dinard, or following first the N176 and then the N12 motorways west from Dinan. Both routes pass the occasional time-forgotten little town or village; few have tourist facilities, but all make pleasant opportunities to stretch your legs.

Jugon-les-Lacs

Tiny old **JUGON-LES-LACS**, 20km west of Dinan, is poised at one end of its own artificial lake – the *grand étang* – which was originally created for defensive purposes during the twelfth century. Peculiarly, the central place du Martray – scene of a market each Friday – is well below the water level, and you have to climb uphill to reach the massive cobblestone dyke that shields it from inundation. At the opposite end of town, the N176 crosses high above the valley on a viaduct. Jugon, nestled cosily between the two, has no room to expand even if it wanted to – it's a subdued but atmospheric place, whose few streets are almost deserted in the evenings.

For most of the way around the **lake**, there's no approach road or footpath, only meadows and trees sweeping down to the water. However, just out of town at the campsite (see p.215), there's a small beach from which you can go swimming.

Lamballe

The fine old market town of **LAMBALLE**, 20km west of Jugon, is crammed into a narrow valley beside a broad river, dominated by a church high up on battlement walls. Its picturesque main square, the **place du Martray**, holds a handful of impressive fourteenth-century half-timbered buildings, while a short walk away there's also an outpost of the French national stud. The town's most famous former citizen was the princess of Lamballe, a lady-in-waiting to Marie Antoinette, who was killed by a revolutionary mob in 1792.

Musée Mathurin Méheut

Place du Martray • April–Sept Tues–Sat 10am–noon & 2–6pm; also open Sun 2–6pm in July & Aug; Oct–Dec Tues–Sat 2–5pm • €3 • ☎ 02 96 31 19 99, ⓦ musee-meheut.fr

The grandest of the medieval houses on Lamballe's central square, the Maison du Bourreau, was once home to the town's public executioner. It now houses the tiny **Musée Mathurin Méheut**, half of which explores the town's history, and features a fascinating model of Lamballe as it looked in 1417, while the rest focuses on the paintings of local-born Mathurin Méheut (1882–1958), which range from Breton landscapes to illustrations for children's books.

Haras National

Place du Champ de Foire • Guided tours only: July & Aug daily 11am–4.30pm, with regular French-language tours, and tours in English at 2.30pm & 4pm; Sept to mid-June daily at 3pm only, in French • €6 • ☎ 02 96 50 06 98, ⓦ haraspatrimoine.com

A branch of the **Haras National** (national stud) all but adjoins Lamballe's main square, in an imposing ensemble in the very heart of town. Though not quite on the same scale as Le Nôtre's dramatic park near Argentan (see p.160), and specializing in any case more in sturdy Breton workhorses than glossy thoroughbreds, it will still delight any horse-lover. Only open for guided tours, which last around 1hr 30min, it's also the focus of a big **horse festival** on the first weekend after August 15.

Moncontour

The attractive little hill town of **MONCONTOUR**, 18km southwest of Lamballe and 23km southeast of St-Brieuc, prospered during the Middle Ages, thanks to its hemp industry. Having been under no pressure to grow since then, it remains largely enclosed by its medieval fortifications – not that you get much impression of them once you're actually in the town, as the houses all face inwards onto the narrow streets.

Moncontour centres on the pretty, triangular **place du Penthièvre**. Here, the Romanesque tower of the church of St-Mathurin gained a delightfully eccentric new belfry with wooden eaves and grey-slate domes in 1902, and now constitutes the highest point on the hill.

PLOUMANAC'H, CÔTE DE GRANIT ROSE (P.225) >

On the first Sunday of August, Moncontour echoes its days of glory by hosting a hectic "medieval fair".

Quintin

QUINTIN, 20km southwest of St-Brieuc, is in the official jargon "a little city of character", still readily recognizable as a seventeenth-century weaving village. Work on the grand **Château de Quintin** began in 1640, and was never completed, but you can tour a few of the rooms, which host temporary exhibitions in summer (late March to June, Sept & Oct daily 2–4.30pm; July & Aug daily 10.30am–noon & 2–6pm; Nov & Dec Sat & Sun 2–4.30pm; €5; ⓦchateaudequintin.fr). The château is at its most imposing, however, when seen from the River Gouët below.

A twenty-minute stroll up from the river can show you the best of Quintin. Follow the rue du Vau-du-Gouët from the east, and climb a stone staircase up through the vestiges of the old town walls, which are overshadowed by the round **Tour des Archives**, covered with creeping wild flowers. At the top is the late-nineteenth-century **Basilique Notre Dame**. Beyond that, you enter the central place 1830, with the rue Grande stretching ahead. Most of its houses are made of elegant grey stone, but a few of their half-timbered predecessors still remain.

Guingamp

The only town of any size along the N12 motorway, as it heads west towards Finistère across the centre of the northern peninsula, is the old weaving centre of **GUINGAMP** – its name possibly the source of the striped or checked fabric "gingham". It's an attractive place of cobbled streets, but there's not much to see beyond the main square – where a fountain bedecked in griffins and gargoyles is overlooked by a splendid pair of lopsided old timber-frame houses propping each other up – and the Black Virgin in the thirteenth-century **basilica**.

Guingamp hosts a big *pardon*, featuring a night procession to the basilica, on the first Saturday in July, while the ten-day **Saint Loup Festival**, celebrating Breton dance, enlivens the middle of August (ⓦdansebretonne.com).

The Menez Bré

A dozen kilometres west of Guingamp towards Morlaix, the "mountain" of the **Menez Bré** is a rounded and exposed monolith that may be just 302m tall, but nonetheless seems a spectacular height amid these plains. In the mid-nineteenth century, the local rector was often observed to climb, laden with books, to the mountain's peak on stormy nights, accompanied only by a donkey. For all his exemplary piety, his parishioners suspected him of sorcery and witchcraft; he was in fact doing early research into electrical forces. Modern visitors hike to the top for dramatic views towards the sea to the north and the rolling hills inland. A footpath

---

A BIG TEAM FROM A LITTLE TOWN

Guingamp has in recent years achieved national fame out of all proportion to its size, thanks to the local football team, **En Avant de Guingamp**. For a community of just over seven thousand inhabitants, it has enjoyed phenomenal success; past players include Didier Drogba, who signed for the club in 2002. At the time of writing En Avant were back in the top French league, Ligue 1, for the third time. Even more significantly, they won the **Coupe de France** in both 2009 and 2014, in each case, remarkably, defeating Rennes in an all-Breton final.

The Roudourou stadium is a short way northwest of the town centre; for fixtures and tickets, which start at just €4 for regular league games, visit ⓦwww.eaguingamp.com.

leads to the Menez Bré from the village of **Tréglamus**, 8km west of Guingamp just off the N12; the round-trip walk is 10km.

ARRIVAL AND INFORMATION

JUGON-LES-LACS
Tourist office Place du Martray (mid-March to mid-Sept Mon–Sat 10am–12.30pm & 2–6pm; also open Sun 10.30am–1pm in July & Aug; mid-Sept to Oct Mon–Fri 10am–12.30pm & 2–5.30pm; Nov to mid-March Mon, Wed & Fri 10am–12.30pm & 2–5.30pm, Tues & Thurs 10am–12.30pm; ☎ 02 96 31 70 75, ⓦ jugon-les-lacs.com).

LAMBALLE
Tourist office 15 place du Champ de Foire, adjoining the *haras* (July & Aug Mon–Wed & Fri–Sun 10am–12.30pm & 1.30–6pm, Thurs 10am–6pm; Sept–June Mon 1.30–5.30pm, Tues–Sat 10am–noon & 1.30–5.30pm; ☎ 02 96 31 05 38, ⓦ www.lamballe-tourisme.com).

MONCONTOUR
Tourist office 4 place de la Carrière (July & Aug daily 10am–12.30pm & 2–6pm; Sept–June Tues, Wed, Fri & Sat

THE INLAND ROUTE

10am–noon & 2–5pm, Thurs 10am–noon; ☎ 02 96 73 49 57, ⓦ tourisme-moncontour.com).

QUINTIN
Tourist office 6 place 1830 (July & Aug Mon–Sat 9.30am–12.30pm & 2–6pm, Sun 10am–1pm; Sept–June Tues, Wed, Fri & Sat 9.30am–noon & 2–5pm; ☎ 02 96 74 01 51, ⓦ tourismequintin.com).

GUINGAMP
By train Guingamp's *gare SNCF*, 500m southeast of the centre, is served by 10 daily trains from Morlaix (35min west), Lamballe (30min east), and Rennes (1hr 10min southeast). A separate branch line runs to Paimpol (2–5 daily; 45min).
Tourist office Place Champ-au-Roy (Tues–Sat 10am–12.30pm & 2–6pm; ☎ 02 96 43 73 89, ⓦ ot-guingamp.fr).

ACCOMMODATION AND EATING

4

JUGON-LES-LACS
Auberge de l'Ecu 25 place du Martray ☎ 02 96 31 61 41. Charming, old-fashioned flower-festooned bar/restaurant with seating on the main square, serving decent traditional food on menus from €12.75 for lunch, and €19 in the evening. Wed–Sun noon–2pm & 7–9pm.
Au Bocage du Lac Rue du Bocage ☎ 02 96 31 60 16, ⓦ camping-location-bretagne.com. Family campsite, out of town along the D52 towards Mégrit, with a heated swimming pool, mini-golf course and pony-riding, plus bikes, boats and windsurf boards for rent. There's even a rental chalet out on the lake itself, perched on stilts. Closed mid-Sept to mid-April. Chalet €164, camping €24.90
La Grande Fontaine 7 rue Penthièvre ☎ 02 96 31 61 29. Attractive Logis hotel, a couple of hundred metres east of the centre on the main road towards Dinan. It has a lively bar with a roadside terrace, and menus at €26 and €38.50. €70

LAMBALLE
Au Boeuf d'Or 12 rue du Dr-Calmette ☎ 02 96 31 31 31. Attractive little restaurant, just beyond the tourist office, that serves a great-value lunch special at €10–12 for three courses, but dinner on Saturdays only; look out for the frogs' legs on the €18 menu. Mon, Tues, Thurs, Fri & Sun noon–2pm, Sat noon–2pm & 7–9pm.
Manoir des Portes La Poterie ☎ 02 96 31 13 62, ⓦ manoirdesportes.com. Very charming sixteenth-century stone-built manor house, in a pretty village 4km northwest of the centre, holding simple but nicely

decorated rooms and a good-value restaurant serving menus from €16.50. €91

MONCONTOUR
A la Garde Ducale 10 place Penthièvre ☎ 02 96 73 52 18, ⓦ a-la-garde-ducale.gitedarmor.com. Beautifully situated B&B, in a sixteenth-century house on the main church square, with three homely, quirky rooms. The friendly owners cook dinner on request, for €25 extra. €60
Chaudron Magique 1 place de la Carrière ☎ 02 96 73 40 34, ⓦ le-chaudron-magique.com. Medieval-themed restaurant very close to the tourist office, where liveried waiters serve decent traditional lunches from €12, and dinner from €22 and upwards; you can even borrow a costume to wear yourself. Tues–Sat noon–3pm & 7–10pm, Sun noon–3pm.

QUINTIN
Commerce 2 rue Rochenen ☎ 02 96 74 94 67, ⓦ hotel ducommerce-quintin.com. Classic little ivy-coated village hotel, on the western fringes of the centre, with tasteful, if far from fancy, rooms. Its solemn but attractive dining room serves good meals from €17.50 upwards, on weekdays only. €87

GUINGAMP
Armor 44–46 bd Clemenceau ☎ 02 96 43 76 16, ⓦ armor-hotel.com. This white-painted, modernized hotel, near the station, is the best-value local option, and has a nice garden around the back. €74

Boissière 90 rue de l'Yser ☎02 96 21 06 35, ⓦrestaurantlaboissiere.jimdo.com. Traditional dinner menus in Guingamp's finest restaurant, in a park northwest of the centre, start at €24, but you can get lunch on weekdays for €14.50. Tues–Fri noon–1.30pm & 7.15–9pm, Sat 7.15–9pm, Sun noon–1.30pm.

Baie de St-Brieuc

While the town of **St-Brieuc** may be more of an obstacle to be avoided than an appealing destination, it serves as a gateway to the series of attractive little resorts that dot its eponymous bay. It also marks the point at which many visitors become aware that Brittany really does amount to something more than just another stretch of French coastline, and has its own very distinct culture and traditions.

As you move northwest from St-Brieuc along the edge of the V-shaped bay towards Paimpol, the countryside becomes especially rich – it's called the **Goëlo** – while the coast itself grows wilder and harsher. The seaside towns tend to be crammed into narrow rocky inlets or set well back in river estuaries, and only a few beaches manage to break out from the rocks.

St-Brieuc

Far too busy being the industrial centre of the north to concern itself with entertaining tourists, **ST-BRIEUC** is an odd-looking place, with two very deep wooded valleys spanned by viaducts at its core. The streets are hectic, with the centre cut in two by a motorway, unrelieved by any public parks, and not much improved either by a mega-shopping complex. Motorists and cyclists, unfortunately, have little choice but to plough straight through rather than attempting to negotiate the back roads and steep hills around.

In late May or early June, St-Brieuc hosts the rather ominous-sounding **Art Rock Festival** (ⓦartrock.org).

Binic

Little **BINIC** has to be the nicest place to stay on the Baie de St-Brieuc. The whole place is on an appealingly small scale, with sandy beaches, a narrow pleasure port crammed with yachts, a jazzed-up little central shopping and dining district, a paved promenade along the seafront, and to either side Devon-like meadows that roll down to the sea. In

---

BRITTANY'S SULPHUROUS SEAWEED

In recent summers, news outlets around the world have published alarming reports of the contamination of Brittany's beaches by **toxic seaweed**. The culprit, **ulva lactuca** – commonly known as sea lettuce – grows offshore in vast quantities, fed by the massive amount of nitrates released into the water system by Breton farmers. Once it dies, it washes ashore in unsightly green piles, to leave beaches lined with thousands of tons of decaying vegetation. As if that weren't bad enough, it produces poisonous hydrogen sulphide as it rots, which builds up beneath a crust then emerges as rotten-egg fumes when the surface is disturbed.

Although almost a hundred Breton beaches have been affected, the problem has been most prevalent on the north coast. In 2009, a horse died at Saint-Michel-en-Grève, after its rider was overcome by fumes, and a council worker was killed in a lorry crash when he passed out after loading up with seaweed at Binic. Two years later, 28 wild boars were found gassed on a beach near St-Brieuc.

Under intense pressure from the French government, local councils in Brittany have instigated clear-up procedures. According to campaigners, however, only extensive restrictions on Breton agricultural practices will eliminate the threat altogether.

INTO THE BRETON HEARTLAND

Plouha, a short way along the D786 from St-Quay, marks the traditional boundary between French-speaking "Upper Brittany" and Breton-speaking "Lower Brittany". As a general indication, you can tell which language used to be spoken in a particular area by its place names. From here on west a preponderance of names begin with the Breton "PLOU" (meaning parish), "TREZ" (sand or beach), "KER" (town) or "PENN" (head). See p.390 for a comprehensive glossary of Breton words.

---

the mid-nineteenth century, Binic was one of the busiest ports in all France; these days it's simply a minor but attractive tourist resort, with a lucrative sideline of selling mud from the River Ic for fertilizer.

The main beach at Binic, the **Plage de la Banche**, stretches away east of the road as you come into town from St-Brieuc. Spacious even at high tide, packed in summer with families, swimmers, children's clubs and groups playing pétanque, at low tide it becomes absolutely vast. On the far side of town, well away from the through highway and out of sight even from the dead-end little road around the harbour, there's another large but much more secluded beach, the **Plage de l'Avant Port**.

St-Quay-Portrieux

ST-QUAY, 5km north of Binic, is a prosperous but otherwise unremarkable place, while its sister town of **PORTRIEUX**, stretching along the waterfront a short way south, has had most of the life sucked out of it since the construction of a new yacht marina to replace its crumbling old fishing harbour. That resulted in its sandy central strand becoming unsafe for bathers; for the best **beaches** hereabouts, head for the Grève d'Isnain and the Grève de Fontenay, both in small bays surrounded by cliffs.

The chapel at Kermaria-an-Isquit

12.5km northwest of St-Quay-Portrieux • Easter–Sept Mon–Sat 10am–noon & 2–6pm, Sun 3–6pm • donation

The little village of **KERMARIA-AN-ISQUIT** is not easy to find, especially if you're coming from the north; the best-signposted of its approaches make their way here along the D21 from Plouha. Nonetheless, a fairly constant trickle of visitors make their way here in summer to see the village's **chapel** and its extraordinary **Dance of Death**, one of the most striking of all French medieval images. The huge series of frescoes – depicting **Ankou**, the skeletal death-figure, leading representatives of all social classes in a *Danse Macabre* – covers the arcades all round the chapel. Painted at the end of the plague-fearing fifteenth century, they were subsequently whitewashed over, not to be rediscovered until 1856. Since then, much of the work has vanished altogether, especially on the ceiling, while in what survives the original colours have faded, and the figures are often no more than silhouettes. However, the fresco has lost little of its power to shock.

In yellow, on a red background, the skeleton alternates with such living characters as a King, a Knight, a Bishop and a Peasant. In verses below, each person pleads for life and laments death, while Ankou insists that all must in the end come to him. A wall to the left of the altar holds a barely discernible representation of the classic medieval theme of the encounter between the *Trois Vifs*, three finely apparelled noblemen out hunting, with the *Trois Morts*, three corpses reflecting in a cemetery on the transience of all things human.

The chapel originally belonged to the lords of the manor of Noë Vert, and is said to be linked by a tunnel, long since flooded, to their manor house 5km away. It was known in Breton as "*Itron Varia An Iskuit*", meaning "Our Lady Who Helps".

A small display case behind the altar contains the skull of one of the lords – Jean de Lannion, who died in 1658 – while a couple of grotesque heart-shaped boxes hold the hearts of another lord and his wife. Just in front of the altar, to the left, a unique statue shows the infant Jesus refusing milk from the Virgin's proffered breast, symbolizing the choice of celestial over terrestrial food.

Abbaye de Beauport

2km south of Paimpol • Daily: mid-March to mid-June 10am–noon & 2–6pm; mid-June to Sept 10am–7pm, with regular 1hr 30min guided tours; also open from 10pm on Wed & Thurs from late July to mid-Aug; Oct to mid-March 2–5pm; closed first fortnight of Dec • €6 • ☏ 02 96 55 18 58, ⓦ abbayebeauport.com

As the D786 north of Kermaria and Binic approaches Paimpol, it meanders back towards the shoreline and passes the substantial ruins of the **Abbaye de Beauport**. Founded by Count Alain de Goëlo in 1202, halfway between St-Brieuc and Tréguier, this was originally a way station for English pilgrims en route to Santiago de Compostela. Much of its income was drawn from thirteen parishes in Lincolnshire, and it never recovered from the English Reformation. A merchant from Paimpol bought the entire estate after the Revolution, and his family owned it until 1992.

The abbey has been sufficiently restored to host major temporary exhibitions each summer. It also reopens for late-night visits, with imaginative lighting effects, during July and August, and hosts regular concerts of Breton and world music concerts; check the website for the latest schedules.

The main appeal for daytime visitors, however, is the sheer romance of the abbey's setting and semi-dilapidated condition. Its stone walls are covered with wild flowers and ivy, the central cloisters are engulfed by a huge tree, and birds flutter about everywhere. The Norman Gothic **chapterhouse** is the most noteworthy building to survive, but wandering through and over the roofless halls you may spot architectural relics from all eras. The monks' refectory looks out across the **salt meadows** where they raised their sheep, and planted orchards on land reclaimed from the sea with an intricate network of dams. Footpaths lead all the way down to the sea, offering the same superb views of the hilltop abbey that must have been appreciated by generations of arriving pilgrims.

Paimpol

An appealing old fishing port that has reinvented itself as a pleasure harbour, **PAIMPOL** focuses on a tangle of cobbled alleyways lined with fine grey-granite houses. During the nineteenth century, it was home to a fifty-strong cod and whaling fleet that sailed for the fisheries of Iceland each February, sent off with a ceremony marked by a famous *pardon*. From then until August or September, the town would be empty of all young men.

The central **place du Martray** is surrounded by an impressive array of sixteenth-century houses. Cobbled streets lead from here down to the port through the peaceful **quartier latin**, an area once filled with bars and cabarets relieving returning fishermen of their money and frustrations.

STEAMING THROUGH THE TRIEUX VALLEY

Between early May and late September, the restored steam train known as **La Vapeur de Trieux** chugs its way on regular excursions from the *gare SNCF* through the Trieux Valley between Paimpol and Pontrieux to the southwest, passing within view of the Château de la Roche-Jagu. The schedule is extremely intricate, but broadly speaking there are no trains on Mondays, and none on Fridays except in July & Aug, but on most other days there's either one daily departure from Paimpol, at 11am, or two departures at 10.15am & 3.52pm (reservations essential; €24.50 return; ☏ 02 96 20 52 06, ⓦ vapeurdutrieux.com).

Thanks to naval shipyards and the like, the open sea is not visible from Paimpol; a maze of waterways leads to its two separate harbours. Both are usually filled with the high masts of yachts, but still also used by the fishing boats that keep a fish market and a plethora of *poissonneries* busy. The tiny port has been very much rebuilt and is rather plain, though it's always lively in summer.

The best **beach** in town, La Tossen, is a short way east of the port, but there are better seaside resorts elsewhere along this stretch of coast, and with its plentiful accommodation, Paimpol is more often used as a base for visits to the Île de Bréhat (see p.221).

The major annual event in the local calendar is the **Festival du Chant de Marin** – sea shanties – held during the second weekend in August (ⓦpaimpol-festival.fr).

Loguivy-sur-Mer

If you find Paimpol too crowded, it's well worth continuing a few kilometres further across the headland to reach the tiny fishing hamlet of **LOGUIVY**. All of the long river inlets along this northern coast tend to conceal tiny coves – at Loguivy a working scallop-fishing harbour manages to squeeze into one such gap in the rocks, with alluring footpaths disappearing up the cliffs to either side. Look out for the local church, on which the weathervane is topped by a fish.

Fresh from three years of forced labour in Siberia, **Lenin**, along with his mother and sister, holed up here for his summer holidays in 1902.

ARRIVAL AND DEPARTURE

BAIE DE ST-BRIEUC   **4**

ST-BRIEUC

By train The *gare SNCF* is 1km south of the centre.
Destinations Paris (5 daily; 3hr); Brest (10 daily; 1hr 20min).
By bus Cap Fréhel (2 daily, 1hr 25min) via Le Val-André (50min) and Erquy (1hr 10min); Carhaix (1 daily; 3hr); Dinan (4 daily; 1hr); Lamballe (3 daily; 1hr 10min) with connections to St-Cast (4 daily; 40min); Lannion (3 daily; 1hr 40min) via Guingamp (45min); Moncontour (4 daily;

1hr); Paimpol (8 daily; 1hr 30min) via Binic (20min) and St-Quay-Portrieux (35min); St-Malo (2 daily; 2hr); Vannes (2 daily; 2hr).

PAIMPOL

By train and bus The *gare SNCF* and *gare routière* are side by side on avenue du Général-de-Gaulle.
Train Destinations Guingamp (2–5 daily; 45min).

INFORMATION AND TOURS

ST-BRIEUC

Tourist office 7 rue St-Gouéno, in the centre (July & Aug Mon–Sat 9.30am–6pm, Sun 10am–1pm; Sept–June Mon–Sat 9.30am–12.30pm & 1.30–6pm; ☎02 96 33 32 50, ⓦbaiedesaintbrieuc.com).
Crafts tours For details of one-day summer tours to visit craft workshops of every variety – taxidermists, bakers, farmers and makers of furniture and of cider – see ⓦcotesdarmor.com.

BINIC

Tourist office Avenue du Général-de-Gaulle (April–June, Sept & Oct Mon–Fri 9.30am–12.30pm & 2–6pm, Sat 10am–12.30pm & 2–5pm; July & Aug Mon–Sat 9.30am–12.30pm & 2–7pm, Sun 10am–12.30pm & 2–6pm; Nov–March Mon–Fri 9.30am–noon & 2–5.30pm, Sat 10am–noon & 2–5pm; ☎02 96 73 60 12, ⓦville-binic.fr).
Boat tours Every Tues from mid-May to mid-Sept, and on

Thurs as well during July and August, Les Vedettes de Bréhat runs day-trips from Binic and Portrieux to the Île de Bréhat (departs Binic 8am, Portrieux 8.30am; €29; ⓦvedettesdebrehat.com).

ST-QUAY-PORTRIEUX

Tourist office 17bis rue Jeanne-d'Arc (July & Aug Mon–Sat 9am–7pm, Sun 10.30am–12.30pm & 3.30–6pm; Sept–June Mon–Sat 9am–noon & 2–6.30pm; ☎02 96 70 40 64, ⓦsaintquayportrieux.com). Ask about late April's Scallop Festival.

PAIMPOL

Tourist office Place de la République, 100m from the pleasure port (July & Aug Mon–Sat 9.30am–7.30pm, Sun 10am–12.30pm & 4.30–6.30pm; Sept–June Mon–Fri 9.30am–12.30pm & 2–6.pm, Sat 9.30am–12.30pm & 2–6.30pm; ☎02 96 20 83 16, ⓦpaimpol-goelo.com).

ACCOMMODATION AND EATING

ST-BRIEUC

L'Arbalaise 12 rue Michelet ☎ 02 96 33 02 30, ⓦ larbalaise.fr. Part bar, part brasserie, and part restaurant in the old quarter, serving everything from a cocktail or coffee to a full meal, with an emphasis on fresh market produce. Full lunch menus from €17, dinner from €19.50. Mon–Wed 8am–6pm, Thurs–Sat 8am–11pm.

Champ-de-Mars 13 rue du Général-Leclerc ☎ 02 96 33 60 99, ⓦ hotel-saint-brieuc.fr. Simple but central and very acceptable rooms, with €8 buffet breakfasts. **€59**

Manoir de la Ville-Guyomard ☎ 02 96 78 70 70, ⓦ fuaj .org/saint-brieuc. Hostel, 2km northwest of the place du Champ-de-Mars, in a magnificent fifteenth-century manor house. Served by bus #A from the *gare SNCF*, it also offers bicycles and canoes for rent. Rates include breakfast. **€21.50**

Youpala Bistrot 5 rue Palasne-de-Champeaux ☎ 02 96 94 50 74, ⓦ youpala-bistrot.com. Upscale contemporary restaurant in the old quarter, behind the cathedral. The menu changes daily, but high-class seafood is guaranteed, with lunch from €23 and dinner from €53. Tues–Sat 12.30–1.30pm & 7.30–10pm.

BINIC

Benhuyc 1 quai Jean-Bart ☎ 02 96 73 39 00, ⓦ en.le -new-benhuyc.com. This very pleasant and extensively modernized hotel, on the north side of the port and affiliated to Best Western, offers the only sea-view rooms in town. **€89**

Le Face à la Mer Plage de la Banche ☎ 02 56 44 28 42, ⓦ restaurant-hotel-binic.fr. Excellent restaurant/bistro with a more formal upstairs dining room enjoying panoramic views across the main beach. Lunch for €20, dinner at €29 or €43. Mon–Sat noon–2pm & 7.30–10pm, Sun noon–2pm.

Les Madières Pordic ☎ 02 96 79 02 48, ⓦ www .campinglesmadieres.com. Secluded, verdant, three-star campsite, set back slightly from the sea 3km south of Binic, off the main road, with extensive lawns and a heated swimming pool. Closed Nov–March. **€19.40**

Le Neptune 11 place de l'Église ☎ 02 96 73 61 02, ⓦ restaurant-hotel-binic.fr. Small family-run hotel, with rather ordinary but good-value rooms, all en suite, above a central bar/brasserie. **€65**

ST-QUAY-PORTRIEUX

Bistrot de la Marine 38 quai de la République, Portrieux ☎ 02 96 70 87 38, ⓦ bistrotlamarine.com. The one bright spot on Portrieux's rundown seafront, this welcoming bar/ bistro serves excellent fish and seafood main dishes for under €20, *moules* for more like €12, and mixed plates of *charcuterie* and shellfish for €19 – plus a steady stream of drinks to neighbours and friends. March–June & Sept–Dec Mon–Sat noon–2pm & 7.30–9pm; July & Aug daily 9am–2am.

Saint Quay 72 bd Foch, St-Quay ☎ 02 96 72 70 48, ⓦ hotel-saint-quay-et-son-restaurant.com. Tasteful,

good-value rooms in the centre of St-Quay, above the classy *Signatures* restaurant, which serves good dinners from €25. Closed Oct–March. **€69**

PAIMPOL

Berthelot 1 rue du Port ☎ 02 96 20 88 66. Small, somewhat kitsch but very hospitable family-run hotel, offering a dozen simple rooms – some en suite, some not, with one of the latter suitable for four people – set slightly back from the pleasure port. **€44**

La Cotriade 16 quai Armand-Dayot ☎ 02 96 20 81 08, ⓦ la-cotriade.com. Paimpol's best seafood restaurant, close to the water on the far side of the harbour, serves a changing daily array of authentic fish dishes, with lunch menus from €26, and a dinner menu at €47. Mid-June to mid-Sept Mon 7.15–9pm, Tues–Sun 12.15–1.30pm & 7.15–9pm; mid-Sept to mid-June Tues–Sat 12.15– 1.30pm & 7.15–9pm, Sun 12.15–1.30pm.

Le Goëlo 4 quai Duguay-Trouin ☎ 02 96 20 82 74, ⓦ legoelo.com. Modern, double-glazed hotel (equipped with a lift) in the ugly new block that lines the inland side of the fishing harbour; several of the rather plain rooms overlook the port. **€68**

★**K'Loys** 21 quai Morand ☎ 02 96 20 40 01, ⓦ k-loys .com. This grand old mansion, overlooking the small boat harbour and crammed with oddities, houses an eccentric but extremely welcoming hotel. The comfortable rooms vary in price according to size and view; the wonderful top-floor Captain's suite, with its retractable ceiling, is highly recommended. A good bistro stretches from the front courtyard into the street. **€130**

Ty Krampouz 11 place du Martray ☎ 02 96 20 86 34. Cavernous restaurant/crêperie just a few steps from the port, with a large terrace on the main square in the heart of town, that's popular with locals not only for its inexpensive €5–11 galettes, but also for its good-value daily bistro specials. Tues–Sat 11.45–2pm & 6.45–9.45pm.

La Vieille Tour 13 rue de l'Église ☎ 02 96 20 83 18. Cosy but sophisticated upstairs dining room, tucked away from the port in the cobbled pedestrian area, and offering top-quality seafood on a quartet of constantly changing menus; the cheapest €33 option usually offers everything you could want. Tues–Sat 12.15–2pm & 7.15–9pm, Sun 12.15–2pm; also closed Wed in low season.

LOGUIVY-SUR-MER

Au Grand Large ☎ 02 96 20 90 18, ⓦ hotelrestaurant -augrandlarge.com. Loguivy's one hotel, right on the waterfront looking out towards Bréhat, has nice sea-view rooms, serves superb fish dinners from €20 to €45 – the chef's speciality is a €20 salad of seared scallops – and has an appealing little outdoor terrace. Closed Jan, restaurant closed Sun eve & Mon in low season. **€60**

Île de Bréhat

Two kilometres off the coast at Pointe de l'Arcouest, 6km northwest of Paimpol, the **ÎLE DE BRÉHAT** gives the appearance of spanning great latitudes. In reality, there are two islands, joined by a tiny slip of a bridge. On the north side lie windswept meadows of hemlock and yarrow, sloping down to chaotic erosions of rock; on the south, you're in the midst of palm trees, mimosa and eucalyptus. All around is a multitude of little islets – some accessible at low tide, others *propriété privée*, most just pink-orange rocks. All in all, this has to be one of the most beautiful places in Brittany, renowned as a sanctuary not only for rare species of **wild flowers**, but also for **birds** of all kinds. Individual private gardens are also meticulously tended, so you can always anticipate a magnificent display of colour, for example in summer from the erupting blue acanthus.

A high proportion of the homes on this island paradise belong to summer-only visitors from Paris and beyond. In winter, the remaining three hundred or so natives have the place to themselves, without even a *gendarme*; the summer sees two imported from the mainland, along with around five thousand temporary residents and countless thousands more day-trippers.

Exploring the island

All boats to Bréhat arrive at the small harbour of **PORT-CLOS**, though depending on the level of the tide passengers may have to follow a concrete walkway for several hundred

4

metres before reaching the island proper. No **cars** are permitted on the island – there's barely a road wide enough for its few light farm vehicles – so many visitors rent **bikes** at the ferry port. That said, it's easy enough to explore the whole place on foot; walking from one end to the other takes just under an hour.

Each batch of new arrivals invariably heads first to Bréhat's village, **LE BOURG**, which stands 500m up from the port and is the centre of all activity. As well as a handful of hotels, restaurants and bars, it also has a limited array of shops, a post office, a bank and an ATM machine, and hosts a small **market** most days. In high season, the attractive central square tends to be packed fit to burst, with exasperated holiday-home owners pushing their little hand-wagons through throngs of day-trippers.

Continue a short distance north, however, and you'll soon cross over the slender **Pont ar Prat bridge** to the northern island, where the crowds thin out, and countless little coves offer opportunities to sprawl on the tough grass or clamber across the rugged boulders. This northern half offers Bréhat's most attractive walking. The main path continues straight across to the **Paon Lighthouse** at the far corner, surrounded by a spectacular chaos of red rocks; to escape the crowds, though, you'd do better to head off along the coastal footpath around the perimeter.

Bréhat's finest **beaches** line the shores of the southern island, however. The pick of the crop is the **Grève du Guerzido**, facing the mainland at its southeastern corner; it might look like a strip of shingle when the tide is high, but the sea retreats to reveal broad sands. While the island no longer has a castle (it was blown up twice by the English), it does have a couple of lighthouses and a nineteenth-century **fort**, in the woods near the campsite.

ARRIVAL AND DEPARTURE ÎLE DE BRÉHAT

By ferry Bréhat is connected regularly by ferry from Pointe de l'Arcouest, which is 6km northwest of Paimpol and served by summer buses from its *gare SNCF*. Parking for the day here costs €6. Broadly speaking, sailings, with Les Vedettes de Bréhat (☎02 96 55 79 50, �🌐vedettesdebrehat.com), are every 30min at peak times between April and September, and every 1hr 30min between October and March, with the first boat out to Bréhat at 8.15am year round (9.30am on Sun in winter), and the last boat back at 7.45pm in summer,

6pm in winter. The direct crossing takes around 10min, and a return trip costs €9.80 for anyone aged over 11, and €8.30 for ages 4–11 (bikes, €16 extra, are only allowed outside peak crossing times). Roughly half the departures in summer, though, cruise all the way around Bréhat before docking at the island after almost an hour; catching one of them, and then returning on a direct ferry costs €15 for over-11s, €11 for ages 4–11. The same company also offers crossings in summer from Erquy, Binic and St-Quay-Portrieux.

INFORMATION AND GETTING AROUND

Tourist office Raised up in one corner of Le Bourg's main square (July & Aug Mon–Sat 10am–1pm & 2–5.30pm, Sun 10am–1pm; March–June & Sept Tues–Thurs & Sat 10am–1pm & 2–4.30pm, Fri 10am–1pm & 2–3.30pm; Oct–Feb Mon & Thurs–Sat 10am–1pm &

2–3.30pm; ☎02 96 20 04 15, �🌐brehat-infos.fr).
Bike rental Cycles are available from outlets at the port, including R. Dalibot (☎02 96 20 03 51) for €13 for a full day, €10 for a half day.

ACCOMMODATION AND EATING

Bellevue Port-Clos ☎02 96 20 00 05, �🌐hotel -bellevue-brehat.fr. This imposing white-with-blue-trim hotel, right by the *embarcadère*, has been nicely modernized; the best of its twenty rooms have sea-view balconies and whirlpool baths. Lunch downstairs costs €16, dinner €26. Compulsory *demi-pension* mid-July to Aug; closed mid-Nov to mid-Feb. **€99**, *demi-pension* **€182**
Camping Municipal Goaréva ☎02 96 20 02 46, �🌐iledebrehat.fr. This wonderful municipal campsite is set in the woods high above the sea at the southwest tip of

the island. Camping wild elsewhere is strictly forbidden. Closed mid-Sept to mid-June. **€11.20**
Men-Joliguet Port-Clos ☎06 88 20 32 88, �🌐locations -brehat.net. Bréhat's best value; this village house beside the *Bellevue* has been modernized to hold five bright, sleek B&B rooms, and has a lovely sea-view garden. Closed Nov–Easter. **€83**
Le Paradis North island ☎02 96 20 03 89. This aptly named spot, just short of the Paon Lighthouse, is in reality no more than a crêpe, ice-cream and hot-dog stand, but

the tables in its ravishing garden makes it an ideal lunch or afternoon break for round-island walkers. Easter to late Sept daily 11.30am–5.30pm.

Shamrock Le Bourg ☎ 02 96 20 06 804. With tables right out on the main square, and a covered terrace to retreat to at the back when the island's too crowded for comfort, this is the best spot for a sit-down lunch, with mussels for €11 and large salads for €13–15. April–Sept daily 11am–8.30pm.

Vieille Auberge Le Bourg ☎ 02 96 20 00 24, ⓦ brehat -vieilleauberge.com. Eighteenth-century privateer's house, on your left as you enter Le Bourg, with simple but very light rooms, the cheapest of which are in an annexe. Closed Dec–Easter. **€79.50**

Côte de Granit Rose

The northernmost stretch of the Breton coast, from Bréhat to Trégastel, is loosely known as the **Côte de Granit Rose**. Great granite boulders are scattered in the sea around the island of Bréhat, and at the various headlands to the west, but the most memorable stretch lies around **Ploumanac'h**, where the pink granite rocks are eroded into fantastic shapes.

Pink granite, glittering sharply but wearing smooth and soft, is an absolutely gorgeous stone – which is just as well, for everything in this area seems to be made of it. The houses are faced with granite blocks, and the streets paved with them; the breakwaters in the sea are granite, and the polished pillars of the banks are granite; the hotels have overgrown granite mini-golfs with little pink granite megaliths as obstacles; and the markets even claim to sell *granit-smith* apples.

Presqu'Île Sauvage

The D786 turns west from Paimpol, crossing a bridge over a green *ria* after 5km to reach the little town of **LÉZARDRIEUX**. Few visitors take the time to explore the peninsula that stretches off to the north from here. Though known as the **Presqu'Île Sauvage**, in truth it's dotted with sleepy villages and holiday homes and while it's certainly pretty, it's no more wild than anywhere else in these parts. However, at its northeastern tip, 10km out from Lézardrieux, it does hold one unusual feature.

The Sillon du Talbert

The **Sillon du Talbert** is a narrow, windswept, curving spit of sand and shingle that reaches out 3.5km into the ocean, and makes for a splendid bracing walk with great opportunities for watching seabirds. At its far end stands the 45m **lighthouse** of Héaux.

Tréguier

Ten kilometres west of Lézardrieux, a bridge across the mouth of the Jaudy river leads into the lovely old town of **TRÉGUIER**. One of the very few hill-towns in Brittany, set at the confluence of the Jaudy with the Guindy river, it was rebuilt on this fortified elevation in 848 AD after an earlier monastery was destroyed by Norman raiders. It does however spread down to include a small commercial and pleasure port beside the Jaudy.

The central unmissable feature of Tréguier is the **Cathédrale de St-Tugdual**, whose geometric Gothic spire, dotted with holes, contrasts sharply with its earlier Romanesque "Hastings" tower. Inside, the masonry blocks are appealingly crude, and dripping with damp that has somehow spared the wooden stalls. The most elaborate of several recumbent tombs is that of **St Yves**, a native of the town who died in 1303 and – for his incorruptibility – became the patron saint of lawyers. Attempts to bribe him continue to this day; his tomb is surrounded by marble plaques and an inferno of candles invoking his aid. An annual *pardon* of St Yves is held on the Sunday closest to his feast day, May 19.

The half-timbered houses of the pretty square outside look down on a portly, seated statue of the writer and philosopher **Ernest Renan**, born here in 1823, whose work formed part of the great nineteenth-century attempt to reinterpret traditional religious faith in the light of scientific discoveries. Worthy Catholics were so incensed at the erection of this memorial in 1903 that they soon built their own "Calvary of Reparation" on the quayside.

During Tréguier's Wednesday **market**, clothes and so on are spread out in the square up by the cathedral, with food and fresh fish further down by the port. The cafés and delis of the main square save their best displays for that day.

Jardins de Kerdalo

Near Trédarzec, 2km east of Tréguier • April–June & Sept Mon & Sat 2–6pm; July & Aug Mon–Sat 2–6pm • €8.50 • ☎ 02 96 92 35 94, ⓦ lesjardinsdekerdalo.com

Originally planted by Russian Peter Wolkonsky, who died in 1997, the **Jardins de Kerdalo** rank among the finest in France. Rare and exotic breeds ramble through the grounds, making a joyful change from the exacting straight-line gardening of so many châteaux.

Château de la Roche-Jagu

D787, 10km southeast of Tréguier • Daily: early May to June plus Sept & Oct 10am–noon & 2–6pm; July & Aug 10am–1pm & 2–7pm; Nov hols 2–5pm • Park access €2, château €4, or €5 during special exhibitions • ☎ 02 96 95 62 35, ⓦ www.larochejagu.fr

Standing on a heavily wooded slope above the meanders of the Trieux river, just as it starts to widen, the fifteenth-century **Château de la Roche-Jagu** is a really gorgeous building, a harmonious combination of fortress and home. The central solid facade is composed of irregular reddish-granite boulders, cemented together, and incorporating one venerable turreted tower at the front and one at the back.

The château plays host to lavish **annual exhibitions**, usually on some sort of Celtic theme. The rooms within are bare, but it's well worth climbing right up to the top of the building. Here you can admire the beautiful woodwork of the restored eaves, and walk the two long indoor galleries, one of wood and one of stone, to enjoy tremendous views over the river. Outside, the modern landscaped park is traced through by several **hiking trails**.

Plougrescant

Perhaps the best-known photographic image of Brittany is of a small seafront cottage somehow squeezed between two mighty pink-granite boulders. Surprisingly few visitors, however, manage to see the house in real life, which stands 10km north of Tréguier, close to the tip of another under-explored peninsula, and just 2km out from

---

THE SEABIRD SANCTUARY OF SEPT-ÎLES

The seven craggy islands that constitute the bird sanctuary of **Sept-Îles** were originally set aside in 1912 to protect puffins – whose population had dropped in the space of twenty years from an estimated fifteen thousand breeding couples to a mere four hundred pairs. The new sanctuary was, however, rapidly "discovered" by other seabirds, and thirteen different species now nest here for all or part of the year. The puffins take up residence between March and July; other visitors include storm petrels (April–Sept), gannets (Jan–Sept), kittiwakes (March–July) and guillemots (Feb–July).

Between February and November each year, **boat trips** out to the islands leave from the *gare maritime* on the Plage de Trestraou in Perros-Guirec (☎02 96 91 10 00, ⓦ armor-navigation.com). Two-hour trips admire the islands from offshore (€18), while a two-and-a-half-hour trip includes a brief landfall on Île aux Moines, the one island that permits human visitors (€21). Precisely what's available on any particular day depends on the tides, and in high season there are additional departures from Ploumanac'h (☎02 96 91 44 40) and Trégastel (☎02 96 15 31 00).

the village of **PLOUGRESCANT**. The precise spot tends to be marked on regional maps as either **Le Gouffre** or Le Gouffre du Castel-Meur, and is signposted off the coastal road a short way west of the Pointe du Château.

Although you can't visit the cottage itself, which actually faces inland, across a small sheltered bay with its back to the open sea, the shoreline nearby offers superb short walks, and a little summer-only café sells snacks and ice creams.

Perros-Guirec

PERROS-GUIREC is the most popular resort along this coast, if not perhaps the most exciting. It has a reputation that seems to attract the retired – its tourist brochures list places where you can get a game of bridge or Scrabble – and an array of shops intended to match: antiques, bric-a-brac and pottery with a big line in granite guillemots and puffins. Perros is also a lot less city-like than it looks on the maps: most of its roads turn out to be tree-lined avenues of suburban villas.

The commercial streets of the centre (up the hill from the port) hold little of interest, and are often jammed solid with traffic in summer. Much more enjoyable is to take a walk around the headland to see the magnificent view from the **Table d'Orientation** at the sharp curve of boulevard Clemenceau.

Perros-Guirec's best beach is the **Plage de Trestraou**, on the opposite side of town to the port, a long curved strand that's speckled with bars, snack bars and crazy-golf courses. The beach itself is made of ordinary sand; the pink granite coast proper lies just beyond its western end, accessed via the Sentier des Douaniers.

4

Ploumanac'h

Although it's much smaller than Perros-Guirec, the village of **PLOUMANAC'H**, 2km west, is a more active resort, largely because the dominant clientele here is families with youngish children. In fact, few places on earth can offer quite such enchantment for energetic kids, who love to scramble around the surreal sandscape revealed when the long tides draw out.

Around the delightful crescent **beach**, glinting pink granite boulders, fringed with green seaweed, erupt from the depths, and rock pools bursting with crabs and other mysteries just wait to be explored. The most obvious focal point is the tiny **Château du Diable**, framing the horizon on one of the countless little islands in the bay – which was where the novel *Quo Vadis* was written around the end of the nineteenth century. When the tide is in, head instead for the pleasantly wild **municipal park** that separates the two halves of Ploumanac'h, the Bourg and the Plage.

The road into Ploumanac'h comes to a dead end at the beach. Just short of the beach, the small lively rue St-Guirec leads to the little square that serves as the main local car park.

WALKING THE SENTIER DES DOUANIERS

A strong contender for the title of Brittany's finest coastal walk, the **Sentier des Douaniers** pathway links the plage du Trestraou in Perros-Guirec with the beach in Ploumanac'h. Originally used by eagle-eyed customs officers on the prowl for smugglers, it winds in and out along the clifftop, passing an astonishing succession of deformed and water-sculpted rocks.

Start from either end, and allow around an hour to walk its full length one-way, assuming you take the time to enjoy the many splendours en route. Birds wheel overhead towards the sanctuary, and battered boats shelter in the narrow inlets or bob uncontrollably out on the waves. There are patches and brief causeways of grass, clumps of purple heather and yellow gorse. Occasionally the rocks have crumbled into a sort of granite grit to make up a tiny beach.

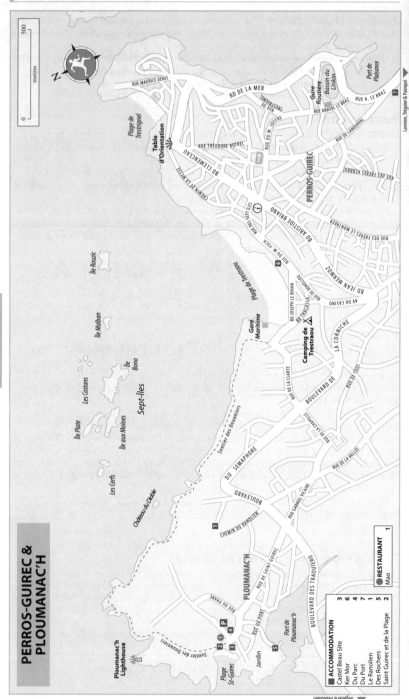

PERROS-GUIREC & PLOUMANAC'H

ACCOMMODATION
Castel Beau Site	3
Ker Mor	6
Du Parc	4
Du Port	7
Le Ranolien	1
Des Rochers	5
Saint Guirec et de la Plage	2

● RESTAURANT
Mao	1

Sept-Îles

Île Rouzic
Île Malban
Île Bono
Les Costans
Île Plate
Île aux Moines
Les Cerfs
Château du Diable

Ploumanac'h Lighthouse

Sentier des Douaniers
Plage St-Guirec
Jardin
Port de Ploumanac'h
PLOUMANAC'H

RUE DU PHARE
RUE DU PORT
RUE DE SAINT GUIREC
BOULEVARD DES TRAOUIÉRO
CHEMIN DU RANOLIEN
BOULEVARD DU SÉMAPHORE
RUE GABRIEL VICAIRE
RUE DE LA VALLÉE
RUE DE LA CHAPELLE
RUE DE TOUL
LA CORNICHE
BOULEVARD DE
RUE DE LA CLARTÉ
BD JOSEPH LE BIHAN
RUE DE BOLLIOU
AV DU CASINO
BD JEAN MÉRAOZ
RUE DU TRAZ VELO

Camping de Trestraou
Gare Maritime
Plage de Trestraou

Plage de Trestrignel
Table d'Orientation

RUE MAURICE DENIS
RUE THÉODORE BOTREL
BD CLÉMENCEAU
CHEMIN DE LA MESSE
RUE DES SEPT ÎLES
RUE DU M. FOCH
BD ARISTIDE BRIAND
BD DE LA MER
RUE TRESTRIGNEL
RUE DU M. JOFFRE
RUE ANATOLE LE BRAZ
RUE A. LE BRAZ
RUE DE LANDERVAL
RUE DES FRÈRES LE MONTREER
RUE DES FRÈRES KERRAHI
Gare Routière
Bassin du Linkin
Port de Plaisance
PERROS-GUIREC

Lannion, Tréguier & Paimpol

Trégastel & Trébeurden

0 — 500 metres

Trégastel-Plage

Three kilometres west of Ploumanac'h along a pretty coastal road, **TRÉGASTEL-PLAGE** boasts a delightful sheltered beach with a couple of huge lumps of pink granite slap in the middle. Sadly, however, the seafront itself is an ugly stretch of concrete, centring on the seafront **Forum**, a swimming pool and leisure complex.

A little way back from the seafront, a small **aquarium** is all but crushed beneath another massive pile of boulders (April–June & Sept daily except Mon 10am–6pm; July & Aug daily 10am–7.30pm; Oct & March daily except Mon 2–5pm; €8.10; ☎02 96 23 48 58 ⓦaquarium-tregastel.com).

Trébeurden

Outbreaks of bizarre red rocks have all but petered out by the time you reach **TRÉBEURDEN**, 11km southwest along the coast from Trégastel, but you do at least come to one more long curving sandy beach, much less developed than most in these parts.

Pleumeur-Bodou

Head inland from Trégastel on the **route de Calvaire**, and you'll come in a few kilometres to a spectacle stranger than anything the erosions can manage: an old stone saint halfway up a high calvary raising his arm to bless or harangue the gleaming white discs and puffball dome of the **Pleumeur-Bodou Telecommunications Centre**. A pink granite "dolmen" commemorates its opening in 1962, when it was the first receiving station to pick up signals from the American Telstar satellite. No longer operational, the centre has been remodelled as the **Cité des Télécoms**.

Cité des Télécoms

Parc du Radôme April–June & Sept plus school hols in Oct–March Mon–Fri 10am–6pm, Sat & Sun 2–6pm; July & Aug daily 10am–7pm • €7.50 • ☎02 96 46 63 80, ⓦparcduradome.com

The Cité des Télécoms holds all sorts of interactive scientific displays, aimed largely at children. Inside the giant golf ball itself, the **Radôme**, spectacular *son-et-lumière* shows explain the history of the whole ensemble, and there's also a smaller **planetarium** alongside.

Gaulish village

Parc du Radôme April–June & Sept Mon–Fri & Sun noon–6pm; July & Aug daily 10.30am–7pm • €6 • ⓦlevillagegaulois.org

Another incongruous note is struck by the reconstructed **Gaulish village**, which is designed to raise money for a French charity working in Africa, and thus incorporates some traditional huts from Togo.

ARRIVAL AND DEPARTURE

CÔTE DE GRANIT ROSE

PERROS-GUIREC

By bus Tibus (☎08 10 22 22 22, ⓦtibus.fr) runs 8 daily buses from Lannion straight to Perros-Guirec, making several stops in town, then loops back to Lannion (1hr) via Ploumanac'h (15min) and Trégastel (25min).

INFORMATION AND ACTIVITIES

TRÉGUIER

Tourist office 67 rue Ernest-Renan, down by the commercial port (early July to late Aug Mon–Sat 9am–6.30pm, Sun 10am–1pm & 2–5pm; late Aug to early July Mon–Sat 10am–12.30pm & 2–6pm; ☎02 96 92 22 33, ⓦtregor-cotedajoncs-tourisme.com).

PERROS-GUIREC

Tourist office 21 place de l'Hôtel-de-Ville (July & Aug Mon–Sat 9am–7pm, Sun 10am–12.30pm & 4–7pm; Sept–June Mon–Sat 9am–12.30pm & 2–6pm; ☎02 96 23 21 15, ⓦperros-guirec.fr).

Sailing and kayaking The Centre Nautique at the plage

de Trestraou (☎ 02 96 49 81 21) offers guided kayaking and sailing tours.

Surfing lessons Ponant Surf School, 2 rue Maréchal-Joffre (☎ 02 96 23 18 38, ⊚ ponantsurfschool.fr).

ACCOMMODATION AND EATING

PRESQU'ÎLE SAUVAGE

Bigouden Blues 57 rue du Sillon ☎ 02 96 22 94 97, ⊚ bigouden.blues.free.fr. Simple café at the start of the Sillon du Talbert, serving lobster and chips on its sea-view terrace for €20, or the more usual *moules frites* for €12. Tues–Sun noon–2pm & 7–9pm; closed mid-Nov to March.

★**Manoir de Troezel Vras** Kerbors ☎ 02 96 22 89 68, ⊚ troezel-vras.com. Irresistibly tranquil rural B&B, set in an old farmhouse, halfway between the Sillon and Tréguier, that has been sensitively converted to a very high standard. The five large guest rooms are splendidly furnished, and sleep 2–5 guests. The friendly hosts serve an excellent nightly dinner for €25; there's no menu, you just get what you're given. No credit cards. Closed mid-Oct to late March. **€88**

TRÉGUIER

Aigue-Marine Port de Plaisance ☎ 02 96 92 97 00, ⊚ aiguemarine.fr. Smart, welcoming hotel down by the port in Tréguier, with swimming pool, private parking, whirlpool spa, good buffet breakfasts for €14.50, and a top-notch restaurant (closed Sat lunch & Mon) where dinner costs €49 and up. **€105**

Château de Kermezen Pommerit Jaudy ☎ 02 96 91 35 75, ⊚ bienvenueauchateau.com. Beautiful little seventeenth-century château, tucked away in a quiet rural location 8km south of Tréguier, where the charming owners offer very pleasant B&B accommodation and big breakfasts. The one snag is that you have to drive out to reach a restaurant. **€120**

Maison d'Hôtes Tara 31 rue Ernest Renan ☎ 02 96 92 15 28, ⊚ chambrestaratreguier.com. Surprising Irish-themed B&B in a splendid old half-timbered house – painted bright blue – between the town and port, with five appealing and comfortable rooms plus a lovely garden. **€65**

★**Poissonnerie Moulinet** 2 rue Ernest-Renan ☎ 02 96 92 30 27. Tasting room above a fish shop just below the cathedral, where you can buy superb seafood platters for €18–50; you can also take them away and eat in the square. The shop itself is open all year. April–Sept daily noon–2.30pm & 6–9pm.

PERROS-GUIREC

Ker Mor 38 rue du Maréchal-Foch ☎ 02 96 23 14 19, ⊚ hotel-ker-mor.com. Hotel based in two modernized Belle Époque villas, overlooking the plage de Trestraou, and holding charming, colourful rooms with spacious bathrooms and in many cases sea views. The dining room that links the buildings serves dinner from €26. **€80**

Du Port Port de Plaisance ☎ 02 96 23 21 79, ⊚ perros-hotel.com. Good hotel, facing the pleasure port, where several of the rather plain, modern rooms enjoy superb panoramas; there's no restaurant. **€72**

Le Ranolien ☎ 02 96 91 65 65, ⊚ leranolien.fr. Four-star campsite in a superb position near a little beach halfway along the Sentier des Douaniers, boasting a great array of swimming pools, waterslides, a spa and a cinema. Rental cabins also available. Closed late Sept to early April. **€45**

PLOUMANAC'H

Castel Beau Site Plage de Saint Guirec ☎ 02 96 91 40 87, ⊚ castelbeausite.com. Lavish, luxury hotel in prime beachfront position, modernized and enlarged to offer 33 ultra-chic sea-view rooms, plus a delicious restaurant that's open for dinner nightly, and lunch on Sundays only, with menus from €41. **€200**

Mao 147 rue St-Guirec ☎ 02 96 91 40 92. Former snack bar that has expanded to take over several adjacent buildings, including a Polynesian-style thatched hut; it offers bargain menus from €12 (even less for crêpes) and, like most places in Ploumanac'h, it has special cheap menus for children. Tues–Sun noon–3pm & 7–11pm; closed Oct–March.

Du Parc 175 place St-Guirec ☎ 02 96 91 40 80, ⊚ hotel-duparc-perros.com. Hotel on the square itself, with no views whatsoever but reasonably priced if unspectacular rooms, and a good-value terrace crêperie/restaurant, *La Cotriade*. Closed Jan to mid-Feb. **€81**

Des Rochers 70 chemin de la Pointe ☎ 02 96 91 67 54, ⊚ hotel-desrochers-perros.com. Very stylish, very friendly modern hotel, beside the port rather than the beach, but still enjoying a fabulous outlook across the harbour, and offering bright, well-equipped rooms. The restaurant downstairs (closed Mon) serves a high-class menu from €20 for lunch, €28 for dinner. Closed mid-Nov to mid-Feb, apart from Xmas/New Year period. **€100**

Saint Guirec et de la Plage Plage de Saint Guirec ☎ 02 96 91 40 89, ⊚ hotelsaint-guirec.com. Freshly upgraded hotel, facing the perfect little beach at Ploumanac'h; all the rooms have wetroom showers, some have spacious private terraces, and there's an excellent family suite. The unfortunately named *Coste Mor* restaurant is actually reasonably priced. Compulsory *demi-pension* mid-June to mid-Sept. *Demi-pension* **€174**

TRÉGASTEL-PLAGE

★**Beau Séjour** 5 plage du Coz-Pors ☎ 02 96 23 88 02, ⊚ beausejoursarl.com. Exceptionally welcoming and hugely eccentric seafront hotel, with all kinds of nautical theming throughout, from portholes in the wardrobes to ropes and lifebelts by the score. The rooms vary enormously, but most have sea views, and one fabulous family suite has boat-shaped beds and a huge balcony. Best of all, though, the owners are also bakers, meaning the €11 breakfast buffet spread is absolutely out of this world. There's also a bar/crêperie, and a good seafood restaurant, *Le Roof* (closed Mon). Closed mid-Jan to mid-Feb & mid-Nov to mid-Dec. **€80**

Tourony 105 route du Poul-Palud ☎02 96 23 86 61, ⓦ camping-tourony.com. Three-star campsite in a verdant beachfront setting, looking across the estuary to the port at Ploumanac'h, with a snack bar and bar. Closed late Sept to mid-April. **€20**

TRÉBEURDEN

Ker An Nod Rue de Pors-Termen ☎02 96 23 50 21, ⓦ kerannod.com. Logis de France hotel, splendidly situated on a bluff above the sea, with fabulous views. Menus from €24. Closed mid-Nov to March. **€80**

Le Toëno 60 rue de la Corniche ☎02 96 23 52 22, ⓦ fuaj.org/trebeurden. Lovely hostel, perched amid the rocks in a peaceful seafront spot on bus route #15, 2km north of town. Closed Oct to early March. Dorms **€19.60**

The Bay of Lannion

Despite standing significantly back from the sea on the estuary of the River Léguer, **Lannion** gives its name to the final western bay before Finistère – and it's the bay rather than the town that is most likely to impress visitors. One enormous beach stretches from **St-Michel-en-Grève**, which is little more than a bend in the road, as far as **Locquirec**; at low tide you can walk hundreds of metres out on the sands.

4

Lannion

Set amid plummeting hills and stairways, **LANNION** is a historic city with streets of medieval housing, and a couple of interesting old churches. As a hi-tech telecommunications centre, it's also one of modern Brittany's real success stories – hence its rather self-satisfied nickname, *ville heureuse* or "happy town".

In addition to admiring the half-timbered houses around the place du Général-Leclerc and along rue des Chapeliers (look out for nos. 3 and 4), it's well worth climbing from the town up the 142 granite steps that lead to the twelfth-century Templar **Église de Brélévenez**. This church was remodelled three hundred years later to incorporate a granite bell tower, and the views from its terrace are quite stupendous.

Ploumilliau

At the trim little inland village of **PLOUMILLIAU**, 10km southwest of Lannion, the weathered granite parish **church** stands surrounded by beds of colourful flowers. Dating from the early seventeenth century, it contains a beautiful pulpit and sculpted wooden panelling, but is really worth a visit for its unique white-painted wooden representation of **Ankou**, the skeletal symbol of death (daily 2–6pm). The statue, carrying a scythe to catch the living and a spade to bury them, was once carried in local processions.

Locquirec

Huge and very inviting beaches lie to both sides of the peninsula that's tipped by the perfect little village of **LOCQUIREC**, across the water from Lannion and officially just within the *département* of Finistère.

Around the pretty port itself, facing the all but circular bay, smart houses stand in sloping gardens, looking very southern English with their whitewashed stone panels, grey-slate roofs and jutting turreted windows. The small sandy beach here is said to be the only one facing south along the entire northern coastline of Brittany, which prompts some brave souls to test the waters as early as Easter.

On the last Sunday in July, Locquirec holds a combined *pardon de St-Jacques* and Festival of the Sea.

Cairn du Barnenez

13km northeast of Morlaix • May & June daily 10am–6pm; July & Aug daily 10am–6.30pm; Sept–April Tues–Sun 10am–12.30pm & 2–5.30pm • €5.50 • ☎ 02 98 67 24 73, ⊕ barnenez.monuments-nationaux.fr

In a glorious location at the mouth of the Morlaix estuary, the prehistoric stone **Cairn du Barnenez** overlooks the waters from the summit of a hill. Laid bare by archeologists, its ancient masonry provides a stunning sense of the architectural prowess of the megalith builders. This is one of the oldest monuments in the world, dating back to 4500 BC; André Malraux called it "the Breton Parthenon". It remained in continuous use for around 2500 years, and was probably used repeatedly as a place of burial, then sealed off and abandoned.

The ensemble consists of two distinct **stepped pyramids**, the older one constructed of local dolerite stone, and the other of grey granite from the nearby Île de Sterec. Each rises in successive tiers, built of large flat stones chinked with pebbles (but no mortar); the second was added onto the side of the first, and the two are encircled by terraces and ramps. Both were long ago buried beneath an eighty-metre-long earthen mound. The whole thing measures roughly 70m long by 15m to 25m wide; the current height of 6m is thought to be smaller than that of the original structure.

While the actual cairns are completely exposed to view, most of the passages and chambers that lie within them are sealed off. Visitors cannot in any case enter the structure, but simply walk around it to admire it from all angles. The two minor corridors that are open simply cut through the edifice from one side to the other, and were exposed by twentieth-century quarrying – which inadvertently provided a good insight into the construction methods, though nothing much was found inside. Each is covered with great slabs of rock; in fact most of the familiar dolmens seen all over Brittany and elsewhere are thought to be the vestiges of similarly complex structures. Local tradition has it that one tunnel runs right through this "home of the fairies", and continues out deep under the sea.

ARRIVAL AND INFORMATION

BAY OF LANNION

LANNION

By train and bus The *gares SNCF* and *routière* (☎ 08 10 22 22 22, ⊕ tibus.fr) stand across the river from the centre, via an attractive little bridge.

Train Destinations St-Brieuc (4 daily; 1hr) via Plouaret (15min) and Guingamp (35min).

Bus Destinations Locquirec (4 daily; 30min) and Morlaix (4 daily; 1hr 20min); Paimpol (3 daily; 1hr); Perros-Guirec (8 daily; 20min) and on to Ploumanac'h (35min) and

Trégastel (45min).

Tourist office 2 quai d'Aiguillon (July & Aug Mon–Sat 9.30am–6.30pm, Sun 10am–1pm; Sept–June Mon–Sat 9.30am–12.30pm & 2–6pm; ☎ 02 96 05 60 70, ⊕ bretagne-cotedegranitrose.com).

LOCQUIREC

Tourist office Place du Port (Mon–Sat 9am–12.30pm & 2–6pm; ☎ 02 98 67 40 83, ⊕ mairie-locquirec.fr).

ACCOMMODATION AND EATING

LANNION

Auberge Les Korrigans 6 rue du 73e Territorial, Lannion ☎ 02 96 37 91 28, ⊕ fuaj.org/lannion-les-korrigans. Well-kept hostel, close to the station. Open year-round, it has a restaurant and bar, and the enthusiastic staff can arrange a wide array of activities, including kayaking. Rates include breakfast. **€21.50**

Ibis 30 av du Général-de-Gaulle, Lannion ☎ 02 96 37

03 67, ⊕ ibishotel.com. The only central hotel in Lannion, facing the station, has seventy well-equipped modern rooms, but no restaurant. **€86**

Tire-Bouchon 8 rue de Keriavily ☎ 02 96 37 10 43, ⊕ letirebouchonlannion.fr. Good traditional restaurant in the heart of town, recently renovated and offering weekday lunches from €11.50, dinner menus from €22. Tues–Sat noon–1.45pm & 7.15–9pm.

LOCQUIREC

Camping du Fond de la Baie Route de Plestin ☎ 02 98 67 40 85, ⓦ mairie-locquirec.fr. Beautifully positioned municipal campsite, 1km south along the corniche and facing across the bay directly back towards Locquirec. Open year-round, with bike and kayak rental. **€14**

Grand Hotel des Bains 15bis rue de l'Église ☎ 02 98 67 41 02, ⓦ grand-hotel-des-bains.com. Grand indeed, this elegant and very expensive seafront hotel stands in private gardens close to the heart of little Locquirec. With its clapboard façade and whitewashed woodwork, it might be more at home in New England, but to French visitors, thanks to its starring role in the coming-of-age movie *Hôtel de la Plage*, it epitomizes Brittany. Spacious rooms, many with terraces, plus a good restaurant and spa. **€244**

4

Finistère

ÎLE DE SEIN, QUAI DES FRANÇAIS LIBRES

5

Finistère

The *département* of Finistère has always been isolated from the French (and even Breton) mainstream: its name literally means "the end of the world". This remote rural landscape was the last refuge of the Druids from encroaching Christianity, and its mysterious forests and elaborate parish closes testify to its role as the province's spiritual heartland. Today, Roscoff has reopened the old maritime links with England, high-speed TGV trains mean that Brest is just four hours from Paris, and the motorway loops around the end of the peninsula. Yet Finistère remains only sporadically touched by modern industry; agriculture and low-key tourism are the mainstays of the economy. Breton survives as a spoken language here, and traditional costumes are still worn in reverence of culture not tourism at many a festival.

Memories of the days when Brittany was "Petite Bretagne", as opposed to "Grande Bretagne" across the water, linger in the names of Finistère's two main areas. Both the northern peninsula – **Léon**, once Lyonesse – and its southern neighbour – **Cornouaille**, the same word as "Cornwall" – feature prominently in Arthurian legend.

A succession of jagged **estuaries** corkscrew deeply into Brittany's wild and dramatic northwestern coastline. Known both as *abers* (as in Welsh place names) and as *rias* (as in Spanish Galicia), each shelters its own tiny harbour and countless deserted coves. Potential overnight halts, interspersed with vast beaches and dunes, punctuate the route all the way west from the delightful old port of **Roscoff** to the picturesque fishing village of **Le Conquet**. A notoriously treacherous stretch of ocean separates the mainland here from **Ouessant** and **Molène**, which can make for an uncomfortable ferry ride, yet those two islands have the mildest winter climate in all France. The one coastal destination you might prefer to avoid is the regional capital, and lone big city, of **Brest**, the base of the French Atlantic fleet. Inland, the **parish closes** lie strung across sleepy little villages southwest of **Morlaix**, each ornate church and its associated ensemble still perpetuating a fierce medieval rivalry.

In the south, Cornouaille's capital, lively **Quimper**, is one of France's most pleasant, and least known, little cities, with plenty to see and a vibrant atmosphere, while thriving resorts such as **Bénodet**, **Loctudy** and **Pont-Aven** (the last made famous by Gauguin) line the south coast. There are surprises everywhere – take the perfectly preserved medieval village of **Locronan**, or the extraordinary world apart that is the tiny **Île de Sein**.

Finistère's most popular region for holiday-makers, the **Crozon peninsula**, juts into the sea between the two ancient realms, beneath the **Menez-Hom** mountain. **Morgat** and **Camaret** here are both ideal for long, leisurely seaside stays, with opportunities for secluded camping all around.

FAÏENCE, QUIMPER

Highlights

❶ Île de Batz Small, car-free island only a few hundred metres offshore from the attractive port of Roscoff and a perfect family destination. **See p.239**

❷ Guimiliau One of the finest parish closes – a remarkable medieval church in a pretty rural village. **See p.245**

❸ Camaret Picturesque port with good beaches, prehistoric sites, interesting architecture and great seafood. **See p.262**

❹ Locronan Jewel-like hilltop village that has hardly changed in five centuries. **See p.266**

❺ Île de Sein Barely rising from the Atlantic, this misty and mysterious island makes a romantic day-trip from Audierne. **See p.270**

❻ Faïence de Quimper For centuries the craftsworkers of Quimper have produced hand-painted ceramics, which make great souvenirs. **See p.276**

❼ Villa Tri Men Ravishing riverfront hotel at Ste-Marine, just across from Bénodet. **See p.279**

❽ Bot Conan Lodge Glamping Breton-style, in luxury safari tents alongside an exquisite sandy beach. **See p.281**

HIGHLIGHTS ARE MARKED ON THE MAP ON P.236

Roscoff

Delightfully small and unspoiled, **ROSCOFF** is on a very different scale from France's other Channel ports. That's partly because the deep-water harbour used by Brittany Ferries, the **Port du Bloscon**, is a couple of kilometres east of the venerable but still lively village centre, focussed around the original fishing port.

Two long, stone jetties enclose the **old harbour**, while pleasure boats bob in the bay behind. Tourists gather all through the day to watch the fishermen at work, and to join the low-key pleasure trips to the **Île de Batz** (see p.239). The island looks almost walkable; a narrow pier stretches over 400m towards it before abruptly plunging into deep rocky waters. The Pointe de Bloscon and the white fisherman's chapel, the Chapelle Ste-Barbe, make a good vantage point, particularly when the tide is in. Below the headland are the *viviers*, where you can see trout, salmon, lobsters and crabs being reared for the pot.

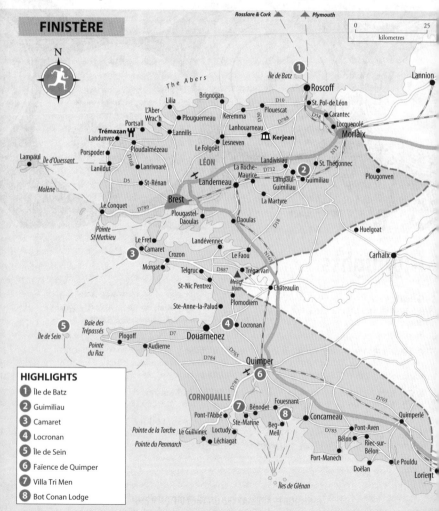

FINISTÈRE

Rosslare & Cork — Plymouth

0 — 25 kilometres

N

The Abers

Île de Batz · Roscoff · Lannion
Lilia · Brignogan · St. Pol-de-Léon
L'Aber-Wrac'h · Plouguerneau · Keremma · Plouescat · Carantec
Portsall · Lannilis · Lanhouarneau · Locquénolé
Trémazan · Landunvez · Ploudalmézeau · Le Folgoët · Lesneven · Kerjean · Morlaix
Porspoder · Lanrivoaré · LÉON · Landivisiau
Lampaul · Île d'Ouessant · Lanildut · St-Rénan · La Roche-Maurice · St. Thégonnec
Molène · Landerneau · Lampaul-Guimiliau · Guimiliau · Plougonven
Brest · La Martyre
Le Conquet · Plougastel-Daoulas · Daoulas · Huelgoat
Pointe St-Mathieu · Le Fret · Landévennec · Le Faou
Camaret · Crozan · Le Faou · Carhaix
Morgat · Telgruc · Trégarvan · Châteaulin
St-Nic Pentrez · Ménez Hom
Ste-Anne-la-Palud · Plomodiern
Baie des Trépassés · Locronan
Île de Sein · Plogoff · Douarnenez
Pointe du Raz · Audierne
Quimper
Pointe de la Torche · Le Guilvinec · Loctudy · Léchiagat · Pont-l'Abbé · Bénodet · Fouesnant · Concarneau · Quimperlé
Pointe du Penmarch · Ste-Marine · Beg-Meil · Pont-Aven · Riec-sur-Bélon
CORNOUAILLE · Bélon · Port-Manech · Le Pouldu · Doëlan · Lorient
Îles de Glénan

5

THE BIRTH OF BRITTANY FERRIES

Roscoff has long been a significant port – Mary Queen of Scots landed here in 1548 on her way to Paris to be engaged to the son of Henri II of France, and so too did Bonnie Prince Charlie in 1746, after his defeat at Culloden. The opening of its deep-water harbour in 1973, however, and the instigation of **Brittany Ferries** services to England and Ireland, had especial significance in the general revitalization of the Breton economy.

Few British holiday-makers are aware of Brittany Ferries' original raison d'être. The routes from Roscoff to Plymouth and to Cork were created not simply to attract tourists, but also to revive the traditional trading links between the Celtic nations of Brittany, Ireland and southwest England – links that were suppressed for centuries as an act of French state policy after the union of Brittany with France in 1532.

Until the 1960s, no direct ferries crossed the Channel to Brittany, and all the cross-Channel operators were British-owned. Brittany Ferries was the creation of **Alexis Gourvennec** (1936–2007), who in 1961, at 24, was the militant leader of a Breton farmers' cooperative. Frustrated by the lack of French government support, the farmers decided to start their own shipping line to find new markets for their produce – the immediate region of Roscoff and Morlaix being particularly noted for its artichokes and cauliflowers. Sailings between Plymouth and Roscoff began in 1973, at first for freight only but swiftly carrying passengers as well.

The company's financial success has allowed it to expand, running services from Britain to St-Malo and the Norman ports of Cherbourg and Caen, as well as to Spain. Above all, however, Brittany Ferries has been an important factor in a resurgence of Breton fortunes, cultural as well as commercial.

Like so many other Breton ports, Roscoff used to make most of its money from piracy. Charming, ornate and playfully embellished grey granite houses along the **medieval lanes**, just inland from the harbour, serve as reminders of that wealth. The sculpted ships and protruding stone cannons of the Renaissance belfry that tops the sixteenth-century church of **Notre Dame de Croas Batz**, at the northern end of rue de l'Amiral-Réveillère, also recall seafaring days. From the side, rows of bells can be seen hanging in galleries, one above the other, like a tall, narrow wedding cake created by the young Walt Disney.

Roscoff's best **beaches** lie to the west of town, beyond the **Thalassotherapy Institute** at Rock Roum, a luxury spa that opened in 1899 and specializes in seawater cures (☎02 57 40 01 20, ⌚thalasso-roscoff.com). The finest of all, at **Laber**, 2km out, is surrounded by expensive hotels and apartments.

Maison des Johnnies et de l'Oignon de Roscoff

48 rue Brizeux • Mid-June to mid-Sept Mon–Fri 11am, 3pm & 5pm; mid-Feb to mid-June & mid-Sept to Dec Tues, Thurs & Fri at 3pm • €4 • ☎02 98 61 25 48, ⌚roscoff.fr

During the nineteenth century, Roscoff turned its back on piracy in favour of earning a more respectable living from exporting **pink onions**. That trade started in 1828, when Henri Ollivier chartered a barge and took the first Roscoff onions over to England, and flourished until the 1930s; until recently, older locals still remembered travelling with their fathers as far afield as Glasgow to sell their produce.

At one time, 1500 "Johnnies" – that classic French image of men in black berets with strings of onions hanging over the handlebars of their bicycles – would set off each year. These days, around twenty still do. The whole story is told by way of hour-long guided tours at **La Maison des Johnnies et de l'Oignon de Roscoff**, near the *gare SNCF*.

Roscoff stages an **onion festival** at the end of August, with such amusements as onion cart-making contests, a vintage tractor parade and onion-soup tasting.

5

Jardin Exotique

Rock Hievec • Daily: March & Nov 2–5pm; April–June, Sept & Oct 10.30am–12.30pm & 2–6pm; July & Aug 10am–7pm • €5 • ☎ 02 98 61 29 19, ⓦ jardinexotiqueroscoff.com

A short walk south along the coast from the ferry terminal leads to Roscoff's tropical garden, the **Jardin Exotique**. In this slightly surreal enclave, cacti, palm trees and flowers of South America and the Pacific flourish in the mild Gulf-Stream climate. It's a favourite halt for migratory birds, and also hosts annual exhibitions of sculptures and installations.

ARRIVAL AND DEPARTURE   ROSCOFF

By boat Brittany Ferries sailings from Plymouth, Cork and Rosslare (☎ 02 98 29 28 13, ⓦ brittany-ferries.com) dock not in Roscoff's original natural harbour, but at the Port de Bloscon, a couple of kilometres east of the town.
By train From the *gare SNCF*, a few hundred metres south of the town centre, a restricted rail service (often replaced by buses) runs to Morlaix (7 daily; 35min),

with connections beyond.
By bus Local buses leave from the *gare SNCF* year-round, and also from the ferry terminal in summer (☎ 08 10 81 00 29, ⓦ viaoo29.fr).
Destinations Lesneven (4 daily; 1hr) via St-Pol (10min) and Plouescat (35min); Morlaix (5 daily; 1hr); Quimper (1 daily; 3hr).

INFORMATION AND TOURS

Tourist office The helpful tourist office is on the quayside just south of the old harbour, at 46 rue Gambetta (July & Aug Mon–Sat 9am–12.30pm & 1.30–7pm, Sun 10am–12.30pm & 2–7pm; Sept–June Mon–Sat 9.15am–noon & 2–6pm; ☎ 02 98 61 12 13, ⓦ roscoff-tourisme.com).
Boat trips The most popular boat trip from Roscoff, available year round, is to the nearby Île de Batz

(see opposite). Between July and mid-Sept, the ferry operators (see p.240) offer cruises of varying lengths around the Bay of Morlaix, typically costing around €15 for 2hr 30min.
Bike and kayak rental Escapades Légendes, in the central car park by the jetty, in summer only (☎ 06 72 10 25 71, ⓦ escapadeslegendes.fr).

ACCOMMODATION

For a small town, Roscoff is well equipped with hotels, accustomed to late-night arrivals from the ferries. However, many are squeezed into ancient houses which may be very charming, but lack lifts, and many also close for some or all of the winter. There's a hostel on the Île de Batz (see p.240).

Des Arcades 15 rue de l'Amiral-Réveillère ☎ 02 98 69 70 45, ⓦ hotel-les-arcades-roscoff.com. Very central sixteenth-century building where 14 of the 20 modernized en-suite rooms have superb sea views, and so, too, does the restaurant, which has menus at €13, and an excellent €29.90 option. Closed mid-Nov to early Feb. €61

Best Western Grand Hôtel Talabardon 27 place Lacaze-Duthiers ☎ 02 98 61 24 95, ⓦ hotel-talabardon .com. This imposing old stone building in the main square faces the church on the inland side, but several of its comfortable rooms have big sea-view balconies. Seafood menus in its attractive dining room, closed Sun eve & Thurs lunch, start at €22. €129

Du Centre 5 rue Gambetta ☎ 02 98 61 24 25, ⓦ chezjanie.fr. Boutique hotel above the venerable *Chez Janie*, entered via the main street but looking out on the port. "Janie" herself is long gone, and what was once a rough-and-ready bar is now much smarter, with modern, tastefully furnished bedrooms – sea views €25 extra – and a decent bistro menu. Closed mid-Nov to mid-Feb. €100

Chardons Bleus 4 rue de l'Amiral-Réveillère ☎ 02 98 69 72 03, ⓦ roscoffhotel.com. Friendly hotel in the heart

of the old town, with simple but comfortable rooms and a good restaurant (closed Thurs & Sun eve Sept–June) where dinner menus cost €24 or €37. Closed three weeks in Feb. €70

Aux Quatre Saisons Perharidy ☎ 02 98 69 70 86, ⓦ camping-aux4saisons.com. Two-star seafront camp-site, 2km west of Roscoff, just off the route de Santec. There's a heated pool, and the adjacent beach is perfect. Closed Oct–March. €15.70

Aux Tamaris 49 rue É-Corbière ☎ 02 98 61 22 99, ⓦ hotel-aux-tamaris.com. Renovated, comfortably furnished rooms in a fine old granite townhouse. Some sleep four, and those that have lovely sea views towards the Île de Batz cost up to €30 extra. Closed 2 weeks in Jan. €85

★Le Temps de Vivre 19 place Lacaze-Duthiers ☎ 02 98 19 33 19, ⓦ letempsdevivre.net. Ultra-stylish contemporary hotel, in an old mansion near the Notre-Dame church. Luxuriously spacious rooms with designer bathrooms, some with wonderful close-up sea views, but no restaurant. Off-season rates are at least €60 lower. €145

EATING AND DRINKING

5

Bonne Étoile 36 rue de l'Amiral-Réveillère ☎06 88 39 94 85, ⓦla-bonne-etoile-roscoff.fr. Jaunty little restaurant, right in the centre near the port, with bright seaside decor and lots of baked goods – pies, tarts and sponges – as well as seafood on menus from €18 to €30. Tues & Sun noon–2pm, Wed–Sat noon–2pm & 7–9pm.

Crêperie de la Poste 12 rue Gambetta ☎02 98 69 72 81, ⓦcreperiedelaposte.fr. Cosy old stone house, just back from the port in the heart of town, offering inexpensive à la carte meals of sweet and savoury pancakes; more exotic seafood crêpes cost up to €11. They also serve fish soup, mussels and other simple meals.

Sept to mid-Nov & mid-Jan to June Thurs–Sun 11.30am until late; July & Aug Mon & Wed–Sun 11.30am until late.

Écume des Jours Quai d'Auxerre ☎02 98 61 22 83, ⓦecume-roscoff.fr. Romantic restaurant in a grand old house 500m south of town along the quayside towards the ferry port, with outdoor terrace seating in summer. Two-course lunch *formules* go for €23 on weekdays, while the *plat du jour* with a glass of wine costs €17; dinner menus, from €35, feature such delights as braised oysters or scallops with local pink onions. Jan to mid-Dec Mon & Thurs–Sun noon–1.30pm & 7–9pm.

Île de Batz

The long, narrow, and very lovely **ÎLE DE BATZ** (pronounced "ba") forms a sort of mirror image of Roscoff across the water, stretching for around 4km parallel to the tip of the headland, and separated from it by a sea channel that's barely 200m wide at low tide, but perhaps five times that when the tide is high. Appearances from the mainland are somewhat deceptive, however; the island's old town, home to a thousand or so farmers and fishermen, may fill much of its southern shoreline, but those parts of Batz that aren't visible from Roscoff are much wilder and more windswept. With no cars permitted, and some great expanses of sandy beach, it makes a wonderfully quiet retreat for families in particular, whether you're camping or staying in its hotels, hostel or B&Bs.

The island's first recorded inhabitant, a "laidly worm", was a dragon that infested the place in the sixth century. Such dragons normally symbolize pre-Christian religions, in this case perhaps a Druidic serpent cult. Allegorical or not, when St Pol arrived to found a monastery he wrapped a Byzantine stole around the unfortunate creature's neck and cast it into the sea. These days, there are no dragons; there are hardly even any trees, just an awful lot of seaweed, which is collected and sold for fertilizer.

Exploring the island

All ferries to Batz pull in at a jetty at the southeast corner of the island's south-facing port. A nice little beach lines the edge of the harbour nearby, though the sea withdraws so far at low tide that the entire port turns into a morass of seaweed. Arriving passengers make the obvious 500m walk towards the town, ranged enticingly along the quayside. Once there, there's nothing particularly to see, but strolling among the beautiful little houses and their radiant gardens is a real joy.

Turning left when you get to the town church will bring you to the 44-metre **lighthouse** that stands on the island's peak, all of 23m above sea level (April–June & first half of Sept Sat & Sun 2–5pm; July & Aug daily 11am–5.30pm; €2.20).

Turning right at the church, on the other hand, leads you in around ten minutes to what's indisputably the finest of the island's many **beaches**, the glorious white-sand **Grève Blanche** at its eastern end, which you may well have spotted already from the boat. Well protected from the wind, backed by soft grass, and lapped by a warm, shallow sea, it's a perfect spot for a day-long family picnic.

Not far south, close to the southeast tip of the island, the **Jardin Exotique Georges-Delaselle** is a 75-year-old garden that takes advantage of the temperate Batz microclimate to sustain its palm trees and other out-of-context flora (April–Oct daily 11am–6pm; €5; ☎02 98 61 75 65).

5

ARRIVAL AND DEPARTURE
ÎLE DE BATZ

By ferry Three rival ferry companies make the 10min crossing from Roscoff to Batz (frequent services daily: July & Aug 8am–8pm; Sept–June 8.30am–6.30pm; 10min; €8.50 return; bikes €8.50). Compagnie Maritime Armein (☎ 02 98 61 75 47, W vedettesbatzroscoff.com), Compagnie Finistérienne or CFTM (☎ 02 98 61 78 87,

W vedettes-ile-de-batz.com), and Armor Excursions (☎ 02 98 61 79 66, W vedettes.armor.ile.de.batz.fr) sell tickets at the landward end of Roscoff's long pier; in summer only, tickets are valid on any ferry. At low tide, the boats sail from the far end of the pier, a good 5min walk further.

INFORMATION AND ACTIVITIES

Tourist office Right beside the ferry dock (April–June & late Aug to Sept Mon & Sat 10am–12.30pm, Tues–Fri 9am–12.30pm & 2–4pm; July to late Aug Mon–Sat 9.15am–12.30pm & 1.30–4.45pm; Oct–March Mon–Thurs 9am–noon & 1.30–4.30pm, Fri 9am–noon; ☎ 02 98 61 75 70, W www.iledebatz.com)
Watersports Rêves de Mer, alongside the campsite,

offers classes in sailing, kayaking and windsurfing (☎ 02 98 61 76 76, W revesdemer.com).
Horseriding In July & Aug, the Ecuries de Batz stables, just north of the Grève Blanche beach, offers horse and pony rides from €11 per hour (☎ 02 98 61 78 91, W ecuriesdebatz .e-monsite.com).

ACCOMMODATION AND EATING
ÎLE DE BATZ

In addition to the options listed below, the island's website, W www.iledebatz.com, holds a wide selection of **rental cottages**, typically costing €550–800 per week in summer.

Auberge de Jeunesse Marine Creach ar Bolloc'h ☎ 02 98 61 77 69, W aj-iledebatz.org. The evocatively named Creach ar Bolloc'h makes a beautiful setting for this hostel, which faces south towards Roscoff from near the port. Two separate cottages hold dorm beds, with a lovely beach just a few steps away. Rates include breakfast. Closed Oct–March. **€17.40**
Les Couleurs du Temps Le Débarcadère ☎ 02 98 61 75 75, W les-couleurs-du-temps.net. Quirky little crêperie-restaurant, near the ferries, which sells sweet and savoury pancakes for €5–7, and prepares the Breton speciality kig ha farz, seafood stew topped by a crêpe. Easter–Sept daily noon–2pm & 6–8pm.
Les Herbes Folles Le Débarcadère ☎ 02 98 61 78 28, W hotel-iledebatz.com. The island's one, simple hotel, on the quay where the ferries come in, is a rambling old place with an open-air wooden deck upstairs, a garden, and abundant nooks and crannies. Seven of its ten en-suite rooms look over the sea back towards Roscoff. It also holds a good restaurant, serving dinner menus from €20.50,

and a very pleasant little bar, the Bigorneau Langoureux ("languorous periwinkle"), stocked with a fine array of Basque wines. **€80**
Terrain d'Hébergement Porz Reter ☎ 02 98 61 77 76, W www.iledebatz.com. Batz's waterfront campsite, at the southeast corner of the island, is about as minimal as they come. There are no set pitches; you simply pick a spot, just back from the beach. It does however hold a small shower block. Closed late Sept to April. **€7.94**
Ti Va Zadou ☎ 02 98 61 76 91, W tivazadou-iledebatz .fr. Run as a B&B, this pretty, peaceful cottage, in sight of the port, offers five attractive and comfortable guest rooms at varying prices, with great views, big breakfasts and cycles for rent. Closed mid-Nov to mid-Feb. **€65**
Ty Yann Bourg ☎ 0298 61 79 31, W creperie.ile.de.batz.fr. While it's basically a crêperie – a very good one – this friendly and spacious place also buys up fresh-caught local seafood, which often includes scallops and lobsters, to serve as €10–15 specials as well as €6–10 pancake toppings. Easter–Sept daily noon–2pm & 6–8pm.

South from Roscoff

The main road south from Roscoff, the D58, swiftly emerges into a heavily agricultural landscape, abounding in fields of the famous Breton artichokes. Motorists soon find themselves, however, entangled in a phenomenally intricate network of bypasses and roundabouts, all designed to keep traffic away from historic **St-Pol-de-Léon**.

Cyclists in particular would do well to get onto the minor roads to the east. That way, you can call in at the appealing little resort of **Carantec**, and then follow the D73 southeast along a narrowing estuary, which at **Locquenolé** becomes the mouth of the River Morlaix. The beautiful deep valley south from here has promenades and gardens along its stone-reinforced banks, and views across to isolated villages such as Dourduff on the other side.

St-Pol-de-Léon

5

The attractive old village of **ST-POL-DE-LÉON**, 6km south of Roscoff, holds two churches that merit a pause. Its **cathedral**, in the main square, was rebuilt towards the end of the thirteenth century along the lines of Coutances' – a quiet classic of unified Norman architecture. The remains of St Pol are inside, alongside a large bell, rung over the heads of pilgrims during his *pardon* on March 12 in the unlikely hope of curing headaches and ear diseases.

Just downhill, the **Kreisker Chapel** is notable for its sharp-pointed soaring granite belfry, now coated in yellow moss. It was originally modelled on the Norman spire of St-Pierre at Caen, which was destroyed in the last war (see p.102); as an elegant improvement on its Norman counterpart, it was itself much copied, and similar "Kreisker" spires are dotted all over rural Brittany. The dramatic view to be seen if you climb this spire (daily 10–noon & 2–6pm; free), out across the **Bay of Morlaix**, should be enough to persuade you to follow the road along the shore.

Carantec

From St-Pol, if you take the foliage-covered lane down to join the D58, you can cross the pont de la Corde to reach the resort and peninsula of **CARANTEC**, studded with small coves and secluded beaches. The nicest of all the local beaches, the **plage du Kelenn**, is the first to the east of the slightly drab town itself. The **Île de Callot**, an enticing hour's walk from Carantec at low tide, is the scene of a *pardon* and blessing of the sea on the Sunday after August 15 – a rather dour occasion, as are most of the religious festivals around Finistère.

This stretch of coast comes alive in summer with a scattering of seasonal **campsites**.

Château du Taureau

Morlaix Bay • Access mid-April to Sept only, via boat trips from Carantec and Plougasnou, which sail to a complicated tide-dependent schedule • €14 • ☎ 02 98 62 29 73, ⊕ www.chateaudutaureau.com

Occupying the whole of a tiny island, the fortified **Château du Taureau** guards the entrance to Morlaix Bay, a short way east of Carantec and 12km north of Morlaix itself. It was built after a succession of skirmishes that began in 1522 when Morlaix pirates raided and looted Bristol. Henry VIII's pride was hurt and, seeking revenge, he sent a sizeable fleet to storm Morlaix. The citizens were absent at a neighbouring festival when the English arrived; when they returned, they found the English drunk in their wine cellars. Once the Bretons had routed their enemies, they built the château to forestall further attacks from the sea. Meanwhile, Morlaix adopted the motto which it keeps to this day: "If they bite you, bite them back."

The château was shaped into its current form by the master military architect Vauban during the eighteenth century, and doubled as a prison until well into the nineteenth century. To get a close-up view, you have to venture onto the water. Summer-only boat trips from Carantec and Plougasnou enable passengers to disembark and spend an hour exploring the actual structure; cruises from Roscoff let you admire it from a distance.

The best vantage point on the mainland is at the tip of the **Pointe de Pen-al-Lann**, 2km east of Carantec. A steep footpath from the car park here leads 300m down to one of the most delightful – and quiet – **beaches** in this region.

INFORMATION   **SOUTH FROM ROSCOFF**

Tourist office Place de l'Éveche, St-Pol (July & Aug Mon–Sat 9.30am–12.30pm & 1.30–6.30pm, Sun 10am–12.30pm; Sept–June Mon–Sat 9.30am–noon & 2–5.30pm; ☎ 02 98 69 05 69, ⊕ saintpoldeleon.fr); 4 rue Pasteur, Carentec (April–June & Sept Mon 2–6pm, Tues–Sat 9.30am–12.30pm & 2–6pm; July & Aug Mon–Sat 9.30am–7pm, Sun 10am–1pm & 2.30–5pm; Oct–March Tues–Sat 9.30am–12.30pm & 2–5.30pm; ☎ 02 98 67 00 43, ⊕ tourisme.morlaix.fr).

5

ACCOMMODATION AND EATING

ST-POL

De France 29 rue des Minimes ☎ 02 98 29 14 14, ⓦ www.hoteldefrancebretagne.com. Friendly, central hotel in a grand old Breton townhouse, with a pleasant garden. Some of the sparse but comfortable rooms have sea views, others look towards the cathedral. **€70**

Passiflore 28 rue Pen-ar-Pont ☎ 02 98 69 00 52, ⓦ hotel-restaurant-lepassiflore.fr. Logis de France, near the station, with simple, brightly painted rooms and a very popular restaurant serving full menus from €20. The hotel reception is closed at weekends, but rooms are still available; the restaurant is closed Sun eve. **€66**

CARANTEC

Cabestan 7 rue du Port ☎ 02 98 67 01 87. This restaurant, right on the waterfront in town, provides the focus of Carantec's nightlife. As well as serving great seafood, often with Asian flavourings, on menus at €17–40, it also puts on live music. Tues–Sun noon–1.30pm & 7–10pm; closed Tues in low season, plus all Jan.

De Carantec 20 rue de Kelenn ☎ 02 98 67 00 47, ⓦ hoteldecarantec.com. Stylish beachfront hotel, where five of the twelve luxurious rooms have terraces with magnificent views of the sea, and all share use of lawns rolling down to the sea. The *Patrick Jeffroy* restaurant, named after the hotel owner and chef, serves very exquisite *nouvelle* menus at €44 for lunch (Wed–Sat only), and €75–132 for dinner. **€182**

Maison de l'Huître Pen-al-Lann ☎ 02 98 67 03 64, ⓦ prat-ar-coum.com. Gorgeous and very clearly sign-posted waterfront spot east of the centre, selling prize oysters from the beds at Prat-Ar-Coum in western Finistère. Mon–Sat 10am–6pm, Sun 10am–12.30pm.

Les Mouettes ☎ 02 98 67 02 46, ⓦ les-mouettes.com. Excellent four-star campsite, where you pay over the usual odds for the benefit of having a supermarket, a pool complex with three impressive water slides, a bar and a club on site. They also offer a wide range of rental cottages. Closed early Sept to mid-April. Cottages **€140**, camping **€50**

Ti Case 9 rue de Maréchal-Foch ☎ 06 62 13 60 67, ⓦ chambreticase.com. Very welcoming B&B, in a central townhouse that holds four brightly refurbished en-suite rooms, two with balconies and two in the attic. All sleep at least three guests. **€69**

Morlaix

During the "Golden Period" of the late Middle Ages, **MORLAIX**, 25km southeast of Roscoff, was one of the great Breton ports, thriving – in between wars – on trade with England. Clustered where the Queffleuth and Jarlot rivers join to flow together into broad Morlaix Bay, its sober stone houses, climbing both sides of a steep valley, were originally protected by an eleventh-century castle and a circuit of walls. Later, as Morlaix grew still more prosperous on piracy and the tobacco trade (both legal and illegal), it spread northwards, down the valley, towards the port.

These days, while many attractive buildings still survive from Morlaix's medieval heyday, it's a strange-looking place, literally overshadowed by a massive pink granite **railway viaduct**, built high above the valley in the 1860s to carry trains en route between Paris and Brest. Despite repeated Allied attempts to bomb it during World War II, it still looms 60m above the central **place des Otages**,

As you enter Morlaix by road from the north, your first view is of shiny yacht masts in the pleasure harbour paralleling the slender pillars of the viaduct. There are few actual sights in town, but it's a pleasure to roam the old centre, with its cobbled streets and half-timbered houses, climb the steep stairways that lead up from the places des Otages and Cornic, or walk up to the viaduct from the top of Venelle aux Prêtres, along an almost rural overgrown path lined with brambles.

In April each year, Morlaix hosts **Festival Panoramas** (ⓦ festivalpanoramas.com), an eclectic festival of contemporary music, from rock to rap by way of electro.

Musée de Morlaix

Place des Jacobins • July–Sept daily 10am–12.30pm & 2–6pm; Sept–June Tues–Sat 10am–noon & 2–5pm, plus first Sun of month 2–5pm • €4.50 • ☎ 02 98 88 68 88, ⓦ musee.ville.morlaix.fr

On her way from Roscoff to Paris in 1548, Mary Queen of Scots stayed at Morlaix's **Jacobin convent**. A contemporary account records that the crush to catch a glimpse of the 5-year-old was so great that the inner town's "gates were thrown off their hinges and the chains from all the bridges were broken down". The convent has long housed the **Musée de Morlaix**, which has no permanent collection on display, but hosts two temporary exhibitions per year.

Tickets also entitle visitors to a guided tour of the nearby **Maison à Pondalez**, at 9 Grand'Rue (same hours), a fabulously restored sixteenth-century house that takes its name from the Breton word for the sculpted wooden internal gallery that dominates the ground floor.

Église St-Mathieu

Off rue de Paris

The austere **Église St-Mathieu**, a short walk southeast of the convent, contains a sombre and curious statue of the Madonna and Child, made in Cologne around 1400 AD. Mary's breast was apparently lopped off by a prudish former priest, to leave the babe suckling at nothing. The whole statue stands open down the middle, to reveal a separate figure of God the Father, clutching a crucifix.

Maison de la Duchesse Anne

33 rue du Mur • April Mon–Sat 2–5pm; May, June & Sept Mon–Sat 11am–6pm; July & Aug Mon–Sat 11am–6pm, Sun noon–6pm • €2 • ☎ 02 98 88 23 26, ⓦ mda-morlaix.com

Duchess Anne of Brittany visited Morlaix in 1506, by which time she had become queen of France. She is reputed to have stayed at the **Maison de la Duchesse Anne**, which, although much restored, does indeed date from the sixteenth century. Its intricate external carvings, and the lantern roof and splendid Renaissance staircase that you see if you pay to go inside, make it the most beautiful of the town's ancient houses, each of its storeys overhanging the square below by a few more centimetres.

ARRIVAL AND INFORMATION — MORLAIX

By train The *gare SNCF* is on rue Armand-Rousseau, high above the town at the western end of the viaduct. It was originally supposed to be linked to town by a funicular railway, but that was never built, so you have to reach it on foot, climbing the steep steps of the Venelle de la Roche. Destinations Brest (20 daily; 40min); Roscoff (7 daily; 35min); St-Brieuc (16 daily; 50min).
By bus All buses depart from place Cornic.

Destinations Carantec (7 daily; 20min); Carhaix (3 daily; 1hr 30min); Lannion (4 daily; 1hr); Quimper (1 daily; 1hr 50min); Roscoff (5 daily; 1hr).
Tourist office 10 place Charles de Gaulle (June & Sept Mon–Sat 9am–12.30pm & 2–6.30pm; July & Aug Mon–Sat 9am–7pm, Sun 10.30am–12.30pm; Oct–May Mon–Sat 9am–12.30pm & 2–6pm; ☎ 02 98 62 14 94, ⓦ tourisme.morlaix.fr).

ACCOMMODATION

Auberge de Jeunesse Éthic Étapes 1 voie d'accès au Port, St-Martin-des-Champs ☎ 02 98 15 10 55, ⓦ aj-morlaix.org. Large, well-equipped, modern hostel, beside the pleasure port just over 1km downstream on the left (west) bank of river from the town centre, with 35 rooms holding four dorm beds each, plus a communal kitchen and large shared space. Rates include breakfast. **€19.40**
De l'Europe 1 rue d'Aiguillon ☎ 02 98 62 11 99,

ⓦ hotel-europe-com.fr. Grand, if eccentric, old hotel in the centre of Morlaix, with a fabulous wooden staircase and nicely refurbished rooms – some plush and some plain, including some cut-rate singles – plus €10 buffet breakfasts. **€99**
Du Port 3 quai du Léon ☎ 02 98 88 07 54, ⓦ lhotel duport.com. Good-value little hotel, facing the port, with presentable, recently refreshed rooms; the quietest are around the back, looking over the pleasant courtyard. No restaurant, but plenty close by. **€85**

EATING AND DRINKING

Atipik Bilig 1 rue Ange-de-Guernisac ☎ 02 98 63 38 63. You'll have to reserve ahead to eat in summer at this unbeatable little central crêperie, with some outdoor

seating and an emphasis on regional ingredients; €10 buys you a crêpe, a galette and a glass of wine. Tues–Sat noon–2pm & 7–9.30pm, plus Mon in July & Aug.

5

Les Bains Douches 45 allée du Poan-Ben ☎02 98 63 83 83, ⓦ restaurant-morlaix-lebainsdouches.fr. This small bistro makes the most of its unusual location – in the beautifully restored former public baths, reached via a little footbridge across a canal – and is an attractive spot for a light €14 lunch or a full €24 dinner. Precise menus change daily. Mon noon–2pm, Tues–Fri noon–2pm & 7.30–10pm, Sat 7.30–10pm.

Dolce Vita 3 rue Ange-de-Guernisac ☎02 98 63 37 67, ⓦ ladolcevitamorlaix.fr. Italian restaurant and take-away at the foot of a pretty central alley, with thin-crust pizzas priced at €8–12, plus pasta, salads and traditional Italian desserts including a great tiramisu. Tues–Sun 10am–10pm.

Tempo Café Quai de Tréguier ☎02 98 63 29 11. Popular bar, with a terrace facing the port, which also serves a daily array of *plats* and *tartes*, costing €10–12, with on occasional live music. Mon–Thurs 10am–10pm, Fri 10am–1am, Sat 5pm–1am.

Ty Coz 10 Venelle au Beurre ☎02 98 88 07 65, ⓦ ty-coz -bar.fr. Venerable half-timbered bar near place Allende, filled with boisterous Bretons playing darts, and serving locally brewed draught Coreff beer. Tues 4pm–1am, Wed–Fri 11am–1am, Sat 10am–1am, Sun 6pm–1am.

The parish closes

The region that's bounded by the valleys of the Elorn and the Penzé rivers, a few kilometres west of Morlaix, is remarkable for the wealth and distinction of its church architecture. Thanks to intense inter-village rivalry during the sixteenth and seventeenth centuries, when each parish competed to outdo the next in the complexity and ornamentation of its village church, this small area holds the most famous examples of what are known as **parish closes**.

It's no coincidence that most such Breton churches date from the two centuries to either side of the union with France in 1532 – Brittany's wealthiest period. A clearly signposted **route** leading past the most famous churches – St-Thégonnec, Guimiliau and Lampaul-Guimiliau – can be joined by leaving the N12 between Morlaix and Landivisiau at St-Thégonnec. Public transport is poor.

St-Thégonnec

At the **ST-THÉGONNEC** *enclos*, just off the N12 10km southwest of Morlaix, the church **pulpit**, carved by two brothers in 1683, is the acknowledged masterpiece, albeit so swamped with detail – symbolic saints, sibyls and arcane figures – as to be almost too intricate to take in. The painted oak **entombment** in the crypt under the ossuary has

---

THE ESSENTIAL COMPONENTS OF A PARISH CLOSE

Although the kind of architectural ensemble specified by the French term **enclos paroissiaux** may not be familiar to most foreign visitors, there is nonetheless a direct English translation: "**parish closes**". It describes a walled churchyard that in addition to the church itself incorporates a trinity of further elements: a cemetery, a calvary and an ossuary.

The **ossuaries** – which now tend to contain nothing more alarming than a few rows of postcards – were originally charnel houses, used to store the exhumed bones of less recent burials. They are the most striking features of the closes, making explicit a peculiarly Breton proximity and continuity between the living and the dead. Parishioners would go to pray, with the informality of making a family visit, in the ossuary chapels where the dead bones of their families were on display. The relationship may have originated with the builders of the megalithic passage graves, which were believed to serve as doorways between our world and the netherworld.

The **cemeteries** tend to be small, and in many cases have disappeared altogether, while the **calvaries** that complete the ensemble are tenuously based on the hill of Calvary. Each is, therefore, in theory surmounted by a Crucifixion, but the definition is loose enough to take in any cluster of religious statuary, not necessarily even limited to biblical scenes, standing on a single base.

more immediate effect. Complete with a stunning life-size figure of Mary Magdalene, it was sculpted by Jacques Laispagnol of Morlaix in 1702. The entire east wall of the church is a carved and painted altarpiece, with saints in niches.

Guimiliau

The showpiece at the pretty flower-filled village of **GUIMILIAU**, 6km southwest of St-Thégonnec, is its **calvary**. This incredible ensemble holds over two hundred granite figures, depicting scenes from the life of Christ and rendered all the more dramatic by being covered with "secular lichen". A uniquely Breton illustration, just above the Last Supper, depicts the unfortunate **Katell Gollet** – a figure from local myth who stole consecrated wafers to give to her lover, who naturally turned out to be the Devil – being torn to shreds by demons.

Inside the church, years of patient restoration have turned the seventeenth-century organ from a tangle of mangled wood back into its original harmonious condition.

Lampaul-Guimiliau

The third of the major parish closes, **LAMPAUL-GUIMILIAU**, is a few kilometres northwest from Guimiliau. Here the painted oak **baptistry**, the dragons on the beams and the appropriately wicked faces of the robbers on the **calvary** are the key components. An unusual stoup depicts a couple of devils squirming as they're doused with holy water.

Landivisiau

LANDIVISIAU, just south of the N12 20km west of Morlaix, makes a good alternative to Morlaix as a base from which to tour the nearby parish closes. There's not much to the town itself, though.

Château de Kerjean

11km northwest of Landivisiau • First half of March, Oct to early Nov & Xmas/New Year Mon & Wed–Sun 2–5.30pm; mid-March to June & Sept Mon & Wed–Sun 2–6pm; July & Aug daily 10am–7pm • €6 • ☎ 02 98 69 93 69, ⊕ cdp29.fr

If not quite the "Versailles of Brittany", as it is promoted, the **Château de Kerjean** is for this remote corner of France a surprisingly classic edifice. Despite being little more than 15km from Roscoff, it's not that easy to find, standing 500m west of the D30, halfway between Landivisiau and the sea.

This moated Renaissance château, set in its own park, was built in the sixteenth century by the lords of Kerjean, with the express intention of overshadowing the mansion of their former feudal overlord, the Carman of Lanhouarneau, who, under some archaic quirk of fealty, made them take an egg, in a cart, each year and cook it in front of him.

Now state property and extensively restored, the building hosts displays on its own history, along with changing annual exhibitions focusing on some aspect of medieval life. In summer, it also hosts open-air musical and theatrical performances.

Le Folgoët

Centring on a well-kept and rather English-looking green, the appealing village of **LE FOLGOËT** stands a couple of kilometres southwest of the slightly larger town of **LESNEVEN**, itself 15km west of Kerjean. Both Le Folgoët's church, and its name, which means "Fool's Wood", stem from a fourteenth-century simpleton called Solomon. After an unappreciated lifetime repeating the four Breton words for "O Lady Virgin Mary", he found fame in death by growing a white lily out of his mouth.

While it doesn't form part of a parish close, the **Notre Dame** church is quite lovely, erected on the site of Solomon's favourite spring, and colourfully garnished with orange moss and clinging verdure (a sign of the penetrating damp inside). Topped by a bumpy and stubbly approximation of a "Kreisker" spire, it has been restored bit by bit since the damage of the Revolution, and an unusual amount of statuary has been placed on the many low niches all around the outside.

On September 8 or the preceding Sunday, Le Folgoët holds a *pardon*, and there's also another *pardon* of St Christopher on the fourth Sunday of July, which involves a blessing of cars that non-motorists may find verging on the blasphemous.

La Roche-Maurice

West of Landivisiau, the N12 races towards Brest, but the lesser D712 and the railway follow a far more pleasant route, along the banks of the pretty Elorn River. After about 12km – not far beyond the chapel of **Pont-Christ**, beside a broad waterfall – the village of **LA ROCHE-MAURICE** occupies a steep high bluff above a curve in the river.

The village's large **parish close** is notable mainly for its rendition of the death-figure **Ankou** (see p.229). This time he's carved above the holy-water stoup on the wall of the ossuary, facing the church, beneath the warning "I kill you all". The interior of the church is gorgeous, the nave divided in two by a lovely green-and-red rood screen, which shows the Twelve Apostles propped up by grotesque animals. Ringed by older carvings, the blue ceiling holds a celestial choir of angels. In summer, the ossuary houses local information and an exhibition on local history.

Château Roc'h Morvan

La Roche-Maurice • Daily 10am–6pm; guided visits July & Aug daily at 3pm, Sept–June 1st Sun of each month, 3pm • ☏ 02 98 85 13 09, ⓦ larochemaurice.fr

Only the solemn, ivy-covered keep now remains of the **Château Roc'h Morvan**, which has occupied the hilltop in La Roche-Maurice since the eleventh century. Once supposedly home to Katell Gollet (see p.245), it was abandoned at the end of the seventeenth century, and its stones used to build the houses that now surround it. Visitors are free to climb the wooden stairway that's rather clumsily attached to the outside, but not to ascend any further inside the ruin itself.

La Martyre

The oldest parish close of all, built in 1460, stands at the heart of **LA MARTYRE**, 7km south of La Roche-Maurice on the road to Sizun (see p.294). This is the most attractive of all the local villages, with stones of its complete **parish close** seamlessly integrated into the walls of its main street.

Above the stoup in the peculiarly lopsided entrance porch, **Ankou** clutches a severed head, watched over not only by a carved red-ochre Virgin, giving birth, but also a nest of house martins. Inside, the church is damp and somewhat faded, but it does have an attractive gilt altar.

Landerneau

The delightful town of **LANDERNEAU**, 20km east of Brest at the mouth of the Elorn estuary, was once a major port, but it's attractive enough to have reinvented itself as a tourist showpiece.

The **pont de Rohan** in the middle of town is said to be, along with the Ponte Vecchio in Florence, one of the last **inhabited bridges** in Europe; as a plaque proudly boasts, it was *re*-constructed in 1510. The bridge itself holds no fewer than four crêperies, along with assorted shops, bars and houses, while streets of fine old mansions climb away to either side of the river.

Plougastel-Daoulas

West of Landerneau, the Élorn broadens dramatically as it enters the Rade de Brest. The city of Brest sprawls along its northern banks at this point, but the southern side holds one final village associated with the parish closes. While the church in **PLOUGASTEL-DAOULAS** was built in 1870 and is far from interesting, the **calvary** just outside it ranks among the finest in Brittany.

This extraordinarily elaborate affair was completed in 1604 to celebrate the passing of an outbreak of the plague – hence the bumps on the shaft of the main cross, designed to recall the sores on the bodies of the victims. Carvings on each side of the base depict scenes from the life of Christ. Sadly, the rest of the village has not been restored so sensitively after the bombing of World War II. A weird shopping mall now overlooks the calvary, equipped with a giant Scrabble board for local senior citizens and a truly awful mural recounting the history of cinema.

| INFORMATION | THE PARISH CLOSES |

Tourist office Zone de Kerven, Landivisiau (Mon–Fri 9am–noon & 2–5pm; ☎02 98 68 33 33, ⓦroscoff -tourisme.com); 9 place de Gaulle, Landerneau (July & Aug Mon–Sat 10am–7pm, Sun 10am–1pm & 2–6pm; Sept– June Tues–Sat 10am–1pm & 2–5pm; ☎02 98 85 13 09, ⓦbrest-terres-oceanes.fr).

ACCOMMODATION AND EATING

ST-THÉGONNEC
★**Auberge de St-Thégonnec** 6 place de la Mairie ☎02 98 79 61 18, ⓦaubergesaintthegonnec.com. A surprisingly smart hotel for such a small village, with comfortable, modern rooms sleeping up to four. Its main building houses a superb restaurant (closed Mon lunch, Sat lunch & all Sun), where menus start at €22.50 and rise to €47 for the gourmet option featuring lobster, crab, sea bass and the like, carefully prepared in original and delicious sauces. *Closed Sun Sept–March, plus mid-Dec to mid-Jan.* **€98**
Du Commerce 1 rue de Paris ☎02 98 79 61 07. Old-fashioned *routier* restaurant, very near the church, and open for weekday lunches only, serving hearty, good-value €12 *formules*. *Mon–Fri 11.45am–2pm; closed 3 weeks in Aug.*
Crêperie Steredden 6 rue de la Gare ☎02 98 79 43 34. Friendly village crêperie that's popular enough to make reservations essentials in summer. Offers numerous speciality pancakes, with menus up to €15. *Wed–Sun noon–2pm & 7–9.30pm; closed Dec & Jan.*

LANDIVISIAU
De l'Avenue 16 av de Coatmeur ☎02 98 68 11 67, ⓦhotel-l-avenue.com. Good-value hotel in the heart of town, with simple but tasteful rooms – pay €5 extra for en-suite facilities – and a nice little restaurant, open for lunch Mon–Sat with a €14, three-course *formule*, and dinner Mon–Thurs only for €22 or €27. **€57**
Le Terminus 94 av Foch ☎02 98 68 02 00. Unprepossessing hotel on the northeast edge of town, where you can get an adequate bed for the night at remarkably low rates; it's more likely to be of interest for its surprisingly good restaurant, which serves weekday workers' lunches for €12 and rich seafood dinners from €20.50. *Restaurant closed Sat lunch, Fri eve & Sun eve.* **€35**

LE FOLGOËT
Le Week-End 8 pont du Châtel, Plouider ☎02 98 25 40 57, ⓦhotelrestaurantweekend.com. The nearest reasonable accommodation to Le Folgoët, near Plouider, 5km northeast of Lesneven, this quiet little Logis de France offers neat, bright en-suite rooms and provides good-value food. *Restaurant closed Mon lunch July & Aug, Sun eve & all day Mon Sept–June.* **€60**

LA ROCHE-MAURICE
Auberge du Vieux Château 4 Grand Place ☎02 98 20 40 52, ⓦauberge-duvieuxchateau.com. Very welcoming, family-run restaurant in the square immediately below the castle, serving weekday lunches for €14, and excellent dinners, featuring the likes of papery scallop parcels or duck with strawberries, from €21.50. *Mon–Thurs & Sun noon–2pm, Fri & Sat noon–2pm & 7.15–9pm.*

LANDERNEAU
Le Clos du Pontic 3 rue du Pontic ☎02 98 21 50 91, ⓦclos-pontic.com. Comfortable old-style villa hotel, set in spacious grounds south of the river, with smart, peaceful rooms and a good restaurant, open Mon–Fri only, where the €29 dinner menu includes locally sourced organic veal. **€55**

5

The abers

Some of the most spectacular shoreline in Brittany lies west of Roscoff. Amid this jagged series of **abers** – narrow estuaries, neither as deep nor as steep-sided as the Norwegian fjords with which they are occasionally compared – several small, isolated **resorts** are heavy on modern holiday homes but relatively short on hotels and other amenities. All have adequate beaches, but it's the coastal scenery that's the real attraction. Conditions can be a little on the bracing side, especially if you're making use of the numerous **campsites**, but in summer, at least, the temperatures are mild enough, and there's more shelter as you move towards Le Conquet and Brest.

Plouescat

The first real resort west of Roscoff, **PLOUESCAT**, is not quite on the sea itself, but there are **campsites** nearby on each of three adjacent beaches. In the town, you'll find a high-roofed old wooden market hall for picnic provisions, and an unexpected, slightly surreal statue of a seahorse with a yin and yang symbol in its tail.

Brignogan-Plages

Pretty little **BRIGNOGAN-PLAGES**, on the first *aber* west of Plouescat, is blessed with a small natural harbour. Once the lair of wreckers, it has beaches and weather-beaten rocks to either side, as well as its own menhir. As the tide here recedes way out towards the mouth of the bay, surreal clumps of seaweed-coated stone bulge up among the stranded boats. The *Café du Port* makes a perfect vantage point. The **plage de Ménéham**, 2km west of town, is a gem of a beach.

Brignogan town centre, 1km inland, is more of a traffic intersection than a destination in its own right – particularly now that its last hotel has closed down.

Plouguerneau

The inland village of **PLOUGUERNEAU**, just north of the main D10 road 20km west of Brignogan, serves as the administrative centre for several smaller communities. Prime among these is **LILIA**, a dramatic waterfront settlement at the tip of a headland 5km northwest.

Vierge lighthouse

Perched, clearly visible, on a tiny rocky islet 1.5km offshore from Lilia, the 82.5-metre **Vierge lighthouse** is considered to be the world's tallest "traditional lighthouse". It also marks the official southwestern limit of the English Channel. It's open to visitors in summer, but can only be accessed on boat trips from L'Aber-Wrac'h (see p.250).

Notre Dame de Grouannec

The church of **Notre Dame de Grouannec**, a small but complete parish close ensemble 4km southeast of Plouguerneau, is an unexpected pleasure. It has been extensively restored, and looks all the better for it, with its fountain, ossuary, mini-cloister and profusion of gargoyles.

L'Aber-Wrac'h

The *aber* between Plouguerneau and the yachting port of **L'ABER-WRAC'H** has a stepping-stone crossing just upstream from the bridge at Lannilis, built in Gallo-Roman times, where long cut stones still cross the three channels of water (access off the D28 signposted "Rascoll", and continue past farm buildings to the right).

L'Aber-Wrac'h itself – which you may well also see referred to as **Landéda**, although strictly speaking that's the name of a separate inland village – is a promising place to

5

DEATH OF A SUPERTANKER

On March 17, 1978, Finistère's rocky northwestern tip was the scene of a defining moment in Breton history, when the sinking of the **Amoco Cadiz** supertanker resulted in an **oil spill** that devastated 350km of the Breton coastline, and threatened to ruin the local economy.

The disaster unfolded barely a kilometre off shore from the small harbour of **Portsall**, 4km northwest of Ploudalmézeau. Displays and films in the **Espace Amoco Cadiz** here (July & Aug Mon–Thurs & Sun 10.30am–12.30pm & 2–7pm, Sat 2–7pm; mid-May to June, 1st half of Sept & school hols Thurs 2–5.30pm, Fri–Sun 10.30am–12.30pm & 2–5.30pm; free; ☎02 98 48 73 19) document not only the immense task of cleaning up the mess, but also the long legal battle to obtain compensation from the "multinational monster" responsible. The French government eventually obtained 1045 million francs in 1992, of which 100 million were passed on to local councils and communities.

The ship's huge **anchor** now stands in the car park across from the hall, while the wreck itself, 1100m offshore, has become a popular dive site.

spend a little time. An attractive, modest-sized resort, it lies within easy reach of a whole range of sandy **beaches** and a couple of worthwhile excursions. Beyond the tiny fishing port, which is home to a busy sailing school, the **Baie des Anges** stretches away towards the Atlantic, with the only sound the cry of seagulls feasting on the oyster beds.

Château de Trémazan

West of Portsall, the coast becomes a glorious succession of dunes and open spaces, with long beaches stretching at low tide way out towards tiny islands. Each little inlet here seems to shelter a treasure of a beach, ideal for family swimming, while bracing walks lead through the heather-covered headlands that abut the open sea.

One especially romantic spot comes just 5km beyond Portsall, where the crumbling walls of the *Sleeping Beauty*-style **château de Trémazan** look down on a magnificent beach. The fleeing Tristan and Iseult are said to have made their first landing in Brittany here, and the cracked ivy-covered keep still stands proud, pierced by a large heart-shaped hole. The castle is not formally open to the public; it's totally overgrown, and to reach it you have to scramble your way through the brambles that fill its former moat. Once you're here, however, it's a real haven for a summer afternoon.

If you are continuing west to Porspoder, pause to look at the exquisite wooden seaside **chapel of St Samson** on the way.

Porspoder

PORSPODER is a sleepy little resort, but does serve as a centre for the many campers who set themselves up on the dunes of the **Presqu'île St-Laurent** that lies opposite. It's an attractive place to be, looking out over the ocean, and relatively busy in season, but rather bleak in winter when many of the surrounding houses are unoccupied.

Le Conquet

LE CONQUET, the southernmost of the *abers* resorts, at the far western tip of Brittany 24km beyond Brest, makes the best holiday base in the region. A wonderful place, scarcely developed, it is flanked by a long **beach** of clean white sand, protected from the winds by the narrow spit of the Kermorvan peninsula, and has ferry access to the islands of Ouessant and Molène. It is very much a working fishing village, the grey-stone houses leading down to the stone jetties of a cramped harbour, which occasionally floods, to the intense amusement of the locals, the waves washing over the cars left by tourists making the trip to Ouessant – so leave your car slightly inland while visiting the island.

5

The **coast** around Le Conquet is low-lying, not the rocky confrontation that one might expect, and Kermorvan, across the estuary, seems to glide into the sea – its shallow cliffs topped by a strip of turf. Apart from the lighthouse at the end, the peninsula is just grassland, bare of buildings and a lovely place to walk in the evening across the footbridge from Le Conquet.

Pointe St-Mathieu

May & June Sat & Sun 2.30–6.30pm; July & Aug daily 10am–7.30pm; 1st half of Sept Mon & Wed–Sun 10am–12.30pm & 2–6.30pm; 2nd half of Sept & school hols Mon & Wed–Sun 2–6.30pm • €3 • ☎ 02 98 89 00 17

A good walk 4km south of Le Conquet brings you to the lighthouse at **Pointe St-Mathieu**, looking out to the islands of Ouessant and Molène from its site among the ruins of the Benedictine **Abbaye de St-Mathieu**. A small exhibition explains the abbey's history, including the legend that it holds the skull of St Matthew, brought here from Ethiopia by local seafarers.

ARRIVAL AND INFORMATION
THE ABERS

PLOUESCAT

By bus Roscoff to Lesneven buses stop at Plouescat before turning inland (4 daily; Roscoff 35min, Lesvenen 25min).

Tourist office 5 rue des Halles (Mon–Sat 9am–12.30pm & 1.30–5pm, plus Sun 10am–noon in July & Aug; ☎ 02 98 69 62 18, ⓦ tourisme-plouescat.com).

BRIGNOGAN-PLAGES

Tourist office 7 av de Gaulle (April–June & Sept Mon 9.30am–noon & 2–5.30pm, Sat 9.30am–noon; July & Aug Mon–Sat 9.30am–12.30pm & 2.30–6.30pm, Sun 10am–12.30pm; ☎ 02 98 83 41 08, ⓦ tourisme-lesneven -cotedeslegendes.fr).

PLOUGUERNEAU

Tourist office Place de l'Europe (July & Aug Mon–Sat 9.30am–12.30pm & 2–6.30pm, Sun 10.30am–12.30pm; Sept–June Mon–Sat 9.30am–noon & 2–5.30pm; ☎ 02 98 04 70 93, ⓦ abers-tourisme.com).

LE CONQUET

By bus Regular buses connect the port and town centre with Brest.

Destinations Brest (10 daily; 45min–1hr); Pointe St-Mathieu (2 daily; 10min).

Tourist office Parc Beauséjour (April–June & Sept Tues–Sat 10am–12.30pm & 2–6pm; July & Aug Mon–Sat 9.30am–1pm & 3–7pm, Sun 10am–1pm; Oct–March Tues–Sat 10am–12.30pm; ☎ 02 98 89 11 31, ⓦ tourismeleconquet.fr).

TOURS AND ACTIVITIES

L'ABER-WRAC'H

Boat tours In summer, to no fixed schedule, pleasure boats take a short cruise from the port to bob at the foot of the Vierge lighthouse (April–Sept; standard cruise €18.50; visits to the lighthouse itself €2.50; ☎ 02 98 04 74 94, ⓦ vedettes-des-abers.com).

Scuba diving The coastal waters nearby are prime territory for divers; boat trips can be arranged through Aber Wrac'h

Plongée (☎ 06 77 78 45 15, ⓦ aberwrachplongee.com).

LE CONQUET

Boat tours In addition to ferries to Ouessant and Molène (see p.254), Finist'Mer runs three or four daily cruises in the Molène archipelago, offering activities such as dolphin-spotting and birdwatching (no fixed schedules; €45–60; ☎ 08 25 13 52 35, ⓦ www.finist-mer.fr).

ACCOMMODATION AND EATING

PLOUESCAT

Camping de la Baie du Kernic ☎ 02 98 69 86 60, ⓦ village-center.com. Very pleasant campsite, 300m from the beach, with indoor and outdoor pools plus sports facilities and live entertainment in July & Aug. Closed Oct–March. **€24**

★ **Camping de Keremma** La Sablière, Tréflez ☎ 02 98 61 62 79, ⓦ campingdekeremma.fr. Lovely little village campsite, inland from the sea on the way between Plouescat and Brignogan, and set on a green avenue lined with meadows of purple-and-yellow flowers. Closed mid-Sept to mid-June. **€11**

Roc'h-Ar-Mor 18 rue Ar Mor, plage de Porsmeur ☎ 02 98 69 63 01, ⓦ rocharmor.com. Basic, bargain-priced hotel, aimed especially at walkers. Only some rooms have showers, and all share toilets; and though it's right on the beach at Porsmeur, none has a sea view. A bright, cheery dining room serves lunch from €13, dinner from €20. Closed Mon & Tues April–June & Sept–Nov, and only open Fri–Sun Dec–March. **€40**

BRIGNOGAN-PLAGES

Camping de la Côte des Légendes Rue Douar ar Pont ☎ 02 98 83 41 65, ⓦ campingcotedeslegendes.com.

Central three-star campsite, beside a good beach on the western side of the bay, north of the centre and 50m from the sailing school. Closed mid-Nov to Easter. **€15.80**

Camping du Phare Route du Phare ☎ 02 98 83 45 06, ⓦ camping-du-phare.com. Two-star campsite, right beside a good beach a short way east of Brignogan. Closed mid-Sept to March. **€12.90**

La Terre du Pont La Terre-du-Pont ☎ 02 98 83 58 49, ⓦ terredupont.com. Attractive fifteenth-century thatched cottage, 100m back from the beach, with bedroom and lounge, currently offered on a B&B basis but liable to be rented out on a weekly basis in future, with a garden and small pool, and bikes available for rent. Closed Nov–March. **€120**

LILIA

Castel Ac'h Plage de Lilia ☎ 02 98 37 16 16, ⓦ castelach .fr. The harbour makes a perfect setting for this low-slung modern hotel, which offers bright, well appointed sea-view rooms, plus a pool and an excellent seafood restaurant with dinner menus at €20 and €30. Closed early Nov to March, except Xmas/New Year. **€135**

L'ABER-WRAC'H

★ **La Baie des Anges** 350 rte des Anges ☎ 02 98 04 90 04, ⓦ baie-des-anges.com. At the start of the bay, a couple of hundred metres past the town's little strip of bars and restaurants, this irresistible hotel commands stunning views out to sea from the start of its vast curve. Consisting of several houses linked by modern extensions, it has a spacious guests-only bar with a small waterfront terrace, but no restaurant. So long as you're happy to pay €40 or so extra for one of the larger rooms, it makes an exceptionally comfortable and peaceful place to stay. Closed Feb. **€108**

Camping des Abers 51 Toull Tréaz, Landéda ☎ 02 98 04 93 35, ⓦ camping-des-abers.com. Three-star municipal campsite, nestled amid the dunes at the very tip of the headland, alongside a long beach and equipped with hedges to ward off the sea breezes, plus a seasonal grocery and snack bar. Bike rental and baby-sitting available. Closed Oct–April. **€17**

Camping Municipal de Penn Enez 551 Penn-Enez, Landéda ☎ 02 98 04 99 82, ⓦ camping-penn-enez .com. Perched atop the dunes, enjoying superb views across the fine beach below and out to sea, this welcoming little campsite has a bakery and grocery in July & Aug only. Closed Oct to mid-April. **€10.85**

Cap'tain 16 rte des Anges ☎ 02 98 04 82 03. Busy but friendly brasserie in the port proper, offering continuous service, especially crêpes and galettes but also any seafood speciality you care to name, with typical daily specials costing €15–20. Mon & Wed–Sun 11.45am–9.30pm; closed Jan to mid-Feb.

Prat-Ar-Coum Lieu-dit Prat Ar Coum, Lannilis ☎ 02 98 04 00 12, ⓦ prat-ar-coum.fr. Clearly signposted 4km west of L'Aber-Wrac'h, on the east shore of the next *aber* along, L'Aber-Benoît, these oyster beds are renowned for producing the best oysters in western Brittany. Although the small restaurant is open in summer only – when a full meal costs around €35 – a quayside stall sells them year round. July & Aug only Mon 7–9pm, Tues–Sat noon–2pm & 7–9pm.

PORSPODER

Château de Sable 38 rue de l'Europe ☎ 02 29 00 31 32, ⓦ lechateaudesablehotel.fr. Beautifully restored hotel, where the large, modern rooms have magnificent panoramic windows and private terraces or balconies; naturally, those that face the sea are very much more desirable. Dinner menus in the gourmet restaurant start at €42, though you can get a two-course lunch on weekdays for €20. **€155**

LE CONQUET

Les Blancs Sablons Kermorvan peninsula ☎ 02 98 89 06 90, ⓦ les-blancs-sablons.com. In July & Aug only, this well-equipped two-star campsite, in the splendid setting of the beach-lined Kermorvan peninsula, offers its own surf school, as well as wood-fired pizzas and a basic grocery. Closed Oct–March. **€16**

Hostellerie de la Pointe St-Mathieu Pointe St-Mathieu ☎ 02 98 89 00 19, ⓦ pointe-saint-mathieu.com. Housed in a thirteenth-century stone structure opposite the abbey entrance, 4km south of Le Conquet, this top-quality hotel has a modern wing of tasteful ocean-view rooms, an indoor swimming pool and a sauna. Its restaurant offers menus from €33 to €88 featuring everything from foie gras to blue lobster. Closed Feb & Sun eve in low season. **€104**

Relais du Vieux Port 1 quai Drellac'h ☎ 02 98 89 15 91, ⓦ lerelaisduvieuxport.com. A handful of inexpensive, attractive and nicely decorated rooms, right by the ferry jetty and mostly facing out to sea, plus a crêperie that also serves good seafood specials, with a full set dinner menu at €31. Closed Jan. **€56**

Ouessant and Molène

The island of **Ouessant** (Ushant in English), 30km northwest of Le Conquet, was first described by the geographer Pytheas as early as 325 BC, under the name of Uxisama, which means something along the lines of "the most remote". Standing at the

5

outermost end of a chain of smaller islands and half-submerged granite rocks, its lighthouse at Creac'h is regarded as the entrance to the English Channel. Most of the archipelago is uninhabited, save perhaps for a few rabbits, but **Molène**, midway between Le Conquet and Ouessant, has a village and can also be visited.

Both islands are served by at least one **ferry** each day from Le Conquet and Brest; however, it is not practicable to visit both in a single day. Ferries can be very crowded in summer, so book your **tickets** in advance if at all possible.

Ouessant

The ride to **OUESSANT** is generally a tranquil affair, though the ferry has to pick its way from buoy to buoy, through a sea which is liable suddenly to become choppy and dangerous. Of the many wrecks among the reefs, the most famous is the *Drummond Castle*, which foundered as the finale to a concert celebrating the end of its voyage from Cape Town to England in June 1896, with the loss of 234 lives. Despite its storms, though, the climate is mild – Ouessant even records the highest mean temperatures in France in January and February.

Ferries arrive on Ouessant at the modern **harbour** in the ominous-sounding Baie du Stiff. There's a scattering of houses here, and a small snack bar, but the only town (with the only hotels and restaurants) is 4km distant at **LAMPAUL**. Everyone from the boat heads there, either by the bus that meets each arriving ferry (€5 return to Lampaul, €15 for a full island tour; ☎06 73 87 82 28, ⓦouessant-voyages.com), by bike, or in a long walking procession that straggles along the one road.

As well as its more mundane facilities, Lampaul has Ouessant's best **beaches** sprawled around its bay. There are few specific sights, but the town **cemetery** is worth visiting, with its war memorial listing all the ships in which the townsfolk were lost, and its graves of unknown sailors washed ashore. A unique Ouessant tradition is also on show in the cemetery chapel – an array of wax *proëlla* crosses, which were used during the funerals of those islanders who never returned from the sea, to symbolize their absent remains.

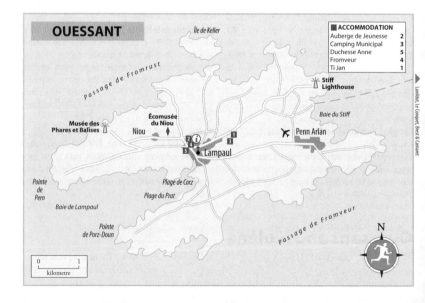

5

COASTAL WALKS FROM CREAC'H LIGHTHOUSE

The Creac'h lighthouse makes a good starting point from which to set out **walking** along the barren and exposed rocks of the north coast. Particularly in September and other migratory seasons, Ouessant is a remarkable spot for **birdwatching**, frequented by puffins, storm petrels and cormorants. The star-shaped formations of crumbling walls that you see everywhere were built so that the sheep – peculiarly tame here – could shelter from the strong winds.

Écomusée du Niou

1km northwest of Lampaul • April–June & Sept daily 11am–6pm in school hols, 11am–5pm otherwise; July & Aug daily 10.30am–6pm; Oct–March Tues–Sun 1.30–5.30pm • €3.50, or €7 for combined admission with the Musée des Phares et Balises • ☎02 98 48 86 37, ⓦ pnr-armorique.fr

Two houses and a few associated outbuildings at **NIOU**, a short walk northwest of Lampaul, collectively form the **Écomusée du Niou**, which is also known as the **Maisons du Niou**. One house contains a museum of island history, detailing how boys from the age of 11 used to embark on sea voyages of up to three years' duration, while the women were responsible for growing crops back home. The other is a reconstruction of a traditional island house, almost entirely filled by massive "box-beds", one of which was for the parents and the other for the children.

Musée des Phares et Balises

2km northwest of Lampaul • April–June & Sept daily 11am–6pm in school hols, 11am–5pm otherwise; July & Aug daily 10.30am–6pm, plus two varying nights each week 9–11pm; Oct–March Tues–Sun 1.30–5.30pm • €4.30 or €7 with Éco-Musée d'Ouessant • ☎ 02 98 48 80 70, ⓦ pnr-armorique.fr

The **Creac'h lighthouse**, towards the northwest corner of the island, was, when this, its third incarnation, opened in 1939, the most powerful in the world, with a 500-million-candlepower beam capable of being seen from England's Cape Lizard. You can't visit the lighthouse tower itself, but the complex at its base holds the **Musée des Phares et Balises**, a large museum about lighthouses and buoys. As well as providing a history of lighthouses from the Pharos of Alexandria and Roman examples, it's crammed with assorted lenses and mirrors, and has detailed displays on shipwrecks in the vicinity. None of the information is in English, however, and photography is not permitted.

Molène

MOLÈNE is quite well populated for a sparse strip of sand. As the port itself is better protected than that of Ouessant, more fishermen are based here. The island's inhabitants derive their income from seaweed collection and drying – and to an extent from crabs and crayfish, which they gather on foot, canoe and even tractor at low tide. Molène owes its name, which comes from the Breton for "the bald isle", to its exceptionally dramatic tides, which halve or double the island's territory at a stroke.

There are no real sights, and few visitors come for longer than an afternoon. Walking the rocks and the coast is the basic activity, though, as on Ouessant, the island **cemetery** is poignant and interesting. The concentration of babies' graves from a typhoid epidemic in the nineteenth century illustrates life in such a small community; marked by silver crosses, they're repainted each November 1.

INFORMATION AND GETTING AROUND | OUESSANT AND MOLÈNE

Tourist office and websites On the main square in Lampaul, Ouessant (mid-July to late Aug Mon–Sat 9am–6.30pm, Sun 9am–1pm; late Aug to mid-July Mon–Sat 10am–noon & 2–6pm; ☎02 98 48 85 83, ⓦ ot-ouessant .fr). Their website holds an extensive list of rental properties on the island. For information on Molène, including rental properties, visit ⓦ molene.fr.

Bike rental Renting a bike from one of the various operators at the port, for around €10–15 per day, is the most convenient way to see Ouessant, which is really too big to explore on foot. Many local tracks are uneven, so it's worth going for a (more expensive) mountain bike, but be warned it's illegal to cycle on the coastal footpaths.

5

GETTING TO OUESSANT AND MOLÈNE

FROM LE CONQUET

Penn Ar Bed offers one to six daily departures from Le Conquet to Ouessant all year, of which up to three stop at Molène. The timetables are extremely intricate, but broadly speaking the first sailing from Le Conquet is at 7.30am from mid-July to late Aug, and at 9am or 9.45am otherwise. **Finist'Mer** sails from Le Conquet to Ouessant three times daily, and to Molène once daily, between mid-July and late Aug only. Otherwise, they offer a single sailing to Ouessant most days between late April and late Sept.

FROM BREST

Penn Ar Bed operates one or two daily services from Brest to Ouessant all year, only one of which usually stops at Molène. The first sailing is always at either 8am or 8.20am.

FROM LANILDUT

Finist'Mer sails to Ouessant from Lanildut, 20km north of Le Conquet, once daily between mid-July and late Aug, and otherwise most Thurs between May and early Sept.

FROM CAMARET

Finist'Mer sails from Camaret to Ouessant on Wed only, at 9.10am, between late April and early July, and during Sept; Mon–Fri at 9.30am for the last 3 weeks of July; and daily at 9.30am in Aug. **Penn Ar Bed** also sails from Camaret to Ouessant at 8.45am daily except Sun, with some additional 11am sailings between mid-July and late Aug. During that same period, they offer one weekly sailing from Camaret to Molène, on either Thurs or Fri, and an additional daily sailing to Le Conquet, where you can pick up a separate boat to Molène. During the fortnights immediately before and afterwards, they offer an occasional departure from Camaret to Ouessant.

FERRY FARES AND CONTACT DETAILS

Penn Ar Bed all round-trip fares June–Sept €34.80, Oct–May €27.80, bikes €15.30 extra; ☎02 98 80 80 80, ⦿pennarbed.fr. **Finist'Mer** fares vary daily €25–34; ☎08 25 13 52 35, ⦿finist-mer.fr.

BY AIR

Finist'Air flies to Ouessant in just fifteen minutes from Brest's Guipavas airport all year – except, frustratingly, between late July and mid-Aug (Mon–Fri 8.30am & 4.45pm, Sat 8.30am; €46.70 each way; ☎02 98 84 64 87, ⦿www.finistair.fr).

ACCOMMODATION AND EATING

OUESSANT

Auberge de Jeunesse La Croix Rouge, Lampaul ☎02 98 48 84 53, ⦿auberge-ouessant.com. Little hostel, north of the centre towards Niou, where rates for beds in the dorms (sleeping two to six) include breakfast. Closed Dec & Jan. **€19.90**

Camping Municipal Penn ar Bed Stang ar Glann, Lampaul ☎02 98 48 84 65. Small municipal campsite, in the walled – and thus wind-free – enclosure of a former barracks on the eastern edge of town, beside the road in from the port and offering only basic facilities. Closed Oct–March. **€13.50**

Duchesse Anne Lampaul ☎02 98 48 80 25, ⦿hotel duchesseanne.fr. Nice little blue-trimmed hotel, just above the port in town (not the ferry harbour). Nine simply decorated en-suite rooms, of which the four that have sea views cost €11 extra, plus a restaurant serving fish-rich menus from €15.60. **€49**

Fromveur Rue du Fromveur, Lampaul ☎02 98 48 81 30, ⦿hotel-fromveur.fr. Hotel set a short walk back from the sea, just up the street near the church. The rooms have been reasonably renovated, and the traditional island cooking is pretty good, even if much of it does consist of attempting to render seaweed and mutton as palatable as possible. Expect to pay €14 for a set lunch. Closed mid-Nov to Jan. **€72**

Ti Jan Ar C'hafé Lampaul ☎02 98 48 82 64, ⦿tijan.fr. This attractively restored village house, in a peaceful setting with a pretty garden, offers eight tastefully decorated rooms but no restaurant. Closed mid-Nov to mid-Feb. **€99**

MOLÈNE

Kastell An Doal ☎02 98 05 15 63, ⦿molene.fr. Simple hotel in an old island house facing the port, where the rooms have great views but can get very chilly in winter. No restaurant, but there is a basic one nearby. Closed mid-Jan to mid-Feb. **€130**

Brest

Set in a magnificent natural harbour, known as the **Rade de Brest**, the city of **BREST** ranks among the great ports of France. Doubly sheltered from ocean storms by both the bulk of Léon to the north, and by the Crozon peninsula to the south, the Rade (or roadstead) is entered by the narrow deep-water channel of the Goulet de Brest, 5km long and 1.5km wide, with steep banks on both sides.

While Brest is a reasonably lively city, and its hilly site offers great sea views, it's not a place where many visitors linger. It sustained extensive damage during World War II, and beautification efforts have additionally been hampered by the fact that, despite the heaviest rainfall in France, Brest is a bit too windswept for flora to flourish. Despite the presence of its modern aquarium, **Océanopolis**, it only really draws in the crowds once every four years, during its spectacular **maritime festival** (due in 2016, 2020 etc).

Brief history

Brest has always played an important role in war, as well as in trade whenever peace allowed. All the great names in French strategic planning – including Richelieu, Colbert,

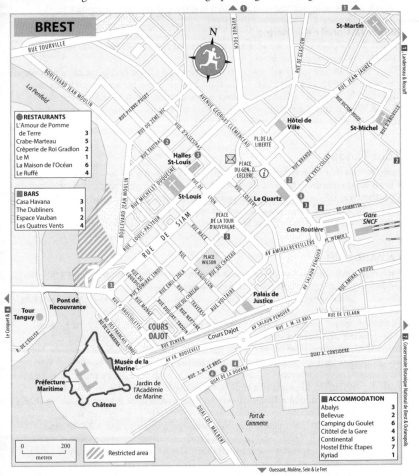

BREST

RESTAURANTS
L'Amour de Pomme de Terre	3
Crabe-Marteau	5
Crêperie de Roi Gradlon	2
Le M	1
La Maison de l'Océan	6
Le Ruffé	4

BARS
Casa Havana	3
The Dubliners	1
Espace Vauban	2
Les Quatres Vents	4

ACCOMMODATION
Abalys	3
Bellevue	2
Camping du Goulet	6
Citôtel de la Gare	4
Continental	5
Hostel Ethic Étapes	7
Kyriad	1

Restricted area

0 200 metres

Ouessant, Molène, Sein & Le Fret

5

Vauban and Napoleon – have been instrumental in developing the port, which is today the base of the French Atlantic Fleet. Its dry dock can accommodate ships of up to 500,000 tonnes, and it remains one of the largest ship-repair centres in the world.

During World War II, Brest was relentlessly bombed to prevent the Germans from using it as a submarine base. When the Americans liberated it on September 18, 1944, after a six-week siege, they found the city devastated beyond recognition. To help normal life resume as soon as possible, rebuilding was rushed at the expense of restoration, and the architecture of the postwar town is raw and bleak, echoing Le Havre in its preponderance of concrete.

Château de Brest

The one major site in Brest's city centre is its fifteenth-century **château**, perched on a headland above the point where the Penfeld River meets the bay, and offering a tremendous panorama of both the busy port and the roadstead. This site has been continuously occupied since at least the third century AD, when it held the fortified Roman camp of Osismis. Not quite as much of the castle survives as its impressive facade might suggest, though new buildings in the grounds still house the French naval headquarters.

Musée National de la Marine

Château de Brest • Feb, March & Oct–Dec Mon & Wed–Sun 1.30–6pm; April–Sept daily 10am–6.30pm; closed Jan • €6, under-26 free • ☎ 02 98 22 12 39, ⊕ www.musee-marine.fr/brest

Three still-standing medieval towers of the Château de Brest house the city's portion of the **Musée National de la Marine**. Collections include some ornate carved figureheads and models, as well as a German "pocket submarine" that was based in Brest during World War II, and visitors can stroll the parapets to enjoy the views. For motorists, there's also the boon of free parking right outside.

Tour Tanguy

Square Pierre Péron • June–Sept daily 10am–noon & 2–7pm; Oct–May Wed & Thurs 2–5pm, Sat & Sun 2–6pm • Free • ☎ 02 98 00 87 93

Down on the opposite bank of the Penfeld to the château, and reached via the **Pont de Recouvrance**, the largest drawbridge in Europe, the fourteenth-century **Tour Tanguy** is topped by a conical slate roof. It's now a museum of local history, where huge dioramas convey a vivid impression of just how attractive a city Brest used to be.

Océanopolis

Port de Plaisance du Moulin-Blanc • Hours vary enormously: 1st half of Feb, mid-March to mid-April, early Sept to mid-Oct & Nov to mid-Dec Tues–Sun 10am–5pm; mid-Feb to mid-March, mid-April to mid-July, late Aug to early Sept, 2nd half of Oct & Xmas/New Year daily 9.30am–6pm; mid-July to late Aug daily 9.30am–7pm; closed most of Jan • adults €18.60, under-18s €12.70 • ☎ 02 98 34 40 40, ⊕ oceanopolis.com • Bus #3

A state-of-the-art complex of **aquariums** and related attractions, Brest's futuristic and ever-growing **Océanopolis** sprawls a couple of kilometres east of the city centre. Its original white dome, now known as the **Temperate Pavilion**, focuses on the Breton littoral and Finistère's fishing industry, with its half-million gallons of water holding all kinds of fish, seals, molluscs, seaweed and sea anemones. The emphasis is very much on the edible, with displays on the life-cycle of a scallop, for example, culminating in a detailed recipe.

To that has been added a **Tropical Pavilion**, with a tankful of ferocious-looking sharks plus a myriad of rainbow-hued smaller fish that populate a highly convincing coral reef; a **Polar Pavilion**, complete with polar bears and penguins; and a **3-D cinema**. Everything's very high-tech, and perhaps a little too earnest for some visitors' tastes, but it's quite possible to spend a whole entertaining day on site – especially if you take the assorted restaurants, snack bars and gift stores into consideration.

Conservatoire Botanique National de Brest

5

52 allée du Bot **Gardens** daily: July to mid-Sept 9am–8pm; spring and autumn 9am–7pm; winter 9am–6pm • **Greenhouses** Easter–June & mid-Sept to mid-Nov Wed, Sat & Sun 2–5.30pm; July to mid-Sept daily 2–5.30pm • Gardens free, greenhouses €5 • ☎ 02 98 41 88 95, Ⓦ www.cbnbrest.fr • Bus #3, #17, #25 or #27, stop "Palaren"

Tucked into a lush valley not far north of Océanopolis, beyond the football stadium, the **Conservatoire Botanique National de Brest** claims to be the second-largest nursery for endangered plants in Europe, after Kew Gardens in London. In the gardens themselves, which form a free public park known as the Parc du Vallon de Stang-Alar, visitors can follow verdant footpaths all the way down to the sea. You can also pay to enter the greenhouses for close-up views of rare species.

ARRIVAL AND DEPARTURE

BREST

By plane Brest's airport, 9km northeast at Guipavas (Ⓦ brest.aeroport.fr), is served by flights from London City Airport on Cityjet, from Gatwick on EasyJet, and from Birmingham and Southampton on Flybe, and also offers local connections to Ouessant (see p.254). An airport shuttle bus runs regularly to the nearest tram stop, Porte de Guipavas (☎ 02 98 80 30 30, Ⓦ bibus.fr; €1.45 one-way). All the major car rental chains have desks at the airport.

By train Brest's *gare SNCF* is on place du 19ème RI at the bottom of avenue Clemenceau.
Destinations Le Mans (2 daily; 3hr 50min); Landerneau (23 daily; 15min); Landivisiau (8 daily; 20min); Morlaix (20 daily; 40min); Paris-Montparnasse (7 TGVs daily; 4hr

20min); Quimper (11 daily; 1hr 15min); Rennes (11 daily; 2hr–2hr 30min); St-Brieuc (10 daily; 1hr 20min).
By bus The *gare routière* stands shoulder-to-shoulder with the train station.
Destinations Brignogan (8 daily; 1hr); Camaret (1–3 daily; 1hr 10min); Le Conquet (8 daily; 45min); Le Faou (2 daily; 1hr); Quimper (5 daily; 1hr 15min); Roscoff (5 daily; 1hr 45min), via Plouescat, Lanhouarneau, Lesneven and St-Pol.
By boat As well as the sailings to Ouessant (see p.254), in summer boats make the 25min crossing from Brest's Port de Commerce to Le Fret on the Crozon peninsula (April–Sept daily 2 sailings each way; €9 one-way; ☎ 07 78 37 03 23, Ⓦ azenor.fr). They also offer trips around the Rade de Brest (1hr 30min €18; 3hr €32).

INFORMATION AND GETTING AROUND

Tourist office Avenue Clemenceau, facing place de la Liberté (July & Aug Mon–Sat 9.30am–7pm, Sun 9.30am–1.30pm; Sept–June Mon–Sat 9.30am–6pm; ☎ 02 98 44 24 96, Ⓦ brest-metropole-tourisme.fr).
By bus and tram Brest's extensive bus network has

recently been complemented by a new tram system, of most interest to visitors for offering quick connections between the city and the airport (☎ 02 98 80 30 30, Ⓦ bibus.fr; €1.45 per journey, €3.95 all-day pass)

ACCOMMODATION

★ **Abalys** 7 av Clemenceau ☎ 02 98 44 21 86, Ⓦ abalys .com. Small but good-value accommodation in a spruce little hotel above a bar near the stations. All rooms have en-suite facilities, though the bathrooms can be tiny, and most have computers with free wifi. **€55**
Bellevue 53 rue Victor-Hugo ☎ 02 98 80 51 78, Ⓦ www .hotelbellevue.fr. Six-storey building, equipped with a lift and bright, modern but not very fancy rooms. A short walk from the *gare SNCF* and well on the way to the lively St-Martin area, near the St-Michel church. Distant sea views. **€65**
Camping du Goulet Ste-Anne du Portzic ☎ 02 98 45 86 84, Ⓦ campingdugoulet.com. This leafy, four-star, year-round campsite, which has a snack bar and a pool with water-slides, is hard to find, on a headland close to the sea on the outskirts of Brest 8km from the centre, across the Pont de Recouvrance and then to the left of the Le Conquet road (D789) – take bus #7 or #14 from the *gare SNCF*. **€21.50**
Citôtel de la Gare 4 bd Gambetta ☎ 02 98 44 47 01, Ⓦ hotelgare.com. Convenient, good-value option very

near the stations. Pay a little extra to get a magnificent view of the Rade de Brest from the upper storeys. Cheaper weekend rates, and buffet breakfast for €8.50. **€64**
Continental Place de la Tour d'Auvergne ☎ 02 98 80 50 40, Ⓦ oceaniahotels.com. Despite the dull concrete facade, this grand hotel has some fine Art Deco features, and is very popular with business travellers. Spotless rooms; several on the fourth floor have large balconies. **€80**
Hostel Ethic Étapes 5 rue Kerbriant, Port de Plaisance du Moulin-Blanc ☎ 02 98 41 90 41, Ⓦ aj-brest.org. Brest's year-round hostel, set in a wooded park, is modern and clean, with beds in four-person dorms and inexpensive meals. Rates include breakfast. It's 3km east of the *gare SNCF*, by the beach and Océanopolis – take bus #3. **€19.40**
Kyriad 157 rue Jean-Jaurès ☎ 02 98 43 58 58, Ⓦ kyriad .com. Although the rooms are on the sterile and small side, this hotel enjoys a good location near the town's nightlife, has good buffet breakfasts, and is close to a free public car park. **€63**

5

EATING AND DRINKING

L'Amour de Pomme de Terre 23 rue des Halles ☎02 98 43 48 51, ⓦamourdepommedeterre.fr. The name says it all: this central restaurant, facing the market *halles*, specializes not merely in potatoes, but in one single kind of potato, the "samba". The most basic dish is simply a baked potato topped with cheese or sausage, but the eccentric owner has also invented all kinds of strange treatments and concoctions, typically costing just under €20, and there are also some tasty Breton stews. Mon–Thurs & Sun noon–2.30pm & 7–10pm, Fri & Sat noon–2.30pm & 7–11pm.

Casa Havana 2 rue de Siam ☎02 98 80 42 87, ⓦcasa-havana.fr. Lively Latin American cocktail bar that offers an extensive tapas menu and puts on free dance classes every night except Sat, with salsa Mon–Thurs, and late-night dancing on Thurs & Fri. Daily 2pm–1am.

Le Crabe-Marteau 8 quai de la Douane ☎02 98 33 38 57, ⓦcrabemarteau.fr. Once again, it's all in the name at this quayside restaurant; take one crab, add one wooden hammer, and there's your meal, costing in its definitive form €23. Dressed and baked crab starters cost €8–12, and they also serve oysters, lobsters and mixed platters by way of variety. Mon–Sat noon–2.30pm & 7–10.30pm.

Crêperie de Roi Gradlon 19 rue Fautras ☎02 98 80 17 28. This friendly and very popular neighbourhood restaurant deserves its sky-high reputation for serving the best savoury and sweet crêpes in the city, with menus starting at just €10. Tues–Sat 10am–3pm & 6.15–10.15pm.

The Dubliners 28 rue Mathieu-Donnart ☎02 98 46 04 98. Lively Irish pub in the St-Martin district, about 10min walk from St-Martin church, with Irish dancing on Mon and live music on Thurs & Sun, and rugby on the TV whenever possible. Mon–Thurs & Sun 3pm–1am, Fri & Sat 3pm–2am.

Le M 22 rue du Commandant-Drogou ☎02 98 47 90 00, ⓦle-m.fr. Smart and very fashionable Michelin-starred restaurant, north of the centre, with a garden terrace, serving daily changing menus of exquisite meat and fish dishes; prices start at €50. Mon–Sat noon–1.30pm & 7.30–9.30pm; closed 3 weeks in Jan and second fortnight in Aug.

★ **La Maison de l'Océan** 2 quai de la Douane ☎02 98 80 44 84, ⓦrestaurant-fruit-mer-brest.com. Blue-hued fish restaurant down by the port, with a terrace facing across to the island ferries. It serves wonderful seafood on menus from €18.55 – which features a mixed shellfish assortment – to €42.40. Daily noon–2pm & 7–11pm.

Les Quatres Vents 18 quai de la Douane ☎02 98 44 42 84, ⓦles-4-vents.com. Busy, friendly and ever-expanding portside café-bar, which also doubles as a brasserie, and has a nautical-themed interior plus a waterfront terrace. Daily 9am–1am.

Le Ruffé 1bis rue Yves-Collet ☎02 98 46 07 70, ⓦle-ruffe.com. Unpretentious, very reliable restaurant between the *gare SNCF* and the tourist office, entirely indoors, which prides itself on serving tasty, traditional French seafood dishes, and a good-value wine list. Weekday lunch *formules* start at €14.80, dinner menus cost €24.90 and €36. Tues–Sat noon–2pm & 6–10pm, Sun noon–2pm.

NIGHTLIFE AND ENTERTAINMENT

During the first weekend of July, Brest hosts an electronic music festival, **Astropolis** (ⓦastropolis.org), while every Thursday from mid-July until the end of August is party night at the port, with free music and other performances on three stages along the quai de la Douane.

Espace Vauban 17 av Clemenceau ☎02 98 46 06 88, ⓦespacevauban.com. Beautifully converted century-old hotel that's now primarily a concert hall, putting on an extensive programme of music and live performance, but also incorporates a bar and restaurant, and still holds a hotel. Tues–Thurs noon–2pm & 7–10.30pm, Fri & Sat noon–2pm & 7–11.30pm.

Le Quartz 60 rue du Château ☎02 98 33 70 70, ⓦlequartz.com. This prestigious national performance space, in the heart of the city, welcomes touring dance, theatre and musical companies.

The Crozon Peninsula

Though the spectacular **Crozon Peninsula**, thrusting out into the Atlantic between Léon and Cornouaille, is almost entirely given over to tourism, its wild beaches and craggy cliffs remain remarkably unspoiled, and it's hard to beat as a family destination. This whole dramatic promontory forms part of the **Parc Naturel Régional d'Armorique**, a protected natural landscape that stretches from the forest of Huelgoat to the island of Ouessant.

Even though the western, oceanward end of the peninsula holds its largest towns and the lion's share of its tourist facilities, nowhere is overrun, and the atmosphere remains

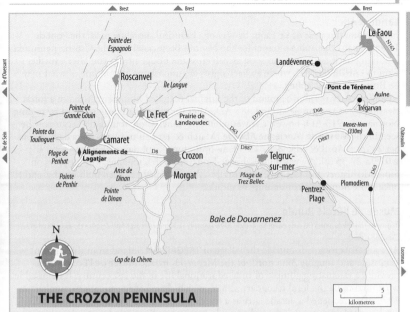

THE CROZON PENINSULA

essentially peaceful. **Crozon** is the largest town, but it makes sense to head straight on either to the classic traditional resort of **Morgat**, arrayed along a splendid curve of golden sand, or **Camaret**, a historic port with a sideline in superlative seafood restaurants.

The inland approaches

Cyclists and pedestrians heading south from Brest can cut straight over to the Crozon Peninsula by **ferry** to Le Fret (see p.263). The ferry doesn't, however, carry cars, so **drivers** have a longer and more circuitous route, crossing the Elorn River over the vast spans of the **Pont Albert-Louppe** (42m high and almost 1km long) and then skirting the estuaries of the **Plougastel peninsula**.

Abbaye de Daoulas

1km south of E60, 20km southeast of Brest • Only open during exhibitions, usually April to early July & Nov to New Year daily 1.30–6.30pm; early July to Oct daily 10.30am–7pm • €7 for abbey, gardens and exhibition • ☎ 02 98 25 84 39, ⓦ cdp29.fr

Although the **Abbaye de Daoulas** was comprehensively destroyed during the Revolution, its former site now holds Brittany's only **Romanesque cloister**, left standing beautiful and isolated at the edge of cool monastery gardens. The abbey gardens make a welcome oasis on a hot summer's day, and also hold a separate, modern museum building, which each year stages a temporary but large-scale exhibition on some historical or archeological theme. There's also a crêperie and a restaurant.

Le Faou

From Daoulas, the motorway and railway cut down to Châteaulin and Quimper. For Crozon, you'll need to veer west at **LE FAOU**, a tiny medieval port that has retained some of its sixteenth-century gabled houses and is set on its own estuary. From beside the pretty little village **church** – whose porch contains some intriguing carved apostles – a sheltered corniche follows the river to the sea, where there are sailing and windsurfing facilities.

5

Landévennec

Nine kilometres west of Le Faou, by way of a beautiful shoreline road, the **Pont de Térénez** spans the Aulne – outlet for the Nantes–Brest canal – to the Crozon peninsula. Doubling back to the right as soon as you cross the bridge brings you after a further 5km to **LANDÉVENNEC**, where archaeologists are uncovering the outline of what may be Brittany's oldest **abbey**.

Nothing survives above ground of the original thatched hut, constructed in a forest clearing by St Gwennolé around 485 AD. After the abbey had been pillaged by raiding Normans in 913 AD, however, it was rebuilt in stone. Those foundations can now be seen in the **Musée de l'Ancienne Abbaye** (March & 1st half of Oct & Nov daily except Sat 2–5pm; April & May daily 10.30am–6pm; June–Sept daily 10.30am–7pm; €5; ☎02 98 27 35 20, ⓦwww.musee-abbaye-landevennec.fr), together with displays on monastic history and facsimile manuscripts. A new abbey has been built nearby, and is once more home to a community of monks.

Musée de l'École Rurale

Trégarvan • Mid-Feb to June & Oct daily except Sat 2–6pm; July & Aug daily 10.30am–7pm; Sept daily 2–6pm • €5 • ☎ 02 98 26 04 72, ⓦ musee-ecole.fr

At a solitary crossroads outside the village of **TRÉGARVAN**, inland from the Crozon Peninsula and roughly 3km north of the Menez-Hom, the **Musée de l'École Rurale** provides a fascinating glimpse of rural educational life in the last century. It's housed in what used to be the local secondary school, which closed owing to lack of numbers in 1974, then reopened a decade later as a recreation of a Breton classroom circa 1920.

A hundred years ago, all the kids would have spoken Breton at home – but they were forbidden to speak it here. The teacher gave a little wooden cow to the first child to utter a word in the mother tongue, and they could get rid of the *vache* only by squealing on the next offender.

The Menez-Hom

For an initial overview of the layout of the Crozon Peninsula, it's worth climbing the **Menez-Hom** at its inland, eastern end. Even if, at just 330m, this is hardly the "mountain" its Breton name suggests, the summit stands sufficiently alone to command tremendous views across the peninsula – a chaos of water, with lakes, rivers and bridges wherever you look, and usually a scattering of hang-gliders dangling in the sky. The exposed and windswept viewing table reveals it to be 300 miles (483km) from both London and Paris. A spur road leads straight to the top from the D887, starting from the opposite side of the hill to Trégarvan, 12km west of Châteaulin.

St-Nic and Telgruc-sur-Mer

Southwest from the Menez-Hom, a magnificent road sweeps down across the heather onto the Crozon peninsula. At the foot of the hill, to the south, **ST-NIC** has excellent beaches (at Pentrez-Plage) – this is the sandy side of the peninsula. The principal village hereabouts, **PLOMODIERN**, stands 5km inland, and offers further accommodation possibilities.

Further round towards Crozon, the village of **TELGRUC-SUR-MER** is poised well above the sea, leaving the gorgeous **Trez Bellec** beach below remarkably pristine for most of the year, though in high summer countless caravans seem to fill the meadows just behind it.

Crozon

The main town on the Crozon Peninsula proper, **CROZON** itself, has a nice little stone-built core that serves as the commercial hub for all the surrounding communities, and plays host to a large-scale **market** on the second and fourth Wednesday of each month. Set well

CLOCKWISE FROM TOP SURFERS, CROZON PENINSULA (P.258); TRADITIONAL BRETON PUDDINGS AT THE MARKET IN CONCARNEAU (P.261); A CARVING OF ANKOU AT THE CHURCH OF LA ROCHE-MAURICE (P.246) >

5

> ### THE GROTTES
>
> The most popular **cruise** from Morgat is the 45-minute tour out to the **Grottes** (April to late Sept daily, departure times depend on tides; €14; ☎ 06 85 95 55 49, ⓦ grottes-morgat.fr). From these multicoloured caves in the cliffs, accessible only by sea but with steep "chimneys" up to the clifftops, saints are said to have emerged in bygone days to rescue the shipwrecked. Even though the boats depart every quarter of an hour in high season, they often leave full, so it's worth booking a few hours in advance.

back from the sea, it's also, unfortunately, a traffic hub, with a one-way traffic system that's always busy distributing tourists among the various resorts, so it's more of a place to pass through than to linger. If you're staying anywhere nearby, however, you'll probably drop in to shop and while away an hour or two in its bars and cafés.

At the end of July and/or the start of August, the Festival du Bout du Monde, a **world music festival**, takes place on the Prairie de Landaoudec immediately north of Crozon (ⓦ festivalduboutdumonde.com).

Morgat

Just down the hill from Crozon, though not separated by any noticeable gap, **MORGAT** makes a more enticing base than its larger, landlocked neighbour. Its long and very sandy crescent **beach**, much loved by windsurfers, ends beneath a pine slope, while the well-sheltered harbour is filled with pleasure boats raced down from England and Ireland.

Other than swimming and sunbathing, the main attractions are **boat trips** around the various headlands, such as the **Cap de la Chèvre**, which can also be reached by a bracing and hugely enjoyable clifftop walk.

Camaret

One of the loveliest seaside towns in all Brittany, the sheltered port of **CAMARET** nestles at the western tip of the peninsula. A long jetty runs parallel to the main town waterfront, sheltering it from the open sea. Beyond the quay at the far end of the harbour, assorted headlands offer pretty **beaches** and fine clifftop hiking, while the heathland to the south boasts some haunting **megalithic alignments**.

In 1801, an American, Robert Fulton, tested the first **submarine** off Camaret. The *Nautilus* was a stuffy, leaking, oar-powered wooden craft, whose five-man crew spent some time scuttling about beneath the waves in the hope of sinking a British frigate. Fulton was denied his glory, though, when the frigate chose to sail away, ignorant of the heavy-breathing peril that was so frantically seeking it out.

Tour Vauban

Foursquare at its far end of the jetty, directly across from the port, the prominent, pink-orange **Tour Vauban** was built in 1689 to guard the approaches to Brest. Walled, moated, and accessible via a little gatehouse reached by means of a drawbridge, it now guards no more than a picturesque assortment of decaying half-submerged fishing boats, abandoned to rot beside the jetty.

At the time this book went to press, the Tour Vauban was closed for extensive restoration; it may have reopened to visitors by the time you read this.

The beaches

The largest and most attractive **beach** near Camaret is a couple of kilometres east, beside the main D8 from Crozon, in the low-lying (and rather marshy) Anse de Dinan. Much closer to town, the small sandy **plage du Correjou**, popular with families, starts on the seaward side of the jetty and stretches west.

COASTAL WALKS FROM CAMARET

A network of wonderful coastal footpaths leads westwards from Camaret's town beach, winding over and/or around successive headlands. The scenery is utterly magnificent, with craggy rocks and sea arches standing just off the heather-topped cliffs, though the dramatic **Plage de Penhat**, just west of the Pointe du Toulinguet, is much too exposed to the ocean to be safe for swimming.

Immediately inland from the Plage de Penhat, the **Manoir de St Pol Roux** was built by Symbolist poet Pierre Paul Roux in 1904, and subsequently smashed into photogenic ruins by the elements. The round-trip walk from the port past the headlands and back into Camaret takes between one and two hours, though a six-hour version continues out to the Pointe du Penhir and back.

Alignements de Lagatjar

D8 · Unrestricted 24hr access · Free

Beside the D8, on the southern fringes of Camaret – and just across a minor road from the *Manoir de St Pol Roux*, stand the megalithic **Alignements de Lagatjar**. Two centuries ago, six hundred standing stones were counted here. Only 65 of those remain, and many of those are now little more than weather-beaten stumps, jutting out amid the brilliant purples and yellows of the heathland. They're still impressive here at the end of the world, however, and starkly beautiful. Their name means "eye of the chicken", and comes from the Breton name for the Pleiades constellation. Archeologists say they were originally arranged in four distinct lines rather than a circle, and suggest that the open area in the middle was used for rituals or even games.

Pointe du Penhir

At the **Pointe du Penhir**, 3km south of Camaret, footpaths lace around the various exposed and windy headlands, frequented mainly by binocular-toting twitchers eyeing up the guillemots and other seabirds that swoop on the **Tas de Pois** rock stacks, scattered out in the sea. Some intrepid individuals abseil their way down similar rock stacks still attached to the mainland; here and there, a few paths pick their way down the sheer cliffs, but most peter out in the little natural amphitheatre that faces the Tas de Pois.

A monument to the Breton Resistance stands nearby, while an intricate set of wartime German bunkers, marked by a row of black anchors, serves as a memorial to the role of merchant ships in the Battle of the Atlantic.

Pointe des Espagnols

Heading north from Camaret or Morgat brings you to the **Pointe des Espagnols**, where a viewing point signals the northern tip of the peninsula. Brest is very close and very visible – without being any the more enticing. Around the cape are several forbidden military installations and abandoned wartime bunkers. You're not allowed to leave the road, and neither are you encouraged to turn the provided telescope towards the nuclear submarine base on the Île Longue.

Le Fret

The diminutive but delightful port village of **LE FRET**, on the northern shore of the peninsula 5km east of Camaret and 5km north of Crozon, is noteworthy mainly for its seasonal **ferry** service to Brest's Port du Commerce. It only has the tiniest of beaches, but the lagoon nearby is much frequented by birdwatchers.

ARRIVAL AND DEPARTURE   THE CROZON PENINSULA

CAMARET

By bus Trains do not serve the Crozon Peninsula, but

Penn-ar-Bed buses (☎08 10 81 00 29, 🌐viaoo29.fr) connect Camaret with Quimper (4–8 daily; 1hr 30min) via

5

Locronan, Plomodiern, St-Nic, Telgruc-sur-Mer and Crozon, and with Brest (4–8 daily; 1hr 30min) via Le Faou, Landévennec, Telgruc-sur-Mer, Crozon and Morgat.

By boat In summer, ferries run from Camaret to the islands of Ouessant (see p.254) and Sein (see p.271).

LE FRET

By boat In summer, passenger-only ferries connect Le Fret with the Port de Commerce in Brest (April–Sept daily 2 sailings each way; €9 one-way; ☎07 78 37 03 23, ⊛azenor.fr).

INFORMATION AND ACTIVITIES

TELGRUC-SUR-MER

Tourist office 6 rue du Menez-Hom (July & Aug Mon–Sat 9.30am–12.30pm & 2–7pm, Sun 9.30am–12.30pm; ☎02 98 27 78 06, ⊛tourisme-presquiledecrozon.fr).

CROZON

Tourist office The peninsula's main tourist office, at 1 bd de Pralognan-la-Vanoise, a little way west of the centre in the *gare routière*, also houses an SNCF ticket office (July & Aug Mon–Sat 9.30am–1pm & 2–7pm, Sun 10am–1pm; Sept–June Mon–Sat 9.30am–noon & 2–6pm; ☎02 98 27 07 92, ⊛tourisme-presquiledecrozon.fr).

MORGAT

Tourist office Place d'Ys (June & Sept Mon 9.30am–12.30pm; July & Aug Mon–Wed 9.30am–12.30pm &

3–7pm, Thurs–Sun 2.30–7.30pm; ☎02 98 27 29 49, ⊛tourisme-presquiledecrozon.fr).

Bike and kayak rental From the splendidly named Crapato Bicyclo, next to the tourist office on the boulevard de la Plage (mid-June to mid-Sept daily 9am–7pm; bike €14 per day, kayak €25 per day; ☎06 88 71 72 22, ⊛crapato.com).

Sailing and kayaking The Centre Nautique de Crozon-Morgat offers summer classes in sailing, kayaking and surfing, and rents the relevant equipment (☎02 98 16 00 00, ⊛cncm.fr).

CAMARET

Tourist office 15 quai Kléber (July & Aug Mon–Sat 9.15am–12.30pm & 2–7pm, Sun 10am–noon; Sept–June Mon–Sat 9.15am–noon & 2–6pm; ☎02 98 27 93 60, ⊛camaretsurmer-tourisme.fr).

ACCOMMODATION AND EATING

DAOULAS

Ar Baradoz Bihan 12 rue de l'Église ☎02 98 85 04 87, ⊛arbaradozbihan.pagesperso-orange.fr. Charming B&B in a seventeenth-century townhouse in the pretty little village of Daoulas, immediately below the abbey, with four-poster beds; the name, meaning "little Garden of Eden", refers to the walled garden. Closed Nov–March. **€60**

LE FAOU

Relais de la Place 7 place aux Foires ☎02 98 81 91 19, ⊛lerelaisdelaplace.com. Reasonable, somewhat faded Logis de France hotel, a few hundred metres south of the river in the newer and much noisier main square. Meals in the restaurant start at €17.80, with a good €29 *Menu du Terroir*. **€63**

★**Viviers de Térénez** Route Térénez, Rosnoën ☎02 98 81 90 68, ⊛lesviviers.fr. Simple roadside seafood shack, in a spectacular spot by the estuary 6.5km west of Le Faou, where they harvest and/or raise oysters, clams, mussels, crabs and lobsters, and also have their own smokehouse. Enjoy plates of whatever you fancy, typically priced at €10–16, at waterfront trestle tables, or buy them by weight to take away. You can also rent kayaks for an after-lunch jaunt on the river. Feb–June & Sept–Dec Mon–Sat 10am–7pm, Sun 10am–noon; July & Aug daily 10am–9pm.

LANDÉVENNEC

Le St-Patrick 16 rue St-Guénolé ☎02 98 27 70 83, ⊛le-saint-patrick.fr. Small but attractive guesthouse in

a former bistro in the heart of Landévennec, where the large, homely rooms share bathrooms. Rates shown do not include breakfast, at €7 per person; evening meals also available in July & Aug. Closed Oct–Easter. **€39**

ST-NIC

Menez Bichen Chemin des Dunes ☎02 98 26 50 82, ⊛menezbichen.fr. Three-star family campsite on lawns beside a lovely, long sandy beach; in July & Aug they offer daily kids' activities plus nightly entertainment and/or themed dinners. Closed mid-Nov to Feb. **€16.75**

PLOMODIERN

★**Auberge des Glazicks** 7 rue de la Plage ☎02 98 81 52 32, ⊛porz-morvan.fr. A real unexpected pleasure; once a blacksmith's workshop, and later the village inn, run by the grandmother of current owner, chef Olivier Bellin, this venerable structure is now an expensive but truly memorable hotel/restaurant. Menus in the dining room, awarded two Michelin stars for its modern French cuisine, start at €55 for lunch, €75 for dinner (closed Mon & Tues, plus Sun eve in low season); the spacious rooms also feature the latest contemporary design. **€200**

Hôtel-Crêperie de Pors Morvan Route de Lescuz ☎02 98 81 53 23, ⊛porz-morvan.fr. Very pleasant little hotel, 3km east, inland, from Plomodiern, with a dozen light, good-value rooms in the converted outbuildings of an old farm, and an inexpensive crêperie in the oak-beamed farmhouse itself. Closed Nov–March. **€56**

TELGRUC-SUR-MER

Panoramic Penquer ☏ 02 98 27 78 41, ⊛ camping -panoramic.com. Four-star campsite, perched on a craggy, heather-covered hillside 1km from the village and 700m above the western end of Trez Bellec beach, with a heated swimming pool, bike rental and a grocery and snack bar. Closed mid-Sept to April. **€22**

Pen Bellec Plage de Trez Bellec ☏ 06 16 55 03 49, ⊛ camping-telgruc.fr. Verdant little two-star campsite at the eastern end of a magnificent unspoiled beach. Closed Oct–May. **€16**

CROZON

De la Presqu'île Place de l'Église ☏ 02 98 27 29 29, ⊛ hotel-lapresquile.fr. Simple, very welcoming Logis de France on the main market square in Crozon, 1.5km from the sea. The rooms are rather small and old-fashioned, but the restaurant, the *Mutin Gourmand*, is truly excellent, serving seafood-rich menus at €26 and €39. Closed Nov. **€80**

MORGAT

Camping Les Pins Route de la Pointe du Dinan ☏ 06 60 54 40 09, ⊛ camping-crozon-lespins.com. Shaded three-star site, well up from the sea above town, with a covered heated swimming pool. Closed Nov–Easter. **€20.50**

Camping Plage de Goulien Kernavéno ☏ 06 08 43 49 32, ⊛ camping-crozon-laplagedegoulien.com. Three-star campsite, just across the headland from Morgat and a few steps from a huge sandy beach. Pitches amid the trees, with an on-site grocery. Closed mid-Sept to mid-April. **€21.50**

De la Baie 46 bd de la Plage ☏ 02 98 27 07 51, ⊛ hoteldelabaie-crozon-morgat.com. Cream-and-blue hotel, in the heart of the main beachfront promenade, that offers plain but good-value en-suite rooms. The cheapest are in an annexe at the back; you'll pay around €20 extra for a sea-view room in the main building, which also holds a tea room. **€49**

Julia 43 rue de Tréflez ☏ 02 98 27 05 89, ⊛ hoteljulia.fr. Neat, quiet hotel in an impressive villa set 300m back from the beach, with comfortable single to family-sized rooms, some of which have sea views. Closed Jan & Feb. **€78**

★ **Kastell Dinn** Hameau de Kerlouantec ☏ 02 98 27 26 40, ⊛ sejour-insolitebretagne.com. Absolute one-of-a-kind B&B, in a gorgeous little village atop the headland, 2km west of Morgat. One "room" consists of a boat equipped with a thatched roof; one's a stone cottage with an upturned boat for a roof; and another is a wheeled wooden caravan. There are also a couple of conventional rooms in a converted granary. Rates do not include breakfast, at €6 per person. **€55**

Kermaria 1 bd de la Plage ☏ 02 98 26 20 02, ⊛ kermaria.com. Luxury B&B, set in a grand, somewhat formal house and featuring high ceilings, leather armchairs and lots of polished wood, with gardens that lead directly onto the beach. Closed Oct–March. **€105**

Saveurs et Marée 52 bd de la Plage ☏ 02 98 26 23 18, ⊛ saveurs-et-maree.com. The pick of Morgat's crop of beachfront seafood restaurants, with the bonus of outdoor seating. Dinner menus €17.50–49. April–Sept daily noon–2pm & 7–10pm; Oct–March Wed–Sun noon–2pm & 7–10pm.

CAMARET

Camping Le Grand Large Lambézen ☏ 02 98 27 91 41, ⊛ campinglegrandlarge.com. Four-star campsite, 2km east of the port and 500m up from the nearest beach, but offering nicely secluded grass pitches, plus a pool with waterslide and great views. Closed Oct–March. **€23.70**

Camping Lannic Rue du Grouannoc'h ☏ 02 98 27 91 31, ⊛ camaret-sur-mer.com. High-quality, two-star municipal campsite, set back from the sea, 1km up the hill in town. Closed Nov–March. **€14**

Côté Mer 12 quai Toudouze ☏ 02 98 27 93 79. All-day brasserie service, with a €17 menu that's available for lunch and dinner on weekdays only, a €29 set menu with options including nine oysters and panfried scallops, and a €56 lobster menu. Daily noon–10pm; closed Wed & Thurs in low season.

Les Frères de la Côte 11 quai Toudouze ☏ 06 78 75 57 54, ⊛ breiz-ile.fr. Camaret's finest seafood restaurant, a funky little place that's open to the harbour and serves fresh fish accompanied by sauces and spices influenced by the owner's Guadaloupe origins. The €13 weekday lunch is a real bargain, while the €27 *Menu Caraïbes* offers a memorable dinner. Mid-March to Sept daily 12.15–1.30pm & 7.15–9.30pm.

Du Styvel 2 quai du Styvel ☏ 02 98 27 92 74, ⊛ hotel-du-styvel.com. Friendly seaside hotel, with a decent restaurant. Ten of the thirteen small but comfortable en-suite rooms have harbour-view balconies. Closed Jan. **€59**

★ **Vauban** 4 quai du Styvel ☏ 02 98 27 91 36, ⊛ hotel vauban-camaret.fr. Plain but exceptionally hospitable and more than adequate quayside hotel, with a simple brasserie (closed Sun eve, all Mon & Tues lunch). Rooms at the front look right out across the bay. Rates remain constant year round; the one family room does not have a sea view. **€45**

LE FRET

★ **Hostellerie de la Mer** 11 quai le Fret ☏ 02 98 27 61 90, ⊛ hotel.hostelleriedelamer.com. Very charming hotel on the pretty quayside, with nicely decorated rooms and a restaurant serving menus from €28 to €76. Restaurant closed Sat lunch, Sun eve & all Mon; hotel closed Jan. **€69**

5

Locronan

The exquisite hilltop village of **LOCRONAN**, a short way from the sea on the minor road that leads southeast to Quimper from the Crozon peninsula, is a prime example of a Breton town that has remained frozen in its ancient form. Owing to a drastic downturn in its economic fortunes, the rich medieval houses at its core have never been superseded or surrounded by modern development.

Now, thanks to steady throngs of tourists, Locronan is thriving once more. The village itself is genuinely remarkable, centring on a postcard-perfect cobbled square, complete with ancient well, from which narrow lanes radiate, lined with gorgeous old cottages bedecked in flowers, and leading into rolling open fields. Small wonder that film directors love Locronan, even if Roman Polanski, to film *Tess*, deemed it necessary to change all the porches, put new windows on the Renaissance houses, and bury the main square in mud to make it all look a bit more English.

Brief history

From 1469 through to the seventeenth century, Locronan was a hugely successful centre for woven linen, supplying sails to the French, English and Spanish navies. Medieval ships would gather in nearby Douarnenez to be piloted together up the treacherous coast of Finistère; as they waited for a convoy to form, they'd repair their sails with cloth from Locronan. As the rival ports of Brest and Lorient rose to prominence, and Louis XIV's minister Colbert forbade the export of sailcloth to England, Locronan declined. The death knell came with the advent of broad-loomed weaving machines during the eighteenth century; its traditional crafts workers simply could not compete.

Église St-Ronan

The fifteenth-century **Église St-Ronan** in Locronan's main square holds the tomb of St Ronan himself, a sixth-century preacher from Ireland who's credited with founding the town's first chapel. Elaborate carvings around the pulpit recount his struggle to establish Christianity in Brittany – look out for the blonde devil-woman, known as the Keben, who attempts to thwart his every move.

Musée d'Art et d'Histoire

Place de la Mairie • Feb–June & Sept Mon–Fri 10am–noon & 2–6pm; July & Aug Mon–Sat 10am–1pm & 2–6pm, Sun 2–7pm • €2 • ☏ 02 98 91 70 14, 🔗 www.locronan-tourisme.com

Locronan's small **Musée d'Art et d'Histoire**, just off the main square, is largely devoted to chronicling the rise and fall of the local linen industry. Beautifully preserved looms and implements illustrate the artistry and expertise of the village's

---

LOCRONAN'S GRANDE TROMÉNIE

Each year, on the second Sunday in July, the Église St-Ronan in Locronan hosts what's arguably Brittany's most famous **pardon**. Usually known as the **Petite Troménie**, the procession expands every sixth year – 2019, 2025 and so on – to become a week-long festival, the **Grande Troménie**.

In Breton, *tro* means "to go round", and *menie* "sacred place". The 12km *Grande Troménie* route is said by some to be St Ronan's favourite Sunday walk; by others, to trace sites associated with a long-vanished Benedictine abbey; and by yet more to be a circuit of pre-Christian megaliths. The six-year cycle is thought to be connected with making the necessary corrections to the Celtic calendar, to compensate for each month lasting exactly thirty days.

Whenever you visit, the *Grande Troménie* makes a lovely half-day hike, up into the hills that surround Locronan, with superb views down to sea. The tourist office can supply a map of the route.

medieval crafts workers, while the "agony and ruin" of the nineteenth century is graphically described. The upstairs galleries display paintings and ceramics from the early twentieth century.

Notre Dame de Bonne Nouvelle

Be sure to take the time to walk 300m downhill along rue Moal from the village centre, to reach the lovely little stone chapel of **Notre Dame de Bonne Nouvelle**. Nestled beside a natural spring that supplied water for hemp manufacturers and also served as a washing place, the church now holds some surprising modern stained glass.

ARRIVAL AND INFORMATION   LOCRONAN

By bus Locronan is on bus #37 between Quimper (8–12 daily; 30min) and Camaret (4–8 daily; 1hr 10min).
By car Motorists visiting Locronan are directed to large car parks on the outskirts, which charge €3 per day.
Tourist office Place de la Mairie, adjoining the museum

(April–June & Sept Tues–Sat 10am–12.30pm & 1.30–6pm, Sun 2–6pm; July & Aug Mon–Sat 10am–6pm, Sun 11am–1pm & 3–6pm; school hols otherwise Tues–Sat 10am–12.30pm & 1.30–5pm; ☎ 02 98 91 70 14, ⓦ www .locronan-tourisme.com).

ACCOMMODATION

Camping Locronan Rue de la Troménie ☎ 02 98 91 87 76, ⓦ camping-locronan.fr. Municipal campsite, in a very pleasant wooded position a few hundred metres uphill along the *pardon* route, and holding lots of rental cabins as well as tent sites and a heated, covered pool. Closed Nov–May. **€20.30**
Du Prieuré 11 rue du Prieuré ☎ 02 98 91 70 89, ⓦ hotel-le-prieure.com. Locronan's one hotel, on the

main approach street rather than in the old town proper, is normally fully booked well in advance. Though not particularly attractive in itself, it's lovely and quiet in the evenings when the day-trippers have gone, and offers well-equipped rooms, including some split-level suites ideal for families. It also has a good restaurant with lunch from €15, and dinner menus from €19 upwards. **€75**

EATING AND DRINKING

Au Coin du Feu Rue du Prieuré ☎ 02 98 51 82 44, ⓦ coindufeu-locronan.com. Pretty little restaurant, beside the main approach road just short of the village core, which serves substantial menus starting at €19.50. Views from its terrace tables reach all the way (just) to the sea. Daily noon–2pm & 7.15–9pm; closed Sun eve & Mon eve in low season.
Crêperie Les Trois Fées 3 rue des Charrettes ☎ 02 98 91 70 23. Cosy, fairy-themed crêperie in an old stone cottage in the heart of town. All the delicious crêpes have "*fée*" in their names, including Fée Ce Book (try saying it aloud). There are plenty of vegetarian options, using tomatoes, caramelized onions and mushrooms, and specials typically cost €8–9. Be sure to try the *chouchan*,

a mead-like apéritif. Mid-June to mid-Sept daily noon–2.30pm & 6–9pm; daily except Wed noon–2.30pm in low season; closed Jan.
Crêperie Ty Coz Place de l'Église ☎ 02 98 91 70 79, ⓦ creperietycoz.com. Good-value crêperie, facing the church on the main square, with a café terrace outdoors and a wide selection of crêpes inside, none costing more then €8. Daily noon–8.45pm; closed Mon in low season.
Ostaliri Ti Jos Place de la Mairie ☎ 02 98 91 70 75. Very friendly bar/café in the small square facing the tourist office; the interior doubles as the village *tabac* and social centre, while the large open-air deck is perfect for watching the world go by. Daily 10am–11pm; closed Wed in low season.

Douarnenez

In 1923, eight hundred fishing boats based at the historic port of **DOUARNENEZ**, in the superbly sheltered Baie de Douarnenez, brought in a hundred million sardines during the six-month season. Ever since then, however the catch has been declining. Although it's still home to large fish canneries, Douarnenez has redefined itself as a living museum of all matters maritime, which centres on **Port-Rhû**, the harbour area on the west side of town. Local seafaring traditions are celebrated at the end of July in the **Temps Fête** festival (ⓦ tempsfete.com).

5

Douarnenez consists of several distinct neighbourhoods amalgamated to form a single community. While there are a couple of nice little **beaches** on the headland close to the town centre, the best of all line the bayfront in **Tréboul**, a pleasant twenty-minute walk west, with the **plage des Sables-Blancs** prime among them. The longer and more exposed **plage du Ris**, east of town, is especially popular with **surfers**.

The seaside village of **Ste-Anne-la-Palud**, north of Douarnenez, holds a large *pardon* on the last Sunday in August.

Port-Musée

Place de l'Enfer • Feb–June & Sept to early Nov daily except Mon 10am–12.30pm & 2–6pm, July & Aug daily 10am–7pm • Feb to mid-April €5.50, mid-April to Oct €7.50 • ⓣ 02 98 92 65 20, ⓦ port-musee.org

The whole area of **Port-Rhû**, on the west side of town, has become the **Port-Musée**, with its entire waterfront taken up with fishing and other vessels gathered from throughout northern Europe. Its centrepiece, the **Musée du Bateau**, houses slightly smaller vessels than those found in the port, including a *moliceiro* from Portugal and coracles from Wales and Ireland, with exhaustive explanations on construction techniques and a strong emphasis on fishing.

The most appealing part of the Port-Musée, however, is back at the waterfront, where, between April and October only, you can roam in and out of four of the boats moored in the port and peer into their oily metallic-smelling engine rooms and cramped sleeping quarters.

Port du Rosmeur

Of the three separate harbour areas still in operation in Douarnenez, the most appealing is the rough-and-ready **port du Rosmeur**, on the east side, which is nominally the fishing port used by the smaller local craft. Its quayside – which is far from totally commercialized, but holds a reasonable number of cafés and restaurants – curves between a pristine wooded promontory to the right and the fish canneries to the left, which continue around the north of the headland. You can buy fresh fish at the waterfront, or go on a sea-fishing excursion yourself, or a tour of the bay.

ARRIVAL AND INFORMATION — DOUARNENEZ

By bus Buses to Douarnenez stop outside the tourist office.

Destinations Audierne (8 daily; 30min); Locronan (July & Aug 2 daily; 20min); Pointe du Raz (July & Aug 1 daily; 50min); Quimper (10–12 daily; 35min).

Tourist office 1 rue du Dr-Mével, a short walk up from the Port-Musée (April–June, Sept & Oct Mon–Sat 10am–12.30pm & 2–6pm, Sun 10am–12.30pm; July & Aug daily 10am–6.30pm; Nov–March Mon–Sat 10am–12.30pm & 2–5.30pm; ⓣ 02 98 92 13 35, ⓦ douarnenez-tourisme.com).

ACCOMMODATION AND EATING

Les Bigorneaux Amoureux 2 bd Richepin ⓣ 02 98 92 35 55, ⓦ bigorneau-amoureux.com. Artfully casual beachfront restaurant, serving good seafood menus from €27, and blessed with a terrace that enjoys a fabulous view over the plage des Dames. Tues–Sun noon–1.30pm & 7.30–9.30pm.

Le Bretagne 23 rue Duguay-Trouin ⓣ 02 98 92 30 44, ⓦ le-bretagne.fr. Welcoming, good-value hotel in the heart of town, offering bright rooms plus a hot tub and sauna. €58

Camping Croas Men 27bis rue du Croas Men, Tréboul ⓣ 02 98 74 00 18, ⓦ croas-men.com. Two-star campsite, a short walk west of town close to the lovely Sables Blancs beach, and offering well-shaded pitches plus rental cabins and fresh-baked bread in summer. Closed Oct–Easter. €12

De France 4 rue Jean Jaurès ⓣ 02 98 92 00 02, ⓦ lafrance-dz.com. Nicely restored central hotel, a short walk from the port, offering 23 large, smart rooms with good bathrooms. Dinner menus start at €31 in the excellent restaurant, *L'Insolité* (closed Sun eve & Mon). €70

Pourquoi Pas 15 quai de Port-Rhû. Friendly bar next to the Musée du Bateau that serves local beers and hosts live café-concerts of Breton music on Fri & Sat. Mon & Tues 3pm–1am, Wed–Sun 3pm–4am.

★Ty Mad 3 rue St-Jean, Tréboul ⓣ 02 98 74 00 53, ⓦ hoteltymad.com. Charming and very stylish seaside hotel, just up from the delightful little St-Jean beach. The spacious rooms have stripped-wood floors and exposed stone walls – only the upper storeys have sea views – while the modern dining room (closed Tues) serves creative and unusual French cuisine, with menus from €29 at lunch, €39 for dinner. Closed mid-Nov to early March. **€95**

Audierne

Though the exposed southwestern extremities of Brittany are not areas you'd normally associate with a classic summer sun-and-sand holiday, **AUDIERNE**, 25km west of Douarnenez on the Bay of Audierne, is something of an exception. An active fishing port, specializing in prawns and crayfish, it squeezes into the narrow inlet of the Goyen estuary, a short way back from the Atlantic. From out to sea, you'd hardly know there was a town here.

L'Aquashow

Rue du Goyen • April–Sept daily 10am–7pm; Oct–March school hols only, daily 2–6pm • €12 • ☎ 02 98 70 03 03, ⓦ aquarium.fr

At the inland end of Audierne, an **aquarium** called **L'Aquashow** holds tankfuls of mostly local fish, captioned as ever with the stress on gastronomy – "the flesh is firm and much enjoyed", or "its flesh is really tasteful". You'll also learn that an octopus can squeeze through a hole as small as its eye, and under-14s can take the "La Tempête" thrill-ride.

While there's no great point watching the fifteen-minute, commentary-free film show of tropical fish in some unspecified South Seas location, it's worth sticking around for one of the regular shows in the open-air riverfront arena, in which captive cormorants and gulls, joined occasionally by their wild brethren, put on aerobatic displays in return for dead sprats.

An on-site snack bar serves simple meals on a pleasant terrace, and there's plenty of open space for picnics just outside.

Ste-Evette

From the centre of Audierne, the road continues just over 1km to the long, curving and surprisingly sheltered **beach** of **Ste-Evette**, which has its own crop of hotels and grand homes. Its southern end, 1km further on and close to the open ocean, is the departure point for boats to the Île de Sein.

Pointe du Raz

Daily: April–June & Sept 10.30am–6pm; July & Aug 9.30am–7pm • Parking €5 cars, €3 motorcycles • ☎ 02 98 70 67 18, ⓦ la-pointe-du-raz.com

The **Pointe du Raz** – the Land's End of both Finistère and France, a slow drive 17km west of Audierne – is a "Grand Site National", and makes a magnificent spectacle. Don't come in summer expecting to get the place to yourself; it attracts a million visitors every year, and they've had to build a huge car park roughly 1km short of the actual headland. Alongside stands a welcome and information complex that in summer seems always to be thronged with visitors. A couple of **cafés** here sell adequate simple meals, but there's no accommodation or camping.

To reach the *pointe*, either catch one of the frequent free shuttle buses (and check the time of the last one back); walk the most direct route, along an undulating, arrow-straight, track; or take a longer stroll along the footpath that skirts the top of the cliffs. However you get there, you'll be glad of strong-gripping shoes as you teeter above the plummeting fissures of the *pointe*, filling and draining with a deafening surf-roar, and look out towards the impressive sequence of lighthouses that march towards the horizon. The winds are often as fierce as the waves, buffeting the thousands of seabirds that make this their home.

5

Baie des Trépassés

The **Baie des Trépassés** (Bay of the Dead), just north of the Pointe du Raz, gets its grim name from the shipwrecked bodies that were once washed up here, and is a possible site of the sunken city of Ys (see p.275). However, it's actually a very attractive spot; green meadows, too exposed to support trees, end abruptly on the low cliffs to either side, there's a huge expanse of flat sand (in fact little else at low tide), and out in the crashing waves surfers and windsurfers get thrashed to within an inch of their lives. Beyond them, you can usually make out the white-painted houses along the harbour on the Île de Sein, while the uninhabited rocks in between hold a veritable forest of lighthouses.

In total, less than half-a-dozen scattered buildings intrude upon the emptiness, including a couple of enticing hotels. There are no facilities for casual visitors on the beach, but the car park just back from the dunes is usually filled with camper vans from all over Europe.

ARRIVAL AND INFORMATION

AUDIERNE

By ferry Île de Sein (1–5 daily; 1hr).

By bus Buses stop beside the port in Audierne, on the quai Anatole-France.

Destinations Douarnenez (8 daily; 30min); Pointe du Raz (July & Aug 1 daily; 15min); Quimper (10–12 daily;

1hr 15min).

Tourist office 8 rue Victor-Hugo, on the main square (July & Aug Mon–Sat 9am–1pm & 2–7pm, Sun 10am–1pm; Sept–June Mon–Sat 9.30am–noon & 2–5.30pm; ☎ 02 98 70 12 20, ⓦ audierne-tourisme.com).

ACCOMMODATION AND EATING

AUDIERNE

Au Roi Gradlon 3 bd Manu-Brusq ☎ 02 98 70 04 51, ⓦ auroigradlon.com. One of the few buildings on the seaward side of the road out of Audierne, this hotel enjoys a superb position facing the mouth of the estuary at the very start of Ste-Evette beach. Its unusual design means that the street-level dining room – where the €25 dinner menu offers changing daily specials (closed Sun eve & all Mon) – is in fact on the top storey, while the rooms are on several further floors, concealed from the road, that drop down below it to the beach. Closed mid-Dec to Jan. €84

De la Plage 21 av Manu-Brusq ☎ 02 98 70 01 07, ⓦ hotel -finistere.com. Aptly named Logis de France, facing the middle of Ste-Evette beach. Many of the more expensive sea-view rooms have balconies, while the restaurant (closed Tues) serves dinner menus from €26. Closed Nov–March. €75

BAIE DES TRÉPASSÉS

De la Baie des Trépassés Baie des Trépassés ☎ 02 98 70 61 34, ⓦ hotelfinistere.com. A truly spectacular hideaway, standing on the grass just behind the magnificent fine-sand beach. The plain, simply decorated rooms come in all sizes and shapes – the cheapest option lacks en-suite facilities, while several sleep three or four – and the restaurant serves menus of wonderfully fresh seafood (€28–62). Closed mid-Nov to mid-Feb. €60

Relais de la Pointe du Van Baie des Trépassés ☎ 02 98 70 62 79, ⓦ hotelfinistere.com. Large hotel, slightly higher up and to the right of the Baie des Trépassés, and run by the same management. All rooms are en-suite, but the cheapest has no views. A brasserie serves sandwiches of all kinds, as well as seafood and meat dishes at €15–23. Closed Oct–March. €60

Île de Sein

Of all the Breton islands, the tiny **Île de Sein**, just 8km west of the Pointe du Raz headland, has to be the most extraordinary. Nowhere does it rise more than six metres above the surrounding ocean, and for much of its 2.5km length it's barely broader than the breakwater wall of bricks that serves as its central spine. Its very grip on existence seems so tenuous that it's hard to believe anyone could truly survive here.

However, the island has in fact been inhabited since prehistoric times. Roman sources tell of a shrine served by nine virgin priestesses, and it was reputed to have been the very last refuge of the Druids in Brittany, who held out here long after the rest of the region was Christianized. It also became famous during World War II, when its entire male population, around 128 men, answered General de Gaulle's call to join him in exile in England. During his first muster of the Free French army, de Gaulle observed that Sein appeared to constitute a quarter of France. He subsequently awarded the island the Ordre de la Libération, and came here in 1960 to unveil a monument to its

5

bravery. Over three hundred islanders continue to make their living from the sea, gathering rainwater and seaweed and fishing for scallops, lobster and crayfish.

According to a traditional saying, "Who sees Sein, sees his death", though that's more because it happens to rhyme in French ("*qui voit Sein, voit sa fin*") than because it holds any particular evil. Setting off to reach the island on a misty morning, however, feels as though you're sailing off the edge of the world; in fact, it's so notoriously inconspicuous that it was described by the French Admiral Tourville as the most dangerous reef in the world.

Exploring the island

Depending on tide levels, **ferries** pull in at one or other of the two adjoining harbours that constitute Sein's one tight-knit village. There are no cars on the island, its few streets being far too narrow for them to squeeze through, and even bicycles are not permitted. A little **beach** appears in front of the village at low tide, and there's also a **museum** of local history (daily: June & Sept 10am–noon & 2–4pm; July & Aug 10am–noon & 2–6pm; €2.50), packed with black-and-white photos and press clippings, and displaying a long list of shipwrecks from 1476 onwards. The basic activity for visitors, however, is to take a bracing walk to enjoy some absolutely ravishing coastal scenery.

The **eastern tip** of the island, barely connected to the rest when high tides eat away at the slender natural causeway, was in days gone by laboriously cleared to create scores of tiny agricultural terraces. These have long been overgrown with sparse yellow broom and left to the rabbits, however, so if you fancy picking your way through the rock pools you'll have the place to yourself.

Heading **west** from town, a somewhat longer walk leads past the Free French Monument and a couple of sandy little bays to the island's main **lighthouse**, the Phare de Goulenez.

ARRIVAL AND DEPARTURE   ÎLE DE SEIN

By boat The principal departure point for boats to Sein is Ste-Evette beach, just outside Audierne; the crossing takes around 1hr. Services are operated by Penn Ar Bed (daily: early July to late Aug 3 daily, with first at 9am; late Aug to early July 1–2 daily, with first usually at 9.30am; ☏02 98 70 70 70, ⓦpennarbed.fr). On Sun from late June to early Sept, Penn Ar Bed also runs trips to Sein from Brest (departs 9am; 1hr 30min) via Camaret (9.40am; 1hr). The round-trip fare on every route is the same (July–Sept €34.80; Oct–May €27.80).

ACCOMMODATION AND EATING

★ **D'Armen** 39 rue Fernand Crouton ☏02 98 70 90 77, ⓦhotel-restaurant-d-armen-ile-de-sein.fr. The nicer of Sein's two good hotels is the very last building as you walk west out of town, which makes it the last restaurant in Europe. All its simple but lovely rooms face the sea, and the excellent €23 dinner menu features mussels in cider, skate, and delicious home-baked bread. Closed early Nov to mid-Feb. €75

Le Men Brial Place de Men Brial ☏02 98 70 90 87.

Crêperie with outdoor tables, right by the picturesque little Men Brial lighthouse, and offering crêpes for €10 plus a €20 menu. April–June, Sept & Oct Mon, Tues Thurs & Fri noon–2pm, Wed, Sat & Sun noon–2pm & 6–8pm; July & Aug daily noon–2pm & 6–8pm.

Trois Dauphins 16 quai des Paimpolais ☏02 98 70 92 09, ⓦhoteliledesein.com. Seven cosy and attractive wood-panelled rooms, not all en suite or with sea views, above a bar in the middle of the port. €48

Penmarc'h peninsula

At one time the **Penmarc'h peninsula** – the southwestern corner of Finistère, which stretches south of Audierne and southwest of Quimper – was one of the richest areas of Brittany. That was before it was plundered by the pirate La Fontenelle in 1597, who led three hundred ships in raids on the local peasantry from his base on the island of La Tristan in the Bay of Douarnenez, and also before the cod, staple of the fishing industry, stopped coming.

5

Now, in the local tourist literature, the region is known as the **Pays de Bigouden**, *bigouden* being the name of the traditional and very elaborate lace headgear worn by the women in the villages around Pont l'Abbé. Often as much as a foot high, these are either very stiffly starched, or supported by half-tubes of cardboard. You're phenomenally unlikely to encounter them on a normal day, though it's said that three women still wear them regularly. Coincide with a *pardon* or festival, however, and you might just spot the white of a *coiffe* swaying in the wind.

Pointe de la Torche

The **Pointe de la Torche**, a slow 40km drive south of Audierne – parallel to the coast but inland through successively small villages – is a windswept headland that's topped by a prehistoric tomb. It marks the southern end of a huge flat beach that's Brittany's top **windsurfing** site, and has frequently hosted international competitions. Whatever time of year you visit, there are likely to be aficionados of the sport twirling effortlessly about on the dangerous water. Swimming is not safe, however.

Phare d'Eckmühl

Penmarc'h • April–Sept daily 10.30–6.30pm, stays open until sunset on Tues in July & Aug; Oct daily 2–6pm; • €2.50, sunset viewing €5 • ☎ 06 07 21 37 34, ⓦ penmarch.fr

The **Phare d'Eckmühl** stands right at the very southwestern tip of Finistère, at the edge of the village of Penmarc'h itself. This 60m-tall **lighthouse** was erected late in the nineteenth century using funds donated by the daughter of one of Napoleon's generals, who, following his role in the French victory over the Austrians at the 1809 Battle of Eckmühl, was awarded the title of Prince of Eckmühl.

Visitors who climb the stunning spiral staircase that wraps around the interior shaft of the lighthouse are rewarded with magnificent views up and down the coast – don't miss the weekly late-night sunset openings if you're around in summer. What's most surprising, though, is the rather extraordinary wood-panelled chamber right at the top, where the lighthouse keepers used to stand watch all night before the light was automated in 2008.

Le Guilvinec

Sheltered in the mouth of a little river, 12km southwest of Pont l'Abbé, **LE GUILVINEC** is a not especially attractive, but surprisingly busy, fishing port, that's home to the fourth-largest fish auction (*criée*) in France; you can learn all about it at the Haliotika museum. Le Guilvinec also holds a small, very pleasant **beach**, just west of the centre, facing onto the open sea.

Haliotika

Late Feb to mid-March, early April to early July & Sept Mon–Fri 10am–12.30pm & 2.30–6.30pm; early July to Aug Mon–Fri 9.30am–7pm, Sat & Sun 3–6.30pm; Oct Mon–Fri 3–6pm • €6, or €7 including guided visit to the auction • ☎ 02 98 58 28 38, ⓦ haliotika.com

Le Guilvinec is playing a pioneering role in a government initiative to turn fishing into a tourist spectacle. To that end, the second storey of the long harbourfront buildings where the fish are landed and sold has been converted to become **Haliotika**, a sort of museum of the fishing industry that combines exhaustive displays on all aspects of the whole messy business, with an open-air terrace offering ringside views as the fleet returns each afternoon from around 4pm, after which there's an early-evening fish auction.

You can also have a day's hands-on involvement with activities of the port, including unloading a boat, as well as attending the auction, for €35, and spend a day out at sea on a working fishing boat for €50.

5

Loctudy

LOCTUDY, 8km east of Le Guilvinec and 6km south of Pont l'Abbé, is well located for boat trips along the River Odet and out to the nearby islands, and also has its own attractive beaches, while at the same time being relatively uncommercial and laid-back.

Musée Bigouden

Mid-April to May & Oct Sat & Sun 2–6pm; June Tues–Fri 10am–12.30pm & 2–6pm, Sat & Sun 2–6pm; July & Aug daily 10am–6pm; Sept Tues–Fri 10am–12.30pm & 2–6pm • €3.50 • ☎ 02 98 66 09 03, ⊛ museebigouden.fr

PONT L'ABBÉ, the principal town of the Penmarc'h peninsula, is home to the **Musée Bigouden**, which spreads over three storeys of the keep of its fourteenth-century **château**. As it's almost entirely devoted to local costumes, you'd need to share that interest to sustain much of a visit. More accessible pleasures lie in a stroll through the woods along the banks of its estuary.

INFORMATION AND ACTIVITIES

LOCTUDY

Tourist office place des Anciens Combattants (July & Aug Mon–Fri 9am–noon & 2–7pm, Sat 9am–noon & 2–6pm; Sept–June Mon–Fri 9am–noon & 2–5pm; ☎ 02 98 87 53 78, ⊛ tourisme.loctudy.fr).

PONT L'ABBÉ

Tourist office 11 place Gambetta (Mon–Sat 9.30am–noon & 2–5pm; ☎ 02 98 82 37 99, ⊛ www.paysdepontlabbe

PENMARC'H PENINSULA

-tourisme.com).

POINTE DE LA TORCHE

Watersports The Twenty Nine shop, among the cluster of snack bars and equipment-rental outlets beside the car park at the Pointe, doubles as headquarters for the École de Surf Bretagne (☎ 02 98 58 53 80, ⊛ twenty-nine.com), and offers instruction in surfing, windsurfing, kiteboarding and other watersports.

ACCOMMODATION AND EATING

LOCTUDY

Hortensias 38 rue des Tulipes ☎ 02 98 87 46 64, ⊛ camping-loctudy.com. Three-star campsite, 3km from the centre of Loctudy but just 300m from the beach, with a snackbar and heated pool. Closed Oct–March. **€19.90**

Porte des Glénan 19 rue du Port ☎ 02 98 87 40 21, ⊛ laportedesglenan.com. Small, good-value hotel, with simple but nicely refurbished rooms in the heart of town, ten minutes' walk from the beach. There's a bar but no restaurant. **€54**

LE GUILVINEC

Poisson d'Avril 19–21 rue de Men-Meur ☎ 02 98 58 23 83, ⊛ lepoissondavril.fr. This stylish, contemporary place, a very short walk from Haliotika, ranks among the very best restaurants in Brittany (closed Mon in low season). Menus priced at €29–42 are rich in oysters and seafood, but also feature hearty meat dishes. If you can't bear to leave, take your pick from the four bright modern guestrooms upstairs, which hold large private terraces and include a family-sized suite. **€105**

Yelloh! Village la Plage 241 Hent Maner ar Ster ☎ 02 98 58 61 90, ⊛ villagelaplage.com. Large family campsite, 1.5km west of Le Guilvinec towards Penmarc'h and 50m back from the beach, with a massive waterpark plus restaurant, bar and grocery. As well as rental cabins and fixed luxury tents, they also offer a genuine, four-person treehouse that's available by the night – generally everything else can be reserved by the week only. Camping **€39.80**, treehouse **€133**

PONT L'ABBÉ

Quatre Saisons 2 rue Burdeau ☎ 02 98 87 06 05, ⊛ creperielesquatresaisons.com. Friendly crêperie just off the main street, where, as well as tasty sweet and savoury pancakes, you can get great local cider and the owner's own onion *compôte*. Tues–Sat 11.30am–2pm & 7–9pm.

Tour d'Auvergne Place Gambetta ☎ 02 98 87 00 47, ⊛ tourdauvergne.fr. Good-value hotel, with simple, well-equipped rooms and a fine restaurant serving lunch from €16 and dinner from €23 (closed Sun & Mon), plus outdoor bar seating, under the trees in a little square in the centre of town. **€49**

Quimper

Pretty, historic, laid-back **QUIMPER** ranks high among the most attractive cities in Brittany. Still "the charming little place" known to Flaubert, it can be crossed on foot in half an hour, though naturally if you take the time to relax in its many bars and cafés

5

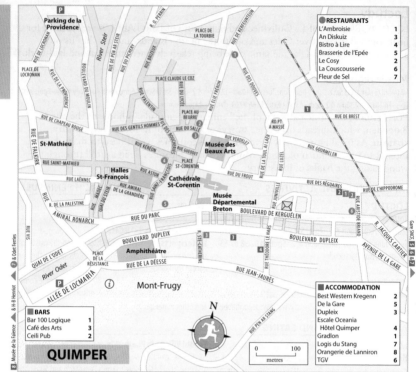

exploration will take considerably longer. It also holds several excellent **museums**, as well as a huge **cathedral**, and hosts a lively programme of annual **festivals**, but perhaps the most enjoyable option of all is simply to take a **river cruise** down the Odet – "the prettiest river in France" – to reach the open sea at Bénodet.

Capital of the ancient diocese, kingdom and later duchy of Cornouaille, Quimper is the oldest Breton city. Its name comes from the Breton word *kemper*, denoting the confluence of the two rivers, the Steir and the Odet. Quimper was originally founded atop the tree-covered **Mont Frugy**, which rises all of 87m above the river junction; follow the footpaths up there, and you can still make out a few vague ruins. The city itself, however, soon moved down to the riverbanks, where the cobbled and largely pedestrianized streets of the medieval quarter now encircle the cathedral.

As the Odet curves from east to southwest, it is crossed by numerous low flat bridges, bedecked with geraniums, and chrysanthemums in the autumn. As you stroll along the riverfront boulevards, several striking modern edifices – most notably, the Bauhaus-style **Ty Kodak** building, constructed for the camera company in 1933 – blend in an oddly harmonious way with their ancient surroundings.

Cathédrale St-Corentin

Quimper's focal point, the enormous **Cathédrale St-Corentin** is said to be the most complete Gothic cathedral in Brittany, though its neo-Gothic spires date from 1856. Looking at its facade, now a sparkling white following several years of painstaking scrubbing, you'll see King Gradlon mounted in perfect symmetry between the spires. Before the Revolution, each St Cecilia's Day a climber would ascend to give the king

5

a drink, and there was a prize of 100 *écus* for whoever could catch the glass, thrown down afterwards. Carvings lower down celebrate the victory of the Montfort family over the Blois family in the War of the Breton Succession (1341–64).

The interior of the cathedral has also been restored and repainted in recent years, but nothing can change its major eccentricity – that the nave is set at an angle to the rest of the church. When the nave was being added to the old chancel in the fifteenth century, the extension would either have hit existing buildings or the swampy edge of the (then) unchannelled river. The deviation is the only solution the masons could come up with.

Musée Départemental Breton

1 rue du roi Gradlon • Mid-June to mid-Sept daily 9am–6pm; mid-Sept to mid-June Tues–Sat 9am–12.30pm & 1.30–5pm, Sun 2–5pm • €5 • ☎ 02 98 95 21 60, ⓦ museedepartementalbreton.fr

Alongside the cathedral, the quirky-looking **Bishop's Palace** nestles against one of the few remaining fragments of Quimper's old city walls. Inside you'll find a wonderful staircase, and the beautifully laid out **Musée Départemental Breton**.

Its collections start with Bronze Age spear- and axe-heads and prehistoric golden jewellery, move rapidly through Roman and medieval statues, and culminate with a remarkable assortment of Breton oddments and *objets d'art*. The highlights are the sixteenth-century statues of polychromed wood, some of which stood originally in the cathedral, but upstairs you'll also find prized examples of regional costumes, furniture, including an ornate nineteenth-century *lit clos* (enclosed bed), and ceramics.

Musée des Beaux Arts

40 place St-Corentin • April–June, Sept & Oct daily except Tues 9.30am–noon & 2–6pm; July & Aug daily 10am–7pm; Nov–March Mon & Wed–Sat 9.30am–noon & 2–5.30pm, Sun 2–5.30pm • €5 • ☎ 02 98 95 45 20, ⓦ www.mbaq.fr

Quimper's compelling **Musée des Beaux Arts** stands across the main square immediately north of the cathedral alongside the Hôtel de Ville. Refurbished to very classy effect, with new floors and suspended walkways, it focuses especially on an amazing assemblage of drawings by Max Jacob – who was born in Quimper – and his contemporaries.

Jean-Julien Lemordant's vibrant murals of Breton scenes, commissioned in 1907 for Quimper's *Hôtel de l'Epée* – which closed in 1974, though the *Brasserie* remains open, albeit remodelled (see p.276) – get a room to themselves, and there's also quite a selection of nineteenth- and twentieth-century paintings from the Pont-Aven school. You'd hardly notice the only Gauguin, a goose he painted on the door of Marie Henry's

---

THE DROWNED CITY OF YS

Quimper's first bishop, **St Corentin**, is said to have arrived with the first Bretons to cross the English Channel to Brittany – the place they named Little Britain – some time between the fourth and seventh centuries. He lived by eating a regenerating and immortal fish all his life, and was made bishop by one **King Gradlon**.

Legend has it that **Gradlon had previously ruled over** the city of **Ys**, which stood out in the Baie de Douarnenez and was protected from the water by gates and locks to which only **Gradlon** and his daughter Dahut had keys. Dahut sounds like a pleasant sort, providing all the citizens with pet sea-dragons to do their errands, but **Saint Corentin** saw decadence and suspected evil. He was proved right: at the urging of the Devil, the princess used her key to open the floodgates, the city was flooded, and Gradlon escaped only by obeying Corentin and throwing his daughter into the sea.

Back on dry land, and in need of a new capital, Gradlon founded Quimper. Ys remains on the sea floor, but will rise again when Paris ("*Par-Ys*", "equal to Ys") sinks. According to tradition, on feast days sailors can still hear church bells and hymns under the water.

5

inn in Pont-Aven itself, but there is a portrait *of* Gauguin, by his friend Paul Sérusier. One room upstairs is devoted to Breton legends, including a terrifying depiction of *Les Lavandières de la Nuit* by Yan'Dargent.

Musée de la Faïence

14 rue Jean-Baptiste Bousquet • Mid-April to late Sept Mon–Sat 10am–6pm • €5, €7 with the H-B Henriot atelier • ☎ 02 98 90 12 72, ⓦ musee-faience-quimper.com

Visiting Quimper, it is impossible to ignore the local ceramic tradition of **faïence**, or tin-glazed earthenware. The **Musée de la Faïence**, beside the river in the southwest corner of town, traces the history of the tradition. First popularized by the city of Faenza in Italy in the sixteenth century, faïence was subsequently produced in Delft in Holland, Majolica in Spain, and then, from 1690 onwards, in Quimper. Local manufacture boomed when the coming of the railways in 1875 brought Brittany's first influx of tourists, and some unknown artisan hit on the idea of painting ceramic ware with naive "folk" designs.

As well as revealing the minerals used to create different colours, such as copper (green), cobalt (blue) and antimony (yellow), the museum includes pieces commemorating such events as World War I, the first automobile accident, and the death of Zola, as well as fascinating specimens from the 1920s. In the age before plastics, fine artists handled commissions such as designing bonnet ornaments for Citroën cars.

H-B Henriot

Rue Haute • Tours mid-April to mid-July Tues–Fri 2.30pm & 4pm; mid-July to mid-Sept Mon–Sat 9.30am, 10.30am, 11.15am, 1.30pm, 2.15pm, 3.30pm, 4.15pm & 5pm • €5, or €7 with the Musée de la Faïence • ☎ 02 98 90 09 36, ⓦ hb-henriot.com

Right next door to the Musée de la Faïence, the major atelier **H-B Henriot** continues to produce hand-painted pottery. Half-hour tours explain the entire process, from design through firing to completion, while the bright, modern **gift shop** alongside sells a superb selection. Sadly, though, the prices, even for the seconds, are similar to those on offer throughout the town.

Halles St-François

Rue Astor • Mon 7am–7.30pm, Tues–Thurs 5.30am–8pm, Fri 5am–8pm, Sat 4.30am–8pm, Sun 7am–1pm

The **Halles St-François** marketplace is a delight, not just for the hugely appetizing food on sale, but for the view beyond the upturned boat rafters through the roof to the cathedral's twin spires. It's open daily, with an extra-large market spreading into the surrounding streets on Wednesdays and Saturdays.

ARRIVAL AND DEPARTURE   QUIMPER

By train Quimper's *gare SNCF* is on avenue de la Gare, 1km east of the centre, on bus #6.

Destinations Brest (11 daily; 1hr 15min); Lorient (18 daily; 40min); Nantes (5 daily; 2hr 30min); Paris-Montparnasse (6 TGVs daily; 4hr 30min); Redon (8 daily; 1hr 30min); Vannes (12 daily; 1hr 15min).

By bus To reach the coast on public transport, buses are your only option (☎ 02 98 90 68 40, ⓦ cat29.fr). The *gare routière* is beside the train station.

Destinations Audierne (10–12 daily; 1hr 15min); Beg-Meil (7 daily; 50min); Bénodet (6–8 daily; 50min); Brest (5 daily; 1hr 15min); Camaret (4–8 daily; 1hr 30min);

Concarneau (7 daily; 40min); Douarnenez (10–12 daily; 35min); Fouesnant (7 daily; 40min); Locronan (8–12 daily; 30min); Morlaix (1 daily; 1hr 50min); Quimperlé (3 daily; 1hr 50min); Roscoff (1 daily; 3hr).

By car Finding a parking space in the centre of Quimper can be difficult; if there's no room in the paying car park beside the river, near the tourist office, head for the free, thousand-place Parking de la Providence, a ten-minute walk north of the centre.

By air British Airways flights from London City Airport serve Quimper's airport at Pluguffan (ⓦ quimper.aeroport .fr), 10km southwest of the city centre on bus #25.

5

THE FESTIVALS OF QUIMPER

Having started in 1923, Quimper's **Festival de Cornouaille** is still going from strength to strength. This great jamboree of Breton music, costumes, theatre and dance is held in the week before the last Sunday in July, attracting guest performers from the other Celtic countries and a scattering of other, sometimes highly unusual, ethnic-cultural ensembles. The whole thing culminates in an incredible Sunday parade through the town. The official programme does not appear until July, but you can get provisional details in advance from the tourist office or at ⓦ www.festival-cornouaille.com.

Not so widely known are the **Semaines Musicales**, which follow in the first three weeks of August (ⓦ www.semaines-musicales-quimper.org). Some events take place in the cathedral, others bring the rather stuffy nineteenth-century theatre on boulevard Dupleix alive. The music is predominantly classical, favouring French composers. There's also a smaller-scale festival of contemporary music and art in March, **Les Hivernautes** (ⓦ hivernautes.com).

INFORMATION AND TOURS

Tourist office 7 rue de la Déesse, place de la Résistance (April & May Mon–Sat 9.30am–12.30pm & 1.30–6.30pm; June & Sept Mon–Sat 9.30am–12.30pm & 1.30–6.30pm, Sun 10am–12.45pm; July & Aug Mon–Sat 9am–7pm, Sun 10am–12.45pm & 3–5.45pm; Oct–March Mon–Sat 9.30am–12.30pm & 1.30–6pm; ☎ 02 98 53 04 05, ⓦ quimper-tourisme.com).

Tours The tourist office arranges an intricate programme of walking tours.

River cruises Between May and September, Vedettes de l'Odet cruise down the Odet from Quimper to Bénodet (1–3 daily departures, except Sun in July & Aug; 1hr 15min each way; €28 return, higher rates for gourmet cruises including meals; ☎ 02 98 57 00 58, ⓦ vedettes-odet.com). Schedules and precise departure points vary with the tide and season; the tourist office sells tickets. The same company also sails between Quimper and the Îles Glénan (see p.280).

Bike rental Torch VTT, 58 rue de la Providence (☎ 02 98 53 84 41, ⓦ torchvttquimper.com).

ACCOMMODATION

Best Western Kregenn 11–15 rue des Réguaires ☎ 02 98 95 08 70, ⓦ hotel-kregenn.fr. Renovated hotel, a block north of the river, with well-appointed modern rooms and off-street parking. There's a smart lobby, and generous buffet breakfasts (€13) are laid out downstairs, but there's no restaurant. €109

De la Gare 17 av de la Gare ☎ 02 98 90 00 81, ⓦ hotel delagarequimper.com. Bright, colourful en-suite rooms arranged around a floral patio and above a no-nonsense snack bar across from the station. €60

Dupleix 34 bd Dupleix ☎ 02 98 90 53 35, ⓦ hotel -dupleix.com. Modern concrete hotel, not very attractive from the outside but airy and bright within, in a good central location overlooking the Odet, with fine views across the river to the cathedral. Some rooms have balconies. The free private garage is a major advantage in this part of town. €65

Escale Oceania Hôtel Quimper 6 rue Théodore Le Hars ☎ 02 98 53 37 37, ⓦ oceaniahotels.com. Comfortable central hotel, next to a parking garage, where the slightly characterless rooms have been spruced up to a pretty decent standard. €10 buffet breakfasts. Rates drop at weekends. €80

Gradlon 30 rue de Brest ☎ 02 98 95 04 39, ⓦ hotel -gradlon.fr. This quiet and exceptionally friendly hotel, a short walk north from the centre, makes an ideal base, and has a pleasant garden. Tastefully decorated rooms, plus a good bar, with an open fire in winter. €98

★ **Logis du Stang** 41 Allée du Stang-Youen ☎ 02 98 52 00 55, ⓦ www.logis-du-stang.com. Delightful B&B, 5km southeast of the centre in a nineteenth-century house, with four well-furnished en-suite rooms and a hortensia-filled garden. €85

Orangerie de Lanniron Route de Bénodet ☎ 02 98 90 62 02, ⓦ lanniron.com. Five-star campsite, 4km south in the grounds of a château, with its own aquapark, restaurant and tennis court, and also chalets and stone cottages for rent. Closed mid-Sept to mid-May. €38.90

TGV 4 rue de Concarneau ☎ 02 98 90 54 00, ⓦ hoteltgv .com. Cheap hotel opposite the station, offering plain but clean rooms with shower and TV at bargain rates. Steer clear of the first-floor ones, though, which can get a bit noisy. €39

EATING AND DRINKING

L'Ambroisie 49 rue Élie-Fréron ☎ 02 98 95 00 02, ⓦ ambroisie-quimper.com. Upmarket French restaurant a short climb north from the cathedral, featuring fine seafood (including tuna) and meat dishes on menus from €29 for lunch on weekday, €43–80 for dinner. Wed–Sat noon–1.30pm & 7.30–9pm, Sun noon–1.30pm.

5

An Diskuiz 12 rue Élie-Fréron ☎02 98 95 55 70. The pick of the crêperies in a city renowned for its pancakes, with outdoor seating just up from the cathedral and a name that means "place to rest". Crêpes and whole-wheat galettes range €4–9. July & Aug Mon, Tues & Thurs–Sat 11.45am–2.15pm & 6.45–10pm, Wed 11.45am–2.15pm; Sept–March Mon & Thurs–Sun 11.45am–2.15pm & 6.45–10pm.

Bar 100 Logique 9 rue des Réguaires ☎06 60 87 44 95, ⓦle100logiquequimper.skyrock.com. Classy little bar that's proud of its status as Quimper's number one gay and lesbian hangout. Tues–Sun 7pm–1am.

Bistro à Lire 18 rue des Boucheries ☎02 98 95 30 86. This café specializes in two things: desserts and detective thrillers. The fruit crumbles are an excellent choice for the former; you can pick the latter off the bookshelves and read while you eat. Lunch time *plats du jour* for €8.20. Mon noon–5pm, Tues–Fri 10am–6pm, Sat 10am–7pm.

Brasserie de l'Epée 14 rue du Parc ☎02 98 95 28 97, ⓦquimper-lepee.com. A glorious Art Nouveau brasserie when Max Jacob brought Picasso here, this Quimper institution, which has outdoor seating facing the river not far from the cathedral, has lost some of its former charm since being modernized, but it still serves excellent food, with *moules frites* for €15, assorted fish and meat dishes for €15–25, a two-course lunch *formule* at €18.80, and dinner menus for €29–46 – and you can get a meal at 11pm, which is rare indeed for Brittany. Daily 10.30am–midnight.

Café des Arts 4 rue Ste-Catherine ☎02 98 90 32 06. Young, sociable café on the south bank of the river, which stays up late nightly with a lively crowd, and has a fine selection of imported whiskys. Daily noon–midnight.

Ceili Pub 4 rue Aristide Briand ☎02 98 95 17 61. This lively and convivial bar is the place to go for all things Breton: a great big ramshackle old place, it offers beer and opinionated conversation, plus live traditional Celtic bands and occasionally jazz. Mon–Sat 11am–1am, Sun 5pm–1am.

Le Cosy 2 rue du Sallé ☎02 98 95 23 65, ⓦlecosy -restaurant.fr. Pretty bistro just north of the cathedral, where the menu proudly insists they serve "*pas de crêpes, pas de frites*"; instead savoury *tartines* or daily *plats* cost €12–19, and set menus cost €16.50 for lunch, €31.50 for dinner. Tues–Sat noon–2pm & 7–9pm.

La Couscousserie 1 bd de Kerguélen ☎02 98 95 46 50. Plush, enjoyable Middle Eastern restaurant by the river, serving couscous platters at €12–26, and tagines for around €17.50, in two Arabian Nights-themed rooms decked out with hookahs and the like. Daily noon–2pm & 7–10.30pm; closed Aug.

Fleur de Sel 1 quai Neuf ☎02 98 55 04 71, ⓦfleur-de -sel-quimper.com. Attractive little restaurant near the riverboat quay, not far west of the centre on the north bank. Despite looking like a chintzy café, it offers gourmet French cooking on largely fish-based menus costing €22 for lunch, €29 and €39 for dinner. Mon–Fri 12.15–1.30pm & 7.30–9pm, Sat 7.30–9pm.

Southeast Finistère

Some of Brittany's finest beaches, and, by no coincidence, most popular family resorts, lie in the southeast portion of Finistère. Following the verdant Odet estuary south from Quimper soon brings you to Bénodet, while the rocky coast to the east, cut repeatedly by deep valleys, holds some ruggedly attractive scenery.

Every little indent and inlet, around **Fouesnant** for example, seems to harbour its own gorgeous pocket **beach**, and there are also a couple of more substantial communities to attract day-trippers: the walled town of **Concarneau**, and the artists' haven of **Pont-Aven**. The inland town of **Quimperlé** and **Le Pouldu** on the coast are the final two stops of any note before you leave Finistère and enter Morbihan.

Bénodet

South of Quimper, and free of its city channel, the River Odet takes on the anarchic shape of most Breton inlets, spreading out to lake proportions then turning narrow corners between gorges. The resort of **BÉNODET** at its mouth has a long sheltered beach on the ocean side. While the town is a little overdeveloped, the beaches hereabouts are splendid, especially for children, for whom there's a lot laid on – including windsurfing and "beach club" crèches (Club Mickey is highly recommended). During its less busy periods, such as spring or autumn, Bénodet is one of the finest spots for a family holiday in the whole of Brittany.

Sainte-Marine

Immediately across the rivermouth from Bénodet, and accessible by regular, five-minute pedestrian-only ferries, its equally attractive little sister port, **Sainte-Marine**, makes a lovely outing. The tiny crescent beach where the ferries pull in, originally a fishing harbour, is lined with cafés and crêperies, while a ten-minute walk south brings you to the long, wide-open **plage du Teven**.

You can also drive to Ste-Marine in a matter of minutes over the graceful **Pont de Cornouaille**, 1km upstream, which offers spectacular views of the estuary.

ARRIVAL AND INFORMATION   BÉNODET

By boat Ferries between Bénodet and Ste-Marine leave every half hour from Cale St-Thomas in the port (*Le Picot*; April–Sept departs Mon–Fri 10.15am–6.15pm, Sat & Sun 1.50–6.15pm; additional departures daily 6.45pm & 7.15pm in July & Aug; €2; ☎06 81 66 78 67). Bénodet is also served by river cruises to and from Quimper (see p.277), and ferries to the Îles Glénan (see p.280).

By bus Buses from Quimper stop in the town centre and at the Kermoor beach (6–8 daily; 50min).
Bike rental Cycletty, 5 av de la Mer (☎02 98 57 18 32, ⓦcycletty.com).
Tourist office 29 av de la Mer (March–June, Sept & Oct Mon–Sat 9am–noon & 1.30–6pm; July & Aug Mon–Sat 9am–7pm, Sun 10am–6pm; Nov–Feb Mon–Sat 9.30am–noon & 2–5pm; ☎02 98 57 00 14, ⓦbenodet.fr).

ACCOMMODATION AND EATING

BÉNODET

Armoric 3 rue Penfoul ☎02 98 57 04 03, ⓦarmoric-benodet.com. Peaceful, family-run Logis de France, set in pleasant gardens near the tourist office and 800m up from the sea. Comfortable, if somewhat old-fashioned, carpeted rooms, and a restaurant serving dinner menus from €27. **€75**
Les Bains de Mer 11 rue de Kerguélen ☎02 98 57 03 41, ⓦlesbainsdemer.com. This down-to-earth hotel, just inland from the port and ten minutes' walk from the beach, has slightly staid but cosy rooms, including large family suites, plus a reasonable restaurant charging €23 and up, and a heated outdoor pool. **€77**
Camping du Letty Chemin de Creisanguer ☎02 98 57 04 69, ⓦcampingduletty-benodet.com. Large and very well-equipped four-star campsite, southeast of the centre alongside the plage du Letty, with an indoor/outdoor aquapark, gym, squash and tennis courts, and super-market/deli. Closed early Sept to mid-June. **€47**
Camping Yelloh! Village Port de Plaisance 7 rte de Quimper ☎02 98 57 02 38, ⓦcampingbenodet.fr. Luxurious five-star campsite, tucked away inland well back from the beach, and hence offering its own extravagant covered water park, as well as a sauna, restaurant, horse riding and nightly entertainment in summer. No tents; mobile-home rentals only. Closed mid-Sept to March. Mobile homes **€112**

Sans Souci 1–3 av de la Plage ☎02 98 57 01 01, ⓦcampingbenodet.fr. Something for everyone, in a perfect setting facing the main town beach; not only is this a good-value seafront restaurant, with three-course weekday lunches for €18.50 and menus from €24 otherwise, but you can also get ice creams and sandwiches all day, or simply drop in for a drink or coffee on the promenade. Mid-Feb to mid-Nov Mon–Thurs & Sun noon–3pm & 7–10pm, Fri & Sat noon–3pm & 7–11pm.

SAINTE-MARINE

Hôtel du Bac 19 rue du Bac ☎02 98 51 33 33, ⓦwww.hoteldubac.fr. Nice little blue-trimmed hotel alongside the ferry jetty, where throwing open the shutters of your jauntily nautical room reveals a perfect seaside scene, and the bistro downstairs is always busy with day-trippers from Bénodet, enjoying high-class meals from €29. **€150**
★Villa Tri Men 16 rue du Phare ☎02 98 51 94 94, ⓦtrimen.fr. Gorgeous villa hotel, set on stately lawns immediately above the ferry jetty in Ste-Marine, and commanding wonderful views back across the river to Bénodet. With their wooden floors and light decor, the spacious rooms resemble those of a New England inn; the best have two balconies, and there are also some suites in separate cottages. The dinner-only dining room (mid-April to Oct; closed Sun) is also excellent, with menus from €39 upwards. **€170**

Îles Glénan

The **Îles Glénan** are a cluster of tiny islands, set in a shallow lagoon that's renowned for its remarkable turquoise waters roughly 16km off the coast of Finistère. If you're lucky enough to own a yacht, or can borrow one, you'll find secluded coves all around the archipelago just waiting to be explored. Commercial day-trips, though, most of which leave from Bénodet or Fouesnant, only go to the largest islet, **St-Nicolas**.

5

Once you're there, the big attraction is a luscious white-sand beach, which is technically a *tombolo*, in that it's a sandspit connecting St-Nicolas to another even tinier outcrop. You can walk around the entire island in under half an hour, along boardwalks laid down to protect plants such as the endemic narcisse de Glénan, which carpets the central meadow with tiny white blossoms in April and May.

ARRIVAL AND INFORMATION   ÎLES GLÉNAN

BY FERRY

Excursions to St-Nicolas are run by Vedettes de l'Odet (€34 return, or €43 with cruise around archipelago; ☏ 02 98 57 00 58, ⊛ vedettes-odet.com).

From Beg-Meil Early July to Aug Mon–Fri 10.30am & 2pm, Sat & Sun 1.30pm.

From Bénodet Mid-April to early July, & first half of Sept Tues–Thurs, Sat & Sun 1.30pm, plus some additional sailings at 10am; early July to late Aug Mon & Sun 11am & 1.30pm, Tues–Sat 10am, 11am & 1.30pm; second fortnight of Sept Tues, Wed & Sun 1.30pm.

From Concarneau Mid-April to early July, & first half of Sept Wed, Thurs & Sun 1.30pm, mid-July to Aug daily 10am, 11am & 2pm.

From La Forêt-Fouesnant Mid-July to Aug Mon–Fri 10am & 1.30pm, Sat & Sun 10am.

From Loctudy Late June to mid-July & first fortnight of Sept Thurs 2pm; mid-July to Aug Tues–Sat 10.15am & 2pm.

BY CATAMARAN

The tourist office in Fôret-Fouesnant offers day-trips to St-Nicolas on a sailing catamaran, including an excellent picnic lunch eaten on board, and chance to help the crew with their tasks (no fixed schedule – call to arrange; €90 per person; ☏ 02 98 51 18 88, ⊛ tourisme-fouesnant.fr).

ACCOMMODATION AND EATING

Sextant St-Nicolas ☏ 02 98 50 68 88, ⊛ sextant -glenan.org. Simple, modern bungalow that serves as a "gîte de mer", holding five dorms with six beds in each, available for maximum stays of three nights per person. With no food or even drinking water available, guests have to bring all they plan to consume from the mainland. Mid-April to mid-Sept daily noon–2pm & 7–9pm.

Les Viviers St-Nicolas ☏ 02 98 50 68 90. Advance reservations, made by 11am for lunch or 6pm for dinner, are compulsory if you want to eat at this family-run restaurant, at the ferry landing. Its €18.50 menu features fish soup followed by either mussels or crab, but you can usually get lobster à la carte. **€16.20**

Fouesnant

Not so much a town as a loose conglomeration of villages, **FOUESNANT**, 9km east of Bénodet, rivals its neighbour as a prime destination for family holidays. While Fouesnant itself is renowned for its cider-makers, and holds a pretty little Romanesque church, most local tourist amenities are gathered in its sister community of **LA FORÊT-FOUESNANT**, which stands at the inland end of the Baie de la Forêt.

This glorious broad bay, formed at the mouth of several minor rivers and fronted by the little resort of **BEG-MEIL** to the west and the walled town of Concarneau to the east, is lined with magnificent beaches. La Forêt-Fouesnant has its own superb expanse, while at **CAP-COZ**, just a couple of hundred metres away on the west side of the bay but around 6km by road, the long sandbar is always busy with kayakers, windsurfers and family bathers in summer. A lovely coastal footpath runs south from here, by way of irresistible little sandy coves like **BOT-CONAN**, to Beg-Meil at the headland.

INFORMATION   FOUESNANT

Tourist office 4 Espace Kernévéleck (July & Aug Mon–Sat 9am–7pm, Sun 10am–1pm; Sept–June Mon–Sat 9am–noon & 2–6pm; ☏ 02 98 51 18 88, ⊛ tourisme -fouesnant.fr).

ACCOMMODATION AND EATING

Belle Vue 30 descente de Bellevue, Cap-Coz ☏ 02 98 56 00 33, ⊛ hotel-belle-vue.com. Classic seaside hotel, poised at the west end of a lovely long beach. Owned by the same family for almost a century, it's been energetically updated, with large and very pleasant sea-view bedrooms and a good-value restaurant. Closed Nov–Feb. **€92**

5

★**Bot Conan Lodge** Hent Lantecost, Beg-Meil ☎06 11 05 19 43, ⓦwww.botconan.com. Not a hotel, despite the name, but Brittany's premier glamping site, using African-style safari tents, permanently fixed on wooden decks, to provide as luxurious a camping experience as it's possible to imagine. The setting is glorious, in rural meadows that roll down to an exquisite little beach, while the tents themselves hold double beds plus separate kitchens and outdoor seating areas. Seven-day minimum stay in high season. Closed late Sept to April. **€99**

Du Port 4 corniche de la Cale, La Forêt-Fouesnant ☎02 98 56 97 33, ⓦwww.hotelduport.fr. Peaceful, smart little hotel, a short walk from the port, with very reasonably priced and brightly furnished rooms and an attractive garden-view restaurant (closed Sun & Mon). **€70**

Concarneau

The historic town of **CONCARNEAU**, on the far side of Fouesnant's Baie de la Forêt, 20km east of Bénodet, ranks as the third most important fishing port in France. Nonetheless, it manages to double as a holiday resort, thanks largely to its walled medieval **Ville Close**, the small and very well-fortified old city located a few metres offshore on an irregular rocky island in the bay.

The main **market** is held in front of the Ville Close on Friday, with a smaller one on Monday; the covered market on the far side of the square is open every morning, and holds plenty of snack stalls. Concarneau hosts an annual festival of Breton music, **Les Filets Bleus** (ⓦfestivaldesfiletsbleus.fr), during the middle weekend in August.

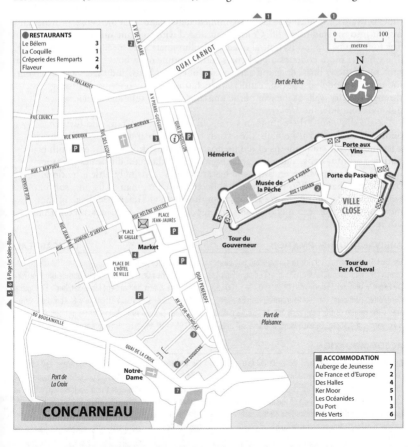

RESTAURANTS
Le Bélem	3
La Coquille	1
Crêperie des Remparts	2
Flaveur	4

ACCOMMODATION
Auberge de Jeunesse	7
De France et d'Europe	2
Des Halles	4
Ker Moor	5
Les Océanides	1
Du Port	3
Prés Verts	6

CONCARNEAU

5

The Ville Close

Even if it can get too crowded for comfort in the height of summer, Concarneau's **Ville Close** is a real delight. You reach it by crossing a narrow bridge and then passing through two successive gateways, marked by a little clocktower and a sundial. Like those of the *citadelle* at Le Palais on Belle-Île, the ramparts were completed by Vauban in the seventeenth century. The island itself, however, had been inhabited for at least a thousand years before that, and is first recorded as the site of a priory founded by King Gradlon of Quimper.

Concarneau boasts that it is a *ville fleurie*, and the flowers are at their most evident inside the walls, where climbing roses and clematis swarm all over the various gift shops, restaurants, ice-cream shops and crêperies. Walk the central pedestrianized street to the far end, and you can pass through a gateway to the shoreline to watch the fishing boats go by, or catch a little *bac* (ferry) across the river mouth. The best views of all come from the promenade on top of the **ramparts**; you can't stroll all the way round to make a complete circuit of the walls, but here and there you can climb up for short stretches.

Musée de la Pêche

3 rue Vauban • Daily: July & Aug 9.30am–7pm; April–June & Sept 10am–6pm; Feb, March, Oct and second half of Dec 10am–12.30pm & 2–6pm • €4.50 • ☏ 02 98 97 10 20, ⓦ musee-peche.fr

By exploring the history and practice of fishing all over the world, from prehistoric times onwards, the **Musée de la Pêche**, immediately inside the Ville Close, provides an insight into the traditional life Concarneau shared with so many other Breton ports. The four rooms around its central quadrangle illuminate four specific aspects of fishing. The whaling room contains model boats and a genuine open boat from the Azores; the tuna room shows boats dragging nets the size of central Paris; and there's also a herring room and a model of a sardine cannery (which this building once was). Passing through the city walls at the rear of the museum, you can tour a genuine trawler moored alongside, the *Hémerica*.

Also on show are a three-thousand-year-old anchor from Crete, and further oddities collected by fishermen; the swords of swordfish and the saws of sawfish; a Japanese giant crab; photos of old lifeboatmen with fading beards; cases full of sardine and tuna cans; and a live aquarium. A small diorama illustrates the story of local man Jean-Marie Le Bris, who has attracted surprisingly little attention considering that in 1856 he managed to become the first man to fly, in a sort of winged boat drawn by a horse and cart, on the beach at Tréfeuntec. Back in the museum shop, you can buy diagrams and models of ships, and stock up on tinned sardines and mackerel.

ARRIVAL AND INFORMATION

CONCARNEAU

By bus There's no rail service to Concarneau, but buses connect the quai d'Aiguillon with Quimper (7 daily; 40min).
By ferry In summer, Vedettes de l'Odet (☏ 02 98 57 00 58, ⓦ vedettes-odet.com) connect Concarneau with Beg-Meil, across the mouth of the bay (early July to late Aug, Wed & Fri 9am and 2.30pm; €6 each way), and also sail to the Îles Glénan (see p.280).

Tourist office Quai d'Aiguillon, just outside the *Ville Close* (May, June & first half of Sept Mon–Sat 9am–12.30pm & 1.30–6.30pm, Sun 10am–1pm; July & Aug daily 9am–7pm; mid-Sept to April Mon–Sat 9am–noon & 2–6pm; ☏ 02 98 97 01 44, ⓦ tourismeconcarneau.fr).

ACCOMMODATION

Auberge de Jeunesse Quai de la Croix ☏ 02 98 97 03 47, ⓦ ajconcarneau.com. Budget travellers will love this very central hostel, which enjoys magnificent ocean views just around the south tip of the headland from the town centre, and has a windsurfing shop nearby. Rates include breakfast; dinner available for €11. **€17.40**

De France et d'Europe 9 av de la Gare ☏ 02 98 97 00 64, ⓦ hotel-france-europe.com. Bright, modernized and very central hotel near the main bus stop, which, as well as well-furnished rooms, offers €12 buffet breakfasts, a garden terrace and a small gym. **€89**

Des Halles Rue Charles-Linement, place de l'Hôtel de

Ville ☎02 98 97 11 41, ⓦhoteldeshalles.com. Spruce, pastel-orange hotel near the fish market, across from the entrance to the *Ville Close*, offering light, recently refreshed rooms, with good showers, at reasonable rates. **€68**

★**Ker Moor** 37 rue des Sables-Blancs ☎02 98 97 02 96, ⓦhotel-kermor.com. Classic, beautifully restored seafront hotel, nautically themed throughout, on the beach 2km west of town. All the rooms have sea views – some via portholes – but you can pay extra for a balcony. **€111**

Les Océanides 3 & 10 rue du Lin ☎02 98 97 08 61, ⓦlesoceanides.free.fr. Good-value place a couple of streets up from the sea, above the fishing port, with plain rooms and a highly recommended and reasonably priced restaurant. **€65**

Du Port 11bis av Pierre Guéguin ☎02 98 97 31 52, ⓦhotelduport-concarneau.fr. Simple, old-fashioned but reasonably priced rooms just outside the *Ville Close*, reached via steep stairs above a bar immediately across from the tourist office. **€54**

★**Prés Verts** ☎02 98 97 09 74, ⓦpresverts.com. This lovely, spacious, well-shaded campsite spreads through green fields at Kernous Plage at the far end of Sables-Blancs beach; facilities include pool and crazy golf. Closed Oct–April. **€21**

EATING AND DRINKING

Le Bélem 15 av du Dr-Nicolas ☎02 30 97 03 42, ⓦlebelemrestaurant.fr. Pretty little restaurant, near the south end of the quayside on the mainland, serving mussels for around €12 and good seafood menus from €25. Mon, Tues, Fri & Sat noon–1.30pm & 7–9.15pm; Thurs & Sun noon–1.30pm.

La Coquille 1 quai du Moros ☎02 98 97 08 52, ⓦlacoquille-concarneau.com. Sophisticated French cuisine, away from the crowds but with views of the *Ville Close* from a quayside terrace across the river, with a bar-bistro as well as more formal dining. The *plat du jour* costs under €10, and a three-course lunch €20, while dinner menus range from €30 to €46.50. Tues–Sat noon–2.30pm & 7–9.30pm, Sun noon–2.30pm.

Crêperie des Remparts 31 rue Théophile Luarn ☎02 98 50 65 66. Slightly off the beaten track behind the main street in the walled city, this place serves good, inexpensive crêpes, either indoors or on a nice terrace. There's also an appealing €15 lunch menu. Daily noon–2pm & 6–9.30pm; low season closed Wed.

Flaveur 4 rue Duquesne ☎02 98 60 43 47. Fabulous fine dining in a cosy Art Deco villa, courtesy of a dynamic young Breton chef. Typical dishes include haddock mousse and spiced local pork belly, with lunch for €15.50 or €19 and dinner menus at €25–47. Tues–Fri & Sun noon–1.30pm & 7–9.15pm, Sat 7–9.15pm; closed Sun eve in low season.

Pont-Aven

PONT-AVEN, 14km east of Concarneau and just inland from the tip of the Aven estuary, is a small port village that's packed with tourists and art galleries. This was where **Paul Gauguin** came to paint in the 1880s, before he left for Tahiti in search of a South Seas idyll. By all accounts Gauguin, who based himself at the still-prominent *Pension Gloannec* (no longer open for business), was a rude and arrogant man who lorded it over the local population, already well used to posing in "peasant attire" for visiting artists. As a painter and printmaker, however, he produced some of his finest work in Pont-Aven, and his influence was such that the **Pont-Aven School** of fellow artists developed here. He spent some years working closely with these – the best known of whom was Émile Bernard – and they in turn helped to revitalize his own approach.

Even though Gauguin is the main reason visitors come to Pont-Aven, the town has no permanent collection of his work. At the time this book went to press, the **Musée de Pont-Aven** in the main square had been closed for major restoration work for several years, and was scheduled to reopen with comprehensive displays on the Pont-Aven School. For the latest news, see ⓦmuseepontaven.fr.

Gauguin aside, Pont-Aven is pleasant in its own right, with countless galleries making it easy to while away an afternoon, and the small neat **pleasure port** boasting a watermill and the odd leaping salmon. Once the day-trippers have gone home, it also makes a tranquil place to spend a night.

If you can't afford to take a souvenir canvas home with you, the town's other speciality is more affordable, and tastes better too. Pont-Aven is the home of two manufacturers of **galettes** – which here means "butter biscuits" rather than "pancakes" – and their products are on sale everywhere.

5

Promenade Xavier-Grall

Just upstream of the little granite bridge at the heart of Pont-Aven – home to perhaps the world's prettiest public toilet – the **promenade Xavier-Grall** crisscrosses the tiny river itself on landscaped walkways, offering glimpses of the backs of venerable mansions, dripping with red ivy, and a little "chaos" of rocks in the stream itself.

A longer walk – allow an hour – leads into the **Bois d'Amour**, wooded gardens which have long provided inspiration to visiting painters – and a fair tally, too, of poets and musicians.

ARRIVAL AND INFORMATION
PONT-AVEN

By bus Pont-Aven is connected by bus with the nearest *gare SNCF*, at Quimperlé (8 daily; 40min; ⓦ breizhgo.com).
By ferry Les Vedettes Aven-Bélon (ⓣ 02 98 71 14 59, ⓦ vedettes-aven-belon.com) run cruises from the pleasure port down to the sea at Port-Manech. Some continue to Port-Bélon near the mouth of the next estuary, where it's also possible to board the boats. Schedules are determined

by the tides (April–June & Sept 1 departure daily; July & Aug 1–3 departures daily; short cruises €13.50, long trips €16.50).

Tourist office 5 place de l'Hôtel de Ville (July & Aug Mon–Sat 9.30am–7pm, Sun 10am–1pm & 3–6pm; Sept–June Mon–Sat 10am–12.30pm & 2–6pm; ⓣ 02 98 06 04 70, ⓦ pontaven.com).

ACCOMMODATION AND EATING

Ajoncs d'Or 1 place de l'Hôtel de Ville ⓣ 02 98 06 02 06, ⓦ ajoncsdor-pontaven.com. The bedrooms inside this very central, blue-and-white-painted hotel are adequate and very ordinary, but it's a great location, and the restaurant (closed Sun eve) is pretty good, offering outdoor seating and serving *moules frites* for €11, a decent two-course weekday lunch or dinner for €20, and full dinner menus from €29. **€68**

Ca'Lidovine 1 promenade Xavier Grall ⓣ 02 98 06 08 99, ⓦ calidovine.com. Italian restaurant, in a delightful river-side position near the start of the walk upstream from the centre, with a full range of antipasti, home-made pasta and meat and fish dishes, as well as set menus from €26. Tues–Sat noon–2pm & 7–9.45pm, Sun noon–2pm.

Castel Braz 12 rue du Bois d'Amour ⓣ 02 98 06 07 81, ⓦ castelbraz.com. Lovely and very good-value B&B, in a charming old townhouse with peaceful gardens, where each of the six rooms is decorated to a different theme from "Jazz" to "Asia", using original artworks. No credit cards. **€70**

Domaine de Pont Aven 6 Rue St-Guénolé ⓣ 02 30 46 80 00, ⓦ hotel-domaine-pontaven.com. Smart hotel, in a former convent high on the riverbank east of the centre; road access is circuitous, but in fact it's just a minute's walk from the port, via a steep staircase. Large, comfortable rooms and suites in a new modern wing, plus a stylish dining room serving dinner from €27. **€148**

Bélon

From the unremarkable village of **RIEC-SUR-BÉLON**, 5km southeast of Pont-Aven, back roads snake down for another 4km to reach a dead end at the **port du Bélon**, on the delightfully sinuous estuary of the Bélon River. The coastal footpath that leads away from here along the thickly wooded shoreline is clearly signposted to offer optional loop trails of 3km, 6km and 8km.

EATING
RIEC-SUR-BÉLON

Chez Jacky Port de Bélon ⓣ 02 98 06 90 32, ⓦ chez-jacky.com. Hugely popular seafood restaurant, in as idyllic a setting as it's possible to imagine, surrounded by the owners' oyster beds near the mouth of the estuary. Once past the well-stocked vivarium at its entrance, you'll find bare wooden benches and tables inside, and beyond

that a lovely waterfront terrace. The ambience is informal, but both the food and the prices are to be taken seriously. Oysters start at €16 per dozen, and a huge platter of mostly raw shellfish costs €44 per person, and there are also various changing but totally fishy menus from €27. Easter–Sept Tues–Sun noon–2pm & 7–9pm.

Quimperlé

The final town of any size in Finistère, **QUIMPERLÉ**, 14km east of Pont-Aven, straddles a hill and two rivers, the Isole and the Ellé. Cut by a sequence of bridges, it's an atmospheric place, particularly in the medieval muddle of streets around **Ste-Croix**

church. This was copied in plan from schema of the Church of the Holy Sepulchre in Jerusalem, brought back by Crusaders, and is notable for its original Romanesque apse. There's a Friday **market** on the square higher up on the hill.

ACCOMMODATION AND EATING   QUIMPERLÉ

Ty Coline Pont Croac'h, St-Thurien ☎ 02 98 35 45 22, ⓦ tycoline.fr. Very pleasant rural accommodation, out in the meadows 10km northwest of Quimperlé, in the form of a nicely furnished gypsy caravan with a private outdoor terrace, and two cute little stone cottages, all capable of sleeping a family of four. Caravan €105,

cottage by the week €470
Vintage 20 rue de Brémond d'Ars ☎ 02 98 35 09 10, ⓦ hotelvintage.com. Elegant rooms individually painted by artists make this the best hotel in town; it also holds a very good restaurant, *Le Bistro de la Tour* (closed Sun & Mon, Sept–June), where full dinner menus start at €37.50. €95

Le Pouldu

At the mouth of the River Laïta, which constitutes the eastern limit of Finistère, the community of **LE POULDU** was another of Paul Gauguin's favourite haunts. It's divided into two distinct sections. The tiny **port**, on one bank of the estuary – most of which has not even a road alongside, let alone any buildings – is shielded from the open sea by a curving spit of sand. The **beach**, more developed than in Gauguin's day but still very picturesque, is a couple of kilometres away, with the headland that separates the two indented with a succession of delightful little sandy coves.

ACCOMMODATION AND EATING   LE POULDU

Grands Sables Le Pouldu ☎ 02 98 39 94 43, ⓦ camping -lesgrandssables.com. Le Pouldu makes an ideal spot to camp for a few days; this well-shaded three-star site is near the beach. Closed mid-Sept to mid-April. €18
Panoramique 2 rue de Kérou ☎ 02 98 39 93 49, ⓦ hotel-panoramique.fr. Good-value, well-kept modern hotel, a short walk up from the lovely Kérou beach. There's no restaurant, but good options are very close at hand. €67

Du Pouldu 75 rue du Port ☎ 02 98 39 90 66, ⓦ hotel -du-pouldu.com. Large, friendly and very busy family-run hotel that stands in a great position next to the port. The plain rooms have fabulous views, and the restaurant does good seafood; the one set dinner menu costs €29 (€5 supplement for a large seafood platter as a starter). Closed Oct–March. €55

Inland Brittany: The Nantes–Brest Canal

ABBAYE DE BON-REPOS ON THE NANTES–BREST CANAL

Inland Brittany: The Nantes–Brest Canal

The meandering chain of waterways known as the Nantes–Brest canal, which interweaves natural rivers with purpose-built stretches of canal, runs all the way from Finistère to the Loire. En route it passes through medieval riverside towns, such as Josselin and Malestroit, which long predate its construction; commercial ports and junctions – Pontivy, most notably – that developed along its path during the nineteenth century; the old port of Redon, on the River Vilaine; and scenic splendours including a string of lakes around the Barrage de Guerlédan. The canal ends by meeting the Loire River at the major city of Nantes, which is currently experiencing a huge revitalization focused on the stunning Machines de l'Île project.

The canal is ideal as a focus for exploring **inland Brittany**, perhaps cutting in to the towpaths along the more easily accessible stretches, and then heading out to the towns and sights around. Enjoyable detours include the **sculpture park** at Kerguéhennec and the village of **La Gacilly** near Malestroit.

According to legend, this area was covered in the distant past by one vast forest, the Argoat. Vestiges of ancient woodland still remain in several areas, like the forests of **Huelgoat**, with its boulder-strewn waterfalls, and **Paimpont**, said in Arthurian legend to have concealed the Holy Grail.

Although for much of the route no road runs adjacent to the canal, the **towpath** is normally clear enough for walking, and it's usually possible to cycle alongside as well. The best way to explore is to rent a **boat**, **barge** or even a **houseboat** along the navigable stretches.

The canal in Finistère

Although the westernmost section of the canal, passing through Finistère, is now one of its least-used stretches, it does hold a number of interesting towns and villages, including peaceful **Châteaulin**, and dynamic **Carhaix**, home to France's largest rock festival.

Châteaulin

CHÂTEAULIN, the first real town on the canal route, amounts to little more than a brief, picturesque waterside strip, overlooked by the pretty little chapel of Notre Dame. It's a quiet place, where the main reason to stay is the River Aulne itself. Enticingly rural, the river is renowned for salmon and trout **fishing**; if you're interested, most bars sell permits. You might also be drawn here by **cycling**: regional championships are held

Highlights

❶ Huelgoat A tangled ancient forest, concealing mysterious ruins and deep caverns, all but surrounds an archetypal Breton village. **See p.295**

❷ Abbaye de Bon-Repos A ruined medieval monastery in a beautiful waterfront setting near Lac de Guerlédan that also holds a gorgeous little hotel. **See p.297**

❸ Kerguéhennec Sculpture Park A sculpture park in the surreal setting of the grounds of an eighteenth-century château. **See p.300**

❹ Forêt de Paimpont A charming forest offering great walks to sites connected with the legends of Merlin. **See p.303**

❺ Malestroit The central square in this quiet medieval town holds fascinating vernacular carvings and sculptures. **See p.306**

❻ Redon A sizeable and likeably lively town at the junction of several major roads and waterways. **See p.309**

❼ Les Machines de l'Île The majestic Grand Éléphant is just one of many mechanical marvels in Nantes' sensational attraction. **See p.314**

HIGHLIGHTS ARE MARKED ON THE MAP ON PP.290–291

each September on a circuit that races through the centre, and on occasion it's used for the French professional championship.

Along the **riverbank**, a statue commemorates **Jean Moulin**, the Resistance leader of whose murder SS officer Klaus Barbie was found guilty in Lyon in 1987. Moulin was *sous-préfet* in Châteaulin from 1930 to 1933; the inscription reads "mourir sans parler" ("to die without speaking").

Canalside walks

Within a couple of minutes' walk upstream from the statue and the town centre you're on towpaths overhung by trees full of birds, with rabbits and squirrels running ahead of you on the path. For the first couple of kilometres, diagrams of corpulent yet energetic figures incite you to join them in unspeakable exercises – if you can resist that temptation, you'll soon find yourself ambling in peace past the locks and weirs that climb towards the Montagnes Noires.

The obvious target for a longer walk is the small village of **PONT COBLANT**, but be warned – it may look just 10km distant on the map, but the meanders make it a hike of several hours. There are no bridges en route, so stay on the north side, to make it easier to take a short cut back by road if you get tired.

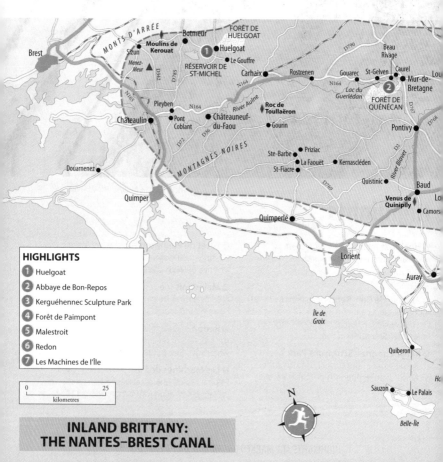

HIGHLIGHTS

1. Huelgoat
2. Abbaye de Bon-Repos
3. Kerguéhennec Sculpture Park
4. Forêt de Paimpont
5. Malestroit
6. Redon
7. Les Machines de l'Île

0 — 25
kilometres

**INLAND BRITTANY:
THE NANTES–BREST CANAL**

Pleyben

PLEYBEN, 11km northeast of Châteaulin and 4km north of the canal at Pont Coblant, is renowned for its sixteenth-century **parish close**. On its four sides the calvary traces the life of Jesus, combining great detail with an appealing naivety. The well-scrubbed church of St-Germain itself – twin-towered, with a huge ornate spire dwarfing its domed Renaissance neighbour – features an altarpiece that's blackened and buckled by age.

Châteauneuf-du-Faou

CHÂTEAUNEUF-DU-FAOU, a little way south of the N164, 25km east of Châteaulin, is much the same sort of low-key destination as Châteaulin and Pleyben, sloping down to the tree-lined river. It's a little more developed, though, and hosts one of Brittany's most enjoyable small-scale festivals, **Fest Jazz** (ⓦ fest-jazz.com), in the final weekend of July, which is known for attracting younger jazz fans and musicians.

The **canal proper** separates off from the Aulne a few kilometres east at Pont Triffen, to make its own way past Carhaix, and out of Finistère.

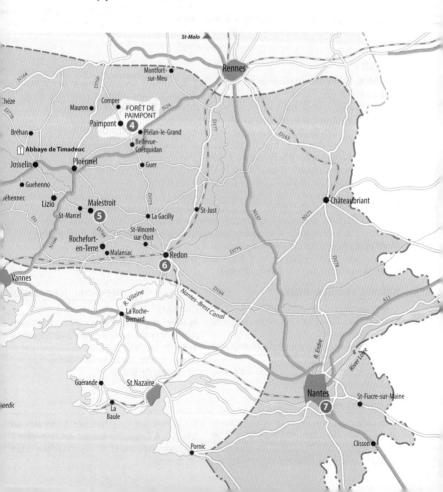

6

THE NANTES-BREST CANAL

The idea of connecting the inland waterways of Brittany dates back to 1627. However, nothing was done to implement the scheme until it became a **military necessity** during the Napoleonic wars, when English fleets began to threaten the ships circumnavigating the Breton coast. To relieve the virtual blockade of Brest in 1810, Napoleon authorized the construction of a canal network to link it with both Nantes and Lorient.

Economic disasters held up its completion, but by 1836 a navigable path was cut and the canal officially opened. It was not an immediate success. It had cost sixty million francs to construct, but the first years of operation, up to 1850, raised a mere 70,000 francs in tariffs. By the end of the nineteenth century, however, business was booming: in the years between 1890 and the outbreak of World War I, the canal carried an annual average of 35,000 tonnes of cargo. In addition to coal, the cargoes were mainly slate from the quarries near Châteaulin, and fertilizer, which helped to develop agricultural production inland.

Then motor transport and improved roads brought swift **decline**. The canal had always been used primarily for short journeys at either end – from Brest to Carhaix and Pontivy to Nantes – and in 1928 the building of a dam at Lac de Guerlédan cut it forever into two sections, with the stretch from Carhaix to Pontivy becoming navigable only by canoe. Plans for the dam were approved on the basis that either a hydraulic lift, or a side channel, would enable barges to bypass it – but neither was ever built. The last barge arrived at Châteaulin in 1945; today, the only industry that has much use for the canal is tourism.

Carhaix

CARHAIX, 25km east of Châteauneuf, is a road junction that started out as headquarters of the pre-Roman Osisme tribe. As Vorgium, from the third century AD onwards, it became the most important Roman town in Brittany. Two lengthy but largely subterranean aqueducts, vestiges of which can still be seen on walking trails, were built to provide it with fresh water.

Behind the most striking building in the modern town – the granite Renaissance **Maison de Sénéchal** on rue Brizeux – Carhaix's spacious Roman street plan remains readily apparent, though it now holds nothing more interesting than a few cafés and shops. During the third weekend of July each year Carhaix stages France's biggest **rock festival**, the massive four-day **Vieilles Charrues** (🌐 vieillescharrues.asso.fr); recent headliners have included Bruce Springsteen and the Arctic Monkeys.

East of Carhaix, the canal – as far as Pontivy – is navigable only by canoe. If that's not how you're travelling, it probably makes more sense to loop south through the **Montagnes Noires** before rejoining the canal at the **Lac de Guerlédan**. Alternatively, to the north – assuming you resisted the detour from Morlaix – you could explore the **Forêt de Huelgoat** and the **Monts d'Arrée**.

ARRIVAL AND DEPARTURE   THE CANAL IN FINISTÈRE

CHÂTEAULIN

By train Châteaulin's *gare SNCF* is on the west bank of the river, 800m from the centre.
Destinations Brest (7 daily; 1hr); Quimper (7 daily; 20min).
By bus Buses stop at the *gare SNCF*.
Destinations Carhaix (5 daily; 1hr); Châteauneuf-du-Faou (4 daily; 30min) via Pleyben (15min).

CARHAIX

By train Carhaix is connected by a spur line to Guingamp (6 daily; 1hr 15min); change there for all other destinations.
By bus Morlaix (3 daily; 1hr 30min), via Huelgoat (30min); Quimper (1 daily; 1hr 20min) via Châteauneuf-du-Faou (30min) and Châteaulin (50min).

INFORMATION

Tourist office Beside the river on quai Cosmao, Châteaulin (April–Sept Mon–Sat 9.30am–12.30pm & 2–7pm, Sun 9.30am–12.30pm; ☎ 02 98 86 02 11, 🌐 chateaulin.fr); rue Brizeux, Carhaix (July & Aug Mon–Sat 9am–12.30pm & 1.30–7pm, Sun 10am–1pm; June & Sept Mon–Sat 9am–noon & 2–6pm; Oct–May Tues–Sat 10am–noon & 2–5.30pm; ☎ 02 98 93 04 42, 🌐 huelgoat-carhaix -tourisme.com).

ACCOMMODATION AND EATING

CHÂTEAULIN

Le Chrismas 33 Grande-Rue ☎ 02 98 86 01 24, ⓦ lechrismas.com. The best value of the town's three or four modest hotels, this Logis de France is a short walk up the road that climbs east of the town centre towards Pleyben, and has a good restaurant (closed Sat eve & Sun in low season), with dinner menus from €22. **€59**

Rodaven ☎ 02 98 86 32 93, ⓦ campingderodaven.fr. Two-star municipal campsite, very attractively situated beside the river, with tent sites tucked under the trees and a wide array of rental cabins. Closed Oct–March. **€13.30**

Run Ar Puns Route de Pleyben ☎ 02 98 86 27 95, ⓦ runarpuns.com. Lively music club and bar, housed in old farm buildings 3km northeast of Châteaulin, serving a wide selection of beers, and specializing in Breton music. They also host a farmers' market on Wednesday evenings. Rock bands from further afield also play here, but there are no concerts in summer. Tues–Sat 6pm–midnight.

PLEYBEN

La Blanche Hermine Place de-Gaulle ☎ 02 98 26 61 29, ⓦ la-blanche-hermine.com. Restaurant in the spacious and grandiose main square, serving à la carte Breton specialities, including a local take on *choucroute*, from around €10. Tues–Sun noon–2pm & 7–9pm.

CHÂTEAUNEUF-DU-FAOU

Penn ar Pont Penn ar Pont ☎ 02 98 81 81 25, ⓦ pennar pont.com. Riverside tourist complex in the grounds of an impressive château, which, as well as tent sites, rental studios and inexpensive *gîtes*, boasts a swimming pool and offers cycle and boat rental. Closed Nov to mid-March. Camping **€11.50**, studios **€50**, *gîtes* **€60**

CARHAIX

Noz Vad 12 bd de la République ☎ 02 98 99 12 12, ⓦ nozvad.com. This very central hotel, near the church, has en-suite rooms, ranging from the tiny, plain "eco" rooms via plush "prestige" options to large family suites. There's a bar but no restaurant, and it also hosts live concerts in spring, plus exhibitions of art, sculpture and photography. **€51**

Montagnes Noires

The **Montagnes Noires**, south of Châteauneuf, delineate the southern borders of Finistère. Despite the name, they are really no more than escarpments, though bleak and imposing nonetheless in a harsh, exposed landscape at odds with the gentle canal path. From their highest point – the stark, slate, 318-metre **Roc de Toullaëron**, between Pont Triffen and Gourin – you can look west and north over what seems like totally deserted countryside.

Le Faouët

The secluded town of **LE FAOUËT**, southeast of Gourin, is distinguished mainly by its large old **market hall**. Above a floor of mud and straw, still used by local traders on market days on the first and third Wednesday of every month, rises an intricate latticework of ancient wood, propped on granite pillars and topped by a little clocktower.

Visitors who come to Le Faouët are generally en route to the twin churches of **St-Fiacre** and **Kernascléden** nearby, built simultaneously, according to legend, with the aid of an angelic bridge.

St-Fiacre

The church at **ST-FIACRE**, 2km south of Le Faouët, is notable for its rood screen, brightly polychromed and carved as intricately as lace. The original purpose of a rood screen was to separate the chancel from the congregation – the decorations of this 1480 masterpiece go rather further than that. They depict scenes from the Old and New Testaments as well as a dramatic series on the wages of sin. Drunkenness is demonstrated by a man somehow vomiting a fox; theft, by a peasant stealing apples.

Ste-Barbe

The fifteenth-century chapel of **Ste-Barbe** perches on a rocky outcrop a couple of kilometres east of Le Faouët, just outside the village of the same name. Accessible only along a very poor road that crosses a bridge over the main D769, it commands views of the deep wooded ravine of the River Ellé. Visitors traditionally ring a large bell in the crude bell tower on the hilltop, before descending a steep stone staircase to the chapel itself, which is the focus of the **Ste-Barbe Pardon** on the last Sunday of June.

Kernascléden

At the ornate and gargoyle-coated church at **KERNASCLÉDEN**, 15km southeast of Le Faouët, the focus turns from carving to frescoes. The themes, however, contemporary with St-Fiacre, are equally gruesome. On the damp-infested walls of a side chapel, horned devils stoke the fires beneath a vast cauldron filled with the souls of the damned, while alongside you should be able to discern the outlines of a Dance of Death, a faded cousin to that at Kermaria (see p.217). The ceiling above the main altar holds better-preserved but less bloodthirsty scenes.

ACCOMMODATION AND EATING	LE FAOUËT

Beg-er-Roch Route de Lorient ☎02 97 23 15 11, ⓦcampingbegerroch.jimdo.com. Three-star municipal campsite in a lovely setting beside the River Ellé, with lush vegetation and mobile home rental, plus footpaths through the woods and mini-golf. Closed Oct to early March. **€13**

Cheval Blanc 5 rue Albert St-Jalmes, Priziac ☎02 97 34 61 07, ⓦhotelrest-cheval-blanc.com. Good-value modernized rooms, 100m up from an attractive lake 7km northeast of Le Faouët via the pleasant (but steep) D132; breakfast costs €5 extra. **€50**

Croix d'Or 9 place Bellanger ☎03 44 54 00 04, ⓦlacroix dor.net. Tasteful if old-fashioned rooms opposite the old market in the heart of town and above the finest local restaurant, which serves lunch from €23 and €40–77 dinner menus featuring seasonal rural favourites like hare *rillettes* and crayfish risotto. Restaurant closed mid-Dec to mid-Jan, plus Sun eve, Tues eve & all Mon in low season. **€101**

Monts d'Arrée

A broad swathe of the more desolate regions of Finistère, stretching east from the Crozon peninsula to the edge of the *département*, is designated as the **Parc Régional d'Armorique**. In theory at least, the park is dedicated to conservation and rural regeneration along traditional lines; in reality, lack of funding means it creates rather less impact. The **Monts d'Arrée**, however, which cut northeast across Finistère from the Aulne estuary, are something of a nature sanctuary; kestrels circle high above the bleak hilltops, sharing the skies with pipits, curlews and great black crows.

Over to the east, the ancient woods of the **Forêt de Huelgoat** can offer an atmospheric afternoon's walking, with the lakeside village of Huelgoat itself making an attractive base if you have the time to linger.

Domaine de Ménez-Meur

Hanvec • March–May & mid-Sept to Oct Wed, Sat, Sun & daily in school hols noon–5.30pm; June to mid-Sept daily 11am–7pm; Nov–Feb school hols only, daily 1–5pm • €3.50 • ☎02 98 68 81 71, ⓦpnr-armorique.fr

The obvious place to pick up information on the Parc d'Armorique is at the **DOMAINE DE MÉNEZ-MEUR**, off the D342 near the Forêt de Cranou. Ménez is an official **animal reserve**, with wild boar and deer roaming free, and a programme of raising rare Breton breeds of sheep and pigs. Rangers at the reserve gate can provide a wealth of detail on the park and all its various activities.

Maison de la Rivière

Moulin de Vergraon, Sizun • Mon–Fri 10am–noon & 2–5.30pm • €4 • ☎02 98 68 86 33, ⓦmaison-de-la-riviere.fr

Eight kilometres north of Ménez-Meur, at **SIZUN**, a research station, **aquarium** and fishing exhibition, known collectively as the **Maison de la Rivière**, sets out to increase public awareness of the significance of Brittany's rivers and inland waterways. Quite apart from its educational value, it's also a good spot for a waterside picnic.

Ecomusée des Monts d'Arrée

Commana • Feb hols & Christmas hols Mon–Fri 10am–5pm; mid-March to May, Sept & Oct Mon–Fri 10am–6pm, Sun 2–6pm; June Mon–Fri 10am–6pm, Sat & Sun 2–6pm; July & Aug daily 11am–7pm • €4.50 • ☎ 02 98 68 87 76, ⓦ ecomusee-monts -arree.fr

After the last inhabitant of **MOULINS DE KEROUAT** – in Breton, Milin-Kerroc'h – died in 1967, the village, on the D764 3km east of Sizun, might have crumbled into indiscernible ruins. Instead, the entire abandoned hamlet has become the **Écomusée des Monts d'Arrée**, with one of its watermills restored to motion, and its houses repaired and refurnished. The largest belonged in the nineteenth century to the mayor of Commana, who also controlled the mills, and its furnishings are, therefore, those of a rich family.

Huelgoat

Best known for its namesake adjoining **forest**, the village of **HUELGOAT**, halfway between Morlaix and Carhaix on the minor road D769, is a pretty little place that has become hugely popular with British holiday-makers and home owners, including a healthy contingent of **mountain biking** enthusiasts. At its core lies a distinguished grey-stone square surrounded by the everyday businesses of rural Breton life, while to the south and west the ever-expanding settlement spreads along the shores of its own small **lake**. A pleasant overnight stop, Huelgoat was also the ancestral home of the Kerouac family, as in Jack Kerouac of *On The Road* fame.

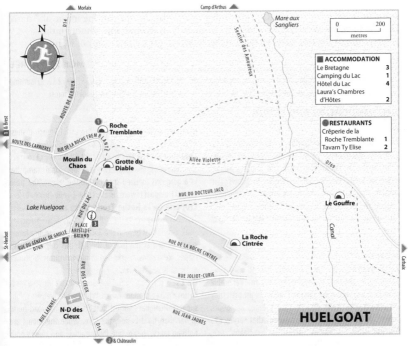

Forêt de Huelgoat

While there may be doubt as to whether the "Argoat", the great forest supposed to have stretched the length of prehistoric inland Brittany, ever existed, the antiquity of the **Forêt de Huelgoat**, stretching north from the village, cannot be questioned. Until 1987, this was a staggering landscape of trees, giant boulders and waterfalls tangled together in primeval chaos. Just how fragile it really was, just how miraculous had been its long survival, was demonstrated by the **hurricane** of that October, which smashed it to smithereens in the space of fifteen minutes.

After almost three decades of restoration, the forest has now returned to a fairly close approximation of its former glories. Once again, it's possible to walk for several kilometres along the various paths that lead into the depths of the woods, and in spring and autumn in particular Huelgoat merits a substantial detour.

A half-hour stroll close to the village enables you to scramble over, among, and even under all sorts of bizarre granite formations, including several inconceivably large tumbled boulders. At the **Grotte du Diable** ("Devil's Cave"), a short way along the main path from the former watermill known as the Moulin du Chaos, just below the road bridge, you can make a somewhat perilous descent, between the rocks, to a subterranean stream.

A hundred or so metres further on, at an open-air auditorium used for occasional performances, the path crosses the stream. Near the top of a small hill on the far side, the **Roche Tremblante** ("trembling rock") is supposed to wobble at the slightest prod; in reality, it seems to remain disappointingly stable despite the strenuous efforts of every passing walker. Just beyond that, in a lovely sunny garden at the foot of the hill is the *Crêperie de la Roche Tremblante* (see below).

Camp d'Arthus

Well into the forest beyond the Roche Tremblante, not far from the waterfall known as the **Mare aux Sangliers**, the **Camp d'Arthus** has been identified as a Gallo-Roman *oppidum*, or hillfort, large enough to be a settlement for a whole community rather than just a military encampment. Until the hurricane, it was also the spitting image of Astérix the Gaul's fictional village. Nowadays it's not nearly so recognizable, although the obliteration of the tree cover enabled archeologists to get a clearer view of its history.

INFORMATION

MONTS D'ARRÉE

Tourist office 18 place Aristide-Briand, Huelgoat (July & Aug Mon–Sat 10am–12.30pm & 2–5pm; Sept–June Mon–Sat 10–11.45am & 2.30–4.30pm; ☎ 02 98 99 72 32, ⓦ tourisme huelgoat.fr), supplies walking maps of the forest.

ACCOMMODATION AND EATING

BRASPARTS

Les Roulottes des Korrigans Rue du Château d'Eau, Goarem Edern ☎ 02 98 81 41 62, ⓦ roulottes-des -korrigans.com. Irresistible, static, and brightly painted gypsy caravans, set on rolling hillside meadows 1km outside Brasparts and 20km southwest of Huelgoat. Capable of sleeping up to five guests, and equipped with kitchenettes, they're normally available for stays of two or more nights only. **€99**

HUELGOAT

Le Bretagne 13 place Aristide-Briand ☎ 02 98 99 83 66, ⓦ le-bretagne-huelgoat.com. Venerable townhouse on the main square, holding eight tastefully restored rooms, decorated to such themes as "South American" or "Asian", plus a restaurant that serves €15 Mexican and Colombian specialities – beans, rice,

plantains, fajitas – as well as the usual French dishes. **€76**

Camping du Lac Le Fao ☎ 02 98 99 78 80, ⓔ contact @lerivieredargent.com. Two-star municipal campsite, in a gorgeous forested spot beside the lake, 800m from central Huelgoat towards Brest. Closed Sept–June. **€12**

Crêperie de la Roche Tremblante Rue de la Roche Tremblante ☎ 02 98 99 98 08, ⓦ creperie-huelgoat -finistere.fr. Just beyond the Roche Tremblante, in a lovely sunny garden at the foot of the hill, this crêperie serves crêpes, ice creams, snacks and drinks to visitors. Summer only; daily noon–7pm.

Du Lac 9 rue du Général-de-Gaulle ☎ 02 98 99 71 14, ⓦ hoteldulac-huelgoat.com. Whatever its website might suggest, Huelgoat's largest hotel is across the road from, rather than right beside, the lake. While the rooms are nothing fancy, they're fine for the price, and there's both a bistro that serves hearty local food on menus at €23 and €32, and a more casual pizzeria. **€60**

Laura's Chambres d'Hôtes 2 Impasse des Cendres ☎ 02 98 99 91 62, ⓦ bnbhuelgoatlauras.vpweb.co.uk. Very welcoming and good-value B&B, at the northern end of the village centre, offering six plain rooms with good en-suite facilities, including some family-sized suites. **€59**

Tavarn Ty Elise Rue Collorec, Plouyé ☎ 02 29 25 01 15, ⓦ crwtynrhifnaw.blogspot.co.uk. Cosy little pub, in a small village 6km south of Huelgoat, and run by a convivial Welshman. Besides serving a wide range of real ales and organic beers, it's well known in these parts for putting on regular evenings of traditional Breton music. Wed–Fri 4–11pm, Sat 3pm–1am, Sun 2–11pm.

Lac de Guerlédan

Between Carhaix and Pontivy, the waters of the **Nantes–Brest canal** are limited to canoeists, but it's worth making the effort to follow its course on land, particularly for the scenery around the artificial **Lac de Guerlédan**, between **Gouarec** and **Mur-de-Bretagne**. Along this 15km stretch the **N164** skirts the edge of the **Forêt de Quénécan**, within which lies the lake, created when the Barrage of Guerlédan was completed in 1928. It's a beautiful section of the river, if a little over-popular with British camper-caravanners, but peaceful enough nonetheless. If you're approaching by road, the canal path is easiest joined at Gouarec. En route, you pass the rather subdued (and unmemorable) town of **ROSTRENEN**, whose old facades are given a little life at the Tuesday **market**.

Gouarec

At **GOUAREC**, the River Blavet and the canal meet in a confusing swirl of water that shoots off, edged by footpaths, in the most unlikely directions. The old houses of the town are barely disturbed by traffic or development, nor are there great numbers of tourists.

Abbaye de Bon-Repos

March–June & Sept–Nov Mon–Fri 10am–noon & 2–6pm, Sat 10am–noon, Sun 2–6pm; July & Aug daily 10am–7pm, plus son et lumière first two weekends of Aug • €5, son et lumière €20 • ☎ 02 96 24 82 20, ⓦ bon-repos.com

Just off the N164 near the village of **ST-GELVEN**, 5km east of Gouarec, the beautiful **Abbaye de Bon-Repos** nestles beside the water at the end of an avenue of ancient trees. Most of the main body of this twelfth-century Cistercian abbey was destroyed during the French Revolution, but many of its former outbuildings survive, including the impressive façade, which now faces onto the canal, and former residences, housing a delightful hotel (see p.298).

The ruins of the abbey are open to visitors, and also play host to *son et lumière* spectacles in August, in which hundred of performers, some on horseback, re-enact scenes from Breton myth and history. In addition, the grounds host a **farmers' and craft market** on Sunday mornings between Easter and late October (ⓦ lepetitmarchedebonrepos.com).

A little further down the lane, a tiny stone bridge crosses the canal, and the towpath squeezes alongside meadows, popular with picnickers.

Beau Rivage

From just west of **CAUREL**, 7km east of St-Gelven, the brief loop of the D111 leads to tiny sandy beaches – a bit too tiny in season. The lovely riverside spot known justifiably as **Beau Rivage** is a very popular location for **waterskiing** (☎ 02 99 21 11 16, ⓦ skiguerledan.fr), and holds a handful of hotels and restaurants.

Mur-de-Bretagne

MUR-DE-BRETAGNE, set back from the eastern end of the lake, is a lively place with a wide and colourful pedestrianized zone around its church. As the nearest town to the barrage – just 2km distant – it serves as the main centre for visitors to pick up information and supplies.

6

INFORMATION

Tourist office 1 place de l'Église, Mur-de-Bretagne (July & Aug Mon–Thurs & Sat 9.30am –12.30pm & 2–6.30pm, Fri 9.30am –12.30pm & 2–7.30pm, Sun 9.30am–12.30pm;

LAC DE GUERLÉDAN

Sept–June Mon–Sat 9.30am –12.30pm & 2–6pm; ☎ 02 96 28 51 41, ⓦ guerledan.fr). They can organize bike rides, horseriding, canoeing and jet-skiing.

ACCOMMODATION AND EATING

GOUAREC

Ty Aven 45 rue du Moulin ☎ 02 96 24 87 99, ⓦ tyaven .com. Cosy little B&B, owned by a friendly couple from Yorkshire. Three bedrooms, one of them family-sized, with British TV and fishing tackle for use on the adjacent river. Rates include continental breakfast; for €5 extra per person, they serve a full English fry-up breakfast. No credit cards. **€55**

ST-GELVEN

Café de l'Abbaye Bon-Repos ☎ 02 96 24 86 56. Rural brasserie, beside the river just across the bridge from the abbey, with nice outdoor seating. Hot dogs and ice creams, plus mussels and chips for €10 and steak and chips for €15. There are open-mic sessions by local musicians on Sundays. Tues–Sun 11am–8pm.

★ Les Jardins de l'Abbaye Abbaye de Bon Repos ☎ 02 96 24 95 77, ⓦ abbaye.jardin.free.fr. Irresistible and inexpensive hotel-restaurant, housed in the cosy slate outbuildings of the abbey. Offering slightly musty, old-fashioned rooms with porthole-style windows, it makes a gloriously peaceful retreat – apart from the hooting of owls in the darkness. The restaurant is a delight, with a panelled dining room filled with china pigs and pig-related knick-knacks, and tables out on the gravel courtyard; the hearty cuisine on menus from €19.50 is reminiscent of Normandy. The owners can be slapdash about answering emails or keeping reservations; be sure to check ahead. **€45**

BEAU RIVAGE

Beau Rivage Site du Beau Rivage ☎ 02 96 28 52 15, ⓦ le-beau-rivage.info. This hotel/restaurant may not be at all prepossessing as a building, and the four bedrooms, though new and well equipped are carpeted all the way up the wall, but it commands magnificent views of the lake

and serves great food, with dinner menus from €20 and even crêpes for breakfast. Restaurant closed Mon eve in July & Aug, all Wed June–Sept. **€55**

L'Embarcadère Site du Beau Rivage ☎ 02 96 28 52 64, ⓦ guerledan.com. Lakefront restaurant serving good meals on its own terrace – menus start at €20, including drinks. It is also the base for two glass-topped sightseeing boats that offer pleasure cruises on the Lac de Guerlédan (€10; July & Aug daily 3pm), as well as three-hour dinner trips (€40–60; schedules vary). April to mid-Oct daily noon–2pm & 6–9pm.

MUR-DE-BRETAGNE

Auberge Grand'Maison 1 rue Léon-le-Cerf ☎ 02 96 28 51 10, ⓦ auberge-grand-maison.com. Hotel/restaurant on the left as you climb towards the centre of town, with nicely spruced-up rooms, and a very good dining room, where weekday lunches cost €30, and otherwise menus start at €58. The chef runs regular half-day cooking classes, as detailed on the website. **€60**

Merlin les Pieds dans l'Eau Anse de Sordan, St-Aignan ☎ 02 97 27 52 36. Ten kilometres west of Mur-de-Bretagne and primarily known as a restaurant/ snack bar, serving drinks, pizzas and full menus, which can be enjoyed at wooden outdoor tables beside the south shore of the lake, this gloriously rural spot also offers camping and three simple double rooms, best reserved well in advance. Bikes, boats, canoes and pedalos are available to rent. Camping **€13.30**, rooms **€60**

Le Point de Vue 104 rue du Lac ☎ 02 96 26 01 90, ⓦ camping-lepointdevue.fr. Lush lakeside campground, 2km west of the town centre, with self-catering cabins, theme nights and access to a full range of watersports. Closed late Sept to mid-May. **€12.25**

The central canal

Beyond the barrage of Guerlédan, the course of the canal breaks off once more from the River Blavet at **Pontivy**, from where you can once again take **barges** – all the way to the Loire. Until you get as far as **Josselin**, with its imposing waterfront ducal castle, none of the towns en route is all that enthralling, but there are some quirky rural attractions nearby, such as the enigmatic statue known as the *Vénus de Quinipily* near **Baud**.

Pontivy

The historic town of **PONTIVY** owes much of its appearance and size to its role as the principal junction of the Nantes–Brest canal. When the waterway opened, the small medieval centre was expanded, redesigned and given broad avenues to fit its new role. It was even renamed **Napoléonville** for a time, in honour of the instigator of its new prosperity, and still uses the name fairly interchangeably. These days, it is a bright market town, its twisting old streets contrasting with the stately riverside promenades.

Château de Rohan

1 rue de Lourmel • Mid-Feb to mid-April & mid-Sept to mid-Nov Wed–Sun 2–6pm; mid-April to mid-June daily 10am–noon & 2–6pm; mid-June to mid-Sept daily 10.30am–6.30pm • €5 • ☎ 02 97 25 12 93

6

Occupying a low eminence above the main through road at the north end of Pontivy, the **Château de Rohan** was built by the lord of Josselin in the late fifteenth century. Used in summer for low-key cultural events and temporary exhibitions, the castle still belongs to the Josselin family. Behind its impressive facade, complete with deep moat and two forbidding towers looking out over the river, the structure rather peters out, though there's a very striking installation of glowing ovals by Koki Watanabe in the basement.

West from Pontivy: along the Blavet

If you choose to follow the **River Blavet** southwest from Pontivy towards Lorient – rather than the canal – take the time to go by the smaller roads along the valley itself. The Blavet connects the canal with the sea, and once linked Lorient to the other two great ports of Brittany, Brest and Nantes.

Quistinic

The D159 to **QUISTINIC** passes through lush green countryside, its hedgerows full of flowers, where by June there's already been one harvest and grass is growing up around the fresh haystacks. The ivy-clad church of **St-Mathurin** in Quistinic is the scene of a *pardon* (in the second week of May) that dates from Roman times. The devotion to the saint is strongly evident on the village's war memorial, too – his name is that of almost half the victims.

Village de Poul-Fetan

3km southwest of Quistinic • Daily: April & May 2–6.30pm; June & Sept 11am–6.30pm; July & Aug 10.45am–7pm • €9.80 • ☎ 02 96 39 51 74

Clearly signposted from Quistinic, the **Village de Poul-Fetan** is an entire Breton village, recreated to how it might have looked in 1850, and peopled by costumed guides who talk visitors through traditional crafts and skills. Various thatched stone cottages hold the likes of a bakery and a smithy; assorted farm animals need feeding and daily care; and children can play long-lost village games.

Vénus de Quinipily

2km southwest of Baud • Daily: May–Oct 10am–7pm; Nov–April 11am–5pm • €3 • ☎ 02 97 39 04 94

The main reason to go on to **BAUD**, a major road junction just east of the river, is to see the **Vénus de Quinipily**. Signposted off the Hennebont road, the Venus is a crude statue that at first glance looks Egyptian. Once known as the "Iron Lady", it is of unknown but ancient origin. It stands on, or rather nestles its ample buttocks against, a high plinth above a kind of sarcophagus, commanding the valley in the gardens of what was once a château. Behind its stiff pose and dress, the statue has an odd informality, a half-smile on the otherwise impassive face. It used to be the object of "impure rites" and was at least twice thrown into the Blavet by Christian authorities, only to be fished out by locals eager to reindulge. It may itself have been in some way "improper" before it was recarved, perhaps literally "dressed", sometime in the eighteenth century.

The **gardens** around the statue are luxuriantly fertile, while the various farmhouses and outbuildings are adorned with splendid flowers.

Josselin

The historic riverside town of **JOSSELIN** is full of medieval splendours, with its gargoyle-studded **basilica** ringed by twisted streets of half-timbered houses. The major attraction for visitors, however, is the **château**, looming high over the Oust.

Château de Rohan

Early April to mid-July & Sept daily 2–6pm; mid-July to Aug daily 11am–6pm; Oct Sat, Sun & hols 2–5.30pm • Tours €8.40, musée €7.50; combined ticket €13.50 • ☎ 02 97 22 36 45, ⓦ chateaujosselin.com

The three Rapunzel towers of the **Château de Rohan**, embedded in a vast sheet of stone above the water, are the most impressive sight along the Nantes–Brest canal. They now serve as a façade for the remnants of the much older castle behind, built by Olivier de Clisson in 1370, the original riverfront towers of which were demolished by Richelieu in 1629 in punishment for Henri de Rohan's leadership of the Huguenots. The Rohan family, still in possession, used to own a third of Brittany; the present incumbent is now a national senator.

Tours of the oppressively formal apartments of the ducal residence are not very compelling, even if it does contain the table on which the Edict of Nantes was signed in 1598. But the duchess's collection of ancient **dolls**, housed in the **Musée des Poupées** behind the castle, is something special. She owns around three thousand, of which she displays a different selection of around six hundred each year.

Notre Dame du Roncier

Josselin's basilica of **Notre Dame du Roncier** was built on the spot where in the ninth century a peasant supposedly found a statue of the Virgin under a bramble bush. The statue was burned during the Revolution, but an important *pardon* is held each year on September 8. As ever, the religious procession and open-air services are solemn in the extreme, but there's a lot of other stuff going on to keep you entertained.

Guéhenno

GUÉHENNO, 10km south of Josselin on the D123, holds one of Brittany's largest and finest **calvaries**. Built in 1550, the figures include the cock that crowed to expose Peter's denials, Mary Magdalene with the shroud and a recumbent Christ in the crypt. Its appeal is enhanced by the naivety of its amateur restoration. After damage caused by Revolutionary soldiers in 1794 – who amused themselves by playing boules with the heads of the statues – all the sculptors approached for the work demanded exorbitant fees, so the parish priest and his assistant decided to undertake the task themselves.

Domaine de Kerguéhennec

Bignan, 7km west of Guéhenno • Daily 8am–9pm; exhibitions late June to late Sept daily 11am–7pm; late Sept to late June Wed–Sun noon–6pm • Free • ☎ 02 97 60 44 44, ⓦ art-kerguehennec.com

The **Domaine de Kerguéhennec**, signposted off the D11 near St-Jean-Brévelay, is an innovatory **sculpture park**, spreading across the lawns, woods and lake of an early eighteenth-century château. Since opening in 1986, it has built up a fascinating permanent collection, and become an increasingly compelling stop. Many of the pieces have been created on the spot by leading international sculptors who have served as artists-in-residence. Among the first to be installed was a massive railway sleeper, painstakingly stripped down by Giuseppe Penone to reveal the young sapling within.

Regular exhibitions are also staged in the château interior, while studios and indoor workshops in the outbuildings are used by visiting artists.

FORÊT DE PAIMPONT (P.303) >

Lizio

The little village of **LIZIO**, off the D151, 9km east of Guéhenno, has set itself up as a centre for arts and crafts, with ceramic and weaving workshops as its speciality. For most of the year, you might pass along its single curving street of stone cottages without seeing a sign of life; on the second Sunday in August, however, it's the scene of a **Festival Artisanal**, featuring street theatre (and pancakes).

Insectarium

Daily: April–June, Sept & Oct 2–6pm; July & Aug 10am–7pm; last admission 1hr before closing • €7.50 • ☎ 02 97 74 94 31, ⓦ insectariumdelizio.fr

If you do take the trouble to stop in Lizio, you may spot that one venerable old cottage, from the outside looking much like the rest, houses an **Insectarium**. Creepy-crawlies within include all sorts of hairy spiders, giant millipedes, huge iridescent butterflies, praying mantises that look like dead leaves and stick insects in amazing colours. It's a little expensive for twenty minutes on the verge of nausea, but kids will probably love it.

Éco-Musée des Vieux Métiers

D174, 4km northeast of Lizio towards Ploërmel • Daily: April–June & mid-Sept to Oct 2–6pm; July to mid-Sept 10am–noon & 2–7pm • €6.50 • ☎ 02 97 74 93 01, ⓦ ecomuseelizio.com

In the countryside surrounding Lizio, various farmers, who welcome visitors, are working to recreate traditional skills such as beekeeping and cider-making, and one is even rearing wild boars for food. The **Eco-Musée des Vieux Métiers** can provide details of them all, as well as an overview of long-lost agricultural techniques and implements.

Ploërmel

Back in the fourteenth century, the English garrison of **PLOËRMEL** was defeated by Josselin in the Battle of the Thirty, a contest that was fought by thirty dismounted knights from either side, halfway between the two towns. Ploërmel is still not quite a match for its rival, partly because it's not on the canal, but it does hold a few attractions, including the artificial **Étang au Duc**, well stocked with fish, 2km north, and an interesting array of houses. James II is said to have spent a few days of his exile in one on rue Francs-Bourgeois, while the **Maison des Marmosets** on rue Beaumanoir has some elaborate carvings.

Spending a night here makes a suitable base for venturing further away from the canal, up into Paimpont forest.

ARRIVAL AND DEPARTURE THE CENTRAL CANAL

PONTIVY

By train Pontivy's *gare SNCF* is ten minutes' walk southeast of the tourist office.

Destinations St-Brieuc (12 daily; 1hr 15min); Vannes (6 daily; 55min).

By bus Buses connect the *gare SNCF* with Rennes (6 daily; 2hr) via Josselin (30min) and Ploërmel (45min).

INFORMATION

PONTIVY

Tourist office On a barge moored beside 2 quai Niémen (June–Sept daily 9.30am–6.30pm; Oct–May Mon–Sat 9.30am–12.30pm & 2–6pm; ☎ 02 97 25 04 10, ⓦ tourisme-pontivycommunaute.com).

JOSSELIN

Tourist office 4 rue des Remparts (April–June & Sept Mon 1.30–5.30pm, Tues–Sat 10am–noon & 1.30–5.30pm; July & Aug daily 10am–6pm; Oct–March Mon 1.30–5.30pm, Tues, Wed & Fri 10am–noon & 1.30–5.30pm, Sat 10am–noon; ☎ 02 97 22 36 43, ⓦ josselin-communaute.fr).

PLOËRMEL

Tourist office 5 rue du Val (July & Aug Mon–Sat 9.30am–6.30pm, Sun 9.30am–12.30pm; Sept–June Mon–Sat 10am–12.30pm & 2–6pm; ☎ 02 97 74 02 70, ⓦ tourisme-ploermel.com).

ACCOMMODATION AND EATING

PONTIVY

Auberge de Jeunesse Île des Récollets ☎02 97 25 58 27, ⓦfuaj.org/Pontivy. Smart hostel, on an island at the north end of town where the river meets the canal, that's very popular with cyclists. Reservation only at weekends in low season. **€15.80**

Europe 12 rue François-Mitterrand ☎02 97 25 11 14, ⓦen.hotellerieurope.com. Charming and very comfortable hotel not far from the river, with modernized rooms and a dining room that's open for dinner only. **€82**

Interhôtel du Château 41 rue du Général-de-Gaulle ☎02 97 25 34 88, ⓦhoteldepontivy.com. Spruce, inexpensive hotel, very near the tourist office, with plain but bright modern rooms and decent €8.50 buffet breakfasts, though no restaurant. **€62**

La Pommeraie 17 quai du Couvent ☎02 97 25 60 09. Lunch menus at this friendly family-run restaurant – certainly the best in town – start at €19, and there's a great €32 dinner menu filled with rich rural specialities such as veal with cèpes. Tues–Sat noon–2pm & 7.30–9.30pm.

QUISTINIC

★**Vallée de Pratmeur** Le Roduic ☎02 97 51 72 02, ⓦvalleedepratmeur.com. Unique and very wonderful accommodation on this wooded estate ranges from individually designed and intricately engineered wooden treehouses to gypsy caravans, yurts and see-through bubble tents, equipped with beds and either raised on platforms or set in the branches of trees. The main house also holds a couple of conventional B&B rooms. Everyone has their own outdoor space, and all share use of an indoor pool. B&B **€70**, yurt or bubble tent **€90**, caravan **€100**, treehouse **€130**

BAUD

Auberge du Cheval Blanc 16 rue de Pontivy ☎02 97 51 00 85, ⓦen.hotelduchevalblanc56.com. Inexpensive

Logis de France in the heart of town, with simple, bright rooms and a good-value restaurant (closed Mon lunch, plus Sat lunch & Sun eve Sept–June), where menus start at €13.50 for lunch, €16 for dinner. **€65**

JOSSELIN

Camping Domaine de Kerelly Bas de la Lande, Guégon ☎02 97 22 22 20, ⓦcamping-josselin.com. Very pleasant little three-star campsite, right beside the river, a 30min walk west from the castle, with a mini-golf course and simple rental chalets, as well as pitches. Closed early Oct to mid-April. **€16**

★**Du Château** 1 rue du Général-de-Gaulle ☎02 97 22 20 11, ⓦhotel-chateau.com. Facing Josselin's fairytale castle from across the river, this lovely hotel makes a perfect place to stay. Though the slightly more expensive rooms, with château views, are not particularly luxurious, they're worth it – the whole place looks fabulous lit up at night – while the dining room, serving lunch from €16 and dinner for €21–45, is first-rate. **€83.20**

PLOËRMEL

Cobh 10 rue des Forges ☎02 97 74 00 49, ⓦhotel -lecobh.com. Fancy and very friendly little hotel, behind a yellow façade in the heart of town, with a dozen cosy rooms – some family-sized – named for characters from Breton legend. At lunch time on weekdays the dining room serves a bistro menu, with a daily *plat* for €9.50; dinner menus start at €27. **€77**

St-Marc 1 place de St-Marc ☎02 97 74 00 01, ⓦhotel -restaurant-saintmarc.com. Good-value hotel near the long-defunct railway station, with plain but acceptable rooms. What they rather charmingly call a "semi-gastronomic" restaurant (closed Sun eve) serves classic Breton cuisine at €15 for lunch, from €22 for dinner. **€46.50**

Forêt de Paimpont

A definite magic lingers about the **FORÊT DE PAIMPONT**. Though now just forty square kilometres in extent, it seems to retain the secrets of a forest once much larger, and everywhere recalls legends of the vanished Argoat, the great primeval forest of Brittany. The one French claimant to an Arthurian past that carries any real conviction, it is just as frequently known by its Arthurian name of **Brocéliande**. Its central village, **Paimpont**, is much the nicest of the little settlements scattered in and around the woodlands.

Paimpont

PAIMPONT village is the most obvious and enjoyable base for exploring its namesake forest. Right at the centre of the woods, backing onto a marshy lake whose shores are thick with wild mushrooms (*cèpes*), it consists of little more than a single little street of stone cottages, leading to a lakeside abbey.

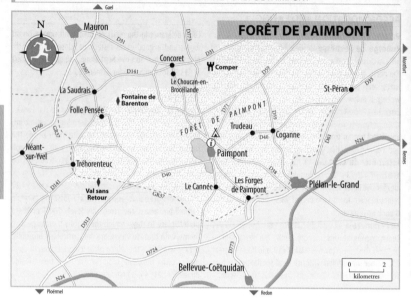

The main square alongside the abbey holds both the tourist office for the whole area and the **Porte des Secrets** (April–Oct daily 9.40–11.40am & 2–5pm; Nov–March Wed–Sun 9.40–11.40am & 2–4pm; €7.50; ☎02 99 07 84 23, ⓦportedessecrets -broceliande.com), a set of converted village houses, inside which fancy interactive displays explain the story of the forest in legend and reality.

Superb **walking** can be enjoyed in almost any direction; the best megalithic site in the vicinity is undoubtedly the **Site des Pierres Droites**, a stone circle not far south.

Château de Comper

7km north of Paimpont · Late March to June, Sept & Oct Mon & Thurs–Sun 10am–5.30pm; July–Sept daily except Wed 10am–7pm · €6 · ☎ 02 97 22 79 96, ⓦ centre-arthurien-broceliande.com

The enchantress Viviane is supposed to have been born at the **Château de Comper**, at the northern edge of the forest near Concoret. Today it serves as the **Centre de l'Imaginaire Arthurien**, hosting different exhibitions and entertainments on Arthurian themes each summer. Only pay to go in if the year's temporary exhibition interests you – the château itself dates largely from the nineteenth century, and the permanent displays of pointlessly posed mannequins are boring in the extreme.

Val sans Retour

Viviane's rival, Morgane le Fay, ruled over the **Val sans Retour** (Valley of No Return) on the western edge of the forest, just off the GR37 footpath from Tréhorenteuc, 11km west of Paimpont. For a round-trip hike that will take up to two hours, depending on how soon you choose to turn back, follow the path south from Tréhorenteuc until you come to a signed junction to the left, leading to a steep valley from which exits are barred by thickets of gorse and giant furze on the rocks above. At one point it skirts an overgrown table of rock, the **Rocher des Faux Amants** ("Rock of the False Lovers") – from which the seductress Morgane was wont to entice unwary and faithless youths.

Maison du Patrimoine

2 rue de Château, Montfort-sur-Meu • School holidays only, all year Tues–Fri 2–6pm, Sun 3–6pm • €5 • ⓦ ecomusee-montfort.com

At **MONTFORT-SUR-MEU**, northeast of the forest and 25km west of Rennes, an illuminating eco-museum, officially known as the **Maison du Patrimoine**, provides background information on the region. Set in the one tower that survives of what in the fourteenth century was a complete walled town, it holds – as well as the usual small-town museum assortment of costumed dolls – fascinating displays on various aspects of local ecology, economy and history. It also runs workshops, where children are taught traditional crafts with materials such as cow dung, and where sculptors explain their work to casual visitors.

6

ARRIVAL AND INFORMATION

PAIMPONT

By bus Regular buses connect the village centre with Rennes (8 daily; 1hr).

Tourist office Place du Roi Judicaël, alongside the Porte des Secrets (April–June, Sept & Oct daily 9.30am–12.30pm & 2–6pm; July & Aug daily 9.15am–7pm; Nov–March Wed–Sun 9.30am–12.30pm & 2–5pm; ☎ 02 99 07 84 23,

FORÊT DE PAIMPONT

ⓦ tourisme-broceliande.com).

TRÉHORENTEUC

Tourist office 1 place Abbé Gillard (Mon–Sat 10am–12.30pm & 2–5.30pm; ☎ 02 97 93 05 12, ⓦ valsansretour .com). They organize regular guided walking tours to the Val sans Retour and Fontaine de Barenton.

ACCOMMODATION AND EATING

PAIMPONT

Camping Municipal 2 rue du Chevalier Lancelot du Lac ☎ 02 97 07 89 16, ⓦ camping-paimpont-broceliande .com. Attractive, well-wooded two-star municipal campsite

on the edge of Paimpont village. Closed Oct–March. **€12.15**

Corne du Cerf Le Cannée ☎ 02 99 07 84 19, ⓦ corne ducerf.bcld.net. Three bright and beautifully decorated B&B rooms in a pretty stone cottage 3km south of

---

SEARCHING FOR THE FOUNTAIN OF ETERNAL YOUTH

Medieval Breton minstrels, like their Welsh counterparts, set the tales of King Arthur and the Holy Grail both in *Grande Bretagne* and here in *Petite Bretagne*. The particular significance of Brocéliande was as the forest where **Merlin** made his home; some say that he is still here, in "Merlin's stone", where he was imprisoned by the enchantress **Viviane**.

The stone is next to the **Fontaine de Barenton**, a lonely spot high in the woods, a dozen kilometres northwest of Paimpont, that's far from easy to find. Turn off the main road into the forest from **Concoret** (a village notable for having once supposedly had the Devil as its rector) at La Saudrais, and you will come to the village of **Folle Pensée**. Go past the few farmhouses, rather than up the hill, and you arrive at a small car park. Follow the wide, gravelled path from its far end, then turn right onto another wide footpath at the first trail intersection. Take the next branch left, and then turn right again at the next junction. The *fontaine* is a couple of hundred metres on, set in a muddy clearing amid the oak trees, and filled with the most delicious water imaginable.

This is the very spot where Merlin first set eyes on Viviane. Sadly, it's not the **Fountain of Eternal Youth** – that's hidden somewhere nearby, and accessible only to the pure in heart. Legend has it, however, that if after drinking from the Barenton *fontaine*, you splash water on to the stone slab, you instantly summon a mighty storm, together with roaring lions and a horseman in black armour. The story dates back at least to the fifth century and is recounted, somewhat sceptically, in Robert Wace's *Romance of the Rose*, written around 1160:

Hunters repair [to the fountain] in sultry weather; and drawing water with their horns, they sprinkle the stone for the purposes of having rain, which is then wont to fall, they say, throughout the forest around; but why I know not. There too fairies are to be seen (if the Bretons tell truth), and many other wonders happen. I went thither on purpose to see these marvels. I saw the forest and the land, and I sought for the marvels, but I found none. I went like a fool, and so I came back. I sought after folly, and found myself a fool for my pains.

The parish priest of Concoret and his congregation are reported nonetheless to have successfully ended a drought by this means in 1835, and a procession endorsed by the church went to the spring as recently as 1925.

6

Paimpont, run by a very friendly pair of artists. Closed mid-Dec to Feb. **€60**

Gîte de Coganne D40 ☎ 02 99 61 88 15, ⊛ gitecoganne. com. Appealing B&B just off the D40 4km northwest of Paimpont, where, with advance warning, they'll cook you a dinner of gourmet crêpes. **€56**

★ **Relais de Brocéliande** 5 rue des Forges ☎ 02 99 07 84 94, ⊛ relais-de-broceliande.fr. Modernized by an energetic new owner, this former coaching inn now has 24 large and very comfortable rooms, plus a spa, sauna and hammam, a bar with pinball machine and jukebox, and an excellent restaurant, with abundant outdoor seating and a cosy interior. Lunch costs €18–23, *croques-monsieurs* and plates of cheese or meat are available all afternoon, and dinner menus range from €30 to €49, with the €30 *Plaisir* option including marbled skate and an amazing avocado-mousse dessert. **€105**

PLÉLAN-LE-GRAND

Auberge des Forges de Paimpont ☎ 02 99 06 81 07, ⊛ restaurant.forges-de-paimpont.com. The best restaurant in the vicinity, in a rural setting beside a little lake 4.5km southeast of Paimpont and 3km southwest of Plélan-le-Grand. Housed in a former ironworks, it serves rich country cuisine from €16 at lunch, €33 for dinner. Wed–Sat noon–2pm & 7–9pm, Sun noon–2pm.

Bruyères 10 rue de Brocéliande ☎ 02 99 06 81 38, ⊛ hoteldesbruyeres.canalblog.com. Hotel in the otherwise unremarkable little village of Plélan-le-Grand, 6km southeast of Paimpont, where the cheapest rooms have no en-suite. The restaurant (closed Tues eve & Wed) offers satisfactory menus from €19.50, and the breakfasts are great. **€45**

MAURON

Brambily 14 place Henri-Thébault ☎ 02 97 22 61 67, ⊛ hotel-lebrambily.com. Reasonable Logis de France in the centre of a rambling, charming country town at the northern edge of the forest. The restaurant (closed Sun eve) serves traditional, well-priced "workers' lunches", including wine, for €10.50, and full dinners from €17. **€60**

Southeast of Josselin

If you follow the canal southeast from Josselin, as opposed to venturing into the Forêt de Paimpont, the next significant town you reach is the small but appealing **Malestroit**. Beyond that, if you are not actually travelling on the canal – which at this stage is the **River Oust** – the D764 on the south bank, or the D146/149 on the north, will keep you parallel for much of its course towards Redon. Along the way, worthwhile detours lead south of the canal to **Rochefort-en-Terre**, and north to **La Gacilly**.

Malestroit

Although not a lot happens in **MALESTROIT**, founded in 987 AD – apart from the **Pont du Rock** music festival (⊛ aupontdurock.com), on the last weekend of July – the town is full of unexpected and enjoyable corners. Houses in the main church square, the **place du Bouffay**, are covered with unlikely carvings – an anxious bagpipe-playing hare looks over its shoulder at a dragon's head on one beam, while an oblivious sow in a blue buckled belt threads her distaff on another. The church itself is decorated with drunkards and acrobats outside, torturing demons and erupting towers within; a placard explains the various allegories. The only ancient walls without adornment are the ruins of the **Chapelle de la Madeleine**, where one of the many temporary truces of the Hundred Years War was signed.

If you arrive in Malestroit by barge – this being a good stretch to travel on the water – you'll moor very near the centre. Beside the grey canal, the matching grey-slate tiles on the turreted rooftops bulge and dip, while on its central island overgrown houses stand next to the stern walls of an old mill.

Musée de la Résistance Bretonne

Rue des Hardys Béhellec, St-Marcel • April–Sept daily 9am–7pm; Oct–March Thurs–Sun 9am–7pm • €7.70 • ☎ 02 97 75 16 90, ⊛ resistance-bretonne.com

The **Musée de la Résistance Bretonne**, in the village of **ST-MARCEL**, just outside Malestroit, marks the site of a June 1944 battle in which the Breton *maquis* (resistance), joined by Free French forces parachuted in from England, successfully diverted the local German troops from the main Normandy invasion movements.

The museum's greatest strength is its presentation of the pressures that made so many French collaborate: the reconstructed street corner overwhelmed by the brooding presence of the occupiers; the big colourful propaganda posters offering work in Germany, announcing executions of *maquisards*, equating resistance with aiding US and British big business; and, against these, the low-budget, shoddily printed Resistance pamphlets.

6

Rochefort-en-Terre

Overlooking the River Arz from a high eminence 17km south of Malestroit, **ROCHEFORT-EN-TERRE** ranks among the most delightful villages in Brittany – even if it is something of a tourist trap, with its little antique shops and expensive restaurants. Every available stone surface, from the window ledges to the picturesque wishing well, is permanently bedecked in flowers, to the extent that Rochefort has been banned since 1967 from taking part in regional and national contests.

At the bottom end of town, the church of **Notre Dame de Tronchaye** holds a Black Virgin that was found hidden from Norman invaders in a hollow tree in the twelfth century, and is the object of a pilgrimage on the first Sunday after August 15. More interesting, though, is the **Lac Bleu**, just to the south, where the deep galleries of some ancient **slate quarries** are the home of blind butterflies and long-eared bats.

Parc du Château
July & Aug daily 9am–7pm; Sept–June in school hols only, daily 9am–dusk • Free

Rochefort's flowery tradition originated with the painter **Alfred Klots**, who was born in France to a wealthy American family in 1875, and bought Rochefort's ruined **château**, perched on its highest point, in 1907.

The castle itself is not open to visitors, but there's free access to its landscaped gardens, terraced on multiple levels and offering magnificent views over the surrounding hills and gorges. Only once you go through its dramatic gateway do you find out that in fact the gateway is all that survives of the original fifteenth-century castle. Instead, what you see was cobbled together by Klots using pieces from other local ruins.

Parc de Préhistoire de Bretagne
Malansac, 2km southeast of Rochefort • April–Jun daily 10am–7pm; July & Aug daily 10am–7.30pm; Sept Tues–Sun 1–7pm; Oct Sat & Sun 1–6pm, last admission always 2hr before closing • Adults €13, ages 4–12 €7.50 • ☎ 02 97 43 34 17, ⓦ prehistoire-bretagne.com

The heavily publicized **Parc de Préhistoire de Bretagne**, outside the small community of **MALANSAC**, is a theme park aimed overwhelmingly at children. Separate landscaped areas contain dioramas of gigantic (if stationary) dinosaurs, and human beings at various stages in their evolution; the story ends shortly after a bunch of deformed but enthusiastic Neanderthals hit on the idea of erecting a few megaliths.

La Gacilly

Fourteen kilometres north of the canal, **LA GACILLY** makes a good base for walking trips in search of megaliths, sleepy villages and countryside. The town itself has prospered of late thanks to a **beauty-products** industry based on the abundantly proliferating flowers in the Aff valley, and very much dominated by the **Yves Rocher** company.

La Gacilly is also a centre for many active craftworkers; a walk down the old stone steps of the cobbled street that runs parallel to the main road between town centre and river is both a pleasure in itself and an opportunity to look in on their workshops. Recent summers have seen the street double as an open-air **gallery**, displaying huge, blown-up photographs and sculptures.

The only real disappointment is that the **riverfront** is not accessible to walkers, though you can enjoy views of it from a couple of restaurants.

Megaliths of St-Just

Around 10km east of La Gacilly, in the vicinity of the village of **ST-JUST**, the small windswept **Cojoux** moor is rich in ancient megalithic remains. Only recently have they received much attention, as archeologists have gradually uncovered all sorts of ancient tombs and sacred sites. It's a rewarding area to ramble around; the larger menhirs and so on are signposted along dirt tracks and footpaths, and you'll probably stumble upon a few lesser ones by chance.

ARRIVAL AND INFORMATION   SOUTHEAST OF JOSSELIN

MALESTROIT

By bus Malestroit is served by buses from Vannes (3 daily; 1hr).

Tourist office 5–7 rue Ste-Anne (May–June, Sept & school hols Mon–Sat 9.30am–12.30pm & 2–5.30pm; July & Aug Mon–Sat 10am–6pm, Sun 2–6pm; ☏02 97 75 45 35, ⓦtourisme.ccvol.com); they can provide details of boat rental.

ROCHEFORT-EN-TERRE

Tourist office 7 place du Puits (Feb, March & Oct–Dec Tues–Fri 10am–1pm & 2–5.30pm, Sat 2–5.30pm; April Tues–Sat 10am–1pm & 2–5.30pm; May, June & Sept Mon–Sat 10am–1pm & 2–5.30pm; July & Aug daily 10am–1pm & 2–6.30pm; ☏02 97 26 56 00, ⓦrochefortenterre-tourisme.com).

ACCOMMODATION AND EATING

MALESTROIT

Cap Horn 1 Faubourg St-Michel ☏02 97 75 13 01, ⓦhotel-malestroit.com. Malestroit's only hotel is a very simple affair, offering half-a-dozen large, somewhat plain, but exceptionally good-value en-suite rooms above a bar. They also have some rental apartments at very similar rates. **€36**

Crêperie Maêl Trech 13 place de Bouffay ☏02 97 75 17 72, ⓦmaeltrech.fr. Pleasant crêperie facing the church, which serves an extensive array of galettes, including vegetarian and seafood specialities for €8–12, as well as substantial salads and standard meat and fish dishes, and a set weekday lunch for €10.50. July & Aug daily noon–10pm; Sept–June Mon & Thurs–Sun noon–3pm & 7–9pm, Tues noon–3pm.

La Daufresne Chemin des Tanneurs ☏02 97 75 13 33, ⓦtourisme.ccvol.com. Two-star campsite, across the river, down below the bridge in the Impasse d'Abattoir next to the swimming pool. Closed mid-Sept to April. **€8.50**

ROCHEFORT-EN-TERRE

Crêperie La Terrasse 8 rue St-Michel ☏02 97 43 35 56. The lovely eponymous terrace makes this village restaurant a good option for a cheap meal, serving crêpes and wood-fired pizzas, with an emphasis on organic ingredients – and local cider. April–Dec daily noon–2pm & 7–9pm.

Le Pélican Place des Halles ☏02 97 43 38 48, ⓦhotel-pelican-rochefort.com. The one hotel in town is a pretty and very central little place with somewhat plain rooms,

and insists guests dine in its restaurant, where dinner menus start at €23. Closed mid-Jan to mid-Feb. Rates include dinner and breakfast. **€132**

LA GACILLY

★ **Europ' Hôtel** 15 place Yves Rocher ☏02 99 08 11 15, ⓦhotel-lagacilly.com. Extremely hospitable Logis, up in the town centre, with quiet and comfortable rooms in what used to be the separate *Hôtel du Square*, reached through the long gardens at the back. **€50**

Grée des Landes Cournon, La Gacilly ☏02 99 70 07 40, ⓦlagreedeslandes.com. Spectacular modern eco-friendly resort and spa, under the auspices of Yves Rocher. Set in lush, flower-filled gardens, across from the village centre on the east side of the river, it offers luxurious suites and cabins, as well as conventional rooms, a full range of health and beauty treatments, and an organic restaurant, *Les Jardins Sauvages*, that serves lunch from €27.50 and dinner from €38.50. **€120**

Manoir de Pommery Sixt-sur-Aff ☏02 99 70 07 40, ⓦmanoir-pommery.com. Sixteenth-century château, 7km east of La Gacilly, which provides ideal countryside B&B accommodation, with three antique-decorated rooms. Rates include breakfast. **€60**

La Vegétarium La Gacilly ☏02 99 08 37 37, ⓦlagreedeslandes.com. Summer-only organic café in the village centre, run by Yves Rocher. Not vegetarian, despite the name, it serves a two-course menu for €12.50. June–Sept Mon–Thurs & Sun 11am–7pm, Fri & Sat 11am–9pm.

Redon

Poised at the junction of the rivers Oust and Vilaine, on the Nantes–Brest canal, linked by rail to Rennes, Vannes and Nantes, and at the intersection of six major roads, **REDON** is not easy to avoid – and you shouldn't try to, either. A wonderful mess of water and locks – the canal manages to cross the Vilaine at right angles in one of the more complex links – the town has history, charm and life.

Until World War I, Redon was the seaport for Rennes. Its industrial docks are therefore on the Vilaine, while the canal, even right in the centre, is almost totally rural. Ship-owners' homes from the seventeenth and eighteenth centuries can be seen in the port area – walk via quai Jean-Bart next to the *bassin* (pleasure port) along the **Croix des Marins promenade**, returning along quai Duguay-Trouin beside the river. The main users of the port now are **cruise boats**, which come from 40km downstream at the Arzal dam.

6

Église St-Sauveur

Founded by St Conwoïon in 832 AD, Redon was a place of pilgrimage until the seventeenth century. Its Benedictine abbey is now the focus of the **Église St-Sauveur** – the rounded angles of the dumpy twelfth-century Romanesque lantern tower are unique in Brittany. All but obscured by later roofs and the high choir, the four-storey belfry is best seen from the adjacent cloisters, now part of the Lycée St-Sauveur. The later Gothic tower was entirely separated from the main building by a fire in 1780.

Under the chapel of Joan of Arc, the church crypt holds the tomb of Pierre l'Hôpital, the judge who condemned **Gilles de Rais** to be hanged in 1440 for satanism and the most infamous orgies. Gilles had fought alongside Joan, burned for heresy, witchcraft and sorcery in 1431, and in both cases the court procedures were irregular to say the least. Legends of Gilles' atrocities were the source for tales of the monstrous wife-murderer **Bluebeard**.

ARRIVAL AND DEPARTURE
REDON

By train Redon's gare SNCF is five minutes' walk west of the tourist office.
Destinations Nantes (10 daily; 50min); Quimper (12 daily;

1hr 45min); Rennes (18 daily; 40min–1hr); Vannes (12 daily; 25min).

INFORMATION AND ACTIVITIES

Tourist office Place de la République (July & Aug Mon–Sat 9.30am–12.30pm & 1.30–6.30pm, Sun 10am–12.30pm & 3.30–5.30pm; Sept–June Mon & Wed–Fri 9.30am–noon & 2–6pm, Tues 2–6pm, Sat 10am–12.30pm & 2–5pm; ☏02 99 71 06 04, ⓦtourisme-pays-redon.com).

River cruises Vedettes Jaunes (☏02 97 45 02 81, ⓦvedettesjaunes.com) run cruises along the Vilaine from the Arzal dam – which is as close as they can get to the sea – upstream past La Roche-Bernard to Redon (July & Aug, Thurs only; departs Arzal 9.30am, Redon 3.30pm; €27).

ACCOMMODATION AND EATING

Asther 14 rue des Douves ☏02 99 71 10 91, ⓦasther-hotel.com. Plain but good-value budget hotel, across (or rather under) the railway tracks from the tourist office, and conveniently set above a brasserie, *des Halles*. **€57**

Chandouineau 1 rue Thiers ☏02 99 71 02 04, ⓦhotel-restaurant-chandouineau.com. Smart hotel close to the station, with just seven comfortable bedrooms at great-value prices, and a gourmet restaurant where dinner menus cost €26–56. **€89**

France 30 rue Duguesclin ☏02 99 71 06 11, ⓦlefrance .chez-alice.fr. Off-white hotel, looking down on the canal; not all rooms are en-suite, but they offer considerable comfort for the price. **€45**

La Grande Oust le Plessis, Bains-sur-Oust ☏02 99 71 18 32, ⓦlagrandeoust.com. Delightful rural retreat, 10km north of Redon, holding two safari-style tents on fixed platforms, each with a double and two single beds, plus an open-air terrace kitchen, and optional €8 breakfasts. Closed Oct–March. **€75**

EATING AND DRINKING

L'Akène 10 rue du Jeu-de-Paume ☎02 99 71 25 15. Crêperie in a flower-bedecked stone house in an alleyway close to the port, serving some of the tastiest €4–9 galettes you're ever likely to find. Daily 11.45am–2pm & 6.45–9.30pm.

La Bogue 3 rue des États ☎02 99 71 12 95. Friendly and good-value fish restaurant, in a flowery mansion in place du Parlement. Lunch costs €17, while the €24 dinner menu features a dozen snails as one of its four courses, and the €62 *Pelegrino* is a sumptuous feast. Tues–Sat noon–2pm & 7–9pm, Sun noon–2pm.

6

Châteaubriant

Sixty kilometres east of Redon, and the same distance north of Nantes, the fortified town of **CHÂTEAUBRIANT** guards the border of Brittany and Anjou. While it's not a place to go out of your way to see, and the flat surrounding countryside holds precious little of interest, a couple of hours spent wandering in and around its venerable **Château** makes a welcome break during a day on the road.

Château de Châteaubriant

Tours May–Sept daily except Tues, 11am, 2.30pm & 4pm; Oct–April Sat & Sun 3.30pm; English tour July to mid-Sept Wed 2pm • €2.50 • ☎02 40 28 20 20

The walls of the **Château de Châteaubriant** still encircle the crest of a knoll just east of the town proper, although only the entrance keep (*donjon d'entrée*) remains of the original tenth-century structure. You can simply stroll through that mighty gateway at any time of day to find a disparate assembly of buildings of different eras, in similarly assorted states of repair, interspersed with peaceful lawns and formal gardens. The most complete edifice is a self-contained Renaissance château, built from 1521 onwards, and equipped with a sort of secular cloisters. To see the apartments inside, join a **guided tour**.

ARRIVAL AND INFORMATION   CHÂTEAUBRIANT

By train Châteaubriant is connected to Rennes (4 daily; 1hr 15min).

Tourist office 29 place Charles de Gaulle (Tues–Sat 9.30am–12.30pm & 2–6pm; ☎02 40 28 20 90, ⓦtourisme-chateaubriant.fr).

ACCOMMODATION AND EATING

Auberge Bretonne 23 place de la Motte ☎02 40 81 03 05, ⓦaubergebretonne.com. Central hotel/restaurant, with eight very comfortable modern rooms and a high-class restaurant serving lunch from €20 and dinner from €28. More expensive menus feature Chateaubriand steaks, which some authorities believe originated here, using high-quality local beef. **€80**

Poêlon d'Or 30 rue du 11-Novembre 1918 ☎02 40 81 43 33, ⓦlepoelondorchateaubriant.com. Excellent little homely restaurant in the heart of town, where the cheapest dinner menu, at €26.50, is replete with hearty traditional meat and fish dishes. Tues–Sat noon–2pm & 7–9pm, Sun noon–2pm; closed first fortnight in Aug.

Nantes

Since the millennium, the rejuvenated, go-ahead city of **NANTES** has transformed itself into a likeable metropolis that deserves to figure on any tourist itinerary. At the heart of this ambitious regeneration project stands a must-see attraction, the **Machines de l'Île** – home of the Grand Éléphant – but the city as a whole is also scrubbed, gleaming and suffused with a remarkable energy.

Although Nantes is no longer officially in Brittany – it was transferred to the Pays de la Loire in 1962 – its inhabitants still consider it to be an integral part of the province.

6

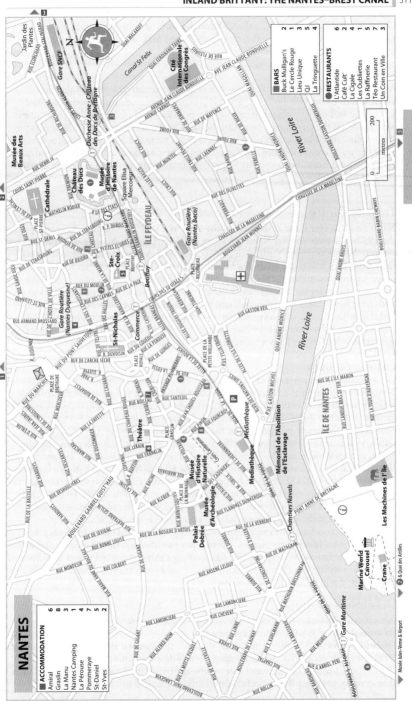

NANTES

■ ACCOMMODATION
Amiral	6
Graslin	8
La Manu	3
Nantes Camping	1
La Pérouse	4
Pommeraye	7
St-Daniel	5
St-Yves	2

■ BARS
Buck Mulligan's	2
Le Cercle Rouge	1
Lieu Unique	3
QJ	5
La Tringuette	4

● RESTAURANTS
L'Atlantide	6
Café Cult'	2
La Cigale	4
Les Oubliettes	1
La Raffinerie	5
Téo Restaurant	7
Un Coin en Ville	3

Once you've seen the machines, the **Château des Ducs** and the **Beaux Arts** museum are well worth visiting, but this is also a place to enjoy a little urban excitement in what otherwise can be a slow-paced region.

Brief history

As capital of an independent Brittany, Nantes was a considerable medieval centre. Great wealth came later, however, when it prospered from colonial expeditions, and was by the end of the eighteenth century the principal port of France. Huge fortunes were made via the city's involvement in the **slave trade**; an estimated 500,000 African slaves were carried to the Americas in vessels based here, and even after abolition in 1817 the trade continued illegally. Subsequently the port declined, and heavy industry and wine production became more important. By the start of the twentieth century the city had become known as "Nantes the Grey".

The city centre

Nantes is no longer quite as defined by the **Loire** as it was in its heyday. As recently as the 1930s, the river crossed Nantes in seven separate channels, but five were filled in by German labour as part of reparations for World War I. Visitors tend instead to orient themselves in relation to two distinct neighbourhoods: the older **medieval city**, concentrated around the cathedral and with the château prominent in its southeast corner, and the elegant **nineteenth-century town** to the west. Many of the streets in both have been semi-pedestrianized, and they abound in pavement cafés, brasseries and shops. Just south, the elongated **Île Feydeau** is no longer an island, being now surrounded not by water, but by busy roads. Even so, its eighteenth-century houses, seen at their best in rue Kervegan, retain a certain Baroque charm.

Château des Ducs

Courtyard and walls July & Aug daily 9am–8pm; Sept–June daily 10am–7pm • Free • ⓦ chateau-nantes.fr

Though no longer on the waterfront, the **Château des Ducs** still preserves the form in which it was built by two of the last rulers of independent Brittany, François II and his daughter Duchess Anne, born here in 1477. Famous people who have been guests or prisoners, defenders or belligerents, of the castle include Gilles de Rais (Bluebeard), publicly executed in 1440; Machiavelli in 1498; the firebrand Scottish preacher John Knox, as a galley slave in 1547–49; and Bonnie Prince Charlie in 1745. The most significant act in the castle was the signing of the **Edict of Nantes** in 1598 by Henri IV, which ended the Wars of Religion by granting toleration to the Protestants, but had far more crucial consequences when it was revoked by Louis XIV in 1685. To their credit, the people of Nantes took no part in the subsequent massacres of the Huguenots.

The stout **ramparts** of the château remain pretty much intact, and most of the encircling moat is filled with water, surrounded by well-tended lawns that make a popular spot for lunch time picnics. Visitors can pass through the walls, and also stroll atop them for fine views over the city, for no charge. Among the incongruous potpourri of buildings within are a major exhibition space used for year-long displays on differing subjects, and a high-tech history museum.

Musée d'Histoire de Nantes

Château des Ducs • July & Aug daily 10am–7pm; Sept–June daily except Tues 10am–6pm • Adults €5, €9 combined with temporary exhibitions; under-18s free • ☎ 08 11 46 46 44, ⓦ chateau-nantes.fr

Spreading through 32 rooms and seven "themes", the **Musée d'Histoire de Nantes** covers local history in exhaustive detail. Highlights include a fascinating scale model of the city in the thirteenth century, and a determined attempt to come to terms with Nantes' slave-trading past, displaying pitiful trinkets that were used to buy slaves in Africa.

Cathédrale de St-Pierre-et-St-Paul

7 impasse St-Laurent • Daily: mid-June to mid-Sept 8.30am–7pm; mid-Sept to mid-June 8.30am–6pm • ☎ 02 40 47 86 64,
Ⓦ cathedrale-nantes.cef.fr

The fifteenth-century **Cathédrale de St-Pierre-et-St-Paul** stands 200m north of the
château. Made to seem especially light and soaring by its clean white stone, it
contains the tomb of François II, the last duke of Brittany, and his wife, Margaret,
the parents of Duchess Anne – with somewhat grating symbols of Power, Strength
and Justice for him and Fidelity, Prudence and Temperance for her. This imposing
monument is illuminated by a superb modern stained-glass window devoted to Breton
and Nantais saints.

6

Musée des Beaux Arts

10 rue Clemenceau • Mon, Wed & Fri–Sun 10am–6pm, Thurs 10am–8pm • €2 • ☎ 02 51 17 45 00, Ⓦ www.museedesbeauxarts.nantes.fr

Nantes' **Musée des Beaux Arts** displays its paintings in excellent modern galleries,
and hosts a high standard of temporary exhibitions. Not all its Renaissance and
contemporary works are on show at any one time, but you should be able to take in
canvases ranging from a gorgeous *David Triumphant* by Delaunay and Léon Comerre's
disturbing *Le Déluge*, a writhing orgy of drowning flesh, to Chagall's *Le Cheval Rouge*
and one of Monet's *Nymphéas*.

Place Royale

Place Royale, at the heart of the nineteenth-century town, was first laid out in the
1790s; damaged by bombing in 1943, it has now been restored. **Place Graslin**, 200m
west, dates from the same period; the Corinthian portico of its **theatre** contrasts with
the 1895 Art Nouveau style of the delightful *La Cigale*, opposite, embellished with
mosaics and mirrors and still a popular brasserie (see p.317).

Passage Pommeraye

A spectacular nineteenth-century multi-level indoor shopping centre, the **Passage
Pommeraye** drops down three flights of stairs towards the river on nearby rue
Crébillon. The scale of its architectural embellishments is extraordinary; each of the
gas lamps that light the central area is held by an individually crafted marble cherub.
The entire complex has been extensively restored, and holds upscale shops and
businesses of all kinds.

Musée d'Histoire Naturelle

12 rue Voltaire • Daily except Tues 10am–6pm • €3.50 • ☎ 02 40 41 55 00, Ⓦ www.museum.nantes.fr

The **Musée d'Histoire Naturelle**, west of place Graslin, centres on an old-fashioned
collection of oddities, including stuffed specimens of virtually every bird and animal
imaginable. Look out for the phenomenal array of different species of wood displayed
as you go up the stairs.

VISITING LOIRE VINEYARDS

Responsible for two classic dry whites, Gros-Plant and Muscadet, the Loire wine region
lies immediately upstream (east) from Nantes. Any vineyard should be happy to give you
a *dégustation*.

Most vineyards operate on a very small scale; the largest, however, the **Chasseloir** vineyard
at **St-Fiacre-sur-Maine**, 17 km southeast of the city (Mon–Sat 9am–6pm; ☎ 02 40 54 81 15,
Ⓦ chereau-carre.fr), is perhaps the most interesting. Occupying the grounds of a former
château, it has fifty acres of vines, some a century old. Although it sells mostly within the
catering trade, anyone is welcome to visit the cellars, which are decorated with painted
Rabelaisian carvings and candelabras made from vine roots.

Musée Jules-Verne

3 rue de l'Hermitage • July & Aug daily except Tues 10am–6pm, Sept–June Mon & Wed–Sat 10am–noon & 2–6pm, Sun 2–6pm • €3 • ☏ 02 40 69 72 52, ⊕ nantes.fr/julesverne

Disappointingly dry despite its proximity to the river, the **Musée Jules-Vernes**, 1km southwest of the centre, commemorates the birthplace of the first serious writer of science fiction.

Mémorial de l'Abolition de l'Esclavage

Quai de la Fosse • Daily: mid-May to mid-Sept 9am–8pm; mid-Sept to mid-May 9am–6pm • Free • ☏ 08 11 46 46 44, ⊕ memorial.nantes.fr

Keen to acknowledge that it owes much of its prosperity and status to its shameful role in the slave trade, Nantes unveiled the powerful **Mémorial de l'Abolition de l'Esclavage** in 2012. Consisting of tiles and placards both along a riverfront promenade, and lining a tunnel immediately below, this Memorial to the Abolition of Slavery spells out the city's involvement, traces a timeline of how it came to an end, and explores the continuing existence of slavery and injustice worldwide.

Les Machines de l'Île

Centring on the fabulous **Grand Éléphant**, the **Machines de l'Île** is a truly world-class attraction. The "machines" of the name are the astonishing contraptions created by designer/engineer François Delarozière and artist Pierre Orefice; the "island" is the Île de Nantes, a three-kilometre-long, whale-shaped island in the Loire that was long home to the city's now-defunct shipbuilding industry.

MACHINES DE L'ÎLE: PRACTICAL INFORMATION

The Machines de l'Île stand roughly ten minutes' walk southwest of the city centre, clearly signposted across the northern arm of the Loire.

OPENING HOURS

Opening hours vary enormously throughout the year; check ⊕ lesmachines-nantes.fr or ☏ 08 10 12 12 25 for details, including the current schedules of elephant and *carrousel* rides.
Early Jan to early Feb: closed
Second half of Feb: daily except Mon 2–7pm
March to mid-April: Wed–Fri 2–6pm, Sat & Sun 2–7pm
Mid-April to early May & late May to June: Tues–Fri 10am–6pm, Sat & Sun 10am–7pm
Middle fortnight of May: Mon–Fri 10am–6pm, Sat & Sun 10am–7pm
July & Aug: daily 10am–8pm
Sept to early Nov: Tues–Fri 10am–6 pm, Sat & Sun 10am–7pm
Early Nov to late Dec: Wed–Fri 2–6pm, Sat & Sun 2–7pm
Late Dec to early Jan: daily except Mon 2–6pm

TICKETS AND RESERVATIONS

Of the two on-site ticket offices, one sells tickets for only the Grand Éléphant and the Gallery, and other only for the Carrousel des Mondes Marins. Both shut one hour before the site closes.

Tickets for the Gallery cost €8 for adults and €6.50 for under-18s; tickets for an elephant ride cost the same. Both tickets include access to the Workshop and the branch of the Heron Tree. Only the Gallery is free with the Pass Nantes (see p.316). Tickets for elephant rides are only sold for same-day rides, but at least one ride per day can be booked online that same day. Note that you can see the elephant close-up – which is actually more exciting than riding it, though kids won't believe it is – without paying for admission.

There are two possible ways to experience the Carrousel des Mondes Marins, which operates to much more restricted hours. At different times you can either visit in "Fairground" mode for €8 adults, €6.50 under-18s, meaning you actually ride twice on the merry-go-round (and can pay €3 extra for additional rides), or in "Discovery" mode, in which case you inspect the merry-go-round but don't ride it for €6 for adults, €5 under-18s.

Part homage to the sci-fi creations of Jules Verne and the blueprints of Leonardo da Vinci, part street-theatre extravaganza, this was launched in 2007 as the lynchpin of Nantes' urban regeneration. Far from an enclosed theme park, it's open to any passer-by, and though you have to pay to enter the various hangars and workshops, you can admire the extraordinary elephant for free, when it emerges for one of its regular walks, and follow it on its pachydermic perambulations along the huge esplanade.

Grand Éléphant

Twelve metres high and eight metres wide, the **Grand Éléphant** is made largely from American tulipwood. Although it's phenomenally realistic, down to the articulation of its joints as it "walks", and its trunk as it flexes and sprays water, its mechanical underbelly is not hidden away; that you can see how it all works is part of the fun. If you're lucky enough to be carried as one of its 49 passengers, you don't have to sit down as you ride; instead you can wander through its hollow belly and climb the spiral stairs within to reach the balconies and vantage points around its canopied howdah.

The exuberant creativity of the whole thing is breathtaking. Originally commissioned to celebrate the centenary of Jules Verne's death, it has a madcap Victorian flavour. Combining Verne's charm and adventure with a modern steampunk aesthetic, its detailing has a crackpot relish, from the intricate sculpting and painting of every wooden surface to the wear and tear on the massive leather ears.

Carrousel des Mondes Marins

A huge stand-alone merry-go-round that's set on the promenade a couple of hundred metres from the main **Machines de l'Île** hangar, the Carrousel des Mondes Marins is a further flamboyant expression of its creators' imagination. Passengers revolve in all sorts of amazing underwater creatures and contraptions, from the Reverse-Propelling Squid to the Giant Crab, arranged in three separate tiers and each equipped with its own hand-operated controls to flap fins, snap teeth and so on. As it's all surrounded by concrete walkways, however, you can't really see what's going on unless you pay to enter.

Workshop and Gallery

The main hangar is home to both the **Workshop**, where employees busy designing and constructing the next generation of machines can be viewed from an overhead walkway, and the **Gallery**, which displays a changing assortment of completed machines that have yet to be assembled into larger constructions.

At the time of writing, pride of place went to the components of **L'Arbre aux Hérons** ("the Heron Tree"), a steel tree 50m in diameter by 22m high, topped by two herons, which will ultimately be erected beside the Loire. Visitors will be able to walk up the branches of the tree, pausing at a café amid the hanging foliage, and ride in baskets suspended from the herons' wings. A full-scale sample branch spreads at the front of the whole complex.

ARRIVAL AND DEPARTURE
NANTES

By train Nantes' *gare SNCF*, a little way east of the château, is on the main line between Paris and Brittany. For most facilities (tramway, buses, hotels) use *Accès Nord*.

Destinations La Baule (12 daily; 55min) via St-Nazaire; Paris (15 TGVs daily; 2hr 15min); Quimper (4 daily; 2hr 40min); Rennes (6 daily; 1hr 40min).

By bus Nantes has two main bus stations. One just south of the centre on allée Baco, near place Ricordeau, is used by buses heading south and southwest; another, where cours des 50 Otages meets rue de l'Hôtel de Ville, serves routes that stay north of the river.

Destinations Pornic (7 daily; 1hr 10min); Rennes (5 daily; 1hr); St-Nazaire (2 daily; 40min); Vannes (1 daily; 2hr 40min).

By air Services to Nantes' airport (⊕ nantes.aeroport.fr), 12km southwest and connected by regular buses, include daily Air France flights from London City Airport.

RIVER CRUISES FROM NANTES

Bateaux Nantais (☎02 40 14 51 14, ⊕www.bateaux-nantais.fr) offer **cruises** on the River **Erdre** from Nantes, departing from the *gare fluviale*, on the quai de la Motte-Rouge a little way north of the centre. Options range from a 1hr 45min sightseeing cruise (€12.50), to a three-hour trip on a floating restaurant for lunch (12.30pm) or dinner (8.30pm), for €51–89.

6

GETTING AROUND

By tram Trams run along the old riverfront, past the *gare SNCF* and the two bus stations. Buy tickets at tram stations, not on board (€1.50 for 1hr, €4.60 for 24hr; ⊕tan.fr).

By bike Under the Bicloo scheme (⊕bicloo.nantes metropole.fr), bikes are available to rent from docking stations all over the city; the first half-hour is free.

INFORMATION

Tourist offices 9 rue des États (July & Aug daily 9am–7pm; Sept–June Mon–Sat 10am–6pm, Sun 10am–5pm; ☎08 92 46 40 44, ⊕nantes-tourisme.com), and at the Machines de l'Île (July & Aug daily 9am–7pm; Sept–June Fri–Sun 2–5pm). Both sell the *Pass Nantes*, available in 24-hour (€25), 48-hour (€35) and 72-hour (€45) versions, which grants unrestricted use of local transport and some car parks, and free admission to several museums and attractions; it can also be bought ten percent cheaper online.

ACCOMMODATION

Amiral 26bis rue Scribe ☎02 40 69 20 21, ⊕hotel -nantes.fr. Well-maintained little hotel on a lively pedestrianized street just north of place Graslin, and perfect for young night owls. All rooms have TV, bath and double-glazing, though some noise still creeps in; ask for a room at the back if that's an issue. Much cheaper rates at weekends. **€96**

Graslin 1 rue Peron ☎02 40 69 72 91, ⊕hotel-graslin .com. Stylish, inexpensive hotel in the city centre, a minute's walk south of place Graslin, in a remodelled older building with some Art Deco touches, with 47 rooms arranged over five floors. Friendly management and good €11 buffet breakfasts, albeit served in a subterranean dining room. **€69**

La Manu 2 place de la Manufacture ☎02 40 29 29 20, ⊕hifrance.org. Nantes' hostel, which has a cafeteria, is housed in a postmodern former tobacco factory a few hundred metres east of the *gare SNCF*, and a 5min ride from the centre on tramway #1. Beds in four- or six-bed dorms; rates include breakfast. Reception daily 8am–noon & 3.30–10.30pm, closed mid-Dec to early Jan. **€21**

Nantes Camping 21 bd du Petit-Port ☎02 40 74 47 94, ⊕nantes-camping.fr. This well-managed, five-star campsite with swimming pool occupies a pleasant tree-shaded setting 4km north of the city centre on tram route #2 (stop "Morrhonnière"). Open all year. **€31.20**

★La Pérouse 3 allée Duquesne ☎02 40 89 75 00, ⊕hotel-laperouse.fr. Superb contemporary building ingeniously integrated into the older architecture that surrounds it – right down to its leaning north-facing side. The interior is decorated with 1930s furniture, stucco walls and high-tech touches. An original, comfortable and friendly place to stay, with excellent breakfasts to boot. **€79**

★Pommeraye 2 rue Boileau ☎02 40 48 78 79, ⊕hotel -pommeraye.com. Extremely good-value, modern, fifty-room hotel with large, designer-decor rooms – some individually designed by artists-in-residence – beautiful bathrooms and free parking; good buffet breakfast for €12. **€89**

St-Daniel 4 rue du Bouffay ☎02 40 47 41 25, ⊕hotel -saintdaniel.com. These very simple but pleasant and well-lit rooms, all en-suite and accessed via steep stairs, are located on a cobbled street just off the place du Bouffay in the very heart of the old city, and are much in demand in summer. Street-side rooms are sound-proofed. Breakfast is just €5.65. **€47**

St-Yves 154 rue du Général Buat ☎02 40 74 48 42, ⊕hotel-saintyves.fr. Very attractive, great-value little ten-room hotel, 20min walk north of the railway station, with friendly staff, a nice garden and big €7 breakfasts. **€61**

EATING AND DRINKING

L'Atlantide Centre des Salorges, 16 quai Ernest-Renaud ☎02 40 73 23 23, ⊕restaurant-atlantide.net. Designer restaurant, with big river views from the fourth floor of a modern block, serving the contemporary French cuisine of chef Jean-Yves Gueho. Fish is the speciality, but expect quirky twists like bananas braised in beer. Menus €38–98. Mon–Fri noon–2pm & 7.30–9.45pm, Sat 7.30–9.45pm.

Buck Mulligan's 12 rue du Château ☎02 40 20 02 72, ⊕buckmulligans.com. Irish-themed bar with genuine Irish owners and a dingy, dungeon-like setting, tucked away close to the château. Plenty of events, from TV sports at weekends to darts competitions, open-mic nights (Mon) and live music (Thurs). Daily 4pm–2am.

Café Cult' 2 rue des Carmes ☎02 40 47 18 49, ⊕cafe-cult.com. Friendly, good-value café in a beautiful old half-timbered house, with a pavement terrace. They serve two-course lunches for €14, dinner for €22, while between mealtimes it progresses from being a tearoom to a cocktail bar to a cheap and lively late-night drinking spot. Mon–Sat noon–2am.

Le Cercle Rouge 27 rue des Carmes ☎02 40 20 16 50. Very simple, very welcoming neighbourhood bar, where the pared-down 1950s decor is a homage to film director Jean-Pierre Melville, one of whose movies was *Le Cercle Rouge*. Tues–Sat noon–2am.

★**La Cigale** 4 place Graslin ☎02 51 84 94 94, ⓦwww.lacigale.com. Fabulous late-nineteenth-century brasserie, offering fine meals in opulent Belle Époque surroundings, with seating either at tiled terrace tables or in a more formal indoor dining room. Fish is a speciality, with lunch options like the €19 beef tartare or the €16 salmon platter. Assorted set menus are served until midnight in keeping with the tradition of providing post-performance refreshments for patrons of the theatre opposite. Daily 7.30am–12.30am.

Les Oubliettes 4 place Marc Elder ☎02 51 82 67 04. Despite the address, this little daytime-only restaurant is splendidly and very spaciously set in the château courtyard, a world away from the city traffic, with seating both indoors and in the open air. Breakfast, tea and good-value lunches, with inexpensive crêpes, and large *plats* and specials for around €10. July & Aug daily 10am–8pm; Sept–June Tues–Sun 10am–6pm.

La Raffinerie 54 rue Fouré ☎02 40 74 81 05, ⓦrestaurantlaraffinerie.fr. Acclaimed modern bistro serving substantial portions of classic French dishes, on seasonally appropriate menus that change daily and feature only a couple of choices for each course, always with both meat and fish as options, on set menus at €19 and €29. Mon–Wed noon–2pm & 7.45–9.30pm, Thurs & Fri noon–2pm & 7.45–10.30pm.

Téo Restaurant 21 quai des Antilles ☎02 40 08 90 28, ⓦrestaurant-teo.fr. Cool, stylish, black-and-white lounge/restaurant in a former banana warehouse, beyond the Machines de l'Île at the southwest corner of the Île de Nantes, with lots of outdoor seating and DJs on Saturdays. Classic French cuisine, complemented by Thai appetizers, with weekday lunch menus from €15 and full dinners from €30, plus a separate snack bar selling pizzas, hot dogs and the like. Tues–Sat noon–2pm & 7.30–10.30pm.

La Tringuette 3 quai de la Fosse ☎02 51 72 39 05. This hip central bar, with indoor and outdoor seating and friendly English-speaking owners, serves *tartines* and *croques-monsieurs* to go with its fine *aperitifs*, and gets especially lively on market day, Sat, when DJs play. Mon–Fri 8.30am–10pm, Sat 8am–8pm.

Un Coin en Ville 2 place de la Bourse ☎02 40 20 05 98, ⓦwww.uncoinenville.com. This hip, cellar-like restaurant sells classic French cuisine with a fusion twist. Lunch time *plats* for around €10, and large salads (in summer only) or set lunch with carpaccio for €14; the full dinner menu costs €28.90. Mon 7.45–10.30pm, Tues–Fri noon–2pm & 7.45–10.30pm, Sat 7.45–11pm.

6

NIGHTLIFE AND LIVE MUSIC

Lieu Unique Quai Ferdinand Favre ☎02 51 82 15 00, ⓦwww.lelieuunique.com. As unique as its name proclaims, this former LU biscuit factory now plays host to concerts, theatre, dance, art exhibitions, a bookshop, a fair brasserie and a great bar, open until late. Mon 11am–8pm, Tues–Thurs 11am–midnight, Fri & Sat 11am–3am, Sun 3–8pm.

QJ 14 rue Alexandre-Fourny ☎02 40 89 48 60, ⓦqjclub.fr. Named in honour of its presiding hostess, Queen Juliana, Nantes' premier gay club, just south of the centre on the Île de Nantes, puts on a wide programme of events and shows. Thurs–Sun midnight–7am.

The South Coast

SAUZON

The South Coast

Brittany's southern coast takes in several of the province's most famous sites, and also offers its warmest swimming. The whole coast is a succession of natural and human wonders. If you have any interest in prehistory, then the concentration of megaliths around the Morbihan should prove irresistible. Carnac, the most important site, may well be Europe's oldest settlement; the sun has risen more than two million times over its extraordinary alignments of menhirs. Locmariaquer, too, has a gigantic ancient stone, perhaps the key to a prehistoric astronomical observatory, while the most beautifully positioned is the great tumulus on Gavrinis, one of the fifty or so islets scattered around the Gulf of Morbihan's inland sea.

In theory, the best of the south's **beaches** are around the Gulf of Morbihan, and at **La Baule**. Not surprisingly, therefore, these areas are very popular with tourists, and you can be hard-pushed to find a room in summer – or to escape the crowds. La Baule is also the one resort in Brittany to be conspicuously affected and overpriced, but excellent, lower-key alternatives can be found close by at **Le Croisic** and **Piriac-sur-Mer**, and all along the south coast: at Carnac and Locmariaquer; at **Quiberon**; and out on the **islands** of **Groix** and **Belle-Île**. The largest Breton island, Belle-Île is a perfect microcosm of the province – a beautiful place with grand countryside and a couple of lively towns.

The south coast is also host to Brittany's most compelling **festival**, the ten-day **Inter-Celtic** gathering at **Lorient** in August.

Lorient

Brittany's fourth-largest city, **LORIENT**, lies on an immense natural harbour that's strategically located at the junction of the rivers Scorff, Ter and Blavet, and protected from the ocean by the Île de Groix. A functional, rather depressing port today, it was founded in the mid-seventeenth century – in what its charter called a "vague, vain and useless place" – for trading operations by the Compagnie des Indes, an equivalent of the Dutch and English East India Companies. Its name was originally

---

THE INTER-CELTIC FESTIVAL

The main reason visitors come to Lorient is for the **Inter-Celtic Festival**, held for ten days from the first Friday to the second Sunday in August. The biggest Celtic event in Brittany, or anywhere else for that matter, it welcomes participants from all the Celtic nations of Europe – Brittany, Ireland, Scotland, Wales, Cornwall, the Isle of Man, Asturias and Galicia. In a genuine celebration of cultural solidarity, well over half a million people come to more than a hundred different shows, five languages mingle, and Scotch and Guinness flow with French and Spanish wines and ciders. There is a certain competitive element, with championships in various categories, but the feeling of mutual enthusiasm and conviviality is paramount. Performances – embracing music, dance and literature – take place all over the city, with mass celebrations around both the central place Jules-Ferry and the fishing harbour, and the biggest concerts at the local football stadium, the Parc du Moustoir.

For full schedules, which are not usually finalized until June, see ⓦ festival-interceltique.com. Tickets for major events should be reserved well in advance.

INSIDE THE CAIRN DU GAVRINIS

Highlights

❶ The Inter-Celtic Festival The world's largest pan-Celtic jamboree, held every August, turns sleepy Lorient into Brittany's liveliest town. **See p.320**

❷ De la Criée A fabulous quayside fish restaurant in Quiberon, serving whatever's freshest from each day's catch. **See p.329**

❸ Sauzon On the lovely island of Belle-Île, this tiny seaside village makes a great refuge from the province's busier summer resorts. **See p.331**

❹ Houat A diminutive offshore island surrounded by sandy beaches and deeply indented coves. **See p.334**

❺ The megaliths of Carnac Said to be the oldest inhabited spot in Europe, Carnac is still surrounded by relics of its ancient past. **See p.335**

❻ Gavrinis Brittany's most impressive pyramid crowns this speck of an island in the land-locked Golfe du Morbihan. **See p.345**

❼ La Grande-Brière Eerie, mist-swathed marshes, just in from the sea, where you can punt from one reed-surrounded village to the next. **See p.352**

❽ Piriac-sur-Mer Utterly unspoiled little seaside village offering simple old-fashioned pleasures in this busy resort region. **See p.354**

HIGHLIGHTS ARE MARKED ON THE MAP ON PP.322–323

L'Orient ("The East"), and came from a mighty trading vessel, the *Soleil d'Orient*, which was the first ship to be built in its nascent dockyards.

As Lorient had to be almost entirely reconstructed following the damage it sustained during World War II, drab concrete facades dominate its central urban landscape. Most of the waterfront is taken up by naval installations, and the one splash of colour is the little pleasure port that serves to separate the old town from the new – not that there's any very discernible difference between the two.

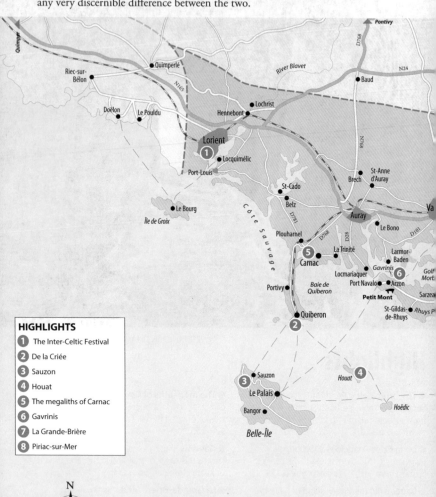

HIGHLIGHTS

1. The Inter-Celtic Festival
2. De la Criée
3. Sauzon
4. Houat
5. The megaliths of Carnac
6. Gavrinis
7. La Grande-Brière
8. Piriac-sur-Mer

0   25
kilometres

BRITTANY'S SOUTH COAST

Cité de la Voile Éric Tabarly

Base de Sous-Marins de Keroman • Check website for the intricate calendar of opening hours, broadly summarized here: mid-Feb to mid-March, mid-April to mid-May daily 10am–6pm; mid-March to mid-April & first half of Oct daily except Mon 2–6pm; mid-May to early July Mon 2–6pm, Tues–Sun 10am–6pm; early July to Aug daily 10am–7pm; Sept Mon–Fri 2–6pm, Sat & Sun 10am–6pm; last admission 1hr 30min before closing • Adults €17.50, ages 7–17 €15 • ☎ 02 97 65 56 56, 🌐 citevoile-tabarly.com

The **Cité de la Voile Éric Tabarly**, a couple of kilometres south of central Lorient at the mouth of the Ter river, is a large, modern, interactive museum of **sailing**. Monsieur

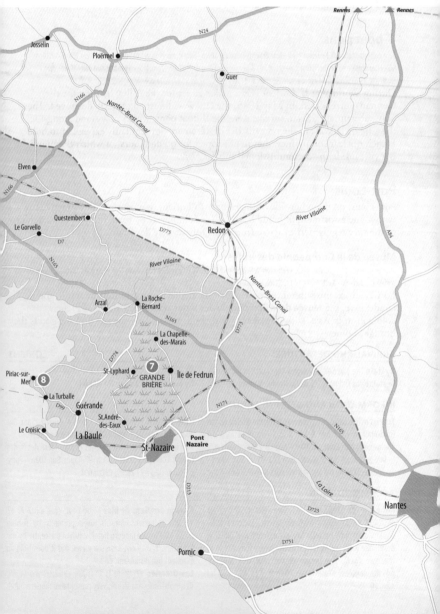

Tabarly himself was a champion yachtsman and Breton hero who drowned in 1998. Several of his yachts – all of which were called *Pen Duick*, meaning roughly "little black head" – are moored alongside, and can be visited.

U-boat pens

Base de Sous-Marins de Keroman • Feb–June & Sept–Dec daily 10am–6pm during school hols, daily except Mon 10am–12.30pm & 2–6pm outside school hols; first 3 weeks of July & last week of Aug daily 10am–7pm; late July to late Aug daily 10am–8pm • €8.80–16.83 depending on various possible visits and tours • ☏ 02 97 65 52 87, ⓦ la-flore.fr

During World War II, Lorient was a major target for the Allies; by the time the Germans surrendered, in May 1945, the city was almost completely destroyed. The only substantial traces to survive were the **U-boat pens**, which now stand alongside the Cité de la Voile in the port district of **Kéroman**. Subsequently expanded to hold French nuclear submarines, they're now open for **guided tours**, of which the highlight is a visit inside the decommissioned sub *La Flore*.

Port-Louis

Port-Louis, on the other side of the estuary to Lorient, is a much more attractive town, with a fine assortment of sandy beaches. It's 20km away by road, but you can catch one of the very regular ferries across from the Embarcadère des Rades.

Musée de la Compagnie des Indes

Avenue du Fort de l'Aigle, Port-Louis • Feb–April & Sept to mid-Dec daily except Tues 1.30–6pm; May–Aug daily 10am–6.30pm; closed mid-Dec to Jan • €8 • ☏ 02 97 82 19 13, ⓦ musee.lorient.fr

Port-Louis retains substantial portions of its medieval fortifications intact. In the citadel here, the **Musée de la Compagnie des Indes** traces the history of French colonialism in Asia, with displays covering both the trading voyages and the goods they brought home.

ARRIVAL AND DEPARTURE — LORIENT

By train The *gare SNCF* is roughly 1km north of the centre. Destinations Quimper (16 daily; 40min); Vannes (16 daily; 30–50min).

By bus Pontivy (2 daily; 1hr 40min).

INFORMATION AND GETTING AROUND

Tourist office Beside the pleasure port on the quai de Rohan (mid-April to early July & late Aug to late Sept Mon–Fri 10am–noon & 2–6pm, Sat 10am–noon & 2–5pm; early July to late Aug Mon–Sat 9.30am–1pm & 2–7pm, Sun 10am–1pm, except during the festival, when it's daily 9.30am–8pm; late Sept to mid-April Mon–Fri 10am–noon & 2–5pm, Sat 10am–noon; ☏ 02 97 84 78 00, ⓦ lorient-tourisme.fr).

Ferries Boats cross from Lorient's Embarcadère des Rades to Port-Louis (Mon–Sat 5.30am–7.45pm, Sun 10am–7pm; €1.40; ☏ 02 97 21 28 29, ⓦ ctrl.fr)

ACCOMMODATION

Auberge de Jeunesse 41 rue Victor-Schoelcher ☏ 02 97 37 11 65, ⓦ fuaj.org/lorient. Lorient's well-equipped, friendly hostel is in a plain, functional building beside the River Ter, 3km west of the centre (bus #21 from the *gare SNCF*). Five-person dorms, plus very minimal private doubles. Closed Jan. Dorms €16.40, doubles €20.50

Maison des Gens de Mer 14 bd Louis-Nail ☏ 02 97 37 11 28, ⓦ lesgensdemer.fr. Used primarily by fishing crews, this spruce modern hotel, south of the centre by the fishing port, may not have sea views, but it does hold an excellent fish restaurant. €63

Les Océanes 17 av de la Perrière ☏ 02 97 37 14 66, ⓦ hotel-lesoceanes.com. Very presentable modern hotel, slightly removed from the centre near the sailing museum, with simple but bright and attractive rooms and some good-value family suites. **€67**

Pêcheurs 7 rue Jean Lagarde ☎ 02 97 21 19 24, ⓦ hotel-lespecheurs.com. Basic but recently renovated and acceptable hotel, close to the town centre, with a pub

(closed Sun) and brasserie downstairs. The cheapest rooms lack en-suite facilities. **€33**

Victor Hugo 36 rue Lazare-Carnot ☎ 02 97 21 16 24, ⓦ www.hotelvictorhugo-lorient.com. Good-value hotel, which, as well as clean, sound-proofed, en-suite rooms, has a pleasant restaurant. **€67**

EATING AND DRINKING

Galway Inn 18 rue Belgique ☎ 02 97 64 50 77, ⓦ thegalwayinn.com. Fine old stone pub, renowned for its fusion of Irish and Celtic traditions, with live music of all kinds at the weekend to go with its draught Guinness and cider. Mon–Sat 4pm–2am, Sun 5pm–2am.

Le Pic 2 bd Franchet-d'Esperey ☎ 02 97 21 18 29, ⓦ restaurant-lorient.com. Just south of the *gare SNCF*, with some outdoor seating, this little restaurant has the air of a classy old-fashioned bistro and serves lunch

from under €15, plus varied, inventive dinner menus of market-fresh produce from €27. Mon, Tues, Thurs & Fri noon–1.45pm & 7–9.30pm, Wed noon–1.45pm, Sat 7–9.30pm.

Tavarn ar Roue Morvan 1 place Polig-Monjarret ☎ 02 97 21 61 57. Infused with all things Breton, this lively old tavern serves good, hearty meat and fish dishes, as well as offering home-made cider and live traditional music. Mon–Sat 11am–1am.

Île de Groix

The steep-sided, eight-kilometre-long rock of the **Île de Groix**, which shields Lorient 10km out to sea from the mouth of the Blavet estuary, is a sort of little sister to the better-known island of Belle-Île. With its own crop of lovely beaches, and its own throngs of summer visitors – not to mention a similar abundance of exclusive holiday homes – it's in no way inferior to its larger neighbour, however, and taking a day-trip out from the Lorient area is well worth the effort.

Groix flourished during the seventeenth and eighteenth centuries in tandem with Lorient, and was even the target of invasions by both the English (in 1663) and the Dutch (in 1774). Subsequently, after the island's first proper port was constructed in 1792, it became a major centre for catching and canning tuna. That industry has long since gone into decline, however, and Groix now makes its living from summer tourism, with beach-lovers joined both by birdwatchers in search of migratory species, and by geologists, who come to study its peculiar rock formations.

Écomusée de Groix

April, Oct & Nov daily except Mon 9.45am–noon & 2–5pm; May–Sept daily 9.45am–12.30pm & 2–6pm; Dec–March Wed, Sat & Sun 9.45am–noon & 2–5pm • €5 • ☎ 02 97 86 84 60, ⓦ ecomusee.groix.free.fr

All ferries to Groix dock at **PORT TUDY**. A former tuna cannery on the quayside houses the **Écomusée de Groix**, chronicling the island's history since the Bronze Age. While the more general displays are interesting enough, the museum's real strong point is in its depiction of the patterns and traditions of individual lives. Countless personal and family sagas are covered in exhaustive detail upstairs, from birth and the acquisition of language – Breton, until World War I – through school, apprenticeship and marriage, all the way to death.

Around the island

The largest of the island's 27 villages, **LE BOURG** (also known as Loctudy, or even, simply, Groix), stands 500m uphill from the port. Although it's attractive enough, with a tuna-fish weathervane topping its little church, a more obvious way to spend a day on Groix is to tour its dramatic coastline. The easiest way to do this is to rent a **bicycle** from one of several outlets at the port, costing around €12 per day. Crossing the island north to south takes barely ten minutes by bike; east to west requires more like an hour, especially as it can be hard to spot which coastal paths will prove negotiable, and which merely peter out into the sand.

At their tallest, at the **Pointe du Grognon** in the northwest, the **cliffs** of Groix rise 50m out of the sea. That may not sound all that high, but only Belle-Île in Brittany surpasses it. Much of the western tip serves as a bird sanctuary; the southeastern corner, by contrast, close to the **Pointe des Chats** and its little lighthouse, is renowned for its unusual green-tinged mineral deposits.

The best **beaches** are also at the eastern end of the island. Locals claim that the **Plage des Grands Sables**, jutting out into the sea, is the only convex beach in Europe. Palpable nonsense that may be, but it is a beautiful little unsheltered strip of sand that offers calm swimming (supervised by lifeguards in summer), with pleasure boats bobbing at anchor just off shore. The next group of beaches to the south are even better, a succession of little sandy coves tucked between the rocks known collectively as **Les Sables Rouges**.

ARRIVAL AND INFORMATION   ÎLE DE GROIX

By ferry from Lorient Compagnie-Océane sails 4–9 times daily all year from the south quay of Lorient's pleasure port. The crossing takes 45min, and in recent years the first departure from Lorient has ranged from 7am in August to 8.05am in winter (adults €31.65 return, under-25s €19.90, bicycles €19.40, small cars €158; ☏ 08 20 05 61 56, ⓦ www.compagnie-oceane.fr).

By ferry from Doëlan Navix sails once daily, in summer only, from tiny Doëlan, 20km west of Lorient and 5km west of le Pouldu (July & Aug daily 9am; adults €31.10 return, under-18s €20; ☏ 02 97 46 60 00, ⓦ navix.fr).

Tourist office On the quayside at Port Tudy (July & Aug Mon–Sat 9.30am–12.30pm & 2–6.30pm, Sun 9.30am–12.30pm; Sept Mon–Sat 9.30am–noon & 2–5pm, Sun 10am–12.30pm; Oct–June Sat 9am–noon & 2–5pm, Sun 9.30am–12.30pm; ☏ 02 97 86 53 08, ⓦ groix.fr).

ACCOMMODATION AND EATING

Auberge de Jeunesse Fort du Méné ☏ 02 97 86 81 38, ⓦ fuaj.org/Ile-de-Groix. Simple but beautifully sited summer-only hostel, a few hundred metres east of town, close to the sea en route towards the small beach at the Pointe de la Croix, with a campsite alongside. Closed Oct–March. **€13.60**

De la Jetée 1 quai Port Tudy ☏ 02 97 86 80 82, ⓦ hoteldelajetee.fr. Hotel at the far right end of the port, which holds somewhat faded rooms with great sea views. Closed Jan. **€69**

De la Marine 7 rue Général-de-Gaulle, Le Bourg ☏ 02 97 86 80 05, ⓦ hoteldelamarine.com. Hotel-restaurant up the hill, in a large, well-furnished house that offers comfortable rooms, most but not all en-suite, and

serves delicious fish dinners in its front garden, including burbot brochettes and fish couscous on menus starting at €17. Closed Nov–March, plus Sun eve & Mon in low season. **€51**

★ **Les Sables Rouges** Port Coustic ☏ 02 97 86 81 32, ⓦ campingdessablesrouges.com. This lovely three-star campsite, poised just above the beaches at the southeast corner, is the nicest on the island. Closed mid-Sept to late April. **€20.50**

Ty Mad Port Tudy ☏ 02 97 86 80 19, ⓦ tymad.com. Fancy hotel, set back behind an attractive lawn by the port, which serves good seafood meals in the open air, and has a pool. Expect to pay €50 extra for the larger, brighter, sea-view rooms. Closed Dec–Feb. **€60**

Hennebont

The old walled town of **HENNEBONT** stands a few kilometres upstream from Lorient, just as the River Blavet starts to widen into the estuary. Its fortifications, especially the main gate, are imposing, and from the ramparts you get wide views of the river below. The old city within, however, is entirely residential.

The one time Hennebont comes alive is at the **Thursday market**, featuring a heady mix of fresh food, crêpes and delicacies from around the world, alongside livestock, flowers, carpets and clothes.

ST-CADO AND THE ÉTEL ESTUARY

No more than a round speck on the waters of the **River Étel**, dotted with perhaps twenty white-painted houses, the delightful islet of **St-Cado** stands just inland of the large bridge on which the D761 crosses the Étel estuary, halfway between Port-Louis and Carnac.

The main feature of the island itself, reached by walking across a spindly little bridge from the mainland, is a twelfth-century chapel that stands on the site of a Romanesque predecessor built by St Cado around the sixth century. Cado, a prince of "Glamorgant", returned in due course to his native Wales and was martyred, but Welsh pilgrims still make their way to this pretty little spot. As Cado is a patron saint of the deaf, it's said that hearing problems can be cured by lying on his stone "bed" inside the chapel. A little fountain behind the chapel only emerges from the sea at low tide. There's nowhere to stay on St-Cado, nor are there any restaurants, but a couple of bars face it from the quayside on the mainland.

North of St-Cado, further upstream, the Étel is much broader; it's among the most beautiful estuaries in Brittany, and its banks barely developed. Navix offers **sightseeing cruises** from the village of Étel, downstream from the road bridge on the east bank (mid-April to early July & first 3 weeks of Sept, 2 departures on Tues, Thurs, Fri & Sun; early July to Aug, 4 departures Mon–Sat; adults €18.50 return, under-18s €11; ☎02 97 46 60 00, ⓦnavix.fr).

Écomusée Industriel des Forges

Inzinzac-Lochrist • June & Sept Mon–Fri 10am–noon & 2–6pm, Sun 2–6pm; July & Aug Mon–Fri 10am–6.30pm, Sat & Sun 2–6.30pm; guided tours 3pm daily July & Aug • €4.40 • ☎02 97 36 98 21, ⓦinzinzac-lochrist.fr

Across the Blavet, just north of Hennebont, the great chimneys of the town's **ironworks** have been smokeless and silent since 1966. It's now **Écomusée Industriel des Forges**, which documents its hundred-year history from the workers' point of view. Some of the redundant employees contributed their memories and tools; for others, turning their workplace into a museum was adding insult to injury, but it is in fact excellent, both in content and presentation.

ARRIVAL AND DEPARTURE   HENNEBONT

Tourist office 9 place Maréchal-Foch (July & Aug Mon–Sat 9.30am–12.30pm & 2–6.30pm, Sun 10am–1pm; Sept–June Tues–Sat 9.30am–noon & 2–5pm; ☎02 97 84 78 00, ⓦlorient-tourisme.fr).

ACCOMMODATION

Ibis Budget Lorient Hennebont Allée Villeneuve ☎08 92 68 32 46, ⓦibis.com. Hennebont's one hotel is this budget motel, just off the motorway 1.5km south of the centre, which has comfortable rooms but no restaurant. €52

The Quiberon peninsula

The **Presqu'île de Quiberon** is as close to being an island as any peninsula could conceivably be; the long causeway of sand that links it to the mainland narrows to as little as 50m in places. The tourists who pack out the peninsula each summer come not so much to visit the towns, which, other than **Quiberon** itself, are generally featureless, but to use them as a base for trips out to **Belle-Île** or around the coastline, which here has two quite distinct characters.

The peninsula has always held strategic military importance. The English held the peninsula for eight bloody days in 1746; Chouans and royalists landed here in 1795 in the hope of destroying the Revolution, only to be sealed in and slaughtered; and the defoliation that threatens the dunes today is in part the result of German fortifications constructed during World War II.

7

Along the peninsula

Just after the D768 curves around the bay outside **PLOUHARNEL**, and starts to descend the peninsula, it crosses the tracks of the Tire-Bouchon train line down to Quiberon.

While safe sandy beaches line the peninsula's sheltered eastern side, the **Baie de Quiberon**, the **Côte Sauvage** that faces the Atlantic to the west is a bleak rocky heathland, lashed by heavy seas. Though it's renowned as a destination for expert **surfers**, it's also notorious as the scene of innumerable drownings.

The slender isthmus of **Penthièvre** stretches for the northernmost three or four kilometres of the peninsula. Windsurfers launch into the bay from the embankment on its eastern side, and kite-fliers perch on the west where the sea's too rough to enter. As the narrow neck finally begins to broaden, the village of **PORTIVY** nestles into the only real shelter along the Côte Sauvage.

Port-Haliguen, near the southern end of the eastern coast, is the only port other than Quiberon itself. Today, it's an active marina, with a little commercial fishing. Boats from the islands occasionally shelter here, and use it for embarkation in rough weather, while this was also the spot where Captain Alfred Dreyfus disembarked on his return from Devil's Island in 1899.

Quiberon

Although much of the Quiberon peninsula has become built up, it still holds only one true town, the eponymous **QUIBERON** at its southern tip. The most active area here, **Port-Maria**, is home to the **gare maritime** for the islands of Belle-Île, Houat and Hoëdic, as well as a fishing harbour, with a lovely sheltered **beach** nearby.

The town proper centres on a busy little park with a miniature golf course, but few of the streets further back hold anything of great interest. The exception is the little hill that leads down to the port from the **gare SNCF**, where you can browse in some surprisingly good clothes and antique shops.

From the ferry terminal and the fishing harbour – once famous for its sardines – a long curve of fine sandy **beach** stretches away east, lined for several hundred metres with bars, cafés and restaurants. The slopes that climb back from the sea are largely residential, with modern holiday apartments scattered amid fine villas.

ARRIVAL AND DEPARTURE   THE QUIBERON PENINSULA

By train The summer-only Tire-Bouchon train – the name, "corkscrew", refers to the bottleneck at the mouth of the peninsula – links Quiberon's *gare SNCF*, just above the town centre, with Auray (2nd half of June & 1st half of Sept 4 trains on Sat & Sun only; July & Aug 6–10 daily; 45min).
By bus Bus #1 runs to the *gare maritime* from Vannes, via Auray and Carnac (8 daily; 2hr; ☎02 97 47 29 64,

ⓦ keolis-atlantique.com).
By car Expect traffic delays all along the peninsula's one narrow road; there's no parking for ferry passengers at the port itself, and few spaces nearby, so you may well have to park at the huge Sémaphore car park at the north end of town, and catch a free shuttle bus for the remaining 1.5km to the waterfront.

INFORMATION AND ACTIVITIES

Tourist office 14 rue de Verdun (April–June & Sept Mon–Sat 9am–12.30pm & 2–6pm, Sun 9.30am–12.30pm; July & Aug Mon–Sat 9am–7pm, Sun 10am–1pm & 2–5pm; Oct–March Mon–Fri 10am–12.30pm & 2–5.30pm, Sat 10am–12.30pm; ☎02 97 50 07 84, ⓦ quiberon.com).

Bike rental Cycl'omar, 47 place Hoche (☎02 97 50 26 00, ⓦ cyclomar.fr).
Sea-kayaking lessons Sillages École de Kayak, 9 av de Groix, St-Pierre (☎06 81 26 75 08, ⓦ kayak-sillages.com).
Surfing lessons École de Surf de Bretagne, 6 av de l'Océan, Plouharnel (☎02 97 52 41 18, ⓦ ecole-surf.com).

ACCOMMODATION

For much of the year, it's hard to get a room in Quiberon. In July and August, the whole peninsula is packed, while in winter it's so quiet that virtually all its facilities close down. The nicest area to stay is on the seafront in Port-Maria, where several good hotel-restaurants face the Belle-Île ferry terminal.

HOTELS

Bellevue 4 rue de Tiviec, Quiberon ☎02 97 50 16 28, ⓦbellevuequiberon.com. A relatively quiet Logis de France, set slightly back from the sea near the casino, 500m east of the port, with its own pool and a dining room, where you pay on a *demi-pension* basis at €30 per person per day. Closed Oct–March. **€84**

Au Bon Accueil 6 quai de Houat, Quiberon ☎02 97 50 07 92, ⓦaubonaccueil-quiberon.com. This freshly spruced-up seafront hotel is Port-Maria's best option for budget travellers. The most basic rooms share bathrooms; pay €20 extra for an en-suite room with sea views. The restaurant downstairs has dinner menus at €22 & €30. **€40**

★**Neptune** 4 quai de Houat, Quiberon ☎02 97 50 09 62, ⓦhotel-neptune-quiberon.com. Great-value hotel, where twelve of the 21 bright, cheery rooms cost €15 extra and have sea-view balconies – though the bathrooms are drab – while larger family suites face inland. **€69**

Port Haliguen 10 place de Port Haliguen, Quiberon ☎02 97 50 16 52, ⓦhotel-port-haliguen.com. Very peaceful seafront hotel facing the pleasure port across the peninsula from the town centre. The modernized rooms have been stripped of superfluities to leave them stylish and still comfortable; it's well worth paying the small supplement for a sea-view balcony. Closed Nov to late March. **€78**

HOSTEL AND CAMPSITES

Auberge des Dunes Avenue Surcouf, Penthièvre ☎02 98 83 55 17, ⓦrevesdemer.com. Secluded hostel complex, on the Côte Sauvage immediately north of the isthmus, with dorms holding two to six beds each, plus a restaurant serving all meals, and a bar. Rates include breakfast. **€24.90**

Camping du Conguel Boulevard de la Teignouse ☎02 97 50 19 11, ⓦcampingduconguel.com. Beach-front four-star site, very close to the southern tip of the peninsula east of Quiberon, where the large pool has elaborate water slides. Closed Nov–March. **€49**

Camping Do-Mi-Si-La-Mi 31 rue de la Vierge, St-Julien Plage ☎02 97 50 22 52, ⓦwww.domisilami.com. Verdant three-star site, 100m from the beach along the sheltered east coast near Quiberon town, with its own supermarket and restaurant in summer. Closed Nov–March. **€14.80**

Camping Municipal de Kerhostin Allée du camping Kerhostin, St-Pierre-Quiberon ☎02 97 30 95 25, ⓦsaintpierrequiberon.fr. Two-star beachfront campsite, looking out over the Baie de Quiberon near the northern end of the peninsula. Closed early Sept to late April. **€17**

Camping Municipal de Penthièvre Avenue Duquesne, Penthièvre ☎02 97 52 33 86, ⓦsaintpierrequiberon.fr. Two-star campsite with direct beach access, plus on-site grocery, bar, bakery and snack bar, and a Monday market alongside. Closed Oct to mid-April. **€14.80**

EATING AND DRINKING

The most appealing area for a good meal is along the waterfront in Port-Maria, where seafood restaurants compete to attract ferry passengers. Morning **markets** are held at Kerhostin at the neck of the peninsula, 5km north of Quiberon, on Wednesday, at St-Pierre-Quiberon just south of Kerhostin on Thursday, and in Quiberon itself on Saturday.

La Chaumine 79 rue de Port Haliguen ☎02 97 50 17 67, ⓦrestaurant-lachaumine.com. This lovely little fish restaurant, away from the sea on the main road into Port Haliguen, serves menus from €20 at lunch, and from €29 for dinner; the latter features salmon braised in champagne. Mid-March to mid-Nov Tues–Sun noon–2pm & 7–9pm; also closed Sun eve except in July & Aug.

★**De la Criée** 11 quai de l'Océan ☎02 97 30 53 09, ⓦmaisonlucas.net. Superb local fish restaurant, serving whatever's freshest from the morning's catch; choose from the overflowing baskets of shellfish, the daily €20–25 specials, or the two great-value set menus, at €18 and €21. Feb–Dec Tues–Sun 12.15–2pm & 7.15–10pm; closed Sun eve in low season.

Le Vivier 12 route du Vivier, Le Manémeur ☎02 97 50 12 60. Very simple café serving quintessentially fresh seafood in a great setting overlooking the Côte Sauvage, just over 1km due west of central Quiberon. Individual *plats* of mussels, smoked fish or shellfish €12–25, full meals from €29. April–Sept daily noon–2pm & 7–9pm; Oct–March Tues–Thurs & Sun noon–2pm, Fri & Sat noon–2pm & 7–9pm.

Belle-Île

The island of **Belle-Île**, 15km due south of Quiberon, is a gorgeous place. Considerably larger than the other Breton islands, it has less of an island feel, with its bus tours and traffic, but its towns – **Le Palais**, **Sauzon** and **Bangor** – are consistently lovely, and it offers wonderful opportunities for walking and cycling.

The physical geography of Belle-Île mirrors that of Brittany as a whole. On the landward side it is rich and fertile, interrupted by deep estuaries with tiny ports; facing

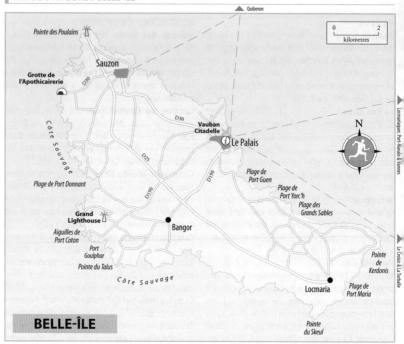

BELLE-ÎLE

the ocean, along its own Côte Sauvage, sparse heather-covered cliffs trail rocky crags out into the sea.

With the island measuring 17km east to west and up to 10km north to south, some kind of transport is essential, even if you just come for a day-trip: rental bikes and cars are readily available at the island port of **Le Palais**, while, for a hefty price, you can also take a small car over on the ferries.

Brief history

Belle-Île once belonged to the monks of Redon, and later to the ambitious Nicholas Fouquet, Louis XIV's minister, whose hubris in buying it in 1658 contributed to his downfall at the hands of the Three Musketeers three years later. It was subsequently captured by the English in 1752, who swapped it for Menorca in 1761 in an unrepeatable bargain deal.

Along the way Belle-Île has seen a fair number of distinguished exiles. The citadel prison at Le Palais closed only in 1961, having numbered among its inmates an astonishing succession of state enemies and revolutionary heroes – including the son of Toussaint l'Ouverture of Haiti, Ben Bella of Algeria, and even, for a brief period after 1848, Karl Marx.

Less involuntarily, such celebrated figures as the painters Monet and Matisse, the writers Flaubert and Proust, and the actress Sarah Bernhardt all spent time on the island.

Le Palais

As you dock at the pleasant little harbour town of **LE PALAIS**, the abrupt star-shaped fortifications of the **Citadelle** are the first thing you see, towering sternly above the port. Once you've explored the few little streets of the town proper, it's well worth crossing the small lock and climbing up to have a closer look.

Citadelle Vauban

Daily: April–June, Sept & Oct 9.30am–6pm; July & Aug 9am–7pm; Nov–March 9.30am–5pm • €8 • ☎ 02 97 31 85 54, ⓦ citadellevauban.com

Now the very picture of tranquillity, the **Citadelle Vauban** is surrounded by lawns, flowers and ornate topiary. Constructed along stylish and ordered lines by the great builder Vauban early in the eighteenth century, the fortress is startling in size – filled with doorways leading to mysterious cellars and underground passages, endless sequences of rooms, dungeons and deserted cells. Parts of it have recently been converted to become a rather opulent hotel, but there's still plenty of scope to roam, and the battlements offer great views over Le Palais.

An informative **museum** documents the island's history, including its involvement in Dumas' tales of *The Three Musketeers* (which feature an account of the death of Porthos on the island). Displays cover Vauban himself, and also the 78 Acadian families who settled here in 1765 after the defeat of French Canada – part of the mass migration that was also responsible for populating Louisiana, in what's now the southern US, with "Cajuns". Very little is translated into English, however, and there's disappointingly little material about the prison's most enigmatic inmates: the La Voisin family of poisoners, incarcerated here in perpetual silence in 1682.

Sauzon

SAUZON, Belle-Île's second town, is also on the island's sheltered north coast. A beautiful little village, it's arrayed along one side of the mouth of a slender estuary, 6km west of Le Palais (and a 20min ride on bus #1). There's next to nothing to see here, but if you're staying any length of time, and you have your own transport, it makes a delightful spot in which to base yourself.

Around the island

Although exploring Belle-Île is an absolute joy, it's too large to see the entire island in a single day. A magnificent **coastal footpath** winds around the entire shoreline, but day-trippers are unlikely to get any further from Le Palais on foot than either Sauzon to the northwest, or the succession of sandy **beaches** like the plage de Port Guen to the southeast.

With a car or bicycle, the best plan is to head to the island's southern side, then hike along at least part of the Côte Sauvage. Note that you can't cycle on the coastal footpath, while many of the officially recommended cycle routes are on dirt roads that can be heavy going. Also, don't put too much faith in island maps that show lots of little villages; most simply don't exist, and only Sauzon, Bangor and Locmaria at the eastern end hold facilities of any kind.

Grand Phare

April–June & Sept Wed–Sun 11am–1pm & 2–6pm; July & Aug daily 1–5pm; Oct Wed, Fri & Sat 1–5pm • €2 • ☎ 02 97 31 83 04

For an overview of Belle-Île, the obvious first stop is the **Grand Phare**, set amid the fields 2km west of Bangor. Dating from 1835, and hollow like a chimney, this 52m-tall lighthouse commands a sweeping panorama of the craggy western coastline just beyond – assuming you have the energy to climb its 247 steps, the last fifty or so of which are up ladders.

Aiguilles de Port-Coton

The only place where a road runs along the Côte Sauvage, and even here just for a few hundred metres, is immediately west of the lighthouse. It ends at the car park for the **Aiguilles de Port-Coton** formation just offshore, where a savage sea foams amid the pinnacles of rock. It's a lovely spot, where you can escape the crowds, and watch the turmoil from different angles, by walking out along any of several spindle-thin cliff-top promontories.

An easy twenty-minute stroll leads to the pretty beach of **Port-Donnant** 1km north, which despite appearances is unsafe for swimming.

Grotte de l'Apothicairerie

The next point where there's access to the coast by road is 5km north of the Aiguilles. A precarious oceanfront cave here, hollowed into the precipitous cliff face, is known as the **Grotte de l'Apothicairerie** because it used to be filled with the nests of cormorants, arranged like the jars on a pharmacist's shelves. Once again it's a ravishing spectacle. Vestiges of ancient stairways to the cave are clearly visible, but none leads all the way down, and signs warn of "mortal danger" should you attempt the descent.

The **D30 inland** from the cave leads along a miniature tree-lined valley sheltered from the Atlantic winds. If you take the **D25** back towards Le Palais you pass the two **menhirs**, Jean and Jeanne, said to be lovers petrified as punishment for wanting to meet before their marriage. Another (larger) menhir used to lie near these two – it was broken up to help construct the road that separates them.

Pointe des Poulains

The **Pointe des Poulains**, at the northwestern tip of Belle-Île where the Côte Sauvage comes to an end, is an exposed little headland that holds a picturesque lighthouse-cum-cottage and is all but separated from the rest of the island at high tide.

The road comes to an end some way short of the slender sandy spit – technically, a *tombolo* – that leads to the point, alongside the country estate where actress and celebrity **Sarah Bernhardt** used to spend her summers. From there, it's an enjoyable ten-minute walk to the very end.

ARRIVAL AND DEPARTURE **BELLE-ÎLE**

FROM QUIBERON

Compagnie-Océane All year, Compagnie-Océane (☎08 20 05 61 56 or ☎02 97 35 02 00, ⓦwww .compagnie-oceane.fr) sends between six and thirteen ferries daily from Port-Maria on the Quiberon peninsula to Le Palais on Belle-Île. The first departure is generally around 8am, and the crossing normally takes 45min, though the high-speed vessel *Kerdonis* makes up to three crossings daily between mid-April and August in just 30min. The return fare is €31.65 for adults, €19.90 for under-25s. Small cars can be taken on the slower crossings only, for €158.40 return, while bikes cost €19.40 return. Reserve in advance during peak periods. Between May and August, the same company also sends the *Kerdonis* from Port-Maria to Sauzon each evening, and from Sauzon to Port-Maria each morning, for the same fare.

Navix In summer, Navix (☎08 25 13 21 00, ⓦnavix.fr) sails to Le Palais on Belle-Île from Port-Maria (mid-April to mid-May Tues–Sun 8.45am; mid-May to June Wed–Sun 8.45am; July to early Sept daily 8.45am & 10.30pm; adults €17, under-18s €11.30; €28/€17 return).

FROM VANNES, PORT-NAVALO AND LOCMARIAQUER

Navix In summer, Navix (☎08 25 13 21 00, ⓦnavix.fr) sails to Le Palais from Vannes and Port-Navalo (mid-April to June and almost all of Sept Tues–Thurs, Sat & Sun; July & Aug daily), leaving Vannes at 9.20am (adults €30 return, under-18s €21.60) and Port-Navalo at 9.45am (€29/€21), with a connecting service from Locmariaquer (€39/€28.50).

FROM LE CROISIC AND LA TURBALLE

Navix Between early July and late Aug, Navix (☎08 25 13 21 00, ⓦnavix.fr) offers daily excursions to Belle-Île that leave Le Croisic at 8.10am, and La Turballe, not far north of La Baule between Piriac and Guérande, at 8.40am (adults €42 return, under-18s €28.40).

INFORMATION AND GETTING AROUND

Tourist office Next to the *gare maritime* in Le Palais (July & Aug Mon–Sat 8.45am–7pm, Sun 8.45am–1pm; Sept–June Mon–Sat 9am–12.30pm & 2–6pm; ☎02 97 31 81 93, ⓦbelle-ile.com).

By bus Belle-Île's bus system offers around six daily connections in summer from Le Palais to each of Sauzon, Bangor and Locmaria (☎02 97 31 81 88, ⓦcars-verts.fr).

By car Locatourisle, at the port in Le Palais (☎02 97 31 83 56, ⓦlocatourisle.com) rents cars from around €70/day in summer.

By bike Several waterfront outlets in Le Palais, including Roue Libre (☎02 97 31 49 81, ⓦbelle-ile-evasion.com), rent bikes at around €12/day, as well as scooters from €45/day.

ACCOMMODATION AND EATING

LE PALAIS

Atlantique Quai de l'Acadie ☎ 02 97 31 80 11, ⓦ hotel -atlantique.com. Cheerful yellow-and-blue hotel in prime position on the quayside facing the ferries, offering good-value accommodation and a decent restaurant with a panoramic terrace, serving lunch from €14 and dinner from €22. The cheapest rooms are in a separate annexe, but even in summer a sea-view room in the main building costs less than €100. €67

Auberge de Jeunesse Haute-Boulogne, Le Palais ☎ 02 97 31 81 33, ⓦ fuaj.org/belle-ile-en-mer. Hugely popular hostel on the heights above town, behind the *citadelle*, a 15min walk from the port. Small dorms, with cooking facilities and breakfast available. Advance bookings essential. Closed Oct–March. €16.50

Camping de l'Océan ☎ 02 97 31 83 86, ⓦ camping -ocean-belle-ile.com. Despite the name, this pleasant, three-star, year-round campsite is 500m directly inland from the port; it offers rental chalets as well as tent camping. Closed Oct–April. €19.80

Château Bordénéo Bordénéo ☎ 02 97 31 80 77, ⓦ chateau-bordeneo.fr. Delightful luxury B&B, 1.5km northwest of town towards Sauzon, with five opulent, pastel-toned rooms and suites, plus a lovely garden and indoor pool. €174

Citadelle Vauban Citadelle ☎ 02 97 31 84 17, ⓦ citadellevauban.com. Sumptuous rooms in a grand mansion within the walls of the *citadelle*, including suites with spectacular sea views; the garden restaurant, the *Table du Gouverneur*, is open to all, serving lunch time *plats* (€15) and *formules* (€19–24), and dinner menus from €35. Closed mid-Oct to mid-April. €145

Le Clos Fleuri Route de Sauzon ☎ 02 97 31 45 45, ⓦ hotel-leclosfleuri.com. This exceptionally welcoming and peaceful hotel, just outside Le Palais on the road towards Sauzon, offers spacious, comfortable and tastefully furnished rooms at reasonable prices, with private terraces but no restaurant. Closed Jan to mid-Feb. €89

Vauban 1 rue des Remparts ☎ 02 97 31 45 42, ⓦ hotel -vauban-belleile.com. Very welcoming Logis de France, a little way back from the port, but still enjoying sea views from its bright, fresh rooms. No restaurant. €80

Le Vivier 4 place de l'Hôtel de Ville ☎ 02 97 31 37 37, ⓦ hotelegalion.com. Modern restaurant below the hotel *Galion*, facing the church and not far back from the port, with indoor and outdoor dining. Three-course lunches for €18, and dinner menus from €24.50, featuring honey-braised ham or mussels, up to a €46.50 option offering both langoustines and lobster, plus à la carte seafood specials. Mid-Feb to June & Sept to mid-Nov 11am–2pm & 6.30–10pm, July & Aug daily 11am–10pm.

SAUZON

Camping La Source La Vallon du Port aux Plages ☎ 02 97 31 60 95, ⓦ belleile-lasource.com. Verdant little three-star campsite, 800m up the valley from the port. Closed Oct to late March. €10.80

Le Petit Baigneur Rampe des Glycines ☎ 02 97 31 67 74. Pretty restaurant set slightly back from the port near the far end, serving à la carte mussels and lunch *formules* for €15, and full dinners from €28. Daily noon–1.45pm & 7–9pm; closed mid-Nov to March, plus Mon in low season.

Du Phare Quai Guerveur ☎ 02 97 31 60 36, ⓦ en.hotelduphare-belleile.com. Inexpensive hotel in a magnificent setting, next to its eponymous lighthouse on the headland at the very tip of the estuary. The rooms are faded and ordinary, though; most have en-suite facilities and cost €10 more. The restaurant downstairs (open April–Sept only) serves fishy menus from €20 at lunch time, €23 for dinner. Closed Nov–March. €55

Villa Pen Prad Rue du Chemin Neuf ☎ 06 49 41 71 43, ⓦ villapenprad.com. Very pleasant B&B, in an unbeatable waterfront location beside the road into Sauzon – a tremendous vantage point for watching activity in the little port – with three charming rooms, a couple of luxurious suites and great breakfasts. €180

THE REST OF THE ISLAND

A l'Îlot Carton Borvran, Locmaria ☎ 02 97 31 73 37, ⓦ alilotcarton.fr. Ten minutes' walk out of Locamaria, this eco-friendly B&B is a genuine one-off – it's made entirely of cardboard. Not just the fixtures and fittings in its single large suite, but the house itself, so you'll just have to hope it doesn't rain. Actually, of course, the friendly owner/builders, who make and sell cardboard artefacts of all kinds, have thought of that; rest assured, it's waterproof. €130

Camping de Port Andro Locmaria ☎ 02 97 31 73 25, ⓦ locmaria-belle-ile.com/heb_campings. Belle-Île holds plenty of fancier campsites, but if you like to camp close to the beach, there's no beating this secluded little municipal site, beside its own perfect strand 3km from Locmaria, towards the southeast tip of the island. Closed mid-Sept to April. €11.80

Castel Clara Port Goulphar ☎ 02 97 31 84 21, ⓦ castel -clara.com. Luxurious spa resort that was a favourite retreat of former President Mitterrand, who came for a farewell visit shortly before his death in 1996. As well as plush rooms, it holds a very fancy restaurant, which puts on a seafood buffet for €39. Closed mid-Jan to mid-Feb. €305

Grand Large Port-Coton ☎ 02 97 31 80 92, ⓦ hotel grandlarge.com. Perched near the ocean just short of the Aiguilles, this orange-pink hotel offers affordable garden rooms, but charges premium rates for its finest sea views. Closed Nov to late March. €81–100

7

Houat and Hoëdic

Houat and **Hoëdic**, two smaller and much quieter islands east of Belle-Île, can also be reached by ferries from Quiberon and elsewhere. Though most visitors come to the islands on day-trips, to seek out their magnificent – and usually all but empty – golden **beaches**, both offer facilities for extended stays.

Île de Houat

The island of **Houat**, which means "duck" in Breton, measures 5km from east to west, and much less than half that north to south. It's an idyllic spot, populated largely by rabbits and lizards, with hardly a tree to its name. Most of what marginally higher ground it has to offer consists of open heathland, with its thin covering of turf petering out at the head of pink granite cliffs which look down on long sandy beaches and lovely little coves.

Boats draw in at **Port St-Gildas**, a not especially picturesque little harbour just below the island's one "town", the flowery village of **HOUAT**. The island is small enough for walking to be a pleasure, and it's not in any case legal to cycle along the coastal footpaths. The finest **beaches** lie to the east and south, in the shape of the sheltered **Tréac'h er Gourèd** that runs the full length of the eastern shoreline, and the **Tréac'h Salus** nearby.

Eclosarium

Daily: Easter–June & Sept 10am–noon & 2–5pm; July & Aug 10am–6pm • €4.50 • ☎ 02 97 52 38 38

During the 1980s, the islanders tried to boost their economy by raising lobsters in tanks in a large shed-like building known as the *écloserie*, 1km southwest of Houat. That experiment never proved profitable, so the structure now serves instead as the **Eclosarium**, a museum dedicated almost exclusively to the microscopic marine world of **phytoplankton**, the organisms responsible for producing eighty percent of the earth's oxygen. It's more interesting than it might sound, with a healthy dose of local history thrown in. Fetid-looking vials demonstrate how algae is cultivated locally for use in products such as shower gel, sun cream, moisturizer and even pasta – if you're tempted, the gift shop sells them at discounted prices.

Île de Hoëdic

At a mere 2.5km end to end, Hoëdic – in Breton, the "duckling" to Houat's "duck" – is that much tinier still. It's such a sleepy place, the story goes, that during the eighteenth century the rector of Hoëdic lost not only his sense of time but also his calendar, and ended up reducing Lent from forty days down to a more manageable three.

The island's sole settlement – **HOËDIC**, naturally – stands right in the centre, a short walk up from the ferry landing at **Port-Argol**. Other than to visit the appealing nineteenth-century church of St-Goustan, the only activity is to walk off in search of **beaches**. The best are to the south and east; take care how far you stroll out at low tide, as some patches become isolated offshore sandbanks when the sea comes in.

ARRIVAL AND DEPARTURE

Ferries from Quiberon All year, Compagnie-Océane (☎ 08 20 05 61 56 or ☎ 02 97 35 02 00, ⏏ www .compagnie-oceane.fr) runs one to six daily ferries to Houat and Hoëdic, to widely varying schedules (40min to Houat, another 25min to Hoëdic; adults €31.65 return, under-25s €19.65, bikes €19.20). They also carry passengers between one island and the other, for an additional one-way fare of €8.25/€6.45.

Ferries from Vannes, Locmariaquer and Port-Navalo Most days in July & Aug, Navix (☎ 08 25 13 21 00, ⏏ navix.fr) sails to Houat from Vannes (8.30am & 10am; adults €34 return, under-18s €23.50), Locmariaquer (9.45am; €34/€23.50) and Port-Navalo (10.45am; €33/€23), and to Hoëdic from Vannes (10am; adults €37 return, under-18s €25.50) and Port-Navalo (noon; €36/€24.70) only.

Day-trips from Le Croisic and La Turballe Most days in July & Aug, Navix (❶08 25 13 21 00, ⓦnavix.fr) sails from Le Croisic at 8.10am, and La Turballe at 8.50am, to Houat (adults €39.10 return, under-18s €26.40) and Hoëdic (€35.90/€23.40).

Day-trips from Port Blanc Once a week between mid-July & late Aug, Izenah Croisières (❶02 97 26 31 45, ⓦizenah-croisieres.com) operates day-trips to Houat and Hoëdic, departing Thurs 8.05am from Port Blanc at Baden (adults €29, under-13s €18).

Day-trips from Port-Navalo It's also possible to reach Houat and Hoëdic aboard the *Krog E Barz*, a replica lobster-fishing boat that runs day-trips from Port-Navalo, on which visitors can help with the actual sailing (adults €59, under-13s €49; ❶02 97 49 07 50, ⓦkrog-e-barz.com).

ACCOMMODATION AND EATING

HOUAT
Camping Municipal Tréac'h er Gouréd ❶02 97 30 68 04. Campsite just back from the Tréac'h er Gouréd beach; note that camping wild in the dunes is illegal, to protect the fragile environment. Closed Oct–May. €10

L'Ezenn Route du Moulin ❶02 97 30 69 73. Hotel on the main road above the Tréac'h er Gouréd beach, which has excellent modernized rooms but no restaurant. Closed Feb. €65

Hôtel-Restaurant des Îles Le Bourg ❶02 97 30 68 02, ⓦrestaurant-des-iles.fr. Small hotel that offers tasteful sea-view rooms and serves good food both indoors and out on its terrace; it's a great spot for lunch, with the main set menu costing €19.50. Closed Nov–Jan. €61

HOËDIC
Camping Municipal Petit Bois ❶02 97 52 48 88. Large, well-equipped site, between the harbour and the village. Closed Sept–June. €10

Les Cardinaux Le Bourg ❶02 97 52 37 27, ⓦhotel-hoedic.com. Several of the plain rooms in Hoëdic's only hotel offer extensive sea views. Menus from €25 are served on its spacious deck. €100

Carnac

It may look at first glance like just another seaside village, but **CARNAC** is the most important prehistoric site in Europe – in fact this spot is thought to have been continuously inhabited longer than anywhere else in the world. Its **alignments** of two thousand or so menhirs stretch over 4km, with great burial tumuli dotted amid them. In use since at least 5700 BC, the site long predates Knossos, the Pyramids, Stonehenge and the great Egyptian temples of the same name at Karnak.

The town of Carnac is split into two distinct halves – **Carnac-Ville**, inland near the alignments, and the beach resort of **Carnac-Plage**. It's an amalgam that can verge on the ridiculous, with rows of shops named Supermarché des Druides and the like. For all that, Carnac is a relaxed and attractive place, and any commercialization doesn't intrude on the megaliths themselves. Fortunately, the ancient builders had the foresight to construct their monuments well back from the sea.

The alignments

Route des Alignements, 1km north of Carnac-Ville • **Site** April–Sept tours only; occasional English-language tours, including Tues 11.30am & Fri 11.30am during July & Aug; Oct–March daily 10am–5pm • April–Sept adults €6, under-18s free; Oct–March free **Maison des Mégalithes** Daily: May & June 9am–6pm; July & Aug 9.30am–7.30pm; Sept–April 10am–5pm • ❶02 97 52 29 81, ⓦcarnac.monuments-nationaux.fr

Carnac's megalithic monuments are arranged in three distinct major alignments – the **Alignements de Ménec**, "the place of stones" or "place of remembrance", with 1169 menhirs in eleven rows; the **Alignements de Kermario**, "the place of the dead", with 1029 stones in ten rows; and the **Alignements de Kerlescan**, "the place of burning", with 555 menhirs in thirteen lines. All three run roughly northeast–southwest, consecutively and parallel to the sea, 1km or so north of Carnac-Ville, but each has a slightly separate orientation.

The alignments themselves are fenced off, with unrestricted public access in winter only. Between April and September, if you want to see them close up you have to sign up for a guided tour from the official visitor centre, the **Maison des Mégalithes**, across the road from the Alignements de Ménec, which also holds interesting displays, plus a model of the entire site.

Although you get a much better sense of the alignments when you're able to walk among them and touch the stones, you can still see them pretty well from outside the fences. That's especially true if you take time to walk the parallel footpaths, like the one

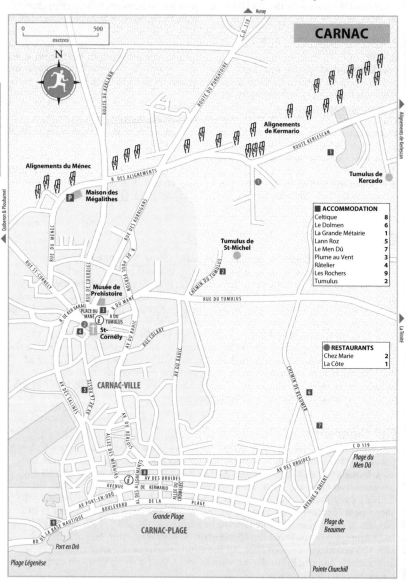

CARNAC

ACCOMMODATION

Celtique	8
Le Dolmen	6
La Grande Métairie	1
Lann Roz	5
Le Men Dû	7
Plume au Vent	3
Râtelier	4
Les Rochers	9
Tumulus	2

RESTAURANTS

Chez Marie	2
La Côte	1

EXPLAINING THE MEGALITHS

All sorts of conjectures have been advanced about the **Carnac megaliths**. One ancient story said they were petrified Roman soldiers; more recently, US soldiers in the last war allegedly believed them to be German anti-tank obstructions. The general consensus today is that they had a religious significance connected with their use as some sort of **astronomical observatory**.

One expert, the late Professor Thom, saw the alignments as part of a unified system for recording such phenomena as the extreme points of the lunar and solar cycles. According to this hypothesis, the Carnac stones provided a grid system – a kind of Neolithic graph paper – for plotting heavenly movements, and hence to determine the siting of other stones (see p.361).

However, it's hard to see real consistency in the size or shape of the stones, or enough regularity in the lines to pinpoint their direction. Local tradition has it that new stones were added to the lines, illuminated by fire, each June. An annual ceremony in which willing participants set up one stone does sound more plausible than a vast programme of slave labour to erect them all at once. In any case, the physical aspect and orientation of the stones may have been subsidiary to their metaphysical significance; perhaps no practical purpose or precise pattern was involved, and their importance was entirely symbolic.

The way you see them today cannot be said to be authentic. Having been used for generations as a source of ready-quarried stone, they were later also surreptitiously removed by farmers attempting to prevent academics and tourists damaging precious crops. Not only is it impossible to say how many stones have disappeared, but those that remain are not necessarily in their original positions – small holes filled with pink concrete at the base of the stones denote those that have been restored or re-erected.

7

---

from the Maison that follows the wilder, northern side of the Ménec and Kermario alignments. That said, from this (or, indeed almost any) distance, the individual stones tend to look like no more than stumps in the heather.

The **menhirs** range in size from misshapen lumps to five-metre-high blocks; some stand alone, others in circles known as **cromlechs**, or in approximate lines. In addition there are **dolmens**, groups of standing stones roofed with further stones across the top, which are generally assumed to be burial chambers.

The complex also includes tumuli, most notably the **Tumulus de St-Michel**, near the town centre, a vast artificial mound containing rudimentary graves. Visitors used to be allowed to enter subterranean passages that tunnelled beneath the St-Michel tumulus, but it's now considered too unstable; the history museum in Vannes has some exquisite jadeite axes found buried within.

Carnac-Ville

The village of **Carnac-Ville**, 1km in from the coast, seems somehow to stand apart from the ancient monuments on its doorstep, and the bustling beach resort immediately south. Its central church, the **Église St-Cornély**, is dedicated to the patron saint of horned animals. Archeologists believe the custom of bringing diseased cattle to Carnac to be cured, still honoured at the saint's *pardon* on the second Sunday in September, dates back as far as the Romans.

Musée de Préhistoire

10 place de la Chapelle, Carnac-Ville • March & Nov daily except Tues 2–5.30pm; April–June & Sept daily except Tues 10am–12.30pm & 2–6pm; July & Aug daily 10am–6.30pm; Oct daily except Tues 10am–12.30pm & 2–5.30pm; Dec–Feb school hols only, daily 2–5.30pm • €6 • ☏ 02 97 52 22 04, ⓦ museedecarnac.com

The rather dry archeological exhibits in Carnac's **Musée de Préhistoire** are likely to leave anyone whose command of French is less than perfect almost completely in the dark as to what all the fuss is about.

Tracing the history of the area from earliest times, it starts with 450,000-year-old chipping tools and leads by way of the Neanderthals to the megalith-builders and beyond.

As well as authentic physical relics, such as the original "twisted dolmen" of Luffang, with a carving of an octopus-like divinity guaranteed to chill the blood of any devotee of H.P. Lovecraft, there are reproductions and casts of the carvings at Locmariaquer, a scale model of the Alignements de Ménec and diagrams of how the stones may have been moved into place.

Carnac-Plage

The seaside resort of **Carnac-Plage** is extremely popular and crowded, swarming with holiday-makers in July and August. For most of these, the alignments are only a sideshow. But, as a holiday centre, Carnac has its special charm, especially in late spring and early autumn, when it is less crowded – and cheaper. The seafront remains well wooded, and the tree-lined avenues and gardens are a delight. The climate is mild enough for the Mediterranean mimosa and evergreen oak to grow alongside the native stone pine and cypress.

Carnac's five **beaches** extend for nearly 3km. The largest – logically enough, the Grande Plage – runs the full length of the built-up resort. For much of the way it's hidden from view by the slightly raised line of dunes that separates it from the boulevard de la Plage, which is in turn very low-key; the parallel avenue des Druides, a couple of blocks inland, is much busier, with shops and restaurants.

Further west, nearer the yacht club, the small **plage Légenèse** is reputed to be the beach on which the ill-fated Chouan royalists landed in 1795. The two most attractive beaches, usually counted together as one of the five, are **plages Men Dû** and **Beaumer**, which lie to the east towards La Trinité beyond Pointe Churchill. They're especially popular with **kite-surfers**.

La Trinité

LA TRINITÉ, 3–4km east of Carnac along the coast, around the sweep of Beaumer bay, is a potential alternative base. A modern and very upmarket yacht harbour that lacks a proper beach, it has achieved fame as the former home of yachtsman Eric Tabarly (see p.323), and thus attracts pleasure-boaters from all over Europe. Less salubriously, it was also the birthplace of Jean-Marie Le Pen, founder of the ultra-right National Front.

ARRIVAL AND DEPARTURE

CARNAC

By train In July and Aug, when the Tire-Bouchon rail link runs between Auray and Quiberon, trains call at Plouharnel, 4km northwest of Carnac.

By bus Buses from Auray (9 daily; 30min) and Vannes (7 daily; 1hr 20min) stop at the tourist office.

INFORMATION AND GETTING AROUND

Tourist office 74 av des Druides, Carnac-Plage (April–June & Sept Mon–Sat 9.30am–12.30pm & 2–6pm; July & Aug Mon–Sat 9.30am–7pm, Sun 3–7pm; Oct–March Mon–Sat 9.30am– 12.30pm & 2–5pm; ☎02 97 52 13 52, ⌨ot-carnac.fr).

Bike rental Le Randonneur, 20 av des Druides, Carnac-Plage (☎06 70 75 42 13).

ACCOMMODATION

HOTELS AND B&BS

Celtique 82 av des Druides, Carnac-Plage ☎02 97 52 14 15, ⌨hotel-celtique.com. Luxurious option, by the beach and affiliated to *Best Western*, with an indoor pool, spa and billiard room. Comfortable modern rooms, some large family suites, and deals on multi-night stays. **€147**

Lann Roz 36 av de la Poste, Carnac-Ville ☎02 97 52 68 00, ⌨lannroz.fr. Very comfortable, very friendly modernized hotel in the heart of town, with rooms of varying sizes, opulent bed linens and fresh-baked breakfasts from the neighbouring boulangerie. **€99**

Ostrea 34 cours des Quais, La Trinité ☎02 97 55 73 23, ⌨hotel-ostrea.com. Hotel-restaurant facing the port in

La Trinité. Some rooms enjoy sweeping sea views – others are rather cramped – and guests in the bistro, which offers continuous service, with typical main courses at €15–20, dine on an expansive outdoor deck. **€95**

★ **Plume au Vent** 4 venelle Notre-Dame, Carnac-Ville ☎ 06 16 98 34 79, ⓦ plume-au-vent.com. Central, welcoming and brilliantly decorated B&B, where the two suites ("low tide" and "high tide") draw tastefully on the nautical theme (for once), with pastel colours and some great found artefacts. **€90**

Râtelier 4 chemin de Douët, Carnac-Ville ☎ 02 97 52 05 04, ⓦ le-ratelier.com. Old, ivy-clad stone hotel with a handful of comfortable rooms, characterized by rustic colours and open wooden beams; the cheapest have showers but not toilets. Top-quality food on menus from €23. Closed mid-Nov to mid-Dec & all Jan. **€58**

Rochers 6 bd de la Base Nautique, Carnac-Plage ☎ 02 97 52 10 09, ⓦ www.les-rochers.com. Well-kept, family-friendly hotel offering the best value by the beach, especially if you are looking for sea-view balconies. Closed Nov–Easter. **€115**

Tumulus Chemin du Tumulus ☎ 02 97 52 08 21, ⓦ hotel-tumulus.com. Fancy hotel, east of town alongside the Tumulus St-Michel, a base for archeologists a century ago, but now entirely modernized, with a heated pool and a fine restaurant where menus, served in the garden in summer, start at €25 for lunch, €45 for dinner. Closed early Nov to mid-Feb. **€175**

CAMPSITES

Camping La Baie Plage de Kervillen, La Trinité ☎ 02 97 55 73 42, ⓦ camping-de-la-baie.net. Attractive four-star campsite, right beside the sea and offering a heated swimming pool, plus a shop, bar and all-day restaurant. Closed late Sept to late April. **€32.85**

Camping Le Dolmen Chemin de Beaumer ☎ 02 97 52 12 35, ⓦ campingledolmen.com. Three-star campsite, just north of Carnac-Plage and an easy walk from the sea, with a grocery, snack bar, and seafood platters on demand, as well as a heated swimming pool. Closed late Sept to March. **€29.50**

Camping Grande Métairie Route des Alignements de Kermario ☎ 02 97 52 24 01, ⓦ lagrandemetairie.com. Upscale five-star campsite, in a lovely tree-shaded spot near the Kercado tumulus, with its own extensive waterpark, its own little farm with llamas and ponies, and children's activities of all kinds. Closed mid-Sept to March. **€47**

Men Dû 22bis chemin de Beaumer ☎ 02 97 52 04 23, ⓦ camping-mendu.com. Two-star site near the sea, just inland from the plage du Men Dû, with a summer-only snack bar. Closed Oct–March. **€24.50**

EATING AND DRINKING

There's a market in Carnac-Ville on Wednesday and Sunday mornings; in the surrounding area, Locmariaquer holds them on Tuesday and Saturday, La Trinité on Tuesday and Friday, and Auray on Monday.

Chez Marie 3 place de l'Église, Carnac-Ville ☎ 02 97 52 07 93. An old favourite in Carnac-Ville, this busy stone-clad crêperie offers good €15 menus with a galette as the main course. Easter–Oct Tues–Sun noon–2pm & 7–9pm.

La Côte 3 impasse Parc-er-Forn, Carnac-Ville ☎ 02 97 52 02 80, ⓦ restaurant-la-cote.com. Inside this venerable stone cottage, a very smart dining room serves inventive, modern gourmet cuisine, which you can sample at lunch for just €26, or from €37 in the evening. Ever more copious offerings stretch up to an €83 all-lobster menu. July & Aug Tues 7.15–9.15pm, Wed–Sun 12.15–2.15pm & 7.15–9.15pm; Sept–June Tues 7.15–9.15pm, Wed–Sat 12.15–2.15pm & 7.15–9.15pm, Sun 12.15–2.15pm.

Locmariaquer

LOCMARIAQUER stands right at the mouth of the Gulf of Morbihan, its cape separated by only a few hundred metres from the tip of the Rhuys peninsula across the water. On the ocean side, it has a long sandy beach, popular not only with swimmers but also with beachcombers and shellfish-scavengers; on the Gulf side, it has a small tidal port. Like Carnac, however, the main reason to go out of your way to visit Locmariaquer is for its fine crop of megaliths.

Site des Mégalithes

D781 • Daily: May & June 10am–6pm; July & Aug 10am–7pm; Sept–April 10am–12.30pm & 2–5.15pm • €5.50, under-18s free • ☎ 02 97 57 37 59, ⓦ locmariaquer.monuments-nationaux.fr

Locmariaquer's principal megalithic site, beside the main approach road 500m northwest of town, was thought until 1991 to hold two monuments – the broken fragments of the largest-known menhir, and a massive dolmen. Then archeologists realized that the car park for visitors had inadvertently been created atop a third, even larger relic. Now known as **Er Grah**, it consists of a series of partially reconstructed stone terraces, the purpose of which remains unknown.

The Grand Menhir Brisé

There's no mistaking the **Grand Menhir Brisé**, a huge column of stone that some believe was the crucial central point of the megalithic observatory of the Morbihan (see p.361). Having originally stood 20m tall, and weighed 347 tonnes, it's thought to have been toppled deliberately around the time the two neighbouring structures were built, and currently lies on the ground in four pieces (a possible fifth is missing). An estimated workforce of between two and four thousand people was required to move it.

The Table des Marchand

Alongside the Grand Menhir, the **Table des Marchand** is a dolmen or table-like structure that when erected stood exposed to the air, but later became covered by a tumulus. It's once more open to the elements; visitors can go inside, along a narrow passage comprised of massive curving menhirs chinked with smaller pebbles, and stand beneath its huge roof. Carvings overhead seem to depict ploughing, which may well have been a recent innovation at the time they were made. During the 1980s, it was discovered that this roof is part of the same stone as that on the tumulus at Gavrinis and on another local dolmen – the carvings match like a jigsaw. That constitutes a fresh puzzle for the archeologists, as it suggests that the builders did not revere the stones in themselves. In addition, the stone at the end of the central chamber was originally erected as a stand-alone menhir, so the "table" must have been built around an earlier monument.

Locmariaquer's other megaliths

As well as the Site des Mégalithes, Locmariaquer holds several other scattered megaliths, which remain open at all times – and open to the weather as well, so watch out for muddy and waterlogged underground passages, and take a torch if you want to explore them thoroughly.

The most interesting are the **Dolmen des Pierres Plates**, at the end of the town beach, with what looks like an octopus divinity deep in its long chamber, and the **Dolmen de Mané-Rethual**, a long covered tunnel leading to a burial chamber capped with a huge rock, reached along a narrow footpath that starts behind the phone boxes next to the Mairie/tourist office. At a third dolmen, the **Mané-Lud**, a horse's skull was found on top of each stone during excavations.

INFORMATION	LOCMARIAQUER

Tourist office 1 rue de la Victoire (July & Aug Mon–Sat 9am–1pm & 2–6pm, Sun 10am–1pm; Sept–June Mon–Fri 9.30am–12.30pm & 2–5.30pm, Sat 9.30am–12.30pm; ☎02 97 57 33 05, ⓦmorbihan-way.fr).

BOATS FROM LOCMARIAQUER

Boat trips set out from Locmariaquer in all directions. Rival companies sell tickets both in the town centre and at the port further down towards the narrow straits; precise departure points depend on the level of the tides. Both Vedettes Angélus (☎02 97 57 30 29, ⓦvedettes-angelus .com) and Navix (☎08 25 13 21 00, ⓦnavix.fr) run gulf tours, as detailed on p.346; the latter also offers day-trips to Belle-Île and Houat.

Between April and September, regular ferries (☎02 97 49 42 53, ⓦpasseurdesiles.com; €8 return) cross to Port-Navalo on the Rhuys peninsula, carrying bikes but not cars.

ACCOMMODATION

L'Escale 2 place Dariorigum ☎ 02 97 57 32 51, ⓦ escale -hotel.com. Small, simple but great-value hotel, right on the waterfront. Its brasserie/restaurant is perched on the sea wall, so you get fabulous views as you feast on oysters, clams and mussels at €10–15 per *plat*. Closed Oct–March. **€55**

Lann Brick Lieu dit Lann Brick ☎ 02 97 57 32 79, ⓦ camping-lannbrick.com. Three-star campsite, set in rich countryside 2.5km northwest of Locmariaquer and 300m from the beach, with a heated pool, grocery and snack bar. Closed late Oct to late March. **€22**

Trois Fontaines Route d'Auray ☎ 02 97 57 42 70, ⓦ hotel-troisfontaines.com. Friendly and attractive modern hotel, looking out towards the bay from across the road into town, not far from the Table des Marchand. Several of the colourful, comfortable rooms have balconies. Closed mid-Nov to mid-Feb. **€90**

Auray

The old town of **AURAY** may not quite have the cachet (or the walls) of its neighbour Vannes, but it's a lot less crowded, and in many ways its medieval streets are just as attractive. Into the bargain, it's also much cheaper than Quiberon and Carnac, while making a good base for visiting the entire area.

Central Auray

The natural centre of Auray these days is the **place de la République**, with its eighteenth-century Hôtel de Ville and adjoining **covered market**. In a nearby square, on rue du Lait, the seventeenth-century **church of St-Gildas** has a fine Renaissance porch, while on Mondays an open-air market fills the surrounding streets with colour – and stops all traffic for a considerable radius.

Abbaye de Chartreuse

Rue Pierre-Allio, Brec'h • Daily except Tues 2–5.10pm; guided visits July to late Aug Sun & Mon 2.30–7pm, Tues–Fri 11.15am–1.15pm & 2.30–7pm • Free • ☎ 02 97 24 09 75, ⓦ auray-tourisme.com

The imposing and evocative **Abbaye de Chartreuse**, 2km northwest of the town centre, houses a David d'Angers mausoleum of black-and-white marble, commemorating the failed Chouan landing at Quiberon in 1795 (see p.327). For Bretons, the event was something more than an attempt at a royalist restoration, with strong undertones of a struggle for independence.

St-Goustan

The ancient riverfront neighbourhood of **St-Goustan**, just a couple of minutes' pleasant stroll down from the centre of Auray, is undoubtedly the town's star attraction. The delightful, albeit restored, fifteenth- and sixteenth-century houses that line its quayside abound in restaurants, brasseries and crêperies, and it's a lively spot on summer evenings.

This bend in the River Loch made a natural setting for a town, and with its easy access to the gulf it was among the busiest ports of medieval Brittany. Today, as you look at it from the Promenade du Loch on the opposite bank, with the diminutive seventeenth-century stone bridge still spanning the river, it's not hard to picture it in its heyday. **Benjamin Franklin** landed here in 1776, on his way to seek the help of Louis XVI in the American War of Independence; Auray is also said to have been the last place Julius Caesar reached in his conquest of Gaul.

Le Bono

The main road down the Auray estuary, the D101, crosses the River Bono on a high bridge 3km south of St-Goustan, still officially within Auray. Visible way below it to the left is a beautiful iron bridge. A side turning before the river leads across that bridge into **LE BONO**, a harbour village that looks almost ludicrously idyllic seen from one of the *vedettes* out in the gulf.

Ste-Anne d'Auray

The satellite community of **STE-ANNE D'AURAY**, 7km northeast of Auray, has been a centre for pilgrimage since 1623, when a local peasant, one Nicolazic, discovered a statue of St Anne (the mother of Mary). He claimed that the saint directed him to the spot where it was buried, and instructed him to build a church. Twenty years later, on his deathbed, the ecclesiastical authorities were still interrogating Nicolazic, but the church had already been built and pilgrims were arriving. Nicolazic was an illiterate peasant who spoke no French; it is a testimony to his obduracy that his claims were eventually accepted against the opposition of sceptical clergy and nobility. To this day, he has not been canonized, but the pilgrimage earned papal approval when Pope John Paul II visited in 1996.

On St Anne's feast day, July 26, the town hosts one of the largest of the Breton *pardons* (ⓦ sainteanne-sanctuaire.com). Well over 25,000 pilgrims gather to hear Mass in the church, mount the *scala sancta* on their knees and buy trinkets and snacks from the street stalls.

Away from the spacious promenades for the pilgrims, though, Ste-Anne is small and drab; not a place for a long stay, although there is no shortage of **hotels**.

Monument aux Morts

Ste-Anne's vast **Monument aux Morts** was erected by public subscription in honour of the 250,000 Breton dead of World War I. One in fourteen of the population died, the highest proportion of any region involved. A crypt topped by a dome with a granite altar, the monument is surrounded by a huge and sombre wall that must be 200m long, covered with inscriptions to the dead. Even that does not have space to list them all by name, often just cataloguing the horrific death tallies of tiny and obscure villages.

Écomusée St-Degan

Rue Park Segal, Brec'h • Mon–Fri 2–5.30pm, in school hols only Nov–Feb • €6 • ⓣ 02 97 57 66 00, ⓦ ecomusee-st-degan.fr

A group of reconstructed farm buildings 6km north of central Auray forms the **Écomusée St-Degan**, which sets out to represent local peasant life a century ago. While it's all a bit determinedly rustic and charming, at least it attempts to avoid the glass cases and wax models of most folk museums.

ARRIVAL AND INFORMATION   AURAY

By train The *gare SNCF* is a 20min walk northeast of the centre; east–west routes run year-round, while the Tire-Bouchon line heads south to Quiberon in summer.
Destinations Quimper (12 daily; 1hr 5min); Vannes (12 daily; 10min); Tire-Bouchon line (2nd half of June & 1st half of Sept 4 trains on Sat & Sun only; July & Aug 6–10 daily) to Plouharnel (20min) and Quiberon (40min).

By bus Buses stop at the *gare SNCF* and in the town centre.
Destinations Quiberon (8 daily; 1hr) via Carnac (30min); Vannes (8 daily; 30min).
Tourist office 20 rue du Lait, alongside place de la République (Mon–Fri 9.30am–12.30pm & 2–5pm; ⓣ 02 97 24 09 75, ⓦ auray-tourisme.com).

ACCOMMODATION AND EATING

CENTRAL AURAY

Celtic 38 rue Georges-Clémenceau ⓣ 02 97 24 05 37, ⓦ celtic-hotel.fr. Nicely refurbished hotel in town, offering small-ish rooms, one of them on the ground floor, and good breakfasts. **€59**

ST-GOUSTAN

★**Marin** 1 place du Rolland ⓣ 02 97 24 14 58, ⓦ hotel-lemarin.com. Very pleasant, welcoming little hotel, a short walk along the quayside from the waterfront of St-Goustan, which offers simple but smart, well-equipped rooms, each named after a Breton island. Closed Jan. **€77**

LE BONO
Alicia 1 rue du Général-de-Gaulle, Le Bono ☎ 02 97 57 88 65, ⓦ hotel-alicia.com. Hotel perched high above the river at the south end of the main bridge, where the very comfortable rooms are equipped with balconies, and several enjoy river views. There's no restaurant, but the downstairs bar spreads across a spacious terrace, and they offer good breakfast buffets for €9.50. Closed mid-Nov to mid-Feb, plus Sun eve & Mon Oct–March. **€91**

STE-ANNE-D'AURAY
Croix Blanche 25 rue de Vannes ☎ 02 97 57 64 44, ⓦ hotel-lacroixblanche.com. Attractively renovated hotel in the heart of town, with a good restaurant serving €12 *plats* and full menus from €18. Closed Jan, plus Sun eve & Mon in low season. **€67**

Moderne 8 rue de Vannes ☎ 02 97 57 66 55, ⓦ hotel lemoderne.com. Good-value hotel in a substantial central townhouse, facing the basilica, with a restaurant that serves a very decent €20.50 dinner menu. Closed Sat in winter. **€70**

Golfe du Morbihan

Beautiful, popular, and yet remarkably unspoiled by tourism, the sheltered **Golfe du Morbihan** – the word means "little sea" in Breton – is one of the loveliest stretches of Brittany's coast. While its only large town, medieval **Vannes**, is well worth visiting, its endlessly indented shoreline is the major attraction, with superb vistas at every turn, and countless secluded **beaches**.

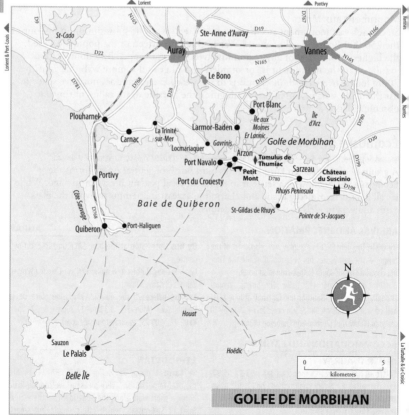

GOLFE DE MORBIHAN

By popular tradition, the gulf holds 365 scattered **islands** – one for every day of the year. For centuries, though, the waters have been rising, and the figure now is more like one for each week. Of these, some thirty are owned by film stars and the like, while two – the **Île aux Moines** and **Île d'Arz** – have regular ferry services and permanent populations, and end up extremely crowded in summer. Others are better, and a **boat tour** around them, or at least a trip out to **Gavrinis**, near the mouth of the gulf, ranks among the most enjoyable activities southern Brittany has to offer.

As the boats thread their way through the baffling muddle of channels, you swiftly lose track of which is island and which is mainland; and everywhere there are **megalithic ruins**, stone circles disappearing beneath the water and solitary menhirs on small hillocks. At the time when they were built, the sea level was around 5m lower than today, and the islands may have been mounds amid the marshlands. Flaubert evocatively described Celtic mercenaries far off in Carthage pining for the Morbihan – *Les Celtes regrettaient trois pierres brutes, sous un ciel pluvieux, dans un golfe rempli d'îlots* – not that the Celts actually set up the stones in the first place.

Larmor-Baden

LARMOR-BADEN, near the eastern tip of the Auray estuary and the departure point for trips to Gavrinis, is a subdued little place, set at the bottom of a long slope of fields of dazzling sunflowers. The port looks out on the tangle of islands in the Gulf of Morbihan, which at this point is so narrow that Arzon on the Rhuys peninsula (see p.350) appears to be on just another nearby island. Neither a resort nor a town, though, it's not an inspiring place to stay.

Gavrinis

The reason to visit the island of **Gavrinis**, which can only be reached on guided boat tours from Larmor-Baden, is its **megalithic site**. The most impressive and remarkable in Brittany, it would be memorable just for its location. But it really is extraordinary as a structure, standing comparison with Newgrange in Ireland and – in shape as well as size and age – with the earliest pyramids of Egypt.

The site is essentially a **tumulus**, an earth mound covering a stone cairn and "passage grave". However, in 1981 half of the mound was peeled back and, using the original stones around the entrance as a basis, the side of the cairn that faces the water was reconstructed to make a facade resembling a step-pyramid. At the time it was built, Gavrinis probably wasn't an island, but a high eminence commanding the mouths of two adjacent rivers. Groups of visitors are now shepherded through the doorway and along a straight passageway that at 14m is said to be the longest known, to reach a slightly enlarged chamber at the far end. The corridor is oriented so that the rising sun at the winter solstice shines directly on the far wall.

Inside, every stone of both passage and chamber is covered in carvings, with a restricted "alphabet" of fingerprint whorls, axe-heads and other conventional signs, including the spirals familiar in Ireland but seen only here in Brittany. The roof is made from the self-same piece of carved stone as covers the Table des Marchand in Locmariaquer (see p.341). No one knows the purpose of the three holes leading to a recessed niche in one of the walls of the chamber. Some medieval monks were buried in the mound, but the cairn itself seems never to have been a grave.

From Gavrinis, you can look across to the half-submerged stone circle on the tiny island of **Er Lanic**, which rests on its skirt of mud like an abandoned hovercraft. It has been identified as a major centre for the manufacture of ceremonial axes, using stone brought from Port-Navalo.

7

GULF TOURS

Izenah Croisières ☎ 02 97 26 31 45, ⓦizenah-croisieres.com. Gulf tours from Port Blanc at Baden in summer (€10–21), and a year-round ferry service to the Île aux Moines (daily every 30min: July & Aug 7am–10pm, Sept–June 7am–7.30pm; €4.70 return).
Navix ☎ 08 25 13 21 00, ⓦnavix.fr. Between May and mid-Sept, cruises from Vannes, Port-Navalo and Locmariaquer include half-day (€21.20) and full-day (€29) trips around the gulf, and also lunch and dinner cruises, where the cost depends on your choice of menu (total €60–70). Between mid-July and late Aug, similar tours at similar prices also depart from Auray, Le Bono and La Trinité.
Vedettes Angélus ☎ 02 97 57 30 29, ⓦvedettes-angelus.com. Up to five gulf tours of varying lengths daily from Locmariaquer and Port-Navalo (mid-April to Sept; €13–23).

ARRIVAL AND DEPARTURE   GAVRINIS

By ferry Gavrinis can be reached April–Sept only. Tides permitting, ferries leave Larmor-Baden at half-hourly intervals, with the last boats of both the morning and the afternoon leaving 90min before the site closes, and the cost includes a 45-minute guided tour of the cairn (April & June–Sept daily 9.30am–12.30pm & 1.30–6.30pm; May Mon–Fri 1.30–6.30pm, Sat & Sun 9.30am–12.30pm & 1.30–6.30pm; €14.40; ☎ 02 97 57 19 38, ⓦ www.gavrinis.info).

Vannes

Thanks to its position at the head of the Golfe du Morbihan, **VANNES** is the major tourist town of southern Brittany. Modern Vannes is such a large and thriving community that the small size of the old walled town at its core, **Vieux Vannes** – largely pedestrianized, in refreshing contrast to the somewhat insane road system beyond – may well come as a surprise.

Brief history

It was from Vannes that the great Breton warrior hero Nominoë (see p.363) set out to unify Brittany at the start of the ninth century; defeating the Franks, he pushed the borders beyond Nantes and Rennes, where they remained until the French Revolution nearly a millennium later. Here too, the Breton *États* assembled in 1532 to ratify the Act of Union with France, in the building known as La Cohue; and here, also, 22 of the royalists captured at Quiberon (see p.327) were executed in the Jardins de la Garrène in 1795. Parisian soldiers fired the shots because local regiments refused.

Vieux Vannes

The focal point of **Vieux Vannes** is the old gateway of the **Porte St-Vincent** on its southern side, which commands a busy little square at the head of the long canalized **port** that provides access to the gulf itself. It's in the delightful tangle of cobbled alleyways within the walls, however – especially those around the cathedral – that most of Vannes' busy commercial life takes place. With their skew-windowed and half-timbered houses – most overhanging and witch-hatted, some tumbling down, some newly propped-up and painted – they amply repay time spent wandering.

Place Henri-IV in particular, with its charming fifteenth- and sixteenth-century gabled houses, is stunning, as are the views from it down the narrow side streets. Here and there, it's possible to climb up onto the **ramparts** to admire the views, though much of the way you have to trace the circuit around the outside instead, from the far side of what used to be the city moat, which now consists of neat and colourful flowerbeds. Near the **Porte Poterne**, the "back gate", an old slate-roofed wash-house survives.

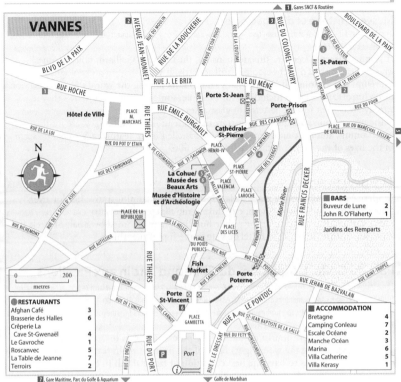

Cathédrale St-Pierre

Place St-Pierre • Daily 8.30am–7pm • ☎ 02 97 47 10 88, ⍟ cathedrale-vannes.cef.fr

The **Cathédrale St-Pierre** is a rather forbidding place, with its stern main altar almost imprisoned by four solemn grey pillars. Light, purple through the new stained glass, spears in to illuminate the finger of the Blessed Pierre-René Rogue, who was guillotined in the main square on March 3, 1796. Opposite this desiccated digit is the black-lidded sarcophagus that marks the tomb of the fifteenth-century Spanish Dominican preacher St Vincent Ferrier. For a small fee, you can in summer examine the assorted **treasure** in the chapter house, which includes a twelfth-century wedding chest, brightly decorated with enigmatic scenes of romantic chivalry.

Musée des Beaux Arts

9 place St-Pierre • Mid-June to early Oct daily 10am–6pm; Oct to mid-June daily except Mon 1.30–6pm • €6.30 with Musée d'Histoire et d'Archéologie; free Sun • ☎ 02 97 01 63 00

Having served at various times over the past 750 years as High Court and assembly room, prison, Revolutionary tribunal, theatre and marketplace, the block-sized building known as **La Cohue**, which takes its name from a word meaning "bustling crowd", currently houses Vannes' **Musée des Beaux Arts**.

Upstairs there's a dull collection of paintings and engravings, heavy on worthy Breton artists such as J.-F. Boucher and Jean Frélaut, while the main gallery downstairs stages temporary exhibitions.

Musée d'Histoire et d'Archéologie

2 rue Noé • Mid-June to mid-Sept daily 10am–6pm; otherwise open to groups only, by appointment • €6.30 with Musée des Beaux Arts; free Sun • ☎ 02 97 01 64 00

A sombre fifteenth-century private mansion, the Château Gaillard, holds Vannes' **Musée d'Histoire et d'Archéologie**. Until recently, it was solely an archeological museum, but although it boasts what's said to rank among the world's finest collections of prehistoric artefacts – including, for example, some elegant stone axes – they're simply arrayed in formal patterns in glass cases.

The upper floors, designed to illustrate daily life in the Middle Ages, are more entertaining, and have an interesting wood-panelled room featuring 57 separate scenes of the lives of the Desert Fathers, painted in 1606.

The new town

Modern Vannes centres on **place de la République**; the administrative headquarters were shifted outside the medieval city during the nineteenth-century craze for urbanization. The grandest of the public buildings here, guarded by a pair of sleek and dignified bronze lions, is the **Hôtel de Ville** at the top of rue Thiers.

Parc du Golfe: L'Aquarium du Golfe and Jardin aux Papillons

21 rue Daniel Gilard • Daily: April–June & Sept 10am–noon & 2–6pm; July & Aug 9am–7.30pm; Oct–March 2–6pm, except school hols 10am–noon & 2–6pm • Aquarium: adults €13, under-12s €8.90; Jardin aux Papillons: adults €11, under-12s €7.90; combined ticket €19.10/€13.30 • ☎ 02 97 40 67 40, ⓦ aquarium-du-golfe.com • Served by free shuttle buses from the port (every 15min; July & Aug daily 9.30am–7.30pm, Sept–June Wed & Sat 9am–1pm)

Vannes' major modern tourist attraction, the **parc du Golfe**, is located roughly 1km south of town, along the west (right) bank of the port. Its main feature is a modern **aquarium** that claims to have the best collection of tropical fish in Europe. Some of its specimens are certainly pretty extraordinary: four-eyed fish from Venezuela that can see simultaneously above and below the surface of the water, and are also divided into four sexes for good measure; cave fish from Mexico that by contrast have no eyes at all; and *arowana* from Guyana, which jump two metres out of the water to catch birds. A Nile crocodile found in the Paris sewers in 1984 shares its tank with a group of piranhas, while elsewhere there's a huge tank of black- and white-tipped sharks. Most species are identified with their French and Latin names, not necessarily their English ones.

Alongside, the separate **Jardin aux Papillons**, or Butterfly Garden, consists of a huge glass dome containing hundreds of free-flying butterflies.

ARRIVAL AND DEPARTURE   VANNES

By train Vannes' *gare SNCF* is on avenue Favrel et Lincy, 25min walk north of the centre.
Destinations Auray (12 daily; 10min); Lorient (16 daily; 30–50min), with connections to Quimper (12 daily; 1hr 40min); Nantes (4 daily; 1hr 20min); Pontivy (6 daily; 55min).
By bus The *gare routière* faces the *gare SNCF* (☎ 02 97 01 22 01, ⓦ lactm.com).

Destinations Arzon (4 daily; 50min); Auray (8 daily; 30min); Carnac (7 daily; 1hr 20min); La Roche-Bernard (3 daily; 1hr); Malestroit (3 daily; 1hr); Ploërmel (3 daily; 1hr 10min) via Elven (20min); Pontivy (9 daily; 1hr 10min); Quiberon (8 daily; 2hr).
By car Parking can be a problem, but there's plenty of space on Quai Tabarly on the port's west side.

INFORMATION AND TOURS

Tourist office Quai Tabarly, on the west side of the port (July & Aug Mon–Sat 9.30am–7pm, Sun 10am–6pm; Sept–June Mon–Sat 9.30am–noon & 1.30–6pm; ☎ 08 25 13 56 10, ⓦ tourisme-vannes.com).
Festivals At the end of July, the open-air concerts of the Vannes Jazz Festival take place in the Théâtre de

Verdure (ⓦ jazzavannes.fr).
Boat tours Boat trips around the gulf, and out to the islands of Belle-Île, Houat and Hoëdic, operated by Navix (☎ 08 25 13 21 00, ⓦ navix.fr), leave from the *gare Maritime*, a little way south of the centre on the parc du Golfe.

ACCOMMODATION

Bretagne 36 rue du Méné ☎ 02 97 47 20 21, ⓦ hotel -lebretagne-vannes.com. Reasonably priced, friendly little hotel, backing onto the walls, around the corner from the Porte-Prison, with a dozen pleasantly decorated, triple-glazed en-suite rooms. €60

Camping Conleau 188 av du Maréchal-Juin ☎ 02 97 63 13 88, ⓦ vannes-camping.com. Very pleasant three-star municipal campsite, the closest to central Vannes, set right beside the gulf, 2km southwest of the centre, with a heated pool and snack bar. Closed late Sept to early April. €21.50

Escale Océania Avenue Jean-Monnet ☎ 02 97 47 59 60, ⓦ oceaniahotels.com. Modern and very dependable upscale chain hotel a short walk northwest of the walled town, offering 65 large, soundproofed en-suite rooms, sleeping up to four, and offering reduced rates at weekends. €105

Manche Océan 31 rue du Colonel-Maury ☎ 02 97 47 26 46, ⓦ www.manche-ocean.com. Ordinary but perfectly acceptable modern rooms between the station and the walled town, used mainly by tour groups. Small-scale

buffet breakfasts for €9.50; no restaurant. €89

Marina 4 place Gambetta ☎ 02 97 47 22 81, ⓦ hotel lemarina.fr. You can't beat the rates for this great location, right by the port with sea views and morning sun, but you need to know what you're getting – small minimally equipped rooms, which, despite double glazing, still catch the noise from the busy bar below. En-suite facilities cost €11 extra. €52

★ **Villa Catherine** 89 av du Président Édouard-Herriot ☎ 02 97 42 48 59, ⓦ villa-catherine.net. Charming five-room B&B, in an early twentieth-century townhouse, restored using ecologically sustainable materials, and serving an entirely organic breakfast; the owners also run a nice crêperie next door. €99

Villa Kerasy 20 av Favrel et Lincy ☎ 02 97 68 36 83, ⓦ villakerasy.com. Luxurious little boutique hotel in an unlikely setting close to the station, with an Asian ambience throughout and its own Ayurvedic spa. The finest rooms lead onto private, miniature Japanese gardens. There's no restaurant. €139

7

EATING AND DRINKING

Dining out in old Vannes can be expensive, whether you eat in the intimate little restaurants on the rue des Halles, or down by the port. Other, cheaper restaurants abound in the St-Patern quarter, outside the walls in the northeast, which also offers the highest concentration of bars. The city's excellent fish market is held in the covered hall on place de la Poissonnerie every morning between Tuesday and Saturday. A general market spreads slightly higher up on the streets towards the cathedral on Wednesday and Saturday.

Afghan Café 12 rue de la Fontaine ☎ 02 97 42 77 77. This excellent, simply decorated restaurant provides a rare opportunity to try good Afghan cuisine, which centres on rice with fish, meat or vegetarian dishes and cardamom tea. At around €6 for a starter, €14–16 for a main course, reckon on €20 a head. Tues–Thurs & Sun noon–1.30pm & 7–10pm, Fri & Sat noon–1.30pm & 7–10.30pm.

Brasserie des Halles 9 rue des Halles ☎ 02 97 54 08 34, ⓦ brasseriedeshallesvannes.com. Lively, inexpensive brasserie, which as well as its jazzy interior manages to squeeze a few tables out onto the pavement. For €11 you can get a bowl of mussels, for €19.50 a seafood *choucroute*, and there's a wide range of mainly fishy dishes at similar prices, plus menus from €15.50 to €29. Daily noon–2.30pm & 7–11pm.

Buveur de Lune 8 rue St-Patern ☎ 02 97 54 32 32. A relaxed and good-natured spot for a fairly priced drink, with the night sky painted across the ceiling. Wed–Sun 6pm–2am.

Crêperie La Cave St-Gwenaël 23 rue St-Gwenaël ☎ 02 97 47 47 94. Atmospheric, good-value crêperie in the cellar of a lovely old house, alongside the cathedral; a meal of one savoury and one sweet crêpe costs €10.50. July & Aug Mon–Sat noon–2.30pm & 6.30–9.30pm; Sept–Dec & Feb–June Tues–Sat noon–2.30pm & 6.30–9.30pm.

John R O'Flaherty 22 rue Hoche ☎ 02 97 42 40 11, ⓦ oflaherty.bzh.bz. A real Irish pub with the right ales on tap, various bits of junk on the walls and traditional Irish folk live on Friday nights. Mon–Sat 6pm–2am.

Le Gavroche 17 rue de la Fontaine ☎ 02 97 54 03 54, ⓦ legavroche-vannes.com. This cheerful, half-timbered, husband-and-wife restaurant is a godsend for meat-lovers in a region dominated by seafood. The steaks are cooked to perfection and original starters such as pig's trotters – along with the complimentary glass of home-made rum – will put hairs on your chest. Menus from €17.90 to €27.50. Tues–Sun noon–2pm & 7–10.30pm.

★ **Roscanvec** 17 rue des Halles ☎ 02 97 47 15 96, ⓦ roscanvec.com. Superb formal restaurant, in a lovely half-timbered house, with some outdoor seating. Lunch at €25 is a bargain, while dinner menus (€48–70) feature unusual dishes such as *carbonara d'huîtres*. Tues–Sat 12.15–2pm & 7.15–9.30pm, Sun 12.15–2pm; closed Tues in low season.

La Table de Jeanne 13 place de la Poissonnerie ☎ 02 97 47 34 91, ⓦ latabledejeanne.com. Smart restaurant, entirely indoors, which faces the fish market and takes its inspiration from the changing daily catch. There's a good-value €16 lunch menu, while dinner is totally à la carte, with most main courses around €20. Tues, Wed & Sun noon–2pm, Thurs–Sun noon–2pm & 7–9.30pm.

Terroirs 22 rue de la Fontaine ☎02 97 47 57 52, ⓦ terroirs-restaurant.com. This friendly little place prides itself on serving changing great-value Breton menus, using local meat and shellfish like mussels and cockles; weekday lunches start at €13.50 for two courses, while dinner costs €24, or €31.50 with wine pairings. They take their wine seriously; the cellar doubles as a wine shop, where you can sample wines and snacks all afternoon. Tues–Fri noon–2pm & 7–9.30pm, Sat noon–2pm; also open Sun noon–2pm in July & Aug.

The southern shore: the Rhuys peninsula

Though the tip of the **Presqu'île de Rhuys** is just a few hundred metres across the mouth of the Gulf of Morbihan from Locmariaquer, it somehow seems to mark a distinctly southwards shift in climate. The Côte Sauvage is lost and in its wake appear pomegranates, fig trees, camellias, even vineyards (Rhuys produces the only truly Breton wine), along with cultivated oysters down below in the mud.

Unfortunately, owing to fierce currents in the gulf, swimming from the north side of the peninsula is very unsafe. The **ocean beaches**, however, make much more promising destinations if you're hoping to sunbathe or play in the water. Fabulously long and sandy, they break out intermittently to either side of **St-Gildas-de-Rhuys**, amid the glittering gold- and silver-coloured rocks.

Château de Suscinio

Route du Duc Jean V, Sarzeau • Daily: April–Sept 10am–7pm; Feb, March & Oct 2–6pm; Nov–Jan 2–5pm • €7.50 • ☎02 97 41 91 91, ⓦ suscinio.info

The D780 runs through the heart of the Rhuys peninsula, with no sea views to speak of. As it starts an extravagant curve south of **SARZEAU**, a short detour south along the D198 leads to the impressive fourteenth-century **Château de Suscinio**, set in marshland at the edge of a tiny village.

Despite its redoubtable size, this completely moated castle never had any defensive purpose or military significance. Originally a hunting lodge of the dukes of Brittany, it has been very heavily restored, and now showcases the extensive remains of a remarkable medieval patterned **tiled floor**, which dates from 1330 and may well be the oldest in all France. You can also stroll around its high ramparts, and visit for musical or theatrical performances on summer evenings.

St-Gildas-de-Rhuys

These days, **ST-GILDAS-DE-RHUYS**, 6km southwest of Sarzeau, combines a pretty little port and a fine stretch of beach, the plage des Govelins. It's best known, however, because **Pierre Abelard**, the theologian/lover of Héloïse, was abbot here for a period from 1126, having been exiled from Paris. "I live in a wild country where every day brings new perils", he wrote to Héloïse, eventually fleeing after his brother monks – hedonists unimpressed by his stern scholasticism – attempted to poison him.

Tumulus de Thumiac

Just north of the main road as the peninsula narrows towards its western tip, the **Tumulus de Thumiac** is also known as the Butte de César, or "Caesar's Mount". Climb its summit to gaze out over the gulf, and you're standing where Julius Caesar supposedly watched the sea battle in which the Romans defeated the Veneti (see p.362) – the only naval victory they ever won away from the Mediterranean and out on the ocean.

Excavations in the nineteenth century revealed a 5000-year-old burial, complete with 32 stone axes and a pearl necklace.

Arzon and Port-Navalo

The pleasant little village of **ARZON** stands at the far western end of the peninsula. Immediately before the centre, however, the **Port du Crouesty** is a desperately unattractive modern marina. On first glance, **PORT-NAVALO** at the very tip has little more character, but there's a cute beach tucked into the headland.

Cairn du Petit Mont

Port du Crouesty • April–June & Sept daily except Wed 2.30–6.30pm, tours 2.45pm & 4.30pm; July & Aug daily 11am–6.30pm, frequent tours • €6.60 • ☏ 06 03 95 90 78, ⦾ petitmont.info

Set in glorious isolation at the tip of a slender promontory that forms the southern side of the Port du Crouesty, the **Cairn du Petit Mont** is an ancient tumulus that has been left entirely undeveloped. There's free access to the footpaths that circle the headland both halfway up – at which level they're lined by high hedges that almost entirely obscure any potential views – and along the coast at its base, which is a longer walk but serves up tremendous views out to sea, across the gulf, and also along the magnificent beaches on the southern shore of the peninsula.

The Petit Mont is topped by an exposed **prehistoric cairn**, much like those at Gavrinis and Barnenez, except that a German bunker was deliberately and destructively built into it in 1943, in order to be inconspicuous from the air. Visitors enter the cairn's deepest chamber, where 6000-year-old carvings can just about be discerned, by way of the bunker, which now holds displays on the site's history.

INFORMATION   **RHUYS PENINSULA**

7

Tourist office Rond-point du Crouesty, Arzon (July & Aug Mon–Sat 9am–12.30pm & 2–7pm, Sun 10am–1pm; Sept–June Mon–Sat 9.30am–12.30pm & 2–6pm, Sun 10am–12.30pm; ☏ 02 97 53 69 69, ⦾ rhuys.com).

ACCOMMODATION AND EATING

SARZEAU

Camping la Ferme de Lann Hoëdic Rue Jean de la Fontaine ☏ 02 97 48 01 73, ⦾ camping-lannhoedic.fr. Very nice campsite, in a rural setting 1km from the busy Roaliguen beach, offering bike rental and basic groceries. Closed Nov–March. **€18.90**

Lesage 3 place Duchesse Anne ☏ 02 97 41 77 29, ⦾ hotelrestaurantlesage.com. Sarzeau's nicest hotel, on the attractive square that faces the church, with smart rooms and a couple of larger suites. Its decent restaurant (daily in summer, closed Sun eve & all Mon in low season) serves lunch from €16, dinner from €30. **€95**

ST-GILDAS-DE-RHUYS

Camping Municipal du Kerver Chemin du Kerver ☏ 02 97 45 21 21, ⦾ campingdukerver.com. Small, slightly exposed campsite in a great beachfront location, which also holds some large, fixed "bungalow" tents, sleeping four people. Closed Oct–April. Pitches **€15.30**, tents per week **€449**

PORT-NAVALO

Glann Ar Mor 27 rue des Fontaines ☏ 06 99 06 91 01, ⦾ glannarmor.fr. Good-value hotel, 150m from the nearest beach, with simple en-suite rooms and no restaurant. Closed mid-Dec to mid-Jan. **€85**

East of Vannes

Though Gavrinis and the Morbihan islands are the most exciting excursions from Vannes, various sights inland, **east of the city**, can fill a day's round-trip. Vannes' **traffic system** will do its damnedest to prevent you leaving the city in any direction, however, so you can't be too choosy about where you end up. Public transport is, as ever, not a viable alternative.

Forteresse de Largoët

Elven • Mid-March to May & school hols in Nov Sat & Sun 2–6.30pm; June & Sept daily except Tues 10.30am–12.10pm & 2.20–6.30pm; July & Aug daily 10.30am–12.10pm & 2.20–6.30pm • Adults €5.50, under-10s free • ☏ 02 97 53 35 96, ⦾ forteresselargoet.free.fr

The ruins of the **Forteresse de Largoët**, also known as the Elven Towers, perch on an eminence in a small forest around 12km northeast of Vannes. Still guarded by its old gatehouse, carved all over with granite bunnies, the castle consists mainly of two stark towers, inside which the wooden flooring has long since rotted away to leave the shafts open to the sky.

The *donjon* proper is topped by a finger-like watchtower, one of the highest in the country at over 45m, where from 1474 until 1476 the Breton Duke François imprisoned the future English king, Henry VII.

Le Gorvello and Questembert

A dozen kilometres due east of Vannes, the D7 passes straight through the beautiful village of **LE GORVELLO**. Bedecked with potted geraniums and huge azaleas, it has at its centre a perfect roadside cross. Another 15km on, larger **QUESTEMBERT** centres on a low-roofed wooden market hall dating from 1675.

La Roche-Bernard

The southern shoreline of the Rhuys peninsula segues imperceptibly into the northern bank of the estuary of the Vilaine, which flows into the sea roughly 30km southeast of Vannes. When Viking longboats used the river to access the heart of Brittany, approaches to the Vilaine were guarded by the fortified settlement of **LA ROCHE-BERNARD** on the south bank, where the harbour continued to serve as what the French call the *avant-port* for Redon and Rennes into the twentieth century. Thanks to a massive dam near **ARZAL**, 5km downstream, sea-going vessels can no longer enter the Vilaine, but La Roche-Bernard remains a pretty little village that's well worth the detour down from the mighty suspension bridge that carries the N165 autoroute towards Nantes.

Most of the village stands atop the rocky headland that gave it its name, and fine medieval buildings cluster around the lovely little central place du Bouffay. Down at water level, a delightful promenade leads beside the river, where assorted quirky sculptures and memorials include a one-third-scale model of the mizzen mast of *La Couronne*, an enormous French naval galleon constructed here at the start of the eighteenth century.

INFORMATION AND TOURS

LA ROCHE-BERNARD

Tourist office 14 rue du Dr-Cornudet (Mon–Sat 9.30am–12.30pm & 2–6pm; ☎02 99 90 67 98, ⓦtourisme-arc-sud-bretagne.com).

River trips In season, boats set off to explore the broad estuary waters as far downstream as the dam, offering close-up views of the densely wooded slopes along the north bank (July to mid-Sept 1–3 times each afternoon, April–June & 2nd half of Sept by reservation only; €12.50; ☎02 97 45 02 81, ⓦvedettesjaunes.com).

ACCOMMODATION AND EATING

QUESTEMBERT

Le Bretagne 13 rue St-Michel ☎02 97 26 11 12, ⓦresidence-le-bretagne.com. Ivy-coated hotel that's a renowned rendezvous for gourmets, with lavish rooms and a sumptuous, Michelin-starred restaurant (closed Mon, plus all of Jan), doing wonderful things with foie gras, sole and truffles on menus at €52–145. **€120**

LA ROCHE-BERNARD

Auberge des Deux Magots 1–2 place du Bouffay ☎02 99 90 60 75, ⓦauberge-les2magots.com. Flower-bedecked hotel up in town, with presentable if old-fashioned rooms, and a restaurant (closed Sun eve & Mon)

that serves bistro lunches from €13, and dinner menus from €20 to €60. Hotel closed Sun eve Sept–June. **€55**

Les Copains d'à Bord Vieux Port ☎02 99 90 81 03, ⓦrestaurant-bateau.fr. Restaurant aboard a permanently moored boat down in the port – in summer, there are tables on deck – where you can get a three-course lunch for €16, or pick from delicious seafood-rich menus at €26 and €34. Mon, Tues, Thurs Fri & Sun noon–2pm, Sat noon–2pm & 7–9pm.

★ **Le Pâtis** Vieux Port ☎02 99 90 60 13, ⓦcamping-larochebernard.com. Charming municipal campsite that stretches along the riverbank, and rents out canoes, kayaks and motorboats. Closed mid-Oct to mid-March. **€16**

La Grande-Brière

South of the **River Vilaine**, you leave the Morbihan, and technically you leave Brittany as well, entering the *département* of Loire Atlantique. The roads veer firmly east and south, to Nantes and La Baule respectively. Inland between them, as you approach the wide Loire estuary, lie the otherworldly marshes of the **Grande-Brière**.

These eighty square kilometres of peat bog have for centuries been deemed to be the common property of all who live in them. The scattered population, the Briérons, make their living by fishing for eels, gathering reeds and – on the nine days permitted each year – cutting the peat. The few villages are known as *îles*, being hard granite outcrops in the boggy wastes. Most consist of a circular road around the inside of a ring of thatched cottages, slightly raised above the waters on to which they back. For easy access to the watery flatlands, filled with lilies and irises and browsed by Shetland ponies, each village is encircled by its own canal, or *curée*. The houses themselves typically consist of two rooms and a stable, with a door on the north side and windows on the south. A few crops are grown in the adjacent fields, which always remain above high water. The most authentic such village, known as both **ST-JOACHIM** and **ÎLE DE FEDRUN**, is filled with traditional dwellings.

Though this can be a captivating region for unhurried exploration, if you're simply passing through, the waterways are not very visible from the road unless you pause on one of the occasional humpback bridges. Instead, the widely touted attractions are taking a tour in either a horse-drawn **calèche** or a **punt**, known as a *chaland* or a *blain*, or simply renting a punt and poling your own way through the bullrushes. Much of the Grande-Brière is a **bird sanctuary**, so expect to see vast numbers of waterfowl.

7

INFORMATION AND ACTIVITIES

LA GRANDE-BRIÈRE

Tourist office Maison du Parc, village du Kerhinet, St-Lyphard (mid-April to Sept daily 10am–1pm & 2–6pm; Oct to mid-April Mon–Sat 10am–1pm & 2–6pm, Sun 2–6pm; ☎ 02 40 66 85 01, ⓦ parc-naturel-briere.com); bike rental available.

Tours and rentals Brière-Evasion, port de la Pierre Fondue, St-Lyphard (☎ 02 40 91 41 96, ⓦ briere-evasion

.com), offer guided tours by *calèche* and punt (€8 each, €14 for both) and punt rental (daily 10.15am–5.30pm; €20), while La Chaussée Neuve, based at St-André-des-Eaux, 6km northeast of La Baule (☎ 02 40 91 59 36, ⓦ brieremahe.free.fr), offers punting tours (€8–16) and rentals (€18–30), plus guided walking and punting tours at 6pm on Thursdays in July & Aug (€10).

ACCOMMODATION AND EATING

Auberge de Kerhinet 10 village de Kerhinet, St-Lyphard ☎ 02 40 61 91 46, ⓦ aubergedekerhinet .com. Simple but well-equipped rooms in a thatched cottage, alongside a charming restaurant (closed Mon & Tues in low season), where you can sample traditional local dishes on menus that start at €20; the €30 option includes a *mélange* of frogs' legs and poached eels. **€70**

Les Chaumières du Lac Rue de Vignonnet, St-Lyphard ☎ 02 40 91 32 32, ⓦ leschaumieresdulac.com. Stylish lakeside hotel where the guest rooms are in traditional thatched cottages, the garden is lush and extensive, and the on-site restaurant, *Les Typhas* (closed Wed lunch, plus

Wed eve & Sun eve in low season), serves weekday lunches from €16 and dinner from €23. **€81**

Le Clos des Bruyères Hameau de Longle, Herbignac ☎ 02 40 88 85 57. Pretty little campsite that's basically a field on a farm and run by an exceptionally friendly couple, with a lake close by. Closed Dec–Feb. **€16**

La Mare aux Oiseaux 223 rue du Chef de l'Île de Fedrun, St-Joachim ☎ 02 40 88 53 01, ⓦ www .mareauxoiseaux.fr. Rather exquisite little hotel, set in beautiful gardens always busy with birds and waterfowl, with impeccable modern rooms, an indoor pool and a gourmet restaurant (closed Mon lunch) serving menus at €45–98. Closed 3 weeks in Jan. **€160**

The coast at the mouth of the Loire

There's something surreal about emerging from the Brière to the coast at **La Baule**. For this is Brittany's most upmarket pocket – an imposing, moneyed landscape where the dunes are bonded together no longer with scrub and pines but with massive apartment blocks and luxury hotels.

Nearby, **Guérande** is a superb medieval walled town, while **Piriac-sur-mer**, and to a lesser extent **Le Croisic**, are less frenetic alternatives. **St-Nazaire**, however, guarding the mouth of the Loire itself, is a run-down industrial port.

Guérande

No visitor should miss the gorgeous walled town of **GUÉRANDE**, inland on the southwestern edge of the marshes of the Grande-Brière. Guérande derived its fortune from controlling the saltpans that form a chequerboard across the surrounding inlets. This "white country" is composed of bizarre-looking *oeillets*, each seventy to eighty square metres, in which sea-water has been collected and evaporated since Roman times, leaving piles of white salt.

Guérande, a tiny little place, is still entirely enclosed by its stout fifteenth-century **ramparts**. A spacious promenade leads right the way around the outside, passing four fortified gateways; for half its length, the broad old moat remains filled with water.

Within the walls, pedestrians throng the narrow cobbled streets during high season; the main souvenir on sale is locally produced salt, but abundant shops sell trinkets from all over the world, and there are lots of restaurants and crêperies. So long as the crowds aren't too oppressive, it makes a great day out, with the old houses bright with window boxes. On Wednesdays and Saturdays, a market is in full swing in the centre, next to the **church of St-Aubin**.

You can only gain access to the top of the walls, and even then only to a short stretch that has no views into the town, via the disappointing **museum** of local history inside Guérande's original main entrance, the **Porte St-Michel** on its east side (April–Sept Mon 2.30–7pm, Tues–Sun 10am–12.30pm & 2.30–7pm; Oct Mon 2–6pm, Tues–Sun 10am–noon & 2–6pm; €4).

ARRIVAL AND INFORMATION   GUÉRANDE

By bus Buses connect the Porte St-Michel with St-Nazaire (10–12 daily; 1hr) via La Baule (20min) and Pornichet (45min).

By car There's metered parking by the tourist office, while the free Guesny car park is a short walk away.

Tourist office 1 place du Marché au Bois, just outside the Porte St-Michel (April & May Mon–Sat 9.30am–12.30pm & 1.30–6pm, Sun 10am–1pm & 3–5pm; June & Sept Mon–Sat 9.30am–6pm, Sun 10am–1pm & 3–5pm; July & Aug Mon–Sat 9.30am–7pm, Sun 10am–1pm & 3–5pm; Oct–March Mon–Sat 9.30am–12.30pm & 1.30–6pm; ☎ 08 20 15 00 44, ⊛ot-guerande.fr).

ACCOMMODATION AND EATING

Remparts 14–15 bd du Nord ☎ 02 40 24 90 69, ⊛hotel desremparts.com. Eccentric little hotel, facing the walls near the tourist office, where the friendly owners have a quirky taste in antiques. There are eight pleasant rooms and a bistro-style restaurant (closed Sun eve & Mon Sept–July) that serves great-value €10 lunch *plats*. **€59**

★**Roc-Maria** 1 rue du Vieux Marché aux Grains ☎02 40 24 90 51, ⊛hotel-creperie-rocmaria.com. Lovely little village hotel, near St-Aubin church, but tucked out of sight behind the market, offering cosy rooms above a crêperie in a fifteenth-century townhouse. Closed Mon in low season. **€67**

Vieux Logis 1 place de la Psalette ☎02 40 62 09 73, ⊛le-vieux-logis.eklablog.com. Central restaurant, set within the walled garden of a grand old house facing the main church doors. There's something to suit every palate, with traditional menus from €17 at lunch, €28 at dinner, plus a separate crêperie/pizzeria. Tues–Sat noon–3pm & 7–11pm, Sun noon–3pm.

Piriac-sur-Mer

Still readily recognizable as an old fishing village, but lively all through summer with holidaying families, **PIRIAC-SUR-MER**, 13km west of Guérande, is a ravishing old-fashioned resort that knocks the socks off its giant neighbour La Baule.

Although the adjacent headland offers fine sandy **beaches** within a couple of minutes' walk from the centre, the village itself turns its back on the Atlantic, preferring to face the protective jetty that curls back into the little bay to shield its small fishing fleet and summer array of yachts.

Piriac's twisting narrow lanes are crammed with **cafés**, **crêperies** and **brasseries**, as well as bucket-and-spade shops and ice-cream and candyfloss stalls. With nothing fancy, pretentious or expensive about it, it's just a lovely place to enjoy the simple pleasures of the seaside.

De la Plage 2 place du Lehn ☎02 40 23 50 05, ⓦhotel delaplage-piriac.com. Quintessential little French seaside hotel on a quiet seafront square. The cheapest rooms are quite rudimentary, lacking en-suite facilities, but most are cheery and comfortable, and almost all have (slightly oblique) views of the sea. A friendly little café takes up most of the ground floor, including the terrace. **€59**

De la Poste 26 rue de la Plage ☎02 40 23 50 90, ⓦpiriac-hoteldelaposte.com. Renovated Logis, in a large corner house a few streets in from the sea, with good rooms, and a terrace bistro (closed Mon in low season) that serves lunch from €15.50, dinner at €26, and snacks in the afternoon. **€68**

Parc du Guibel Route de Kerdrien ☎02 40 23 52 67, ⓦpguibel.com. Well-shaded four-star campsite, 4km northeast of the centre and 1.5km in from the sea, with its own waterpark, plus a grocery, bar and restaurant. Closed Oct–March. **€22.40**

★**La Vigie** 1 quai de Verdun ☎02 40 60 39 62, ⓦrestaurant-la-vigie.fr. Highly recommended brasserie/restaurant right beside by the port, with a smart indoor dining room plus outdoor seating, some right at the water's edge. Set menus offer two courses for €20.50 and three for €27, but there are plenty of à la carte treats too, such as marinated octopus or quail fillet salad. Mon noon–2pm, Tues–Sun noon–2pm & 7–9.30pm.

La Baule

7

LA BAULE is certainly a place apart from its rival Breton resorts, almost any of which can seem appealingly rustic and shambolic by comparison. Sited on the long stretch of dunes that link the former island of Le Croisic to the mainland, it owes its existence to a violent storm in 1779 that engulfed the old town of Escoublac in silt from the Loire, and thereby created a wonderful crescent of sandy beach that's sometimes claimed to be the largest in Europe. That has survived, albeit now lined for several kilometres with a Riviera-style spread of palm-tree-fronted hotels and residences.

Neither La Baule's permanence nor its affluence seems in any doubt these days. This is a resort that very firmly imagines itself in the south of France: around the crab-shaped bay, the rich and/or beautiful stride across the sands against a backdrop of cruising lifeguards, horse-dung removers and fantastically priced cocktails. It can be fun if you feel like a break from the more subdued Breton attractions – and the beach is undeniably impressive. It's not a place to imagine you're going to enjoy strolling around in search of hidden charms, however; the backstreets have an oddly rural feel, but hold nothing of any interest.

By train The main *gare SNCF*, La-Baule-Escoublac, is on place Rhin-et-Danube.
Destinations Nantes (12 daily; 55min) via St-Nazaire; Paris (2–12 TGVs daily; 3hr 15min).
By bus The *gare routière*, on avenue des Ondines near the tourist office, is connected with Guérande (20min) and

St-Nazaire (10–12 daily; 40min).
Tourist office Away from the seafront at 8 place de la Victoire (July & Aug daily 9.30am–7.30pm; Sept–June Mon & Wed–Sat 9.30am–12.30pm & 2–6pm, Tues 10.30am–12.30pm & 2–6pm, Sun 10am–1pm; ☎02 40 24 34 44, ⓦlabaule.fr).

ACCOMMODATION AND EATING

Lutetia 13 av Olivier Guichard ☎02 40 60 25 81, ⓦlutetia-labaule.com. Central hotel, set back less than 50m from the sea and not far from the tourist office, with fancy rooms, some in the Art Deco villa and others in a new annexe, and a spa. The summer-only restaurant (closed Nov–May) offers dependable fish cookery on full menus from €28. **€125**

Mascotte 26 av Marie-Louise ☎02 40 60 26 55, ⓦla-mascotte.fr. Well-priced hotel in a quiet street less than 100m back from the beach, given the feel of a country house by its garden terrace and white columns, with slightly faded rooms but a very good restaurant

(closed Mon) serving lunch from €17 and dinner from €30. **€96**

La Plage 32 bd Hennecart ☎02 40 11 11 51, ⓦlaplage -labaule.fr. Irresistible in summertime, this restaurant is surprisingly affordable considering that it's planted right on the beach, offering a wide range of crêpes for well under €10, plus a €14 lunch menu and plenty of daily seafood specials for €12–20, all served in a friendly atmosphere. Daily except Wed noon–9.30pm.

La Roseraie 20 av Sohier ☎02 40 60 46 66, ⓦlaroseraie.com. The fanciest of the many local campsites, this four-star place, 2km directly inland from

the centre of the beach, has its own extensive waterpark, plus a restaurant and grocery. Closed Oct–March. **€35**
Villa Cap d'Ail 145 av Maréchal-de-Lattre de Tassigny ☎02 40 60 29 30, ⓦvillacapdail.com. Neat, very

presentable pastel-toned rooms in a nicely restored century-old villa, set in lush gardens one block back from the beach, and offering buffet continental breakfasts for €10.50. **€93**

Le Croisic

The small port of **LE CROISIC**, sheltering from the ocean around the corner of the headland, but stretching right across the peninsula, is an attractive alternative to La Baule. These days it's basically a pleasure port, but fishing boats do still sail from its harbour, near the very slender mouth of the bay, and there's a modern **fish market** near the long Tréhic jetty, where you can watch the day's catch being auctioned. The hills to either side of the harbour, Mont Lenigo and Mont Esprit, are not natural; they were formed from the ballast left by salt-trading ships.

For equally good beaches, you could alternatively go east from La Baule to **PORNICHET** (though its overpriced, aseptic marina is worth avoiding) or to tiny **ST-MARC**, where in 1953 Jacques Tati filmed *Monsieur Hulot's Holiday*.

ARRIVAL AND DEPARTURE
LE CROISIC

By train La Baule (10 daily; 15min); Nantes (10 daily; 1hr 10min); Paris (4 daily TGVs; 3hr 15min); St-Nazaire

(10 daily; 30min).

ACCOMMODATION AND EATING

Castel Moor Baie du Castouillet ☎02 40 23 24 18, ⓦcastel-moor.com. Old-fashioned seaside hotel, 500m beyond the town centre towards the end of the headland, on the sheltered side, with simple good-value rooms and a decent dining room (daily in summer; lunch Tues–Sun, dinner Fri & Sat only in low season) where the full three-course menu costs €25. **€70**
Les Nids 15 rue Pasteur ☎02 40 23 00 63, ⓦhotel lesnids.com. Appealing modern hotel, set slightly back

from the ocean side of the peninsula, which has its own small indoor swimming pool and a bar but no restaurant. Closed Oct–March. **€76**
Océan 15 route de la Maison Rouge ☎02 40 23 07 69, ⓦwww.camping-ocean.com. The pick of several camp-sites that line the rocky sea coast known as the Grande Côte, just outside Le Croisic, with a children's waterpark, plus a restaurant and shop. Closed late Sept to early April. **€40**

St-Nazaire

Poised on the northern side of the mouth of the Loire, 60km west of Nantes, the historic port of **ST-NAZAIRE** – where the shipyards had been in more or less continuous operation since they built Julius Caesar's fleet – was almost entirely obliterated by Allied bombing during World War II. Of course, it's unfair to criticize it on that basis, but it's really not a place to spend your holidays; its central streets are extraordinarily drab and run-down.

There is, however, a certain fascination in the colossal, obscene bulk of the former Nazi **U-boat base** that lines the waterfront, a vast mass of solid concrete no bombing could destroy. Visitors are free to follow the walkways up to its derelict rooftop for views out over the post-industrial wasteland that surrounds it, while part of the interior now holds the **Escal 'Atlantic** museum of ocean liners.

Incongruously enough, St-Nazaire also holds some fine **beaches**, in the shape of the sandy coves that lie out on the outskirts, 1km west.

Escal'Atlantic

Boulevard de la Légion d'Honneur • Feb to early July & Sept–Oct daily except Mon 10am–1pm & 2–6pm; early July to Aug daily 10am–7pm; Nov & Dec Sun 10am–1pm & 2–6pm • Adults €13, under-15s €6.50 • ☎02 28 54 06 40, ⓦsaint-nazaire-tourisme.com

Housed in St-Nazaire's forbidding former German bunkers, **Escal'Atlantic** is a museum-cum-themed attraction that seeks to evoke the heyday of trans-Atlantic travel aboard the great French ocean liners. Everything is entirely indoors; you enter by stepping aboard a reproduction of the *Normandie*, as she looked on 29 May, 1935, at the start of her maiden voyage from Le Havre to New York, and you wander thereafter through replica cabins, decks and dining rooms from that and other ships. Even the promenade decks are still enclosed, though artificial breezes blow. It's all very upbeat – you won't find a mention of the *Titanic*, for example – and quite fascinating, albeit expensive for an hour or two's diversion for a family group. The surprise ending, though, provides a rousing finale.

ARRIVAL AND INFORMATION   ST-NAZAIRE

By train A dozen daily trains connect St-Nazaire's *gare SNCF* with La Baule (15min) and Nantes (40min).

Tourist office Immediately below the bunkers on boulevard de la Légion d'Honneur (mid-Jan to early Feb daily 2–5.30pm; early Feb to April Tues–Sun 9.30am–12.30pm &

1.30–5.30pm; May to early July & Sept–Oct Mon 1.30–6pm, Tues–Sun 9.30am–12.30pm & 1.30–6pm; early July to Aug daily 9.30am–6.30pm; Nov & Dec Tues–Sat 2–5.30pm, Sun 9.30am–12.30pm & 1.30–5.30pm; ☎ 02 20 22 40 65, ⓦ saint-nazaire-tourisme.com).

ACCOMMODATION AND EATING

Brit Hôtel Korali 4 av du Commandant l'Herminier, place de la Gare ☎ 02 40 01 89 89, ⓦ hotelkorali.fr. Large, soundproofed hotel opposite the station, which offers presentable rooms at discounted rates Fri–Sun. **€75**

Touraine 4 av de la République ☎ 02 40 22 47 56, ⓦ hotel-le-touraine.fr. Basic, inexpensive hotel in the heart of town, with simple but adequate rooms and some larger family suites. **€38**

South of the Loire

From St-Nazaire you can cross the mouth of the Loire via an inspired piece of engineering, the **Pont St-Nazaire**. This is a great elongated S-curve of a suspension bridge, its lines only visible at an acute angle at either end.

From this high viewpoint (up to 131m), you can see that the **Loire** is a definite climatic dividing line (a point regularly confirmed by French television weather bulletins). To the north of the river, the houses have steep grey-slate roofs against the storms; to the south, in the Pays de Retz, the roofs are flat and red-tiled. Nonetheless, vast deposits of Loire silt have affected both banks of the huge estuary – they buried the ancient town of Montoise on the southern side just as they did Escoublac to the north.

As you continue **south** along the coast, Brittany begins to slip away. Dolmens stand above the ocean, and the rocky coast is interspersed with bathing beaches, but the climate, the architecture, the countryside and, most obvious of all, the vineyards make it clear that this is the start of the south.

Pornic

The **Pays de Retz** coast is developed for most of its length – an almost unbroken line of holiday flats, Pepsi, *frites* and crêpes stands. **PORNIC**, the nicest of the resorts, has a functional fishing port and one of "Bluebeard" Gilles de Rais' many castles. It is a small place: you can walk beyond the harbour and along the cliffs to a tiny beach where the rock walls glitter from phosphorescent sea water.

ARRIVAL AND DEPARTURE   PORNIC

By train The *gare SNCF* is near the harbour and is served by trains from Nantes (2 daily; 1hr).

ACCOMMODATION

Beau Soleil 70 quai Leray ☎ 02 40 82 34 58, ⓦ hotel-beausoleil-pornic.com. Charming little nautically-themed

hotel, facing the port and château; the crisp modern rooms aren't fancy, but for the location they're great value. **€77**

LA BELLE ANGÈLE, PAUL GAUGUIN

Contexts

History

Although both Brittany and Normandy have belonged to the French state for almost five hundred years, they have maintained distinct identities throughout recorded history, and their traditions and interests remain separate.

Brittany, for most of the five millennia during which its past can be traced, drew its cultural links and influences not inland, from the rest of France, but from the Atlantic seaboard. Isolated both by the difficulty of its marsh and moorland terrain, and its sheer distance from the heartland of Europe, it was nonetheless at the centre of a sophisticated prehistoric culture intimately connected with those of Britain and Ireland. It is populated today by descendants of the Celtic immigrants who arrived from Britain and Ireland around the time that the Romans were leaving Gaul. The "golden age" of Brittany came in the fifteenth century, when it was ruled as an independent duchy, shortly before being absorbed into France.

Breton nationalists wholly attribute the economic decline of the province in subsequent centuries to the union with France. While other factors were also at play, it's certainly true that the rulers of France often ignored or oppressed their westernmost region, and even the recent revival of Brittany's fortunes owes much to the conscious attempt to revive the old pan-Celtic trading routes.

Normandy has no equivalent prehistoric relics, and only very briefly was it an independent nation. Its founders were the Vikings who raided along the Seine in the ninth century. These Northmen gave the region its name, and brought it military glory in the great Norman age of the eleventh century, when William conquered England and his nobles controlled swaths of land as far afield as Sicily and the Near East. They were also responsible for the cathedrals, castles and monasteries that still stand as enduring monuments to Normandy's lost might.

The Normans blended into the general mass of the population, both in France and in England, and Normandy itself was surrendered to Louis IX by Henry III of England in 1259. After the Hundred Years War, the province was firmly integrated into France, and it all but disappears from history until the Allied invasion of 1944.

The megaliths of Brittany

Megalithic sites can be found all around the Mediterranean, and along the Atlantic shoreline from Spain to Scandinavia. Among the most significant are Newgrange in Ireland, Stonehenge in England and the Ring of Brodgar in the Orkneys. However, there was not one, single megalith-building "civilization", and neither did the practice necessarily originate in the Mediterranean and spread out to the "barbarian" outposts of Europe. In fact, the tumuli, alignments and single standing stones of Brittany are of pre-eminent importance.

Late Stone Age settlements had been established along the Breton coast by around 6000 BC. Soon afterwards, the culture responsible either began to build megaliths, or was displaced by megalith-building newcomers. Dated at 5700 BC, the tumulus of

5700 BC	4500 BC	56 BC
Stone Age megalith builders erect Europe's first known stone construction, the tumulus of Kercado, near modern Carnac	The first stepped pyramid of the Cairn du Barnenez is built in northwest Brittany; it remains in use for the next 2500 years	Julius Caesar watches his Roman fleet defeat the Veneti in a major sea battle off the coast of Morbihan

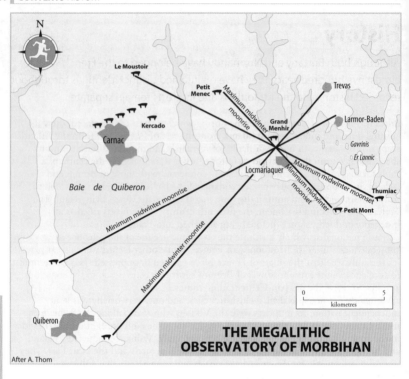

N

**THE MEGALITHIC
OBSERVATORY OF MORBIHAN**

After A. Thom

Kercado at **Carnac**, in southern Brittany, appears to be the earliest stone construction in Europe, predating even the Egyptian pyramids.

Little is known of the **people** who erected the megaliths. The few skeletons to have been found seem to indicate a short, dark, hairy race with a life expectancy of around 35 years. All that's certain is that their civilization was long-lasting; the earliest and the latest constructions at Carnac are over five thousand years apart.

As for the **purpose** of the stones, there are far more theories than definite conclusions. Flaubert commented: "Those who like mythology see them as the Pillars of Hercules; those who like natural history see here a symbol of the Python…lovers of astronomy see a zodiac". In the eighteenth century, for example, enthusiasts managed to see snakes in everything, and declared the megalithic sites to be remnants of some Druidic serpent cult; in fact the stones were ancient long before the Druids appeared.

In any case, archeologists argue that the stones date from the great period of transition when humankind was changing from a predatory role to a productive one, and can only have been put in place by the coordinated efforts of a large and stable **community**. Some suggest that the megaliths were erected by Neolithic settlers, who, generation by generation, migrated across Europe from the east,

654	709	799
St Philibert establishes the Abbaye de Jumièges on the banks of the Seine	High tides floods Mont-St-Michel Bay, permanently drowning the ancient forest; Aubert, bishop of Avranches, establishes an island monastery	Charlemagne unites Brittany under the Franks

bringing advances in agriculture. Whether these technologically advanced newcomers displaced Brittany's previous inhabitants, or simply taught them new skills, remains unknown. The worldwide pattern, however, seems to be that people do not simply learn to plant seeds and grow crops, but they acquire a whole cultural package in the process, taking in prayers, beliefs and rituals, along with new forms of social organization.

It takes a substantial community, with a settled economy and the capacity to create a large agricultural surplus, to erect large monuments. Their construction could also have demonstrated that the group responsible was "favoured" by the gods, and thus of "pure" or "noble" lineage.

An experiment in 1979 demonstrated that it takes 260 people, using rollers, to set up a 32,000-kilogramme stone, together with a large number of auxiliaries to provide food and shelter. It's surely inconceivable that entire alignments like those at Carnac could have been erected in one go. Instead, each stone or small group was presumably shaped, transported and put in place during a quiet period in the farming calendar. Perhaps the process involved an annual festival, to celebrate a successful harvest; or perhaps it was a more sombre, fearful ritual. Either way, the social significance of constructing these lines, mounds and circles may well have been of greater importance than any physical characteristics of the arrangements themselves.

That certain megalithic structures are aligned with astronomical phenomena may simply show their builders knew about astronomy, not that that was the purpose of their monuments. What's more, how we see them today, as cold bare stones, may bear little resemblance to how they originally looked, surrounded by wooden huts or temples, daubed with ochre or lit by fire, or festooned with pelts and hunting trophies.

THE MEGALITHIC OBSERVATORY OF THE MORBIHAN

These days, the most fashionable theories about the megaliths of Brittany – with the general public at least – see the megaliths as part of a vast system of **astronomical measurement**, record-keeping and prediction. As elaborated by Alexander Thom, the argument goes that in Brittany, the now fallen **Grand Menhir of Locmariaquer** was erected, using a standard measure of length known as the "megalithic yard" (and equivalent to 83cm), as a "universal lunar foresight". Its alignments with eight other sites are said to correspond to the eight extreme points of the rising and setting of the moon during its 18.61-year cycle.

The **Golfe de Morbihan** made an ideal location for such a marking stone – set on a lagoon surrounded by low peninsulas, the menhir was visible from all directions. Once the need for the Grand Menhir was decided upon, it would then have taken hundreds of years of careful observation of the moon to fix precise positions for all the relevant sites. Supposedly, this was done by lighting fires on the top of high poles at trial points on the crucial nights every nine years. The alignments of Carnac are thus explained as the graph paper, as it were, on which the lunar movements were plotted.

While certainly appealing, the notion of this **megalithic observatory** is by no means universally accepted. Controversy rages as to whether the Grand Menhir ever stood or, if it did, whether it fell or was broken up before the eight supposedly associated sites came into being. In addition, advocates are accused of ignoring the fact that the sea level in southern Brittany 6600 years ago was 10m lower than it is today.

845	911	1066
Nominoë becomes Brittany's first independent ruler, after defeating the Frankish leader Charles the Bald in the Battle of Redon	The Viking warrior Rollo becomes Duke of Normandy, and lays out the city of Rouen	William the Conqueror successfully invades England

In any case, the stones at Carnac have been so greatly eroded that perhaps it is little more than wishful thinking to imagine that their original size, shape and orientation can be accurately determined. They have been knocked down and pulled out by farmers seeking to cultivate the land; they have been quarried for use in making roads; they have been removed by landowners angry at the trespass of tourists and scientists; nineteenth-century pseudo-scientists have tampered with them, re-erecting some and shifting others; and what may have gone on in much earlier periods is anyone's guess.

Despite the pervasive legends, the megaliths cannot be attributed to the Celts. Even so, theological parallels have been drawn between ancient and modern **Breton beliefs**. It is argued that there is a specifically Breton attitude to death, dating back thousands of years, in which the living are in everyday communication with the dead. The phenomenon of the "parish close" (see p.244) is said to mirror the design of the ancient passage graves, with the Christian ossuary serving the same function as the buried passageways of the old tombs – a link between the place of the dead and the place of the living.

Celts and Romans

While Brittany in particular prospered during the **Bronze Age**, manufacturing bronze axes that were distributed throughout Atlantic Europe, its peoples were left behind by the technological advances of the **Iron Age**, and became increasingly peripheral from 700 BC onwards. The economy turned instead towards supplying raw materials to the more developed cultures of Germany and southern France, and both the Bretons and the Normans first appear in recorded history as traders in **tin and copper**. Small trading ports emerged all along the Atlantic coast, and the routes went up the rivers Loire and Seine. The tin itself was mined in both Brittany and Cornwall, and the Seine became important as the "Tin Road", the most direct means for the metals to reach the heart of Europe. Iron Age forts, such as the one of which traces survive in the forest of Huelgoat, show evidence of large-scale, stable communities even far inland.

That was why the **Romans**' top priority, when they came to Gaul centuries later, was to control the Seine valley and tie the province firmly into the network of empire. Brittany, less accessible to the invading armies, put up more spirited resistance, although sadly there was no such last-ditch rebel stronghold as Astérix's fictional village. The **Breton Gauls**, descendants of a first influx of Celts, were divided into five major tribes, each controlling an area roughly corresponding to a modern *département*.

The most powerful tribe, the **Veneti**, were based in the Morbihan, with what's now Vannes as their capital. The decisive sea battle in which they were defeated in 56 BC took place around the Golfe du Morbihan, and was the only major naval battle the Romans ever won outside the Mediterranean. Ocean-going expeditions beyond the Pillars of Hercules were not among the Romans' strong points – hence their predilection for roads and foot-slogging – but their galleys, built somewhere near St-Nazaire, proved far more manoeuvrable than the leather-sailed ships of the Veneti. The cost of defeat for the tribes was severe; those who were not killed were sold into slavery, and their children mutilated. Julius Caesar was there to see the battle; he went no further than Auray, but the whole Breton peninsula was swiftly conquered.

1120	**1135**	**1172**
The 17-year-old heir to the English throne, William Aetheling, is drowned as he attempts to sail home from Barfleur	Henry I of England dies of a surfeit of lampreys at Lyons-la-Forêt	Henry II of England performs public penance in Avranches for the murder of Thomas à Becket

Roman Armorica, which also incorporated much of Normandy, experienced five hundred years of peace, if little actual prosperity. While the Roman roads were the first efficient means of land communication, they served mainly to channel wealth away towards the centre of their empire. Walled cities such as Rennes, Vannes, Rouen and Caen were founded, but little changed, let alone improved, life for the native population. During the fourth century, a couple of Bretons, Magnence and Maximus, managed to become emperors of Rome, but by then pirate incursions had made fortifications essential along the coast.

Christianization and the Franks

Any civilizing effect that the Romans may have had disappeared during the **barbarian invasions** at the start of the fifth century. The one thread of continuity was provided by the **Christian** Church. The first Christians had already arrived in Normandy during Roman rule, and the bishopric at Rouen was established by St Mellon as early as 300 AD. They were followed in the fifth and sixth centuries by waves of **Celtic migrants** crossing from Britain to Brittany. Traditional history considered these to be "Dark Ages" of terror and chaos throughout Europe, with the immigrants as no more than panic-stricken refugees. However, evidence of ongoing diplomatic and trading contact across the Channel suggests a more ordered process of movement and interchange.

The vigorous Welsh and Irish missionaries named their new lands **Little Britain**, and their Christianity supplanted the old Celtic and Roman gods. That process is remembered in myth in terms of the confrontation of elemental forces – the Devil grappling with the Archangel Michael from Dol to Mont-St-Michel, St Pol driving out the "laidly worm" from the Île de Batz – which surely symbolize the forcible expulsion of paganism. Often the changes were little more than superficial: crosses were erected on top of menhirs, mystical springs and wells became the sites of churches, Christian *pardons* traced circuits of megalithic sites, and ancient tales of magic and witchcraft were retold as stories of Jesus and the saints. Place names commemorated numerous Celtic religious leaders – Malo, Brieuc and Pol – who were never officially recognized by the Church as saints.

The region as a whole was split into two separate petty monarchies, **Dumnonia** in the north and **Cornubia** (the basis of Cornouaille) in the south. Charlemagne amalgamated the two by force under **Frankish control** in 799, after they had consistently failed to pay tribute. When the Frankish Empire began to fall apart, their appointee as governor, **Nominoë**, seized the opportunity to become the first ruler of an independent Brittany, by defeating the Frankish leader Charles the Bald in the Battle of Redon in 845.

ARTHURIAN LEGENDS

Cultural links with Britain and Ireland meant that Brittany played an important role in **Arthurian legends**. Breton minstrels, like their Welsh counterparts, did much to popularize the tales in the Middle Ages. None of the local sites that claim to be Arthur's Camelot carries much conviction, although Tristan who loved Iseult came from Brittany (the lovers may have hidden at Trémazan castle in Finistère), as did King Ban and his son Lancelot. Sir Galahad found the Holy Grail somewhere in Brocéliande Forest, said also to be the home of such diverse residents as Merlin, Morgane le Fay and the Fisher King.

1197	**1415**	**1431**
Richard the Lionheart constructs the Château Gaillard beside the Seine	Henry V of England successfully besieges Harfleur, en route to victory at the Battle of Agincourt	Joan of Arc is tried and executed in Rouen

Without Celtic immigration on anything like the same scale, it took longer for **Normandy** to become fully Christianized. It was only when it, too, came under the control of Charlemagne's **Carolingian** dynasty that the newly founded monasteries of Jumièges and St-Wandrille became pre-eminent.

Over the succeeding centuries, as the authority of the Franks weakened, the **Vikings** repeatedly raided along the Seine, while similar raids on the Breton coast drove many monks into exile across the Channel. Major Viking incursions took place in the second half of the ninth century, interspersed with attempts to conquer England. The Vikings came more often and for longer, until in 911 King Charles the Simple acknowledged the inevitable and granted their leader **Rollo** formal title to the **Duchy of Normandy**. In their adopted French homeland, the pagan Scandinavians acquired the culture, language and religion of their new subjects so rapidly that spoken Norse died out in Rouen by the time of Rollo's grandson, Duke Richard I. Even so, they were still seen as a people apart.

A few years later, in 932, the Breton prince known as Alain Barbetorte returned from England to re-establish control over Brittany, and many of its monasteries were subsequently rebuilt in the new Romanesque style.

The Normans

During the eleventh century, **the Normans** became one of the most significant forces in Europe. Not only did the dukes of Normandy invade and conquer England, but Norman mercenaries and adventurers fought to gain lands for themselves wherever they could. They insinuated themselves into the wars of Italy, individually acquiring control of Aversa, Apulia and Calabria, as well as most of Sicily, their greatest prize. They took part in the Church's wars, too, fighting in Greece against Byzantium, and in the First Crusade – which in 1098 saw the Norman leader Bohemond take Antioch.

The Bayeux Tapestry portrays Duke William's **invasion of England** as a just struggle, the result of William's conviction that he was the rightful heir to Edward the Confessor, as acknowledged under oath by Harold. Be that as it may, the sheer speed of what proved to be a permanent conquest indicates the extent of Norman power at the time. Having crossed the Channel to defeat the usurper Harold in September 1066 in the **Battle of Hastings**, the Conqueror was crowned king in Westminster Abbey on Christmas Day, and by the next Easter was secure enough to return to Normandy. Almost paradoxically, the Norsemen from France finally freed England from the threat of invasion from Scandinavia, which had persisted for centuries. English attention was thus reoriented towards the mainland of Europe – a shift that had a major impact on history.

The Norman capacity for **organization** was primarily responsible not just for these military triumphs, but also for the consolidation of power and wealth that followed. The Domesday Book, which catalogued the riches of England, was paralleled by a similar undertaking in Sicily, the *Catalogus Baronum*. William's son Henry introduced trial by jury in the king's courts, while Henry II established the Exchequer to collect royal revenue.

Intellectually, too, the Normans were dominant; the Abbey of Bec-Helloin was a renowned centre of learning, inspired first by Lanfranc and then by the theologian

1491	1517	1524
Duchess Anne of Brittany marries Charles VIII of France	François I, the new king of France, founds Franciscopolis, which as Le Havre swiftly becomes northern France's main trading port	Giovanni da Verrazzano sails from Dieppe to found what is to become New York

Anselm, each of whom moved on to become archbishop of Canterbury. And **architecturally**, the wealth and technical expertise of the Normans made possible the construction of such lasting monuments as the cathedrals of Bayeux, Coutances and Durham, and the monasteries of Mont-St-Michel, Jumièges and Caen.

The twelfth-century "**Anglo-Normans**" who invaded Ireland were recognizably descended from the army of the Conqueror, and Norman French remained the legal and administrative language of England until 1400. Elsewhere the mark of the conquerors was less distinct. The Norman kings of Sicily ruled a cosmopolitan society dependent largely on the skills of Muslim craftsmen. Their architecture barely resembles what is thought of today as "Norman", and the Norman bloodline soon vanished into the general population of Sicily.

However, for the duchy and the kingdom on either side of the Channel, the shared rulers made close connections inevitable. The Norman lords in England required luxury items to be imported. Flemish weavers were encouraged to settle in London and East Anglia, and gradually the centre of affluence and importance shifted away from Normandy. By the time Henry II, great-grandson of William the Conqueror, inherited the throne, England was a major power and the seeds of the Hundred Years War had been sown. Fifteen years later Château Gaillard on the Seine was taken by **Philippe Auguste**, and Normandy became part of France for the first time.

The Hundred Years War

While Normandy was at the height of its power, **Bretons** lived in constant fear of being invaded by their belligerent neighbours. Their own leaders had only managed to prevent a Viking takeover of Brittany by enabling numerous **warlords** to set up their own private strongholds. Their emergence seriously weakened the authority of Nominoë's successors, and the resultant anarchy devastated the Breton economy. Frequent power bids by the Norman English and the kings of France – now referred to as the **Hundred Years War** – hardly helped the situation.

Bertrand du Guesclin, born in 1321 in Broons, south of Dinan, ranks among the outstanding medieval military geniuses. After an ignominious start, when his father disowned him because of his ugliness, he developed his novel approach to war as an outlaw chief in the heart of Brittany. With little truck for chivalric conventions, he simplified the chaotic feudal map, and in a bewildering succession of French and Spanish campaigns earned the command of the French army. Eschewing prearranged battles in favour of ambush and general guerrilla tactics, he taught the French to fight dirty. Nobles were forced to dismount and fight on foot, while paying his soldiers ensured they did not alienate the peasantry by plundering. This formidable man also developed the use of gunpowder, in tandem with new assault techniques capable of devastating the strongest fortresses.

Thanks to du Guesclin, the English had been driven almost completely out of France by 1377. Virtually every town and castle in Brittany and Normandy seems to have some du Guesclin connection; not only did he live, besiege or fight almost everywhere, but after his death in 1380 parts of his body were buried in no fewer than four different cities. Yet, despite his myriad intrigues and battles, Brittany benefited very little from his activities.

1532	**1532**	**1598**
François I meets Jacques Cartier at Mont-St-Michel, and charges him with exploring the shores of Canada	The permanent union of Brittany and France is sealed in Vannes	Henri IV of France signs of the Edict of Nantes, ending the Wars of Religion by granting toleration to the Protestants

The Hundred Years War resurfaced after du Guesclin's death, with much of the fighting in Normandy. Henry V of England recaptured the province step by step, until by 1420 he was in a position to demand recognition of his claim to the French throne. Eight years later, the French were defending their last significant stronghold, Orléans on the Loire, when the extraordinary figure of **Joan of Arc** (see p.72) appeared on the scene and relieved the siege of the city. Through moral inspiration as much as military leadership, she ensured that the mass of ordinary, miserable peasants, not to mention the demoralized soldiers of the French army, made the enemy occupation untenable. Within two astonishing years, the Dauphin had been crowned, to become King Charles VII of France. Joan herself was captured by the Burgundian allies of the occupiers, tried by a French bishop and an English commander, and burned at the stake as a witch in Rouen. Nonetheless, in 1449, Charles VII was able to make a triumphal entry into the regional capital. Within twelve months this latest 32-year English occupation of Normandy was at an end.

The Duchy of Brittany

As the second phase of the Hundred Years War began, Breton involvement was minimal. Between 1399 and 1442, **Duc Jean V** remained neutral, allowing the economy of the province to prosper. Fishing, shipbuilding and sail manufacture developed, accompanied by a flowering of the arts exemplified by the construction of the Kreisker chapel and the church of Folgoët.

Although involvement in the Anglo-French conflict was inevitable, Jean's heirs for a time continued to rule over a successful and **independent duchy**. Arthur III, duke in the mid-fifteenth century, had fought alongside Joan of Arc, but used his connections with the French army to protect Breton autonomy. His successor, Duc François II, was less astute. Brittany, the last large region of present-day France to resist agglomeration, was a very desirable prize for King Louis XI. In looking for allies beyond France, François antagonized and alarmed the French. A pretext was eventually found for the royal army to invade Brittany, where the Breton army was defeated at St-Aubin-du-Cormier in 1488. Duc François was forced to concede to the French king the right to determine his own daughter's marriage, and died of shame (so the story goes) within a few weeks.

François's heiress, **Duchess Anne**, was the last ruler of an independent Brittany. At first she defied the treaty of 1488, and attempted to forge an alliance against the French, first by becoming engaged to the Prince of Wales, and then by marrying Maximilian of Austria by proxy in 1490. However, Charles VIII of France (himself in theory married to Maximilian's daughter) demanded adherence to the treaty, captured Nantes, advanced north and west and proposed to Anne.

By and large the population preferred a royal wedding to death by starvation or massacre, and it duly took place on September 16, 1491. Anne bemoaned, "Must I thus be so unfortunate and friendless as to have to enter into marriage with a man who has so ill-treated me?" – and then, to the amazement of all, the couple actually fell in love. Despite the marriage, the duchy remained independent, but Anne was contractually obliged to marry Charles's successor should he die before they produced an heir. Charles did indeed bump his head and die in 1498, whereupon his successor,

1690	1720	1752
Faïence – decorated pottery – is first manufactured in Quimper	A huge fire destroys most of Rennes	Belle-Île is captured by the English, who swap it for Menorca in 1761

Louis XII, divorced his wife and married Anne. This time Anne's position was considerably stronger, and in the contract she laid down conditions that remained a source of Breton pride and frustration for many centuries. The three main clauses stipulated that no taxes could be imposed without the consent of the Breton *États*; conscripts were only to fight for the defence of Brittany; and Bretons could only be tried in their own courts. When Anne died, Bretons mourned a genuinely loved leader.

In 1514, the still independent duchy passed to Anne's daughter Claude, whom the future François I of France married with every intention of incorporating Brittany into his kingdom. This he did, and the permanent **union of Brittany and France** was endorsed by the Breton *États* at Vannes in 1532. In theory, the act confirmed Anne's stipulations that all the rights and privileges of Brittany would be observed and safeguarded as inviolable. However, it was rarely honoured, and its violation by subsequent French kings and governments has been the source of conflict ever since.

The ancien régime

As the French Crown consolidated its power and began to centralize its economy, the ports of the two western provinces developed, serving the **colonial interests** of the state. As early as 1364, sailors from **Dieppe** had established Petit Dieppe in what is now Sierra Leone. **Le Havre** was founded in 1517 to be France's premier Atlantic port and, between attacks and takeovers by the English, became a centre for the coffee and cotton markets. Sailors from Granville, Dieppe and Cherbourg set up colonies in Brazil, Canada, Florida and Louisiana.

In Brittany, **St-Malo** and **Lorient** were the top trading ports; the latter benefited whenever the English harassed Channel ports and shipping. **Jacques Cartier** of St-Malo sailed up the St Lawrence River and added Canada to the possessions of France. Nantes, too, was an important base for trade with the Americas, India and the Middle East, with **slaves** an especially profitable "commodity". Though the business of exploitation and battles with foreign ships was motivated by private profit, the net result was very much to the advantage of the state.

Thanks to its early contacts with England, and the cosmopolitan nature of its Channel ports, Normandy became one of France's principal centres of **Protestantism**; Caen in particular had a very active Huguenot population. The region was in the front line when the **Wars of Religion** flared up in 1561–63 and 1574–76. When the Edict of Nantes, with its privileges and immunities for Protestants, was revoked, large-scale Huguenot emigration seriously damaged the local textile industry.

Brittany on the other hand had a minimal Protestant presence, and the Wars of Religion were only significant as a cover for a brief attempt to win back independence. Breton linen manufacture had taken advantage of the lack of French tolls and customs dues, and only declined much later, when England, post-Industrial Revolution, flooded the market with mass-produced textiles.

Although the power of the French kings increased over the centuries, outlying regions were not always entirely under royal control. Rural nobles were persistently lawless, and intermittent **peasant revolts** took place. In 1675, Louis XIV's finance minister put a tax on tobacco, pewter and all legal documents to raise money for the war with Holland. The ensuing "Stamped Paper" revolt, which started with riots in Nantes, Rennes and

1776	1793	1790s
Benjamin Franklin lands at Auray, seeking French help in the American War of Independence	Terror reigns in Nantes, as Carrier, representative of the post-Revolutionary National Convention, massacres 13,000 victims in three months before he is himself guillotined	Marie Herel invents Camembert at her Normandy farm

Guingamp, soon spread to the country, with the peasants making very similar demands to those of the revolutionaries over a hundred years later. The aristocracy brutally crushed the uprising, pillaging several towns and stringing up insurgents and bystanders from every tree.

The reign of **Louis XIV** saw numerous infringements of Breton liberties, including the uprooting of vines throughout the province on the grounds that the people were all drunkards. If the Bretons could not get revenge they could at least be entertained by court scandals. In 1650, Louis's Superintendent of Finance, **Nicolas Fouquet**, bought the entire island of Belle-Île and fortified it as his own private kingdom. The alarmed king sent D'Artagnan and the three musketeers to arrest him before his ambitions went any further.

While taxes on Brittany increased in the early eighteenth century, Normandy found new prosperity by feeding Paris. Lacemaking, too, became a major industry, and several abbeys that had been closed during the Wars of Religion were now revitalized. However, by 1763 France had lost Canada and given up all pretensions to India. The ports declined and trade fell off as England became the workshop of the world.

Revolution

At first, both Brittany and Normandy welcomed the **French Revolution**. Breton representatives at the États Généraux in Paris seized the opportunity to air Brittany's grievances, and the "Club Breton" they formed was the basis of the **Jacobins**. Caen, meanwhile, became the centre of the bourgeois **Girondist** faction. In August, 1789, it was a Breton *député* who proposed the abolition of privileges. However, under the Convention it became clear that the price for the elimination of the *ancien régime* included further reductions in local autonomy and the suppression of the Breton language.

Neither province was sympathetic to the execution of the king – thirty thousand people took to the streets in Rouen to express their opposition. The Girondins came out worst in the factional infighting at the Convention. Some Girondist deputies managed to flee the edict of June 2, 1793 that ordered their arrest, but the army they organized to march on Paris was defeated at Pacy-sur-Eure. The final major Norman contribution to Revolutionary history was provided that same day by **Charlotte Corday** of Caen, when she stabbed Jean-Paul Marat in his bath.

The concerted attack on religion and the clergy was not happily received, particularly in Brittany where the Church was closely bound up with the region's independent identity. An attempt to conscript an army of 300,000 Bretons was deeply resented. The popular image of the Revolution in Brittany was now further damaged by the brief **Reign of Terror** in 1793 of Carrier, the Convention's representative in Nantes. Under the slogan "all the rich, all the merchants are counter-revolutionaries", he killed perhaps thirteen thousand people in three months, by such methods as throwing prisoners into the Loire tied together in pairs. This was done without Tribunal sanction or approval, and Carrier was himself guillotined before the end of the year.

Brittany was an inevitable focal point for the Royalist **counter-revolution** known as the *Chouannerie*. A vast invasion force of exiled and foreign nobility, backed by the

1810	1843	1848
Napoléon authorizes construction of the Nantes–Brest canal	Queen Victoria becomes the first English monarch to make an official visit to France since Henry VIII	The railway from Paris reaches Dieppe, prompting the start of daily cross-Channel service from England

English, was supposed to sweep through France, rallying all dissenters to the royalist flag. In the event, only eight thousand landed at Quiberon in 1795, and they failed even to escape the self-imposed trap of the peninsula, devastating what little they could before being massacred. Much local support was motivated by the desire to win back independence, but Breton *Chouans* ("screech owls") fighting elsewhere found themselves abandoned to years of doomed, quixotic guerrilla warfare.

A rebel army continued to fight sporadically in the Cotentin and the Bocage until 1800, while in Brittany another **royalist revolt** in 1799 was easily crushed. In 1804, Cadoudal, "the last *Chouan*", was captured and executed in Paris, where he had gone to kidnap Napoléon – having refused the emperor's offer of a generalship if he surrendered.

The nineteenth century

Normandy at the start of the nineteenth century remained wealthy, despite the crippling of its ports by the European blockade against Napoléon. Proportionally, five times as many of its people were eligible, as property owners, to vote as in the impoverished mountain areas of the south, while its agriculture accounted for eleven percent of France's produce on six percent of its land. Only industry remained relatively unadvanced.

When protectionist tariffs were removed from grain in 1828, forcing Normandy to compete with other producers, widespread **rural arson and tax riots** ensued. But the deeply conservative Catholic peasantry showed little enthusiasm when the revolution of 1848 offered the prospect of socialism. Even the re-emergence of a rural textile industry in the 1840s, relying on outworkers exploited by the capitalists of Rouen, added no radical impetus.

The advent of the **railways** and the patronage of the imperial court encouraged the development of Normandy's resorts, while watermills along the Seine powered spinning centres at Louviers, Évreux and Elbeuf. Serious decline only came in the 1880s, when **rural depopulation** was brought on by emigration combined with a low birth rate – and a high death rate, in which excessive drinking played a part.

Nineteenth-century Brittany was no longer an official entity, save as five *départements* of France. The railways were of negative benefit, submitting the province to competition from more heavily industrialized regions, while the Nantes–Brest canal did not achieve the expected success, and **emigration** increased from here, too. Culturally, the century witnessed a revival of Breton language, customs and folklore, but the initiative came from intellectuals rather than from the mainly illiterate masses.

Around the turn of the **twentieth century** both provinces experienced a surge of artistic creativity, thanks to painters such as Gauguin in Pont-Aven and Monet in Giverny, and writers like Marcel Proust in Normandy and Pierre Loti in Brittany.

As everywhere in Europe, this idyll was shattered by the **Great War**. Although far from the actual front, both Brittany and Normandy were dramatically affected. Brittany, for its size, suffered the heaviest death toll of anywhere in the world. The vast memorial at Ste-Anne-d'Auray is testimony to the extent of the loss, while a parallel spiritual grief can be seen in the dramatic growth in Normandy of the cult of the not-long dead Thérèse of Lisieux.

1849	1864	1883	1886
Delphine Couturier, later immortalized as Flaubert's *Madame Bovary*, commits suicide in Ry	As part of the US Civil War, the Union ship *Kearsarge* and the Confederate *Alabama* fight a naval battle off Cherbourg	Claude Monet moves to Giverny	Paul Gauguin first paints in Pont-Aven

World War II and the Battle of Normandy

That the **beaches of Normandy** were chosen as the site of the Allied invasion of Europe in June 1944 was by no means inevitable. Far from the major disputed areas and communication routes of Europe, Normandy had seen almost no military activity since the Hundred Years War. During that blazing summer, however, six armies and millions of men fought bloody battles across the placid Norman countryside. By the time Hitler's defensive line was broken and the road to Paris cleared, much of the province was in ruins.

France had surrendered to the Germans in 1940. A year later, the fascist armies turned east to invade the Soviet Union. America and Britain declared full support for the Soviets but resisted Stalin's demand for a second front. In 1942, the two western powers promised a landing in northern France, but all that ensued was an abortive commando raid on Dieppe (see p.48). By the time the second front materialized, the tide of the war had already been turned at Stalingrad.

The Germans had meanwhile fortified Europe's entire northwestern seaboard. Their **Atlantic Wall** was constructed from spring 1942 onwards by the Todt organization, previously responsible for building the German *Autobahn* network. Although it used thirteen million cubic metres of concrete, and 1.2 million tons of steel, it was never an unbroken continuous line, and the senior German officer in France later described it as a "giant bluff".

From the Allied point of view, any invasion site had to lie within range of air support from Britain, which meant anywhere from Rotterdam to St-Malo. Nonetheless, the Nazis expected the attack to come at the Channel's narrowest point, across the Straits of Dover. The **D-Day invasion** of June 6, 1944, was presaged by months of intensive aerial bombardment across Europe, without concentrating too obviously on the chosen landing sites. In the event, the Nazis vastly overestimated Allied resources – two weeks after D-Day, Rommel still thought the Normandy landings might be no more than a preliminary diversion to a larger-scale assault around Calais.

A British photographic survey of the whole Norman coast – even prewar holiday snaps had been requisitioned – conclusively established that none of the Norman channel ports was susceptible to easy capture. Amphibious craft therefore stormed Normandy's **beaches** rather than its ports. On Utah Beach, the Atlantic Wall lasted for little more than five minutes; on Gold, Juno and Sword beaches, it was overrun in about an hour; and even on Omaha, where the sea turned red with blood, it took less than a day for the Allies to storm through.

Albert Speer summed up the failure of the wall by saying: "A fortnight after the first landings by the enemy, this costly effort was brought to nothing by an idea of simple genius…the invasion forces brought their own harbours with them". These "**Mulberry**" **harbours** proved the key to the Allied victory.

The basic plan was for the British and Commonwealth forces under Montgomery to strike for Caen, the pivot around which the Americans – whose **General Eisenhower** was in overall command – were to swing, after themselves landing further west. Not everything went smoothly. Appalling stories describe armoured cars full of men plunging straight to the bottom of the sea as they rolled off landing craft unable to get close enough to the shore. Many early objectives took much longer to capture than originally envisaged – the British took weeks rather than hours to reach Caen, while

1897	1899	1902
A young Carmelite nun, Thérèse Martin, dies in Liseux. She becomes a saint in 1925, and France's joint patron saint, with Joan of Arc, in 1944	Captain Alfred Dreyfus is court-martialled in Rennes for the second time… and is found guilty once again	Lenin holidays with his mother in Loguivy-sur-Mer

American hopes of a rapid seizure of the deep-water port at Cherbourg were thwarted. Most notorious of all, the opportunity to capture the bulk of the German army, which was all but surrounded in the "Falaise pocket", was lost for various and complex reasons still being debated by historians.

Almost five thousand of the 156,000 soldiers who landed on D-Day itself were killed. In all, between June 6 and August 22, 1944, a total of 124,400 US soldiers and 82,300 from the UK and Canada lost their lives.

Military historians say that, man for man, the German army was the more effective fighting force, but with their sheer weight of resources the Allies achieved a fairly rapid victory. Crucially, the concentration of German air power on the eastern front meant that there was never a significant German air presence over Normandy. Parachutists, reconnaissance flights and air support for ground troops were all able to operate virtually unimpeded, as, too, were the bombing raids on Norman towns and on every bridge across the Seine west of Paris. Furthermore, the muddled enemy command, in which generals at the front were obliged to follow broad directives from Berlin, caused an American general to comment, "One's imagination boggled at what the German army might have done to us without Hitler working so effectively for our side."

Within a few days of D-Day, the leader of the Free French, **General de Gaulle**, was able to return to France, making an emotional first speech at Bayeux, while a seasick Winston Churchill sailed up to Deauville in a destroyer and "took a plug at the Hun". At the end of July, General Patton's Third Army broke out across Brittany from Avranches with the aid of thirty thousand **French Resistance** fighters, and on August 25, Allied divisions entered Paris, where the German garrison had already been routed by the Resistance.

Though the war in Europe still had several bloody months to run – Hitler made a desperate last attempt to smash the western front during the Ardennes offensive of December 1944 – the road to Berlin was finally opening up.

Postwar: the Breton resurgence

The war left most of **Normandy** in ruins: while the province remained relatively prosperous in terms of its produce, decades of reconstruction were required. The development of private transport also meant that Normandy became ever more filled with the second homes of the rich. This has often been resented –in 1962, for example, the movie actor Jean Gabin was literally besieged in his new country house east of Sées by hundreds of peasants insisting that he had "too much land", and was obliged to sell some of it off.

Meanwhile, very little was happening in **postwar Brittany** save ever-increasing migration from the countryside to the main towns, and from there, often, out of the province altogether. By the 1950s, some 300,000 Bretons lived in Paris, industry was almost exclusively limited to the Loire estuary, and agriculture was dogged by archaic marketing and distribution.

However, since the late 1960s, Brittany has experienced considerable economic regeneration, thanks in part to the initiatives of the late **Alexis Gourvennec**. He first came to prominence at the age of 24, in 1961, when he led fellow farmers into Morlaix to occupy the government's regional offices in an effective (if violent) protest at exploitation by middlemen. The act set the pace for his lifetime's concern – to obtain

1912	1922	1942
The *Titanic* calls at Cherbourg during her one and only voyage	Pablo Picasso paints *Deux Femmes Courant Sur La Plage* in Dinard	Almost a thousand Canadian soldiers die in Operation Jubilee, a commando raid on Dieppe that establishes the futility of a head-on attack on Normandy's ports

the best possible price for Breton agricultural produce. To this end he lobbied Paris for a deep-water port at Roscoff, and once that was built his farmers' cooperative set up **Brittany Ferries** to carry Breton artichokes and cabbages to English markets.

Brittany Ferries has prospered, thanks in part to the British and Irish entry to the EU upon which Gourvennec had gambled. Yet, despite Gourvennec's enthusiasm for his Celtic cousins, there were several instances of ugly **protectionism** – attacking British lorries importing meat, violently breaking up strikes in Brittany and forcibly preventing Townsend Thoresen from starting a rival ferry service to St-Malo.

In 1973, a semi-decentralized **regional administration** was set up to provide an intermediate level between the *départements* and the State. Normandy, being rich, became two regions – *Basse*, with its capital in Caen, and *Haute*, centred on Rouen – while Brittany was a single entity, but lost the Loire-Atlantique *département*, which included what was traditionally its principal city, **Nantes**. The new boundaries had little impact on people's perception of the provinces, but had practical consequences when the Socialist government increased regional powers in 1981.

Fishing and **agriculture** remain the mainstays of the Breton economy, though the former has never benefited from an equivalent to Gourvennec. Both arenas have been subject to increasingly bitter intra-European disputes. The economic survival of Breton fishermen in particular has been seriously threatened by a flood of cheap imports from the factory-fishing trawlers of the former Soviet Union. When five thousand fishermen rioted in Rennes in 1994, a stray flare set light to the roof of the ancient Breton Parliament.

Thirty percent of fish caught by British vessels are exported to Europe through French ports, and Channel ports have been repeatedly blockaded, with hypermarkets being ransacked and Scottish fish landed at Roscoff destroyed by angry mobs. In response to a threat by trawlermen wishing to fish for scallops and spider crabs, to blockade the Channel Islands, the French government reduced the tax burden on self-employed fishermen, and set minimum prices for cod, haddock, coley and monkfish.

Despite the loss of its traditional industrial centres on the Loire estuary, Brittany has nonetheless expanded its manufacturing base, with the Citroën/Peugeot plant at Rennes among the highest-profile examples. The development of the ultra-fast Paris–Brest TGV rail link also made a considerable difference. Growth in Normandy has been less spectacular, but the region entered the twenty-first century with something of a resurgence, spearheaded by the high-tech facilities of Caen.

Brittany's separatist movement

Politically, Bretons always used to supply an above-average proportion of the national conservative vote, with the most traditional, rural, areas being the most conservative of all. In recent national elections, however, the region has come to favour the left.

Brittany's **separatist movement** has never been all that powerful. In 1932, a bomb in Rennes destroyed the monument to Franco-Breton unity, but the wartime collaboration of **Yann Goulet** and the Breton National Party with the Nazi occupiers – they even had their own stormtroopers, Bagadou Stourm, who hunted down resistance fighters – permanently alienated many potential sympathizers. From 1966 onwards, the Front de Libération de Bretagne intermittently attacked such targets as

1944	1966	1973
On June 6, D-Day, the world's largest-ever seaborne invasion storms onto the beaches of Normandy	The first tidal power station, the Barrage de la Rance, goes into operation between St-Malo and Dinard	Brittany Ferries starts sailing from Roscoff to Plymouth; administrative reforms mean that Nantes and the Loire-Atlantique no longer officially form part of Brittany

the nuclear power station in the Monts d'Arrée, and the Hall of Mirrors at the palace of Versailles in 1978. They were joined in 2000 by the shadowy **Breton Liberation Army** (ARB), which carried out a succession of bombings that culminated with an explosion that killed an employee at a *McDonald's* restaurant outside Dinan.

The emphasis for most Breton activists these days is on cultural pride rather than militancy. The idea is to establish a clear and vital sense of national identity – to create, as one leader put it, "the spiritual basis for a new political thrust". Although overall use of the Breton language may be declining, it is taught in schools, and great stress has been placed on its historical and artistic significance.

The environment and tourism

Perhaps the biggest ongoing story in recent years has been the catastrophic succession of **oil spills** along the coastline. Ever since the foundering of the *Torrey Canyon* off Ouessant in 1967, and the devastation when the *Amoco Cadiz* sank off northern Finistère in 1978, Bretons have come to dread the coming of the *marées noires* or "black tides". Another major disaster came in 1999, when the Maltese super-tanker *Erika* sank off southern Brittany, releasing around 23,000 tonnes of pollutants into the Atlantic.

Controversy has also centred on the AREVA (formerly Cogema) nuclear reprocessing plant at **Cap de la Hague**, near Cherbourg in Normandy. The state-owned facility "reprocesses" spent nuclear fuel from power stations all over the world, and in doing so discharges a hundred million litres of nuclear waste each year into the Atlantic. Analysis of the ocean floor in the vicinity has shown it to be so contaminated that legally the stones on the sea bed should themselves be classified as controlled nuclear waste. **Greenpeace** researchers labelled the La Hague plant as "the single largest source of radioactive contamination in the European Union", and also "the single largest source of aerial radioactivity in the world".

Tourism to both regions remains strong, despite such factors as the recession, the decline in cross-Channel ferry routes since the advent of the Channel Tunnel and the "toxic seaweed" crisis (see p.216). More visitors than ever seem to be touring Normandy's invasion beaches, even though 2014's commemorations of the 70th anniversary of D-Day were inevitably attended by fewer veterans than before.

1978	1995	2014
The *Amoco Cadiz* supertanker is wrecked off the coast of Finistère	The Pont de Normandie spans the mouth of the Seine	World leaders gather for the 70th anniversary of D-Day

Books

Both Brittany and Normandy have been written about extensively, in literature and history. Books that played a helpful or enjoyable role in preparing this guide are listed below; those marked ★ are especially recommended.

PREHISTORY AND MEGALITHS

Aubrey Burl *Megalithic Brittany*. Detailed guide to the prehistoric sites of Brittany, area by area. Very precise on how to find each site, and what you see when you get there, but little historical or theoretical overview.

★**John Michell** *Megalithomania*. General popularizing work about megaliths everywhere, with a lot of entertaining descriptions of how visitors have reacted to them.

Mark Patton *Statements in Stone*. Sober, scientific account of Brittany's megalithic heritage, reappraised in the light of archeological discoveries.

A. Thom and A.S. Thom *Megalithic Remains in Britain and Brittany*. A scientific rather than anecdotal account of the Thoms' extensive analysis. The mathematics and astronomy can be a bit overpowering without necessarily convincing you of anything.

★**Uderzo and Goscinny** *Astérix the Gaul*. Breton history, brewed to the boil in a magic cauldron.

HISTORY AND POLITICS

John Ardagh *France in the New Century: Portrait of a Changing Society*. Detailed journalistic survey of modern France, with an interesting and relevant section on "Brittany's revival".

Alfred Cobban *A History of Modern France*. Very thorough, three-volume political history from Louis XIV to de Gaulle.

Patrick Galliou and Michael Jones *The Bretons*. Accessible and illuminating account of Breton history from the megaliths, through the Romans, as far as the union with France.

★**Frank McLynn** *1066: The Year of The Three Battles*. Myth-busting exploration of what really happened in 1066, which reveals how close the Norman invasion came to failure.

François Neveux *A Brief History of the Normans: The Conquests That Changed the Face of Europe*. Accessible overview of who the Normans were, how they rose to prominence and what became of them.

Graham Robb *The Discovery Of France*. Captivating study of the evolution and "civilization" of France since the Revolution, which makes a superb antidote to conventional narratives of kings and state affairs.

Barbara Tuchman *Distant Mirror*. A history of the fourteenth century as experienced by a French nobleman. Makes sense of the human complexities of the Hundred Years War.

★**Mark Twain** *Joan of Arc*. Little-known fictionalized biography of Joan by America's greatest nineteenth-century writer; quite extraordinarily hagiographic considering his normal scorn for religion.

Ian W. Walker *Harold: The Last Anglo-Saxon King*. This first full-length biography puts flesh on the bones of the man whom William defeated at the Battle of Hastings.

Theodore Zeldin *France 1845–1945*. Five thematic volumes on French history.

THE NORMANDY LANDINGS

Stephen Ambrose *D-Day*. Six hundred-page extravaganza by the doyen of American historians, chronicling the minutiae of the Normandy landings.

★**Anthony Beevor** *D-Day: The Battle For Normandy*. This consistently absorbing reappraisal instantly became the definitive account of the Allied invasion of Normandy.

Paul Fussell *The Boys' Crusade: American GIs in Europe – Chaos and Fear in World War Two*. This short reflection on the lives of the young American soldiers who took part in the D-Day campaign is heavily coloured by Fussell's own wartime experiences, which makes for a fascinating polemic.

Max Hastings *Overlord*. Balanced and objective history of D-Day and its aftermath; Hastings distances himself thoroughly from propaganda and myth-making.

John Keegan *Six Armies in Normandy*. A fascinating military history, which combines the personal and the public to original effect. Each of the participating armies in the Battle of Normandy is followed during the most crucial phase of its involvement; some of the lesser details of the conflict are missed, but the overall sweep is compelling.

★**Studs Terkel** *The Good War*. Excellent collection of interviews with participants of every rank and nation, including civilians, in World War II.

ART AND ARCHITECTURE

Henry Adams *Mont-St-Michel and Chartres*. Extraordinary, idiosyncratic account of the two medieval masterpieces, attempting through prayer, song and sheer imagination to understand the society and the people that created them. A tribute to Norman wisdom.

John Ardagh *Writers' France*. Entertaining anecdotes about most of the writers mentioned in this book, with colour photos.

Christina Björk *Linnea in Monet's Garden*. A Swedish book for children, which tells the story of a young girl achieving her unlikely lifetime's dream of visiting Monet's home in Giverny. A well illustrated introduction to the Impressionists.

★ **Claire Joyes** *Monet at Giverny*. Large-format account of Monet's years at Giverny, combining biography with good reproductions of the famous waterlilies.

BRITTANY IN FICTION

Honoré de Balzac *The Chouans*. A hectic and crazily romantic story of the royalist *Chouan* rebellion shortly after the Revolution, set mainly in Fougères.

Alexandre Dumas *The Three Musketeers*. Brilliant swash-buckling romance with peripheral Breton scenes on Belle-Île and elsewhere.

Victor Hugo *Ninety-Three*. Rather more restrained, but still compelling, *Chouan* novel.

Jack Kerouac *Satori in Paris*...and in Brittany. Inconse-quential anecdotes.

Pierre Loti *An Iceland Fisherman*. Much-acclaimed nineteenth-century realist novel (filmed in 1924), focusing on the whaling fleets that sailed from Paimpol, and now available in translation.

NORMANDY IN FICTION

Julian Barnes *Flaubert's Parrot*. A lightweight novel that rambles around the life of Flaubert, with much of the action taking place in Rouen and along the Seine.

Peter Benson *Odo's Hanging*. Delicate but dramatic fictionalized account of the human stories behind the creation of the Bayeux Tapestry.

Gustave Flaubert *Bouvard and Pécuchet*. Two petits-bourgeois retire to a village between Caen and Falaise and attempt to practise every science of the time. Very funny or dead boring, according to taste.

★ **Gustave Flaubert** *Madame Bovary*. "The first modern novel", by the Rouennais writer. Drawn from a real-life story from Ry (see p.81), it contains little that is specifically Norman, however.

Marcel Proust *In Remembrance of Things Past*. Dense, dreamily disturbing autobiographical trilogy, evocative of almost everything except the places in Normandy and Brittany to which his memories take him back.

★ **Julian Rathbone** *The Last English King*. Lyrical and extremely readable fictionalized version of the Norman Conquest, as told by King Harold's one surviving bodyguard. The Normans themselves are depicted as heartless villains.

Jean-Paul Sartre *Nausea*. Sartre's relentlessly gloomy description of just how unpleasant it was to drag out one's existence in Le Havre (or "Bouville") in the 1930s.

★ **Henry Treece** *Hounds of the King and Man with a Sword*. Classic children's fiction that provides a vivid picture of the Normans and their world.

BRETON MYTH AND FOLK TALES

Pierre-Jakez Hélias *The Horse of Pride*. This deeply reactionary and sentimental account of a Breton childhood in the Bigouden district of the early twentieth century has sold over two million copies in France.

★ **Professor Anatole Le Braz** *Celtic Legends of the Beyond: A Celtic Book of the Dead*. The definitive text on Breton myths centred on Ankou and the prescience of death.

F.M. Luzel *Celtic Folk-Tales from Armorica*. A collection of timeless Breton fairy stories, in English, and complete with commentaries.

W.Y. Evans Wentz *The Fairy Faith in Celtic Countries*. Bizarre survey of similarities and differences in folk beliefs and religion between Celtic nations, with extensive details about Brittany.

Breton music

Drawing richly in its themes, style and instrumentation on the common Celtic heritage of the Atlantic seaboard, Breton music has for centuries played a unifying and inspiring role in the culture of the province. It has survived the union with France and the general attempt by the French state to suppress indigenous art and language.

However, it's hard to pin even an approximate date on the origins of traditional Breton music. No literature in the native tongue survives from before the fifteenth century, although wandering Breton minstrels, known as *conteurs*, had enjoyed great popularity abroad long before that. Many of the songs they wrote were translated into French, being otherwise unintelligible to audiences outside Brittany, but unfortunately both versions have vanished with time. Only a few Norse and English translations, probably dating from the twelfth century, escaped destruction. These tell of romances won and lost, acrimonious relationships between fathers and their sons, and the testing of potential lovers.

The historical record of Breton music begins with the publication of **Barzaz-Breiz**, a collection of traditional songs and poems, in 1839. Compiled by a nobleman, Hersart de la Villemarqué, from his discussions with fishermen, farmers and oyster-and-pancake women, it has come to be acknowledged as a treasure of Breton folk culture. Serious doubts have been raised as to its authenticity – sceptics believe Villemarqué doctored those parts of the material he found distasteful, and even composed portions himself – but it is unquestionably a work of linguistic brilliance and great beauty, and its appearance triggered the serious study of popular Breton culture. Following in La Villemarqué's footsteps, the far more scrupulous folklorist **Francois-Marie Luzel** (1821–95) published four large volumes of ballads and songs, and three volumes of folk tales, between 1868 and 1890.

Since World War II, Brittany's music and folk culture has been a major vehicle for the expression of Breton identity. Breton music and dance clubs have thrived all over Brittany and beyond (notably Paris). Like its Irish and Scottish counterparts, Breton music remains popular with all ages.

To bequeath this rich heritage to future generations, huge effort has been put into collecting and recording Breton music. The best single source of information is **Dastum**, a central library of music, song and folklore (Ⓦdastum.net).

Styles and instrumentation

According to harpist Alan Stivell, "Breton music is a Celtic music… While other Europeans favour a diatonic scale, Celtic musics have a tendency to go back to a pentatonic scale". Produced for example by playing just the black keys on a keyboard, the pentatonic scale has five tones to the octave. Its widespread use is what gives not only traditional Breton music, but also Gregorian chant and traditional Scottish, Irish and Chinese music, their distinctively melancholy, minor-key sound.

Until the 1960s, Breton **songs** were normally sung unaccompanied, often by solo performers. Performances and recordings of either unaccompanied, or minimally accompanied, singing remain common. Traditional songs fall into several distinct categories, including **gwerziou**, sombre or serious ballads; **soniou**, lighter songs about love, for instance, or drinking; and sacred songs, known as **kanticou**. Deeply rooted and beautiful, this last style has been enhanced by the twentieth-century development of combining **church organ** with *bombarde* to produce haunting renditions of religious music. At the same time, Breton **singer-songwriters** are producing original material of high quality. Pre-eminent among them is **Gilles Servat**, who sings in both Breton and French, and mixes his own protest songs and modern chansons with long-established Breton pieces.

Breton bagpipes

Perhaps the most quintessentially Breton instrument, the **bombarde**, is a double-reed descendant of the medieval shawm. While it looks like a shortened version of the oboe, its tone is more vigorous and bracing; depending on your mood, it can sound like either a hypnotic trance-inducing paean to the gods, or a sackful of weasels being yanked through a mincer. Traditionally, the *bombarde* is played either solo or as part of a duet or *couple*, alongside a **biniou** or bagpipe. Brittany boasts two principal kinds of bagpipe: the **biniou braz** or "big bagpipe" is the Scottish bagpipe with three drones, while the **biniou koz** or "old bagpipe" is much smaller, has a single drone, and its piercing sound is an octave higher. In a *couple*, the *bombarde* can be played in unison with the *biniou* or in a call-and-response alternation known as *kan ha diskan*, in which the opening and closing phrases overlap. Other than the drone(s) of the *biniou*, there are no harmonies.

Pipe-bands or **bagadou** are very popular, and pipe-band competitions attract large crowds. The first-ever Breton pipe band was only put together in the 1940s, but there are more than a hundred on the circuit today. Their precise size and make-up varies, but as a rule they consist of around twenty-five musicians: eight *biniou* (*braz*), ten *bombardes*, and seven drums (four snares, two tenors and one bass). Most *bagadou* include both traditional and composed material in their repertoire, and the most accomplished are renowned for their innovation and range. Thus **Bagad Men ha Tan** have collaborated with Senegalese percussionists, while **Bagad Kemper** have expanded to include a brass section, and have recorded with traditional vocalists, jazz musicians and rock groups.

The Breton harp

While the *biniou* and *bombarde* were traditionally played outdoors, the **telenn** or **Breton harp** began life in the Middle Ages as an indoor, courtly instrument. Its use had dwindled almost to extinction before the Breton cultural resurgence. Although Jord Cochevelou achieved local fame as both a maker of, and a composer for, the Breton harp, it was his son **Alan Stivell** who brought it to worldwide fame, with his milestone 1972 recording *Renaissance of the Celtic Harp*. Other Breton harpists worth looking out for include the group **Triskell**, which features the virtuoso brothers Pol and Hervé Quefféléant, **Dominig Bouchaud**, **Kristen Nogues** and **Myrzhin**, who has played with Afro-Celt Sound System among others.

Violin and guitar

Instruments more familiar to outsiders include the **violin**, which is descended from the medieval rebec (*rebed* in Breton), and returned to prominence with the folk revival of the 1960s, with the increasing influence of Irish bands. The best-known Breton practitioners are **Jacky Molard**, **Fanch Landreau**, and **Christian Lemaître**, who plays with the pan-Celtic ensemble Celtic Fiddle Festival.

The **guitar** too has become ubiquitous, whether played solo or as part of larger groups; **Dan Ar Braz**, **Soïg Siberil** and **Jacques Pellen** are equally renowned in both roles. In addition, the **accordion** has enjoyed a certain popularity ever since it was brought to Brittany by soldiers returning from the trenches of World War I; **Yann-Fañch Perroches** is the best-known modern practitioner.

Traditional dance music

Each of the many different rhythms in **Breton dance tunes** tends to be associated with different dance steps, and to originate from a distinct region of Brittany. The most common form of dance music has long been that performed by **sonneurs de couple**, a pair of musicians playing *bombarde* and *biniou*. While following the same melody line, with a drone from the *biniou*, they pursue a steadily accelerating tempo, each taking turns in call and response. The second player chimes in with the last three or so notes of the first player, and then vice versa, each musician overlapping and covering as the other pauses for breath.

The purely vocal counterpart to this, known as **kan ha diskan**, is performed by a pair of "call-and-response" singers. In its basic form, the two unaccompanied singers – the *kaner* and the *diskaner* – alternate phrases, joining each other at the end of each phrase. As there were no amplifiers in the past, singers used a high-pitched nasal tone to ensure that their voices would carry. They might also give dancers the odd break by performing a *gwerz*, or ballad, again unaccompanied.

Such traditional accompaniments have been increasingly supplanted by four- or five-piece **folk groups**, who add fiddle and accordion, and sometimes electric bass and drums, to the *bombarde*, and less often the *biniou*. As the tunes are reinterpreted, the *gwerz* singers are giving way to folk-style singer-songwriters, with guitar backing. Purists might regret such changes, but they have probably ensured the survival of *festou-noz*, with the enthusiastic participation of musicians and dancers of all ages.

Festou-noz

The liveliest setting in which to hear traditional Breton music is a *Fest-Noz* or "Night Feast", a night of serious dancing (and drinking). A *Fest-Noz* (plural *Festou-noz*) was originally an outdoor music-and-dance event, and thus especially suited to summer. Nowadays, however, *Festou-noz* take place year round, usually in large halls but also in barns in rural areas. Once the evening gets underway, people dance in great circles, often in their hundreds, hour after hour, sometimes lively and leaping, sometimes slow and graceful with their little fingers intertwined. Joining in is an exhilarating experience – it's easy to learn, just copy what everyone else does.

Festou-noz have nurtured successive generations of Breton musicians, and served as a springboard for bands such as **Strobinell**, with their line-up of *bombarde, biniou*, violin, flute and guitar, who eventually move on to join the festival and concert circuit. Over the years, an electrified *Fest-noz* sound has also developed, complete with drum kit, as epitomized by bands like **Bleizi Ruz** (Red Wolves) and **Sonerien Du** (Black Musicians).

The most musically innovative band of all, **Gwerz**, started out by making several CDs of traditional songs and instrumentals, using *bombarde, biniou*, clarinet, violin and guitars; members these days concentrate on solo projects.

Festou-noz are well publicized locally with posters and leaflets, and you can find up-to-the minute listings online at ⓦtamm-kreiz.com.

LIVE MUSIC AND FESTIVALS

Visitors to Brittany get the chance to enjoy Breton music at several annual festivals. The most famous of these is the Lorient Festival inter-Celtique. Others include Quimper's Festival de Cornouaille (mid–late July), Rennes's Tombées de la Nuit (early July), and the intimate Printemps de Châteauneuf-du-Faou (Easter Sunday).

In addition, most Breton towns and villages have cafés and pubs that offer live music. Try:

Brest *The Dubliners.*
Douarnenez *Le Pourquois Pas.*
Lorient *Galway Inn* and *Tavarn ar Roue Morvan.*

Plouyé *Tavarn Ty Elise.*
Plouhinec (near Lorient) *Café de la Barre.*
Quimper *Ceili Pub.*
Rennes *Barantic.*

RECOMMENDED DISCOGRAPHY

COMPILATIONS

Breton Music For Dummies (Keltia Musique)
Fest Vraz (Keltia Musique)

BOMBARDE AND BINIOU

Youenn Le Bihan (*bombarde*) and **Patrick Molard** (*biniou koz*) *Er Bolom Koh*
Patrick Molard (*biniou braz*) *Deliou*

BAGADOU (PIPE-BANDS)

Bagad Bleimor *Sonerezh Geltiek*
Bagad Kemper *Hep Diskrog; Azeliz Iza*
Bagad Men Ha Tan & Doudou N'Diaye Rose *Dakar*

TELENN

Dominig Bouchaud *L'Ancre d'Argent*
Alan Stivell *Renaissance of the Celtic Harp; Trema'n Inis; 1 Douar*
Triskell *Rowan Tree*

VIOLIN

Christian Lemaître, Jacky Molard, Fanch Landreau et al. *Archétype*
Jacky Molard, Patrick Molard & Jacques Pellen *Triptyque*

GUITAR

Dan Ar Braz *Xavier Grall chanté par Dan Ar Braz*
Jacques Pelenn *Les Tombées de la Nuit*
Soig Siberil *Gwenojenn*

CHURCH MUSIC

Anne Auffret, Jean Baron & Michel Ghesquiere *Sacred Music from Brittany*
Anne Auffret, Daniel Le Feon & Loik Le Griguer *Pardoniou*
Yann-Fanch Kemener & Anne Auffret *Roue Gralon/Ni ho Salud!*

VOCAL

Annie Ebrel *Tre ho ti ha ma hini*
Yann-Fanch Kemener & Didier Squiban *Enez Eusa*
Erik Marchand & Thierry Robin *Songs of Central Brittany*
Denez Prigent *Live Holl a-gevret!*
Marthe Vassallo & Philippe Ollivier (aka "Bugel Koar") *Ar Solier*

DANCE MUSIC

Various *Kan ha Diskan*
Various *Voix de Bretagne*

FESTOU-NOZ

Bleizi Ruz *En Concert*
Frères Guichen *Dreams of Brittany*
Gwerz *Live*
Pennou Skoulm *Fest-noz*
Sonerien Du *Steir*

SINGER-SONGWRITERS

Louis Capart *Patience; Rives Gauches de Bretagne et d'Ailleurs*
Gilles Servat *Les Albums de la Jeunesse; Je Vous Emporte Dans Ma Coeur*
Triskell/Gilles Servat *L'Albatros Fou*

CONTEMPORARY BRETON SOUNDS

Denez Abernot *Tri Miz Noz*
Bernez Tangi *Eured an Diaoul*
Cheb Mami *Meli Meli*
Kerhun et les Gnawa *Lila-Noz*
Erik Marchand *Kan*
Erik Marchand et le Taraf de Caransebes *Dor; Sag an Tan Ell*
Ozan Trio *Prizioù*
Les Ramoneurs de Menhir *Dañs an Diaoul*
Red Cardell *Le Banquet du Cristal*
Storlok *Stok ha Stok*
Tayfa *Assif*

Contemporary Breton music

Breton music has come a long way since **Alan Stivell** led one of Europe's first folk-rock bands in the late 1960s. Stivell played harp and bagpipes alongside Dan Ar Braz on electric and acoustic guitar, performing a repertoire that drew on wider Celtic traditions. Both artists still perform and record in the folk-rock idiom.

Since then, groups such as Gwerz and latterly **Skolvan** have added subtle jazz and Eastern European touches to their interpretations of Breton music, while Gwerz's singer **Erik Marchand** has been even bolder, performing *gwerziou* with a Romanian gypsy band and playing with Sardinian and Gallego musicians. Marchand is emblematic of a steady modern flow of innovative cross-cultural music from Breton musicians, due in no small part to the fact that more Bretons live in Paris – one of the great hubs of world music – than in any city in Brittany. Notable collaborations include those of **Kerhun** with Moroccan Gnawa musicians, and the

Breton/Algerian confluences to be found in the music of Cheb Mami, Thalweg, Mugar, Idir and Tayfa.

An exhilarating creativity pervades Breton "roots" music. **Manau** and **Denez Prigent** have mixed techno and club sounds with traditional airs and ballads, while Prigent has also presented contemporary messages within the ancient tradition of *gwerziou*. His work with Lisa Gerrard (for the movie soundtrack *Black Hawk Down*) and Nabil Khalidi has produced thrilling blends and textures. Similarly, **Bagad Kemper** have performed and recorded with the South African Zulu rock group Johnny Clegg & Savuka, as well as splicing together jazz horns including saxophone, guitarists and a singer with a full pipe band. Meanwhile **Didier Squiban's** *Breton Piano Trilogy* displays classically polished solo piano jazz variations on traditional Breton themes.

Breton singing too has explored new territory, from the dramatic Brechtian cabaret delivery of **Marthe Vassallo's** *gwerziou*, with their stark and lurid accordion accompaniment, to the bluesy, surreal, satirical, darkly poetic songs of **Bernez Tangi** and **Denez Abernot**.

By Paul Matheson, drawing on an original piece by Raymond Travers.

French

Although Breton (see box, p.390) is still a living language, every encounter you have with local people in both Brittany and Normandy will almost certainly be conducted in French.

Thanks to the number of words and structures it shares with English, French can seem deceptively familiar, but it's not a particularly easy language to pick up. The bare essentials, however, are not difficult to master, and can make all the difference. Even just saying "Bonjour Madame" or "Bonjour Monsieur" when you go into a shop, and then pointing, will usually get you a smile and helpful service. People working in hotels, restaurants and tourist offices almost always speak some English, and tend to use it even if you're trying in French – be grateful, not insulted.

Pronunciation

One easy rule to remember is that **consonants** at the ends of words are usually silent. *Pas plus tard* (not later) is thus pronounced "pa-plu-tarr". But when the following word begins with a vowel, you run the two together: *pas après* (not after) becomes "pazaprey".

Vowels are the hardest sounds to get right. Roughly:

a as in hat	i as in machine
e as in get	o as in hot
é between get and gate	o, au as in over
è like the ai in pair	ou as in food
eu like the u in hurt	u as in a pursed-lip, clipped version of toot

More awkward are the combinations **in/im**, **en/em**, **an/am**, **on/om**, **un/um** at the ends of words, or followed by consonants other than **n** or **m**. Again, roughly:

in/im like the **an** in a**n**xious	on/om like the **on** in D**on**caster said by someone with
an/am, en/em like the **on** in D**on**caster when said with	a heavy cold
a nasal accent	un/um like the **u** in **u**nderstand

Consonants are much as in English, except that: *ch* is always "sh", *c* is "s", *h* is silent, *th* is the same as "t", *ll* is sometimes like the "y" in yes, *w* is "v" and *r* is growled (or rolled).

BASIC WORDS AND PHRASES

French nouns are divided into masculine and feminine. This causes difficulties with adjectives, whose endings have to change to suit the nouns they qualify – you can talk about *un château blanc* (a white castle), for example, but *une tour blanche* (a white tower). If you're not sure, stick to the simpler masculine form – as used in this glossary.

ESSENTIALS		good night	bonne nuit
hello (morning or	bonjour	goodbye	au revoir
afternoon)		thank you	merci
hello (evening)	bonsoir	please	s'il vous plaît

PHRASEBOOKS AND COURSES

Rough Guide French Phrasebook (Rough Guides). Mini-dictionary-style phrasebook with English–French and French–English sections, along with cultural tips for tricky situations and a menu reader.

See ⓦ bbc.co.uk/languages/french for a free, 24-part online audio course.

sorry	pardon/Je m'excuse	21	vingt-et-un
excuse me	pardon	22	vingt-deux
yes	oui	30	trente
no	non	40	quarante
OK/agreed	d'accord	50	cinquante
help!	au secours!	60	soixante
here	ici	70	soixante-dix
there	là	75	soixante-quinze
this one	ceci	80	quatre-vingts
that one	celà	90	quatre-vingt-dix
open	ouvert	95	quatre-vingt-quinze
closed	fermé	100	cent
big	grand	101	cent-et-un
small	petit	200	deux cents
more	plus	300	trois cents
less	moins	500	cinq cents
a little	un peu	1000	mille
a lot	beaucoup	2000	deux mille
cheap	bon marché	5000	cinq mille
expensive	cher	1,000,000	un million
good	bon		
bad	mauvais	**TIME**	
hot	chaud	today	aujourd'hui
cold	froid	yesterday	hier
with	avec	tomorrow	demain
without	sans	in the morning	le matin
entrance	entrée	in the afternoon	l'après-midi
exit	sortie	in the evening	le soir
man	un homme	now	maintenant
woman	une femme (pronounced "fam")	later	plus tard
		at one o'clock	à une heure
		at three o'clock	à trois heures
NUMBERS		at ten-thirty	à dix heures et demie
1	un	at midday	à midi
2	deux		
3	trois	**DAYS AND DATES**	
4	quatre	January	janvier
5	cinq	February	février
6	six	March	mars
7	sept	April	avril
8	huit	May	mai
9	neuf	June	juin
10	dix	July	juillet
11	onze	August	août
12	douze	September	septembre
13	treize	October	octobre
14	quatorze	November	novembre
15	quinze	December	décembre
16	seize	Sunday	dimanche
17	dix-sept	Monday	lundi
18	dix-huit	Tuesday	mardi
19	dix-neuf	Wednesday	mercredi
20	vingt	Thursday	jeudi

Friday	vendredi	July 14	le quatorze juillet
Saturday	samedi	November 23	le vingt-trois novembre
August 1	le premier août	2015	deux mille quinze
September 6	le six septembre		

TALKING TO PEOPLE

When addressing people a simple *bonjour* is not enough; you should always use *Monsieur* for a man, *Madame* for a woman, *Mademoiselle* for a young woman or girl. This isn't as formal as it might seem, and it has its uses when you've forgotten someone's name or want to attract someone's attention.

Do you speak English?	Parlez-vous anglais?	I understand	Je comprends
How do you say it in French?	Comment ça se dit en français?	I don't understand	Je ne comprends pas
What's your name?	Comment vous appelez-vous?	Can you speak more slowly?	S'il vous plaît, parlez moins vite
My name is…	Je m'appelle…	How are you?	Comment allez-vous?/ Ça va?
I'm…	Je suis…	Fine, thanks	Très bien, merci
…English	…anglais[e]	I don't know	Je ne sais pas
…Irish	…irlandais[e]	Let's go	Allons-y
…Scottish	…écossais[e]	See you tomorrow	À demain
…Welsh	…gallois[e]	See you soon	À bientôt
…American	…américain[e]	Leave me alone (aggressive)	Fichez-moi la paix!
…Australian	…australien[ne]	Please help me	Aidez-moi, s'il vous plaît
…Canadian	…canadien[ne]		
…a New Zealander	…néo-zélandais[e]		
…South African	…sud-africain[e]		

FINDING THE WAY

bus	autobus/bus/car	I want to get off at…	Je voudrais descendre à…
bus station	gare routière	the road to…	la route pour…
bus stop	arrêt	near	près/pas loin
car	voiture	far	loin
train/taxi/ferry	train/taxi/bac	left	à gauche
boat	bâteau	right	à droite
plane	avion	straight on	tout droit
shuttle	navette	on the other side of	à l'autre côté de
train station	gare (SNCF)	on the corner of	à l'angle de
platform	quai	next to	à côté de
What time does it leave?	Il part à quelle heure?	behind	derrière
What time does it arrive?	Il arrive à quelle heure?	in front of	devant
		before	avant
a ticket to…	un billet pour…	after	après
single ticket	aller simple	under	sous
return ticket	aller retour	to cross	traverser
validate your ticket	compostez votre billet	bridge	pont
valid for	valable pour	town centre	centre ville
ticket office	vente de billets	all through roads (road sign)	toutes directions
how many kilometres?	combien de kilomètres?		
how many hours?	combien d'heures?	other destinations (road sign)	autres directions
hitchhiking	autostop		
on foot	à pied	upper town	ville haute/haute ville
Where are you going?	Vous allez où?	lower town	ville basse/basse ville
I'm going to…	Je vais à…	old town	vieille ville

QUESTIONS AND REQUESTS

The simplest way to ask a question is to start with *s'il vous plaît* (please), then name the thing you want in an interrogative tone of voice. For example:

Where is there a bakery?	S'il vous plaît, la boulangerie?	bed and breakfast	chambre d'hôte
Which way is it to the Eiffel Tower?	S'il vous plaît, la route pour la tour Eiffel?	Can we camp here?	On peut camper ici?
		campsite	camping/terrain de camping
Can we have a room for two?	S'il vous plaît, une chambre pour deux?	tent	tente
Can I have a kilo of oranges?	S'il vous plaît, un kilo d'oranges?	tent space	emplacement
		hostel	foyer
		youth hostel	auberge de jeunesse

QUESTION WORDS

where?	où?
how?	comment?
how many/how much?	combien?
when?	quand?
why?	pourquoi?
at what time?	à quelle heure?
what is/which is?	quel est?

ACCOMMODATION

a room for one/ two persons	une chambre pour une/ deux personne(s)
a double bed	un grand lit
a room with two single beds/twin	une chambre à deux lits
a room with a shower	une chambre avec douche
a room with a bath	une chambre avec salle de bain
for one/two/three nights	pour une/deux/trois nuits
Can I see it?	Je peux la voir?
a room on the courtyard	une chambre sur la cour
a room over the street	une chambre sur la rue
first floor	premier étage
second floor	deuxième étage
with a view	avec vue
key	clef
to iron	repasser
do laundry	faire la lessive
sheets	draps
blankets	couvertures
quiet	calme
noisy	bruyant
hot water	eau chaude
cold water	eau froide
Is breakfast included?	Est-ce que le petit déjeuner est compris?
I would like breakfast	Je voudrais prendre le petit déjeuner
I don't want breakfast	Je ne veux pas de petit déjeuner

DRIVING

service station	garage
service	service
to park the car	garer la voiture
car park	un parking
no parking	défense de stationner/ stationnement interdit
petrol/gas station	poste d'essence
fuel	essence
unleaded	sans plomb
leaded	super
diesel	gazole
(to) fill it up	faire le plein
oil	huile
air line	ligne à air
put air in the tyres	gonfler les pneus
battery	batterie
the battery is dead	la batterie est morte
spark-plugs	bougies
to break down	tomber en panne
gas can	bidon
insurance	assurance
green card	carte verte
traffic lights	feux
red light	feu rouge
green light	feu vert

CYCLING

to adjust	régler
ball bearing	le roulement à billes
battery	la pile
bent	tordu
bicycle	le vélo
bottom bracket	le logement du pédalier
brake cable	le cable
brakes	les freins
broken	cassé
bulb	l'ampoule
chain	la chaîne
cotter pin	la clavette
to deflate	dégonfler

dérailleur	le dérailleur	chemist/pharmacist	pharmacie
frame	le cadre	hospital	hôpital
gears	les vitesses	condom	préservatif
grease	la graisse	morning-after pill/	pilule du lendemain
handlebars	le guidon	emergency contraceptive	
to inflate	gonfler	I'm allergic to…	Je suis allergique à…
inner tube	la chambre à air		
loose	déserré	**OTHER NEEDS**	
to lower	baisser	bakery	boulangerie
mudguard	le garde-boue	food shop	alimentation
pannier	le pannier	delicatessen	charcuterie, traiteur
pedal	le pédale	cake shop	pâtisserie
pump	la pompe	cheese shop	fromagerie
puncture	la crevaison	supermarket	supermarché
rack	le porte-bagages	to eat	manger
to raise	remonter	to drink	boire
to repair	réparer	tasting, eg wine tasting	dégustation
saddle	la selle	camping gas	camping gaz
to screw	visser/serrer	tobacconist	tabac
spanner	la clef (mécanique)	stamps	timbres
spoke	le rayon	bank	banque
to straighten	redresser	money	argent
stuck	coincé	toilets	toilettes
tight	serré	police	police
toe clips	les cale-pieds	telephone	téléphone
tyre	le pneu	cinema	cinéma
wheel	la roue	theatre	théâtre
		to reserve/book	réserver

HEALTH MATTERS

doctor	médecin
I don't feel well	Je ne me sens pas bien
medicines	médicaments
prescription	ordonnance
I feel sick	Je suis malade
I have a headache	J'ai mal à la tête
stomach ache	mal à l'estomac
period	règles
pain	douleur
it hurts	ça fait mal

RESTAURANT PHRASES

I'd like to reserve a table	Je voudrais réserver une table
for two people, at eight thirty	pour deux personnes, à vingt heures et demie
I'm having the €30 set menu	Je prendrai le menu à trente euros
Waiter!	monsieur/madame!/ s'il vous plaît!
the bill/check please	l'addition, s'il vous plaît

A FOOD GLOSSARY

BASIC TERMS

l'addition	bill/check	à emporter	takeaway
beurre	butter	entrée	starter
bio or biologique	organic	formule	lunch time set menu
bouteille	bottle	fourchette	fork
carafe d'eau	jug of water	fumé	smoked
la carte	the menu	huile	oil
chauffé	heated	lait	milk
couteau	knife	menu	set menu
cru	raw	moutarde	mustard
cuillère	spoon	œuf	egg
cuit	cooked	offert	free
emballé	wrapped	pain	bread
		pimenté	spicy

plat	main course
poivre	pepper
salé	salted/savoury
sel	salt
sucre	sugar
sucré	sweet
table	table
verre	glass
vinaigre	vinegar

SNACKS

un sandwich	a sandwich
une baguette	
au jambon	with ham
au fromage	with cheese
au saucisson	with sausage
à l'ail	with garlic
au poivre	with pepper
au pâté (de campagne)	with pâté (country style)
croque-monsieur	toasted cheese and ham sandwich
croque-madame	a croque-monsieur with an egg on top
pain bagnat	bread roll with egg, olives, salad, tuna, anchovies and olive oil
panini	toasted Italian sandwich
tartine	buttered bread or open sandwich
œufs	eggs
au plat	fried
à la coque	boiled
durs	hard-boiled
brouillés	scrambled
omelette	omelette
nature	plain
aux fines herbes	with herbs
au fromage	with cheese

PASTA (*PÂTES*), PANCAKES (*CRÊPES*) AND FLANS (*TARTES*)

nouilles	noodles
pâtes fraîches	fresh pasta
crêpe au sucre/aux œufs	pancake with sugar/ eggs
galette	buckwheat pancake
socca	thin chickpea flour pancake
panisse	thick chickpea flour pancake
pissaladière	tart of fried onions with anchovies and black olives

tarte flambée	thin pizza-like pastry topped with onion, cream and bacon or other combinations

SOUPS (*SOUPES*)

baudroie	burbot or monkfish soup
bisque	shellfish soup
bouillabaisse	fish soup Mediterranean-style
bouillon	broth or stock
bourride	thick fish soup
consommé	clear soup
garbure	potato, cabbage and meat soup
pistou	parmesan, basil and garlic paste added to soup
potage	thick vegetable soup
potée auvergnate	cabbage and meat soup
rouille	red pepper, garlic and saffron mayonnaise served with fish soup
soupe à l'oignon	onion soup with gruyère cheese topping
velouté	thick soup, usually fish or poultry

STARTERS (*HORS D'ŒUVRES*)

assiette anglaise	plate of cold meats
assiette composée	mixed salad plate, usually cold meat and vegetables
crudités	raw vegetables with dressings
escargots	snails
hors d'œuvres	combination of the above plus smoked or marinated fish

FISH (*POISSON*), SEAFOOD (*FRUITS DE MER*) AND SHELLFISH (*CRUSTACES* OR *COQUILLAGES*)

amandes de mer	clams, cockles
aiglefin	small haddock or fresh cod
anchois	anchovies
anguilles	eels
barbue	brill
bar	bass
baudroie	monkfish or anglerfish
bigorneau	periwinkle
brème	bream
bulot	whelk
cabillaud	cod

calmar	squid
carrelet	plaice
claire	type of oyster
colin	hake
congre	conger eel
coques	cockles
coquilles St-Jacques	scallops
crabe	crab
crevettes grises	shrimp
crevettes roses	prawns
daurade	sea bream
écrevisses	crayfish
éperlan	smelt or whitebait
favou(ille)	tiny crab
flétan	halibut
friture	assorted fried fish
gambas	king prawns
hareng	herring
homard	lobster
huîtres	oysters
julienne	ling
langouste	spiny lobster
langoustines	saltwater crayfish (scampi)
lieu	pollock
limande	lemon sole
lotte	burbot
lotte de mer	monkfish
louvine, loubine	similar to sea bass
loup de mer	sea bass
maquereau	mackerel
merlan	whiting
moules (marinière)	mussels (with shallots in white wine sauce)
oursin	sea urchin
palourdes	clams
poissons de roche	fish from shoreline rocks
praires	small clams
raie	skate
rouget	red mullet
saumon	salmon
sole	sole
St Pierre	John Dory
thon	tuna
tourteau	crab
truite	trout
turbot	turbot
violet	sea squirt

FISH DISHES AND TERMS

aïoli	garlic mayonnaise served with salt cod and other fish
anchoïade	anchovy paste or sauce
arête	fish bone
assiette de fruits de mer	seafood platter
assiette de pêcheur	assorted fish
beignet	fritter
darne	fillet or steak
la douzaine	a dozen
frit	fried
friture	deep-fried small fish
fumé	smoked
fumet	fish stock
gigot de mer	large fish baked whole
grillé	grilled
hollandaise	butter and vinegar sauce
à la meunière	in a butter, lemon and parsley sauce
mousse/mousseline	mousse
pané	breaded
poutargue	mullet roe paste
raïto	red wine, olive, caper, garlic and shallot sauce
quenelles	light dumplings
thermidor	lobster grilled in its shell with cream sauce

MEAT (*VIANDE*) AND POULTRY (*VOLAILLE*)

agneau (de pré-salé)	lamb (grazed on salt marshes)
andouille/andouillette	tripe sausage
bavette	French cut of beef equivalent to flank
bifteck	steak
bœuf	beef
boudin blanc	sausage of white meats
boudin noir	black pudding
caille	quail
canard	duck
caneton	duckling
contrefilet	sirloin roast
coquelet	cockerel
dinde/dindon	turkey
entrecôte	rib steak
faux filet	sirloin steak
foie	liver
foie gras	(duck/goose) liver
gibier	game
gigot (d'agneau)	leg (of lamb)
grenouilles (cuisses de)	frogs (legs)
grillade	grilled meat
hâchis	chopped meat, mince or hamburger
langue	tongue
lapin/lapereau	rabbit/young rabbit
lard/lardons	bacon/diced bacon
lièvre	hare
merguez	spicy, red sausage

mouton	mutton
museau de veau	calf's muzzle
oie	goose
onglet	French cut of beef steak that makes a prime steak
os	bone
poitrine	breast
porc	pork
poulet	chicken
poussin	baby chicken
ris	sweetbreads
rognons	kidneys
rognons blancs	testicles
sanglier	wild boar
steak	steak
tête de veau	calf's head (in jelly)
tournedos	thick slices of fillet
tripes	tripe
tripoux	mutton tripe
veau	veal
venaison	venison
volaille	poultry

MEAT AND POULTRY DISHES AND TERMS

aïado	roast shoulder of lamb stuffed with garlic and other ingredients
aile	wing
au feu de bois	cooked over wood fire
au four	baked
baeckoffe	Alsatian hotpot of pork, mutton and beef baked with potato layers
blanquette, daube, navarin, ragoût, estouffade, hochepôt	types of stew
blanquette de veau	veal in cream and mushroom sauce
bœuf bourguignon	beef stew with Burgundy, onions and mushrooms
canard à l'orange	roast duck with an orange and wine sauce
canard pâté de périgourdin foie gras	roast duck with prunes and truffles
carré	best end of neck, chop or cutlet
cassoulet	casserole of beans, sausages and duck/goose
choucroute	pickled cabbage with peppercorns, sausages, bacon and salami
civet	game stew
confit	meat preserve

côte	chop, cutlet or rib
cou	neck
coq au vin	chicken slow-cooked with wine, onions and mushrooms
cuisse	thigh or leg
épaule	shoulder
en croûte	in pastry
farci	stuffed
grillade	grilled meat
garni	with vegetables
gésier	gizzard
grillé	grilled
hâchis	chopped meat or mince hamburger
magret de canard	duck breast
marmite	casserole
médaillon	round piece
mijoté	stewed
pavé	thick slice
pieds et paques	mutton or pork tripe and trotters
poêlé	pan-fried
poulet de Bresse	chicken from Bresse – the best
râble	saddle
rôti	roast
sauté	lightly fried in butter
steak au poivre (vert/rouge)	steak in a black (green/ red) peppercorn sauce
steak tartare	raw chopped beef, topped with a raw egg yolk
tagine	North African casserole
tournedos	beef fillet with foie gras rossini and truffles
viennoise	fried in egg and breadcrumbs

TERMS FOR STEAKS

bleu	almost raw
saignant	rare
à point	medium rare
bien cuit	well done
très bien cuit	very well done
brochette	kebab

GARNISHES AND SAUCES

américaine	white wine, cognac and tomato
arlésienne au porto	with tomatoes, onions, aubergines, potatoes and rice in port
auvergnate	with cabbage, sausage and bacon

béarnaise	sauce of egg yolks, white wine, shallots and vinegar
beurre blanc	sauce of white wine and shallots, with butter
bonne femme	with mushroom, bacon, potato and onions
bordelaise	in a red wine, shallot and bone-marrow sauce
boulangère	baked with potatoes and onions
bourgeoise	with carrots, onions, bacon, celery and braised lettuce
chasseur	white wine, mushrooms and shallots
châtelaine	with artichoke hearts and chestnut purée
diable	strong mustard seasoning
forestière	with bacon and mushroom
fricassée	rich, creamy sauce
mornay	cheese sauce
pays d'auge	cream and cider
périgourdine	with foie gras and possibly truffles
piquante	gherkins or capers, vinegar and shallots
provençale	tomatoes, garlic, olive oil and herbs
savoyarde	with gruyère cheese
véronique	grapes, wine and cream

VEGETABLES (*LÉGUMES*), HERBS (*HERBES*) AND SPICES (*ÉPICES*)

ail	garlic
algue	seaweed
anis	aniseed
artichaut	artichoke
asperge	asparagus
avocat	avocado
basilic	basil
betterave	beetroot
blette/bette	Swiss chard
cannelle	cinnamon
capre	caper
cardon	cardoon, a beet related to artichoke
carotte	carrot
céleri	celery
champignons, cèpes, ceps, girolles, chanterelles, pleurotes	mushrooms
chou (rouge)	(red) cabbage
choufleur	cauliflower
concombre	cucumber
cornichon	gherkin
echalotes	shallots
endive	chicory
épinards	spinach
estragon	tarragon
fenouil	fennel
férigoule	thyme (in Provençal)
fèves	broad beans
flageolets	flageolet beans
gingembre	ginger
haricots	haricot beans
verts	string beans
rouges	kidney beans
beurres	butter beans
laurier	bay leaf
lentilles	lentils
maïs	maize (corn)
menthe	mint
moutarde	mustard
oignon	onion
panais	parsnip
pâte	pasta or pastry
pélandron	type of string bean
persil	parsley
petits pois	peas
piment rouge/vert	red/green chilli pepper
pois chiche	chickpeas
pois mange-tout	snow peas
pignons	pine nuts
poireau	leek
poivron (vert, rouge)	sweet pepper (green, red)
pommes de terre	potatoes
primeurs	spring vegetables
radis	radish
riz	rice
safran	saffron
salade verte	green salad
sarrasin	buckwheat
tomate	tomato
truffes	truffles

VEGETABLE DISHES AND TERMS

aligot	puréed potato with cheese
allumettes	very thin chips
à l'anglaise	boiled
beignet	fritter
duxelles	fried mushrooms and shallots with cream
farci	stuffed
feuille	leaf
fines herbes	mixture of tarragon, parsley and chives

gratiné	browned with cheese or butter	parmentier	with potatoes
à la grecque	cooked in oil and lemon	petits farcis	stuffed tomatoes, aubergines, courgettes and peppers
jardinière	with mixed diced vegetables	râpée	grated or shredded
mousseline	mashed potato with cream and eggs	sauté	lightly fried in butter
		à la vapeur	steamed
à la parisienne	sautéed potatoes, with white wine and shallot sauce	en verdure	garnished with green vegetables

BRETON

Breton belongs to the Celtic family of languages, linked with Welsh and Gaelic even if it's not mutually comprehensible, and especially closely tied with Cornish. Its strong oral tradition ranges from medieval minstrels to modern singers and musicians.

Current estimates put the number of people who understand spoken Breton at between 400,000 and 800,000. However, only perhaps a third of those actually speak the language with any fluency or frequency. You're very unlikely to find it spoken as a first, day-to-day language; the only conceivable possibilities are among the very old, or in exceptionally remote parts of Finistère. As an oral language, Breton was spoken in different dialects in different regions; there were at least five distinct dialects in Western Brittany alone.

For centuries Breton was efficiently suppressed by the state; its use was forbidden for official and legal purposes, and even Breton-speaking parents sought to enhance their children's prospects by bringing them up to speak French. Although Breton is now taught in some schools once again, and there is even a Breton regional bank, learning the language is not really a viable prospect for visitors who do not already have a good grounding in another Celtic language.

However, as you travel through the province it's interesting to note the roots of Breton **place names**, many of which have a simple meaning in the language. The list of Breton words below includes some of the most common, as well as a few everyday words and greetings.

BRETON VOCABULARY

aber	estuary	**lann**	heath
avel	wind	**lech**	flat stone
bihan	little	**loc**	isolated, holy place
bran	hill	**mad**	good
braz	big	**men**	stone
Breizh	Brittany	**menez**	mountain
creach	height	**mario**	dead
cromlech	stone circle	**menhir**	long stone
dol/taol	table	**meur**	big
dour	water	**mor**	sea
du	black	**nevez**	new
enez	island	**parc**	field
gavre	goat	**penn**	end, head
goat/coat/koat	forest	**plou**	parish
goaz	stream	**pors**	port, farmyard
gwenn	white	**roch**	stone
hen	old	**ster**	river
heol	sun	**stivel**	fountain, spring
hir	long	**ti**	house
kastell	castle	**traez**	sand, beach
kenavo	goodbye	**trugarez**	thank you
ker	town, village	**trou**	valley
koz	old	**wrach**	witch
lan	church, holy place	**ya**	yes

FRUIT (*FRUIT*) AND NUTS (*NOIX*)

abricot	apricot
acajou	cashew nut
amande	almond
ananas	pineapple
banane	banana
brugnon, nectarine	nectarine
cacahouète	peanut
cassis	blackcurrant
cérise	cherry
citron	lemon
citron vert	lime
datte	date
figue	fig
fraise (de bois)	strawberry (wild)
framboise	raspberry
fruit de la passion	passion fruit
grenade	pomegranate
groseille	redcurrant
mangue	mango
marron	chestnut
melon	melon
mirabelle	small yellow plum
myrtille	bilberry
noisette	hazelnut
noix	walnuts; nuts
orange	orange
pamplemousse	grapefruit
pastèque	watermelon
pêche	peach
pistache	pistachio
poire	pear
pomme	apple
prune	plum
pruneau	prune
raisin	grape
reine-claude	greengage

FRUIT DISHES AND TERMS

agrumes	citrus fruits
beignet	fritter
compôte	stewed fruit
coulis	sauce of puréed fruit
crème de marrons	chestnut purée
flambé	set aflame in alcohol
fougasse	bread flavoured with orange-flower water or almonds (can be savoury)
frappé	iced

DESSERTS (*DESSERTS* OR *ENTREMETS*) AND PASTRIES (*PÂTISSERIE*)

bombe	moulded ice-cream dessert
brioche	sweet, high yeast breakfast roll loaf
calisson	almond sweet
charlotte	custard and fruit in lining of almond fingers
chichi	doughnut shaped in a stick
clafoutis	heavy custard and fruit tart
crème Chantilly	vanilla-flavoured and sweetened whipped cream
crème fraîche	sour cream
crème pâtissière	thick, eggy pastry filling
crêpe suzette	thin pancake with orange juice and liqueur
fromage blanc	cream cheese
gaufre	waffle
glace	ice cream
Île flottante/ œufs à la neige	whipped egg-white floating on custard
macaron	macaroon
madeleine	small sponge cake
marrons Mont Blanc	chestnut purée and cream on a rum- soaked sponge cake
mousse au chocolat	chocolate mousse
omelette norvégienne	baked alaska
palmier	caramelized puff pastry
parfait	frozen mousse, sometimes ice cream
petit-suisse	a smooth mixture of cream and curds
petits fours	bite-sized cakes/ pastries
poires belle hélène	pears and ice cream in chocolate sauce
tarte tatin	upside-down apple tart
tarte tropézienne	sponge cake filled with custard cream topped with nuts
tiramisu	mascarpone cheese, chocolate and cream
yaourt/yogourt	yoghurt

Glossary

abbaye abbey

aber estuary

accueil reception

arrêt d'autobus bus stop

Assemblée Nationale the French parliament

auberge de jeunesse (AJ) youth hostel

autobus city bus

autoroute motorway/freeway

banque bank

bassin harbour basin

Beaux-arts fine arts school (and often museum)

bibliothèque library

bistro small restaurant or bar

bois wood

boulangerie baker

brasserie café/restaurant

bureau de change money exchange

calvaire ("calvary") a cluster of religious statues standing on a single base, usually topped by a Crucifixion, as found in many Breton churchyards

car coach, bus

cave (wine) cellar

centre ville town centre

chambre d'hôte B&B

charcuterie delicatessen

chasse/chasse gardée hunting grounds beware/ keep out

château castle or mansion

cimetière cemetery

citadelle fortified city

cloître cloister

confiserie sweet shop

consigne left luggage

couvent monastery

crêperie pancake restaurant

dégustation tasting

département administrative division equivalent to an English county

dolmen megalithic stone "table"

donjon castle keep

église church

enclos group of church buildings

enclos paroissial ("parish close") a walled churchyard that incorporates a church, a cemetery, a calvary and an ossuary

entrée entrance

fermeture closing time/period

forêt forest

formule lunch time set menu

fouilles archeological excavations

foyer residential hostel for young workers or students

gare routière bus station

gare SNCF train station

gîte d'étape countryside hostel

grotte cave

halles covered market

hôpital hospital

hôtel hotel – but also used for an aristocratic townhouse or mansion

Hôtel de Ville town hall

île island

jours fériés public holidays

mairie town hall

maison literally a house – can also be an office or base of an organization

marché market

menhir single megalithic stone

office du tourisme (OT) tourist office

ouverture opening time/period

pardon religious procession

pâtisserie pastry shop

pharmacie chemist

place square

plage beach

plat du jour daily special on menu

porte gate

poste post office

presqu'île peninsula

privé private

PTT post office

quartier quarter or district of a town

Relais Routier truck-stop restaurant

rez-de-chaussée ground floor (UK), first floor (US)

RN route nationale main road

salon de thé tearoom

SI tourist office (see syndicat d'initiative below)

SNCF French railways

syndicat d'initiative (SI) tourist office

tabac bar or shop selling stamps, cigarettes, etc

tour tower

traiteur delicatessen

Vauban famous seventeenth-century military architect

zone bleue parking zone

zone piétonnière pedestrian zone

Small print and index

Rough Guide credits

Editor: Ruth Reisenberger
Layout: Nikhil Agarwal
Cartography: Lokamata Sahu
Picture editor: Raffaella Morini
Proofreader: Stewart Wild
Managing editors: Natasha Foges, Alice Park
Assistant editor: Sharon Sonam
Production: Janis Griffith

Cover design: Nicole Newman, Raffaella Morini, Nikhil Agarwal
Editorial assistant: Rebecca Hallett
Senior pre-press designer: Dan May
Programme manager: Gareth Lowe
Publisher: Joanna Kirby
Publishing director: Georgina Dee

Publishing information

This twelfth edition published June 2015 by
Rough Guides Ltd,
80 Strand, London WC2R 0RL
11, Community Centre, Panchsheel Park,
New Delhi 110017, India
Distributed by Penguin Random House
Penguin Books Ltd,
80 Strand, London WC2R 0RL
Penguin Group (USA)
345 Hudson Street, NY 10014, USA
Penguin Group (Australia)
250 Camberwell Road, Camberwell,
Victoria 3124, Australia
Penguin Group (NZ)
67 Apollo Drive, Mairangi Bay, Auckland 1310,
New Zealand
Penguin Group (South Africa)
Block D, Rosebank Office Park, 181 Jan Smuts Avenue,
Parktown North, Gauteng, South Africa 2193
Rough Guides is represented in Canada by Tourmaline
Editions Inc. 662 King Street West, Suite 304, Toronto,
Ontario M5V 1M7
Printed in Singapore
© Greg Ward 2015

Maps © Rough Guides
Contains Ordnance Survey data © Crown copyright and
database rights 2014
No part of this book may be reproduced in any form
without permission from the publisher except for the
quotation of brief passages in reviews.
408pp includes index
A catalogue record for this book is available from the
British Library
ISBN: 978-0-24100-974-1
The publishers and authors have done their best to
ensure the accuracy and currency of all the information
in **The Rough Guide to Brittany & Normandy**, however,
they can accept no responsibility for any loss, injury, or
inconvenience sustained by any traveller as a result of
information or advice contained in the guide.
3 5 7 9 8 6 4 2

MIX
Paper from
responsible sources
FSC™ C018179

Help us update

We've gone to a lot of effort to ensure that the twelfth
edition of **The Rough Guide to Brittany & Normandy** is
accurate and up-to-date. However, things change – places
get "discovered", opening hours are notoriously fickle,
restaurants and rooms raise prices or lower standards. If
you feel we've got it wrong or left something out, we'd like
to know, and if you can remember the address, the price,
the hours, the phone number, so much the better.

Please send your comments with the subject line
"**Rough Guide Brittany & Normandy Update**" to
🅔 mail@uk.roughguides.com. We'll credit all contributions
and send a copy of the next edition (or any other Rough
Guide if you prefer) for the very best emails.
Find more travel information, connect with fellow
travellers and plan your trip on Ⓦ roughguides.com.

ABOUT THE AUTHOR

Greg Ward has been writing the *Rough Guide to Brittany & Normandy* since the first edition back in 1986. He has also written and photographed several other Rough Guides, including those to the USA, Southwest USA, Hawaii, Las Vegas, the Grand Canyon, Blues CDs and US History; edited many more, including those to India and the USA, Blues, Soul and Elvis; written books for other publishers; and spent a number of years working in the Rough Guides office. For more details, visit ⓦgregward.info.

Acknowledgements

Author: Thanks and love to my wife Sam, for everything. Thanks, too, to my editor Ruth Reisenberger, for her great and exceptionally patient work, and to Alice Park, Natasha Foges, Raffaella Morini, James MacDonald, Nikhil Agarwal and everyone at Rough Guides for their help and input. And thanks to all those who helped to make my travels in France so enjoyable, including Assal Baktashian, Céline Badde, Lionel Besnard, Amy Buckingham, Christopher Jones, Wendy Mewes, Maggie McNulty, Beverley Morrison, Chelsey Palmer, Arnaud Polaillon, Daragh Reddin and Alison Weatherhead.

Readers' updates

Thanks to all the readers who have taken the time to write in with comments and suggestions (and apologies if we've inadvertently omitted or misspelt anyone's name):

Edmond Barry, Nicole Booth, Monica Budden, Laurie Chertock, Dick Conroy, Valerie Davies, Leslie Engler, M. Gillick, Rod Gray, Kathrin Greve, Richard Griffiths, Gill Gustar, Moire Lennox, Gwyn Lloyd, Chris Onions, Geneviève Pérennou, Sheila Smith, Adrian Stevens, Gill Thomas, Lelia Thornton, Louisa Tunstall, Hilary Vincent, Merriall Wearen and Ian Wilson.

Photo credits

All photos © Rough Guides except the following:
(Key: t-top; c-centre; b-bottom; l-left; r-right)

p.1 Corbis/Olivier Leclercq/Hemis
p.2 Corbis/Bertrand Rieger/Hemis
p.4 Getty Images/Teolc Eniger/Flickr Open
p.5 Corbis/Atlantide Phototravel
p.8 Alamy Images/Hemis
p.9 Alamy Images/Hemis (tl, b); Getty Images/Gisèle Tellier (tr)
p.11 Corbis/Francis Leroy/Hemis (t); Corbis/Juliane Lancou/The Hell Gate (c); Alamy Images/travellinglight (b)
p.12 Getty Images/Fred Tanneau/AFP
p.13 Getty Images/Nicolas Thibaut/Photononstop RM (t); Corbis/Hervé Hughes/Hemis (c); Alamy Images/Gilles Rigoulet/Hemis (b)
p.14 Getty Images/Oric1-Flickr/Flickr RF (t); Corbis/Jon Boyes/incamerastock (c); Getty Images/Martine Mouchy/Photolibrary (b)
p.15 The Bridgeman Art Library (tl); 4Corners/Günter Gräfenhain (tr); Corbis/Hans Georg Roth (c); Getty Images/Fabio Nodari/Flickr RM (bl); Alamy Images/Les. Ladbury (br)
p.16 Corbis/Doug Pearson/JAI (tl); Dreamstime.com/Robert Zehetmaye (tr); Latitude/Andia (bl, br)
p.17 Corbis/Guy Thouvenin/Robert Harding World Imagery (t); Corbis/Atlantide Phototravel (c); Corbis/Gilles Rigoulet/Hemis (b)
p.18 Getty Images/David Martinelli/www.maverick-photos.net/Flickr Open
p.20 Alamy Images/Hemis
pp.42–43 Corbis/Ivan Vdovin/JAI
p.45 Getty Images/Tim Gartside
p.67 Getty Images/Magdalena Jankowska/iStockphoto

pp.86-87 Getty Images/Frans Sellies/Flickr Vision
p.89 Getty Images/M. Seemuller/DeAgostini
p.115 Corbis/Peter Langer/Design Pics (t); Corbis/Walter Bibikow/JAI (b)
pp.142–143 Corbis/Francis Cormon/Hemis
p.145 Dreamstime.com/Cavaudon
p.161 Alamy Images/Patrick Forget/Sagaphoto.com (t); Alamy Images/Hemis (b)
pp.176–177 Alamy Images/Cro Magnon
p.179 Getty Images/Ian Cumming/Axiom RM
p.197 Alamy Images/Hemis (t); Getty Images/Anger O. (b)
p.213 Getty Images/Visions Of Our Land
pp.232–233 Corbis/Stéphane Lemaire/Hemis
p.235 Corbis/Jean-Pierre Lescourret
p.261 Alamy Images/Hemis (t)
pp.286–287 Corbis/Jon Boyes/incamerastock
p.289 Alamy Images/mediasculp
p.301 Getty Images/Philippe MANGUIN Photographies/Flickr RF
pp.318–319 Getty Images/Miemo Penttinen – miemo.net/Flickr Open
p.321 Corbis/Marc Dozier
p.339 Alamy Images/Gary Dyson (t); Alamy Images/age fotostock Spain, S.L. (b)
p.358 Getty Images/G. Dagli Orti/DeAgostin

Front cover & spine Mont-St-Michel © 4Corners/Stephane Compoint/Onlyfrance/SIME
Back cover Baie des Trépassés © Latitude/Andia (t); Mussels, Rennes market © Alamy Images/David Burton (bl); Le Bec-Hellouin © 4Corners/Günter Gräfenhain (br)

Index

Maps are marked in grey

T

U

V

Map symbols

The symbols below are used on maps throughout the book

Main road	✈ Domestic airport	Church (regional)	Carousel
Minor road	Ⓜ Metro/subway	Synagogue	Menhir standing stone
Motorway	Ⓣ Tram stop	Place of interest	Lighthouse
Pedestrianised road	✉ Post office	Castle	Bridge
Step	✚ Hospital	Gate	Building
Railway	ⓘ Information centre	Zoo	Market
Path	P Parking	Viewpoint	Church (town)
Wall	Campsite	Megalithic site	Stadium
Ferry	Abbey	Mountain peak	Park
Tram line	Stately home/palace	Cave	Christian cemetery
✈ International airport	Chateau	Swamp	Beach

Listings key

■ Accommodation
● Restaurant
■ Bar
● Shop

A ROUGH GUIDE TO
ROUGH GUIDES

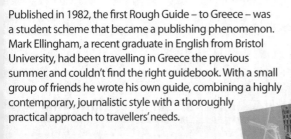

Published in 1982, the first Rough Guide – to Greece – was a student scheme that became a publishing phenomenon. Mark Ellingham, a recent graduate in English from Bristol University, had been travelling in Greece the previous summer and couldn't find the right guidebook. With a small group of friends he wrote his own guide, combining a highly contemporary, journalistic style with a thoroughly practical approach to travellers' needs.

The immediate success of the book spawned a series that rapidly covered dozens of destinations. And, in addition to impecunious backpackers, Rough Guides soon acquired a much broader readership that relished the guides' wit and inquisitiveness as much as their enthusiastic, critical approach and value-for-money ethos.

These days, Rough Guides include recommendations from budget to luxury and cover more than 120 destinations around the globe. We also as produce an ever-growing range of ebooks. Visit ⓦ roughguides.com to see our latest publications.